Resistance

A Radical Political and Social History of the Lower East Side

A Seven Stories Press First Edition

Seven Stories Press
140 Watts Street
New York, NY 10013
http://www.sevenstories.com

In Canada: Publishers Group Canada, 559 College Street, Suite 402, Toronto, ON M6G 1A9

In the UK: Turnaround Publisher Services Ltd., Unit 3, Olympia Trading Estate, Coburg Road, Wood Green, London N22 6TZ

In Australia: Palgrave Macmillan, 627 Chapel Street, South Yarra, VIC 3141

College professors may order examination copies of Seven Stories Press titles for a free six-month trial period. To order, visit http://www.sevenstories.com/ textbook or send a fax on school letterhead to (212) 226-1411.

Book design by Nancy Calef   http://nancycalefgallery.com

A radical political and social history of the Lower East Side / editor, curator, producer Clayton Patterson ; editors, Clayton Patterson, Joe Flood, Alan Moore ; associated editors, Nancy Calef ... [et al.]. -- Seven stories press 1st ed.
p. cm.
Includes index.
ISBN-13: 978-1-58322-745-9 (pbk. : alk. paper)
ISBN-10: 1-58322-745-8 (pbk. : alk. paper)
1. Lower East Side (New York, N.Y.)--Politics and government. 2. Lower East Side (New York, N.Y.)--History. 3. Lower East Side (New York, N.Y.)--Social conditions. 4. New York (N.Y.)--Politics and government. 5. New York (N.Y.)--History. 6. New York (N.Y.)--Social conditions. I. Patterson, Clayton. II. Flood, Joe. III. Moore, Alan, 1951- IV. Calef, Nancy.

F128.68.L6R33 2007
974.7'1--dc22

2006037811

Printed in Canada
9 8 7 6 5 4 3 2 1

Resistance

A Radical Political and Social History of the Lower East Side

editor/curator/producer
Clayton Patterson

Editors: Clayton Patterson, Joe Flood, Alan Moore
Associate editors: Nancy Calef, Michael Carter, Jim Feast,
Jan Herman, Ron Koln, John McMillian, Howie Seligman,
Laura Tuchman, Jody Weiner

Acknowledgments:

It would have been impossible for me to have made this book alone. All the authors and people involved in this tome supplied the true grit, intelligence, energy and vitality that made this reference book come to life. There are volumes of people who must be thanked, but room is limited so I can only name the few who did a lot of extra work, or added necessary missing ingredients: Elsa Rensaa, Lars Reilly, Dan Simon, Phoebe Hwang, Jon Gilbert, Crystal Yakacki of Seven Stories Press, The Solo Foundation, Howie Seligman, Angel Orensanz Cultural Foundation, Al Orensanz, Shalom Neuman and Deborah Fries of Fusion Arts Museum, David McWater, Michael Rosen & Leslie Gruss, Aaron Sosnick, Robert Perl, David Leslie, Richard Kusack, Roland Legiardi-Laura, Colin Moynihan, Darren Bloch, Jim Feast, Ron Koln, Laura Tuchman, Steven Watson, Rebecca Moore, Jerry Pagane, Michael Carter, Nancy Calef, Jody Weiner, John McMillian, Jan Herman, Eric Miller, Alan Moore, Joe Flood, Richard Kostelanetz and Jeff Ferrell. There were periods of both darkness and light. It was during the darkness that people came out and helped, pushed, guided. For this help I am truly grateful. You all know who you are and what you have done . . . the struggle continues . . .

Editors-- Clayton Patterson, Alan Moore, Joe Flood
Associate editors: Nancy Calef, Michael Carter, Jim Feast, Jan Herman, Ron Koln, John McMillian, Howie Seligman, Laura Tuchman, Jody Weiner

AUTHORS:

Al Orensanz
Fred Good
Thomas McEvilley
Christopher Mele
Lynne Stewart
Joe Flood
Aldo Tambelli
Steve Zehentner
Janet Abu-Lughod
Yuri Kapralov
Peter L. Wilson
Colin Moynihan
Seth Tobocman
Clayton Patterson
Richard Kostelanetz
Eric Miller
Seth Farber
Sarah Ferguson
Joanne Edelman
JoAnn Wypijewski
Daniel Edelman
Chris Brandt
Aaron Jaffe
Carolyn Ratcliffe
Richard Kusack
Roland Legiardi-Laura
David Pultz
Laura Zelasnic
Tom Savage
Interview by Clayton Patterson
Will Sales

Peter Missing
A. Kronstadt
Ron Casanova & Steven Blackburn
Ellen Moynihan
P.O. John Mellon
Joshua Rothenberger
Chief Michael Julian
Bill Weinberg
Alan Moore with Alan Antliff
Elsa Rensaa
Richard Porton
Aaron Jaffe
Chris Flash
Kenny Tolia
Alfredo Irizzary
Mary McCarthy
Cheryl Guttman
Eve Hinderer
Hanon Reznikov
Interview by John Beresford
John McMillian
Michael Rosen
Virginie Rocky
Jay Blotcher
Jim Feast
Mac McGill
Fly
James Cornwell (aka Jim C.)
Osha Neumann
Steve Dalachinsky

Table of Contents

Table of Contents

PHOTO SECTION   261

SECTION THREE - TOMPKINS SQUARE

SECTION FOUR - MEDIA

SECTION FIVE - BIOGRAPHY

Foreword

**Resistance: A Radical Political and Social History of the Lower East Side
By Jeff Ferrell**

Rarely does a book come along with politics as vivid as its people. Clayton Patterson and the many contributors to *Resistance* pull it off. With a fine mix of fondness, humor and critique, they document the hodgepodge of incendiary politics and interpersonal engagement that defined decades of New York's Lower East Side. More to the point, they show us that for the Lower East Side at its best the people were the politics. Making your way through *Resistance*, you might as well be wandering the political landscape of the neighborhood back in the day, stopping to dig the street players, putting up a poster or pushing a copy of *The Shadow* newspaper, pitching in to defend a squat or a collective garden, cutting through the crowd in Tompkins Square Park, sidestepping a junkie or a cop. *Resistance* swarms with the movement and emotion of the Lower East Side's people, revealing a politics invented out of their daily battles with police, landlords, developers — hell, sometimes with each other. Reading the book, you feel like a flaneur, lost to the rhythms of the neighborhood streets and learning something new at every turn.

This emerging dynamic of uncertainty animating the Lower East Side (LES) was anything but politics as usual. Needless to say corporate developers and law-and-order devotees didn't have much use for the its long efflorescence of radical politics — but as *Resistance* makes clear, neither did the (old) "New Left," "The Nation," or the Democratic Party machinery of New York City. Whether withholding support or just not paying attention, the caretakers of conventional politics kept the Lower East Side at arm's length; as Clayton says, they weren't particularly interested in making sense of the "ugly rank collective," the oddball assortment and association of people that made up the neighborhood and its history.

And yet, as *Resistance* reveals time and again, making sense of that 'ugly rank collective', understanding the sorts of people who constituted it, is just the point — because to appreciate the mongrel beauty of the Lower East Side's inhabitants is to appreciate the vibrant militancy of its collective politics. Appropriately enough, the shape of this outcast collective keeps shifting throughout the chapters of *Resistance* — but in one configuration or another, the Lower East Side's beggars' banquet keeps feasting on its own sideways energy, and the ragtag choir keeps singing loud and proud. There's Sarah Ferguson, describing the motley rabble of Tompkins Square Park and the Lower East Side: squatters and hippies, anarchist bike messengers, homeless agitators and soap-boxing radicals. Or Joshua Rothenberger, on the crowd standing up to the cops in that same park in 1988: "the homeless, local residents, activists, artists, anarchists, communists, and various marginalized groups joined together'

ix

A Radical Political and Social History of the Lower East Side

x

. . . ." There's squatter activist Jerry the Peddler, explaining his attraction to the Lower East Side: "I like hanging out with hippies, punks, beatniks, and freaks . . . " And Jay Blotcher, ACT UP activist, recalling that "Black and Latino poor were mixing it up with upper middle class people with AIDS," adding, "We were artists, writers — mostly hungry, certainly pissed off . . . . I made friends with seers, madmen, angels and lost souls."

Seers, squatters, agitators, angels, lost souls — man, I hear echoes of the past. I hear Ginsberg, the best minds of a generation howling against cops and developers and occupying squats empty of all save the mental furniture. I hear Dylan and Desolation Row, Good Samaritans and the carnival and everyone famous long ago, and The Clash, calling us out to riot on our own. Most of all, I can't help but hear the old angelic cacophony of the Paris Commune, the "festival of the oppressed" that occupied the streets of Paris a century or so before the Lower East Side's festival of the oppressed occupied Tompkins Square Park. In fact, accounts of the 1870s Paris Commune, written by its participants, could easily enough be mistaken for reports in *Resistance*. While it lasted, the Commune — or for that matter the Lower East Side — ran on the "free and spontaneous cooperation of all individual energies." It interlaced "heroism and laughter," mixed "fighting and singing," reveled in loudly sung lyrics like "They're the Rabble! Well, I'm one of them!" And it — the Paris Commune, that is, or the Lower East Side — erupted in defiance of a centralized government and an urban redevelopment scheme designed to push the poor and la boheme out of the City's central districts.

If confusing the Paris Commune and the Lower East Side is easy, it's also instructive — because just as the Paris Commune is today remembered as an historic moment of anarchic uprising, the Lower East Side may one day be remembered as another. *Resistance* commemorates Emma Goldman as the godless godmother of the Lower East Side, her anarchist politics honed in local immigrant and labor cultures; it also documents the ways in which Wobblies, Situationists, and Punks continued over the years to infuse the Lower East Side with Emma's ethos, with sensibilities of direct action, do-it-yourself politics, and street-level defiance.

But as important as they are, it's not simply these "radical artifacts," to use Richard Porton's chapter title, that attest to the Lower East Side's anarchism; it's also the enduring will to innovation and autonomy. After all, anarchism by definition and by practice operates less as a received ideology than as an ongoing experiment, an open road toward defiant self-determination. Recalling the war to save Tompkins Square Park from cops and curfews, for example, Seth Tobocman explains that, "Most of us didn't think of ourselves as anarchists. It was our actions that made us anarchists. We were the riff raff out on a mission" — and so provides a perfect definition of anarchism. Alan Moore and Alan Antliff argue that Clayton Patterson's aesthetic politics are " . . . pure punk . . . the revenge of life experience over corporate art . . . a do-it-yourself approach that echoes the anarchism at the core of the punk ethos." Clayton counters that "I do not think of myself as an anarchist . . . I consider myself to be an artist. Being an artist to me means seeking original answers" — and so reminds us that good art and good anarchy are never far apart. Frank Morales remembers modestly that there wasn't "really any squatter movement per se," because it wasn't 'a centralized thing' — and so describes an anarchist squatter movement.

Throughout the book, this lovely sort of slippery, surreptitious anarchism keeps surfacing-and sometimes comes full circle. Serving a year in jail for inciting a riot in Tompkins Square Park, Kenny Tolia gets a gift: a copy of Emma Goldman's autobiography *Living My Life*, from which he learns that she served a year in jail for the same crime.

As must already be obvious, the politics of the Lower East Side were also the politics of urban space — its use, meaning, and control — and as suggested by Kenny Tolia's year in the slammer, among the most sacred of Lower East Side spaces was Tompkins Square Park. An earthbound embodiment of the Lower East Side's "legacy of rebellion," with its century-old history of draft protests, folk parties, and outsider encampments, the park in 1988 reproduced its own politics, and with a vengeance. The spark that year was a heavy handed attempt by the city to impose a park curfew; the explosion was a running street battle between rogue cops and park defenders that spilled out of the park and ultimately engulfed the whole of the Lower East Side in its politics. Out of that explosion the park curfew was killed — but beyond that, as resident after resident remembers in *Resistance*, the explosion offered a moment of profound and ongoing radicalization.

That spirit of radicalism and spatial autonomy exploded into other situations as well, especially the self-made squats that sprang up inside abandoned buildings, and the collective community gardens that blossomed around the neighborhood. The garden that Jerry the Peddler tended behind his squat, for example, served not just as a garden but as a "communal meeting place . . . where people could come and go as they pleased . . . a real autonomous zone." With their parks, squats, and gardens, the people of the Lower East Side fought a political economy of absentee landlords and intentional neglect. Later, defending those same spaces, they stood up to schemes of sanitized gentrification that, as Seth Tobocman says, treated the people of the Lower East Side "like outsiders on streets where they had lived for years." Carving out spaces for innovation and community, people found themselves banded together in defense of their shared existential turf.

Of course, these spaces and these politics were mediated as well. Essential to the battle for Tompkins Square Park and its radicalizing aftershocks, for instance, was a brilliant bit of cinema verite: an attentive, hand-held video that Clayton Patterson shot while wandering amidst the action. The video became a kind of founding document for Lower East Side rebellion — and it became a legal document as well, used by Clayton to challenge court cases and force changes in the New York City Police Department. As a "documentarian of deviant behavior," Clayton continued this strategy in other cases, and not surprisingly often found himself tangled up in his own legal blues for the trouble. Others on the Lower East Side likewise confounded art, media, and activism to good effect. The anarchist *Shadow* newspaper reported on Lower East Side events, sure, but also functioned as a form of mediated activism. Seth Tobocman and others plastered the neighborhood with cut-and-paste posters and graffiti, all of it "independent of any organization." And then there was "Up Against the Wall, Motherfucker" — a notorious "art gang" whose staged public events teetered dangerously between performance art and propaganda-of-the-deed provocation.

Today, though, the performances are over, the posters have all come down, Jerry the Peddler's garden has become a parking lot. And like low rent urban bohemias from Boston to Denver, the Lower East Side has pretty much gone to hell, finally overrun by the political economy of privilege. As the contributors to *Resistance* carefully document, police harassment and shrinking city services did some serious damage to the Lower East Side over time, and so softened it up for subsequent up-scale urban redevelopment. In fact, Alan Moore and Alan Antliff note in their chapter that Clayton and others are today "haunted by the erasure of the scenes of the past in the meat grinder of New York City development" — and that this sense of lost history has been a primary motivation for the book itself. But in any case, as David Boyle argues at the end of Sarah Ferguson's chapter on the squatter movement, "If you're gonna change the world, you're not going to change it by hanging out on the Lower East Side and talking to the same people, because the Lower East Side is not the world."

Yeah, well, maybe not. But as the contributors to *Resistance* also record, at least some of the Lower East Side's radical history remains, and in the form of significant material accomplishments: homeless co-ops, low income housing, surviving squats, the ABC No Rio collective space. The politics that fired that radical history also remain. *Resistance* reminds us that the fight for community and autonomy remains always underway, pushed underground one moment, bubbling back up the next. For that matter, it seems to me, *Resistance* itself constitutes such a moment of radical effervescence. A passionate history of the Lower East Side is also its own sort of provocation, an unfinished handbook on the possibilities of radical politics. After all, as Emma herself said, anarchism isn't "a theory of the future" — it's a "living force in the affairs of our life, constantly creating new conditions." Or as Seth Tobocman writes, reflecting on a fight now two decades old, "I hope that the Tompkins Square uprising was a prelude to a story not yet written."

A prelude to a story not yet written — yeah, that's it. That's *Resistance*.
Man, I hear echoes of the future.

Intro

By Clayton Patterson

History is made by those who write it. *Resistance* is intended to save some of that history which is too easily lost. The Lower East Side (LES) has always been a hotbed of high energy politics and charged-up political idealists; that is changing as the death grip of gentrification pulls the community around an economic corner that financial gold diggers have been trying to turn for decades. Money, greed and the value of real estate have replaced idealism, creativity, temporary autonomous zones, liberated lifestyles, and struggling masses of newly arrived immigrants. The Lower East Side has been tamed, not likely to go back to its old wild ways.

Much of the information in this book is hard to find or simply not available elsewhere. These hidden histories and related facts reflect the struggles of the poor, the defenseless, the outsiders, those with a poor education or limited access to the system. Imagine how history might have changed if the characters depicted in Herbert Asbury's *Nineteenth Century Gangs of New York* had written articles voicing their positions on poverty and social problems! Aldo Tambellini, an artist/activist poet, extols the virtues and qualities of Joe Colombo; and even though Joe was a leader of an organized crime family, his was a strong voice for Italian-American civil rights, a person who rallied his people against Italian discrimination.

In August 1988, the New York Police Department planned an attack on Tompkins Square Park several days in advance, seeking revenge on the small group of anarchists who had driven 9th precinct officers out of the park the week before. Ron Casanova, a homeless man living in Tompkins Square Park records his perspective on the riot, dispelling the myth that it began after an eviction attempt on the homeless in the park.

The political period I documented, and my years of turmoil, began in 1988 with my 3 hours 33 minute videotape of the Tompkins Square Park police riot. After the tape hit main stream TV, I was involved with court cases rolling on, one after another, for the next seventeen years. While each case was different, they most often involved police brutality or other misconduct, intellectual property rights, and ownership of the original videotape recording. What constitutes best evidence possible? What are the rights of the person who shot the tape? Can the government seize an artist's property? What are the perimeters for documenting on the streets? The impact of my Tompkins Square Park police riot tape started a trend using hand-held video cameras during protests and other interactions with authorities. Little brother watching big brother: the idea became a force to be reckoned with. We were the first video *"Cop Watch."*

My editorial choices include as many active participants as possible. I wanted a multitude of voices, not just one recognized group of expert opinions. *Resistance* gives an overview

A Radical Political and Social History of the Lower East Side

of radical LES political history, highlighting a few individuals and concentrating more on the period of the 1980s up to the millennium. History that is still fresh in the minds of people who contributed to this book.

Resistance includes some new and ongoing wars against gentrification. For example, the ongoing battle to save recently land-marked PS 64 from being turned into a "dorm"; the effort to stop demolition of 158-year-old St. Brigid's Church; the Communities' petition to remove five stories from an over-built residence on E. Third Street; will tenants of 47 East Third Street win their lawsuit finally enabling them to keep their homes? These are the new front-lines that define the real estate conflict.

One victory has been the "ABC No Rio" struggle. After years of negotiating, they recently purchased the building title from the City. Let's see if an anarchist collective can retain the charm of the present building and not end up looking like a dentist's office.

My partner and I have built a photography, video, and paper archive that reflects in depth people struggling to make it in society. By generating some interest in this period, I'm attempting to grease the wheels of written history before this prolonged struggle disappears and is lost forever from our records.

In a gross sense, history comes from two directions: from the academy (the book) or from the street (word of mouth). Each level of society has an outlook but the one at the top has the greatest influence. The bottom has a whole set of social beliefs as well, and those beliefs rightly or wrongly govern that section of society. A big part of the social machine moves in this way. Truth is complex. Conspiracies are complex.

Resistance crosses many lines and points of view. I have included people who made a difference: scholars, writers, journalists, cops, photographers, film/video people, poster-makers, the homeless and other people who deal in word of mouth on the street. Academics deal with facts and an objective eye according to a method.

I am lucky that *Resistance* has a two-tier police point of view, one by John Mellon, a patrolman studying to become a sergeant, who gives us his observations after studying the 1988 police riot. He notes how the police went from community policing to a paramilitary model after the riot proved to be a catalyst for change. The other point of view is from retired chief, Michael Julian, who gives us his side in dealing with those difficult times. Thoughtful officers such as these two give us hope that not all government is lost or corrupt, and that there are good people on all sides of the battle.

I tried to find some balance between defenders of government bureaucracy and wild-eyed leftist intellectuals; a number of them once looked like conspiracy theorists voicing ideas based on fear or distrust of government, theories of discriminatory practices by government based on poverty or class, and accusations about police corruption covering the alleged relationship between police and the street drug trade. Yet, with all of these limitations and omissions, a number of speculations voiced about government corruption turned out to be true. It is easy to marginalize the lone critic no matter how valid their point, especially if they are without status, social position or money.

In 1975, President Gerald Ford told New York City, who had asked for federal help for its fiscal crisis, to "Drop dead!" Certainly by Mayor Koch's third term, the City was a parody of the capitalist system. It was a world economic center, where not much worked, in moral and economic collapse. The City looked and functioned like a member of the failed Eastern Communist bloc. Even the Rolls Royce dealership had left town. Koch's government was filled with hustlers, thieves and corrupt people who milked the system for anything they could get.

By 1988, the Koch party years were now almost over, government corruption and junkies had won — it was their city. I saw Mayor Koch walking on Ave. A and I asked him the question that was his old famous slogan: "How'm I Doing?" But he never answered, looking unhappy and forlorn.

Many LES struggles were against the status quo, which for decades was controlled by the democrats; too much control by one party and not enough alternative debate or the option to make a change. The power elite had become stagnant, lacked creativity with no sense of direction. Corruption was business as usual while the Big Apple was overripe and rotting.

Mayor Dinkins, elected after Koch, started to clean up and restructure the police department. His Mollen Commission on police corruption helped illuminate a deep and troubling systemic relationship between narcotics, the NYPD, and the criminals on both sides who sold the drugs. The 9th Precinct, frequently in the news, became such a focus that it had its own chapter in The Mollen Report. Sadly, the 7th and 5th Precincts, also a part of the LES Golden Triangle, were never investigated. Many of the positions that the protesters took, in the end, proved not only ethical but right; whenever I went to court, I would bring up the relationship between police and drugs. The NYPD now had two black eyes: one from the police riot and the other from the public's conclusion that NYPD participated in the drug trade. The Dinkins administration started to clean up, reorganize, retrain and implement a paramilitary model. Dinkins' changes gave Giuliani a much more cleaned-up force, allowing Giuliani to carry out his law and order authoritarian point of view.

In 1988, the cops could not close a 10 1/2 acre park on the LES On 09.11.01. in a couple of hours, the NYPD closed down the whole city: bridges, tunnels, subways, buses, airports, ferries, and most of the traffic in lower Manhattan. During the Koch period, people believed that the City could never be "controlled." Now some say, we are close to a police state. We have moved from one extreme to the other.

I thought it was important to have scholars contribute to the book. Al Orensanz's chapters about Dorothy Day and Emma Goldman give context to these women in the community and an understanding of struggles common to the LES. Janet Abu-Lughod and Christopher Mele are leading experts on the sociological and economic life of the LES. John McMillian, also helpful with editing, has been instrumental in preserving the history of the LES '60s radical group "The Motherfuckers."

A Radical Political and Social History of the Lower East Side

The LES has always had a heavy influence on American culture and politics. History has been changed many times by the people who lived here or passed through. The backbone of these creative times was cheap rent and the constant flow of the brightest and most unique of the newly arriving immigrants. Records of these influences are scattered, and there is little remaining evidence because it was either a youthful scene that moved on, an anti-social scene, or too working-class to matter. The LES community has always been about difficulties; so many of those influential ones did not leave a recorded history.

In the early '80s, in anticipation of the transfer of Hong Kong to mainland China, a Tsunami-like wave of Chinese currency flooded New York, absorbing blocks of real estate on the Bowery and practically all of Little Italy until it was no longer an Italian stronghold. Although Little Italy has retained it's name as a tourist stop, individual properties were also bought below 14th Street and so began one of the first real gentrifying factors in the LES.

Recently, New York Law School and New York University, with their insatiable appetite for more land and with student dorms presently under construction, have begun to flood the LES with transient students and all that entails. LES is starting to look like Greenwich Village following the '60s: bars and restaurants catering to people from other places looking to get drunk or well fed. The destructive effect of gentrification can also be seen in SoHo, not an important art center for twenty years, and recently the art galleries have moved out. Now the LES has so many of these tourist places that I wonder if anything creative will ever happen here again? Kill the anarchy and you kill the spirit.

There is no heaven on earth. When you clean out the drugs and street crime, what you get in return are yuppies and narcissistic self-obsessed values. Our community now suffers under a different kind of unethical and immoral behavior. Street robberies were once done by desperate, raggedy people. Robbers now come dressed in expensive suits carrying fat real estate portfolios stuffed with court papers, and then come lawyers, followed by politicians who overturn rent and real estate laws, while government agencies encourage citizens to rat out their neighbors with anonymous, malicious 311 calls.

We have entered a different period. In the old days, street dealers flaunted the law and got a free ride. Richard Kusack's chapter details a developer who deliberately went against building department rules and regulations and was still rewarded by being allowed to keep the additional five stories that he'd illegally added in violation of zoning laws. For connoisseurs of irony, the best part of this flagrant disregard for the community and zoning laws is that New York Law School put their seal on the deal by agreeing to rent the building as a law school dorm.

What seems like the Law School's contradiction of ethics may give credence to the low opinion a lot of regular people feel about the law, lawyers and the government. Or maybe the school teaches an alternative point of view: all laws are alleged, so there are no real standards. Any law can be put in flux, so now there is a thirteen story building on a tenement block zoned for five stories and Con Ed cannot keep up.

Clayton Patterson

As the community loses it's working class, it's creative artistic edge, and it's anarchistic stance, it is no longer a ghetto. The police are no longer in the background, instead sitting in parked police vehicles or patrolling in paramilitary uniforms carrying submachine guns. In 2006 LES, the foreground noise is real-estate, zoning, skyscrapers, demolition of landmark buildings, rent, and an over-developed entertainment zone sporting shoulder-to-shoulder bars, restaurants, and night spots.

Expensive rents have nearly stopped the influx of the tired huddled masses. Now all we see is the bourgeois immigrants who have careers or the money to integrate their way into the system. For the most part, the young today are not the mesmerized starry-eyed youngsters looking to find a way to be artists or musicians. It is too expensive to live here. Now the youth who are showing up en masse are transient students paying high college tuitions, trying to develop a career and then go back to where they came from. The LES has become a full-scale entertainment zone for people from outside the neighborhood. The blue collar working class has almost been pushed out, and people are too wrapped up in their own careers, or survival, to be involved with anything anti-social, or anti-authoritarian, or anything that seriously questions the system.

Nothing has permanently changed the LES as much as gentrification. Not Jacob Riis, not the fires, not the Slocum disaster, not the riots. All the social changes and disasters were absorbed into the texture of the neighborhood and the community went back to being somewhat the same. Gentrification has left a mark that will permanently change this community forever.

A Radical Political and Social History of the Lower East Side

Avenue A, 1991

Tompkins Square Park, 2003

Photographs By Clayton Patterson

A Radical Political and Social History of the Lower East Side

HOWL performance in Tompkins Square Park, 2003

Jim "Mosaic Man" Power is ripping the mosaics off his Veterans at War and Lesko lamp post at 7th Street & Ave A. Jim is homeless and says he was cheated by HOWL.

HOWL/Feva (Federation of East Village Artists) was formed to fight against gentrification. Its Mission Statement promised to protect, support and promote local artists, celebrating creative venues, thereby strengthening the sense of a creative community. HOWL/Feva promised artists housing, health care, a Smithsonian of the counter culture. It was just a con. *HOWL*, the title of the poem by Allen Ginsberg, was the brand, and the artists became a front to attract private investment. In the end, HOWL/ Feva nailed the coffin lid shut on 150 years of a struggling creative community. HOWL/Feva became the demarcation line for the Death of Bohemia.

                                    - Clayton Patterson

A Radical Political and Social History of the Lower East Side

ATTENTION

XX

CONGRESS OF RESISTANCE

The worldwide Political, Business and Cultural Power is trying to control all spheres of human activity: social, cultural, scientific, and life itself! The mass media, controlled and led by the same Power determine the quality and fairness of the social and cultural phenomena as well as of the scientific research, medical practices and pharmacological control. They are trying to usurp the right to declare some social arrangements positive, i.e. good, and others negative, i.e. evil. Thus they manipulate the morals and conscience of the human community. They promote people advancing their ideologies to be the cultural idols and use television and drugs to control our minds and beings. The triumph of the theatrical democracy is the demise of Democracy. The triumph of the Avant-garde has consigned its achievements to the museums, thus abolishing the avant-garde; all under the guise of the now outdated concept of modernism. They may have abolished the avant-garde, but they could not abolish its traditions — the traditions of free thinking and spirit. All the institutions have been monopolized: the press, television, communications, culture, etc. The society is facing an abyss. That's why we are appealing to all the free thinking people — the dissidents and individuals — to the political and cultural human being of the Earth! to come together and create an action. All come together to create a peoples congress.

We need a Congress of Resistance!
We need to mobilize all the progressive forces to conduct a Congress of Resistance.
Resistance to what?
Resistance to massive lies, corruption, imperialism, violence, body and mind control. We will build the Congress of Resistance with the goal of defending human dignity freedom of thought and creativity, human individuality. All out for the Congress of Resistance! and to create an action.

Clayton Patterson, NYC - L. Pinchevsky, NYC -- Alexander Brener Moscow.

Supporters:
Ferderico G. Pommier Vincelli, Historian, Rome, Italy / Konstantin Simun, Artist, Boston / Mark Kramer, Writer, NYC / Robert D. Brown, Artist, NYC / Anne Ardolino, Poet, NYC / Elsa Rensaa, Artist, NYC / Ralph Feldman, Photographer, NYC / Jim Power, Mosaicman, NYC / Vagrich Bakhchanyan, Artist, NYC / Charles Gatewood, Photographer, SF / Boris Lurie, Artist, NYC / Sasha Bourdo, Actor, Paris / Eleen Ribire, Journalist, Paris / Dietmar Kirves, Artist, Berlin / Mathilda Wolf, Artist, Berlin / Manwoman, Artist, B.C., Canada.

Published in: Manhattan Mirror, New York, 1997

Intro

Welcome to Our Resistance: The What and Why of the Tompkins Square Park Rebellion
By Alan W. Moore

In Tompkins Square Park today, the tousle-haired children play in their yards, the dogs romp in theirs, and young people lounge on the grass during warm weather. Most people seem prosperous, well groomed, and carefree. It's another world from fifteen years ago, when the park was a graffiti-smeared battleground for squatters and cops, and the surrounding streets were still game zones for the street hustler poets that Miguel Piñero wrote about: poverty-driven and drug-related.

By the late 1980s, the housing crisis for low income people had become intolerable. Epidemic AIDS and homelessness beached thousands on the city's streets. Dozens of vacant city-owned properties were squatted. As property values rose, the city moved to retake these buildings. The squatters, many of them anarchists, organized a spectacular protest. That moment was the last great effulgence of resistant culture on the Lower East Side. Its spirit is at the heart of this book. That is its reason to be, to recall, explain and to memorialize that resistance.

This book is the result of Clayton Patterson's dogged persistence. He is an artist, a documentary photographer, and a gallery entrepreneur. While he is not a bookman, his years in the neighborhood have given him the knowledge and feeling for the people who make it up, and he has beaten the bushes for years to get their stories.

These essays were written by sociologists, art historians, anarchists and theorists, housing activists, psychologists, political prisoners, journalists and police. They tell the stories of sweeping economic and demographic changes, of buildings abandoned and reclaimed, and of the people who lived to lead resistance in New York. In this book you'll find careful analysis next to polemic and coup-counting, episodes of desperate poverty, the glamour of fierce struggle and numbing legalism. Here, art and politics are blended in a cannibal stew. While the variety of writing may seem bewildering, it is a true reflection of a part of the world that has contributed so much to American urban culture.

The first part of *Resistance: A Radical History of the Lower East Side* is historical. Cultural historian Al Orensanz recounts the story of the anarchist Emma Goldman and Catholic Worker founder Dorothy Day. These two extraordinary women embody the paradigms of the radical alternative culture in the United States. Goldman arrived in New York in the 1880s during the charged days following the Haymarket Riot in Chicago, a high water mark of militant

A Radical Political and Social History of the Lower East Side

working class anarchism in the United States. Dorothy Day worked for peace and "Catholic communism" until her death in 1980. In Orensanz's view, both women's radical experiments failed, recalled today only as "vignettes in the mainstream development of American life."

He roots Goldman's anarchism firmly in Jewish internationalism, and examines Day's work in the political climate of the New Deal and post-war anticommunism. Goldman's influence faded with the anarchist movement itself during the years of strong state socialism and capitalism. Day, Orensanz maintains, failed to realize the possibilities of alliance with the Puerto Rican labor movement and the 1960s counterculture. Overall, Orensanz seeks to discern the drive towards a synthetic revolutionary potential in the mixture of ethnicities and agendas on the Lower East Side.

Fred Good's essay is a dense, concisely written memoir by a close participant in the many utopian and cultural projects begun on the Lower East Side of the 1960s and '70s. Born to Belgian parents, Fred Good became a compadre of young Puerto Rican activists on the Lower East Side in the mid-1960s. He describes the genesis of their group "Real Great Society," and tells of its leader former gang member Chino Garcia. Good wrote grants and coordinated publicity for the RGS. Their first big undertaking was "University of the Streets," a storefront open education project eventually lodged in a building donated by a wealthy Dutchman. Good sketches in the political background of President Lyndon Johnson's "War on Poverty," as it played out on the Lower East Side, and he details the ethnic nationalist currents that broke and reformed the group.

Central to Good's tale is the story of the Nuyorican poets. The most famous of them was Miguel Piñero, but it was Miguel Algarin who started the Nuyorican Poets Café in 1975. Good describes the utopian undertakings of the "11th Street Movement," in which buildings reclaimed through "sweat equity" became centers of solar and wind power and basement fish farms. CHARAS, the successor organization of RGS, took over a large abandoned school on 10th Street and ran it as the El Bohio cultural center until 2001, when the city took control under Mayor Rudolph Giuliani. (The struggle to regain community control of this building continues as this book goes to press.) Good, in passing, discusses a score of other community-based arts groups.

Philosopher and art historian Thomas McEvilley's memoir of two decades living on the Lower East Side describes the transformation of the neighborhood. The open air drug trade and prostitution marked the neighborhood when he moved into it, and he tells one sad story of child slavery. At the same time, the East Village art movement and cocaine-fueled nightclub scene was developing in the environment. Like many in this book, McEvilley comments drily on the ways in which the neighborhood's art scene promoted gentrification, how the 1980s fever for art "spread the idea that the neighborhood was entering or about to enter a new era." At present, McEvilley sees a neighborhood "poised between two worlds"— the "soul-destroying gentrification" which continues to transform streets, competing with the neighborhood's tradition as a center of culture and creativity.

Sociologist Christopher Mele's essay, "Making Art and Policing Streets: The Early Years of Gentrification on the Lower East Side," is a fact-laden socio-political account of a complex story. It moves from its genesis in abandoned buildings and urban decay during the 1970s through the consummation of the area during the administration of Mayor Giuliani as a "branded" settlement area for young urban professionals. Mele minutely charts the economic conditions and political maneuvers that fed these trends. He details how the subversive anti-establishment and working class past of the area was co-opted by gentrification forces and fashioned, with the aid of artists and other cultural actors, into an edgy but depoliticized identity.

Before beginning her career as a preeminent radical lawyer, Lynne Stewart worked in the 1960s as a New York City school librarian. In her essay, she tells of the 1967 city-wide teachers' strike from the point of view of the activists on the Lower East Side who sought community control of schools. This is a committed account of days when a multi-ethnic mobilized community struggled with the striking teachers' union to keep their schools open, and Black Panthers guarded the steps.

Joe Flood tackles the complex problem of "Homelessness and the Lower East Side." He discusses the waves of building abandonment by landlords, the closure of state mental hospitals, and job loss due to de-industrialization. The Bowery, on the western edge of the Lower East Side, acted as a funnel for the region's homeless into the district. Flood spices his account with harrowing stories from the area's notorious shelters, such as the stabbed man who was required by staff to clean up his own blood. The influx of cheap smokable cocaine called "crack" in the 1980s combined with police corruption to create neighborhoods seemingly out of control.

In a recollection of the extensive early Italian presence on the Lower East Side, the video artist Aldo Tambellini writes of documenting the meetings of the Italian-American Civil Rights League, and videotaping the aftermath of the assassination attempt on leader Joe Colombo.

Steve Zehentner writes of the 1998 demolition by city authorities of a largely rent-controlled tenement building in defiance of a judge's order. The tactic of demolition was used repeatedly by the city against buildings occupied by squatters and low-income tenants. In meticulous detail, Zehentner describes the lightning demolition and the case as it wound through the courts, laying direct blame for this radical dispossession at the feet of Mayor Giuliani.

The distinguished urban sociologist Janet L. Abu-Lughod writes "Money, Politics and Protest: The Struggle for the Lower East Side." In this memoir, Abu-Lughod recounts how, as the result of a teaching appointment in 1987, she became involved in local politics and residents' efforts to fight the ongoing gentrification of the area. Through her experiences with the research center she helped to create, she describes the different agendas united under the umbrella of the "Joint Planning Council," its successful mobilization of local energies and its eventual fragmentation and failure. Alternating between a "sidewalk's-eye view" of the residents' struggle and a description of the neighborhood's wider sociological context, she deftly mixes the personal and the historical in an engaging and hopeful narrative.

A Radical Political and Social History of the Lower East Side

Yuri Kapralov, novelist and artist, writes *"Christodora, The Flight of a Sea Animal,"* on the great high-rise built as a settlement house for the poor. The place saw four years of occupation by radical activists before police stormed it and sealed it for 14 years. (It was later renovated as a high-income condominium.) In his inimitable style, Kapralov evokes the daily life of poor residents on the streets in 1960s and '70s.

An essayist and radical historian, Peter Lamborn Wilson (aka Hakim Bey) recently moved out of New York City to live in the country. His memoir is partly about the series of changes that led to that decision, with detailed asides on the Lower East Side's radical past and the role that movements as diverse as "French Situationism" and "Beat Culture" played in the recent life of NYC Bohemia. Wilson uses his experience as a jumping off point to trace the complex intellectual and cultural history of the Lower East Side.

Journalist Colin Moynihan defines a squat, writing a concise and straightforward explanation of the backgrounds, situations and ideals of these resistant urban homesteaders. He describes the rough politics — electoral and otherwise — that led to the squatters' millennial deal with the city government, and speculates on why it came to pass.

Renowned graphic artist Seth Tobocman writes from inside the movement of anarchist squatters. In this memoir, Tobocman describes his experience during the Tompkins Square riots and the general climate of the neighborhood. He insists that only by understanding the larger political backdrop of the years of Ronald Reagan's presidency can one understand what occurred on August 6th, 1988. He describes his life in the neighborhood and his evolution into an "irresponsible community organizer." His group put together the effective "eviction watch" phone tree and the 1986 New Years' Eve rock concert in the park, while supporting squats and interacting with other local housing groups.

The conversation between Father George Kuhn and editor Clayton Patterson reveals the continuity between the work of Dorothy Day and today's activist clergy. Kuhn understands himself as a Christ-centered contemplative, a peacemaker and justice seeker through his religious commitment, confronting today's neo-feudal order through the time-tested principles of the Catholic church. This discussion ranges over an extensive discussion of the police, their leadership, corruption investigations, and their conduct during the 1988 riot in the park. Kuhn worked against the rampant drug trade, trying to direct it away from sensitive areas, like the entrance to schools. He and other religious leaders were arrested after they delivered food to besieged squatters who had taken over a building as a community center. The prosecution in their subsequent trial was founded on systematic misrepresentation by testifying police officers.

The widely-published author and artist Richard Kostelanetz points directly at the anarchist roots and leanings of leading Lower East Side cultural figures, including novelist Henry Miller, Lee Baxandall (an avowed marxist), The Living Theatre (led by Judith Malina and Julian Beck) and the vastly influential composer John Cage.

Eric Miller, a folklorist and media artist, shares his thoughts about the public lives of people in the East Village neighborhood that he knew. Commencing with a personal self-positioning, including his current anthropological work with nomadic people in India, Miller describes the characters who hung out at Ray's newsstand on Avenue A across from Tompkins Square Park. These vignettes look at the people whose presence was essential to the maintenance of resistance, although they invariably vanish from most historical reckonings. Miller carefully describes the social ecology of the park before its "cleansing" by city police. He extends his consideration of the interstitial lives of marginal people through a psychogeographical description of his favorite walk along the East River down the island's edge to south Manhattan.

The second section of *Resistance*, on housing, is the guts of this book, directly concerning the incidents and mechanics of what anarchist propaganda called the "total war for living space" being waged on the Lower East Side.

Sarah Ferguson, a journalist who covered much of the squatter resistance story for the *Village Voice*, pens a close consideration of the period in the light of present realities. She begins with a sketch of the historical role that Tompkins Square Park played as the open-air "living room" for a community of poor people living in densely crowded tenements. She discerns that what happened in the last decades was the forcible erasure of that history and what Pierre Bourdieu calls "habitus." The set of local public practices, carried from generation to generation, was forcibly uprooted, disrupted and replaced with a new set of practices — those of the returning suburban bourgeoisie.

Being an engaged reporter, Ferguson understands her story now as that of "the last generation of activists to conceive of the Lower East Side as oppositional space." A key figure in this understanding was Frank Morales, an Episcopal priest who explicated what activists charged was the government policy of "spatial deconcentration" — the systematic withholding of services from poor communities to clear them for the middle class. For the squatter activists of the district, taking over buildings was a counterattack in the war of government upon the urban poor.

(In recent years, the work of the urban sociologist team of Deborah and Rodrick Wallace have fleshed out what was then widely regarded as paranoid exaggeration. Their book *Title of It* documents the think-tank studies that encouraged cities nationwide to allow their urban centers to turn into wastelands.)

Ferguson recounts the political history of Tompkins Square Park as a center of resistance. She calls it a "mythos," a key locale in the conception of "political and economic exceptionalism" that guided many on the Lower East Side. She describes in detail the homesteading programs developed under President Jimmy Carter's administration that were leading to reclamation of abandoned buildings as low income housing — programs scrapped by President Ronald Reagan. She sees squatting as a logical reaction to the city and federal refusal to build low income housing.

Ferguson's interview with David Boyle reveals the ways in which the homesteading, community garden and squatting movements evolved as the political climate turned chilly for tenants and warm for speculators. She describes the "corridor of squats" on East 8th Street,

A Radical Political and Social History of the Lower East Side

whose residents brought with them tactics and politics from the vast European urban squatting scene and openly defied the city government. Squatting on the Lower East Side became part of a comprehensive lifestyle of social activism, and, as rental prices spiked in the mid-1980s, the graffitied slogans and posted broadsides of the movement pointed the finger at the gentrifiers.

Her account of the riot is balanced, describing both the acts of provocation and the clear intent of the police to crack down on the boisterous cadre of radicals. She describes the relationship between older housing activists and the younger squatters, and details the consequences of the election of the neoconservative councilman Antonio Pagan. The militancy of the squatters was met by a full-scale militarization of police tactics.

Seth Farber, a psychologist, recalls his early years as a committed student on the Lower East Side. The mounting homeless crisis, he asserts, was rationalized by the corporate media as a flood of the deinstitutionalized mentally ill — in fact it was a housing crisis as the city abandoned the poor. Farber is committed to structural family therapy as a means of treating the mentally ill, not relying upon neuroleptic drugs and striving to free the mad from their "assigned role" as patients. Public mental health does not accept these methods, so Farber began to work with networks formed by activist patients themselves. He names well-known artists who were part of this movement, and describes how the squats of the Lower East Side helped people to successfully deinstitutionalize themselves. Farber concludes with a critique of the conservative ideologues who "medicalized" the homeless problem, calling it "madness in the streets." This position strengthened medical institutions, another instance of psychiatry in service of the emerging urban status quo.

Joanne Edelman's stories of her life in a squat on East 7th Street are a bizarre blend of normal domestic life and episodes of high drama involving machetes. JoAnn Wypijewski's account of her legal victory over a shyster middleman selling fake leases reflects an earlier period when activist agencies and the city government worked together. She reminds us that the squatter rebellion and police confrontation belongs to a period of backlash against people's power. Daniel Edelman recollects his legal work on behalf of an East 7th Street building, revealing the complexity of each building's situation and the personal relationships that move city real estate cases.

Cooper Square is one of the oldest tenant action groups on the Lower East Side. Chris Brandt's narrative begins with an anecdote about garbage which illustrates the practical politics of the group. Cooper Square, which included academics and city planners in its number, began in the 1950s to contest New York's master planner Robert Moses and his plans to displace thousands of low-income tenants to build an expressway. The group used theatrical tactics to dispute state-driven urban renewal, dressing up as Indians and encamping along Houston Street in teepees. While market-driven redevelopment is more difficult to oppose since it's less easy to personify and therefore may appear "natural," the theatrical elements of resistance by activists remained a key part of the housing battles of later years.

Frank Morales was a leader of the squatter resistance in the '80s and '90s, and in Aaron Jaffe's interview, he discusses the theories of "spatial deconcentration," the removal of the poor from urban areas, (as reported by government and in the writings of prominent conservatives). The squatting movement began simultaneously in the Lower East Side and the South Bronx. Activists perceived that HPD, the city's housing agency, was allowing vacant buildings to deteriorate. They were "land banking." Morales describes in detail the procedure for taking over a building in New York, and the network of mutual support that helped prevent evictions.

Like Mike Davis, in his recent book *Planet of Slums*, Morales' analysis of the housing crisis in New York is global. He regards the city homeless shelter system as "low intensity detention." He distinguishes the squatters' position from that of other neighborhood housing activists, and describes both the political and legal work they undertook and the day-to-day struggles with police.

Fly, an artist and writer, tells of her life in the squats in a 1999 piece, and her involvement with the activist art and community center "ABC No Rio" on Rivington Street. This collectively managed building, a stalwart venue for hardcore Punk music, is closely identified with the squatter and anarchist movements, and other resistance movements.

The crucial subject of zoning is addressed in Richard Kusack's exhaustive text, which is essentially a legal brief concerning one building. Legal and political contests over land use are paramount in what is to be done, as Roland Legiardi-Laura points out in his text "Soul War for the East Village." His mission now is to preserve the "communal and creative qualities" of the District, the "poetry, politics, passion, proud poverty" and tradition of struggle that make it a place where creative people want to live. Fights over zoning are crucial to stem the "attack of the giant towers," that is, over-sized apartment buildings. Legiardi-Laura's report on current issues facing local activists today includes the tasks of historical preservation and the protection of the many community gardens developed simultaneously with the homesteads and squats.

The next section of the book deals with the backgrounds of the central event of the resistance to gentrification, the Tompkins Square Park riot of 1988. In fact, the confrontations between activists and police extended over many years, climaxing in the 1988 riot and continuing into the 1990s.

Anarchist activist A. Kronstadt writes under a nom de guerre, backgrounding what he calls the "Tompkins Square Rebellion." What drove many of the activists in this battle, he writes, was not only ideology but their personal experience of some of the harsher tactics landlords used to empty buildings of low-rent tenants.

Kronstadt tells the story of implementating "quality of life" policing under Mayor Ed Koch, beginning with a crackdown on pot smoking in Washington Square Park. Here the curfew was first established, a practice police used later in Tompkins Square Park. Kronstadt describes the concerts and rallies that anarchist squatters organized at the bandshell in the park. (The bandshell was later demolished by the city.) The radicals — and Kronstadt details their differences and squabbles with liberal housing activists — were united by two main principles, opposition to gentrification and resistance to increasing police repression.

A Radical Political and Social History of the Lower East Side

The "Heterodox Movement" was anchored by the "Anarchist Switchboard" and "Sabotage Books." It was made up of many "kitchen table cabals," cellular organizations that organizers today might call "affinity groups." Fire barrels around which the homeless congregated became important rallying places for activists, who plastered their propaganda messages regularly around the park. Kronstadt describes the squats defense against eviction, and the sensational reporting of television journalists, smearing the scruffy movement with the charge of satanism.

In his detailed blow-by-blow insider account of the park activists, Kronstadt marks a beginning for the large encampment of homeless in Tompkins Square Park, and describes every major encounter of the period. He differentiates between the different detachments of police who worked the park, some tolerant and others "mean," and describes the struggle up to the point of the park's closure.

The Tent City story in Tompkins Square Park is told by Ron Casanova, a lifelong Lower East Sider who became the spokesman for the homeless living in the park. His is a strong, colorful account of the texture of homeless life, and of the alliance with the black-clad chain-smoking anarchists. His "Tent City" group, held themselves apart from many other drug-users in the park. Like Kronstadt, Casanova tells the sad story of the homeless Polish man, Ed, who froze to death the night a policeman kicked over his fire barrel, and of many incidents in the epic struggle with police. This story is about the strong personal relationships that undergirded homeless activism, including the inspiring trip to Philadelphia to participate in the national homeless organizing campaign "Survival Summit" and the subsequent march on Washington, D.C.

Ellen Moynihan writes of the May Day Riot of 1990, resulting when police peremptorily shut down a music concert organized by squatters in Tompkins Square Park. This riot resulted in numerous prosecutions targeting squatter leaders for inciting to riot, and represents the state's success in criminalizing the resistance movement. The event was the fourth annual concert in the park on May Day, and Moynihan tells some of the local history of the date's significance for the labor movement. May Day was also the time leases expired for tenement dwellers in the 19th century.

A perspective on the 1988 riot is provided in the essay by John Mellon, a police officer. Mellon reviews the events of the evening with attention to the question of leadership, concluding that the presiding commander was unprepared to lead police in the confrontation with protesters. In fact, Captain MacNamara "bit the onion" for the riot, in that he was blamed for the debacle and relieved of his command. But, Mellon observes, the police department as a whole was unfamiliar with the broader political issues behind the protests, and tactically impoverished.

Joshua Rothenberger discusses the famous three hour and thirty-three minute long video-tape shot the night of the riot by the editor of this book, Clayton Patterson. Rothenberger brings the precepts of media theory to bear on Patterson's work in the park, understanding it as grassroots alternative media. The stark, uncontestable document of police misconduct countered the consistently pejorative presentation of the East Village resistance movement in the mainstream media, both television and newspapers. In his close reading of the filmic "text," Rothenberger discusses Patterson's positioning, the verbal reactions to his presence by members of the crowd in the park that night, and the dialogues he had during the lulls in the action.

Rothenberger notes that "police brutality" stood in for the broader warfare on the poor mandated by shifts in late capitalist modes of production, that is, displacement of the working class from their historic district due to deindustrialization of the City. As the Lower East Side was transformed into the "bedroom of Wall Street," police brutality became a stand-in for this process, both necessitated by it and representing it.

One of the more unusual pieces in this collection is the reflection by Michael Julian on his years commanding the 9th Precinct. The direct voices of police are rarely heard in histories of resistance. Julian offers disturbing testimony on the disorder of the Tompkins Square Park encampment of homeless, and sharp criticism of the squatters as self-serving and intimidating. He recounts the spike in thefts and drug sales that accompanied the encampment, and describes the regular open-air markets of stolen goods.

Julian is hard on his own troops as well, describing the entrepreneurial overtimers and bad arrests with which he had to contend. An intelligent and skillful policeman, he describes his methods of dealing with the "cop baiting" activists through restraint, communication, and small squadrons of police rather than the prevailing strategy of the top brass, "calling out the army." The belligerent, planless resolve of city bureaucrats who did not have to do the dirty work of evictions often made his work difficult. Julian also says that he was called in by one group of anarchists to protect them from another during the demise of the "Anarchist Switchboard."

Finally, in an instance of intertextual drama, Julian's account of the May Day Riot of 1990 directly contradicts Ellen Moynihan's above. He appeals to the video evidence . . .

In the preface to his collection of period articles in this section, journalist Bill Weinberg reflects that declamations of the "annoyingly apocalyptic" anarchists of the day seem to have proven correct — Tompkins Square was a "social laboratory of the new security state." He also notes a resurgence of the activist spirit in the neighborhood in this new century, and the deep persistence of "deviationism" in human environments.

This is the topic of his first piece describing the legacy of rebellion. In a concise and colorful historical account, Weinberg traces the oppositional history of Tompkins Square Park and the Lower East Side neighborhood it serves since its establishment in 1834.

He next dissects the May Day riot of 1990, discussed above by Moynihan and Julian, in a thoughtful, interview-laced piece written a few weeks after the event. The police shut down the last moments of the four-day "Resist 2 Exist" festival. Was it a provocation? If so by whom? Weinberg talked to all the principals, including an arrested activist who had heard police in another precinct criticizing the commander of the 9th for being soft — "in South

A Radical Political and Social History of the Lower East Side

Korea they turned water cannons on 'em." The diversity of the movement becomes clear in his mention of the Revolutionary Communist Party, whose Maoist members staged a re-occupation of the evicted ABC squat.

Weinberg explicates the anarchist critique of the liberal housing activists' settlement with the city, the "50-50" plan in which private market-rate development would fund low-income housing. He also discusses the "Missing Foundation" rock band, the group that provided a soundtrack to the riot by continuing the park concert banging on metal after the electricity had been shut off. MF graffiti was ubiquitous in the neighborhood, promising class war in the police state, and threatening the bourgeoisie moving in. This was insurrectionary political culture intended to slow gentrification: "In the Nihilist equation, more flying bottles translates into fewer homeless."

A year later, Weinberg's reporting has turned committed. In "Police State," he pinpoints the looting of a small store as the pretext police needed to close the park, which would remain closed for two years. (The looting also moved anarchist activists toward a policy of nonviolence.) He reports the outrage of the local community board, the civic group Mayor David Dinkins did not consult in his plans to reconfigure Tompkins Square Park. He then penetrates the maze of housing politics on the Lower East Side, describing the conservative pro-development group (whose leader Antonio Pagan would soon win a seat on the city council) and the tension-wracked liberal housing coalition. Behind this antagonism is the larger reality of redistricting, redrawing electoral lines to link the low-income communities of the Lower East Side with adjacent wealthy areas.

As children accessed their playground through police barricades, this writing evokes the sense of a neighborhood under siege by arbitrary city authority. Weinberg reveals the extent to which mainstream community governance was entwined with the homeless and squatter resistance. He mentions the post clearance homeless encampments that sprang up on vacant lots near the park, and quotes a citizen who fears what eventually happened – wholesale removal of the homeless to shelters on the city's outskirts where they have been forgotten.

Weinberg describes the new shadow-and-arrest tactics that undercover police were using against activists, and an attempted push-in by cops on the St. Brigid's church, which was supporting the homeless and the demonstrations against the closure, across from the park. At this point, during the first Gulf War, which many in the community were protesting, the cautious Julian is relieved of command at the 9th precinct, and FEMA is consulting with local law enforcement on the heavily-surveilled closed park. Demolition of recently-built facilities is underway in the park because it is the kind of "renovation" that is impossible to stop.

In the next section of the book: "Politics," Clayton Patterson speaks directly. In my profile of this book's editor, Clayton discusses his longtime freelance documentary work in the context of mainstream television. As a photographer of demonstrations and police work, Clayton was always aware of the danger and ambivalence of his position absent press credentials as a pure observer, authorized only as citizen and artist. As an artist he is caustic on the 1980s East Village art scene participants who abandoned the neighborhood and in retrospect, were obviously (and casually) complicit with gentrification. He well understands the consistent radical activists and the dynamics of the squatter movement, and is unsparing in his critique of the degenerated traditional Democratic political apparatus in the neighborhood.

Clayton discourses at length about the police, alleging their complicity with the long-running broad-based community drug trade. (Was this overt corruption, as in other precincts, or more largely the kind of "bureaucratic entrepreneurialism" Julian notes, in which cops learned how to milk the system with minimal exposure to hazard and a minimal effect on the trade?) Clayton's central contention about the effect of the Tompkins Square movement on the police, however, is that fighting this resistance schooled the New York police in paramilitary methods, the kind they use today to contain and suppress demonstrations. These methods were in full effect during the 2004 Republican National Convention here.

For his part, in this piece, Allan Antliff situates Clayton's politics in terms of classical anarchism. His reply: "I am an artist." Rather than seeing this as an evasion of political allegiance, Clayton's position accords better in the artistic arena.

Clayton has certainly paid the price many times for his insistent police videotaping. In "Trial and Error," Clayton's partner Elsa Rensaa writes a close account of his legal damages action after being assaulted by numerous police outside a city property auction at police headquarters. The photographer is well known to the force, since he was present at many police brutality trials growing out of his videotape of the 1988 Tompkins Square Park riot. Rensaa discusses the numerous fabrications by police during the failed civil suit, and the irregular behavior of the jury.

In his piece on Patterson's video, written not long after the riot, film historian and journalist Richard Porton contexts the tapes in relation to the traditions of documentary filmmaking. Patterson's work is engaged, not encumbered by a pretense of neutrality. In his close reading of the tape, Porton reflects on various recorded statements in terms of revolutions past — the 1789 French, the Paris Commune and the 1874 Tompkins Square Riot. In an analysis of late 20th century anarchist political history, Porton pinpoints what he calls the "transclass" nature of contemporary urban movements based in the "anarcho-punk" alliance. These contemporary international developments contradict orthodox Marxist political analysis.

Porton further expands his view of anarchist history in a brief introduction to what Patterson had planned as the original version of this book — a collection of the Tompkins Square anarchist posters and flyers put up around the park. Porton discusses Emma Goldman, Hyppolyte Havel and the anarcho-syndicalist Sam Dolgoff. Porton observes that anarchists on the Lower East Side, unlike the more doctrinaire Marxists committed to the pursuit of state power, "were often the primary mediators between political and artistic subcultures." (This close connection in early 20th century New York has been recently explored in Allan Antliff's book *Anarchist Modernism*, and for turn of the last century Paris in David Sweetman's *Explosive Acts*.) The Tompkins Square Rebellion, as Kronstadt termed it, had support from anarchists worldwide.

A Radical Political and Social History of the Lower East Side

Aaron Jaffe interviews Chris Flash, editor of the anarchist newspaper *The Shadow*. This voice of the anarchist squatter resistance was published by "activist-journalists," a tabloid precursor of today's international web-based Indymedia. The long-running paper is named for the radio drama character Lamont Cranston — (cue long, echoing maniacal laugh.) Chris Flash is versed in the history of underground press — in New York that includes *The East Village Other*, *The Rat*, and briefly The *Village Voice* — and its fate. Jaffe is a good foil to Flash, asking adversarial questions which lead Flash to clearly explain his position.

"The squatters are heroes," Flash says. If so, among these must be counted Kenny Tolia, the only activist to serve time in prison for his role in the 1990 May Day Riot. Tolia tells a compelling story of his initiation as a young man into a squat on 5th Street, "wearing a bike lock for a necklace and homemade bloody shirt reading: EAT THE RICH." He settled in well with his strange comrades and soon "took to preaching the reformed gospel of the European squatters." He defended the homesteader Adam Purple's remarkable "Garden of Eden" (it was destroyed), handled press relations for his own building's struggle to survive city eviction (successful), and opened a number of buildings to set up squats. While Tolia is proud of his role in Lower East Side history, he observes finally, that all signs of that era have today been erased from the streets.

The next section is Biography. In a sense, this has all been biography -- the story of activism of this era is intensely personal, and only the personal stories of a succession of individuals can tell it in its proper dimensions.

The Latino activist tradition on the Lower East Side, and the latter-day gentrification resistance, were closely connected at many points, although that relationship remains to be explicated. The interview with Alfredo Irizarry is one of too few Puerto Rican voices in this book. The road to Irizarry's career in grass roots media production began with his work with Paul Goodman, anarchist philosopher and educator. The interview sketches a subsequent career of '70s utopian community activism in the teeth of one of the district's lowest periods. The "Loisaida movement" took over buildings as community centers, and Irizarry published periodicals and produced video covering the action.

Cheryl Guttman's interview with Yippie activist Dana Beal sketches in the contentious background of the groups organizing the youth rebellion in the '60s and '70s. Beal, inspired by the "Dutch Provos" group, worked with Abbie Hoffman and Jerry Rubin on the Lower East Side, putting together absurdist theatrical demonstrations to drive home political messages. Beal and his friends produced the *Yipster Times* underground journal from their base on Bleecker Street. Beal speaks about the internal politics of the anti-Vietnam War movement. As it swelled, some factions turned to violence. While he was involved in organizing drives marked by violent incidents, Beal preferred "alternative cultural actions." His concerns revolved around drugs, and his groups have sponsored the annual "Smoke-In" demonstrations. Beal agitates for medical marijuana use and promotes the African herb ibogaine as a cure for heroin addiction.

In her report of a meeting with Ben Eagle, formerly Ben Morea of "Up Against the Wall Motherfucker," Eve Hinderer records the bare facts of his biography as Ben related them. A career Lower East Side radical during the 1960s, Ben's group the Motherfuckers did many spectacular actions on the Lower East Side, as well as basic relief work. As the '60s confrontations escalated, the Motherfuckers were the Black Bloc of their day, taking part in riots and specializing in "breakaways" -- gaining entry to protected buildings during demonstrations.

xxxiii

These precursors of the direct action squatters of the end of the century receive a good deal of overdue attention in this book. Historian John McMillian recounts his pursuit of the Motherfuckers story and what can only be called the legend of Ben Morea. Finally he meets Morea in a coffee shop, and writes a charming account of their conversation.

Osha Neumann's account of his time in the Motherfuckers group called "Taking the Plunge" reveals the times and the dynamics of the group. For Neumann, writing theory and making art in a Lower East Side apartment, the "plunge" begins with the Angry Arts week in 1967 to protest the war in Vietnam. This led to a banner action in St. Patrick's Cathedral, and afterwards Neumann helped form Motherfuckers. Under Ben Morea's leadership, group involvement became an identity, a family-like army of long-haired urban guerrillas.

Ben Morea was mentored into the Lower East Side scene by Judith Malina and Julian Beck of the Living Theatre. Hanon Reznikov writes of the period when, after living abroad for many years, after the death of Beck, the Living Theatre reopened in Lower East Side New York in 1989. For a few years, the group offered their brand of issue-oriented committed theatre to a neighborhood in the throes of transition.

John Beresford profiles Jerry the Peddler, the squatter "conductor." Beresford follows Jerry Holtzclaw's life through his childhood in Texas, his stint in the Army (he was ultimately jailed then discharged for refusing to go to Vietnam), and his later experiences in '70s student groups. As one of the many who eked out a living selling stuff on the sidewalks of the neighborhood, Jerry began his organizing career on behalf of street peddlers. Later he became a regular stentorian street voice at housing demonstrations, helped open buildings and instructed neophytes in squatting techniques. As part of that struggle, Jerry also worked to try to save the neighborhood's garden spaces from development, most notably Adam Purple's lost "Garden of Eden."

In a very different vein is the recollection by Michael Rosen of the job he had building the Red Square luxury housing complex, one of the first large constructions in the East Village at the end of the '80s. Rosen recalls a childhood visit to his Orthodox Jewish great-grandfather, part of his family roots on the Lower East Side. In building "Red Square," even as he lived in a penthouse of the oft-attacked Christodora residential tower, Rosen was a developer with deep community roots and a clear consciousness He worked with local artists on the interior décor as well as with famed designer Tibor Kalman on the exterior of the building. Rosen today is an engaged proponent of neighborhood cultural organizations and is active in landmarking buildings and maintaining zoning restrictions.

Mary McCarthy's story of her initiation and involvement with the free magazine *Quality of Life* in Loisaida complements Irizarry's story of his career in community media. As the rough

A Radical Political and Social History of the Lower East Side

conditions of life, and frequent macho confrontations throughout this book, necessarily become the focus of interest, McCarthy reminds us of the rich texture of positive striving, altruism and achievement marking the poor denizens of the Lower East Side. She notes in passing that the now-defunct Cuando community center had the first passive solar energy array in the United States. There oughta be a plaque over the new apartments now under construction there.

In the suavely titled "Land Without Lords," jazz bassist and organizer William Parker talks with friends about his life. Parker moved to the Lower East Side in the mid-1970s — "There were a lot of interesting people doing interesting things . . . sculptors, poets, walking around, carrying things, going from here to there." He describes the process of homesteading his building with his young family. As a jazz musician, he played in many living rooms, squats, community centers, clubs — the many varied places that make up an artistic neigh-borhood, mostly gone today.

The final section of the book is devoted to the crisis of AIDS. For the Lower East Side this will always be about those who are no longer with us. The plague decimated the boldest among a generation of artists and performers, and went a long way to make contemporary culture anemic and academic. What got stronger by far, though, during the years AIDS raged in downtown New York, was the culture of resistance.

Jay Blotcher's vivid account of the life and death struggle of the infected and their allies in the organization ACT UP recalls the urgency of the era. The "charismatic, good-looking bunch of young queers" who found themselves on the front lines of a brilliantly coordinated cam-paign against government and medical establishments learned to form alliances with the poor people among whom they lived, alliances that have become increasingly key as the fronts of the fight against this disease have turned global. Today, in talking to neighborhood newcomers, Blotcher feels nostalgia for the passion of that activism period — "How do you explain to an arriviste that hopelessness is sometimes the only thing that engenders hope?"

Jim Feast's consideration of AIDS on the Lower East Side ties together the "planned shrink-age" program of withdrawing government services (documented in Deborah and Rodrick Wallace's work) with the spreading epidemic. The destruction of social networks as the area was degraded made the district an incubator for disease. It is easy to forget the cruelty of this moment, when public voices argued that those dying of AIDS — the drug-addicted and homosexual — deserved their fate.) Feast offers a picture of the ACT UP movement's contribu-tion to the structure of protest movements — direct democracy, surgically targeted protests, and a deeply informed membership. Some of these were characteristic of the squatters move-ment as well: "This was the period of the radical street expert." Feast argues that lower Manhattan gave the world a new mode of "radical street combat" — "streets" in the case of ACT UP including the television studios of the information superhighway. (The thesis that the methods and ethics of AIDS activism seeded the new period of protests against global capitalism is at the heart of Benjamin Shepard and Ronald Hayduk's anthology *From ACT UP to the WTO, 2002*.) Feast describes the needle exchange program in which addicts were given clean "works" in an effort to stem a nexus of AIDS transmission. Opposed and retarded by

Alan W. Moore

government, including President Bill Clinton, activists took the job to the streets. When they were arrested, their defense was "necessity" actions undertaken to save lives.

Clayton Patterson's anthology is a full dress treatment of subject matter that usually remains obscure. But for this book, much of the Lower East Side of the late 20th century would remain such a shadowland, known primarily to historians, artists and outlaws curious about their heritage. It would be as lost to the general public, Kenny Tolia observes, as the recently excavated Five Points, down in contemporary Chinatown, the real life scene of the film and much of the book *Gangs of New York*.

This book talks from all sides, in discourse that is activist, artistic, writerly, academic, sharply focused, wobbly and meandering. Finally, an extraordinary picture of a signal period in American activism emerges, a fight for place as urban space for ethnic and working-class communities and with them artistic bohemias disappears. This Lower East Side which has been so productive of poetry, music and art, so thriving with hard-luck social schemes of utopian intent, with this book has begun the task of truth telling about itself.

-- Alan W. Moore

The Center of the Fringe World
By Richard Kostelanetz

For over a century now, the Lower East Side has been the most fertile incubator for not only New York City but all radical America. Just as Emma Goldman met Alexander Berkman on Suffolk Street here, so did Allen Ginsberg live east of First Avenue his entire adult life. Dorothy Day's *Catholic Worker* began on East First Street, becoming the liberal conscience for Catholic America. Free Schools of various kinds began here, often finding not only pupils but teachers among nearby residents. On Houston Street, at a rooftop theater late in 1958, I saw Zero Mostel, then still black-listed, play Leopold Bloom in *Ulysses in Nighttown*; it was a masterful performance remembered still. Just as Off-Off-Broadway thrived in the East Village, so was the legendary Fillmore East located on lower Second Avenue and then CBGB's a few blocks away on the Bowery. Lower Second Avenue has likewise housed the legendary Café Royal (until 1953 the intellectual heart of the Yiddish-speaking world), the Poetry Project, the composer Phillip Glass, and the Anthology Film Archives for most of its history.

The Russian revolutionary Leon Trotsky worked in a print shop in the same St. Marks Place building where the Anglo poet W. H. Auden later resided for decades. The Hell's Angels have owned a building and lived on East Three Street since the 1960s. The New York Libertarian Party still has its monthly dinners at a Ukrainian restaurant on lower Second Avenue. Jerry Rubin lived at 5 St. Mark's Place and Abbie Hoffman in the basement of # 30 until his family moved to East Fifth Street, a few doors away from the police station he frequently entered, sometimes involuntarily. 6 St. Marks Place has been at various times the anarchist Modern School, whose board of directors included Emma Goldman, and a differently anarchic gay bathhouse.

In this outlaws' heaven called the LES were published alternative newspapers more radical than the *Village Voice*, including Emma Goldman's *Mother Earth*, Dorothy Day's *Catholic Worker*, *The East Village Other* and *The Rat*, as well as experiments in non-authoritarian editing such as the annual *Assembling*. Here squatters have inhabited empty buildings with no objections from their immediate neighbors, creating models for urban homesteading. During the late 1980s, Tompkins Square Park became a refuge for homeless people who were evicted from other city parks and public spaces.

For over a century now the LES has been a low-rent cultural bohemia hospitable to radicals of all kinds, as distinct from an artists' colony, such as Woodstock or SoHo, or a college campus. The question raised by this book is whether the Lower East Side, even on the verge of appalling gentrification, is still radically incubating?

Over fifty years ago, I was bussed every weekday from the Upper West Side to a "progressive" elementary school on 11th Street near Second Avenue, when "bums," as we used to call them, would inhabit the small park in front of St. Mark's Church. Forty years ago, I

A Radical Political and Social History of the Lower East Side

moved from Harlem near Columbia University, where I was trying to become a scholar, to East Fifth Street between Second and Third Avenues. Since nearly everything important to me was within walking distance, obstacles against participating and enjoying, even for a shy person, such as myself (then), were few.

Here I became a writer, a radical writer some say, because that's what the neighborhood atmosphere fostered in me. The building next to me was owned by the publisher of the old-left National Guardian weekly newspaper. Among his basement tenants was the legendary radical photographer Paul Strand. Down the block lived David Peel, reportedly, along with his collaborators in a rock group called The Lower East Side; among their records were Have a Marijuana, American Revolution, and The Pope Smokes Dope. (In the mid-1970s, I moved to SoHo where I became an artist, thanks in part again to the atmosphere around me; but that's another story, recalled in my *SoHo: The Rise and Fall of an Artists' Colony* [Routledge, 2003].) Had I not resided in the Lower East Side, I probably would have been a different kind of writer (and a different person as well) and certainly not have written this preface. Inhabiting a hothouse influences receptive people to be what they've not been before and would not otherwise be. One truth of *Resistance* is that the Lower East Side has recently been (and perhaps still is) a neighborhood with such a fertile culture.

When I was a disaffected suburban teenager, we congregated on McDougal Street between West Third and Bleecker to find an alternative world. By the sixties, those a decade or so younger would gather on St. Mark's Place, three blocks north of where I then lived. (Now the alternative drag seems to be Ludlow Street, further south within the LES.) One measure of difference between the East Village and the West (of Broadway) in my time is that self-consciously bourgeois people wouldn't want to live among us. The apartments were too small and too shabbily appointed. Some still had bathtubs in the kitchen, yes. This wasn't SoHo, which benefited from ownership and the arts of renovation.

Something on the street would shock proper people, such as bums sleeping on the pavement or a guy pissing or someone selling merchandise obviously pilfered only a few days before; my neighbors coolly ignored all of them, reflecting their profoundly libertarian attitude. (Now the newcomers call 311 or 911.) The only other place in the world where I found a similar resistant atmosphere was Kreuzberg in West Berlin. When Ronald Reagan came to Berlin the second time, City police, recalling earlier demonstrations against him, simply closed off the whole sector, forbidding everyone from leaving it until Reagan left, and literally locking out potential protesters!

For me the surest measures of gentrification are that the bums are long gone from the park in front of St. Mark's Church and that since the 1990s yuppies have wanted to live on the LES rather than just visit. One turning point was the renovation of the imposing Christodora House, vacant for so long, on the east side of Tomkins Square; another, the construction of a new apartment building in the early 1990s, wittily called Red Square on east Houston Street. With a statue of Vladimir Lenin on its roof, it offered 130 rentals that weren't cheap. Indeed, rent in the LES would never be a New York City bargain again. A few years ago, a friend working for a company abroad paid over five thousand dollars per month for a duplex between Avenues B and C — over five grand, which paid several years' rent on the same block

A Radical Political and Social History of the Lower East Side

only a few decades before, and a year's rent into the early 1980s. Nonetheless, for me the Lower East Side has been, and still is, paradoxically, the center of the fringe world.

The best anthologies achieve with many authors what cannot be (or is not) done by one. Until individual scholars do their thing, the books of Clayton Patterson's collaborators, here over three dozen in number, become the richest guides to radical activities on the Lower East Side. If recent "East Village" and "Downtown" gallery exhibitions suffered from leaving too much out, implicitly diminishing their rich subjects, one virtue of Clayton's book(s) reflects his inclusive generosity. Mightily, he tries to incorporate everything and everyone, from artists to professors, activists to absentee intellectuals, among many others, all of them acknowledging that the LES has indeed been a "hood" with a special culture.

SECTION ONE - HISTORY

Chapter 1

Revolution Elsewhere
By Al Orensanz

The lives of Emma Goldman and Dorothy Day span the last hundred years of American social history. These two women are paradigms of the radical experience on the Lower East Side. They were participating witnesses to the expectations and struggles of the working class, as well as the ambitions and failures of radical consciousness in America. These two anarchist women — one an atheist and the other a Catholic — both based their lives in the Lower East Side of Manhattan. By using their life stories as a focus, it is possible to explore the revolutionary perspective of anarchism, its weaknesses and failures in challenging the American State. Biographies point to larger social and historical movements. The differences in politics formed by Goldman's Jewish atheism and Day's Catholicism are explored. And because Manhattan's Lower East Side is more than a backdrop to their stories and politics, because its history dramatizes their experiments and failures, the Lower East Side is the third actor. Its people and history are the touchstone for Goldman's and Day's anarchism.

Manhattan's Lower East Side

The Lower East Side is a distinctive geographical neighborhood in Lower Manhattan, covering approximately one thousand acres from 14th Street, which is its upper boundary. This boundary separates the area's poor proletarian, fast changing, immigrant communities from the middle-income districts north of 14th Street. Broadway is its boundary to the west. To the south, the Brooklyn Bridge ramps act as barriers between the Lower East Side, Wall Street and the Civil Centre section. To the east, the East River forms a continuous border along a gently curving shoreline of parks and piers. The social composition and social history can be compared to East London.

Encounters on the Lower Last Side 1889-1937
Emma Goldman and Alexander Berkman[1]

On a hot Sunday, August 15th 1889, Emma Goldman, a young Russian Jewish girl, twenty years of age, arrived at the Lower East Side from Rochester, New York, after checking her sewing machine at Grand Central Station's baggage room. Hours later, a friend took her to Sach's Cafe on Suffolk Street, a local hang-out for radicals, poets and working-class intellectuals. Here she was introduced to Alexander Berkman, another young Russian immigrant, eighteen years old, who demanded attention from everyone by his exuberant manner. That evening they both attended a lecture by Johann Most, the editor of *Freiheit*, an anarchist paper.

1

A Radical Political and Social History of the Lower East Side

The topic of Most's lecture was the Haymarket Riot: a conventional designation for the imprisonment, trial and execution of four Chicago anarchists in November, 1887, charged with throwing a bomb into a rally on May 4th, 1886. It had since been a heated topic of discussion among working circles and progressive leaders. Johann Most had been in America for six years, arriving from an English prison where he had served sixteen months hard-labor for an article he'd written praising the assassination of Czar Alexander II. Most, a follower of the anarchist, Bakunin, and a strong advocate of "propaganda by deed," made an angry denunciation of the social conditions that had caused the Haymarket Riots.

To Emma and to Alexander Berkman, as to another 130,000 Jews in the Lower East Side, both the martyrs of Chicago and the assassination of Czar Alexander II were spiritual landmarks.[2] Berkman was a boy of eleven in St. Petersburg, when from his classroom, he heard bombs exploding. Emma Goldman was thirteen years old, and to join her father in St. Petersburg, she left her school in Konigsburg, Germany and was smuggled into Russia with her mother and two young brothers (as Jews were not allowed to enter legally). When Emma arrived in St, Petersburg, the city was in a state of terror. The new Czar Alexander III was determined to eliminate all the *narodniki* (populist) leaders and issued a package of new, harsher laws against Jews all over Russia. So the pogroms began.

Emma Goldman arrived in America in the spring of 1883, and Berkman in the winter of 1888. From the time of their meeting on Suffolk Street in 1889, until Emma's death in 1940 in Canada, the labor movement in America, the civil liberties movement and the texture of American social life would feel their profound contribution. And she remained permanently connected with the Lower East Side.

The Lower East Side Jewish Culture[3]

By 1890, the Jewish community consisted of 135,000 people; by 1900 it had increased to 150,000. It was a fairly homogeneous community in terms of ethnic identity, religion, employment, economic class and language (Yiddish), drawn from the pogroms in Lithuania, Ukraine, Germany, Romania, Poland and Hungary. Its economy was based on small factory production and employment in cigar shops, garment shops, laundries, food stores, butchers shops and other workshops, as peddlers and cart vendors. Wages were very low — 50 cents a day on average. The busy and bleak sweatshops of the Lower East Side depended for their trade on a generation of German Jews in uptown Manhattan, with names such as Seligman, Kahn, Goldman, Sachs, Lehman, Lewishon, Loeb and Guggenheim, some of them with previous experience peddling and push-carting on and around Grand Street.

The Jews of the Lower East Side developed one of the most intense and extensive cultural networks ever created by an immigrant group, and Yiddish acquired the status of a major creative language. By 1920, one hundred and fifty newspapers and publications were in existence in the Lower East Side, in several languages: Yiddish, German, Russian, English, Romanian, Ladino and Hebrew. Some twenty theatres around the Bowery offered renewed Yiddish repertory. East Broadway was dubbed as *Nevsky Prospect*, the affluent boulevard in St. Petersburg. A generation of sweatshop poets like Morris Winchesky, David Edelstadt and Morris Rosenfeld produced one of the most genuine working-class poetry movements of all time. Dozens of small halls and back room cafés were the daily meeting place for lectures and heated political and philosophical discussions on Karl Marx, Michael Bakunin, and the intricacies of social democracy, Marxism and Anarchism, as early as 1882.

The Jews moved into an area populated also by some 80,000 Irish, 60,000 Germans and 90,000 Italians in the 1890s. The Lower East Side portal to America was plagued by unemployment, poverty, disease and poor housing. As Bishop John Hughes put it, "it was the poorest and most wretched population that can be found in the world." The City Committee on Housing, in 1880, described it at length as the: "dim, undrained courts oozing with pollution, dark narrow stairways decayed with age, reeking with filth, overrun with vermin, rotted floors, ceilings begrimed . . . inhabited by gaunt shivering forms and wild ghostly faces."[4]

Encounters on the Lower East Side 1932-1980
Dorothy Day and Peter Maurin[5]

Dorothy Day's apartment on East 15th Street was a few blocks from the old address of Goldman and Berkman. (By the time Day lived there, Berkman was exiled in southern France and Emma was traveling through Scandinavia alerting the world to Hitler). Dorothy Day was born in Brooklyn, had spent her early years traveling around the country following her father, a journalist always looking for employment. In 1916, Dorothy arrived on the Lower East Side to live on Cherry Street, not far from the old Sach's café and was employed on several progressive papers like *The Call, The Masses* and *The Agitator*.

The night of December 8th, 1932, Dorothy Day, 30 years old, was just back from an assignment for *Commonweal* covering a Communist sponsored hunger march of the unemployed to Washington. She had been to the National Shrine of the Immaculate Conception in the Capital, praying that she might find something to do in the social order besides report conditions, writing, "I wanted to change them, not just report them, but I had lost faith in the revolution. I want to love my enemy, whether capitalist or communist."

That night, a French working man was waiting for her at home. He was Peter Maurin, 57 years old, a vagabond in Canada and the Midwest, and for some time a hobo on the Bowery just a few blocks from 15th Street. From that night on, Peter Maurin would indoctrinate Dorothy Day, a four-year convert, with his vision of Catholic tradition. Maurin had the idea of publishing a paper he insisted on calling the *Catholic Radical*, but Dorothy Day won out, naming it *The Catholic Worker*. Its offices were in the basement of the same building on East 15th Street.

A Radical Political and Social History of the Lower East Side

The Lower East Side Today

4

At the time of Dorothy Day's death in 1980,[6] the urban landscape of the Lower East Side was practically the same as it was a hundred years before. The municipal reports of the day do not use the Dickensian language of the 1880s, but their content is similar. One quarter of the residential buildings were in poor to critical condition. The old German and Jewish streets of the Lower East Side were practically vacant, a haven for junkies and drug dealers. The Lower East Side was second only to Harlem in the sale of narcotics. The number of mental patients was double the New York average. Approximately five thousand alcoholics and vagrants populated the Lower East Side and the "deinstitutionalized mental patients" were being dumped by the thousands into the area. Unemployment affected forty percent of the population, and crime was rampant.[7]

Certainly, conditions for the Lower East Side had changed little, but the population was different. Dorothy Day's experiment in "houses of hospitality" coincided with the Jewish flight from the area. In 1980, only 25,000 Jews, were entrenched in a small area of public housing called "Cooperative Village." More than 100,000 Jews, as well as thousands of Italians and Irish, had left the area in a process of upward and onward mobility. Hispanics and some Blacks filled the gap, and more recently 100,000 Chinese. This was one of the most dramatic demographic dislocations in America.

While Dorothy Day's experiment was going on, another major revolution took place. The recent flight from the area made space available to accommodate a floating community of 10,000 to 100,000 youths, who, during the '60s and early '70s, gathered in the Lower East Side, experimenting with poetry, drama, films, drugs, communal lifestyles, religion, mystic and metaphysical cults, and alternative press. Allen Ginsberg, William Burroughs, Bob Dylan, Gary Snyder, Timothy Leary and Andy Warhol were among the many who attracted the middle class and unsatisfied youth from all over the country to the biggest counter-culture community outside of San Francisco.[8]

Nowhere At Home . . . On The Edge Of Mainstream American History

Emma Goldman, the émigré, was to grow within a culture of Jewish internationalism, during a period when the Jews were "nowhere at home." Her anarchism spoke to her sense of exile from the dominant culture. The attempt to produce "the deed" (the assassination attempt on Henry Frick, for which Berkman was imprisoned and she was deported) that would inspire and raise the masses was a spiritual action.

In the 1930s, Dorothy Day and Peter Maurin were cultural and ethnic foreigners on the Lower East Side. They used Church tradition to criticize the present . . . both the New Deal and McCarthyism. Their "exile" was also internalized and spiritualized, exiled from the Hispanic labor movement and the counterculture which grew before her eyes.

Praiseworthy comments have been written about both women despite that today their radi
cal experiments tend to look like vignettes in the mainstream development of American life
After all, American history is loaded with reformers and radicals, both individuals and communities, although it is difficult to find a country with a steadier course of affairs. Why is it
that Emma Goldman and Dorothy Day now look like two fascinating yet isolated and obsolete
characters? To understand the *failure* of these two radical experiments, the Lower East Side
will be used as a sample, a condensation, of the entire American urban society which both
Goldman and Day failed to revolutionize.

Emma Goldman

Emma was living in the Lower East Side at the time of a radical, secular culture among the
thriving Jewish immigrants. When the pogroms took place in Russia, the Jews were confronted with the choice of leaving for Palestine (a choice for Zionism and nationalism) or leaving
for America (a choice for internationalism). The leaders, at least, were well aware of this
double choice and they opted for America. They had a conscious understanding that they
were headed to establish a universal socialist society, beyond the barriers of nationality,
ethnicity and religion.

The first Jewish labor leaders of the Lower East Side identified themselves above all as proletarian workers.[9] They had an overwhelming tendency to identify themselves with the Russian
Narodnaya Volya martyrs, and they were determined to establish a free, revolutionary society.
Many people living in the Lower East Side were associated with the St. Petersburg heroes,
and the Bund (Algemeiner Yiddisher Arbeiterbund in Lita, Polen und Rusland) was tightly
associated with the Lower East Side, in terms of moral, intellectual and financial support.
For a few years, during the 1880s and '90s, anarchism captured the imagination of the class-
conscious immigrants. It was an anarchism with a total rejection of other values, with an
absolute intellectual system and fervor almost theological in its assault on traditional culture and theology. It spoke to the Jewish sense of being utterly adrift and without ties to
the old world or the new, and at the same time it developed traditional seeds deeply
ingrained in Jewish theology and culture, as we will see later on.

Emma Goldman saw herself at the head of the radical movement to which thousands of people and hundreds of groups were contributing. She was drawing from and contributing to a
mental climate. The Lower East Side provided her with the appropriate atmosphere. Nowhere
else, outside of Vilna or St. Petersburg, could she have felt more at home than here.
Nevertheless, Emma was always an exile in America, and although she was expelled to Russia
with Alexander Berkman in 1919, she worked within a framework of friends, small institutions and, above all, in a climate of revolutionary hope until the very moment that her
American citizenship was withdrawn and she was deported.

By the 1890s, it was clear that the Jewish immigrant masses were not to establish a radical
society on the Lower East Side, let alone in America as a whole. Socialists like Abraham
Cahan and Joseph Barondes would safely ride the aspirations of the masses into the moderate shores of American trade unionism, which joined professionalism with a total disavowal
of politics.

A Radical Political and Social History of the Lower East Side

When Emma returned to America, in 1934, she was neither a prophet nor a threat. Franklin D. Roosevelt, who gives his name to the farthest East Drive of the Lower East Side, had been elected president on the basis of the New Deal, which included strong government control of the country's economic life, increasing nationalistic upswing and a return to well-established principles of order and authority. Communists who wanted a state socialism as hard as in Russia boycotted Emma's lectures. Anarchism looked irrelevant, silly and hopelessly out of date. Alexander Berkman, ill, poor and unable to live by his own means, was suffering the endless harassment of the French authorities, which kept him secluded in his village on the Côte d'Azur.

Dorothy Day

Dorothy Day commenced her experiment on the Lower East Side together with Peter Maurin in the New Deal climate of the 1930s and continued to the McCarthy atmosphere of the '40s and '50s. Anarchism was a ghost, and the only "black sheep" were the disciplined, centralized state-oriented American Communists. But not for long.

Three major social forces created the backdrop for Dorothy's experiment. There was World War II, the Hispanics in New York, and the counterculture. Dorothy would maintain a strong, uncompromised stance against war in Spain (1936-1939) and World War II (1939-1945). The *Catholic Worker* would suffer the anger of many church people ready to accept just sides in all wars. Pacifism, support of strikers, opposition to nuclear weapons, equal rights, non-violence, the dignity and value of work, and the general cause of the poor and oppressed were the horizon of Dorothy Day's and Peter Maurin's concerns. Unlike Emma Goldman and Alexander Berkman, however, they would never count on their own people.

Dorothy and Peter Maurin were both foreigners on the Lower East Side, foreigners ethnically, among Hispanics, Jews, Italians and Irish, and culturally. Peter Maurin was born French/Catalan Catholic and Dorothy, who was fascinated and amazed by a local Irish American Catholic church on the Lower East Side, was a late convert to the Catholic Church. Both became anarchists through the unlikely path of the Catholic Church. Rather than developing through the stream of immigrant people, like Emma and Alexander, they would move through a stream of tradition. The Catholic tradition was a means of criticism of the present and of participation in the lot of oppressed people throughout the world. Because of this, revolution was internalized and spiritualized. Unlike the atheist Emma, Dorothy would never go to Union Square to address the masses or visit the anarchist villages of Aragon to participate in the realization of revolution. She would share with the saints of the past, with her friends and with the destitute who came her way.

Besides the challenge of war, there were two other challenges that could have given Dorothy Day the connection to her movement to the masses. The first was the installation of 70,000 Puerto Ricans in the neighborhood. There is a silenced history of the Hispanic Labor Movement in New York. It is astonishing that Dorothy Day never knew of Bernardo Vega,[10] the great Puerto Rican labor organizer in New York, while she was quite familiar with Cesar Chavez and his Chicano United Farm Workers' struggles in California. The Hispanic immigration into the Lower East Side during the late '40s, '50s and '60s and the response of the Catholic Church, is in striking contrast to the response that the German Jews gave to East European Jews from 1880 to 1920.[11] For the last 30 years the church has been unable to incorporate this vast community of a million and a half into the church itself and into the mainstream of America. Day ran to California and to Cuba but missed the fact that a nation of derelicts invaded her own sidewalks and thresholds.

The other revolution that Day seems to have missed was the counterculture exploding in her own streets. Saint Mark's in the Bowery, an Episcopal Church with a long tradition in acceptance of the Arts, played a key role in making the counterculture possible. Together with Judson Memorial Church in Washington Square, it helped create a powerful creative explosion for youth and arts in the American scene. Poets and artists had been regular members of Mary House Community and regular contributors to the *Catholic Worker*. Yet Dorothy Day's Houses of Hospitality persisted as yet another separate, un-melted group in the same neighborhood, in a country where "the melting pot" never went beyond a title of a play.

Both movements, the Hispanic and the counterculture, were revolutionary tendencies with which Day could have connected, through which her experiment could have been associated with popular struggles. But they were missed in part because neither came in the form of the worker and the poor in the classic concept of revolution.

The Politics Of Writing

In the face of their movements' failure to become vehicles for mass politics, both Goldman and Day became passionately involved with writing and educational activities. Anarchists are well known for their passion for the written word. After all, starting with Karl Marx himself, no one has written and speculated so much about changing the world as revolutionaries. Curiously enough, given their commitment to collective processes, anarchists have always been great autobiographers. This passion for writing and educating reaches a remarkable summit in the four characters of our story. They founded publications, wrote books and became involved in educational projects. In Dorothy Day's books and articles, this trend reaches a peak, since her writing becomes a self-confession. We are not given her account of the facts, experiences and feelings, but the repercussions that these facts and experiences bore on her psyche. Dorothy Day lines up radical writing with the traditional genre of mysticism. Writing is a self-confession and religious experience. Her autobiography starts with a sensory description of the Catholic confession experience, and concludes: "Going to confession is hard. Writing a book is hard because you are giving yourself away." Emma Goldman, on the other hand, used writing as a consciously revolutionary device, as she herself says in her preface to *Anarchism and Other Essays*:

> I came to see that oral propaganda is at best but a means of shaking people from their lethargy: it leaves no lasting impression. The very fact that most people attend meetings only if aroused by sensational newspapers, or they expect to be amused, is proof that they really have no inner urge to learn. It's altogether different with the written modes of human expression.

A Radical Political and Social History of the Lower East Side

Writing is a constant in the lives of both women, and in the lives of American revolutionaries like John Reed and Max Eastman. They all acted as witnesses to revolution elsewhere, seeming to have accepted the fact.

Emma Goldman spent a year as a manager for Paul Orleneff, a Russian theater director who staged Chekhov and Dostoevsky, in Russian, on the Lower East Side. When he could not cope with the American pace of life and returned to Russia, he staged a performance and gave all the proceeds to Emma for her magazine *Mother Earth* (March 1906 - August 1917).[12] The living room at 210 East 13th Street was the office of the magazine. Alexander Berkman had just come out of prison, after fourteen years inside for the assassination attempt they had planned together. He lived with Emma and dedicated himself to work on the publication. Articles on anarchism, patriotism, love and prudery, poems, book reviews and news reports uniting revolutionary and artistic impression were contributed by writers from America and elsewhere.

Both Emma Goldman and Alexander Berkman were prolific writers. Writing was always a reflection of their experience and didactic commitments. *Anarchism and Other Essays* (1911) conveys her personal convictions on women's emancipation, on Francisco Ferrer, secular education and the Catholic Church in Spain, patriotism and love. The facts and experiences are a point of departure for radical reflection. The *Social Significance of Modern Drama* (1914) was the result of her lectures on playwrights and plays, many of which were then staged by Guido Bruno at the Thimble Theater in the Village and by Paul Orleneff in the Lower East Side. *My Disillusionment in Russia* (1923) was the result of one year in the Soviet Union and the sad discovery that a dictatorship of the state had taken supreme rule of all life. While in Russia, she and Berkman took the commission of gathering art for the Museum of the Revolution, and this gave them the opportunity to visit the country and see, among many other scandals, how the anarchist army of Nestor Mahkno was destroyed, when they met secretly with Mahkno's wife in Kiev, and seeing too how 18,000 revolutionary sailors were crushed at Kronstadt. Finally, the multi-volume *Living My Life* (1931) was her personal memoirs.

Alexander Berkman also cleaved to the memoirs genre. *Prison Memoirs of an Anarchist* (1912) and *Now and After: The ABC of Communist Anarchism (What is Communist Anarchism?)* (1912) are major educational accomplishments. Emma Goldman wrote the preface to the 1937 edition:

> The superior quality of anarchist literature as compared with the writings of other social schools is its simplicity of style. Michael Bakunin, Élisée Reclus, Peter Kropotkin, Enrico Malatesta and others wrote in a way as to make their ideas easily understood by the workers. . . . Yet it would be true to say that even they hardly had the average man in mind — the average man of Anglo-*Saxon* mentality. There is no getting away from the fact that there is a vast difference between the mind of the Latin worker and that of his brother in the United States and in England. The former has been steeped in the Revolutionary traditions and struggles for freedom and other causes, while the latter had been brought up on the "blessing" of parliamentarianism.

Alexander Berkman's *The Bolshevik Myth* (1925) is a personal account and reflection on the failure of the Russian Revolution. Finally, *Nowhere at Home* (1975) is a collection of letters in exile. It gives detailed accounts of their lives and conceptual processes from the days of Emma's last imprisonment in America to the death of Berkman in Nice.[13]

Besides this written educational mission, they held other forms of educational commitment. In 1910, Emma Goldman opened the Francisco Ferrer Modern School at 104 East 12th Street as an experiment of the foremost progressive education for children, an example followed by schools throughout the country. Besides the school, Emma became engaged in a continuous cross-country lecture tour dealing with freedom of speech, sexual freedom, birth control and other libertarian campaigns.[14]

Dorothy Day's educational activities included the publication of three volumes *Loaves and Fishes* (1936), *The Long Loneliness* (1952) and *On Pilgrimage: The Sixties* (1972), which tightly intertwined her life with the surrounding condition of America.

Peter Maurin was a born teacher, and for him any park bench, coffee shop counter or lodging house was a place to teach. He only published through the *Catholic Worker* which ran, over and over again, his *Easy Essays,* as he called his articles, collected and published for the first time in 1949 under the title *Catholic Radicalism*.[15] Since his very first meeting with Dorothy Day, he had proposed the publishing of a periodical. Dorothy Day pulled together seventy-five dollars from several priests' donations and stipends, and the paper was on sale in Union Square on May 1st, 1933, competing with the *Daily Worker*, the American Communist newspaper. Peter Maurin lived in the *Catholic Worker* office, and every month he turned in a few Easy Essays.[16]

Dorothy recalled: "He was the kind of teacher who believed in a repetition, restatement and the continual return to first principles. He ran all over Manhattan indoctrinating whoever he could get. He never preached, he taught."

Like Emma, Dorothy Day and Peter Maurin instigated other educational campaigns. They carried on the experiment of Houses of Hospitality, first on Mott Street and Christie Street, and later at 55 East Third Street and 36 East First Street. There were also the farming communes on Staten Island, Newburg and Marlboro.

Peter Maurin was insistent on the rediscovery of the village agrarian economy and the rediscovery of the crafts. He was always talking about the agronomic universities. The Friday night meetings, together with the farm communes and the Houses of Hospitality, continued to be the three planks of Dorothy Day and Peter Maurin's platform.

This enormous body of educational work brings home some of the meaning in their story. Both Emma and Alexander and Dorothy and Peter seem to have turned their anarchism from a movement of the masses into a radical educational reflection process.

A Radical Political and Social History of the Lower East Side

Revolution Elsewhere: The Visits To The Revolution

10

Emma Goldman fled America returning to Russia and Ukraine to see the revolution dying,[17] and to Barcelona and the near region of Aragon in 1936.[18] She visited the factories to be met by an amazing spectacle:

> Not only had the brave Spanish workers united to stop fascism, but had evident-
> ly united to stop capitalism as well. Not only had capitalism been overthrown
> but this revolution, unlike Russia's, was being made by anarchists. This was a
> revolution model that could serve. The Barcelona workers, mostly anarchistic,
> were in charge of the city. The gas, electric, water, telephone and public trans-
> port services, the factories, trades, and small shops, the barbers and the waiters
> . . . all had organized themselves into collectives and had enlisted in the revolu-
> tion.

Emma went to the battlefront in Aragon, in the same villages visited by Orwell and reported in *Homage to Catalonia*, to find both a war and an amazing revolution. In Calande, Caspe, Hijar, Fraga and throughout the Argonese countryside, Emma saw collectives and individuals living peacefully. Barbershops were free for everybody, as were butchers' shops, transport from one village to another, schooling and entertainment. Money bills were thrown into the street and all the farming work was being carried on a rotating basis on common organized land.

Emma Goldman would see churches turned into warehouses or completely destroyed in Barcelona. In anarchist Aragon, priests and bishops were killed on a massive scale, and religion was banned. As in the days of Francisco Ferrer and the "tragic week" in Barcelona (from July 26th to August 1st, 1909), the hatred of the masses against organized religion would explode in one of the bloodiest and most destructive religious persecutions.

During 1961 and 1962, Dorothy Day wrote extensively about Cuba and its revolution, visit-ing Cuba to see for herself another ambivalent but excruciating experience of revolution and change with intolerance and repression. She also visited Mexico and was very alert to the struggles of the Hispanics in California and the situation in Latin America. Contrary to Emma Goldman's disillusionment with the Russian Revolution, Dorothy Day's attitude towards Cuba can be summarized in these comments from November 1962:

> I am trying not to be the occasion of sin for our opponents in future. Which
> means that I will try again to think things out, study, read more, and find more
> authorities for our positions, stimulate others to that same study, and so to
> express myself that I will invoke in others what is really there to be evoked — a
> desire to do what is right, to follow conscience, to love one's brother and to find
> what there is of God in every man [sic].

Summing up her view of the Spanish revolution, Emma, now an old woman, would write at the time when Communists were destroying anarchists' achievements and strategies, and were finally overcome by Franco's troops, who entered Barcelona in January 1939: "It is as though you had wanted a child all your life, and at last, when you had almost given up hoping, it had been given to you — only to die soon after it was born. "

11

The Prophetic Breath: A Spiritual Politics

In New York Jewish life of the 1880s and '90s, public avowal of apostasy, atheism and agnosticism was a vital phenomenon. There was the sober secularism of William Frey and Felix Adler, the founder of the New York Ethical Culture Society; Abraham Cahan the editor of the (socialist) *Jewish Daily Forward*; and the Education Alliance, a stronghold of Americanization of Jews in the Lower East Side, where Hebrew and Yiddish were not allowed for many years. The anarchists went far beyond this current of secularism and anti-clericalism. There was also an aggressive secularism. For a long time, there were balls and parades, very popular on the Lower East Side, to celebrate, in a secular mood, the great festivals of Rosh Hashanah and Yom Kippur. The announcements ran as follows:

> Grand Yom Kippur Ball, with theater, arranged with the consent of all new rabbis
> of Liberty, Koll Nydre night and day. In the year 5651, after the invention of the
> Jewish idols and 1890 after the birth of the False Messiah . . . The Koll Nydre will
> be offered by Johann Most: music, dancing and buffet, Marseillaise and other
> hymns against Satan.

Emma Goldman, like the rest of her family, had never been especially religious. Her recollections of her professor of religion at Koeningsberg were very negative. On the other hand, her relationship with Christianity in the new world was not good. Through her study and identification with the educational work and ideas at Francisco Ferrer, Emma received a deep anti-Catholic sensitivity. In one essay she wrote:

> On September 1st, 1909, the Spanish government at the behest of the Catholic
> Church, arrested Francisco Ferrer . . . The killing of Francisco Ferrer was not the
> first crime committed by the Spanish government and the Catholic Church. The
> history of these institutions is one long stream of fire and blood. Still, they have
> not learned through experience nor come to realize that every frail being slain by
> the Church and State grows and grows into a mighty giant who will someday free
> humanity from their perilous hold.[19]

Emma identified herself with Ferrer in his rejection of the Catholic Church ("The hideousness of that black monster"):

> The Catholic Church is the target of the Republican regimes in Europe. Together
> with despotism, the Church has been the enemy of progress and liberalism from
> the very beginning. It takes more than one brave effort to split that rock of ages,
> to cut off the head of that hydra monster, the Catholic Church and the Spanish
> throne.[20]

A Radical Political and Social History of the Lower East Side

Alexander Berkman wrote a short insightful chapter in his *What Is Communist Anarchism?* in which he asked: "Can the Church help you?" He used the same polemical language as Emma, in the tradition of Bakunin. It is a language developed with the concepts of Ludwig Feuerbach, attacking a supposedly dehumanizing Christian mysticism, but owing nothing to a biblical approach, either to the Old or New Testaments.[21]

During his long years in prison in Pennsylvania, Berkman recalled his adolescent days in St. Petersburg and the messianic hope that the old rabbi transmitted to the young Russian Jews. On one occasion, student and rabbi opened up a conversation on the time and possibility of the coming of the Messiah. What if all the Jews in the world would not commit any sin for just a second, would not the Messiah come then, as tradition had it? This messianic attitude was profoundly ingrained in Emma and Alexander. Their project of "propaganda by deed" was nothing but a secularized continuation of the prophetic breath. Both radicals' attitude to religion can be summarized in this comment of Berkman in his *Prison Memoirs Of An Anarchist*:

> With a sense of sobering sadness, I think of the new hope, the revolutionary Messiah. Truly, the old Rabbi was wise beyond his ken: it is given to no man to hasten the march of the delivery. Out of the people's need, from the womb of their suffering, must be borne the hour of redemption. Necessity, necessity alone, with its iron heel, will spur numb misery to effort and awaken the living dead. The process is torturously slow, but the gestation of a new humanity cannot be hurried by impatience. We must bide our time, meanwhile preparing the workers for the great upheaval.[22]

The Jewish religious environment of the days of Emma Goldman and Alexander Berkman was in disarray. At the turn of the century, only twenty five percent of that city's workmen rested on the sacred day of rest. Hester Street storekeepers shamelessly exhibited their wares on the Sabbath and some dared to do so on the Penitential Days. By 1912, it was estimated that sixty percent of the stores were open on the Sabbath. *The Jewish Daily Forward* appeared on Saturday. At the Yiddish theaters, Friday night and Saturday matinee performances were sellouts and Bowery music halls lured youngsters even on the high days of Purim. The feast of the Maccabees passed almost unnoticed, for every night was festive at the theater. There was no place for Succoth (the Feast of the Tabernacles) to erect the booth of rushes gathered on the roof of the crowded tenements. Rabbis were men of neither preparation nor piety. In the 1887, an association of downtown congregations invited the great Rabbi of Vilna, Jacob Joseph, to fill the office of chief rabbi. Synagogues sprouted everywhere around the area. Until very recently, there were eight great synagogues and eleven small ones, most of them erected and maintained according to the geographical origins of the people.

So, although there were young radicals who led the community at large leaving their imprint for many decades, the Lower East Side changed drastically from the open, secular attitude to a stronghold of Jewish orthodoxy, where the Sabbath and all major and minor festivals are observed faithfully. More pertinent to this story, the cosmopolitan internationalism of the Jewish Lower East Side evolved slowly but irreversibly into a prevailing support for the State of Israel.

In the breaths of the lay radicals like Goldman and Berkman, we can hear strongly, and powerfully, the biblical spirit of the prophets and the uncompromising stance of the Jewish religion. The claim of total power and lordship by human institutions or individuals is idolatry, and the primary commitment is justice and compassion for the oppressed and the poor. Being radical, Peter Maurin would say, is going back to the roots.

Dorothy Day and Peter Maurin had an altogether different approach to religion. Peter Maurin was a former Christian Brother and had a close acquaintance with French theology that he summarized as "cult, culture and civilization." His range of reading was broad and consistent. Dorothy Day was brought up in a shallow Episcopalian tradition. Her conversion to Catholicism was wrapped in the most popular pious terms and concepts. Throughout her life, Dorothy developed an amazingly devotional, traditional approach to faith. She was fascinated by the most elementary forms of cult and devotion (such as "picketing St. Joseph," the nightly prayer vigils when they were in need of money). She developed a very wide range of reading, both from the anarchists, such as Malatesta, Kropotkin, Tolstoy and Proudhon, and Catholic authors such as Maritain, Merton, Guardini, and Eric Gill, and the classics as St. Augustine and St. Thomas Aquinas. On the Lower East Side, there was still a heavily Irish American style of Catholic Church. By "Irish Catholic" we mean a model of church in which all intellectual and secular debates are kept at bay.

Since the days of Bishop John Hughes, when St. Patrick's Cathedral was at Mulberry Street, the Church on the Lower East Side has carried an imprint that remains. There are some twenty parishes that cover, on a rigorous geographical basis, the whole of the Lower East Side, as well as a few national parishes (Polish, Ukrainian, etc.). Parishes operate as isolated entities, accommodating very tight primary relationships of religion, leisure and education for their people. The goals and strategies of each parish derive from the parish priest's world view and flair. There is no relationship between parishes, no common strategy, and all religious institutions and groups, such as convents and associations, are referred to and accountable to the parish. This is a model of the church totally different from that in European Catholic countries.

American Catholics, like all other American Christians, perceive themselves first and foremost as members of their parish community. There is a lifelong loyalty to one's church in terms of self-identification with a community and solemnization of one's highest life moments to a point that Christianity never knew in Europe. In America, a church has many functions that correspond, for most people, to their entire public life. Churches are the place where they are recognized and identified as members, but this identification and recognition is, paradoxically, exclusively *private*, since there is no national or prevalent form of religion.

In the end, all churches tend to accommodate a very familiar set of attitudes that cannot be totally equaled with the main theory of Will Herber in his *Catholic, Protestant, Jew*. The European Catholic, on the other hand, and to some extent the Protestant, perceives her/himself as a member of the Church as such, believing and shaping her/his behavior on a very

A Radical Political and Social History of the Lower East Side

broad and general terms. As a matter of fact, most Catholics, both in Europe and Latin America, do not consider their relationship to their parishes as a central feature of faith. The Irish American tradition, on the other hand, strongly identifies Church membership with the local parishes.[23]

The personal, non-local community that Dorothy Day and Peter Maurin established for themselves on the Lower East Side did not coincide with those characteristics. It was more tailored to the European mind. The spirit of Peter Maurin's French Catholicism was very much at work there. The sense of communion with people from all over the world, the theoretical debates at the Friday night meetings and at *The Catholic Worker* and, above all, the concern for problems and issues of universal cultural bearing and a willingness to bring radical change to society were unusual in an American Catholic context.

In the Irish Catholic tradition, religion itself is considered a major vehicle of reform, and charity is the key to such social reform. The Society of St. Vincent de Paul is the oldest lay Association in Catholic New York, and has been established throughout the area since the mid 1880s. Charity is expressed by works of mercy and such "works of mercy" were a key practice for Dorothy Day in setting up the Houses of Hospitality. In no other form of Catholicism, does visiting the sick, and a prayer for the dead, appear with such emphasis, alongside temperance and the personal aspect of faith.

Conclusion: Back to the Lower East Side: consensus and revolution

Why did the revolutionary aspirations of these two revolutionary women fail? Why were they doomed always to be witnesses of revolution elsewhere, never at home or in their own time? The preceding pages have suggested that both their atheism and religion and the Zionist developments of Judaism were marginal to the American social process, although Goldman was imprisoned and finally exiled.

At the time this conclusion is written, the Lower East Side appears as a successive series of immigrant waves, in many cases simultaneous waves, living side by side for decades, developing and contributing to mainstream America. Sometimes the immigration was marginal in its political effects (Italians, Hispanics and Chinese), sometimes powerful. The immigrant waves enter and then leave the neighborhood for higher economic and urban status in the city and the country. But the neighborhood, the Lower East Side, has remained run down from the Irish days of Bishop John Hughes in the 1840s and '50s, to the anarchist period of Johann Most in the 1880s and '90s, to the civic Judaism of Judah Magnes in the 1910s, to countercultural years of the Hispanic Young Lords in the '60s, to the present Chinatown Planning Council.

It is this changing proletarian horizon that made the development of radicals like Emma Goldman and Dorothy Day possible: witnesses to revolutions elsewhere in the world and agitators in limited social circles at home. Their stories suggest a shorthand as to why they did not succeed in transforming American society in general.

In this respect, Dorothy Day's attempts to convey a revolutionary message through Catholicism seems precarious to say the least. There was no long Catholic American tradition of public political involvement to draw on and she had to rely on experience from elsewhere, from a universal church (a borrowed concept from Europe), vaguely appealing to American Catholic Church members.

On the other hand, Emma Goldman's attempt to convey a revolutionary message clothed in secular, atheist language could not be popularly accepted by American urban society, since it would imply a reconstruction of the atheistic worldview established in the founding of the revolutionary constitution. And American Judaism, long before the Holocaust, cast its lot with the emergence and the consolidation of the state of Israel, giving up any claim to establishing in America the early dream of the universal fraternity of the proletariat. Jewry was soon assimilated into the American dream, according to American goals and means.

It would not be too much to see the problems of the American state mirrored in the problem of religion. The lack of contradiction in a diversity of religious expression appears in other aspects of American society. Americans perceive the state as something essentially good, permanent and enduring. Latin and Slavic countries know that their states are recent, disputable and transient. Even the visibility of the American state appears very thin and unassuming.

To Americans, America appears to be a country without basic inner contradictions, unlike most European countries. In America, there is no structural conflict between the church and state, between state and civil society, between center and periphery, between organized labor and political power, between national language and regional/minority language. Or at least these conflicts are not expressed, but accommodated to the consensus of individualism and freedom.

At the very heart of the American Constitution, religion is designated as the foremost area of self-expression and manifestation of civic freedom. Religion is not defined as a national/public characteristic as in the Church of England and the Scandinavian churches, or as a parallel power to the state, as in France, Italy, Spain, Poland or Russia. It is instead the foremost area of the exercise of individual freedom. The various religious bodies represented in America act as guarantors of the American separation of church and state. Religion in America has given up any possibility of pursuing major change in society, and accepts and takes for granted the present framework of the social and political machine.

While in Europe, the church has pre-existed the state in most of its forms and structures. In America, common wisdom insists that nothing predates the Constitution. No institution can claim legitimacy based on anteriority. It can safely be said that all churches and religions in America have internalized the idea of America as the chosen nation of God to bring democracy, freedom and equality to the rest of the world.

No part of the vast American territory has ever made any claim to secession or independence since the Civil War. Critique of the center is best detected and blunted by the central government itself, effectively robbing such a critique of any possible cutting edge.

A Radical Political and Social History of the Lower East Side

16

Emma Goldman tried revolution through the labor movement, freedom of expression, educational and sexual freedom. Dorothy Day tried the same through religion and civic commitment. Like the Lower East Side itself, both remained marginal to the dominant culture; Emma exiled and Dorothy self-exiled. Their struggles were later incorporated into the dominant centralized system, legitimated but robbed of their revolutionary vision.

It might be possible, however, to still glimpse how the seeds of revolution are continued and how an alternative legitimacy might be reconstructed. Since the 1970s, Emma's rejection of the suffrage struggle and the promotion of sexual freedom for women has been recalled and understood by a new generation of radical feminists. Dorothy's radicalism has inspired a new generation of the Catholic Left as well as evangelical radicals of the Sojourners movement.

 Women who have no country have a way of discovering that in the end their country must be the whole world.

Endnotes:

1. For Emma Goldman and Alexander Berkman's biographies see Emma Goldman's Living My Life (2 volumes, New York, Knopf, 1931), reprinted by Dover Publications 1970; and Richard Drinon Rebel In Paradise (New York, Beacon Press, 1970). William D. Miller has published his Dorothy Day (New York, Harper and Row, 1982). But her own three books The Long Loneliness (New York, Harper and Row, 1952), Loaves And Fishes (New York, Harper and Row, 1963) and On Pilgrimage: The Sixties (New York, Curtis Books, 1972) give a thorough account of her pilgrimage. For an in-depth account of Peter Maurin's main turning points see Dorothy Day's The Long Loneliness and her introduction to Peter Maurin, Easy Essays (Chicago, Franciscan Harold Press, 1977).

2. Emma Goldman is buried in Chicago's Waldheim Cemetery, near the graves of the revered Haymarket martyrs and that of Voltairine de Cleyre. At one time, Emma placed a wreath of flowers on their grave and wrote moving comments about their sculptural monument. Her last wishes were to be buried near them. Alexander Berkman shot himself on June 28th, 1936 in Nice, where he is buried. Had he remotely anticipated the advent of the Spanish Revolution, he would have made an effort to continue living despite his shattered physique and many handicaps, as described in the preface to the 1937 edition of his What Is Communism Anarchism? (Now and After: the ABC of Communist Anarchism) (New York, Dover Publications, 1972).

3. Jewish immigration to New York's Lower East Side has been well documented. Some accessible books, with abundant complementary bibliography, are Jacob A. Riis, How the Other Half Lives: Studies Among the Tenements of New York (New York, Hill and Wang, 1957); Ronald Saunders, The Downtown Jews: Portraits of an Immigrant Generation (New York, Harper and Row, 1969); Moses Rischin, The Promised City, New York's Jews 1870-1914 (New York, Harper and Row, 1970) and Irving Howe, World of Our Fathers: The Journey of the East European Jews to America and the Life They Found and Made (New York, Harcourt Brace Jovanovitch, 1976).

4. New York State, State Assembly Report of a Select Committee to Examine into the Condition of Tenant Houses in New York and Brooklyn 1857, Vol. 3 no. 205 p. 14. Charles Dickens in his American Notes and Pictures of Italy (London 1888) describes at length the loathsome, drooping and decayed " heart of the Lower East Side. Does the quote start with loathsome?

5. Dorothy Day never met Emma Goldman, and only briefly Alexander Berkman. William D. Miller mentions, in his recent biography of Dorothy Day, a late exchange of letters between the two women. Throughout Dorothy Day's books we get the feeling that Dorothy was little familiar with the ideas of Emma and that many of them were quite displeasing to her, such as the open attitude to sensuality and birth control.

6. Peter Maurin died at Maryfarm, Newburg, New York, on May 15th, 1949 and is buried in a donated grave in St. John's cemetery in Brooklyn. Dorothy Day died on November 29th, 1980, and is buried in Staten Island, not far from where she was baptized into the Catholic church.

7. See Harry Schwartz Planning for the Lower East Side (New York, Praeger Publishers, 1973); Portfolio An Information System for Community Districts, Manhattan Community District No. 3 (New York City Hall, New York, 1979).

8. There is an extensive bibliography about the counterculture in the '60s in the Lower East Side. Prof. Harry Silverstein contacted a research project at the time of the events, published as Creative Arts Alienated Youth Project. Final Report, Research and Evaluation (Center for New York City Affairs/New School of Social Research, New York, 1971) see also Allen De Loach, The East Side Scene: American Poetry 1960-1965 (New York, Doubleday and Co., 1972).

9. Labor rights were virtually unknown in law in the 1880s. Of 232 New York City labor unions in 1900, many of them just benevolent societies, only 45 had been founded before 1880. The first Jewish Union in the Lower East Side was established in 1882 (The Propaganda Verein) on Rivington Street by very young Russian workers who, soon after, founded the Ruska Rabochi Soyouz (Russian Workers' Union) stressing their proletarian, trans/Jewish class identification. By 1888, there were two well-differentiated lines: the anarchistic and the social democrat. The United Hebrew trades (led by Jacob Migidoff, Bernard Weinstein, Morris Hillkowitz, Abraham Cahan, etc.) represented the social spirits, till the moment of its absorption by the American Federation of Labor in the 1920s. The anarchistic union movement started with the Jewish workers union, founded in 1885 by two teenage brothers from Odessa, Mitya and Nyuma Gretch. From the Jewish Workers Union grew Pioneers of Liberty, headed by Johann Most, from Orchard Street. But the Haymarket affair (1887), and then the attempted assassination of Henry C. Frick by Alexander Berkman (1895), the assassination of President McKinley (1901), the alleged murder of the paymaster of Braintree, Massachusetts, by Sacco and Vanzetti, and other murders indirectly traceable to anarchists, would lead to their estrangement from the masses and the labor movement.

10. Bernardo Vega (1885-1965) spent his life among his fellow Puerto Rican working men in small tobacco factories in Harlem, Chelsea, and the Lower East Side. He founded publications, labor groups and political parties, among them the Partido Comunista Puertoriqueno in 1934. His book, Memorias de Bernardo Vega: Contribucion a la Historia de la Comunidad Puertoriqueno en Nueva York, (Ediciones Huracan, Rio Piedras, Puerto Rico, 1977) is a basic source of knowledge of the labor history of Hispanics in New York.

11. The uptown Jews help to the proletarian Eastern European Jews reached its peak through the attempt of Rabbi Judah Magnes, incumbent of Emmanu-El synagogue on Fifth Avenue. He summoned east side leaders and uptown magnates to the convention in Clinton Hall in 1908, to create a Kehillah (communal council) "to wipe out invidious distinctions between East European and West European, foreigners and natives, uptown and downtown Jew, rich and poor; and make us realize that the Jews are one people with a common history and common hopes." The extreme Orthodox groups were hostile to any structure that claimed to transcend religion, while the Socialists were hostile to any that claim to transcend class interests. For a decade the Kehillah, and the generosity of Jacob Schiff and other wealthy uptowners, developed bureaus of education, social morals, industry, philanthropic research and social relief. The reports produced by these bureaus are among the most remarkable pieces of documented information from any immigrant community about the Lower East Side. In November 1913, a report disclosed the existence of 914 hangouts, 423 disorderly houses and 374 pool parlors as well as drug dealing, horse poisoning and many other forms of crime. See Arthur Goren New York Jews and the Quest for Community (New York, New York University Press, 1970).

12. Mother Earth printed contributions and artwork from Kropotkin, Voltairine de Cleyre, (who translated for the magazine The Modern School by Francisco Ferrer), Hyppolite Havel, Man Ray, Alfred Stieglitz and many others; reports from The Modern School and other anarchist schools in the country. Another outlet of Emma's educational commitment was The Modern School magazine. The lectures and performances of the modern school were attended by Eugene O'Neill, John Reed, Theodore Dreiser and Mike Gold among many artists and bohemians from the neighboring village. Mother Earth was reprinted by Greenwood Press, in 1968.

13. Alexander Berkman defended in the pages of Blast the life of Thomas Mooney, a San Francisco anarchistic, charged in 1916 with the throwing of a bomb during a massive parade in favor of the First World War American intervention. Berkman and Goldman managed to mobilize thousands of workers in front of the American Embassy in St. Petersburg chanting "Mooney, Mooney." Demonstrations spread throughout Europe until President Wilson intervened.

14. Founded by the Francisco Ferrer Association, the school opened at 6 Mark's Place. Later it moved to 104 East 12th Street, and then, in 1912, to 63rd East 107th Street and finally to Stelton, New Jersey. The idea of joining education and farming would reappear in the radical experiment of Peter Maurin and Dorothy Day in the 1940s and after. There were 21 "Modern Schools " throughout the country between 1909 and 1961, and 12 more related

A Radical Political and Social History of the Lower East Side

schools, based on the model of the Escuela Moderna of Barcelona. See Paul Avrich, The Modern School Movement: Anarchy and Education in the United States. (Princeton University Press, 1980).

15. The first edition of Peter Maurin's Easy Essays came out in 1936 with illustrations by Ade Bethune. In 1949 the work was published in an expanded version, with illustrations by Ed Willcock, under the title of Catholic Radicalism: Phrased Essays for the Green Revolution (The Catholic Worker Books). Dorothy Day herself directed the Franciscan Herald press edition of Easy Essays, with splendid woodcuts by Fritz Eichenberg, in 1977.

16. Professor William D. Miller is the author of a book about The Catholic Worker: A Harsh and Dreadful Love. The Catholic Worker (New York, Liverlight, 1970). Today, the Catholic Worker with more than 100,000 copies in circulation, continues printing with contributions from writers and artists from all over the world. This tradition of writers and artists include names like the English distributionalists distributors? Distributionists? from Ditchling and Eric Gill, Charles Mounier, Maritain, etc.

17. Emma Goldman's and Alexander Berkman's disappointing experience of revolutionary Russia coincided with the active, enthusiastic participation by John Reed and Louise Bryant in the same events. John Reed went to Russia as reporter of The Masses and The Call (two papers in which Dorothy Day had been involved). John Reed died in 1920, and Emma and Alexander continued in Russia for one year more. Trotsky had put a harsh end to the possibility that Ukraine that might be allowed to develop along anarchistic lines, crushing the anarchistic army. See Michael Palij The Anarchism of Nestor Mahkno 1918-1921: An Aspect of the Ukrainian Revolution, (University of Washington Press, Seattle, 1976). Emma and Alexander attended the burial of John Reed in Moscow. Max Eastman, editor of The Masses, joined the American Revolutionary writers in their survey of the Revolution, utterly disappointed. For this lower Manhattan/St. Petersburg connection see John Reed's Ten Days that Shook the World in one of the four editions available (International Press, Penguin Books, the New American Library and Vintage) and the autobiographical volumes of Max Eastman Enjoyment of Life (New York, Harper and brother, 1948) and Love and Revolution (New York, Random House, 1964).

18. Neither the first nor the second World War exacerbated the feelings of people and literary and intellectual exploration as did the Spanish Civil War, and particularly the events in Catalonia and Aragon, where the final battles were fought. Among the witnesses to the Spanish war and revolution there are Andre Malraux, Georges Bernanos, François Mauriac, Paul Claudel, Jacques Maritain, Antoine de Saint-Exupery, Louis Aragon and Paul Eluard in France; George Orwell, W. H. Auden, Stephen Spender, C. Day Lewis and Herbert Read in England; Ernest Hemingway, John Dos Passos, Theodore Dreiser and Archibald MacLeish in America. For the active participation in the Spanish Civil War by Americans see Robert A. Rosenstone, Crusade of the Left, The Lincoln Battalion in the Spanish Civil War (New York, Pegasus, 1969) and Edwin Rolfe The Lincoln Battalion (New York, Random House, 1939). For a thorough description of the anarchistic revolution in Aragon villages see George Orwell's Homage to Catalonia (several editions) and, for a detailed information of this anarchist agrarian revolution, Burnette Bolloten, The Grand Camouflage, The Communist Conspiracy in the Spanish Civil War (New York, Frederick A. Prager, 1961) An unusual angle of observation is given by an Aragonese priest, Mosen Jesus Arnal, in Porque tui secretario de Durruti (Edicions Mirador del Pirineu, Andorra la Vieja, Camps, Calmett Editor, Terrega, 1972). Arnal acted as secretary to the anarchist militia commander Buenaventura Durruti.

19. Emma Goldman Anarchism and Other Essays, p. 150-51. For the role of Francisco Ferrer in the Spanish rationalistic approach to education, and for his role in the events known as "the tragic week " that led to his execution, see Joan Connelly Ullman The Tragic Week (Harvard University Press, Cambridge, Massachusetts, 1968). The violence of the proletariat in Barcelona during the "tragic week" against churches and church educational institutions would be a prelude to the massive destruction of temples and mass killings of priests and bishops during the Civil War.

20. Emma Goldman, ibid, p. 153.

21. Current philosophical world views about religion, and most specifically about Christianity, during the 19th century knew nothing about eschatology and the eschatological dimensions of the biblical faith. But revolutionaries are not to be blamed since only half a century later did political thinkers (Ernst Bloch) and theologians (Jurgen Moltmann) began to develop the consequences of the theological discovery of concepts like eschaton and "kingdom of God." These were brought to the forefront of modern sensitivity from such unexpected corners like liberal theology (Johannes Weiss and Albert Schweitzer) and the English radical theologians (F. D. Maurice, Thomas Hancock, Stewart Headlam, Conrad Noel, Percy Widdrington, etc.). For a sociological approach to the theological and philosophical framework of anarchism and Christianity see Aurelio Orensanz Anarquia y Cristianismo (Madrid, Manana editorial, 1978). This draws heavily on the anthropologist Andrews Ortiz-Oses Comunicacion y Experimencia Inter-Humana (Bilbao, Desclee de Brouwer, 1977.

22. Alexander Berkman Prison Memoirs of an Anarchist, pp 226-227.

23. An excellent picture of the early Irish and German Catholic Church and Lower East Side in Jay P. Dolan The Immigrant Church: New York's Irish and German Catholics 1815-1865 (John Hopkins, University Press, Baltimore, 1975). There is complementary material in Thomas F. O'Dea "The Catholic Immigrant and the American Scene " (Chapter III of his Sociology and the Study of Religion, New York, Basic Books, 1970). Nathan Glazer and Daniel Patrick Moynihan in their Beyond the Melting Pot, the Negroes, Puerto Ricans, Jews, Italians and Irish of New York City (Cambridge, the M.I.T. press, 1970) bring fascinating facts and approaches about religion in urban New York. Last, but not least, see the classic by Will Herberg, Catholic, Protestant, Jew, An Essay in American Religious Sociology (New York, Doubleday & Co., 1960). For the Jewish history of the Lower East Side see Jo Renee Fine and Gerald R. Wolfe, The Synagogues of the Lower East Side (New York, Columbia University Press, 1977) and Gilbert Klaperman The Story of the Yeshiva University, The First Jewish University in America (New York, Macmillan Co., 1969).

19

Bibliography:
Emma Goldman and Alexander Berkman
Emma Goldman: *Living My Life* (2 volumes), New York, Dover press, 1970.
  Anarchism and Other Essays, Port Washington, NY, Kennikat Press, 1969.
Alexander Berkman: *Prison Memoirs of an Anarchist*, New York, Schocken Books, 1970.
  What is Communist Anarchism? New York, Dover press, 1972.
  Mother Earth (a reprint), New York, Greenwood Press, 1968.
Paul Avrich: *The Modern School Movement: Anarchism and Education in the United States*, Princeton University Press, 1980.
Richard and Anna Maria Drinon *"Nowhere at Home: Letter from Exile of Emma Goldman and Alexander Berkman*. New York, Schocken Books, 1975.

Dorothy Day and Peter Maurin
Dorothy Day: The Long Loneliness, New York, Harper and Row, 1952.
  Loaves and Fishes, New York, Harper and Row, 1952.
  On Pilgrimage, The Sixties, New York, Curtis books, 1972.
William Miller: *Dorothy Day*, New York, Harper and Row, 1982.
  A Harsh and Dreadful Love, New York, Liverlight, 1970.
Mel Piehl: *Breaking Bread: The Catholic Worker and the Origin of Catholic Radicalism in America*, Philadelphia, Temple University Press, 1982.
Peter Maurin: *Easy Essays*, Chicago, Franciscan Herald press, 1977.

Jewish Background on the Lower East Side
Jacob Riis: *How the Other Half Lives, Studies Among the Tenements of New York*, New York, Hill and Wang, 1957.
Ronald Saunders: *The Downtown Jews, Portraits of an Immigrant Generation*, New York, Harper and Row, 1969.
Moses Rischin: *The Promised City, New York's Jews 1870-1914* New York, Harper and Row, 1970.
Arthur Goren: *New York's Jews and the Quest for Community*, New York, New York University, 1970.
Irvin Howe: *World of Our Fathers the Journey of the East European Jews to America and the Life They Found and Made*. New York, Harcourt Brace Jovanovitch, 1976.

A Radical Political and Social History of the Lower East Side

Hispanic Proletarian New York

Bernardo Vega: *Memorias de Bernardo Vega, Contribucion a la Historia de la Communidad Puertoriqueno en Nueva York*, Ediciones Huracan, Rio Piedras, Puerto Rico, 1977 .

Joseph Fitspatrick: *Puerto Rican Americans,* New York, Prentice Hall, 1971.

Piri Thomas: *Down Those Mean Streets*, New York, Knopf, 1967.

Counterculture in New York's East Side

Allen De Loach: *The Lower Side Scene American Poetry 1960-1965*, New York, Doubleday and Co., 1972.

Ed Saunders: *Tales of Beatnik Glory*, Stonehill Publishing Co., New York, 1975

Harry Silverstein: *Creative Arts Alienated Youth Project*, New York, Center for New York City Affairs, The New School for Social Research, 1971

Other

Alice Wexler: *Emma Goldman: An Intimate Life*, Virago Press, 41 William IV Street, London WC2, 1985

20

Chapter 2

THE ORIGINS OF LOISAIDA
Fred Good

Introduction

Interpreting past events is always, to an extent, a subjective matter. We see the world from our own point of view. This is particularly true when we ourselves have been involved in shaping those events. So before exploring some of the specific situations and events which shaped life on the Lower East Side during the sixties and seventies, I will first try to give you, the reader, an idea of what the neighborhood was like when I first arrived there as well as introduce myself to you.

Located directly east of Greenwich Village, between Stuyvesant Town to the north and Chinatown to the south, the southern part of the Lower East Side included Little Italy, the Bowery with its wholesale outlets and cheap hotels which catered to the down and out, the low-income housing projects along the East River and a mixed area known as the Two Bridges neighborhood, which has been improved through urban renewal efforts over the past two decades. The northern part from Houston to Fourteenth Street between Avenue A and the East River has come to be referred to as Alphabet City, and for some, as Loisaida, a name coined by my friends, activists Chino Garcia and Bimbo Rivas, in the early seventies. This part of the Lower East Side was rapidly deteriorating. Prior to World War II, the Lower East Side was settled by Eastern Europeans, mostly Jewish. There were pockets of middle class housing projects throughout the neighborhood, including a large urban renewal effort around Cooper Union on the western edge between Broadway and Second Avenue. During the sixties, this area, extending to Avenue B, came to be referred to as the East Village, The influx of artists and hippies into the area gave it an avant garde image, which was briefly exploited by landlords hoping to improve property values.

After the war, many poor Puerto Ricans came to the eastern part of the Lower East Side, replacing Jews, who moved to better neighborhoods throughout the city and America. Their shops and restaurants remained for some time. Together with city service workers, social workers and teachers, these shop owners commuted into the neighborhood by day. In the evenings, the Puerto Ricans, who worked in menial jobs around the city, returned to their apartments in the public housing projects along the East River or to their tenement build-ings between Avenues A and D. They were joined by a smattering of writers, artists and musicians who moved into the low-income apartments the neighborhood provided. Starting in the sixties, suburban drop-outs, college students, mostly in their late teens and early twenties, and young professionals also migrated to the neighborhood. A large contingent of hippies came and left between 1964 and 1968. They gave the "East Village" a high national, even international, profile. But their exodus, caused to some extent by the murder of two

A Radical Political and Social History of the Lower East Side

young people in an apartment on Avenue B in 1967, had the effect of depreciating real estate values as landlords "disinvested" in the neighborhood.

By the late sixties, most of the real estate owners on the Lower East Side were absentee landlords, living as far away as Florida and California. They treated their real estate as income property, frequently allowing their buildings to deteriorate while accumulating back tax liabilities as well as building violations imposed by city inspectors. They would collect rents from poorer and poorer tenants for as long as they could. Eventually they abandoned their properties, which were then repossessed by the City of New York. By the late '70s, there were hundreds of abandoned buildings in the Lower East Side. These buildings were fertile ground for drug dealers and the heroin addicts to whom they catered. Known as "shooting galleries," many of these buildings provided a place for addicts to congregate and "shoot up" drugs.

In my role as a community organizer on the Lower East Side from 1965 through 1981, I came to know hundreds of people at many levels (both within and outside of the neighborhood), who in one way or another influenced what was going on there at the time. I owned and lived in a brownstone on East Seventh Street between Avenues C and D and worked on dozens of neighborhood projects during those years. These included being a part of creating The Real Great Society, or RGS, as it came to be known, the founding of the University of the Streets in 1967, managing the Seven Loaves Arts Coalition during the late '70s and helping many other neighborhood groups such as Kenkeleba House and Mothers in Action. In 1981, I moved to North Carolina to devote my time to painting and family life. I sold my brownstone on Seventh Street to a fellow artist, a woman, who has since moved. I had bought the building for $45,000 in 1971, made some renovations while owning the property and sold it for twice that in 1983. Today that brownstone is worth well over $1 million.

The first of three boys, I was born in Pittsburgh, Pennsylvania, of Belgian parents. They had temporarily moved to the United States just after being married in 1938. My father was doing a three-year internship for Gulf Oil, which had bought our family oil business a decade earlier. With the outbreak of World War II, my parents were unable to return home. When Hitler invaded Belgium in 1940, my father volunteered in the American Army, was immediately nationalized and commissioned into the Officers Strategic Services, which later became the CIA. He spent the next three years in Europe as an intelligence officer.

Growing up as first generation Americans was for my brothers and me quite different than it was for most immigrants who came to America seeking a better life. We lived in affluent neighborhoods and attended both public and private schools in Philadelphia, then Greenwich, Connecticut, Jacksonville, and finally Savannah. In 1958, during my first year in college at Georgetown University, my parents moved back to Philadelphia, where they live to this day. Every summer starting in 1946, we boarded an ocean liner and traveled to Belgium to spend the summers on our grandparents' estate.

My brothers and I grew up speaking both English and French and assimilated most of the cultural and social skills that were part of the education of any affluent European at the time. Our upbringing included travel throughout Western Europe, visiting old towns, castles and museums. An appreciation of history, art and literature were ingrained in us from an early age. Our parents read the English and American classics to us nightly as we were growing up. They didn't buy a television set until we were in our teens. We rarely watched it.

Only in my mid-twenties did I come to realize how unique our upbringing was. While privileged, we had also been sheltered. After spending two years as a lieutenant in the United States Army Artillery, I was ready for a change and decided to join my brother Mike who had dropped out of his last year in college at Villanova and moved to the Lower East Side. As a teenager, he had begun to question some of the social attitudes and values with which we had been raised. Unlike me, he did not try so hard to conform; by the time he was twenty, he decided to drop out of college and strike out on his own.

Forming the Real Great Society

On the Lower East Side we found many of the characters we came to know so well from Oliver Twist and other Dickens' novels our parents read to us as children. Suddenly, poverty and crime became a real part of our daily existence. Now, the people described in Oliver Twist were not just storybook characters. They took on slightly different faces than those English ones. The props were a little different. But the injustices and inequalities in the London that Dickens was writing about were essentially the same as those we found in New York's Lower East Side. We became immersed in the life and times of our newfound neighborhood, convinced that there was something that could be done about the conditions we found there. I abandoned any lingering thoughts of going to work in a bank or returning to Europe to make a living as a businessman.

Mike and I easily made friends with the young Puerto Ricans of the neighborhood. They had never met "rich white kids," and we had never met Puerto Ricans, rich or poor. Most of them were members of street gangs — primarily a matter of survival in the hostile environment of the inner city. Up until then, the musical West Side Story was our only exposure to New York City youth gangs. We were now face to face with the living versions of characters we grew up to think of as existing in a world we would never experience. It was, we were led to believe, an underworld of people who had marginalized themselves; who had chosen evil over good.

To our surprise, we discovered that our new friends were not much different from ourselves and that we could get along fine. We also discovered that we shared many of the same dreams in life. We wanted to create a better world. It had to begin with us, we reasoned. We had to live what we dreamed. It did not take us long to discover that there were opportunities for us out there; we simply had to promote ourselves and our new way of life. We believed that the first step was to come to know and trust one another. We shared our life stories.

Chino Garcia was three years old when his family moved to the Lower East Side to seek a better life. By the time he was twelve, he was a well-developed, six-foot youngster who appeared quite a bit older. He had not been able to learn to read and write in school, where the classes were too crowded for individual attention. By the ninth grade, he dropped out of

A Radical Political and Social History of the Lower East Side

school and spent his time learning to survive in the streets. There his natural social and physical skills gave him an edge. He was handsome and self-assured for his age. He found himself in leadership roles, eventually becoming the head of the Assassins, one of the dominant gangs in Manhattan.

When Chino was fifteen, the police gave him an ultimatum: Go back to Puerto Rico or go to jail. Pressure from his mother sent him back to his native country. There he found a menial job and decided to reform his ways. The conditions of poverty he encountered in Puerto Rico had a profound and lasting effect on him. By 1964 he returned to New York with new goals in mind.

Chino found a somewhat different environment than the one he had left. The gangs had largely dissipated as a result of a concerted effort on the part of the police and New York social agencies to get rid of them. A friend, Angelo Gonzalez, who led a gang named the Dragons, had just been released from prison after three years and was also thinking about turning over a new leaf. Together they came up with the idea of starting a social club where they could keep their peers out of trouble while earning a little money in the process.

The two former gang leaders convinced a Catholic priest who ran a youth center to let them use his basement to set up their club. There they met my brother Mike, who was exchanging work for room and board. Within months, however, they were caught with liquor on the premises and were back in the streets. By then, Mike had rented a fourth floor railroad apartment at 605 East Sixth Street between Avenues B and C. His apartment became a hangout for Chino, Angelo and their friends. I moved in with Mike in the spring of 1965.

Within days of joining my brother, I was spending my time painting large abstract expressionist canvases on the rooftop of 605 East Sixth Street. Often I was joined by Chino and others. Getting to know these young Puerto Ricans was a revelation to me. They were not at all like what I had imagined juvenile delinquents to be. They had the same dreams and ambitions I had. They were creative and fun-loving. They were easy to get along with. I resolved to devote myself to changing the conditions in which these young people found themselves. We rented the downstairs storefront and hired ourselves out to paint local apartments and take on small moving and cleaning jobs in the neighborhood. At night, we hung around talking about how we would build a better world. We decided to call ourselves the "real" Great Society in contrast to President Johnson's "Great Society." We saw ourselves as personifying the American Dream.

It did not take long before we discovered others who were interested and inspired by our idealism. Some of these people became important advocates for us. Charles W. Slack, a former Harvard professor, was now teaching at Columbia Teachers College. He had worked with Chino and other gangs in the early sixties. He and his friend, Frank Ferguson, who was attending graduate school and living with his wife on the Lower East Side, helped us learn about government and foundation funding and how to write grant proposals. We were introduced to the Moreno Institute by John Huntington. We befriended its founder, Jacob

Moreno, the creator of psychodrama and father of group psychotherapy. A number of corporate executives became interested and involved in what we were doing.

Slack was helping corporations obtain government funding to set up Job Corps Centers. He began sending Chino and Angelo around the country to talk to college students and business executives about how they had transformed themselves from juvenile gang leaders into neighborhood activists committed to rebuilding their neighborhood. "Gangs are dead in New York," ran one headline on the front page of a newspaper in Madison. Angelo's picture below the headline implied that this was the result of the work of the Real Great Society. Wherever they made speeches, newspapers carried articles about these reformed New York gang leaders, often inflating reality. Chino and Angelo were turning into media celebrities. Middle class college students were inspired by their rhetoric. Executives and government bureaucrats were impressed by the press they were getting. While Chino and Angelo were making appearances at campuses, rotary clubs and boardrooms around the country, I began to explore my newfound community, its people and its institutions.

By the summer of 1965, I was working with Judge Mary Kohler, helping to set up the Neighborhood Youth Corps program in New York City. The program hired poor youth to work in government and non-profit agencies during the summer. As an employee for Neighborhood Youth Corps and subsequently the New York City Youth Board and Job Corps, I quickly learned the ropes of government, non-profit agencies and private foundations. At every opportunity, I worked to further the Real Great Society. I found a lawyer to help us establish the Real Great Society, Inc., a non-profit, tax-exempt corporation. We elected Chino Garcia, president, Angelo Gonzalez, vice-president, Carlos Troche, secretary, and me as treasurer. We were now ready to apply for grants, operate programs and raise money from the public.

Promoting the Real Great Society (RGS) became an all-consuming cause for me. The theme we espoused was empowerment. Former juvenile gang leaders, we argued, were best equipped to help their peers turn their lives around to become productive, active citizens. I was focused and determined. Within a few years, we had begun to be noticed. We landed our first grant for $15,000 in January 1967. We had been invited a month before to meet with Allan Betts, Executive Director of the Astor Foundation, in his office on Park Avenue. He had read our proposal and was intrigued. The foundation's primary focus at the time was delinquency prevention. Mr. Betts later explained, "I was attracted to them because of their sincerity, their enthusiasm and their self-confidence. I felt that they might learn. At least they would have a valuable experience. This was the first time I had seen ghetto people like them, really wanting to make good, and I was deeply impressed." (Poston, 1970).

While the Real Great Society had no formal program during these formative years, we came to agree on some common beliefs and attitudes that helped shape our future. Several themes emerged. We could learn from one another by doing. Forming an organization together to improve our community would require us to learn about and to interact with government and a host of other institutions in the community. Working together to formulate goals and objectives and to articulate a program for achieving them would enable us to play a leadership role in the emerging War on Poverty. Chino came up with a kind of preamble for the Real Great Society. "For a long time in America people have been saying that 'all men are created equal.' We say, 'all men are created great.'" The RGS looked more like a political movement than a program.

26

Joining the War on Poverty

The Astor Foundation grant enabled us to begin implementing some of our dreams. Within a few months, three projects were up and running.

On the surface we were looking good and the future seemed bright. The Leather Bag, a retail storefront selling leather crafts made by young neighborhood people, was open and doing business. A small storefront daycare center watched over the children of some of the neighborhood's working mothers, but had no source of income. The Fabulous Latin House, a dance club on 14th Street, became a popular nightclub for Puerto Rican youth. Although it was doing a hefty business, the income seemed to disappear as quickly as money was collected at the door. It's not that money was being siphoned off, but that we were not keeping very close tabs on what was spent. The truth is that we spent money unrealistically, thinking that as long as we were doing the right thing, it was okay.

Whether these projects actually had an impact on curtailing juvenile delinquency was a matter of conjecture and nobody seriously tried to find out. None of these three projects lasted much beyond the life of the Astor grant that initially funded them. But the projects gave us momentum in the public eye.

By the summer of 1967, the RGS was well on its way. Life Magazine published a long article with pictures about us, and other publications were following suit. The Boston Sunday Herald ran a feature article covering our visit to Harvard University where we talked to an enthusiastic audience of some 200 students. We were no longer a ragtag bunch of idealists having a good time. The press was paying attention to us. Without realizing it, we were quickly turning into very effective politicians, making inflated claims and giving the impression that we were able to do things far beyond our real capabilities. The influx of money and attention was deceiving. We were able to claim credit for things that were not entirely of our making.

A second grant for $25,000 from the Vincent Astor Foundation later that year fueled our sense of success. We had proposed an educational program without knowing much about how to create one. We were not even required to submit a written proposal. Our three initial projects appeared to be successful on the surface, and our publicity could not have been better. Mr. Betts was willing to go to his board and ask for another grant on our behalf. We wanted to start a school. I had recently met Robert Theobald, a British economist and author (The Guaranteed Annual Income) at Columbia University. He had some ideas about creating a radical new kind of university.

The design was simple. We would rent a storefront, then send out a mimeographed flyer around the neighborhood asking for "resource" volunteers and students to enroll in whatever subjects they might want to explore. When there was a resource person and at least a few interested students in any subject, we would gather them together, find an appropriate time and space for them to meet, and let the group go from there. It would all be offered for free. The grant would just pay for space rental, some flyers, office materials and other necessary incidentals.

The University of the Streets emerged on the scene in the summer of 1967, with a picture and article on the front page of the *New York Times*. Because of its high profile, hundreds of middle class students, many of whom had been part of the civil rights and anti-war movements, as well as a large number of hippies, flocked to the project. Organized student groups such as the SDS (Students for a Democratic Society) sought us out. We rented a large street-level storefront on the corner of Avenue A and East Seventh Street and, due to the response we got, negotiated with the landlord to rent additional floors. Owen Watson, a karate black belt who had recently returned from military service in Vietnam, came to an RGS board meeting and got approval to set up a School of Martial Arts on the second floor.

Within a month, we had enrolled 1,600 students and resource people and had rented three more floors in the building. A wide variety of groups were meeting during the day and evenings. A bulletin board on the street level listed class offerings and a schedule of when they met. Classes included drama, music, tutoring, various languages, different kinds of arts and crafts, radio and television repair, philosophy and many others. Initially, the majority of participants in the University of the Streets were middle class, many drawn to the neighborhood for the summer because of its reputation as the center of hippie activity.

By the fall of 1967, most of these people had gone on to other things. But each of the five floors were spoken for. A teen center was established in the basement. It acted as a kind of recruitment center for kids wanting to participate in our tutoring program. An art gallery was opened on the street level. It served as a venue for local artists who were just starting out and offered art classes for aspiring artists. The karate school, popular with local youth, was thriving on the second floor. It had an enrollment of well over 100 students. The third floor became a music center with such notable musicians as Kenny Dorham, Jackie McLean and Bill Dixon working as teachers and mentors to younger musicians. Bill Dixon also rehearsed an orchestra of some forty musicians two times a week. The fourth floor became a daycare center which was a model for many community daycare centers around the city. The fifth floor, which housed our offices, is where we tutored youth, published a newsletter and organized neighborhood activities, including a football team, which practiced in the East River Park and played other teams from around the city.

While the University of the Streets was focused on building a solid program on the Lower East Side, the RGS leaders continued traveling around the country, speaking and making inflated claims about what they were doing in their neighborhood. They were also now making trips to Washington, D.C. where they were meeting with officials at the Office of Economic Opportunity, the Department of Labor and the Department of Health, Education and Welfare. With the encouragement and help of a former State Department official, they had formed a new national organization called Youth Organizations United and were lobbying for a large government grant.

A Radical Political and Social History of the Lower East Side

Chino and Angelo were now joined by several former gang leaders from uptown who had started an East Harlem branch. Their influence on Chino and Angelo eventually led to a schism within the RGS. Unlike our personnel on the Lower East Side, the East Harlem leaders were all Puerto Rican and had adopted the rhetoric and attitudes of the Young Lords, a Puerto Rican version of the Black Panther Party. Their style was confrontational and less idealistic than that of the Lower East Side leaders. They had connected with the RGS for pragmatic reasons; namely, to help them obtain grants from foundations and government.

Chino and Angelo initially resisted this influence. But the lure of myth-making combined with ethnic pride and the tacit support of officials in Washington, led them to turn against those of us who were operating on the home front. It was almost as if there were two separate organizations. One group, entirely made up of Puerto Ricans, was focused on promoting themselves outside of the neighborhood and consolidating their power and influence in East Harlem; while another, ethnically and educationally diverse, was engaged in grassroots community development on the Lower East Side. As long as these two groups remained apart and independent, and there was not much money involved, there was no cause for conflict. That changed when we joined the War on Poverty.

A hallmark of Lyndon Johnson's Great Society, the War on Poverty was the result of legislation developed by John F. Kennedy and his administration after he read a book by Michael Harrington called *The Other America*, which exposed widespread poverty in America. Kennedy's assassination created the conditions whereby Congress felt compelled to pass his legislation. The Office of Economic Opportunity (OEO) was created in 1964 with Kennedy's brother-in-law, Sargent Shriver, chosen to administer the new agency. The OEO contracted mostly with big businesses, local governments and established nonprofit organizations to design and operate programs to help the poor. It had twice turned down our proposals to support our efforts on the Lower East Side. A serendipitous event changed that.

Robert Kennedy became New York State's junior senator in 1966. Returning from Washington on the air shuttle to New York City, Frank Ferguson was seated next to the Senator. After gaining his attention, Frank talked to him about the work we were doing on the Lower East Side. Kennedy told Frank to call one of his assistants, Adam Walinsky, in Washington. Within a few weeks, Frank and I were sitting with Walinsky telling him all about the Real Great Society. After an hour of conversation, Walinsky called Shriver to tell him that Senator Kennedy would appreciate favorable action on the proposal from the Real Great Society.

Within a few days, on February 28, 1968, our proposal was approved. The grant assured the project's survival. It also led to conflict and a split between the Puerto Rican leaders and the rest of us who ran the University of the Streets. At a national level, a number of social and political forces were colliding, creating a charged and chaotic political environment. The anti-war and civil rights movements and the anti-poverty program were each having an effect on the national scene. The emergence of the counter-culture was also influencing the mood of the country.

Following the assassination of Martin Luther King in early April, 1968, riots broke out in cities across the country. Youth Organizations United, designed to be a national coalition of inner-city youth groups similar to the RGS, had captured the attention of the vice president's office in Washington. It was negotiating a multi-million dollar federal grant to be distributed to inner-city youth groups around the country. The riots following the Martin Luther King, Jr. assassination stopped that.

Coming to Grips with Reality

The extensive publicity that had surrounded the Real Great Society during its formative years not only drew people to us, but had an impact on our own sense of who we were and what we could do. A feeling of euphoria surrounded our first several foundation grants and the opening of the University of the Streets in the summer of 1967. The sense of empowerment engendered by the cooperation of so many different kinds of people gave us the impression that this was the way things could really be. Our success, however, was not always viewed favorably.

Rather than applying for anti-poverty funds through local channels, namely, the Lower East Side Community Corporation, the Real Great Society had applied directly to the Research and Demonstration section of the Office of Economic Opportunity in Washington, which was empowered to bypass local structures. Thus, we came to be viewed with suspicion by some in the neighborhood who did not understand how we had gained such special status. Our grant was larger than the annual budget of many of the other new agencies in the community. So, by the time we actually began to spend money from our federal grant, we were not always perceived locally with the same enthusiasm with which many outside of the neighborhood perceived us. Our real problems, however, were within our own organization.

Almost from the beginning, the University of the Streets operated independently of the Real Great Society. Muhammad Salahuddeen, an African-American social worker, was the project's director. A convert to Islam and a musician, he was middle-aged and not part of the inner core of the RGS. He was viewed with suspicion by the East Harlem leaders, who sought to eliminate non-Puerto Ricans from key roles within the organization.

The reason the East Harlem leaders befriended us was to gain quick and easy access to resources such as the Astor Foundation and government. They did not go through the long and sometimes difficult learning process we had gone through on the Lower East Side. Their agenda was quite different from ours. Unlike the idealistic, multiethnic, cross-cultural, economically diverse group of people on the Lower East Side who had created the Real Great Society, the East Harlem leaders espoused Puerto Rican power. Despite this, or perhaps because of it, they were able to form an alliance with Columbia University, and this gave them immediate credibility. They obtained much larger grants from the Astor Foundation ($50,000) and other private and local governmental sources than we had.

On the Lower East Side, we achieved credibility on our own over a period of three years of working together. Our inspiration sprang from the experience of being able to live and learn

A Radical Political and Social History of the Lower East Side

together even though we had come from very different backgrounds. We sought to share this experience with others and to encourage them to join us on the journey.

By the time the University of the Street's grant money began to flow, the East Harlem leaders had managed to have a portion of it designated for use by East Harlem. By that time too, as noted, funding for Youth Organizations United had been curtailed because of the riots following King's assassination. As a result, the RGS leaders were back in their respective neighborhoods. On the Lower East Side, they needed something to do. They decided to rent a storefront on Ludlow Street and became more interested in the affairs of the University of the Streets. The OEO proposal, while acknowledging the eclectic nature of the University of the Streets, focused primarily on aspects of the project aimed at young Puerto Rican former gang members. This gave the East Harlem leaders a rationale for convincing Chino and Angelo to remove those of us who were not Puerto Rican from leadership roles in the organization. This effort came to a head on the morning of January 28, 1969.

The RGS leaders called Muhammad to their Ludlow Street storefront headquarters and announced to him that he and his staff were fired. At the same time, they sent a dozen young men, some reputed to have been carrying firearms, to the building on the corner of Avenue A and East Seventh Street and loaded every piece of furniture and office equipment, as well as tools and musical instruments, from each of the five floors, onto trucks and drove away. Left with an empty building and no money, Muhammad called the staff together late that afternoon. Within a few hours, we had not only resolved to start over, but had devised a plan to do so. The University of the Streets was now publicly its own organization. Months before, in anticipation of the possibility that we might have to sever relations with the RGS, we had established a separate non-profit corporation, which held the lease for the space we occupied.

Within a year, the University of the Streets had established itself as a viable vocational training program and was receiving private grants and federal money. The building which it occupied on the corner of Seventh Street and Avenue A was purchased by a wealthy Dutch industrialist, Oscar Van Leer, who had learned about the project through New York's senior senator, Jacob Javits. Van Leer deeded the building to the non-profit corporation (U.O.T.S., Inc.), managed by Muhammad. Over the next three decades, the project has gone through a variety of changes. Muhammad continues to live on the seventh floor of the building and manages it as best he can. The karate school and a music program continue to this day.

(Incidentally, relatively soon after the takeover, the downtown RGS disassociated itself from uptown RGS. Chino went on to start CHARAS. Even after the split, I remained friends with him, although the closeness and shared idealism we felt in the heady first days of the RGS could, of course, never be recaptured.)

Self-help and Community Control

Starting in the mid-'60s, a trend towards community self-help began to replace the network of settlement houses and social agencies, like Mobilization for Youth, which were created by outsiders to address problems within the neighborhood. The War on Poverty, as well as state and local governmental agencies, private foundations and corporations, provided the money for dozens of new organizations to come into being. Community action became synonymous with community control and the idea of community control spread to all facets of life-social, educational, cultural and economic.

The decentralization of the New York City Board of Education by the Lindsay Administration into 32 locally elected school boards had an important impact on the Lower East Side in the early '70s. The first District One School Board elections pitted entrenched, mostly Jewish interests aligned with Albert Shanker's United Federation of Teachers Union, against a multi-ethnic slate of representatives referred to as the "community" board. Young idealistic Puerto Rican, black and white activists, who worked in the neighborhood in dozens of social agencies, joined forces to mobilize neighborhood residents to defeat entrenched interests loyal to the teachers' union.

The community slate of candidates gained control of the District One School Board for two short years, during which time they hired the controversial Puerto Rican superintendent, Luis Fuentes. In the long run, however, they were not able to sustain what seemed at the time to be a unified, grassroots coalition devoted to empowering local residents. Establishment forces were able to corrupt the election process a few years later, enabling a majority of union supporters to regain control of the school board. The District One School Board struggle did set the tone for the activism of the next several decades on the Lower East Side. Activists came to know one another, learning to cooperate around common agendas.

Part of the effort to take control of the local school board involved the registration of thousands of new voters, mostly Puerto Rican. Local people began to understand how the system worked. They came to a better understanding of the role of government in their lives and how to manipulate it to their own benefit. Arturo Santiago (who ran the Association for Community Services), Dora Colazo-Levy and Armando Perez (one of the original leaders of the RGS) are examples of Puerto Rican residents who found their way into mainstream politics, serving as district leaders in the Democratic Party.

Economic control was manifested in the sweat equity movement, which was pioneered by Interfaith Adopt-a-Building. Robert Nazario, one of the original RGS leaders, was the director of this group during its formative years, prior to his becoming a housing advisor to President Carter and later settling in Baltimore, where he continued promoting sweat equity homesteading. Adopt-a-Building played an advocacy role on the Joint Planning Council to get the support of New York City government for sweat equity homesteading. The broader homesteading movement of the '80s and '90s is a descendant of these earlier efforts.

By the early '70s, activism within the Puerto Rican community on the Lower East Side turned inward. This took the form of self-expression through the arts. During the summer, the streets came alive with conga drums. Groups of conga players were often joined by guitar players and other musicians. Throughout the summer, poets recited their lyrics, and there was lots of singing in the streets and parks around the neighborhood. Abandoned buildings were torn down by the city and turned into small "vest pocket" parks by locals who grew

A Radical Political and Social History of the Lower East Side

flowers and vegetables and congregated in them for special events. While "poverty pimps" continued to work in the neighborhood's many anti-poverty agencies, a community spirit took hold, with residents creating their own particular solutions to the conditions they faced. Amidst the physical deterioration, drug addiction and crime, there was a spirit of survival and pride.

The Nuyoricans

Three Puerto Rican poets, Miguel Algarin, Lucky Cienfuego and Miguel Piñero, were making a name for themselves in New York City and beyond. As the Nuyorican Poets, they performed throughout the city, usually with congas and other instruments accompanying them. They were often joined by other young, aspiring Puerto Rican poets. Their language came directly from the streets. It combined English and Spanish into what they called "Spanglish." Their themes were taken from street life. Their lyrics were down and dirty, with explicit references to sexual experience, drugs, crime and poverty. One common archetype was a capitalist oppressor pushing drugs to maintain poverty and suffering in the ghetto. The lyrics were political, blunt and confrontational.

As a group, the trio did not last long. Piñero, who was also a heroin addict and small time thief, was convicted in the late sixties of sexually assaulting a minor and spent three years in jail. During that time, he wrote the play, *Short Eyes*. Produced by Joseph Papp and enacted by the theater group "The Family," the play won the New York Drama Critics Award in 1973. Following that success, Marvin Felix Camillo, the group's artistic director, asked his board of directors to hire me as its business manager. During the next two years, I worked closely with Marvin and his board, which was headed by the famous actress Colleen Dewhurst. Joseph Papp continued to support The Family for years.

A movie based on Piñero's life appeared in 2000. It is an inaccurate version of his life and gave a distorted impression of Piñero himself. Rather than the flamboyant character depicted in the film, Miguel was a quiet, kind and sensitive soul, caught in the grips of debilitating addictions and conflicting influences. He was an extraordinarily talented poet and playwright. He was a tragic character who came to be exploited by mainstream television interests.

One of the more disturbing stories to emerge from Piñero's involvement with Hollywood was how television producers would supply him with cocaine to encourage him to work on scripts for them. Luis Guzman, among others, was a beneficiary of Piñero's connections to the film and television establishment. Fortunately, Guzman resisted the temptation of drugs and became a successful actor in his own right. Guzman continues to remain friends with Chino Garcia, although he no longer has much of a connection to the neighborhood in which he grew up-the place where he initially became interested in acting.

Algarin and Piñero remained close friends until Piñero's death in 1988. At the time, with the help of others, Algarin organized a memorial procession that wound through the streets of Loisaida, growing larger as it moved along. Piñero's ashes were spread through the streets in an enactment of one of the poet's more famous poems in which he describes his funeral. It was Nuyorican at its best. Sadness turned into artistic expression and celebration. Ugliness made into beauty.

Algarin, who taught English at Rutgers University, was the most educated of the three poets. He was a close friend of Allen Ginsberg and other literary figures of the time. He lived on a relatively good block in a ground floor apartment on East Sixth Street between Avenues A and B, rode the subway to work and back and led a relatively structured life. With a friend, Richard August, he established the now famous Nuyorican Poets Café in a storefront across the street from his apartment on East Sixth Street. It was 1975.

The Café became a regular venue for local aspiring poets and performers and sometimes for some more famous established poets like Ginsberg and his friend, William Burroughs. Performers at the Café were as young as 9 years old. I will never forget the performance by Luis Guzman when he was 15. Alone, on stage, he portrayed a drag queen talking to herself as she puts on her makeup in front of a mirror. It stands as the most hilarious single act I have ever seen.

The late Bimbo Rivas was a regular at the Café. A poet and actor, he led a group known as Teatro Ambulante. Their plays were performed in the streets, at block parties and in community centers. They often included dance and music. Luis Guzman was among his young, up-and-coming actors. Together with his younger friend, Chino Garcia, who introduced Bimbo to community activism, they coined the name "Loisaida," Spanglish for Lower East Side. The name became adopted and popularized by the Seven Loaves and its member groups as well as by a band named "A Band Called Loisaida." The band's lead guitar player, Edwin (Pupa) Santiago, has recently reorganized the group, which now has a website and easily purchasable CDs.

Gentrification vs. Loisaida

The neighborhood arts coalition known as Seven Loaves was established in the early '70s. It was formed by seven community arts groups, which had sprung up in the '60s and early '70s. They came together to share resources, coordinate fundraising efforts and undertake specific community projects together. Each group had its own board of directors and a particular mission and purpose. The Seven Loaves coordinator was a professional who helped the member groups with their grant applications and provided other kinds of technical assistance on an ongoing basis. These groups, together with several others who joined the coalition in the early '80s, played an important role in communicating the spirit and culture of activist minority communities. The best known of these groups was CHARAS.

Formed in the early seventies by Chino Garcia and five other individuals as a community development effort, CHARAS became most known for building geodesic domes. R. Buckminster Fuller had inspired them to apply modern technology to solving inner city problems. This idea was later extended to the Eleventh Street Movement, a project sponsored by Adopt-a-Building, in which aqua culture, solar energy and wind power were introduced into the design of several sweat equity buildings on Eleventh Street. Following up on a sugges-

A Radical Political and Social History of the Lower East Side

tion by my friend Frank Ferguson, I flew to San Francisco in the fall of 1967 to meet Fuller and invite him to visit us on the Lower East Side. When he came to the University of the Streets in 1968, he met Chino and they agreed to collaborate. CHARAS, in effect, became the successor of the original Real Great Society.

In the late '70s, CHARAS moved into a large, five-story, abandoned public high school on East Ninth Street, which Adopt-a-Building had obtained from the City of New York. They began the process of renovating the basement auditorium, heating system and first floor. CHARAS was given the responsibility of managing the building, naming it El Bohio. As a show of support for the project in 1980, more than 100 artists and performers from throughout New York City collaborated to produce one of the more interesting art exhibitions in the city that year. Using almost every room in the first three floors of the building, artists were free to do whatever they wanted in their allocated space. Known as The Survival Show, it received excellent publicity and was well attended. However, its young, white organizers were disappointed in their relationship with CHARAS and almost all of them disappeared when the show was over.

The Survival Show was emblematic of a trend which would characterize CHARAS for the next two decades. Activists, inspired by the causes CHARAS espoused, would become involved in El Bohio, often putting large amounts of time, energy and money into it, only to become disenchanted and eventually leave the project. One Native American group, which wanted to occupy and renovate two entire floors, decided not to join the effort because they were refused equal representation on the El Bohio board of directors. Consequently, the building was only partially occupied over the two decades CHARAS managed it. This undermined their efforts to reverse the sale of the building by the city to a developer.

In 2002, the Giuliani Administration was finally able to prevail in a long and expensive legal battle for control of El Bohio. Gentrification of the neighborhood, which symbolically had begun with the community's inability to successfully convert the Christodora House into a community center and housing for low income people, was exposed as the de facto policy of the New York City administration starting with the Giuliani administration and lasting to the present. CHARAS moved to East Harlem.

Adjacent to El Bohio facing Tompkins Square Park, the Christodora House was a 16-story building which had been abandoned and taken over by the city. It was occupied in the late '60s by one of the more visible community activists at the time, Bob Collier, whose reputation had been his calling card in the streets. He had spent three years in prison for trying to blow up the Statue of Liberty. Many of the neighborhood's juvenile delinquents and activists became involved with him in attempting to persuade the City of New York, which had taken possession of the building, to repair its in-door swimming pool and to provide resources to repair the heating system and renovate its rooms. Dozens of the building's apartments came to be occupied by squatters and homeless people, many of whom were being released to the streets from mental institutions.

Despite concerted attempts on the part of community activists to prevent it, the city sold the Christodora House for $63,000 to a real estate speculator in 1973. The speculator methodically vacated the building by hiring thugs to intimidate the people who were living there. Authorities blatantly ignored persistent community protests, in effect siding with the speculator. Gentrification had begun with the City of New York turning a blind eye to its insidious incursion into the neighborhood. It would continue into the next century.

In addition to CHARAS, six other groups were part of Seven Loaves. *The Fourth Street i* was a magazine run by a group of young people who were part of a youth group associated with St. Brigid's Catholic Church on Avenue B, just across from the eastern edge of Tompkins Square Park. Forming a closely knit group, these teenagers were seriously involved in music, writing and photography.

The Fourth Street i was distributed throughout the neighborhood. It consisted of articles, photographs and poetry about life on the Lower East Side. The parish, which also ran a school, was led by two priests, who were eventually forced out of the church because of their open relationships with women, whom they eventually married, and grassroots involvement. They encouraged Puerto Rican parishioners to organize their own anti-poverty efforts, including an alternative high school for young people who dropped out of regular public school. The Ninth Street School operated throughout the '70s. It was one among several independent "alternative" schools formed on the Lower East Side in response to the inability of the public schools to handle some of the area's teenagers. Superintendent Luis Fuentes was a great supporter of the Ninth Street School.

CITYarts was dedicated to painting murals on the faces of buildings. These panels, often conveying political messages, can still be seen on some of the buildings around the neighborhood. The Printshop focused on teaching the production of cards and posters.
The Children's Arts Workshop taught children a variety of visual arts. The Basement Workshop in Chinatown focused on teaching printing and other reproduction techniques.
The Darkroom was focused on photography and the development and editing of film. These groups often worked directly with local schools. They focused on the expression of neighborhood themes.

In 1980, a number of other community groups joined the Seven Loaves Coalition, which became the Lower East Side Arts Network. These groups included Kenkeleba House, Actors' Directors' Writers' Coalition, Black Maria, the Chicano Raza Group of the Performing Arts, East River Park Amphitheater Restoration Corporation, Lower East Side Community Music Workshop, Musicians United Unlimited, Quality of Life in Loisaida (Calidad de Vida en Loisaida), Scavenger Theater, and Tylis Photo and Documentation Project. Although these groups were usually small, centering around a few practicing artists, they each played a part in promoting a particular community identity, which came to be manifested in the naming of Avenue C as Loisaida Avenue and Avenue B as Charles Parker Avenue.

Of the new groups joining the Lower East Side Arts Network, Kenkeleba House had the most ambitious program. Joe Overstreet, an accomplished painter, with his partner, Corrine Jennings, a gifted writer and educator, established Kenkeleba House as a collective of artists and educators, incorporating in 1975. The group's stated purposes were to help promote cultural awareness in the community, to engage in cultural exchange programs with other com-

A Radical Political and Social History of the Lower East Side

munities and to help develop young artists through educational opportunities. They were able to obtain the old Mobilization for Youth building on East Second Street in the latter part of the '70s, where they converted the bottom floor into a large art gallery, which held art exhibits and performing arts events on a regular basis. The upper floors were converted into live-in studios for artists.

Any article about this period of Loisaida history would be remiss without at least a mention of Steve Cannon and the group of poets and writers with which he was associated (known as the Umbra Poets), which included Ishmael Reed and David Henderson. His organization, A Gathering of Tribes, located on East Third Street, is still active today. A retired professor of literature at Medgar Evers College, Steve continues to be a regular at the Nuyorican Café. He edits and circulates a magazine, *The Gathering of the Tribes*, which has been influential among artists and activists for more than twenty years.

The perspective offered in this chapter, as I noted at the outset, is personal. Many other individuals and organizations, as well as local agencies and politicians not mentioned here, contributed to the life and times of that part of the Lower East Side now commonly referred to as Loisaida. There were also outside forces impacting the community which shaped its future. Only by recording what we know and how we saw it can we arrive at a better understanding of history, thereby reconciling our own particular prejudices with a broader, more comprehensive understanding. Viva Loisaida!

Bibliography:

Good, Fred. *Poems*. Chapel Hill: New View Publications, 1999.

Von Hassell, Malve. *Homesteading in New York City, 1978-1993: The Divided Heart of Loisaida*. Westport, Connecticut: Bergin & Garvey, 1996.

Mele, Christopher. *Selling the Lower East Side*. Minneapolis: University of Minnesota Press, 2000.

Poston, Richard. *The Gang and the Establishment*. New York: Harper and Row, 1970.

Chapter 3

TWENTY ONE YEARS ON THE LOWER EAST SIDE by Thomas McEvilley

21 Years on the Lower East Side
Thomas McEvilley

21 years on the Lower East Side of Manhattan, always within 100 yards or so of the same
intersection, Second Street and Avenue B. In 1982, Maura Sheehan and I rented two storefronts at 9 Clinton Street. A few years later, we moved to a building at 245 East Second,
about at the intersection with Avenue C. The *New York Times* put the façade of the building
on the front page of the Metro section one day in about '85, with the caption: "A Building
on One of the Worst Blocks in New York." The rest of the building, we soon found out, was
on rent strike. The tenants were mostly associated with the club/art center ABC No Rio, a
building they had somehow gotten from the city by going on rent strike and getting a
lawyer. They had hoped to do the same with 245. Walter, the apparent landlord (no one
knew who really owned it), was in despair. The rent-strikers would register complaints — like
no functioning mailboxes. He would put in new (used) mailboxes, and within a day they
would be smashed. The tenants began breaking holes in the walls to merge spaces — holes
large enough to step through.

On the top floor was a shooting gallery where junkies would go with ten bucks and get a hit
of heroin and, for a couple of extra bucks, get a place to do it and nod in for a while. If
they didn't have the couple extra bucks, they would shoot it up on the stairs immediately
outside my door. Through the peephole I would see sometimes as many as three people —
always black or Latino — shooting up on different stairs, nodding off with the needles still in
their arms, the syringes hanging. On Clinton Street there were pits in front of the storefronts, giving access to the basement; these pits were always filled with garbage, about
three feet deep. Junkies would descend into the pits and, standing waist deep in garbage,
tie off and shoot up. One wild woman from the islands would hold the syringe in her teeth,
like Carmen's rose, as she used both hands to tie off her arm and raise her head to scan the
horizon.

At that time the intersection at Second and B was one of two or three open-air drug markets
in the city (one in Harlem, another in the Bronx) that were tolerated by police. It kept the
drug business — and the violence and robberies that accompanied it — out of middle class
neighborhoods. All day and all night the vendors called out their wares around and in the
middle of that intersection. Sales were completely in the open. One dealer had found a way
inside an abandoned building and broken out a few bricks to create a hole in the wall big
enough to reach through. Ten-dollar bills would go in and the little glassine packets would
come out. After AIDS became known, the idea of sealing syringes so they would look like
new hospital materials added a new level to the business. Through the peephole I saw

37

A Radical Political and Social History of the Lower East Side

junkies with a heat-sealing device sealing works in the hallway without even wiping them off, then selling them as new to those coming to the shooting gallery.

Along with drug trade came prostitution. Young women, mostly Puerto Rican or Dominican, would perform in doorways or in halls in tenements. Once AIDS became widely known, the commodity was mostly the blowjob. One of our neighbors, Norma, was in the business and would often show up wounded by knives. She explained that the Puerto Rican girls resented swallowing the customer's cum, and as soon as they tasted it in their mouths, would pull off, leap up, and run. It was a matter of pride with them. Angry customers would strike out, sometimes with knives.

Maura and I befriended Norma's six-year-old son, Alex, who would come over after school to play or hang around. After a couple of years of this, Norma came over one day with a proposition. Her parents in Puerto Rico, she explained, had sold her to an older man when she was six or so. It was understood that he would use her as a sex object, and also that he would take care of her. Now Norma offered Alex to us on the same terms. We could do whatever we wanted with him, she said, as long as we promised we would make him go to school. She thought he'd have a better chance with us than with her. She was surprised when we turned the offer down.

In 1982 and 83, the so-called Lower East Side art movement got underway. Galleries opened here and there in small storefronts. The principal commodity was appropriation painting, which hadn't yet caught on in the mainstream. Young artists like Rick Prol, Mike Bidlo and Philip Taaffe exercised their wit on art and history. A club scene developed in tandem with an upsurge of performance art. Great centers included the Pyramid Lounge, which was already venerable, and new clubs like 8 BC (on Eighth Street between avenues B and C). The Pyramid was a great center of performance art by Iris Love and others. At 8 BC the Japanese performance group Popo and the Gogo Boys would start at 2 a.m. Cocaine was everywhere at the time, and people kept late hours. A different kind of culture prevailed at the University of the Streets, where incredible jazz sessions took place every weekend night.

The whole thing lasted no more than five years. Then the successful dealers, like Pat Hearn, moved into spaces in Soho and took the more successful artists with them. Now Bidlo shows with Bruno Bischofberger. Appropriationism passed fully into the mainstream and then more or less ran its course.

The Lower East Side art fever spread the idea that the neighborhood was entering or about to enter a new era. By the mid-'80s, one heard constant rumors of gentrification. Supposedly the city government wanted the area to undergo development and become a gentrified white neighborhood. Meanwhile the islander population would move to other boroughs or other towns. This is what they called Manhattanization. When the city planted trees up and down Clinton Street from Delancey to Houston, it seemed certain that it would happen overnight. In fact, year in year out there was virtually no sign of it. Occasionally a single tenement building would be renovated, but on the whole the population remained the same and the street culture did too. This remained the case through most of the '90s.

Only in the last three years or so has gentrification really happened visibly, and even now it has limits. The neighborhood now is balanced between the traditional island population and young white people who often move here after college. Avenue B between Second and Third street, for example, is significantly gentrified right now, with three restaurants with ropes and a newly built apartment house that commands $2500 for a one-bedroom. The corresponding block of Avenue C, however, is just as it was twenty years ago, except that the liquor store, which used to stay open illegally after midnight and on Sundays, no longer does so. The proprietor would keep the gate halfway down and the lights off in the front of the store. You would duck under the gate to make an illegal purchase. Outside, a sign proclaimed this defiantly: We are always open for boozeness. Those days are over, as is the open-air drug market, which the Giuliani administration got rid of or moved elsewhere.

The history of the Lower East Side is of course much older than the art movement of the '80s. It was a center of the Beatnik era, and during the Black Power movement, massive rallies were held in the bandshell in Tompkins Square Park. In fact, the area has been a center of left activism at least since 1849, when a huge influx of Jews fled Germany due to their involvement in the socialist revolution that had failed the year before. This tradition has endured from the Henry Street Settlement House to Kenkelaba House to the anarchist bookstore on Avenue B (which closed recently as the rents on the block rose).

The last great phenomenon was the homeless movement's center in Tompkins Square Park in the late '80s and early '90s. At its height there were several hundred people living in the park in what appeared to be an orderly community. Like street communities in Bombay, there were acknowledged leaders, places were assigned, things were clean. The denouement is even better known — how the city came in with bulldozers one morning before dawn and dozed the shacks and tents down, then enforced a curfew on the park and tore down the bandshell. It was widely believed that this too was the result of the city's desire for gentrification and the higher property values and taxes it would bring with it. But aside from the notorious Christodora building on the park at Eighth and B (where Cher was said to have bought the penthouse, although she never moved in after protesters demonstrated against her; it's where George Gershwin lived once, too) the park area has remained much as it was before the homeless movement settled into it.

Today, despite the weight and clarity of its history, the neighborhood is somewhat undefined. Poised at the edge of two worlds, it could go any direction. One significant new force is the Orensanz Foundation on Norfolk Street, an old gothic revival synagogue reclaimed as a venue for art and culture and still serious about those matters. I heard a singer with a lute sing the *Beowulf* poem in Old English there, a baritone with a chamber orchestra perform an oratorio of Oscar Wilde's *De Profundis*. Indeed, the Lower East Side is a place suited to serious culture. History hangs over it all, more than most neighborhoods, and it is a history that is meaningful politically, socially, and artistically. If the neighborhood undergoes the kind of soul-destroying gentrification that has long been ominously predicted for it, that history will be over. It will be necessary to efface it not only from the streets but from memory. Only this book will be left.

Chapter 4

Making Art and Policing Streets
By Christopher Mele

Gentrification on the Lower East Side is a complex story that, in many ways, is still unfolding. As recently as November 2002, a *New York Times* article characterized the Lower East Side as "the underground's underground, a radical alternative to most alternatives you can name."[1] Such assertions mimic almost verbatim the descriptions of the East Village authored over two decades ago, as Kenny Scharf, Keith Haring and Jean-Michel Basquiat captured press attention with the conspicuous promotion of "downtown" fashion, music, performance, video and painting. But surely all is not the same and it is more than worthwhile to revisit those early years when a host of different forces came together to produce much of what we know and see today: an upscale, high-rent neighborhood that gestures toward an inclusion of elements of its working-class past. In this essay, I pay particular attention to two forces that came into play and, together, helped bring about the rampant gentrification of the Lower East Side north of Houston Street in the critical period of the early 1980s: the link between the culture industry and real estate and the "quality of life" policies that restricted *public expressions* of social, political, and cultural diversity. Before discussing each of these forces, I first address the critical juncture in the neighborhood's recent past — the late 1970s and early 1980s — when the ravages of community abandonment and the beginnings of redevelopment briefly coexisted.

From Disinvestment to Reinvestment

Heading east on foot or by cab from Fifth Avenue to the East Village and on to Loisaida in the late 1970s was a journey from the center of Manhattan to its so-called margins, from a landscape of townhouses and boutiques to one of tenements, bodegas and carnicerías. Just before reaching the imposing phalanx of public housing projects on Avenue D, the remnants of 1970s wide-scale abandonment were visible in blocks of buildings with bricked-up windows and doorways and overgrown lots strewn with debris. But sandwiched between these spaces of destruction were pockets of freshly painted and renovated boutiques, art galleries and restaurants that foreshadowed the development that would come.

At that time, the East Village and Loisaida in particular seemed unlikely venues for investors, banks, and developers to commence middle-class redevelopment. Many streets and avenues remained plagued with drug dens and a high incidence of crime unnerved even the most thick-skinned New Yorkers. The housing stock and population table included here clearly shows the damaging social effects of abandonment. Within a decade in the relatively small area of Loisaida, we see an extraordinary exodus of residents and a reduction in the number of tenement apartments. Yet the significant changes in Manhattan's economy and the extensive redevelopment of the adjacent areas of Lower Manhattan suggested the potential payoff of gentrification would outweigh its risks.

Christopher Mele

**Changes in Housing and Population in Loisaida,
East of Avenue B[2], 1970-1980**

	1970	1980	1970-1980 (% Change)
Loisaida Housing			
Total private housing units	10,944	5,725	- 48%
Loisaida Population			
Total Population	40,145	24,093	- 40%
As a percent of all East Village	46%	38%	
Total residents living in:			
Private Housing[3]	26,290	11,283	- 57%
Public Housing	13,855	12,810	- 8%
Loisaida Latinos[4]			
Total	18,031	16,492	- 9%
In Private Housing	11,075	6,536	- 41%
As a percent of all private housing	42%	57%	
In public housing	6,956	9956	+ 43%
As a percent of all public housing	50%	78%	
Loisaida Non-Latinos:			
Total	22,114	7,601	- 66%
In private housing	12,215	4,747	- 69%
As a percent of all private housing	58%	42%	
In public housing	6,899	2,854	- 59%
As a percent of all public housing	50%	22%	

Source: United States Bureau of the Census, 1970 and 1980.

After the city's near bankruptcy in the late 1970s, and with considerable help from a corporate-friendly political administration, New York emerged as a global city in finance, banking, insurance and real estate. Growth in the specialized services sector created more skilled occupations and mid-level positions in finance, insurance, international commerce, law and communications. In the midst of recovery euphoria, however, the divisions between the city's richest and its poorest classes widened. The increase in the number of new corporate service positions was outmatched by the disappearance of semi-skilled jobs, creating a condition that drove parts of the city's poor and minority labor force into an expanding formal and informal low-wage service economy. In nearby SoHo, a mix of real estate capital, government development incentives and an expanding art market spurred development from a light manufacturing district into the beginnings of an upscale residential and retail district.[5] In addition, favorable changes in immigration laws and the growth of the Pacific Rim economy brought about tremendous population growth in Chinatown and the expansion of its borders well into the southern tier of the Lower East Side.[6]

The growth of the service economy and the contraction of Manhattan's middle-class housing supply directed the attention of developers and municipal leaders toward the borough's remaining low-income housing markets. There was a significant drop in dilapidated vacant

A Radical Political and Social History of the Lower East Side

housing units within the city between 1981 and 1984. During the same time period, rents for substandard housing rose a staggering 20%.[7] Citywide, nearly a third of apartments vacated by Puerto Ricans and blacks were rented to non-Puerto Ricans and non-blacks while the proportion of white single-person households increased.[8] Overall, the city's housing market tightened as increases in luxury conversions removed middle-class rental units from the housing stock.[9] As the supply of middle-income rental units dwindled, existing housing in low-income neighborhoods within or near the core became targeted for upgrading, push-ing those who could no longer afford Manhattan rents to "less desirable" areas within the city. Within the context of these housing market changes, the Lower East Side emerged as the last low-income residential enclave south of 96th Street.

With considerable assistance from the Koch Administration, the real estate industry turned to redevelopment of the Lower East Side's century-old "cold water" flats, occupied by low-income residents paying regulated rents. In the 1980s, the means for displacing low-income tenants, converting apartments into co-ops or condominiums, renovating Old Law and New Law tenement units, circumventing rent regulations and obtaining mortgages from banks and savings institutions, developed as a specialty industry within New York real estate. Periodicals geared toward developers of low-income neighborhoods, such as the *Apartment Law Insider*, featured articles such as "What to Do When Rent-Controlled Tenant Vacates" (March 1985), "17 Improvements That Get You a Rent Hike" (June 1986), and "How to Evict Drug Dealers from Your Building," (September 1988).

Political leaders and policymakers drew lessons from the fiscal crisis, which was reconfig-ured as a crisis of disincentives for urban investment, rather than the city's inability to address or contain mounting social problems. With respect to low-income neighborhoods in particular, the city's position was to encourage and subsidize efforts by the middle-sized and large developers and lending institutions to enter and transform working-class housing markets for middle and upper-class consumers. City agencies with any degree of authority over private or public land use and development were brought in line with an aggressive entrepreneurial and pro-growth ideology. Municipal and state urban redevelopment incen-tives were made available to developers with access to capital rather than to individual owners, small landlords or local housing cooperatives.[10] Tax abatement programs required expensive renovations and improvements to be made to properties. In the absence of low-interest loans, small-time property holders were incapable of embarking on ambitious reno-vation projects and therefore were ineligible for many of these programs' benefits. Rehabilitation loans, which could have been utilized by individual owners or tenant-man-aged buildings, were phased out by the early 1980s. Consequently, small-scale or single "mom and pop" tenement owners were increasingly replaced by brokerage firms, property management corporations and individuals with extensive property holdings within the neighborhood and in similar neighborhoods, such as Harlem or Hell's Kitchen.[11]

The economic conditions in Manhattan that produced a favorable real estate investment environment (that included low-income housing markets) and the city's extensive package of redevelopment subsidies positioned the Lower East Side — still reeling from the effects of abandonment — for the gentrification that has enveloped the neighborhood since the early 1980s. In addition to the investment environment and incentives, however, we need to consider two other factors that are somewhat distinctive to the Lower East Side and that facilitated its middle-class development: 1) the fabrication of an East Village arts district amenable to development, and 2) municipal restrictions on public expressions of social, political, and cultural diversity that promoted a middle-class neighborhood identity over a working-class one.

Fabricating and Marketing East Village Culture

The Lower East Side has a long history of hosting various political movements and serving as incubator for new forms of music, art, fashion and literature. The late 1970s, with its landscape of abandoned buildings, empty lots, graffiti and a thriving drug economy, was no different. The East Village proved an agreeable place for the emergence and growth of rebellious "underground" art and music scenes. The union of art and the urban, built environment, for example, was realized in the transformation of graffiti from street expression to celebrated art form. Artists made use of the underground scene, incorporating music and performance in exhibitions held in alternative galleries, clubs and makeshift storefronts across the neighborhood. In 1979, the painter Kenny Scharf organized a single-night art exhibition at the nightclub Club 57 on St. Marks Place; in 1980, Keith Haring followed suit.[12] Similar one-night shows were held at the Pyramid Club on Avenue A. In addition to exhibitions at clubs, paintings and sculpture were displayed in small, unpolished galleries that artists began to operate in the ground-floor storefronts of tenements.

The linkage between culture and economy was well in place by the early 1980s, when the national media began to speak of the various cultural forms emanating from the East Village as belonging to a "culture of insurgency."[13] Critics, dealers and buyers began to speak of a particular style, an East Village "look" and wrote ethereal references to the Lower East Side as "a state of mind . . . an open, unwalled ghetto of talent and understanding."[14] And when the more successful artists migrated from the East Village to 57th Street or SoHo, they elevated awareness of the East Village and its "rogue" cultural scene among elites and the more curious of the middle class. The obscurity of the East Village art scene quickly disappeared. References in East Village music and art to "urban decay" remained the same but the reactions from the larger population shifted from fear and repulsion to curiosity and desire.

Real estate developers were quick to make the most of the growing popularity of the "underground" scene as *cultural capital* to facilitate gentrification (as they continue to do today). Real estate investors viewed such publicity as a means to draw mostly white, middle and upper-income, well-educated renters downtown. Developers easily tapped into the images, symbols, and rhetoric that characterized an East Village "brand" or "style," deploying them in their marketing efforts and in the design of renovated apartments and buildings. What constitutes the East Village "brand" is a de-politicized and imitated subversion borrowed from references to past and present protest, resistance and artistic experimentation. Meanwhile, the area's dominant population of working class and impoverished families functions as a cast of background players in an abstracted "hip" environment, themed around carefully managed representations of dysfunction and difference. Their lifestyles and everyday activities exist to contribute the necessary ambiance stripped of politics and resistance,

44

but filled with excitement and the thrill of the unanticipated. Poverty, crime and despair, as such, do not sell clothes, makeup, music or housing, but sanitized and playful symbolic references to them can and do. Consequently, the production of the built environment for middle-class consumption begins to resemble less the harsh realities and more the sugar-coated representations of a subversive and alternative East Village.

Municipal "Street-Level" Policies and "Quality of Life" Initiatives

In tandem with the efforts among the real estate industry to market a concocted Lower East Side "hip" identity were the city's efforts to reassert control over public space and the character of street life. As we have seen, the new urban initiatives and policies developed in the 1980s were shaped and defined by a post-fiscal crisis mandate that emphasized increasing tax revenues though development incentives and the rollback of governmental provision of low-income housing. Along with economic incentives, the city took an aggressive stance toward changing the low-income, working-class character of the Lower East Side through the use of municipal and police powers.

In the 1980s, the city administration sought to undo most of the programs that had transferred some control over neighborhood private and public space to low and moderate-income residents. Ostensibly created to protect low-income neighborhoods from the ravages of disinvestment, the Department of Housing Preservation and Development (HPD), became the institutional strong arm for private revitalization. Many of the city's tenant self-management and ownership programs were severely curtailed, under-financed or totally eliminated to promote private redevelopment rather than community empowerment.[15] Throughout the 1980s, HPD demolished city-owned buildings (some occupied by squatters), leaving empty parcels that were more attractive to developers seeking to construct new housing. In the 1970s, the city was supportive of gardens, often leasing unkempt lots to residents to grow vegetables and flowers. With the rebound of the housing market, however, the city placed a moratorium on leasing lots to gardeners in the 1990s.[16]

The Koch administration's pro-development agenda also comprised draconian policies to rid the neighborhood of its "unsavory elements," to sanitize its public spaces, and to reign in the area's free-wheeling, chaotic social environment. In the early 1980s, the police mounted an anti-drug effort called Operation Pressure Point, sending over 230 officers and 40 detectives along with numerous vehicles and helicopters to begin what locals described as a military invasion of Loisaida. To drive out the entrenched two-decade old drug economy, the police occupied streets, corners, empty lots and parks. In the first month, the police made over 2,000 drug-related arrests, an average of 67 per day. After five months, the arrest total was close to 7,000, and after seventeen months, 14,000 people were arrested on drug-related charges citywide.[17] Operation Pressure Point was a public relations victory for the Koch administration as sensational scenes of drug busts and police occupation were widely circulated by the media and played well into the image of a neighborhood renaissance.

The NYPD also periodically cracked down on ad hoc outdoor flea markets along St. Mark's Place, Second Avenue and Avenue A that were sources of income for some residents and many homeless persons. Anti-loitering campaigns along neighborhood streets and corners, which ostensibly would curb the drug and prostitution trade, restricted a long east side tradition of "hanging out," especially among youth. In the mid-1980s, the area's many lots were fenced in, preventing their use as gardens or makeshift junkyards, or sites for nefarious drug transactions.

Long neglected, surveillance and regulation of activities within Tompkins Square Park escalated throughout the 1980s, culminating in local resistance in 1988. Like most urban riots, the events of August 1988 in Tompkins Square were a watershed that reflected the frustrations of past and present social conditions and unleashed new social forces to atone or address community grievances. The melee revealed political, economic and cultural tensions among class and ethnic-based resident factions over ways to deal with or combat real estate intentions and actions and the city's local development policies. The real estate sector, pro-development community associations, the police and city leaders presented the uprising as a result of differences in opinion over quality of life concerns, respect for law and order and appropriate uses of public space.

In the 1990s, the Giuliani administration increasingly employed city agencies to regulate and modify the uses of public space, from sidewalks to empty lots. With the power of effective new policies, both significant and banal (such as public passageway laws, park regulations, and even jaywalking ordinances) the city has systematically regulated and controlled public spaces, fundamentally excluding many of Loisaida's low-income and minority residents from the "revived" east side. In addition to efforts to "clean up" East Village parks, empty lots and sidewalks, the city deployed a "zero tolerance" strategy for dealing with neighborhood squatters. Typically under the pretense of protecting public safety, HPD has systematically condemned and issued evictions to squats throughout the Lower East Side. Demonstrations and violence over the status of occupied abandoned buildings continued through the 1990s as private developers and service providers (whom squatters disparagingly referred to as "poverty pimps") pressured officials to utilize city-owned property.

The Giuliani administration's drive to purge the public landscape of uses, practices, and behaviors labeled deviant, unpleasant or simply unorganized fit squarely into the themed development purported by the real estate sector. Driven from the streets, parks, lots and sidewalks, the expression of East Village cultural and political radicalism is plainly enduring in its most contrived forms in bars, nightclubs, restaurants and themed apartment buildings. The political regulation of public space and social behavior has advanced the commercialism of the East Village legacy of subversion and counterculture. Under the guise of "improved quality of life," city policies have driven the once *public* expression of cultural radicalism and subversion into the *private* realm —most notably, into commercial and residential real estate spaces where desirable references to difference are employed to theme development. "Quality of life" improvements, such as those made to parks, streets, and public buildings, are used to justify and exculpate the social cost of residential displacement that is the consequence of redevelopment efforts. By controlling the use of public space, the city seeks to rid the East Village of its "free-wheeling" reputation and help construct an identity more inclined toward the middle-class residents that developers seek to attract.

46

Conclusion

As I have briefly pointed to here (and, more fully, elsewhere),[18] the gentrification story on the Lower East Side involves much more than an assessment of real estate investments flowing into (or, as history has shown, out of) the neighborhood or a cataloging of city development incentives. A central part of the story is the real estate marketing of the neighborhood's artistic reputation coupled with the city's policies of cracking down on the public expressions of social, political and cultural diversity. These may seem contradictory, but they are not. Municipal policies and "quality-of-life" initiatives further redevelopment through surveillance and regulation of public expressions of cultural and political differences. Thus while the police enforce mandates to eject squatters from city-owned buildings and drug dealers, prostitutes and the homeless from sidewalks and other public spaces, private developers can gesture toward these very same "social ills," providing a sanitized and commercialized sensibility of urban despair to the young, affluent middle-class drawn to the Lower East Side's "alternative" allure.

Endnotes:

1. "Where Witty Meets Gritty."" *The New York Times*, November 15, 2002.

2. By the late 1950s, the geographic borders of Loisaida were Houston Street north to 14th Street and Avenue A east to the East River Park. Unfortunately, census tract boundaries do not correlate with Loisaida's borders. The data in this table are for the area between Houston Street to 14th Street and Avenue B and the East River Park.

3. The term "Private Housing" intends the area's stock of apartment houses as distinct from the large-scale Riis and Wald public housing projects. In the course of the 1970s disinvestment, a significant number of tenements became *in rem* (city-owned) or tenant-managed and thus no longer owned or controlled by private landlords.

4. Due to changes in definitions and undercounting of illegal immigrants, longitudinal comparisons cannot be exact. In the 1970 census, "Persons of Puerto Rican Birth or Parentage" included persons born in Puerto Rico and persons born in the United States or an outlying area with one or both parents born in Puerto Rico. (U.S. Census of Housing and Population, 1970, Appendix B). In 1980, "Persons of Hispanic Origin"" were those who classified themselves in one of the specific Hispanic origin categories listed on the questionnaire — ""Mexican," "Puerto Rican," or "Cuban" — as well as those who indicated they were of "other Spanish/ Hispanic"" origin. Persons of "Other Spanish/Hispanic" origin were those whose origins are were from Spain, the Spanish-speaking countries of Central or South America, or the Dominican Republic, or they were persons of Hispanic origin identifying themselves generally as Spanish (U.S. Census of Housing and Population, 1980, Appendix B).

5. Sharon Zukin, *Loft Living* (Rutgers University Press, 1989).

6. Jan Lin, *Reconstructing Chinatown* (University of Minnesota Press, 1998).

7. Michael A. Stegman, *"Housing in New York City."* Report prepared for the City of New York, Department of Housing Preservation and Development, 1984, 105.

8. Stegman *op cit.*, 53.

9. Stegman *op cit.*, 37.

10. The city's pro-development programs provided incentives and subsidies for owners to make substantial renovations upon units in their buildings. Because of the design of the incentive programs, they were profitable to landlords only if they could charge substantially higher rents for the renovated units. A program offered by the Division of Housing and Community Renewal (DHCR) called the Major Capital Improvement (MCI) subsidized building-wide improvements such as new windows, furnaces and boilers. The program allowed owners to pass on all the all direct and indirect costs of improvement to tenants by increasing regulated rents gradually and permanently (once the costs were paid, rent hikes remained as profit). Two tax reduction programs, J-51 for old buildings and 421-a for new construction, also promoted neighborhood upgrading. J-51 offered two forms of benefits to owners in return for certain improvements: [1] tax abatements that lowered the amount of property tax for a period ranging from 12 to 20 years; [2] exemptions from any tax increases that resulted from reassessments based upon capital improvements made. The Section 421-a program was part of the State of New York's Real Property Tax Law. For properties constructed under the 421-a subsidy, property taxes were phased in incrementally over a 10-year period, including a total exemption during construction and the first two years of operation. Eligible owners agreed to offer rent rent-stabilized units during the period in which the tax abatement was applied.

11. *A Sanborn Real Estate Directory* survey of East Village property owners who bought buildings and lots between 1983 and 1986 was cross-checked against the *Real Estate Directory* of Manhattan which listed individual owners and their holdings in the borough of Manhattan. Developers with multiple East Village holdings were found to have invested in similar neighborhoods within the city.

12. David Hershkovits, "Art in Alphabetland." *ARTNews*, September, 1983, 90.

13. Robert Siegle, *Suburban Ambush: Downtown Writing and the Fiction of Insurgency*. (The Johns Hopkins University Press, 1989).

14. Nicholas Moufarrege, "East Village." *Flash Art*, 111, 37, March, 1983, 37.

15. William Sites, ""Public Action: New York City Policy and the Gentrification of the Lower East Side."" In *From Urban Village to East Village: The Battle for New York's Lower East Side*, Janet Abu-Lughod et al. (Cambridge: Blackwell Publishers, 1994), 201.

16. Schmelzkopf 1995: 377.

17. Lynn Zimmer, "Proactive Policing Against Street Level Drug Trafficking, *American Journal of Police*, 1990, pp. 43-74.

18. Christopher Mele, *Selling the Lower East Side: Culture, Real Estate, and Resistance in New York City* (University of Minnesota Press, 2000).

Chapter 5

Beginning My Political History
By Lynne Stewart

I came to the Lower East Side by accident. It was l961. It was cheap and my then husband and our new baby wanted to live in Manhattan. We paid $71 a month for a one-bedroom in an upscale tenement (it had an elevator) at 128 Broome Street overlooking the Williamsburg Bridge. Having received my degree in History/Political Science the preceding June, I was interested in local grassroots organizing in this new (to me!) urban enclave that was now my home. Naive, not yet radicalized, I somehow ended up at the local Democratic Club on East Broadway. These old hands took one look at me and decided I should go to Little Italy and gather signatures for one "Duke" Viggiani. Later, I realized that I had become a "tool" of Carmine DeSapio's Tammany Hall but I faithfully went to Mott and Mulberry and had a great time going door to door. These folks looked at me like I had just beamed down, but once they heard who "sent" me, they were warm and welcoming.

In September, l962 I got a job as librarian in Harlem. This was my great awakening about all the things they didn't teach in the Queens schools and colleges I had attended. My focus changed from electoral politics to in-the-streets/movement/internal strategy to get to the beast to accomplish real change for these suffering children. By 1964, I had moved (2nd baby) with a recommendation from an activist community priest at St. Mary's church on Grand Street. They were planning to take down my building on Broome to build the Fort Pitt police/firehouse, so I was eligible and became, with my two children, one of the first tenants at Gompers Houses on Pitt Street. I was to remain there for thirty years.

By 1964, the political pot was boiling all over the city. The war. Black/Puerto Rican rights. For me, this all coalesced around the Community Control of Schools movement. Starting in Harlem and IS 20l, parents and community opted out of the forced bussing "integration" and demanded autonomous control of the neighborhood schools. Ralph Poynter (my husband of almost 40 years, a black man) was a teacher in my school at Lenox Avenue and he became during the '60s and still counting, one of the outstanding voices against the Central Board of Education and champion of all the city's children.

I left Harlem and came to PS 64 on Ninth Street near Avenue B. In 1965, that school had almost 5,000 children (a comment on the "new demographics" of the LES). I was there to organize the sympathetic teachers to the Teachers' Freedom Party that had started as opposition within the United Federation of Teachers union to president Al Shanker. As it became more and more obvious that the union was aligning itself with management, the Board of Education, against the righteous demands of unrepresented minority communities, this group became independent and worked with a city-wide group led by Ralph Poynter, Concerned Parents and Community Organizations, which was broken down school district by school district. Of course, District 1 was the locus for the LES. The boundaries were, North-

14 Street, East-River, West — the Bowery and South — Allen/Pike Street. It was a perfect piece of pie, encompassing the predominantly Puerto Rican and black and liberated white community. The opposition was an entrenched voting bloc in the Grand Street apartments, that were originally built by a great union for their workers and which had become, by the '60s and thereafter, an overtly racist all white minority.

In 1967, there was a one-week strike by the UFT primarily concerning wages but galvanizing the newly formed community control movement. Schools were opened by community groups even in the face of union picket lines. The main grievance?? The UFT supported the right of any teacher to permanently "remove" disruptive (translation: black/latino) students from this school system that was unable or unwilling to educate the majority of city children.

The powers that be, recognizing that an attack on the educational system to achieve local control could lead to real black and latino power, quickly moved and set up Demonstration Districts in Harlem (IS 201), Ocean Hill/Brownsville and Two Bridges (LES but really Chinatown). These districts gave voting to parents but no power over the budgets and no accountability to the School Boards. We met and decried this as a pacification plan. We wanted real control. When Ocean Hill tried to transfer (NOT fire) 13 teachers in 1968 the UFT, acting out its role as race-baiter and defender of the status quo, sided with the Board of Ed and called a city wide strike against the communities. It was a time of confrontation as the Police were sent to protect the picket lines (when the teachers dared in the face of solid community HOSTILITY) while activists opened schools and claimed them on behalf of the children, parents and community. Schools were chained shut to keep us out and arrests were regular. We targeted the schools where we had the most power — PS 63 on Third Street between A and First Avenue, PS 140 on Ridge and Rivington, and my school, PS 64 on Ninth between B and C. Several of the Junior Highs (JHS 22 and 71) were opened. At JHS 71 at Sixth Street and Avenue B, a large crowd of parents and junior high school students had gathered to open up the school. A larger group of NYPD had gathered. A standoff with no school seemed to be the outcome. Some of the men, including Ralph, began verbal harassment of the police. As the voices escalated, a young girl darted through the barricade and made it to the doorway before they grabbed her. At that point the confrontation was on and within a half hour the school was opened due in part to an African American teacher by the name of Ali, who joined the community and forced the issue.

Other schools became similar battlegrounds as the community attempted to assert its rights over the 9-week strike. 11,000 teachers citywide crossed the picket lines and served the true community. At PS 63, a custodian armed with a hammer tried to attack a black parent, Barbara Jackson, who had her baby in her backpack carrier. A melee ensued, involving Ralph Poynter and the NYPD as well as the students who were there to attend, one of whom was my daughter (that baby who first came to the LES in 1961), Brenna. This day of struggle was duly recorded in the picture centerfold of the *New York Daily News*. The scenario was repeated all over the city as more and more people called for community control in the face of the entrenched and institutionalized racism of the UFT. At PS 64, we opened the school and had daily classes. The front steps were frequently guarded/patrolled by the local cadre of Black Panthers led by Bob Collier, who was living on Eighth and B. Other names from that struggle are Susan Ribner, Brad and Bobbi Chambers, Mona Collier, Helene Caldwell, Roz

A Radical Political and Social History of the Lower East Side

50

Weiner, Dolphy Hazel, Susan Mulgrav, Joe Jackson, Jack Jackson, Danny Mallea, Cathy Mallea, Ruth Winds, Cathy Prensky, Carmen Diaz, Henry Ramos, Willimae Adams, Charlie Moffat (who got arrested at PS 140 for the crime of "impersonating a plumber"!!!), Norie Wilson, Ernesto Martinez, and many more that my aging memory can't dredge up.

After the strike, the teachers were rewarded by the city and earned more money with make-up time than ever before. But the battle lines had been drawn and nowhere in the city did it rage more fiercely than the Lower East Side. After the Ford Foundation and McGeorge Bundy's pacification plan had failed, the legislature "allowed" the formation of local school districts. In all of the elections that followed during the 70s, the community control candidates (denominated Por Los Niños, For the Children) were always opposed by a well-funded slate of candidates supported by the UFT. In 1972-73, there was a board of Por Los Niños elected and, as one of their first acts, they hired Luis Fuentes, the FIRST Puerto Rican to be a superintendent. They also appointed 14 parent-selected principals. They installed a true bilingual program and began black studies. In 1974, the UFT slate won and undid all of the above. In addition, the district budget was "re-aligned." Instructional supplies were cut $50,000 to ensure patronage jobs for a defeated UFT candidate and a former UFT employer. The community fought back. There were public school board meetings that were disrupted at PS 20 and Seward Park High School. Members of the UFT Board were ejected and dragged off the stage. The microphone was seized. Outrage spilled over but all of this was overcome by the late '70s. Puerto Ricans and blacks were hired in administrative school posts. The Local School Board had become a non-entity corrupted by politics as usual. Many of the activists including Artie Santiago and Ernesto Martinez had succumbed to the lure of Poverty Pimpism and had jobs and "perks." Christodora House, the building on the corner of Ninth and B, which had once housed the Panthers and countless other grassroots organizations after the city gave it to the community, became derelict and then — via the mysteries of gentrification —a high-scale condominium with apartments overlooking the Park.

During the '60s and '70s, the Lower East Side Community was on the march, fueled by righteous anger. I have only recalled a few of the struggles. There were many —around housing, welfare, etc. There was a militancy that now, alas, is no more. The history of those days should not be forgotten among the fancy restaurants and boutiques of 2005. The people, yes.

Chapter 6

Lynne Stewart: Convicted
A "Chilling Effect" for Legal Community
        By Bill Weinberg

Newly appointed US Attorney General Alberto Gonzales hailed the Feb. 10 conviction of activist attorney Lynne Stewart and her co-defendants, saying the verdicts "send a clear, unmistakable message that this department will pursue both those who carry out acts of terrorism and those who assist them with their murderous goals." *The New York Times* coverage of the Justice Department victory called it "one of the country's most important terror cases since the Sept. 11 attacks." But supporters of Lynne Stewart say the case had more to do with a dangerous erosion of attorney-client privilege than with terrorism.

After 12 days of deliberations, Stewart was convicted on all five charges she faced — including "providing material support" to terrorism, conspiracy to abet terrorism, and lying to the government about her actions. She faces up to 30 years in prison. At 65, this means she will almost certainly die in prison.

This was actually the second set of indictments brought against Stewart. The first indictments, brought in April 2002 when federal agents raided her downtown Manhattan office, were dismissed by US Judge John Koetl in July 2003 as unconstitutionally vague. But that November, the Justice Department filed fresh charges that Stewart and her co-defendants — postal worker Ahmed Sattar and translator Mohammed Yousry — had conspired to provide material support to Egypt's Gama'a Islamiyya, or Islamic Group, which is designated a terrorist organization by the State Department. Judge Koetl let these charges stand, and the case wound up in his Manhattan courtroom.

Stewart was initially charged with passing messages between her client, Sheikh Abdel Rahman, and Egyptian supporters from his Minnesota prison cell, where he is serving a life term on charges of conspiring to blow up several New York landmarks. Abdel Rahman — the notorious "Blind Sheikh" — was said to be the mastermind of the 1993 World Trade Center attack (although he was never convicted of that), and was barred from communicating with the outside world by Special Administrative Measures, or SAMs, which Stewart had to sign on to in order to continue representing him.

The new indictments charged that Stewart helped disguise prison conversations in which Rahman passed messages to his translator and assistant. The indictment said Stewart "pretended to be participating in the conversation with Abdel Rahman by making extraneous comments such as 'chocolate' and 'heart attack.'"

Stewart guessed that the conversations were being monitored, and the charges against her bore that out. Stewart and her defense team argued that this electronic eavesdropping, and

A Radical Political and Social History of the Lower East Side

the strictures placed on facilitating Sheikh Rahman's communications, violated the spirit of the Sixth Amendment, which guarantees the right to legal counsel. In a Feb. 17 interview with Jose Santiago of WBAI Radio news, Stewart said the wiretapping at the prison was an unconstitutional "incursion into the attorney-client right to confidentiality by the government."

The prosecution argued that her own words indicated she knew she was breaking the law. At one point she said, "Well, I don't think I can hide this from Pat Fitzgerald," the federal prosecutor who headed the 1995 case against Sheikh Rahman (today US attorney for Chicago).

Stewart was not accused of any direct links to acts of violence, nor of speaking with Islamic Group leaders in Egypt — only to the press. She acknowledged that in June 2000 she called a Reuters reporter in Cairo to read him a press release from the Sheikh. Although the press release apparently broached the Islamic Group breaking its ceasefire with the Egyptian government, there were no subsequent attacks. Stewart maintained that speaking to the press on behalf of her client was a legitimate and indispensable part of her legal representation. "I did what a good and vigorous lawyer does," she would tell WBAI.

The prosecution worked hard to create the image of a major terrorist case. Sattar, facing a life sentence on terrorist conspiracy charges, admitted that he urged Egyptian exile Rifai Taha in a phone call to Afghanistan to write an edict which was released to the Internet under the Sheikh's name, calling for "killing the Jews where ever they are found." But he insisted his intention was to keep the Sheikh's name pubic, not to advocate breaking the ceasefire. He also admitted to corresponding with and sending money to Ramzi Yousef, indicted ringleader of the 1993 World Trade Center attack. A front-page New York Times story last Oct. 2 said the tap on Sattar's Staten Island home phone provided investigators with a virtual map to terrorist networks all over the world. But co-defendant Yousry — also convicted on terrorist conspiracy charges — was himself a government collaborator, admitting he kept FBI agents updated on the Sheikh's communications.

Assistant US Attorney Christopher Morvillo said in his in opening statement in June 2004 that Stewart was complicit in a virtual "jail break." Invoking the Islamic Group's deadly 1997 attack on tourists at Luxor and the 2000 kidnapping of tourists in the Philippines — both apparently carried out on behalf of Sheikh Rahman — Morvillo said: "His words and speeches were as dangerous as weapons."

Not surprisingly, Stewart's own political views became a key part of the case. This line of questioning resulted in a tense back-and-forth between assistant US attorney Andrew Dember and Stewart's own lawyer Michael Tigar. Stewart — who had previously represented David Gilbert, an ex-Weather Underground militant convicted in a 1981 armored car robbery in Rockland County, and Richard Williams, convicted in a string of bombings at military sites and corporate offices in the early '80s — said she sought to be a "very adversarial" lawyer. Describing her politics in classically Jeffersonian terms, she said, "I believe government is best when government is little," and called herself a "revolutionary with a small r." While explicitly disavowing attacks on civilians, she did decry the "voracious type of capitalism" now in the world and said "I believe entrenched institutions will not be changed except by violence." Asked by Tigar Oct. 28 if she would have done the same for her client knowing the consequences, Stewart — a wife, mother and grandmother — tearfully said, "Sitting here today, it's a very difficult question."

Former US attorney general Ramsey Clark, who was co-counsel with Stewart in Sheikh Rahman's 1995 trial, was called to testify on her behalf, saying he also used the same media contacts to keep their client's name in the press as part of their defense strategy. "The lawyers had a duty in representing him and helping to protect all his rights to remind the world of his existence," he said.

Judge Koetl reminded the jury repeatedly that the case — being heard in a courthouse just blocks away from Ground Zero — was not related to 9-11. But in September, the jury was shown a video of a 2000 al-Jazeera TV broadcast of Osama bin Laden, his deputy Ayman al-Zawahiri and other al-Qaeda figures speaking on behalf of Sheikh Rahman and other imprisoned militants. In the video, which al-Jazeera captioned "bin Laden, Others Pledge Jihad to Release Prisoners in US, Saudi Jails," a voice identified as that of the Sheikh's son is heard off-camera exhorting "Avenge your leader! Let's go spill blood!"

Stewart was cynical about the judge's instructions to ignore 9-11 while allowing the video of bin Laden to be shown in court. "You can't throw a skunk in the jury box and ask the jurors not smell it," she told reporters.

Sattar's lawyer Kenneth Paul accused the prosecution of scare tactics. "This is really a case about words and nothing more," he told *Newsday*. "Nothing ever happened, ever! It is all talk." He said the use of Osama's face in the courtroom served to distract attention from the "oppressive" human rights situation in Egypt, which is the real context for the Islamic Group's violence. Stewart would tell WBAI News that the video was aired "to intimidate this jury, to make them feel there was us and there was them . . . that by reason of doing the work I do, I had somehow become the enemy."

New York's media had a field day with the case. When the name of Yusuf Islam — the singer formerly known as Cat Stevens who was inexplicably put on an official "terrorist watch list" — came up in the recorded prison conversations as a prospective member for a defense committee for the Sheikh, *Newsday* seized on this as evidence of the singer's "possible terrorist connections." But the tape reveals Stewart and the Sheikh had only the vaguest idea who Islam was, referring to him as "one of the Beatles."

The media also touted a dubious Stewart case link to the January slaying of an Egyptian Coptic Christian family in their New Jersey home, with New York's ABC News airing sketchy claims that a relative of the family had helped prosecutors in translation work for the case.

The case also raised questions about reporters' rights as well as attorney-client privilege. In June 2004, the prosecution agreed to drop a subpoena seeking the testimony of *Newsday* reporter Patricia Hurtado regarding her interview with Stewart pending a judge's decision on whether or not her testimony could be legally compelled. The Justice Department also

A Radical Political and Social History of the Lower East Side

threatened to subpoena other journalists who had interviewed Stewart — including this reporter. Despite threats, no subpoena was brought after WW4 REPORT declined to cooperate.

The jurors in the case were anonymous and sequestered, escorted by federal marshals to and from the courtroom. On Jan. 25, the defense team asked Judge Koetl to declare a mistrial when the jurors' van driver steered through a crowd of reporters and Stewart supporters outside the courthouse and exchanged angry words. The same driver had apparently made racist remarks. Jurors were disturbed by the incident and asked to discuss it with the judge. But the mistrial request was denied.

Mistrial was also requested after the Jewish Defense Organization left a flyer at Stewart's home calling her a "traitor to America." The flyer had a phone number for a message giving Stewart's home address and saying "she belongs in a cage." The message also urged callers to "reach out" to the jurors to demand her conviction — raising questions about potential jury tampering.

Stewart is now awaiting sentencing, and pledges to appeal her case. In her post-conviction interview with WBAI, Stewart said Judge Koetl "is empowered to give me a sentence of probation, and that is the only appropriate thing he can do while we are fighting the appeal."

Stewart said Koetl has the opportunity to make a real statement — one way or the other. "If this judge gives me a substantial sentence . . . that will send a further message to the bar. Lawyers right now are aware that the government has laid down a standard for lawyers to toe the line, and if they don't toe the line they could be subject to indictment . . . and face imprisonment. This puts a chilling effect out in the whole legal community."

RESOURCES:

Justice for Lynne Stewart homepage:
http://www.lynnestewart.org/

FindLaw's Legal Commentary on the Lynne Stewart verdict:
http://writ.news.findlaw.com/cassel/20050214.html

WORLD WAR 4 REPORT interview with Lynne Stewart:
http://ww3report.com/stewart.html

Special to WORLD WAR 4 REPORT, March. 7, 2005
Reprinting permissible with attribution

http://ww4report.com

Chapter 7

Homelessness and the Lower East Side
By Joe Flood

In the mid-1980s, no city in the country had a more recognizable homeless problem than New York, and no neighborhood bore the weight of destitution and homelessness more than the Lower East Side. Hundreds of people were shipped in and out of the Third Street Men's Shelter on a daily basis. Tompkins Square Park resembled a refugee camp, with tents, lean-to's and even semi-permanent structures housing people. Hundreds more slept in abandoned buildings, vacant lots, shelters and the Second Avenue subway station and tunnels leading to it. All but un-policed in some areas, the neighborhood was overrun with drugs and the crime that paid for them.

"Man, at night you could walk around Tompkins Square Park and it was like fire-flies from all the lighters and the pipes," says Michelle Jean, who once lived in the Park. "Everyone had a different section. In the drug section, people were smoking like they had a license for that shit."[1]

Yet for all the attention paid to this complicated issue, the rhetoric of most politicians and pundits missed the point, particularly regarding the roots of the crisis. Homelessness was not simply a creation of the 1980s, of Ronald Reagan and Ed Koch. It was rooted in two decades of housing policy and economic and social trends, a confluence of factors that created a metropolis beset by destitution, violence and substance abuse. Everything from a massive fire epidemic, to de-institutionalization of the mentally ill, to the early stages of gentrification combined to create a city that reporters and even city officials dubbed "New Calcutta."[2]

CREATING A CRISIS

By 1968 a strange thing was occurring in New York's most overcrowded neighborhoods: they became dotted with abandoned buildings. In most cases landlords, seeing signs of decline, simply walked away from their buildings, not paying taxes or the building superintendents. When the checks stopped coming, many supers stopped working, and buildings fell into decay and abandonment. Because reports of landlord abandonment are not kept, the trend went largely unnoticed by those not confronted by the specter of boarded up and crumbling buildings in their own neighborhood. By 1970 though, the estimated 100,000 abandoned housing units in the city could no longer be ignored.[3] That year *New York Daily News* stories on the rash of abandonment brought the issue to light, and Assistant City Housing Administrator Neal Hardy warned that without more federal housing funds, many city neighborhoods would turn into "ghost towns."[4]

A Radical Political and Social History of the Lower East Side

A significant problem for years, the abandonment trend was turned into a crisis by a massive fire epidemic that swept through New York's poorest neighborhoods. Combined with abandonment, the fire epidemic destroyed 600,000 housing units during the 1970s. Parts of the South Bronx lost 80% of their housing and population; a section of Alphabet City lost 57% of its housing stock and 68% of its population; and there were similar results in neighborhoods like Harlem, Brownsville and Bushwick.[5] Yet for a brief period of time, the loss of housing was balanced by the "white flight" phenomenon of the 1970s. The spread of the fires — and the spikes in crime, drug abuse, and disease that followed — chased 1.3 million white New Yorkers from the city in just ten years. Most of these people came from blue-collar, traditionally Irish, Italian and Jewish neighborhoods near poorer black and Latino communities experiencing the worst fire problems. So even as thousands of burnout victims from Bushwick, Bedford-Stuyvesant and the South Bronx moved to places like Flatbush, East New York, and the West Bronx, these neighborhoods actually saw an *increased* vacancy rate between 1975 and 1978.[6] But by the late 1970s, most of the middle-class families that could move to the suburbs already had, and fires and abandonment spread to these areas.

Tens of thousands of buildings were abandoned by their landlords, and by the late 1970s, 9% of the apartments that did remain were in remittance to city ownership for failure to pay taxes.[7] A cash-strapped City Hall was hardly the appropriate landlord to maintain decaying apartment buildings where people still lived, never mind rehabilitate those that had been boarded up and often taken over by drug dealers and the homeless. Embarrassed by occasional 'city-as-slumlord' exposés, City Hall decided to board up many buildings, and more low-income residents were turned out on the streets. While unable to find the money to rehabilitate crumbling buildings, the city did find enough to wallpaper over thousands of boarded up windows to give the impression of normalcy in abandoned buildings visible from highways and elevated subways. Commuters on the Cross Bronx Expressway were treated to the tranquil outline of a cat grooming itself, or sprouting potted plant, in the windows of hundreds of buildings, but this poor-man's gilding could do little to hide the housing crisis. By the late 1970s, the vacancy rate had dropped to 1%. With a diminished supply and increasing demand, rent prices soared 24% from 1976 to 1979, leaving the thousands who had been burned out of their homes with few options.

Further swallowing up available housing was the closure of state mental hospitals without the promised opening of halfway-houses and other services for the mentally ill. While often overplayed, de-institutionalization did have a serious impact on housing in the city. Between 1965 and 1977, New York State released 126,000 patients from its mental hospitals. By 1980 an estimated 47,000 of those lived in New York City, along with an additional 8,000 people who would have been admitted to hospitals under the old guidelines but were turned away.[8] Many lived in the most precarious situations, often in flophouses and Single-Room Occupancy (SRO) hotels, the highest concentration of which were on the Bowery on the Lower East Side. Yet between 1975 and 1981, two-thirds of low-cost residential hotels were demolished, abandoned, or converted to condos and co-ops to promote and prepare for gentrification.

"Urban renewal in the '80s was one of the first factors in creating homelessness," says Beverly Cheuvront, a reporter who covered housing issues during the 1980s and is now the communications manager for the Partnership for the Homeless. "We started clearing out the very low-income, the Bowery type communities, tearing down all these structures that were housing people, and then never did the rebuilding. A lot of low-income housing was torn down for this great rebirth that didn't quite happen."

The housing market was bleak for the city's poor. Between 1978 and 1987, more than a quarter of low-rent units disappeared. There were 60% fewer apartments affordable for people on public assistance (or earning a similar amount of money). Almost 20% of apartments were subject to owner neglect, such as failure to pay taxes, mortgage defaults, and the stripping of essential services from the building, nearly all of this occurring in poor neighborhoods with a high concentration of minorities.[9]

This local change in the housing market combined with larger national trends that proved particularly deleterious to those same struggling neighborhoods. During the 1960s the country first became familiar with the term 'de-industrialization,' as millions of jobs were lost to plant closings, particularly in the cities of the Northeast and the 'Rust Belt.' Just two generations after the "Great Migration," when millions of black people moved from the South to work in northern factories, those same jobs rapidly disappeared. More than a million jobs were lost overseas while many more, ironically enough, moved to the cheaper, non-union South.

No city lost more jobs during the period than New York, 600,000 manufacturing jobs disappeared during the 1960s alone.[10] In addition to the national trends, New York's industry was being actively pushed out by government policies. Robert Moses' Slum Clearance Committee and highway projects bulldozed countless businesses and small manufacturers from the 1940s to the late 1960s. Shipping expenses became prohibitive for many companies when the city's port was moved to Elizabeth, New Jersey to make way for the World Trade Center, and changes in zoning laws in 1961 made industry illegal in much of the city.

Between 1969 and 1975, the city lost an additional 500,000 jobs,[11] as many companies left the city because it was literally burning and falling to the ground, and the fire and abandonment decimated neighborhood economies. Black communities were hit hardest by the job losses, but the increased need for employment and low-cost housing was not met with aid, but rather was interpreted as proof that such aid would be useless. Unemployment was seen as a sign that many black neighborhoods were in the midst of an irreversible decay, and politicians saw it as further proof of what Daniel Patrick Moynihan called the "social pathology . . . which slums produce."[12] As Martin Luther King once said, "When there is massive unemployment in the black community, it is called a social problem. But when there is massive unemployment in the white community, it is called a depression."

The trend was exacerbated by federal policies that shifted money away from the struggling cities of the North and Midwest, to the suburbs and to the expanding Sunbelt region. To shore up the recent swing of southern states to the Republican side, Nixon made the 1970s a decade of uneven federal spending, with states south of the Mason-Dixon line receiving

$1.25 in federal money for every dollar they sent to Washington, compared with 81 cents for the rapidly de-industrializing states of the Northeast and Midwest.[13] Much of this additional aid encouraged suburban construction at the expense of urban maintenance. The Housing and Community Development Act of 1974 re-allocated money formerly used to maintain urban communities through housing initiatives like the Model Cities program, to a Community Development Block Grant for growing communities, spurring suburban construction that outpaced even the rising demand.[14]

These national trends contributed to the already dismal state of housing, employment and city services in New York's poor neighborhoods. Many families were forced to double and triple up in decaying apartments and the projects. Yet as the housing market continued to worsen, thousands who either had no support network or had overstayed their welcome with friends and family were forced onto the street. The most attractive options for the new homeless were found in the same neighborhood that had been a magnet for the down and out for decades: the Lower East Side.

HOMELESSNESS AND THE LOWER EAST SIDE

If you took a survey of most of the homeless people in this area, the majority of them don't come from this area. It was a magnet, it had a reputation.
— Lower East Side homeless man, to the author

The city shelter system was completely unprepared for the spike in homelessness caused by de-institutionalization, unemployment and fire and abandonment, with just a single intake center serving a homeless population that was estimated at 36,000 people in 1979.[15] Fittingly enough, this intake center — the Third Street Men's Shelter — was located in the heart of the Lower East Side, between Second Avenue and the Bowery. The Lower East Side was a natural option for many homeless men, who for years had found shelter on the Bowery, with its seedy residential hotels and SRO's, shelters and soup kitchens. For just a few dollars a night you could still rent a chicken wire-walled cage large enough for a bed and a few belongings in one of the remaining Bowery flophouses. The neighborhood was home to a number of soup kitchens and clinics and an informal economy of odd jobs and piecemeal labor that could provide extra cash for food, shelter, drugs or alcohol. Aside from these tangible benefits, the Lower East Side became something of a safe haven for people with few options.

"The Lower East Side was full of homeless people, it attracted them from all over," says Gerry Howard, a Queens native who lived in Lower East Side shelters and subway tunnels in the mid-1980s and early-1990s. "When you're miserable and you find a group of people that have that same misery, the intensity of your misery automatically diminishes. It's like screaming and hollering that you can't get a pair of shoes, and then you see someone that doesn't have no feet . . . You can throw in misery loves company, and you could throw in birds of a feather, and it would probably all be valid because birds of a feather *do* stick together, and misery *does* love company."[16]

The combination of a rising homeless population, a flourishing drug trade, and nascent stirs of gentrification made the neighborhood a study in disparity. Some flophouses were renovated and converted into apartments for artists and professionals, while others rented out their first floors to punk-rock clubs like CBGB's and Great Gildersleeves. On the corner of Bond Street and the Bowery, one could hear jazz music drifting from the Tin Palace nightclub while watching heroin addicts come and go from the shooting gallery behind it. Within a block of the Bowery, you could see experimental dance productions at New York University's Tisch School of the Arts, get a free bowl of soup at one of two Catholic Worker hospitality houses, or check out the latest skull-motif artwork on the front stoop of Hell's Angels headquarters.

In 1979 a class action suit, Callahan vs. Carey, was filed by three homeless men against the city and state for failing to provide them with shelter. To the surprise of many, the judge found in favor of the plaintiffs and ordered the city to provide shelter access for any man who wanted it. With thousands of homeless people taking up residence in subway tunnels, public parks, street corners and wherever else there was space, City Hall fought the perception of a city on the brink by opening new shelters, ranging from small church basement bunkhouses to former hospitals that could house hundreds.

The Third Street shelter remained the nerve center of the system though, with anyone seeking refuge needing to first report there before being bussed out to a shelter and then bussed back when their night or weeklong stay was up. Up to a thousand people came in and out of Third Street each day, and as the homelessness crisis worsened so did the conditions in and around the shelter. The building served alternately as a sort of informal winter drop-in center for anyone looking to get warm (including alcoholics, junkies and drug dealers) and as a makeshift shelter, guards herding the men into the building's "Big Room" where they slept on floors, chairs and couches when the shelters they were supposed to be sent to were full. The building was a miserable place, known amongst homeless men for its readily available drugs and alcohol, mentally and physically ill patrons, and the ever-present threat of assault and robbery.[17]

"Oh man, back in the mid-'80s, [Third Street] was notorious with capital letters, NOTORIOUS," says Gerry Howard, who stayed at Third Street between other shelter assignments. "I've seen murders inside the place. I saw a guy walk right in and put a gun to a guy's head and just Boom! Blew him away while I was sitting right there. I even knew the guy that did it. He's dead now too."

Nearby residents and city officials shared the same grim opinion of the shelter. Sociologist and cofounder of the New York and National Coalition For the Homeless Kim Hopper worked for more than a decade as a court-appointed observer at the shelter. In his book, *Reckoning With Homelessness*, Hopper recounts numerous scenes of violence, substance abuse and callous, even brutal treatment by the overwhelmed staff:

> A little over a month ago [James, an intake worker, informs me], one of the
> clients was badly beaten by a staff on security rounds. The attack, on his
> account, was entirely unprovoked. The assailant was a staff member of some eight

A Radical Political and Social History of the Lower East Side

years' standing. No attempt was made to break it up, either by other staff or by the security force, until blood began to pool around the man's head, as the staff member smashed it repeatedly on the floor. The cops, it should be noted, do not intervene unless called upon to do so by one of the staff; no such request was made. [I checked the logbook.] A whitewash report has been logged in the record. It notes only that an "altercation" had occurred in which a staff member claimed that a client "took a swing at him and he retaliated. (May 26, 1980)

[I went] into the bathroom, where I found a man cleaning the floor. The man's shirt was stiff with dried blood from, it turned out, two stab wounds he had received the night before. Both wounds were open, though the bleeding had stopped. He was mopping up the blood at the staff's instruction, and there was no way he could have received his assignment and gotten his mop and bucket out of the closet without having passed in close view of a number of staff members. (February 1, 1990)[18]

Given the Dickensian-poorhouse nature of the shelter, the streets were a more attractive option for many who came to Third Street. They were often safer than the shelter itself, and provided an odd kind of stability for men who didn't know which borough they were going to be sleeping in from night to night. The blue-collar Lower East Side, long accustomed to homelessness, was a natural fit for people coming in and out of Third Street.

As urban renewal, fires, abandonment and a bad economy continued to turn people out onto the streets, the number of homeless men in the Lower East Side spiraled out of control. Tompkins Square Park began to resemble a refugee camp, with hundreds of homeless people camping out each night. Many who took refuge in the park say they came because police officers told them it was the one place in the city they could go and not be hassled or rousted awake by police. The Board of Education even began special training for teachers in Lower East Side schools, where it was common for half of the students in a class to be homeless.[19] The neighborhood had always been home to large numbers of homeless people but they more closely fit the skid-row stereotype: white, alcoholic men, often war veterans, who stayed in flophouses and kept out of trouble. But the new population was in more dire straits, turning to panhandling, crime and the oblivion of drugs in much higher numbers. Police records at one point showed that 12% of those arrested in the entire Ninth Precinct gave the shelter as their address.[20]

Making matters worse, in 1983 a new smoke-able form of cocaine arrived on the streets. Previously the only way to smoke cocaine was to freebase it, mixing cocaine hydrochloride-basic powdered coke — with ether and boiling it off, leaving behind a smoke-able powder. The problem was that ether, a highly unstable chemical, becomes even more volatile when boiled, and is prone to explosion. It was a freebasing accident that nearly killed comedian Richard Pryor in 1980, leaving him severely burned.

The complexity and danger of freebasing proved a deterrent, but the immediate, explosive high created by smoking cocaine was popular, and the new method provided a cheaper, safe alternative to freebasing. It involved mixing cocaine with baking soda and water, then dry-ing it into hard pieces that could be broken up into single serving rocks by dealers. Rocks could be bought for as little as a few dollars and the crackling sound it made when smoked gave the drug its most notorious nickname, crack. The drug took to the poverty and desperation of post-burnout New York like a match to a tinderbox, sparking an unprecedented epidemic. The mainstream media did not even pick up on the new drug for almost two years, and then only after it had spread to white neighborhoods and the suburbs. The first *New York Times* reference to crack appeared in November of 1985 in an article about a cocaine abuse program in wealthy, suburban Westchester county.[21]

Crack starts out cheap but the high, lasting just a few minutes, leaves the user desperate for more, often willing to turn to crime to get another hit. The physical effects of the high are also linked to anger, violence and sexual promiscuity. Even the most seasoned veterans of Lower East Side poverty were caught off-guard by the drug and the homelessness crisis. Soup kitchens and shelters like the Bowery Mission and the Catholic Worker, which had been in the neighborhood since the Great Depression, were put under immense strain.

"We did an enormous amount of work," said Carmen Trotta, who has lived as a volunteer at the Catholic Worker on East First Street since the mid 1980s. "All my life, when everybody is talking about the drug problem with the homeless, [I say] I don't know what the drug problem could possibly have been prior to crack. We know a number of heroin addicts and it's terrible to see what happens to their body, what they do sometimes to get money for drugs, but we don't have that much trouble with them. But crack is different. There is a lot more violence associated with crack."[22]

Initially, understaffed police departments in poor neighborhoods were unable or unwilling to do much about the spread of crack, but soon many became directly involved in its dissemination and the further destruction of ghetto neighborhoods. Police corruption and involvement in the crack trade first came to light in 1986 when 11 officers from Bedford-Stuyvesant's 77th Precinct were arrested for raiding known drug spots, then stealing money and drugs. Twenty-seven supervisors were subsequently transferred to other precincts but Police Commissioner Benjamin Ward decided no further investigations needed to be done into possible citywide police corruption. Things quieted down at first, but in 1991 evidence of years of ignored corruption came to light, beginning with the arrest of six NYPD officers in Long Island for trafficking cocaine. The head of the operation, Officer Michael Dowd, was eventually brought up on a variety of federal charges, including making as much as $8,000 a week from drug dealers in return for protection from police raids. In Harlem's 30th Precinct, police involvement with drug organizations allowed for open dealing on nearly every corner of Broadway between 135th and 155th Streets. 14 officers from the "Dirty Thirty" were arrested after videotapes showed them beating up Harlem residents and stealing drugs and cash. Dozens of officers were eventually implicated in the scandal.

The 1994 Mollen Commission Report on police corruption paints a chilling picture of highly organized groups of renegade police officers dealing drugs, falsifying documents and brutalizing citizens in scenes reminiscent of the corruption brought to light two-decades earlier by Officer Frank Serpico. The report describes residents more afraid of police than criminals, and clean officers unwilling to report corruption because they felt "the department did not want them to report corruption, that such information was often ignored, and that their careers would be ruined if they did so."[23] Arrests were made and investigations undertaken in scores of precincts, including the Lower East Side's own Ninth Precinct, where more than a dozen officers were involved in "protecting narcotics dealers, robbing dealers and snorting cocaine and drinking while on the job."[24] Few charges were brought to court though, as the rug was swept out from under corruption investigators when the ringleader of the group was arrested on drug charges before sufficient evidence could be gathered against the rest of the operation.

With even the police directly involved in the sale of crack, the drug spread like wildfire. Interviews with numerous neighborhood residents, homeless shelter staff and homeless people who lived in the neighborhood at the time all tell the same story of a neighborhood overrun with drugs and violence.

"I remember when crack hit the city," said Carmen Trotta. "We can all certainly remember it on our block because whole sections of the soup line would suddenly disappear. The guys lined up outside, whatever it was 100 people or so, and 20 people would suddenly walk out of the line and walk down the street to buy crack and they were buying it openly, they would just line up, somebody would take the money and just hand out crack."

With an exploding homeless population, open drug dealing and the crime and violence associated with it, the Lower East Side to many seemed a neighborhood on the brink. Dealers ran street corners. Many playgrounds and small parks became unusable for residents and their children, filled with sleeping homeless people at night and littered with "works," used drug paraphernalia like hypodermic needles, during the day.

THE TIMES THEY ARE A-CHANGIN'

Over the last decade visible homelessness in both the Lower East Side and city at large has dramatically decreased. The change has had nothing to do with a drop in homelessness — the population has actually increased, with new records set almost annually in post-millenial New York. One cause of the decreasing visibility of destitution is the changing face of homelessness — single mothers, children and the working poor have for years been the fastest growing segments of the homeless population. Another cause is increased policing of the parks, subways and streets, pushing many further to the fringes of the city.

As gentrification took hold in the Lower East Side attempts to decrease homelessness in the neighborhood — both in terms of raw numbers and visibility — had a powerful effect. The closing, renovation and curfewing of Tompkins Square Park was symbolic of attempts to overhaul the neighborhood's blighted reputation during the 1990s. Neighborhood groups like BASTA (Before Another Shelter Tears Us Apart), politicians like Antonio Pagan helped close the Third Street Men's shelter and Mayor Rudolph Giuliani's "Quality of Life" campaign used occasionally draconian measures to marginalize homeless people in the neighborhood. The trend even affected charitable organizations that provided relief to the poor.

"The Catholic Worker came to be seen as something of a threat to some people and businesses on the block," says Trotta. "They saw the soupline as an obstacle to developing the neighborhood. Nowadays, we're almost like a novelty, a quaint reminder of what the neighborhood used to be like."

Recent years have seen a small uptick in homelessness in the neighborhood, and anecdotal evidence suggests increased tolerance from the police. Yet this seems less of a return to the 'old days' than the more relaxed demeanor of a neighborhood secure in its status as an expensive, gentrified entertainment zone. In some ways the continued presence of the Catholic Worker, Bowery Mission and handful of remaining flophouses is beneficial to the neighborhood's reputation, lending it a certain 'street-cred.' Poverty is an important compo nent of the profitable "East Village aesthetic" (see Christopher Mele's earlier chapter "Making Art and Policing Streets,") and the specter of an occasional panhandler provides a veneer of grittiness to what is now one of the most expensive neighborhoods in the city.

Two decades ago New York's loss of housing and jobs, and increase in violence and drugs, created an unforeseen crisis in the Lower East Side, setting the stage for the political, social and artistic upheaval of the 1980s. Yet for all the changes these trends brought to the Lower East Side, they were somehow sown into the social fabric of the neighborhood. Since its origins as a German farming community, the Lower East Side has been swept by new waves of immigrants, artists, bohemians and radicals, always altering but rarely transforming its essential character. So too the homeless, but recent trends may prove more dominant. As the old cliché goes, only time will tell where the gentrifying wave of trendy bars, sky-high rents and New York University dorms will lead.

Endnotes:

1.   From an interview with the author, July 2002. Michelle is a pseudonym.

2.   "New Calcutta" was the heading for a series of editorials in the *New York Times* about the lack of services for the homeless, beginning on July 15, 1987, and City Comptroller Harrison Goldin remarked at a press conference in 1985 that "New York doesn't have to look like Bombay."(Albany Times Union, September 23, 1985).

3.   Metzger, John T. 2000, "Planned Abandonment: The Neighborhood Life-Cycle Theory and National Urban Planning" *Housing Policy Debate, Vol. 11*, Fannie Mae Foundation, 2000, page 16.

4.   Mortiz, Owen "Sees City Full of Ghost Towns," *New York Daily News*, August 3, 1970.

5.   U.S. Census Bureau, Census 1970 and 1980. Alphabet City statistics are derived from New York County census tracts 22.02, 26.01, and 26.02, covering Ave.'s B-D from East Houston Street to 9th Street.

6.   Wallace, Deborah and Rodrick, *A Plague on Your Houses: How New York Was Burned Down and National Public Health Crumbled*. 1998, Verso, New York, page 56.

7.   Hopper, Kim. *Reckoning with Homelessness*, 2003, Cornell University Press, page 77.

8.   Hopper, Kim, page 77.

9.   Hopper, Kim, page 163.

10. Leondar-Wright, Betsy, "Black Job Loss Déjà vu" *Dollars and Sense*, issue 253, June/July 2004.

11. Sterne, Michael, "City Fiscal Crisis Feeds on Itself," *New York Times*, Oct. 27 1975, page 22.

12. "Text of the Moynihan Memorandum on the Status of Negroes," *New York Times*, Jan. 30, 1070, page 3.

A Radical Political and Social History of the Lower East Side

13. Leondar-Wright, Betsy.

14. Metzger, John, pages 16-17.

15. This estimate, like any estimate of homeless persons within a given area, is fraught with difficulty. The figure was arrived at by combining an internal memo from the State Office of Mental Health that estimated a homeless male population of 30,000, with a report from the Manhattan Bowery Corporation, which estimated there to be between 6,000 and 6,500 "periodically homeless women" in the city. Both estimates though are merely best guesses and many estimates are much higher.

16. Howard, Gerry, interview with the author, tape recording, August 2002.

17. Hopper, Kim, page 93.

18. Hopper, Kim, page 97.

19. Gill, Jonathan, "Homelessness Under Study," *New York Times*, April 10, 1988.

20. Jaynes, Gregory, "Where Liberals Feel Under Siege From Homeless," *New York Times*, November 11, 1987.

21. Boundy, Donna, "Program for Cocaine-Abuse Under Way," *New York Times*, Section 11WC, page 12, Nov. 17, 1985.

22. Trotta, Carmen, interview with the author, tape recording, August 2002.

23. Krauss, Clifford "Command Failures: Mollen Report Blames Gap in Responsibility for Rogue Officers," *New York Times*, July 7, 1994, page A1.

24. Selwyn Raab, "Witnesses Tell Of Cover-Up In Police Graft" *New York Times*, Sep 29, 1993, page B1.

Chapter 8

Documenting the Italian-America Civil Rights League
By Aldo Tambellini

In 1971, I was invited to present one of my "electromedia" (multimedia) performances at a conference sponsored by the New York State Department of Education, Division of Humanities and the Arts. My wife Elsa and I, returning home, decided to qo to a meetinq of the Italian-American Civil Rights League which was convened at the Park Sheraton Hotel Ballroom in Manhattan. The activities of the league had come to my attention through the continuous negative coverage by the New York media.

In 1970, Joe Colombo had organized "a small but courageous group of Italian-Americans to picket the FBI (on 69th Street) and demanded that the FBI and the mass news media end the harassment, discrimination and defamation against the Italian-Americans." The group, made up of mostly working class and grass-roots people, later became the Italian-American Civil Rights League which was created to "ensure and guarantee the Civil Rights and Constitutional Liberties of all Italian-Americans." The league also encouraged the boycott of movies, television programs and commercials which stereotyped and degraded Italians. Colombo was the founder of this movement. General open meetings were held monthly on Wednesday night.

Elsa and I entered the filled-to-capacity ballroom at the Park Sheraton Hotel. We saw several men sitting on stage and one of them was at the microphone addressing the audience. I learned later that the speaker was Nat Marcone, the president, a former union leader. He was delivering a report on the league's recent activities. Anthony Colombo, the vice president, spoke and then Joe Colombo addressed the audience. Here was a short, energetic, very charismatic man in his mid-forties who in a reasonable tone had the audience's total attention. As he spoke, he became larger than life-size. "There is a conspiracy in this country against all Italian people. It was because of this we formed the Italian-American Civil Rights League right on 69th Street and Third Avenue (NYC), right out in the open and under God's eyes — under the stars." The audience clapped giving him a long ovation; all chanting "ONE-ONE-ONE," the league's "Unity" slogan. He continued talking about specific incidences of discrimination correcting the many distortions in the press. After that, the meeting progressed to the reports from different committees such as the one on education where it was documented that in New York City there was practically no Italian-American representation in the ranks of administration in the public school system. Likewise, other committees reported the scarce visibility of this ethnic group in high-level positions in other areas. This mirrored my artistic and cultural experience in New York City. I found the meeting to be highly informative, heightening my awareness and providing supportive data of the realities of the time. I was carrying my video porto-pac inside a shoulder bag but I refrained from using it, not wanting to record the meeting without having prior approval.

65

A Radical Political and Social History of the Lower East Side

At a later date, I made an appointment to see Joe Colombo and to ask his permission for what. Elsa and I went to the new League's Headquarters at 635 Madison Avenue and it was there, sitting around a conference table, that I talked to Joe Colombo. I told him I was an artist who had a theater on Second Avenue and Tenth Street and was very active in the arts of the Lower East Side and that I wanted to document future activities and the development of the league. "You're doing something good for the Italian-Americans and I approve of it." Joe replied. From then on, Elsa and I became card-carrying members of the league and videotaped most of the meetings and activities such as: the demonstrations outside the FBI Headquarters; the demonstration at the Board of Education Offices in downtown Brooklyn and the tragic event at the Unity Rally in Columbus Circle.

Sometimes, at the meetings, there were humorous anecdotes as the one about the purchase of a 250-acre piece of land with several buildings and two large lakes located 90 miles from New York City which was to be the home of Camp Unity, a summer camp free to children of all races and ethnic backgrounds. Part of the money for the purchase of this parcel of land was raised through a benefit where Frank Sinatra and many stars performed at Madison Square Garden in November 1970, raising $500,000. It seems that Joe's biggest concern, at the time, was that someone would have planted a dead body in one of the lakes to discredit the efforts of the league and emphasize the mob image projected by the media. A diver and undersea consultant was hired, she searched the lakes and reported that "no dead bodies were found."

The league grew to 150,000 members with over 50 chapters around the country. Colombo had become a celebrity and he appeared as a guest in several TV Shows including the Dick Cavett Show and the Tonight Show. The league went after those institutions and companies which were defaming the Italian-Americans. Through the pressure of boycotts and demonstrations, the league was successful in stopping the airing of the Alka-Seltzer popular commercial which characterized Italians saying, "Mamma mia, datsa some spicy meat-a-ball." Furthermore, it stopped General Motors from calling one of its cars the "Godfather's Oldsmobile" and was instrumental in having Macy remove the Godfather Game from its shelves. The Civil Rights League got the attention of many politicians and people in powerful positions. Among them, Nelson Rockefeller, the then Governor of New York was quoted as saying, "Words such as Mafia or Cosa Nostra, whether intended or not, inevitably slur an entire people." John Mitchell, US Attorney General said, "There is nothing to gain by using the term Mafia and Cosa Nostra except to give gratuitous offense to many Americans of Italian descent." Despite all of these positive activities and a swelling of membership drawn from blue-collar workers and family people, the New York media had unleashed a defamatory attack on the League to discourage participation and membership.

The Second Unity Day Rally to be held at Columbus Circle on June 28, 1971, was going to be a show of pride and unity among Italian-Americans and serve as a continued protest against defamation. The league meetings concentrated on preparations for the rally. Joe acknowledged the meaning and importance of this event as a demonstration of strength and unity to the city and the nation. As time drew closer, I felt a sense of anxiety at the meeting, as if something dangerous was going to happen. At one of the last meetings, Colombo angrily said, "There are people in this organization that are betraying us." He looked very concerned, but he insisted on proceeding with the plans. With his great sense of organization, Colombo prepared for the big event and inspired us to persist as a show of strength and defiance against the increasing opposition from the New York media. Several well-known political dignitaries and performers, in support of the league, were going to be on stage. Major television network journalists (ABC, CBS, NBC) and photographers were to be present. Every detail was carefully tended to and personally supervised by Joe Colombo.

June 28, 1971, Second Unity Day Rally, Columbus Circle, New York City

I was in Brooklyn at a hardware store buying parts which would allow me to position the camera on my shoulder making it easy for me to record for an extended time. I knew it was going to be a long day. At about 11 or so in the morning, I took a train at Atlantic Avenue Station in Brooklyn to go to Manhattan. I was going to meet Elsa at the Circle who was waiting for me there with the Sony recorder and my press pass, approved by Colombo the previous day, which would get me into the press circle in front of the concert stage. As I got off at the 59th Street stop, I saw a man running in my direction being chased by the police. The police were yelling, "That's him. That's him." As I exited, I saw, under bright sunlight, red, green and white — the Italian Flag colors, stretching around the circle. I saw the commotion of a huge crowd, heard an ambulance siren followed by police sirens, and then, Nat Marcone, at the microphone shouting, "Do not leave. That's what they want you to do. Stay together. We must show unity. Stay together, nothing has happened." I made my way through the crowd towards the press circle looking for Elsa. I came upon a group of men with their arms locked forming a human chain. I told them I wanted to get through, that my wife was on the other side. Someone said, "No one crosses this line." I kept on moving around them looking for Elsa. I finally saw her. "They shot Joe. They shot Joe," she said in a total daze. "What the hell are you talking about?" I asked. "They shot Joe; he was a few feet from me. I saw him falling to the ground. Colombo was shot." "Pass me the recorder," I said. She passed it over and I yelled, "I've got to start documenting." I left her inside the chain of men and I moved further away. I found a van and climbed on top of it in order to position myself in full view of the circle. Two men just below me started a fight. Another member of the league said, "Don't pay attention. They are doing that intentionally to disrupt." I started to record, immediately. I saw the police on horses divide the crowd in half. A man with a mohawk hair cut, suddenly took two hatchets out of his unbuttoned shirt, raised them above his head letting out a warrior yell. Instantly, the "League Captains" disarmed and carried him over their shoulders. The man's head was bleeding profusely. I remembered seeing this strange man, many times, wondering on the streets of downtown Brooklyn.

Some people began to leave. Marcone, was back at the microphone, "They want you to disperse, stay together. We are here to show unity and strength." The crowd remained surprisingly very orderly. I continued recording the rest of the program and the rally went on as scheduled with several dignitaries speaking. Connie Frances, the singer, was supposed to perform but she sent a message that she could not attend. By that time, it was clear what had happened. Colombo had been taken to the hospital between life and death. His alleged assassin, Jerome Johnson, had been shot dead. Father Gigante, the league's Priest, led the

A Radical Political and Social History of the Lower East Side

crowd in payer. "Let's pray to God and Saint Jude to save the life of Joe Colombo." Toward the end of the rally, Elsa joined me, the crowd was dispersing and piles of the *Daily News* were dropped to the ground. The headlines read, "Colombo Shot at the Rally," with a large photo of Joe Colombo on the floor, blood flowing from his mouth.

Elsa reconstructed the scene from inside of the press circle. She wrote:

> Then there was a crack in the air. 'Oh God,' I thought. 'Trouble. No, it must be a fire cracker.' I turned and a figure was lying in the ground. He looked so small and still. Then more cracks in the air and I saw from the corner of my eye, men ducking for cover and then they pushed me in one direction, everyone running. The police, blue uniforms, shoved me and others against the wall of the stand. I couldn't see anything more than a confusion of men and policemen. I looked up to the stand. Anthony (Colombo) came forward crying, 'My father, is my father ok?' 'He's ok," someone said. Women were shrieking and crying. Some men ran under the stand after someone. 'Stop them!" yelled the police. 'What do you expect?' Anthony shouted. Saw Noral. He spoke moving his lips. 'They got Joe. They got Joe 3 times in the head.' I turned to the man next to me. 'They shot Joe.' I said. 'Naw,' he said, 'couldn't be.'

The word came around that there was a bomb under the concert stage that did not go off. Colombo was taken to the nearby Roosevelt Hospital. Late that evening, Elsa and I went there and found out that a group of bodyguards was protecting the ward where he was. They were afraid that he might be shot again. Colombo was in a coma with two bullets lodged in his brain and one in his jaw. Outside the hospital men and women were holding a candlelight vigil in a continuous circular procession chanting, "God save Joe Colombo, Saint Jude save Joe Colombo." I recorded the ritual.

The league continued the monthly meetings which I attended. At one of them, I met T. Grace Atkinson, a major leader of the feminist movement of that time. She delivered a paper in which she presented Joe Colombo as a leader of the working class and a victim to its cause. When she found out that I had been documenting the league, she asked to see the tapes. She came to my loft with a female friend. As the sun disappeared in the sunset, she watched the tapes of the rally.

A year later the Italian-American Civil Rights League disbanded. The year after Joe Colombo, reduced to a vegetable state, died. For me, Joe Colombo will always be remembered as the Malcolm X of Italian-Americans.

Chapter 9

The Midnight Demolition of 172 Stanton Street
By Steve Zehentner

On Saturday, January 24th, 1998 at approx 9:00 a.m., bricks loosened by record rainfalls and inadequate maintenance broke away from a small section of the north facade of 172 Stanton Street. No other visible shift of the rest of the building's facade occurred, nor did any debris fall from the building in any other location. Located on the corner of Clinton and Stanton Streets, 172 Stanton Street was a building privately owned by Ruth and Nat Weisberg and 172 White Mountain Ltd. Built in the 1870s, it housed approximately 25 low-income tenants in 12 rent stabilized and rent controlled apartments. On the ground floor there was a thriving bodega.

A tenant called the fire department (FDNY) and by 9:30 a.m., the police and fire departments ordered the tenants to immediately evacuate the building, saying, "Just put on your clothes, leave now, and later on, after we inspect the building, you'll be able to return." Tenants in adjacent buildings at 176 Stanton Street and 28-30 Clinton Street were also evacuated. By 10:00 a.m., the Office of Emergency Management (OEM), a division of the Mayor's office that coordinates all inter-city emergency operations, was on site. By 11:00 a.m., New York City Mayor Rudolph Giuliani arrived and inspected the building. By 1:30 p.m., all the streets leading to the site were closed. By 2:30 p.m., the demolition contractor, NBI Equipment, hired by the Housing Preservation and Development Authority (HPD), moved in with a boom crane.

A few blocks away, the Red Cross set up a relief center for the tenants of the three buildings, and affidavits were taken from all the residents of 172 Stanton Street:

> I, Muhith Mohammad Ahmed, hereby swear: I reside at 172 Stanton Street, 1D. Our building is right now being destroyed. My possessions are still inside the building, including my schoolbooks, homework, clothing, money and other personal belongings. The police will not let us reclaim our things. They say that only after the building is demolished then they will allow us to dig through the rubble, after our things are lost and destroyed. And yet, I have seen men going in and out of the building all day, even as we have been refused entry. City workers, police, others come in and out, run up and down the stairs, everybody is allowed in, it seems, except for us, the people who live there. Please order the City to allow us to get our things before they destroy the building. Signed on the 24th day of January 1998 under the penalties and pain of perjury.

As the police (NYPD), fire department, and the demolition contractor workers moved throughout the building all day to shut off the utilities, residents pleaded with the police to be allowed to retrieve their pets, which were killed during the subsequent demolition. At approximately 4:00 p.m., Marc Friedlander, a.k.a. Marc Zero, a resident of 172 Stanton Street, broke through the police perimeter and entered his apartment. Mr. Friedlander stated,   69

The City told me all day that we would be allowed to get our stuff out. Then they started saying that they were just going to gently tear the building down and carefully remove possessions with the crane." Mr. Friedlander is an avid collector and award winning video and filmmaker whose last 14 years of work and collecting included: an international film, video, and photography archive; video cameras and other production equipment; rare movie cameras; audio recording masters; rare manuscripts and books; and antique clothes. After gathering up one box of video cameras and recent video work, he was promptly arrested in his own apartment and escorted from the building.

On the street, community activists worked to organize the paperwork for a Supreme Court Justice who was waiting at their home to issue a temporary restraining order against the demolition. When word that the imminent arrival of this court-ordered injunction reached the press area, several witnesses reported that Jerry McCarthy from the OEM made a call on his cell phone, and that immediately afterwards, at about 8:00 p.m., the demolition of 172 Stanton Street began.

Ironically, last February 1997, at 537-39 East 5th Street, two injunctions from New York State Supreme Court judge Barbara Kapnick had been served on the City to halt demolition and the cartage of the residents' possessions. The "law and order" Mayor ignored the injunctions, and New York State law as well as Federal law, and demolished the building. Jacqueline Bukowski, the lawyer representing the residents of 537-39 East 5th Street, said, "When the City ignores the laws of the State, it forces its citizens to live in a state of fear and unpredictability. Even homeless people living under a bridge have Federal law protection regarding the seizure of their property.

On Saturday night, the tenants of 172 Stanton Street were driven out of Manhattan to a hotel near LaGuardia airport, approximately five miles from their neighborhood. The City, as it has done in similar cases, put them up in this hotel for three days. After that time, they were categorized as "homeless" and were put into the shelter system, then onto an emergency list for housing.

By Sunday noon, the building was gone. Demolition crews worked continuously through the night with the crane and a large scoop, taking bite after bite of the building. Debris dumped in the barricaded street was collected and hauled away. Many witnesses to the demolition reported that at no time during the 17 hours of pounding did the building, which was described by Ted Birkham, a spokesmen for the Department of Buildings, "as in danger of collapsing," further collapse. It was simply dismantled floor by floor until the demolition crew reached the ground.

The speed and efficiency of the operation and the well-managed control of the site and of the press, coupled with the surreal quality of the crane scoop repeatedly attacking the building all night long under the glare of spot-light, left many onlookers in shock. Neighborhood residents reported the feeling of having an arm or leg cut off without any explanation or diagnosis. The life of the corner of Stanton and Clinton Streets — the social scene, the bodega, the bank of phones, the familiar neighbors — all disappeared.

> I, Marcelino Garcia, hereby swear: I reside at 172 Stanton Street. The building is right now being demolished. It is still safe to enter — there are many men inside right now. I and my neighbors are losing everything, a lot of valuable things, including money, jewelry, important papers and medicines. There are two cats and two pets birds on three floors that are still stranded in the building. Signed on this 24th day of January 1998 under the penalties and pain of perjury.

New York City's Administrative Building Code

Several provisions within New York City's Administrative Code contemplate the possible need for City officials to order the demolition of a privately owned building.

Title 26/Subchapter 3/Article 8: Unsafe Buildings and Property; 26-235 through 26-243, state that city officials must serve written notice upon the people with an interest in the building, the owner and the tenants; conduct a survey of the premises with no less than three licensed architects/engineers — one of whom should be appointed by the owner; place their Unsafe Building report before the state Supreme Court; and receive a court order granting them permission to act. Only then may they proceed with a building demolition.

While Article 8 does not specifically authorize the City to demolish a building without a court order from the supreme court, under the DOB's Operations Policy and Procedure Notice #16 from 1993 (OPPN 16/93): "When a building has suffered life threatening structural damage, or is in imminent danger of collapse, the DOB may issue an Immediate Emergency Declaration, which expects work to begin by the day after the declaration." When the Department of Buildings proceeds under the OPPN, unless requested by HPD on a site-specific basis, it does not have to issue an Unsafe Building notice, nor obtain a court order. It is, however, required to send a notice to the interested parties stating, "Because of the severity of the condition, the work to repair or demolish must begin immediately. If you fail to do so, the City will perform the necessary work and seek to recover the expenses from you." OPPN 16/93 also authorizes the HPD to retain a contractor through an expedited-bid process, or in the case of 172 Stanton Street, a no-bid process.

It's important to note that while the Administrative Code is legislated by the City Council and is periodically revised, the Administrative Code's Rules and Regulations allows individual agencies, in this case, the Department of Buildings, to issue operational policies such as the OPPN 16/93 without oversight of any governmental body.

However, within OPPN 16/93 there is no technical criteria to guide the DOB Commissioner or his/her inspectors as to what situations warrant an override of standard procedures as delineated in Article 8, and, of course, the subsequent suspension of the New York Sate and Federal constitutionally-protected due-process guarantees. Borough Commissioner of the DOB, Ron Livian, said at the time that simply by the mandate of their office, "we can

A Radical Political and Social History of the Lower East Side

authorize the demolition of a building when we decide that a building is in imminent danger of collapse."

Information recently provided by the Building Department's General Counsel states:

> Pursuant to the City's general police powers, the Department of Buildings is the agency charged with the authority and responsibility to protect the health, safety and welfare of the public from harm due to dangerous buildings in the City of New York. The police powers authorize the Department to determine when emergency conditions exist with respect to a building or structure such that there is an imminent threat to safety that requires immediate action to abate the emergency conditions. The Building Code does not specify who can make this determination. The authority rests with the Commissioner, the Borough Commissioner, or his/her designee or representative.

While there may be real disasters where safety concerns might justify foregoing the legal procedures as delineated in Article 8, there is no procedure that requires the city to prove that it operated in good faith when acting under OPPN 16/93. Such requirements reported to the Community Board could act as a safeguard against the arbitrary use of OPPN 16/93.

At present, the law still allows for the city to act first and, if necessary, defend its actions in court later. To that end the city has at its disposal the more than 600 lawyers of the Corporation Counsel. In 2003, the Building Department's General Counsel confirmed that, "Of the approximately 66 emergency declarations the Department issued, 22 emergency declarations recommended demolition of the building."

> I, Paula Berson, hereby swear: I am a resident of 172 Stanton Street, Apt. 2C. The firemen banged on my door early this morning and told me I had to get out. They gave me five minutes. I am unable to save any of my possessions including my Medicare card, money, artwork and all of my files. I can't even prove that I live in the building without this identification. Signed on this 24th day of January 1998 under the penalties and pain of perjury.

Vacate and Demolish: An Escalation of Tactics

Throughout the 1990s, leading up to the demolition of 172 Stanton Street, there was an escalation of the use of immediate emergency declarations and demolitions on the Lower East Side: 316 East Eighth Street; 319-21 East Eighth Street; 27 Second Avenue; 26 East First Street; 535 East Fifth Street; 537-39 East Fifth Street; and East 13th Street between Avenues A & B. Two of these demolitions occurred in 1997:

537-39 East Fifth Street, demolished Feb 1997

The city-owned building occupied by more than 20 squatters for years was said to be in danger of "imminent collapse" after a fire on the second floor. Independent architect John Shuttleworth testified in court that the fire was contained in one corner and that the building appeared to be structurally sound. Police and city officials were walking throughout the building after the fire without hard hats or any other precautions. One person, Brad Will, made his way into the building and onto the roof. When the police failed to apprehend him, they continued demolition, knowingly endangering his life. Two NY State Supreme Court injunction orders to cease demolition and cartage of property were ignored by the city. Residents' possessions were needlessly destroyed, their pets killed.

26 East First Street, demolished July 1997

The city-owned building occupied by legal rent-paying tenants was said to have been in danger of "imminent collapse" after a rainstorm caused plaster to fall in the building's stairwell. The tenants were given a half-hour to vacate and were never allowed back in. An independent architect who sought to assess the structural condition of the building was refused entrance. City workers moved throughout the building and removed some of the tenants' possessions. Most possessions, as well as peoples' pets, were lost in the demolition. Tenants were housed for one night by the Red Cross, three days in a welfare hotel and then were placed in the homeless shelter system.

City Councilwoman Margarita Lopez fully grasped the odious intentions of the city regarding 172 Stanton Street when she told the *New York Press*, "If they can't get rid of rent control and rent stabilization . . . then they tear the buildings down." Another community leader, Jose Rivera, stated, "If 172 was in such bad shape, why was the Mayor walking in and out of it?" (*New York Press*)

Photographs taken that morning by Clayton Patterson show Giuliani, along with a group of City officials, standing casually, without even the protection of hard hats, in *The Shadow*s of a building allegedly in "imminent danger of collapse."

This coordinated effort between the Mayor, NYPD, FDNY, OEM, DOB, HPD, the Corporation Counsel and the New York media who protect them, had become increasingly sophisticated, swift and brutal. In earlier demolitions, real efforts were made to remove people's possessions. Sometimes days would pass as the city hired movers to pack possessions and videotape apartments. Eventually squatters, some of whom were in city-run programs, became aware of the real intent of phony vacate orders and refused to leave their homes.

In response, the city stepped up its actions and employed riot troops, sharpshooters on roofs, and at 13th street, a HPD tank, to intimidate and remove tenants of buildings. Eventually, the city decided it was more efficient and much easier to use the Department of Buildings to declare an Immediate Emergency, and tear the building down before the community could react and organize.

"The City under Giuliani was never willing to limit itself to judicial processes in its efforts to achieve its master plan," said community activist Frank Morales. He continued:

> As they sensed the community was organizing, they evolved a direct action
> approach that bypassed legal constraints. It was a policy that was the logical
> extension of arson for profit, disinvestment and land banking. From their perspec-

A Radical Political and Social History of the Lower East Side

tive, and that of real estate interests, they much prefer the open space than a building with low-income tenants. Long-term low-income tenants are an anathema to speculation. They want to create a landscape of exploitable terrain.

Barry S. Gedan, a lawyer for Wantanabe Realty in the case, Wantanabe Realty vs. City of New York --- another case involving Mayor Giuliani, similar in its violation of due process guarantees, and resulting in the demolition of Coney Island's Thunderbolt roller coaster-stated,

> From the depositions in the Watanbe case, it became apparent that, at least at that time, the city was not following its own law and believed that even if [time existed within which] an unsafe building proceeding could be commenced and the owner given notice and an opportunity to be heard in court, the city could nevertheless demolish a structure without bothering with the UB proceeding and without getting a court order. Under that way of thinking, the city believed that it could show up at anyone's building and flatten it to the earth without a court order even though there was no immediate danger.

According to John Shuttleworth, an independent licensed architect and former Community Board 3 member:

> Judging from photographic evidence of the north facade of 172 Stanton Street, and site observations of the Stanton and Clinton Street facades, the building could have easily been braced and made safe in order to allow tenants to retrieve their possessions. The restoring of facades is standard procedure and is happening right now all over the city. The vacate order was responsible, but the owner should have been given the opportunity for independent inspection and repair.

The Settlement

In March of 1998, 21 tenants, represented by the Jacob D. Fuchsberg Law Firm, filed an action for damages in the US District Court. The complaint listed the defendants as: Richard Roberts, Commissioner HPD; Jerome Hauer, Director OEM; Jerry McCarthy, Director and Assistant Director OEM; Mayor Rudolph Giuliani; Ronny A. Livian, PE, Borough Commissioner, DOB; Thomas O'Flaherty, Building Inspector, DOB; The City of New York; and Ruth and Nat Weisberg.

The wrongful demolition action, presided over by Judge Richard M. Berman, charged due process violations against the city and failure of the landlord to properly maintain the building in a safe and proper condition.

The tenants' case alleged that "the decision and policy determination by the City to demolish 172 Stanton Street was made in an arbitrary and capricious manner in that the City and its employees failed to abide by Article 8, 26-235 through 26-243 of the New York City Administrative Code and consequently there was a direct abuse of process."

The tenants maintained that only licensed engineers or architects from the DOB possess the authority to declare an Immediate Emergency and order a demolition. Yet in an early morning on-site press conference, Mayor Rudolph Giuliani declared to the media that the DOB had determined the building had to come down. Significantly, at no time prior to this announcement did any licensed engineers or architects from the Department of Buildings inspect 172 Stanton Street. It was only hours later that two licensed architects, Thomas O'Flaherty and Joseph Trivisonno, arrived on the scene, and both deny ever declaring an immediate emergency or giving any order to demolish the building. (Thomas O'Flaherty signed the Emergency Declaration Form requesting the demolition on Sunday, Jan 25th, the day after the demolition began). "More than one dozen City witnesses have been deposed, including the Commissioner of the Department of Buildings, and not one person can say who authorized the demolition.

Alan L. Fuchsberg, the tenants' lawyer said, "The City had placed in motion the machinery to take down that building before even an engineer had looked at it. Our architect and other experts with whom we've consulted are definite that the building was not in danger of imminent collapse."

On behalf of the owners, attorneys Dowd and Marotta alleged, "The City failed to obtain a court order as required by the New York City Building Code and failed to provide the owner of the building with any opportunity to inspect the building or correct any conditions short of total demolition." Citing this as a "violation of substantive and procedural due process rights guaranteed by the Fourteenth Amendment of the United States Constitution, the suit challenged the City's procedure in emergency demolition operations, claiming that the procedure had been changed over the years to dispense with procedural safeguards. For example, the current Department of Buildings policy does not allow for community board notification as it did in prior years."

In November of 2002, a settlement between all parties was reached simultaneously. Lawyers for the tenants and owners declined to comment on the settlement amounts, though the *New York Times* reported that the tentative agreement on behalf of the tenants called for the city to pay the tenants a total of $2.3 million, and for the landlord's insurer to pay the tenants $500,000. Dowd and Marotta's website reported that settlement discussions had resulted in a monetary settlement compensating the owner for the costs of rebuilding and removing all liens affecting the property. (The fee from demolition contractor was between $300,00-400,000). Daniel Marotta, the lawyer for the Weisbergs, said, "The settlement fairly compensated my client and it was enough money to settle the case, but is not enough to deter the City from future abuses." Rough estimates of the cost of rebuilding a five-story building on that lot range from $1.9 to $2.5 million.

A City Law Department official, Gabriel Taussig, said at the time that the overall settlement would "stipulate that the city stands by its decision to demolish the building as a safety hazard." Though the City never admitted any wrongdoing, Daniel C. Marotta, lawyer for the landlords, offered, "After getting depositions from all the City officials, none of whom admitted to ordering the demolition, and getting a ruling from Judge James C. Francis IV that Mr. Giuliani submit to a deposition, all fingers pointed to Mayor Giuliani." The City filed a statement by Mr. Giuliani in which he denied knowledge of how the decision was made. "I do not know the details of how the decision to vacate the building or the decision to demolish the building were made," the Mayor said.

A Radical Political and Social History of the Lower East Side

Alan Fuchsberg believes that the City settled because the judge appreciated that the psychiatric evaluations of the tenants clearly showed that they had suffered post-traumatic stress disorder. "We had well presented evaluations of the tenants that obviously affected the judge, who encouraged settlement."

A spokesperson for the Weisberg family said:

> My sense from off the record conversations I had with city officials was that they thought they had reacted properly, but after much review, that things could have been done differently. Nonetheless, the settlement is not enough for us to rebuild. We hope we can put something together, but if we can't, we may have to sell the property. Right now, we have no plans for the site. Our lawyer felt that we could have pushed on, but we were primarily concerned with our tenants whose lives were destroyed.

> I, Stanley Kleinkopf, hereby swear: I and my wife Ann, reside at 172 Stanton Street, apartment 1C. Around nine o' clock this morning my neighbors heard a rumbling. Now our building is being demolished and we have not been allowed to reclaim our possessions, including jewelry, our medication, our pet cat named "Honey" and everything else we own. I am 75 years old and Mrs. Kleinkopf is 71. We have lived in our apartment for forty years. My bankbook and financial papers are still in the apartment. My medical bills, everything. Please stop the demolition and allow us to reclaim our things and our lives. Sincerely and signed under the penalties and pains of perjury on this 24th day of January 1998.

A Collusion of Interests and the US Constitution

The demolition of 172 Stanton Street was clearly not an isolated case, nor did it happen in a political vacuum, but why did it happen?

There have been theories offered about possibility of political patronage and paybacks to the demolition contractor, Anthony Noto of NBI Equipment, whose company was on site within twelve hours after the first bricks fell (*New York Press* 1/1999). DOB and HPH policy state that when an immediate emergency is declared, the demolition is expected to commence within 24 hours. In these cases, HPD administers a no-bid contract. "Without a full competitive bidding process, opportunity for corruption is ripe," said lawyer Daniel Marotta. A spokesperson for HPD said they currently have 12 demolition contractors in their database and when an emergency is declared, a contractor is selected randomly by a computer. NBI Equipment does seem to be unusually busy servicing HPD contracts (the Seward Park parking garage in 1999, the Thunderbolt roller coaster, and many others), but attempts to find a simple motivation to tie all the facts of the case together as to why 172 Stanton Street was brought down is ultimately unsatisfying. Regarding the possibility of political patronage and money changing hands, Marotta continued, "Giuliani is more powerful than that."

As Councilwomen Margarita Lopez puts it,

This was a conspiracy of many, not just one. Giuliani is a mayor that New Yorkers have yet to see clearly. He was clearly protected by the media and he ruled the city with his own rules. There was fear of retribution from those who disagreed and everyone bowed down to him; the legislature, the judicial, the executive. This was an action that was a reflection of the city at that time, but it was a series of interrelated conditions that made it possible.

Rudolph Giuliani's take-charge, get-things-done persona and arbitrary application of the law is legend and well-documented. His frequent attacks on the 1st Amendment led to dozens of lawsuits and according to the New York Civil Liberties Union, the City lost 25 out of 26 federal cases. His order to strip search protesters at NYPD headquarters was against department policy. His decision to build his Emergency Command Center at 7 World Trade Center overrode the recommendation of his City Council. His war against street artists, vendors, *New York Magazine* and the Brooklyn Museum of Art kept the Corporation Council busy and cost the taxpayers of New York City heavily.

His orchestrated rise to power in the '90s — with real estate interests as his largest campaign contributor — happened when the conditions were right for a man of his personality, connections and agenda to be in charge. His reign coincided with the international ascendancy of unregulated capitalism, deification of marketplace solutions, stock market mania, increased militarization of the police, erosion of civil liberties, and the influence on local New York City politics of the neo-conservative research group, the Manhattan Institute (MI).

Founded by former head of the CIA, William Casey, the MI was Giuliani's think tank. Richard Schwartz, a former senior advisor to Giuliani and Institute fellow, called the MI an "integral part of the new urban agenda for the 1990s." MI Fellows and affiliated scholars have published a flurry of studies attacking rent regulations, and promoting the militarization of the police and the strategy of "spatial deconcentration," a policy developed in response to the riots of the 1960s. It is a racially prejudiced philosophy which says that inner urban areas would be better if cleared of services and residents, and land-banked. Later on, the white middle class would be allowed to repopulate these areas through a process known as gentrification. The goal in essence is to execute popular resistance preemptively, before rebellion has a chance to grow, in order to protect themselves and their profits. (Morales: *ReSearch and Destroy* 1997, http://mail.interactivist.net/housing/war_2.html)

A Senior Fellow at MI, and author of *The Ecology of Housing Destruction*, Peter Salins states that New York City's "raging," "destructive," "inferior surplus housing stock" should be "retired." According to the professor, "housing destruction is simply the housing market's way of ridding itself of the most unsatisfactory component of the housing stock." He realizes these will be "hard" and "painful choices," which are bound to be "controversial, unpopular and fraught with peril." Nonetheless, the time has come to bite the bullet" (Morales)

Perhaps there are moments in time when the conditions are right for all the forces of the powerful to collude in such a way that they reach an unstoppable critical mass that tips into new terrain. Perhaps the demolition of 172 Stanton Street was such a moment: when a mayor, well known for his disregard of the law and at the height of his power, and a city

78 government, infiltrated at every level with the interests of corporate real estate, met at a building in a neighborhood historically known as a community of resistance. The result, in the words of councilwomen Lopez, was "a situation so blatant in its disregard of the rule of law, that the decorum of the city was at stake."

Perhaps this was a situation in which — under the guise of the mandate to "protect the health, safety and welfare of the public from harm due to dangerous buildings" — an autocratic leader had enough power to orchestrate all of his city agencies to do just the opposite while stepping on the United States Constitution's due process guarantee.

In explaining the importance of due process safeguards, Lawyer Barry Gedan said:

> The essence of the relationship between different levels of government and its citizens is found within constitutional due process requirements which in their most basic form protect the citizens from arbitrary government action by requiring the government to guarantee its citizens the opportunity to have a hearing before they are deprived of their life, liberty or property. In that is your right to stand up to your government and say you're right and they're wrong, and to have an independent judge conduct a hearing. That's democracy.

United States Constitution

AMENDMENT IV
The right of the people to be secure in their persons, houses, papers and effects against unreasonable searches and seizures, shall not be violated, and no Warrants shall issue, but upon probable cause, supported by Oath or affirmation, and particularly describing the place to be searched, and the persons or things to be seized.

AMENDMENT V
No person shall be deprived of life, liberty, or property, without due process of law; nor shall private property be taken for public use without just compensation.

AMENDMENT XIV
All persons born or naturalized in the United States and subject to the jurisdiction thereof, are citizens of the United States and of the State wherein they reside. No State shall make or enforce any law which shall abridge the privileges or immunities of citizens of the United States; nor shall any State deprive any person of life, liberty, or property; without due process of law; nor deny to any person within its jurisdiction the equal protection of the laws.

> I, Steven Fleischer, residing at 172 Stanton Street, Apt. 3D, request that we be allowed to retrieve our belongings as promised by members of the Fire Inspectors and Building Inspectors. In my apartment are precious antiques, photo equipment, diplomas, awards, family photos, optical equipment, locksmith equipment, electrical, many tools of my trade, all my clothes, TV's, appliances, etc, etc, etc, etc. My whole life is there. Signed on this 24th day of January 1998 under the penalties and pain of perjury.

Chapter 10

Money, Politics and Protest:
The Struggle For The Lower East Side
          By Janet L. Abu-Lughod

Names are Important:

The terms East Village, Alphabet City, Loisaida, The Lower East Side, and Lower Manhattan roughly delimit an historic zone with elastic boundaries and the even more elastic ideological stances of the people who use them.

The name "East Village" is of very recent origin and is preferred by real estate developers, speculators and gentrifiers (as the enscripted in the slogan, "Die Yuppie Scum"). Its boundaries encompass the old 11th and 17th Wards that stretch from 14th Street on the north toof Houston Street on the south, and from east of the diagonal equivalent to Fourth Avenue and its southern extension, The Bowery. Its eastern boarder approaches but does not include the massive public housing projects east of Avenue Dd. During the second half of the 19th nineteenth century, the streets were laid out to mesh with the 1811 Manhattan grid, once landfill and draining rescued this somewhat swampy farmland and transformed it into an infamous tenement reception area for New York City's newest immigrants. First came the Germans [(it was then known as "Kleindeutschland")], later joined and then supplanted by southern Italians and Jews from Eastern Europe. Puerto Ricans came in the 1950s, and in the 1960s, it was a magnet for "hippies" (hardly an ethnic group). As the most recent wave of gentrification began to move from west to east, the term "village" was introduced to borrow prestige from Greenwich Village west of Broadway.

Alphabet City has a more limited reference. The eastern edge of lower Manhattan bulges out into the East River, requiring a modification of the north-south grid that runs from 10th Avenue on the west to First Avenue on the east. Avenues A through D had to be added as a kind of sub-zero account, taking in about half of the zone. In common parlance, it is considered to be the poorer, more outré, and artier zone. Once again, it terminates symbolically on the west side of Avenue D, opposite the "projects." In particular, Avenues C and D (including the projects) came to be called to Loisaida by the Puerto Rican community, reflecting how the words "Lower East Side" sounded to them.

The Lower East Side is the largest zone and is the name most favored by its politically — committed residents, who eschew terms such as the effete "East Village" and the trendy "Alphabet City." Its use indicates commitment to the historic heritage of a working-man's immigrant quarter and to the preservation of its affordable housing.

In short, the name of the district varies with the ideological position of the speaker.

A Radical Political and Social History of the Lower East Side

How We Became Involved:

But I didn't know any of this when I blundered into the area the first week I arrived in New York, drawn by its remarkable history and fascinated by its overly-decorated architecture, which belied its origin as a working-class tenement district. In the fall of 1987, I had come to live in Lower Manhattan, having accepted a teaching job in the Graduate Faculty of the New School. Originally trained at the University of Chicago as an urban sociologist and planner, I had been teaching urban sociology in various universities since 1958; just before moving to New York I had spent some twenty years at Northwestern University teaching about the city of Chicago and directing its Urban Studies Program. I had never lived in New York, which meant that I had a lot to do a week before classes began. I needed a "field work area" for my urban research class, and I needed it in a hurry!

I selected for my "urban laboratory" what my first informants called the "East Village." It was near the New School and accessible to all; this was important because I planned an experiment to involve my students in a collective research project rather than to allow them to scatter across the city.in [collective teach research — what does that mean? Remember, you're not talking to a primarily academic audience]

in collaboration with my graduate students. Early on, however (perhaps it was beginner's luck), I discovered that the zone was seating seething with conflicts, opposing factions, and issues that, although common to inlying areas of big cities throughout the country, were perhaps more extreme and transparent here. Furthermore, such conflicts were certainly not new to the area; it had a long history of activism.

The process of gentrification, however, was already well advanced by the time we still naïve "researchers" entered the area and stepped into a hornet's nest of contention. In the coming years, we had to learn everything, from the history of the area, the sources of its population, its changing economic base, its position within the geographic and fiscal terrain of the city, and the prior attempts to reconfigure its housing and uses.[1]

We had bitten off more than we could chew. It was then that I asked for help from the Alfred P. Sloan Foundation. We received a modest grant to set up a small research center (REALM, an acronym for Research About Lower Manhattan[2]) at the New School and to begin collecting data and sources. We also initiated an informal seminar to which we invited more knowledgeable persons.! [why the exclamation point?] Participants were eventually drawn from universities all over the city. Once a month we served them seltzer and potato chips, and in return, volunteers reported on their work and joined in the lively discussions. (The maximum number of people ever assembled was the day when some 70 persons turned out to view the remarkable videotape Clayton Patterson had produced on the "Riot of Tompkins Square."[3])

From Participant Observers to Active Participants

But we had barely progressed in our data gathering and understanding when matters came to a boil, requiring our full-time attention and, as it developed, our active participation as well. In early August 1988, the Tompkins Square "police riot" erupted into a full-scale battle, as residents protested the imposition of a nightly curfew on the park and were savagely chased and beaten in return. None of us (my students and myself) could remain disinterested "researchers" any longer. Marching with the community, we knew which side we were on, although, in the years to come, it turned out that there were many sides even on "our side." Through a rare coalition of progressive forces that would eventually fragment, the riot galvanized disparate groups. This unity allowed the neighborhood to win this first struggle to keep the park open through the night, but the victory was to be only temporary. By 1991, the city closed the park entirely, surrounding it by a high wall of fences, generously sprinkling the grounds with rat poison, and then redesigning the abandoned space. Over the course of the next year, the park was reconfigured to make it into a more easily controlled and curfewed place. [The recession of 1991 slowed down the steamroller of gentrification, but as the housing market recovered in subsequent years, it picked up speed again.]

Background

In the fifteen years between 1976 and 1991, the outcome of the struggle for turf seesawed from side to side, sometimes favoring coalitions of defending activists, sometimes favoring the forces of gentrification. There were periodic campaigns by the police to dislodge the homeless (some 150, mostly men, at peak population) from their jerry-built shacks in Tompkins Square Park at the core of the area. There were squatters who had occupied and were fixing up buildings that had been deserted by their previous owners or forfeited to city ownership by tax arrears.[4] The Housing and Preservation Department (HPD) had rented some of these tenements to "temporary" groups under a variety of inventive mechanisms, hoping to later auction them off to their advantage and put them back on the tax rolls. There were protest movements organized to protect the homeless and the squatters from eviction. There were also old-time working and middle class residents who valued and wanted to preserve the neighborhood's intimate qualities, the range of small businesses, the diversity of its ethnic mix and its affordable prices. Many of these groups were organized, and their organizations united under the umbrella of the Joint Planning Council, whose prime focus was to resist displacement and guarantee that affordable housing would not be eliminated.

By 1986, significant threats to the neighborhood's continuity were becoming more visible and opposition more vocal. In that year, a major achievement of a broad but loose coalition of neighborhood groups was to staged a rally at City Hall, under the perennial slogan "This Land is Our Land." This forced the City to declare a moratorium on sales of its properties until suitable plans to expand the supply of affordable housing could be agreed upon.

But the coalition of powers working against them was formidable and much damage had already been done. Long before signs of gentrification had become visible on the streets,

A Radical Political and Social History of the Lower East Side

"flippers" (speculative investors) had been buying up derelict properties with the intent of making quick profits by reselling them. Arsonists had torched other buildings, leaving owners to collect insurance and leaving bare ground that was actually worth more than any occupied rent-regulated structure. Petty real estate investors entered the market in search of bargains. They were buying cheap, making shoddy repairs, and then illegally evicting tenants whose rents were still protected under old rent control or rent regulation laws. Other, larger developers then bought these buildings, fixed them up more elaborately, and then sold them whole or piece-by-piece, in some cases breaking them up into condominiums. Still other developers, after escaping rent controls, displaced poorer tenants and re-rented the vacant units at much higher prices.[5]

Pressures to end the moratorium were building, but so was the population of homeless living the park. It was in the context of this complex struggle for turf that the "sanitizing" and "gentrification" of Tompkins Square Park became a key strategy for developers (in league with city government), and that defense of an open park became a rallying focus for advocates seeking to preserve and expand the supply of affordable housing in the surrounding area.

Why the Coalition Broke Down, or How the Developers Won . . . Somewhat

After the first victory in the summer of 1988, which succeeded in rescinding the curfew on the park, the number of persons making their homes in the park increased to a peak of some 250. By winter, emboldened by the fact that the park workers tended to look the other way, by winter some had moved to seek shelter in the covered band shell that had formerly hosted rock concerts. Many others began to build more permanent, although rickety, makeshift "houses" over the benches they had formerly used for sleeping. Sympathetic neighbors distributed blankets and some food, and the churches flanking the square continued to offer free meals.[6] In the meantime, squatters were able to invade and take over more derelict structures, in many cases using their sweat equity to supplement their expenditures to make these dwellings habitable.[7]

This intensified the motivation of gentrification forces. Clearly, in order to make the area more attractive to middle class buyers and tenants, the park need to be "cleaned up." A series of failed attempts to remove the homeless had left them in place. Officers of the Parks Department had learned that so long as the park remained open, structures would be rebuilt. Surprisingly, it was only after the election of New York's first and only black mayor that the final foray was made, in the beginning of 1991, and the settlement was dislodged. (It moved to a vacant lot farther east and ironically named "Dinkinsville".)

At the same time, there were pressures to lift the moratorium on the sale of tax delinquent properties. As a result of continuing negotiations between the leaders of the Joint Planning Council, working through Community Board 3, and the City (HPD), a compromise was reached via a cross-subsidy plan. The plan was apparently straightforward. According to the agreement reached, the city would be "allowed" (that is, the moratorium would be lifted) to sell off the vacant lots in its possession to developers wishing to build new, market rate housing. In exchange, titles and subsidies would be given to mutual housing associations and charitable organizations to allow them to upgrade existing tenements for persons of low to moderate means. Although a Memorandum of Understanding between the Community Board and HPD had been signed as early as 1987, it was now ready to be implemented. But it was too late.

The negative effects, on the ground, of the cross-subsidy agreement were already apparent. These were consequences that should have been easily foreseen. The compromise created greater incentives, on the part of the City as well as developers, to convert buildings into vacant lots and thus "free them up" for sale to developers. In fact, the City condemned and demolished as "unsafe" a number of structures that were occupied by squatters who had been repairing them. Other tenements suffered from "unexplained" arson.

Furthermore, the community gardens that had sprouted and flourished on the cleared lots — providing cooperating neighbors with vegetable crops, floral beauty, and places for communal activities — could be targeted for removal. (The most important threatening loss was the clearing of the corner lot that had hosted Plaza Cultural, which the community had earlier equipped with a small amphitheater where celebrations, both formal and informal, were held. This cultural institution and others had occupied valuable corner lots containing communal gardens that now became fair game for developers. They were scarcely "vacant," but the city determined that these could be sold under the cross-subsidy agreement.

In addition, a listing of buildings eligible for upgrading for charitable organizations and mutual housing associations compiled by the Community Board revealed that many were already occupied by squatters who had rehabilitated them but had no legal title. This put the housing "reformers" on a collision path with their former reluctant allies, the squatters, who now recognized that they would lose their "affordable" housing to the interests of providing "affordable" housing for others. In fact, "affordable housing" was largely built for institutional uses (e.g. AIDS hospices and church-related housing) or assigned in open competitions to families new to the neighborhood.

In short, the coalition that had mounted its successful protest at City Hall in 1986, under the slogan "This is Our Land" (routinely chanted in protests and placed on buildings, together with a skull and crossbones), was breaking apart. By 1991, it appeared that the developers might win, especially after the City made its final assault on the people living in Tompkins Square Park. When the park was finally reopened after a year, gone were the crevices that had provided some privacy and had permitted the ecological subdivisions the homeless had used to segregate into compatible subgroups with assigned turf. Gone was the band shell that had hosted rock concerts. Gone were the open spaces neighbors, including protesters, had used to organize events.

By this time, however, New York was undergoing one of its periodic economic contractions, tied to setbacks in the stock market. Although all other conditions for further gentrification were in place, the large developers developed cold feet. A New York State sponsored housing program went ahead, building subsidized public housing (low rise cement block minimum standard units). These were located primarily on the vacant lands between Avenues C and D, which market-rate developers had rejected because they were too close to the existing high rise public housing projects on the east side of Avenue D.

As the local economy recovered during the high-flying years of corporate excess and dot-com exuberance in the second half of the 1990s, building began again on the remaining vacant lots. That was when the community gardens and Plaza Cultural were targeted, and then, in violation of the City's commitment not to destroy or assign existing buildings to developers, the vacated city school building that had housed artists, community groups, and hosted dramatic and artistic events was finally closed and sold.

Publishing Our Research

In our collective book, *From Urban Village to East Village: The Battle for New York's Lower East Side*, we ended our account in the early 1990s. This volume had grown quite naturally from the research we conducted, supplemented by chapters contributed by various researchers we met through the REALM seminars. In many ways, the book is unique — both in content and in methods.

The most common model for a community study is for a single researcher to live in an area for several years, observe its life, and describe its conditions. Almost inevitably, the researcher comes to affiliate with certain groups in the area and to internalize its values and its views toward other "Less-sympathetic" groups. This is particularly pernicious in areas such as the Lower East Side, which are fragmented by conflicting interests and opposing views. This is why in our research collective we were careful to try to fairly represent the positions of the various groups. (Only the landlords were ignored!) We did this through a division of labor: each one of us working through informants with their own definitions of the situation, joining their meetings and informal activities, sitting with faction members at the contentious community board meetings, marching in the protests they organized. In our weekly debriefing meetings, we shared information but, even more so, perspectives.[8]

Despite this, we feel our findings are tentative and inadequate. First, limitations arise out of the limited time of the study, only five years out of more than a hundred years of the neighborhood's life. To what extent is it fair to evaluate its achievements without acknowledging the traditions of resistance that provided a model and gave continuity, even though the actual resisters had no living links to earlier residents? Struggles over the future of the Lower East Side go back to its very origins, when shoddy developers put up the original tenements and housing reformers sought to institute minimum design standards for light and air.[9] Conflicts among residents of different ethnicities and varying economic interests were also not new. And in the depressed 1930s, planners were already envisaging the rebuilding and "gentrification" of this last low-rent quarter so conveniently close to Wall Street.[10] Just as there were precedents before the 1970s, there will be other contests ahead for this changing neighborhood. And the relative success or failure of resistance depends on larger economic factors that cannot be predicted.

There is a second problem, and that is whether the events described over our brief period of study apply to other areas? We began by claiming that the forces of burnout and gentrification operating on the Lower East Side were somewhat similar to those operating in other parts of New York City and in certain inner areas of other cities. But the fact is that in many of those other areas, residents were in the end utterly displaced. Unlike the East Village, they had been unable to mobilize enough and in time to minimize the impact of these general forces of capitalist real estate. It would therefore be wrong to dismiss the degree to which the social mobilization that was achieved in the East Village during the crucial period between the late 1980s and the mid-1990s was just another case. How much did the success of resisters depend upon previous traditions of organization and on the skills and commitments of its leaders, including elected officials?

The geographic characteristics of the East Village also contributed to the relative success of the resistance. The presence of the projects set a natural limit to the desires of gentrifiers, as did the expansion of Chinatown from the south. In addition, the existence of Tompkins Square Park as a natural focus and site for organization was also an important factor in defending the neighborhood. The fact that the area just south of Houston Street experienced an onslaught of gentrification in the next decade without eliciting the complex protests and multiple organizations of the East Village warrants explanation. Was it something special in the history and mix of peoples or was it something special about the particular era of New York politics (or a combination of both) that yielded such a rich flourishing of community solidarity and activism?

I like to think that the East Village was able to slow down gentrification and to achieve its modest successes largely because of the quality of its various leaders and activists, and their continued commitments, assets not commonly shared by other areas under "attack." Whether these efforts can be sustained in the future is open to questions. For a while, plans for building the Second Avenue Subway, a long-delayed project, were being revived; this would have deprived the zone of the natural protection of its relative isolation from the mass transit system of the city. The destruction of the World Trade Center has imposed such heavy financial burdens on the City that these plans have again been put on hold. And the economic repercussions on the city's population, and thus the decreased demands for yuppie housing at a time when the needs for affordable housing have skyrocketed, may yet yield continued life for this part of the Lower East Side.

Endnotes:

1. Eventually, some of this research yielded fine doctoral dissertations which were later published as outstanding books.

2. Its original name was *Research/Action Lower Manhattan*, but the then president of the New School thought it too incendiary to mention "action" and we were required to rename it!

3. My "*The Battle of Tompkins Square Park*," chapter 11, in Abu-Lughod et al., *From Urban Village to East Village:The Battle for New York's Lower East Side* (Oxford UK: Blackwell,1994, pp. 223-66) depends heavily on Clayton Patterson's remarkable video-filming of the riot over a period of four "real time" hours. REALM was able to help sponsor the editing of his tapes down to a one-hour presentation that was widely shown throughout the city.

4. During New York's fiscal crisis in the mid-1970s, the City, hoping to collect long-overdue real estate taxes, had shortened the time between tax arrears and foreclosures. The unintended consequence was that the City found itself the default owner of such properties - almost 500 of them, according to records we uncovered.

A Radical Political and Social History of the Lower East Side

5. For a deeper analysis of this process, see Christopher Mele, *Selling the Lower East Side: Culture, Real Estate, and Resistance in New York City* (Minneapolis: University of Minnesota Press, 2000). Maps of the expanding range of "gentrification" appear in Neil Smith, Betsy Duncan and Laura Reid, *"From Disinvestment to Reinvestment: Mapping the Urban "Frontier" in the Lower East Side,"* pp. 149-168 in Abu-Lughod et al. (1994).

6. See Dorine Greshof and John Dale, *"The Residents in Tompkins Square Park,"* in Abu-Lughod et al., 1994, pp. 267-284.

7. See Andrew Van Kleunen, *"The Squatters: A Chorus of Voices . . . But Is Anyone Listening?"* in From Urban Village to East Village, pp. 285-312.

8. These innovative methods are described in my article, *"Diversity, Democracy, and Self-Determination in an Urban Neighborhood: The East Village of Manhattan,"* in Social Research (Spring 1994).

9. Richard Plunz and Janet Abu-Lughod, *"The Tenement as a Built Form,"* pp. 63-79 in Abu-Lughod et al., 1994.

10. Suzanne Wasserman, *"Déjà vu: Replanning the Lower East Side in the 1930s,"* pp. 99-120 in Abu-Lughod el al., 1994.

Chapter 11

Christodora

The Flight of a Sea Animal
By Yuri Kapralov

An inquiry into the rise and fall of one of the finest settlement houses in urban America. Christodora House on Avenue B, established in 1887 as The Young Women's Settlement House and later known in the neighborhood as the "Little House by the Side of the Road."

Frozen Stiff During Summer Heat Wave
(One version of an introduction)

Oh boy, it's now ninety-six degrees and still rising. Not a single leaf moves above us, not one pigeon, not one squirrel. The dogs lie ominously quiet, perhaps they are already boiled. Even the concrete of our chess tables is hot. The tall cans of Rolling Rock which we buy at the Arab bodega on Avenue A become undrinkable in exactly seven minutes. The men and women sitting at the tables across from us are drinking blackberry brandy, washing it down with rum and Coke. They are playing Hearts. We are playing chess, not too seriously. Our special little oasis, the chess tables near Avenue B, is a place where dreams and hopes are long lost and forgotten. We are exhausted Bedouins sitting under a pyramid of sorts — Christodora House on Avenue B.

It is still by far the tallest building in our sea of tenements. To me, it will always remain a mystery. A proud monument to noble aspirations. Built to serve the poor, now accommodating the rich. This pyramid, perhaps more than anything else, reflects the changes in the East Village, a neighborhood I love and have lived in for many years. Looking at it, I realize that it will be casting its shadow over the park long after I am gone. And the future Bedouins will be sitting in our oasis, wondering.

For us, this is the final encampment. We've run out of places to go. This is it, and the air is gray. A strangling curtain of gray lace. It's harder and harder to breathe. We try not to move, but we must. We are playing chess, after all. We have to make our moves. On the patches of dry grass behind our benches rest the relative newcomers to Tompkins Park — the homeless. To me, they are defeated and wounded soldiers, prisoners of war behind impenetrable barbed wire. Although I am a Bedouin, I feel kinship with them. Especially in the cold sweat of sleepless nights when I attempt to climb the barbed fences of my own concentration camps.

It reaches ninety-eight degrees. We are not zombies yet. We are reasonably intelligent beings. We sometimes talk politics. One young, black guy next to me who lives in the Men's

A Radical Political and Social History of the Lower East Side

Shelter and speaks Russian quite fluently sums up the policy of Glasnost and tells us a few Russian anecdotes. No one really pays much attention.

My chess opponent is a Chinese scholar and translator. He is a white man, a former hippie who recently sent the daughter he had with a black woman to an upstate college. He strokes his long reddish beard and thoughtfully explains the current trends of Chinese literature. We pretend to be listening but our thoughts are on something else. Now that we seem to be surviving through this afternoon, we wonder: *what about tonight*? We dread it.

It's an all-consuming fear. Are we going to make it?

As soon as I close my eyes and try to relax, the projectionist starts running my reels again. Faster and faster. The years are out of sequence. Who cares? I don't. One summer my dog would die, another summer my son would grow up and walk away down the melting pavement. Why walk? Why walk away? Oh, yes, today the streets are also melting. My eyes are open. I do remember that everything in the East Village begins and ends on street level. It was like that in the misty, idealistic '60s when I first moved here and sat with thousands of hippies right where the homeless now sleep. We listened to Jefferson Airplane playing from the bandshell. All through the fires and muggings and the heroin of the '70s to the present—our empty, deadly '80s.

This one thing never changed. People still find their friends, their wives, their dogs and cats, their lovers, their books. Once I found a lady's gold watch in an envelope stuck into an old book thrown out on Avenue A. People get ripped off and drink their Colt 45 and Night Train Express and buy their drugs and do whatever is necessary to ease their pain. Sometimes, they die on street level. Enough. I make my move and realize I made a fatal error. I drink my beer and watch my opponent. He is in no hurry to finish me off. He lets me off the hook. Then we finish our lukewarm beer. The heat is finally getting to me. My mind keeps spinning even with my eyes wide open. Yet I know I am frozen. I am on a snow-covered steppe north of Stavropol, a frightened Russian boy, barely alive, listening to the thunder of artillery fire. I look across the table. I look sideways. All of us here in this park are frozen. Frozen in time and space and some of us are already dead. Sure, the chess pieces we are playing with belonged to Paul, our writer friend who used to walk in a funny way, so open and naive. In his apartment, he used to stack newspapers until they reached the ceiling. Not just any newspapers but *The Wall Street Journal*. Why? Nobody knew. There were at least 10 million cockroaches in his place. You couldn't even sit down. Paul was the greatest bartender at Max's Kansas City until he had a stroke. And for quite a few years, he sat frozen with us. He is long gone now, but we still play with his chess set. Paul's typewriter, his only valuable possession, was given to me. And it still types, as far as I know. I gave it to another writer. So many writers here and not enough typewriters. Another friend's system broke down, and he left to die near his parents, someplace in the Midwest. What's left? An unfinished canvas, a few pieces of furniture, a dog and a cat.

Our oasis itself is frozen. Only minor changes occur. Someone nods until his head hits the concrete chess table. Someone walks to the bodega to get more cold beer. Someone goes behind the tree and takes a leak.

Yuri Kapralov

Our chess tables are very special. So different from the rest of the park. The realities of life don't matter here. Never did. We listen to a man from Ecuador talk about his village and the earth there, so fertile you plant a seed and in three days, it grows into a bush. We've heard his story many times before. It's the only story he knows. A couple of tables away, the elderly Ukrainians talk about sunflowers and the earth of their dreams. That's the only problem we have. Our spinning minds. The projectionist has gone berserk. Our reels run with the speed of twenty thousand frames per second. And it's ninety?eight degrees.

I look at another summer, one of the years that stretch into centuries. The afternoon sun is reflecting in the shattered windows of Christodora House. I watch myself climbing old stairs and roofs. I walk precariously on planks made from two by fours. I climb through a broken, boarded-up window. I am inside the Pyramid. It's a long walk to the top floor. What a view. I am astounded.

I stand there for an hour, at least. Then I walk down through endless rooms and mountains of bottles and cans and hypodermic needles and women's purses ripped open. I see a giant black hole where the elevators once were. There are weird noises. I want to leave as soon as I can. I walk through what was once a magnificent oak-paneled library with a huge fireplace. Many piles of partially burned books lie on the floor. I pick one up. "Poetry is a journal kept by a sea animal living on land and wanting to fly the air." Perhaps this amazing building, this pyramid, had been such an animal all along. I think I should at least try to reconstruct its journal.

I see myself going insane for the next couple of years, talking to dozens of old-timers, sitting in libraries, sorting out the who, what, when, and how, and trying to answer some of the why. Thank God I did it when I wasn't entirely frozen. I ask the projectionist to rerun this part of my reel a bit slower. The projectionist reminds me that every morning during the summers, a handsome elderly black gentleman with a long silvery beard carries his bag of laundry into the park toilet. He washes his belongings in the sink and hangs everything on the fence to dry. He sits next to it with his eyes closed. Once his laundry dries, he folds it neatly and leaves the park. He never speaks to anyone. And why should he? He is the Great Pharaoh. In his native ancient Egypt, he has seen many groups of colorfully dressed, bearded architects spread out their plans for his pyramid.

In the East Village, just before the turn of the century, in August of 1887 to be precise, two very unlikely architects, both young women, began building their pyramid. They began, just as everything in the East Village begins and ends, then and now, on street level in a storefront: 167 Avenue B. Outside their door, they put a simple wooden sign: YOUNG WOMEN'S SETTLEMENT HOUSE — EVERYONE IS WELCOME.

The Early Settlement

Walking through the burned-out sections of the East Village between Avenues B and D, it is very difficult to imagine that at the turn of the century over 4,000 people lived on each and every one of these devastated and mostly empty blocks.

A Radical Political and Social History of the Lower East Side

90

When you add all the thousands of horses, pigs, chickens, sheep, cows, geese, goats, and dogs, every square foot of space was used. So were the alleys, roofs, basements, and streets.

The density was unreal. The area was landfill over a swamp. Swarms of mosquitoes were so thick that horses would collapse from sheer loss of blood when left unattended. Hundreds, perhaps thousands, of people were dying each year from malaria alone. God only knows how many died from other diseases and hunger.

From 1881 through 1889 close to six million immigrants from Europe and Turkey arrived in New York. About one third of them settled on the Lower East Side for a period of ten years or more.

The nation could not easily absorb this flow of humanity. There were intense debates in Congress and everywhere in the country for and against immigration.

The opposing views changed little over the following decades. Even today, one could substitute the dates and nationalities of the immigrants and hear the same arguments.

For example, writing in the 1883 issue of the *North American Review,* Honorable W. B. Chandler (Chairman of the Senate Committee on Immigration) states that, "We cannot safely undertake the assimilation of the ignorant and debased human beings who are tending toward us." He also raises the familiar question of whether other countries were sending us their criminal and "low life element" so that we could feed and care for them.

Cautiously arguing against the suspension of immigration, Senator Henry Hansbrough of North Dakota wrote in the same issue: "The strong, healthy and honest immigrant brings more than the paltry dollars in his pockets." Nevertheless, Frederick Knapp (Commissioner of Immigration of the State of New York) placed a definite economic value of $1,125 on each immigrant. And the debates continued.

To the average new immigrant who had just given away his last penny and all his valuable icons, rings, or silverware to various immigration officials as bribes to get off Ellis Island, such high appraisal would seem a cruel joke.

It was very difficult to survive on the Lower East Side in 1893. For the young immigrant woman, life was a continuing nightmare.

Aside from getting married, she had three basic choices. If she was pretty she could become a prostitute. If she was strong, she could work in a sweatshop or as a maid. If she did not have these qualities, she could become a nun.

There was also the East River, the gas stoves, and the roofs of the tenements. Many young women chose those routes, too.

It was against this background that two young women, Christine McCall and Sara Carson, pulled together their meager resources, barely enough to cover a month's rent, and took a three-room flat and an unfinished storefront at 167 Avenue B between Tenth and Eleventh streets. This was the site of the original Young Women's Settlement House, known in the neighborhood later as the Little House by the Side of the Road. It opened its doors in the summer of 1887.

Miss McCall, a slight, intense woman in her late twenties, had been a YWCA worker uptown. Both she and her friend, Sara Carson, were active in the Suffrage movement. The Settlement House they founded was unique in several ways. First, there were no other Settlement Houses in the area (the nearest was the University Settlement on Eldridge Street). Second, although it was non-denominational, it followed a grass roots Christian philosophy. Third, its work was restricted to young immigrant women, their parents, and children.

Many programs that originated at the Young Women's Settlement became models for social programs nationwide some 60 years later. After-school daycare programs for working mothers; women's awareness groups, a program providing medical and psychiatric help for unwed mothers; even services to make the tenement flats more livable for single women.

They also pioneered sending social workers to city jails to tutor illiterate children, 10 to 14 years of age, who were imprisoned.

This program was very important because there were thousands (some estimates range over ten thousand) such children in prisons or in the so-called "work camps." Some of these children were actually executed for crimes ranging from ordinary burglary to murder. In cases involving these children, miscarriage of justice was the rule rather than the exception.

The needs of all people of the neighborhood gradually changed the primary purpose of the Settlement House, and the programs within it became more generalized. When the House moved into a large three-story brownstone on Avenue A and Ninth Street, it became somewhat like the Henry Street Settlement, a cultural/social/educational community center.

Its social program was still a priority but, as time went on, it was eclipsed by the new cultural programs. The Settlement now had an established music school with over 250 students, a glee club, a theater club. There were citizenship classes for adults, dances, concerts, lectures and poetry readings by the members of its famous Poetry Guild.

On March 21, 1914, one of the more promising students of its Music School, George Gershwin, age 15, gave his first public concert. The reviews were mixed. George's brother, Ira, was active in the glee club and Poetry Guild.

That Poetry Guild, which boasted the smallest theater in America (rear bedroom, their "Magic Casements"), produced not only some of the great American poets, but a whole string of popular novelists, Jerome Weidman among them, who often used the Settlement House as a background for their novels. Some of the biggest names in film and theater, producers and actors (Edward G. Robinson and Tony Curtis among them) were in the theater club. An estimated 5,000 people visited the Little House by the Side of the Road, as it was sometimes affectionately called, every week.

During the summer, hundreds of kids went to their Bound Brook Camp in New Jersey or spent weekends as guests of Mrs. Arthur Curtiss James on her vast estate in Tarrytown. Mrs. James was the institutions president and Chairman of its Board of Managers. A lot of money began flowing into various Settlement House activities.

Toward the mid-'20s, the neighborhood changed completely. So, once again, did the emphasis of the Settlement's work. Miss McCall stepped down as Director and Herbert Beal was brought in. The main activities were now the Music School, the adult citizenship classes, the Boy Scouts (Troop 202 was stationed there), and the Nature clubs. Many of the meaningful social programs were quietly dropped. There developed a kind of wall between the Settlement and the community it served. A couple of scandals involving some staff workers and local women further alienated the neighborhood.

Jerome Weidman describes the settlement in one of his novels as "an outpost of the Uptown world planted in their midst, an oasis founded and operated by strangers for reasons never quite understood and trusted by their beneficiaries."

These strangers included some super-wealthy and powerful people. Mr. and Mrs. Arthur Curtiss James had given the Settlement its three-story brownstone in the first place and were now committed to building a huge 18-story building on its site. It would be the largest Settlement House ever built in America.

The Super Rich

Arthur Curtiss James and his wife, the former Harriet Eddie Parsons, were not merely super rich, but the absolute cream of the crop of New York society. Mr. James, a railroad tycoon, financier, and owner of several huge companies, was estimated to be worth 300 million dollars in the mid-'20s — he was in the class of J.P. Morgan and the Rockefellers. He lived in a twelve-story mansion on Millionaires' Row at 998 Fifth Avenue. There was a mansion of equal magnitude in Newport, Rhode Island, and an estate in Tarrytown, New York. During World War I, Mrs. James, always a civic-minded lady and from all accounts a very sensitive person as well, entertained over 1,200 soldiers on some weekends at their Tarrytown estate.

Mr. James was eccentric and contradictory, as idiosyncratic in some respects as Howard Hughes. He was an avid yachtsman. He sailed across the Atlantic, down the Nile and the White Nile. He was an art collector with tastes ranging from the English masters (George Romney, Joshua Reynolds) to Touraine tapestries and Roman sarcophaguses in which, it was rumored, he liked to take a nap from time to time.

He was also a great and intelligent philanthropist in his time and was active in his church, the First Presbyterian on Fifth Avenue and Eleventh Street. He was active in politics. His support was valued highly by the mayor, the governor, as well as those in the Senate and White House.

His favorite charities were as diverse as his art collection. He gave to the Metropolitan Museum (he was a trustee), the Union Theological Seminary, and a wide range of unrelated organizations in between. It was his wife who interested him in the work of the Young Women's Settlement House and the Christodora House.

For a time, he became obsessed with poverty and the Settlement's work. One of the legends was that he used to park his Packard north of 14th Street and, dressed as a pushcart peddler, walk down Avenue B to his Settlement House, talking to people along the way. He would later sit at a meeting of the Board of Managers and astound everyone with his knowledge of the neighborhood and its problems.

When the new Christodora House was dedicated to him in December of 1928, Mr. James admitted to his friends that he considered it his greatest achievement.

In the '30s, he must have felt the depression. He sold his Fifth Avenue mansion to move into a smaller six-story townhouse at 39 East 69th Street. This townhouse was called one of the most elegant in the city by several newspapers and periodicals.

In 1931, Mrs. James became an invalid. She died ten years later. Mr. James died the following month.

The couple had no children. The estate was divided in accordance with Mr. James's will between numerous relatives and friends. The James Foundation was set up to continue charitable work. The principal benefactors were the Christodora Foundation and the YMCA. About a dozen other organizations received lesser amounts of the foundation's shares. It was a very complicated arrangement. The James Foundation was set up for a period of 25 years. It apparently ceased to function in the mid-'60s. The Christodora Foundation still exists. It was after a long conversation with Mr. Steven Slobodin, the present director of the Christodora Foundation, that I decided to do some serious research for this book.

The Pyramid

To people living in lower Manhattan, this building is a familiar sight. For decades, it stood abandoned. Among other firsts, the building had the dubious distinction of being the first slum skyscraper. I suspect that the reason it wasn't torn down was that nobody knew how to do it. Like a pyramid, it was built to last forever

In 1928, it officially opened as the new Christodora House, replacing the Little House at the Side of the Road. It was then, and is now, a true palace amidst the tenements of the East Village. It was built on a floating foundation —an architectural first.

It had everything. A large swimming pool, a gymnasium with parquet floors and handball court, a concert hall that held three hundred people, a restaurant, and a solarium. The library was paneled in oak and had a large working fireplace. Early American furniture bought at Sloane's was installed throughout the entire building. A few masterpieces from the legendary Arthur Curtiss James art collection hung in the lobby and in the classrooms of the Music School. It was indeed the biggest Settlement House ever built in America.

The new Christodora House was a gift from Mr. and Mrs. Arthur Curtiss James. It cost them almost two million dollars to erect it. In 1928, that was a lot of cash.

During the years that followed, it became the in place for New York society figures to visit and donate money to. Long lines of Rolls Royces, Packards and Cadillacs were observed parked on East Ninth Street near the side entrance. The neighborhood children, barefoot and dressed in rags, often besieged the car occupants and chauffeurs, begging for pennies. Although the Settlement's work went on during those years, the activities, instead of expanding, began to contract. The importance of the Residence Club for young men and women occupying the upper floors was stressed.

Handsome advertising flyers from the Christodora Residence Club detailed "elegant living," convenience and good service. The rates were from $7 to $10 a week; $1.50 a day for transients. Breakfast and supper were included. The guests also had the use of the swimming pool, gymnasiums, the library and the solarium. No tipping was allowed throughout the building.

The people occupying the Residence Club were mostly young executives, teachers, legal secretaries, doctors, nurses and New York University graduate students with trust funds. The yuppies of that time. There were no neighborhood people living in the building, but cleaning women and other low-paid help were recruited from the area.

During World War II, the building housed some refugees from Nazi Germany on a very select basis: professors, lawyers, journalists, scientists, etc.

For a very brief time after the war, some upper floors were used to house (under armed guard) Soviet citizens, primarily prisoners of war from Fort Dix who refused to go back to Russia. Under the Yalta agreement, they were to be forcibly repatriated to the Soviet Union anyway. This was done in total secrecy. No member of the Settlement's staff knew the details or purpose of this operation. In the summer of 1946, two of these prisoners jumped out of the windows of Christodora House. One died, the other managed to escape. There were eyewitnesses, but the incident was not reported in any of the New York papers. The operation moved elsewhere immediately afterward.

What transpired in 1947 has all the elements of mystery, suspense, political intrigue, and human drama. It makes today's anti-poverty rip-offs seem like child's play.

The city fathers suddenly decided that what the city needed was a Youth Detention Facility. They thought the Christodora House would be perfect for that purpose. Christodora leadership at that time was floundering. The city made an offer for the building which was difficult to resist: $2.6 million in cash and adequate space in the newly constructed Jacob Riis housing complex on Avenue D. The only catch was that the Settlement had to go to two buildings: one on Eighth Street and one on Tenth Street along Avenue D. It was a most devious offer.

A big split developed among the Christodora Board of Managers. The conservative faction with whom the director, Mr. Beal, was thought to be aligned, argued for the sale, citing the ever-rising maintenance costs and rising deficits (the Residence Club was not paying for itself). The liberals argued that leaving the building and going to another neighborhood would be a terrible blow to a community served so long and with such dedication by the Settlement staff. Still another group of managers, the realists, tried to convince city officials that it would simply be too costly to convert the building into, basically, a jail.

The Board of Managers rejected the city offer by a slim majority. Then the city pulled a fast one. They came in and condemned the entire building, citing some minor violations. This was a sham, of course. The building was in fine shape. At the next board meeting, after intensive maneuvering, the realists caved in. The city's offer was accepted and the Settlement House moved soon thereafter to two locations on Avenue D.

After the city took possession of the building, they conducted an extensive study and found that what the realists were telling them was true. Converting the building to a secure facility would indeed be too costly. So they decided to build the Youth Detention Center from scratch in the Bronx (on Spafford Avenue). However, they were now stuck with an empty skyscraper.

Enter all the elements of a Marx Brothers movie. Incredibly, the city offered to sell the building back to the Christodora House. The same officials who only a few months before were trying to push the Settlement House out, were running around begging and pressuring the Board members into buying back the building. Only it just wasn't possible for the Settlement House to move back for many reasons.

A big scandal was in the making. The city had to do something, and fast. First, they clamped the lid of secrecy over the entire matter. Some of their records vanished; some were falsified; key officials were quietly shifted to other boroughs.

The city then moved a unit of the Welfare Department, called the Department of Employment and Training, into the building. It was an unadulterated whitewash to get the reporters from the *Journal American*, who were close to cracking the story, off the scent.

That welfare "operation" was a "paper operation," but the woman in charge of it was an able, seasoned, and crafty bureaucrat. She wrote glowing, reports about her achievements. In time, everyone forgot that the building was virtually empty. As far as the city was concerned, it was used to full capacity.

The woman in charge was also farsighted enough not to allow anyone from the neighborhood into the building. The use of the gymnasiums and the pool were now denied to local kids. She would even order that the donated used clothing be burned rather than distribute it to the local poor. Some residents say she feared that clothing donated by the uptown whites would fall into the hands of the Puerto Ricans and blacks who were moving into the area.

Neighborhood people, as well as community groups, knew that there was nothing happening in the building. In 1951, St. Brigid's Church, a large Catholic congregation in the community, decided to offer the city one million dollars with the idea of using part of the Christodora building to replace its ancient and overcrowded parochial school.

The city indignantly refused the offer since they still pretended that the building was being used. So the Welfare Department "operation" worked out of the nearly empty building for over six years. Eventually, someone in the city looked at the maintenance costs and was horrified. The city quietly closed the building and retired the "dedicated public servant" who ran her "paper operation." The building remained closed for over ten years. It was, however, in very good shape and everything in it was working. It was a ship in mothballs.

The Displaced Settlement House

After moving from the Avenue B building, the Christodora Settlement House was in a new neighborhood. It was also now divided into two parts: two floors of the Jacob Riis housing complex on 10th Street and Avenue D, and almost three floors on Eighth Street and Ave. D.

The Jacob Riis housing complex was originally build for the returning World War II veterans and their families, but even as early as 1947, it already had a sizeable welfare population, many of whom were elderly.

There were strong tenant organizations in the crowded housing complex who resented the free space that the city had allocated to the Settlement and immediately demanded meaningful programs from its staff.

These demands were for improving services to the elderly women in particular, establishing expanded daycare facilities for preschoolers, after-school tutoring for public and private school children, expansion of their daycare and summer camp facilities, hiring of neighborhood residents, and so on.

The floundering and somewhat demoralized leadership of the Christodora House, not used to any demands from the politically naive community around Tompkins Square Park, was further demoralized and divided by this unexpected and strong pressure.

They shifted the main focus back to social problems. The music school was closed. A few arts-related programs were also dropped. They expanded their summer camp and daycare facilities. But the demands continued.

In an effort to expand their area of service, they acquired a brownstone on 151 Avenue B, two doors from their old building, and the former Recreation Rooms Settlement on First Street near First Avenue.

They departed from their former philosophy and trained and hired social workers who were community residents.

According to one former Christodora social worker whom I interviewed, the problem was partly their inertia, their unwillingness to promote outreach into the community. That worker thought it originated with their director, Mr. Beal, who appeared to be a remote and inaccessible man, trying to run the settlement as if it were a business.

With Mr. Slobodin assuming the directorship of the Christodora House in 1958, the Settlement experienced a brief renaissance. There were, however, many new factors on the Lower East Side scene. The neighborhood changed radically, once again. There was a large influx of Puerto Rican and Slavic immigrants. The veterans in Jacob Riis housing project moved out. It became housing for people on welfare and other forms of public assistance. New York City's social services had improved considerably. Some of their social programs were the exact duplicates of Christodora's former programs. Many Christodora workers began working for the city.

When the Mobilization for Youth project (MFY) was launched on the Lower East Side by Henry Street Settlement and five other Settlement Houses, including the Christodora House, the Board of Managers expressed concern that they were in direct competition with one of the projects they had helped to launch. The decision was made to get out of the city altogether and put their efforts into their Bound Brook Summer Camp activities.

They argued that federal, state, and city governments, who were now supporting youth activities in the ghettos of the inner cities, did not give any support to summer camps or activities, leaving it to private foundations, like the Christodora House. Presently, the Christodora Foundation supports three summer camps for city kids in northern New Jersey.

Whether the decision to leave the East Village was the right one or a cop-out, the departure of the Settlement House left a great void in our East Village community. It certainly contributed to the neighborhood's rapid deterioration, especially east of Avenue B.

I have tried not to rely too much on just the available research material. I have found some of the newspaper and magazine accounts pertaining to the Christodora House to be misleading, or downright erroneous. The *New York Times* for example, made basic errors in its 1928 article; and then again in 1969 and 1971.

Personal accounts give a more accurate picture. A seventy-year-old Vista volunteer working in the area remembered living at the Christodora Residence Club at the time Hitler invaded Norway. A Ukrainian woman who worked as a maid in the same residence recalled some fascinating details of day-to-day operations of the House. And many others shared their memories: A local businessman who played basketball in the old brownstone and belonged to their famous 202 Boy Scout troop. Several former teachers and social workers. A former World War II veteran who organized their "One to One" Club working with retarded children. A well-known composer who went to their music school. An actor who vividly remembers their Christmas and Halloween celebrations, and who learned to swim in the Christodora pool.

A Radical Political and Social History of the Lower East Side

Several mothers who had children enrolled in various activities. A former welfare official. A Russian soldier who was held there briefly after World War II and escaped before he could be forcibly repatriated to the Soviet Union. A retired Italian city sanitation worker who was born next door to the original Young Women's Settlement (167 Avenue B), and many more.

So far, I have interviewed over thirty people, including the current director and administrator of the Christodora Fund, Mr. Steven Slobodin. I have plans to interview about a dozen more people whose lives have been touched in some way by this unique Settlement House. Actor Tony Curtis's entire life was changed when he was brought to the Settlement House as a juvenile delinquent, and fell under the influence of Paul Schwartz. Paul was one of the House's best social workers, and he introduced Tony to the Theatre Club.

The dead characters are just as important as the living. People like Christine Isobel McCall and Sara Libby Carson; Mr. and Mrs. Arthur Curtiss James; Dr. Stanton Coit and Lillian Wald; George and Ira Gershwin; Jacob Riis and Jane Addams; Bird C. Coler and Henry Pelton; Commissioner Rhatigan and Mayor O'Dwyer; Mrs. Roosevelt and Mrs. Hall; Governor Dewey and Governor Harriman; and Moise, the famous doorman, handyman and jack-of-all-trades at both the old and new houses.

The Radicals Take Over Tompkins Square Community Center

This particular period I remember only too well. Actually, I was only peripherally involved with the Tompkins Square Community Center (TSCC), helping out with their food co-op in the late '60s. But many of my friends, both radicals and simple people trying to help our already disintegrating community, were deeply involved in running the center. Some of the radicals who were young then are still making headlines. People involved in the Brinks job, Joanne Chesimard, Antony La Borde, Donald Weems; just about all of the Who's Who of the black/white radical establishment was at one time or another inside the Christodora House, which they controlled for four years.

Many plots against "imperialist Amerik-k-ka" were hatched in the building. Some, such as one to kidnap Lyndon Johnson, were too fantastic to go beyond the talking stage. Others, such as the "Panthers 21" plot to blow up the Statue of Liberty, have received nationwide attention and resulted in trials, frame-ups, convictions, reversals, and so on.

There might have been a large cache of weapons hidden in the building, probably in the flooded sub-basement. The infamous .9mm pistols, some sub-machine guns, grenades and probably some plastic explosives. It's hardly a coincidence that after the radicals had finally been evicted from the building, patrolmen Rocco and Laurie were massacred with .9mm pistols on the corner of 11th Street and Avenue B, only two blocks from the Christodora House.

"Evicted" in this case is not exactly the right word. I recall vividly hundreds of Tactical Force police in battle gear surrounding the building, positioning themselves on nearby rooftops. A helicopter buzzed near the Christodora roof, its machine gun trained on the building. Avenue B and East Ninth Street were closed to traffic. All the people in Tompkins Square Park were forced to leave. The park was sealed off completely.

From the roof of my building on Seventh Street and Avenue B, a couple of friends and I watched this doomsday scenario unfold. We were led to believe by local radical mouthpieces that there were four hundred teenagers inside who had sworn to defend the building to their death. They were prepared to fight room by room and then blow themselves up, rather than surrender to "the pigs." It was supposed to be another Stalingrad. Everyone anticipated a huge battle.

We did see what looked like machine gun barrels sticking out of the top floor windows. The loudspeakers blared back and forth as various city officials scurried around the building trying to negotiate something. Suddenly the loudspeaker stopped.

There was a brief battle. Later, one of the kids who was inside told me what happened in detail. From my roof, we could see the helicopter drop a few tear gas grenades into the upper windows. A platoon of cops stormed the building from the roof of P.S. 64. Simultaneously, another unit burst through the front door. I saw a group of about a dozen frightened teenagers run out from the side entrance with their hands in the air. They were handcuffed quickly and hustled into a bus waiting along East Ninth Street. Then the cops led a few men and women, some of whom were screaming, out of the building. The adults were not handcuffed. They seemed to be arguing with the police and city brass. There were a few cops left by the entrance, but the radical era was definitely over. The next morning, city workers boarded up the doors. This happened in 1972 and the building remained shut for fourteen years.

The radical era began with the Lindsay administration in 1966. When Lindsay was sworn in as Mayor, the East Village from 14th Street to Houston Street, and Avenue A to Avenue D was a cohesive, bustling neighborhood with a mixed lower-income population. There were over two thousand small businesses owned and operated mostly by local residents. Along Avenues C and D, there were many vegetable markets, butcher shops, fish stores, dozens of bakeries, clothing stores, shoe stores and shoe repair shops, pharmacies, delis, candy stores, restaurants and even small toy factories. Anything and everything could be bought and sold.

In terms of quality of life, 1966 wasn't so bad. There was practically no crime and no abandoned or burned-out buildings. The children were safe even in the public schools. There was little racial or ethnic animosity, mainly because all the working poor were from many ethnic and racial backgrounds. There were about fifteen hundred people living on each block. Puerto Ricans and Slavs (Polish, Russian, Ukrainian and Carpatno Russians) comprised the major population, followed closely by Bohemians, Jews, Blacks and Albanians. There were still a few small Irish and Italian enclaves. Rent was cheap. In just a few years, an average family could save enough money to move to Greenpoint, Brooklyn or New Jersey. Many of the people, especially the elderly, did not want to move anywhere. They had their friends and relatives right in the neighborhood. It was their small village.

A Radical Political and Social History of the Lower East Side

Actually, the area was more like a town. It also served the sprawling Jacob Riis and Lillian Wald housing complexes between Avenue D and FDR Drive.

This not-so-little town became one of America's Hiroshimas, destroyed by human greed and the corruption of "poverty-pimp" politics first introduced by Mr. Lindsay. I and many of my friends living in the area had voted for him in 1965.

As we watched our community being destroyed during his administration, the truth of one proverb often came to mind: "The road to hell is paved with good intentions."

The intentions *were* great. Community control, an infusion of massive anti-poverty funds into the area to create new youth projects, rehabilitation of the old tenements, and many other plans.

The only problem was that the Lindsay Administration Commissioners in charge of these various great projects were like Lindsay himself-wealthy, white, liberal politicians. They were unaware of the fact that in addition to Blacks and Puerto Ricans, there were also poor whites living in New York. In our area of the East Village, these poor Whites accounted for over 60 percent of the population.

Everything the Lindsay administration introduced was done on a racial basis. It did not work even in predominantly Puerto Rican and Black areas, such as the South Bronx and Williamsburg. In the East Village, it was a disaster.

Let me give a mild example of how such a policy worked at the street level. Two teenagers I knew lived in the same house on my block for at least ten years. One was Polish and one Puerto Rican. Every year the two of them got summer jobs with the Parks Department. In 1966, the Puerto Rican kid got the job but the Polish kid did not because he was white. When he got home, his Puerto Rican friend suggested that he change his name from Robert to Roberto and the ending of his last name from -ski to -oz. He did and got the job. But this story has no happy ending. The seeds of racism . . .

[Editor's note: This is where the article ends, Mr. Kapralov passed away before he was able to finish this piece, or the book he planned on expanding it into.]

Chapter 12

Under the Tar the Beach
By Peter Lamborn Wilson

When I got back to New York City in 1980 after twelve years away (North Africa, Lebanon, Turkey, Iran, India) I re-settled on the Upper West Side. In the '60s it'd had its own boho community, but now most of the old crowd were gone, dead, or grown up. After a few years it began to get boring and expensive, and I decided to emigrate — no weaker word can express the sense of departure — to the Lower East Side.

Got a real chap apartment on East 7th Street. Later I learned that in the '50s, Ginsberg and Kerouac had roomed together in my tenement, and Ginsberg showed me old famous photos of Jack on the fire escape and "tar beach" roof. This was before Ginsberg moved to 12th Street with Peter Orlovsky.

In the '80s the Lower East Side still seemed like the edge of things — the "Margin." Performance art was born then, and I spent a lot of time at the Alchemical Space, an anarchist coal cellar theater on East Ninth. Ginsberg, Herbert Huncke, Orlovsky, Harry Smith, the Living Theater, lunch with Quentin Crisp, jam sessions with Don Cherry, riots in Tompkins Square Park, all were part of life down there. Very traditional là-bas, "down there": coffee at Life Café, meetings at the LBC (Libertarian Book Club), one of the oldest anarchist orgs in America, founded by comrades of Emma Goldman. Some of them were active into the 1990s, for example, Sam Dolgoff, Mel Most, "Brand" Arrigoni, and so on.

An American historian once quipped that "there's no such thing as the New Age" because in the 19th century, America already had Spiritualism ("channeling"), new religions, feminism, alternative medicine, yearnings for the mystic East and so on. He might've added that there's no such thing as "New Left" either, since the 19th century also always had riots in Tompkins Square Park. Some of the same organizations were still around and functioning, like the IWW (International Workers of the World).

Politically the really "new" admixture in the 1980s came from European Situationism, that possibly poisonous and certainly intoxicating flower dropped from the vine of May 1968, which had finally percolated through the language barrier and begun to influence the old American New Left or its shattered remnants. Aside from Situ influence on theory it also generated a praxis of Debordian intransigence, Deleuzo-Guattarian "molecularity," the old, old Romantic program of deliberate derangement of the senses, a Late Punk mentality and style-negation of the negation of the negation . . . ad infinitum.

In an odd way, I consider the 1980s to be almost a lost or forgotten decade. I don't have the sense that many social historians are aware of (or are willing to discuss) the radical cultural ferment and political heat of that era. In part, this weird amnesia must be due to the peculiar nature of the abrupt and maybe "tragic" end of the decade (1989-91) -when Global

A Radical Political and Social History of the Lower East Side

Capital in its great triumph buried the whole Idea of the Social under the cacavalanche of consumer ecstasy and eternal terror. Almost never do I hear or read any indication that for some of us aging hippies, the '80s were nearly as interesting as — in some ways more interesting than — the Holy Sixties. I see the *New York Times* Lifestyle section (or some similar oracle) has recently declared that the '80s are "In" but I'm sure they haven't the foggiest notion of *our* '80s. Their bleats of nostalgia are all for commodities and commercial popcult drek, not for the Marginal Scene and its ethic of resistance.

So — the '80s were a sort of utopian era, and the LES was a utopian zone (with extensions in Brooklyn). For me, the local nodes of this time/zone included the LBC ("plumbline" anarchism), the John Henry Mackay Society (Individualist/Philosophical anarchism), Mel Most's Living Theater "Arts Section" of the IWW (anarcho-syndicalism), Autonomedia/Semiotext (no particular "line" but publishers of French PoMo and Situ material, and with links to independent Marxism as well as anarchism), and "spaces" like the Alchemical, and later the Gargoyle Méchanique on Avenue B.

Elsewhere in this book you'll find plenty of other nodes — these were my own coordinates. Non-locally, the pattern included certain places but even more certain zines-the Factsheet Five movement, the zine scene and alternative press world — such as *Popular Reality* or *Dharma Combat*, and of course the various editions of the *Moorish Science Monitor*; collage art by James Koehnline, Freddy Baer or Winston Smith; WBAI radio (I call it "non-local" because it broadcasts beyond Manhattan, but the station itself was always a local node of radical something-or-other); and strongholds of the old BeatnikWorld such as the Jack Kerouac School of Disembodied Poetics in Boulder, Colorado, or City Lights Books in San Francisco. Again, I mention only the ones that counted for me personally. Needless to say there were thousands more, and — believe it or not, children — there was a real network then, even Before the Internet!

In general, this "world" was saturated with good drugs thanks to the work of the young "Third Generation" psychedelic movement — and with good sex-at least until around '85 or '87 when the NeoCon Body Hatred movement and the War on (some) Drugs began to impinge more and more on everyone's goodtime consciousness. I never squatted — it would've cost more than my rent, believe me — but of course the squat movement and the community garden movement always seemed to me the very bedrock praxis of the era: *act loca*, spatial concentration rather than mediated experience and spatial deconcentration. Resistance to gentrification/capitalization of neighborhood communities — through strategic alliances between working class and lumpenprole activisms.

Around '86-'87, there was a massive attempt to invade the LES on behalf of real estate speculators and Reagan/Thatcherite freemarket ideologues — art galleries bloomed overnight, junkies were rounded up and deported, squats were attacked, etc. This putsch failed because the Market (stretched tight, no doubt, by the final econo-war drive against the Evil Empire) collapsed ignominiously in '87.

Not just the '80s but the whole 20th century (and Second Millennium) came to a premature end in 1989 with the fall of the Berlin Wall. Suddenly the *Spectacle* — the false dialectic of the USA vs. USSR — ground to a halt. The "institutional Left," which for fifty years had based its politics on this situation (pro, con, or neutral) also seemed to collapse. The "margin" between the two stupid superpowers disappeared, and along with it the cultural and political marginality of the LES, the zine world, and even anarchism itself seemed to implode. The last and largest Anarchist Gathering, San Francisco 1989, marked the end of an era, though most of us failed to realize it at the time. The same year saw the first "Pure" or postmodern war, the Gulf War, and the universal apotheosis of neo-liberalism.

It's true that a new movement is trying hard to *appear*, to carry the movement of the Social into the global era. The Zapatista uprising in '94 emerged as the first real armed resistance to Globalism, hence the first postmodern revolt, as the *New York Times* called it sneeringly. The Anti-Globalization movement, if it is a movement, is trying to focus the struggle and gather up the remnants. The prospects, however, remain grim. As for the LES, the forces of McDisneyfication began a new assault around 1995 — or at least that's when I began to notice it. Squats were attacked with *tanks*. Rents began to skyrocket. Bohemia was holding on by the skin of its teeth. Precious gardens were bulldozed and cheap shitty yuppie housing was jacked up in the old sad vacant lots.

There was an old Dominican guy who had a tiny garden next to my building, with flowers, Virgin Mary, chairs, strange white "Chinese" chickens, and afternoons of rum and dominoes. He got swept away. After a few months of hideous pile-driving construction, a big new apartment building appeared. In the lobby I saw artsy b&w photos of picturesque LES people like crusty-punk girls and old Dominican guys — the very people displaced to raise this deluxe lazarette — like trophies in some rod 'n' gun club of bourgeois splendor. "Everything that once was real moves away into representation."

Everyone knows that Capital uses artists and bohemians as pioneers of gentrification. Art must somehow share complicity in this. Somewhere there's blame to be meted out. Maybe I didn't want to look too closely into this. In any case I'd run out of energy. I couldn't take the *noise* anymore, the sheer cacophony of gleeful Business-Zone triumphalism as it plowed under all the former No-Go Zones and planted its money-trees, its media-fungus, its neo-racist algae-slime. Death by advertising.

So I left NYC and moved to the country. Kept my apartment however-the rent was still so low (since we tenants were in fact the "landlord") that I could afford to. I happened to be there on September 11, 2001. A friend phoned and told me what was going on. I witnessed the buildings' collapse from my roof, from the old tar beach where Jack once posed in virile white teeshirt. Oddly, there was no noise.

Not that I ever liked the buildings, those cloned slabs symbolizing the aesthetic emptiness of greed and the arrogance of Wall Street brutalism. But I don't want to deal with that symbolism now. Just to say — the destruction and absence of the towers poisoned the view even more than their presence. The cloud of ghost dust drove me away. I don't know what that "means." If anything.

Peter Lamborn Wilson   April, MMII

Chapter 13

Squatting
By Colin Moynihan

Passersby who stroll down the newly gentrified blocks of Avenue C that stretch from East 14th Street to Houston Street are sometimes puzzled as they pass by an old brick tenement on the west side of the avenue just below East 10th street. The building has a weathered brick façade and a black metal door. The door has no windows and there is no intercom system. Displayed in an upstairs window of the building is a sign that reads "This land not for sale." As recently as the mid-90s many of the people who now pause to gaze at this building and wonder aloud what goes on inside, would have been unlikely to venture deep into the Lower East Side. But these days, the same new restaurants and shops that lure visitors from other areas provide a heightened contrast that makes the unusual building stand out more than ever.

The building in question is a squat. Throughout the 1980s and 1990s, dozens, perhaps as many as hundreds of squats dotted the Lower East Side. During those decades, countless buildings in the neighborhood were abandoned by tenants and landlords. Fires, some set accidentally, others the result of arson, were a common occurrence. Rubble strewn lots dominated parts of the landscape. On some blocks, detritus and crumbled brick and mortar filled the majority of the lots with only an occasional, solitary building standing intact. Some of the buildings that remained became occupied by drug dealers or were turned into shooting galleries. At the same time corner drug bazaars operated openly throughout the day and night.

While many buildings were destroyed or otherwise uninhabitable, landlords shut down still more. They were employing a practice known as "warehousing," in which buildings in a blighted area are held empty until a time in the future when their value might rise. The City of New York also took over control of hundreds of properties in the neighborhood, most of which were seized through tax foreclosure, and kept them vacant. The result of this combination of factors was to create a housing shortage on the Lower East Side, while increasing rent in the existing housing stock.

Then the squatters came. They were inspired by a range of influences, including the Dutch Provos of the 1960s, who took over empty buildings, and further back to 19th Century utopian communes such as those organized in France by Charles Fourier. Other influences were more contemporary: a punk rock-style approach that extolled the virtues of DIY (or "do it yourself") culture, combined with a natural stance of anti-authoritarianism, both driven by a desire for affordable housing.

The squatters were a mixture of working families, artists, skilled tradesmen and anarchists. They used sledgehammers to knock down bricked up doorways to city-owned buildings and then moved in. Most of the buildings were in poor shape. There was no heat or hot water. The roofs were punctured by holes or nonexistent and often pigeons had taken to nesting inside. At times entire floors had been removed or had caved in, leaving behind only ghostly joists spanning the width of a building on upper floors. The squatters repaired the buildings as they lived inside, patching roofs, repairing drainlines and repointing brick facades.

But as the squatters proliferated, they drew unwelcome attention from the city. Officials considered the squatters little more than trespassers and during the '80s and '90s evicted dozens of buildings. Some of the evictions involved prolonged sieges and conflicts. In 1995 the evictions culminated on East 13th Street when hundreds of police wearing visored helmets and supported by an armored personnel carrier flooded onto the block between Avenue A and Avenue B and evicted residents from three squats there. The eviction was broadcast on television and reported the next day in newspapers.

In August 2002, the City of New York made a startling announcement. The Department of Housing Preservation and Development, which held the deeds to the thirteen remaining squats on the Lower East Side, said that they had reached an agreement with the squatters and with the Urban Homesteaders Assistance Board, a non-profit organization. The agreement stipulated that the city was turning over ownership of twelve of the buildings to UHAB. After the squats were brought up to code, UHAB would then turn possession over to the squatters, with the proviso that the buildings would be maintained as low-income dwellings.

The squats were to be turned into a specific style of low-income housing co-op, known as HDFCs. Such buildings were established throughout the city in the late 1980s and the 1990s under the aegis of the Housing Development Fund Corporation. Strict income guidelines governed who was eligible to live in those buildings. The buildings payed low tax rates, and maintenance charges for those who live in them is also low — generally ranging from $300 to $600 per month.

HDFC buildings are also different from more conventional co-ops in that they are not intended to be speculative investments. Owners of apartments in such buildings are expected not to sell their dwellings at market rate. They must also use such apartments as their primary residences, which means they must stay there at least 183 days per year. Many HDFC buildings also do the work of managing the building — paying water bills and taxes, organizing repairs, making decisions on who will move into available apartments — on their own, without the help or guidance of a management company.

In most respects the proposed transfer was welcomed by the squatters. Although there were those who opposed legality on philosophical grounds, thinking that ownership of private property is wrong, there were many others who said their goal as squatters all along had merely been to establish low-income housing that could be sustained for generations. The fact that the HDFCs, with their emphasis on community, democratic decision-making and commitment to remaining outside the mainstream real estate market, seemed to operate already in ways the squats could easily adapt to, made the plan seem logical to them.

A Radical Political and Social History of the Lower East Side

It comes as little surprise that squatters who had spent years living under the threat of eviction, some of whom went to bed each night with a packed knapsack of clothes and valuables next to their mattresses, would greet the city's proposal with relief. It's an altogether more interesting and complex question, however, to wonder why the city was motivated to enter into a compromise with the squatters.

Throughout the 1980s and the 1990s, city officials, real estate developers and local landlords regularly criticized the squatters as criminals, saying that their raffish, disorderly presence kept property values low and impeded the rejuvenation of the neighborhood. Some of the most ardent enemies of the squatters were the non-profit housing groups that competed with them for city-owned buildings. The local political champion of these interests was Antonio Pagan, a conservative Democrat who represented the neighborhood on the City Council, and helped funnel many buildings into programs controlled by political allies. In response, squatters held angry demonstrations at local community board meetings. One squatter hurled a cream filled cake into the face of the board chairman. Others lit off stink bombs at a meeting, then after rushing outside, secured the exits behind them with bicycle locks. One of the most significant disturbances occurred at a community board meeting at the Great Hall at Cooper Union, the same hall where Abraham Lincoln delivered a famous campaign speech in 1860. There in 1993, a melee took place after squatters protesting the eviction of the Glass House squat on Avenue D ignited a smoke bomb and pulled a fire alarm. A dozen people were arrested, including a board member named Margarita Lopez, who later beat Antonio Pagan in an election and took over his city council seat. While the city negotiated with UHAB over the future of the squats, Lopez was one of the council members who helped to hammer out the resulting agreement.

Theories about the city's eventual change of heart abound, but there is little hard evidence to support any of the ideas. The transfer was not announced formally by the city. Instead it was leaked by UHAB, in the form of an internet story on the website of City Limits magazine, which shares an office with UHAB. That day, a spokeswoman for the Department of Housing Preservation & Development, the agency that had official control over the squats, explained the decision to make the deal to a reporter by saying that the squatters who lived in the buildings at the time of the agreement were different from the ones who had clashed with the city in earlier times. The statement was inaccurate, as the official who made it perhaps knew, but the nature of the falsity underscores the fact that the city was not eager to broadcast their agreement with former foes.

There are some familiar with the squatter community who insist that the only reason that any squats remained into the year 2000 was through the promise of disruption and the threat of violence. That is to say, the squatters of the Lower East Side had for years made evictions a difficult, expensive and unpopular exercise for the city. By barricading themselves inside their buildings, rather than surrendering peacefully, the squatters ensured that blocks surrounding their buildings would be blocked off and filled with police, emergency services officers, ambulances, arrest vans and various heavy-duty trucks containing police equipment. The drama entailed in the evictions also made the events newsworthy. And while reporters were not partisans working on behalf of the squatters, there are few readers or viewers who take kindly to the idea of armed evictions, no matter how grungy in appearance the evictees. Not to mention the fact that it's difficult for any police department to seem sympathetic when rolling an armored personnel carrier through the streets.

The thought follows that as the once blighted blocks of the Lower East Side, where drug bazaars, stabbings and arson were formerly common, came to be dotted by restaurants and boutiques, as rents rose, and as politically disconnected residents were replaced by those with a more developed capacity for official-style outrage, it became less viable for the city to shut down entire blocks in the area. A populace that once suffered such spectacles without loud complaint was replaced by a populace that while not entirely sympathetic to the idea of sweat equity, might sum up their discontent with evictions by declaring "If I'm paying $1,800 a month to live on this street I damn well want to be able to come and go as I please. And I want to do so without cops on my roof, without angry crowds making noise outside my window"

In short, the demographic and economic changes on the Lower East Side during the second half of the 1990s created a reality in which squat evictions were no longer politically feasible for the city. The irony that underlies this idea is that the gentrification that the squatters accurately considered a threat to their own existence, might in the long run have played a role in their preservation.

It is now certain that the squats have a future on the Lower East Side. It is not yet clear, however, what that future holds. Work has been going on slowly since the transfer of the buildings and some squats, like Umbrella House and 209 East 7th Street, now have new boilers. Others have become disenchanted with UHAB and are angry about what they perceive as a delayed timetable for the transference of building deeds.

Probably the most crucial issues that the squatters will face in the coming years will center upon how they define themselves and run their own buildings. HDFC buildings in Manhattan have notoriously been places where internecine disputes and lawsuits are common. For the squatters, who are used to making decisions outside of the mainstream legal system, it may not be easy to begin resolving differences in front of court-appointed referees or housing court judges. There are also those who fear that the squats will somehow lose their unique characteristics now that they have become legitimate in the eyes of the law. That seems unlikely, though, at least in comparison to the urban landscape that nowadays surrounds the squats.

New York City, after all, is a place of change, rebirth and evolution. And nowhere over the last decade or so has rapid, drastic change been more evident than on the Lower East Side. That the squatters have survived the gentrification that has suffused the area over the last several years is surprising. The fact that they have a history and a culture of their own to draw upon makes them unique regardless of what course they take next. In 2003, a group of squatters received a grant from New York State and began assembling an archive that aims to document and preserve their history. Included in the collection are diaries, fliers, posters, legal papers and artifacts recovered from the buildings they live in. During that time, one squatter, who lives on East 7th Street, reflected on the future and the present. "We're still here," he said. "And we're not going anywhere."

Chapter 14

The Tompkins Square Anarchists
(Prologue to a story not yet written)
By Seth Tobocman

At 11 pm on the night of August 6th 1988, a small group of us gathered at the 8th Street entrance to Tompkins Square Park on the Lower East Side of New York City. We embraced one another, greeting each other warmly. There was an air of fear and anticipation. I knew every face in that crowd. Soon a ring of police in riot gear had formed around us. The park was full of police vehicles. Sharpshooters looked down from rooftops. A helicopter swooped low over our heads. We were not only there to protest a midnight curfew on Tompkins Park, we were there to take a stand on the totality of American politics and culture at that time. What followed would be known as the 1988 Tompkins Square Riot, and would make headlines around the world. The papers would attribute the Riot and the movement that followed it to a mysterious group of Tompkins Square anarchists who had come out of nowhere. But in truth, the situation had been developing quietly for at least ten years.

To understand the Tompkins Square riot, you have to understand the 1980s. Let us first dispense with this notion that the '80s were a big-spending era of easy money and optimism. To see the '80s this way is to look at the world through the eyes of the very small section of the population who did well in a declining economy. President Ronald Reagan was not your lovable, but senile grandfather. Reagan put nuclear weapons in Europe (a policy started by Carter) and publicly joked about starting a war with Russia. He sponsored death squads in El Salvador, overthrew the government of Grenada and undermined the government of Nicaragua. Through overt aid to rebels in Afghanistan and covert aid to Iran he built up the Islamic fundamentalist movement that has caused so much suffering in recent years. It was on Reagan's watch that Israeli general Ariel Sharon invaded Lebanon, resulting in a massacre of Palestinian refugees.

While Reagan raised the American flag overseas, he was anything but an economic nationalist. His 'free trade' policies opened the borders to foreign goods. Whole American cities shut down as industries either went belly up, or moved to foreign countries where U.S.-backed dictators had kept labor costs low by crushing unions. Reagan's patriotism was a cover for the first wave of what is now called economic globalization.

In inner city ghettos like Manhattan's Lower East Side, we had already been hit hard in the '70s by a policy called "benign neglect." The budget for the fire department and other city services had been cut, allowing slumlords to burn their buildings. Open drug dealing was tolerated. The urban environment became a wilderness, ripe for exploitation by a new type of real estate pioneer. In the '80s we saw the second phase of what we came to see as a deliberate policy. The neighborhood was renovated, but not for the poor people who lived there. A new urban middle class attached to the booming stock market moved in. Rents went up. Many people became homeless. Others found themselves in a changed environment, suddenly treated like outsiders on streets where they had lived for years.

It is not surprising that these conditions would breed resistance. It is surprising there wasn't more. There was nothing on the scale of today's anti-globalization movement. Part of the blame must fall on the liberal media and so called progressive politicians, who took a defeatist position right from the start.

For example: In fall of 1982, I was part of a group of about 12 people who staged a sit-in in the offices of Senator D'amato to protest the U.S. bombing of El Salvador. There was a *Village Voice* intern who sat with us singing along with us and taking notes. When the police came in, he got up. The rest of us were dragged out in brutal fashion. Days later I went to the Voice to find out about the article I had assumed he was writing. The intern told me that he had pitched the story to his editor, who said that the Voice had published lots of stories like that in the '60s but that the '60s were over. I wonder how many actions took place in the 1980s that we will never hear about because of editors like that. For sure, a lot of people died in Latin America in the 1980s and there should have been a stronger response.

As young men and women who were angry about the direction our country, city and neighborhood was headed in, it was hard to know where to turn. Most of the activist groups we encountered were top heavy with older folks who survived the '60s and now fancied themselves leaders. It was hard to get our peers interesting in working with such groups.

Josh Whalen, Eric Drooker, Paul Hewitt and I formed an affinity group of sorts. We put up our own political posters and graffiti independent of any organization, and developed an analysis linking foreign wars to the war on the poor here in the city. Other small crews, most notably the nihilist industrial band Missing Foundation, took a similar approach.

In 1986, Josh persuaded us to help him organize a New Year's Eve rock concert by telling us that at the end of the show the rock 'n' rollers would pour out into the street and smash the doors of the Christodora House (a much-hated condominium). The concert happened, much radical propaganda was distributed, and radical statements were made from the stage, but no riot ensued. It is hard to believe we put faith in such a scenario. It is harder to believe that in 1988, exactly that scenario would take place. In the 1988 police riot, the punks would trash the Christodora. No responsible community organizer would put stock in the idea that white hardcore kids could be frontline troops in the battle against gentrification. Let's hear it for irresponsible community organizers!

Every popular movement of the 20th century has promised to expropriate wealth from those who are hoarding it and give it to people who need it. The squatters were actually doing this. Because of many years of arson and neglect, the City owned many abandoned buildings and was doing nothing with them. The squatters would break into these buildings and make them into homes. Likewise, gardeners would squat vacant city owned lots and make them green. Eventually the City would try to evict these people and there would be confrontations.

A Radical Political and Social History of the Lower East Side

Through working on and defending the squats, we got a chance to put our ideas into practice and we created a network of activists who were tested in real situations and could be relied upon in a crunch. We organized the Eviction Watch phone tree, which would be called when cops came to evict a building. This phone tree would eventually be used to organized other types of actions as well.

One of the early uses of the phone tree was in defense of homeless people who were being brutalized by guards in the shelter system. Homelessness became a word in the 1980s as economic conditions got worse. This new category of being defined entirely by what he or she did not have, began to organize themselves, creating groups like the Union of the Homeless and the Revolutionary Homeless Organization. We sought to ally ourselves with this new movement. New squats were being opened all the time and many of us had messianic visions of housing all of the homeless in city-owned abandoned buildings.

Long before we started to slug it out with the cops we were attacked by local political hacks. Not-for-profits wanted the buildings squatters lived in and the lots gardeners cultivated for their projects. Many of these projects involved renovating buildings, providing some units for low-income tenants, then renovating the rest as luxury units. In other words, cash cows for the not-for-profits. But even if you accept the altruistic-sounding names of these groups at face value, the fact is that at that time there was plenty of abandoned property to renovate. It was a City policy to get different groups fighting each other over a few plots of land while offering the rest to developers. Charles King, president of Housing Works, told me, "When we went to the City and asked them for a place to build housing for people with AIDS, they said, 'What do you want, a squat or a garden?'"

Those allied with the not-for-profit housing groups have commented ad nauseum on our alleged "whiteness." To be sure, we could have done a better job of outreach in the Puerto Rican community. It would have been easier to do that without interested parties spreading rumors and lies against us. But the Tompkins Square movement had an odd type of diversity. It included people of all ages although a significant section were in their early 20s. There were construction workers, cab drivers, drug addicts and sex workers, ex-cons and musicians. Every nationality was represented. And probably every sexual preference. There were very few college students. Most of us didn't think of ourselves as anarchists. It was our actions that made us anarchists. We were the riff raff out on a mission.

Being hated by liberals, ignored by the press and harassed by the cops had its good side. We had no reputations to protect, no allies to alienate. We were regarded with complete contempt by city officials, but that didn't stop us. We were free to act. We had no shame. I came to think of a good activist as someone who didn't care if a bucket of shit was dumped on his head.

So we arrived at August 6th 1988 as a small, marginal group of people with a lot of pent-up frustration. But the police riot would change that. That night the NYPD ran through the streets of the Lower East Side recruiting new anarchists with their nightsticks. After one night of rioting the beleaguered mayor lifted the curfew and we had the proof we needed. Direct action had worked! We had taken the powers that be by surprise and over the next two years it felt like we had them on the run. Some of us would talk of putting a barbed wire fence in the middle of 2nd Avenue and declaring the Lower East Side an independent state.

There would be a series of confrontations over the eviction of squats, over the rights of the homeless and I think over something more abstract. Whose park, whose streets, whose buildings? To whom did the city belong? To those who own it on paper, or those who live in it?

Capitalism rolls over whole countries and it would be unrealistic to think that a state of insurrection could persist on the Lower East Side forever. Eventually, the establishment came to understand and take us seriously. So they chose to expand the resources necessary to put us down. We were a very small movement facing big capital with deep pockets and backed by government power. When the curfew was enforced, the homeless were driven into hiding and two-thirds of the squats were evicted. Of the thirty squats open in 1989, only 11 still exist. The city has wisely chosen to leave these hardy squatters alone. And so there is quiet in this gentrified neighborhood.

What survives is the image of an anarchist movement in the streets of an American city. This idea seemed way out in the 1980s, but since Seattle it no longer does. Today's anti-globalization movement is much bigger than the Tompkins Square movement ever dreamed of being. And more organized. It is less diverse, but that has its good side as well as its bad side. There was a lot of Dutch courage in our movement. Today's activists are more sober and a lot braver. There has been a frightening escalation in the level of violence people are facing. Rubber bullets in Quebec, real bullets in Genoa, tanks in Ramallah. But through all of this, the young anarchists have not become discouraged. And so I hope that the Tompkins Square uprising was a prelude to a story not yet written.

Chapter 15

An Interview with Father George Kuhn, former pastor of St. Brigid's Church. Interview by Clayton Patterson

GK - My name is Father George Kuhn and I was born in 1939. I came to the Lower East Side in the summer of 1986, assigned as pastor of St. Brigid's church and was happy to be here because I was looking for a relatively small parish with an Hispanic population.

CP - So you were in your 40s and an activist Catholic priest.

GK - I know I'm considered an activist priest but I see myself more as a contemplative, one who has to try to put into action the fruits of ones contemplation and I don't particularly relish the idea of being an activist. I cannot preach the gospel and try to live my own faith without dealing with issues of justice and have been compelled into speaking up and acting on behalf of people who are suffering or abused, and consequently have been considered an activist.

CP - You were an admirer of Dorothy Day, another Lower East Sider.

GK - Exactly. I think of her as a mentor. She also did not see herself as an activist but primarily as a disciple of Jesus, very involved in prayer, in regular liturgies, prayer groups, and the Friday night meetings, but always related with gospel. She would be a good example of how I would consider myself. She always said you could not become goal-oriented or you would be destined to burnout. You have to see your work as part of the process: peace is not a goal, it's a process. In dealing with justice and peace you have to see it as part of your spiritual growth. Learning how to deal with adversity and learning how to deal with injustice. But if I think I'm going to conquer injustice or think of myself as peacemaker, I'm not, the only peacemaker in terms of our faith is Jesus, we are the instruments, the disciples, and we're only here for a short time and we do what we can. My problem with people who are merely activists is that they burn out after awhile.

CP - So that's how you avoid becoming a dropout, a burnout or an alcoholic?

GK - That is an important part of it. Many priests who burn out lose their sense of spirituality, of prayer, of reflection. It is easy to do that when so many people are hurting or impoverished and have no place to live. Not just the homeless but people who are barely surviving after paying their rents and this is not restricted to one area, it is all over the country.

Father George Kuhn - Interview by Clayton Patterson

CP - When I was a child a person who was considered rich wasn't all that wealthy. The discrepancies now are huge. Like Bloomberg who is worth 40 billion opposed to people earning below minimum wage.

GK - It is pure unadulterated greed but not all that shocking in terms of the history of spirituality. Avoiding greed was an issue in the Jewish scriptures. The Prophet Isaiah speaks out strongly against impoverishment of the poor by people who are just thinking about themselves. This phenomenon seems more rampant than ever. But in an historical perspective, reading Isaiah seems like he is talking about what is happening today.

CP - We can certainly go back to the feudal system of kings and serfs with no middle ground, especially where there are masses of poor and people with extreme wealth and no social support system to fall back on (as what happened after hurricane Katrina). Bush's Iraq Democracy and Freedom rhetoric, with proposed universal health care and schools, should also be relevant to America. We have basically a class war rather than race or nationality war, not that coming from Guatemala isn't a hindrance, but social position now is based on money rather than on race. Powell cares as little for the poor blacks as does Bush.

GK - That's where we are removed from the pure Marxist dialectic of class struggle. You take people like Condoleeza Rice and Powell who learned how to say yes to the whole system and if they had a brain in their head and knew how to manipulate the structures they too could get up there to control the dominated and oppressed. The thing is that when you get there you don't realize how far you have strayed because people usually start out with a good will but they get in structures that destroy their sense of humility, of compassion, of gentleness that are all biblical in both the Old Testament and the New Testament.

CP - Once in awhile along comes an unusual person like you, or like Deputy Inspector Julian. I've never met a cop like Julian who was in a position of authority who was straightforward, honest and dedicated to the neighborhood and had real values. At Umbrella Squat when HPD (Housing, Protection and Development) ordered the cops to go in and evict all squatters Julian knew that some of the people had lived there more than 30 days because they had shown him letters and other documents. Julian told HPD "I'm not risking my men to get into this fight for you to take over the building when you don't have a plan." For Julian, an individual cop, to say this was to a city authority was unheard of. Julian later showed me notes from the Nuremberg trial where Eichman said he was following orders, and in reality any other cop would have listened to HPD rather than to listen to squatters.

GK - I think Julian was a lawyer, he also went to John Jay College so he was very sensitive to issues of law pertaining to the police. The problem is a commanding officer who is not sure of himself or doesn't have the brains, who can become influenced by men under him and so as not to offend them becomes part of a mob mentality. Julian had a good sense of himself, a good sense of what his mission was, what his authority was, where it came from in terms of the law, he felt a lot of confidence in that.

A Radical Political and Social History of the Lower East Side

CP - Before becoming head of the Ninth Precinct I think Julian taught at the [police] academy so he wasn't instilled with all the negative values of the precinct, having not spent a lot of time in precinct houses. One of the issues that he had when he took over the Ninth was that if cadets came directly from the academy and into a precinct they immediately learned the game.

GK - They had to stop that program because the cadets were coming back with all distorted values, the precinct's values. You wouldn't want to bring a kid in there, the language was appalling, it was a terrible scene to walk into.

CP - The Seventh and Fifth Precincts missed condemnation in the Mollen Commission Report but only because the Ninth precinct was spotlighted in the news, but in reality there was just as much corruption and drugs in the Seventh and Fifth. When the Mollen Commission Report came out the Ninth Precinct had their own chapter including the July 4th drug party, and I'm sure it was drugs they picked up in the community. I believe it was Chief Sullivan who busted Detective Brown on the Friday and the party was on the Monday so all of a sudden the cat was out of the bag, one cop was caught and the party never happened. Had it not been for this the feds or whomever was in charge of the sting would have swooped in and caught everybody stoned with illicit drugs. Talk about scandal and illustrating what police culture was actually like.

We met for the 1st time on August 6-7, 1988, the night of the riot. How did you come to be on Avenue A at Tompkins Square Park?

GK - Like any historical event this didn't happen in a vacuum, there are other issues, there was a huge police presence that night in the park because Captain McNamara felt that the police were beaten in a previous incident a week before. I came across him in the park in one of those vans that had a desk and spoke to him to find out what was going on. He said they would not allow the police to be beaten again so he was formulating plans concerning deployment of cops from outside the area and who was going to hide where. He was strategizing a battle. Of course at the time I didn't know what he had planned but we later saw the results. If he was a general in the Army he would probably have been fired for the mess the police made that night. As a matter of fact he did get moved to another precinct in another Borough as a result of his actions.

CP - After the riot, city officials said skinheads and punks from Westchester caused the "melee," but during the trials an officer from Highway Two said "We were told several days in advance to prepare to be stationed at Tompkins Square Park." The prosecutor insisted, "You didn't know that you would be there," and he said more than once, "Yes we knew a week before." So you can't tell me the police Commissioner didn't also know. What time did you arrive?

GK - Father Pat telephoned around 1AM. When I arrived there were bloody people and they wouldn't let ambulances through. That was one of my first attempts at intervention to try to find someone in charge of this operation so I could get an ambulance. Yuri Kapralov's skull was cracked open and Rudolph Pipkin, owner of the Tunnel Club was bleeding from the

Father George Kuhn - Interview by Clayton Patterson

head. Both were covered in blood. I got to one of the white shirts who eventually let the ambulances in. Yuri was a great friend of mine after that, and credited me with saving his life, but this may have been an exaggeration.

And another thing I noticed was that many cops had their badges off. I tried to take a picture and almost lost not only my camera but my hands and arms. I saw an officer coming at me with a club. This happened several times.

CP - Did you ask the commanding officer about missing badges?

GK - No, there were sergeants around but they paid no attention.

CP - They also switched badges so the numbers did not identify the officer. Chief Darcy, several captains, deputy inspectors and inspectors were there and this event went on for at least six hours, so how can it be a commanding officer who is uniform-aware did not see his men with their hats off or on backwards, badges missing, and numbers taped over?

GK - Father Pat and I also tried to get in touch with City Hall, Mayor Koch, but nobody knew where he was. It turned out he was in the Hamptons. Whether by design or what I don't know, but you couldn't locate anybody in authority. At the riot some of the white shirts told me "You have influence with these people, get them to move back." I said, "You get your troops out of here, you are the instigators, you caused it, when you pull your troops, it's over but as long as you stay here you are provoking this."

CP - The police left at six in the morning. Do you know what time the curfew was over? It was six in the morning. So once again, as the previous week, the police were in retreat. You said before you thought McNamara had screwed the whole thing up but I think the whole police department was completely out of control and drugs had taken over the city. There was no central authority and the chain of command wasn't working in the precincts.

GK - At that time I mentioned that the New York City police was much like the National Guard in Latin American countries who get their orders from higher up, but have no sense that they are there for law and order but only to obey superiors so they just do it. I asked officers, "do you realize what you are doing down here?" They said "what can I do? I'm just paying the mortgage," "I got a house," "I got a family," and "you can't speak up, if you speak up you're out." It doesn't matter if you're patrolman or the captain of the precinct you are just following orders.

CP - And then throw in drugs and corruption, you've got the whole gangster mentality.

GK - This is what happens when there is an eclipse of God in society, then everybody is autonomous and there is no sense of local or world community. Basically that's what they teach kids now in school, nobody tells you what to do, you decide yourself and are treated as a mature person who must determine right from wrong and take personal responsibility for your actions. That is values clarification. The idea of removing any sense of God ultimately leads to totalitarianism: those who have more power and more weapons will constantly control the vulnerable.

CP - Where were you before coming to St. Brigid's in 1986?

GK - I was ordained in 1964. I was in a rural parish upstate, I taught in a Catholic high school for three years, and I was in a wealthy parish in Larchmont, New York, for seven years which was an incredible defining experience in my priesthood in the sense that you could see how money controls everything, even values, where you can have opposition even among religious people. For example, against a group home for retarded children because it would lower real estate values. And of course, even to suggest there might be moral problems with bombing children and women in the Vietnam War raised fury, but not with all of them, some people were conflicted, and even organized a march called "Capitalists for Peace" that some local medical people and even some wealthy people joined. But the sense of anger against the protest coming from generally devout people was absolutely incredible.

Then I did two years in campus ministry at a college and discovered how all aspects of education are taken over by marketing people who determined admissions. I heard teachers refer to students as product, and this was basically a liberal arts college that had Catholic roots although it was no longer Catholic. Alumni who had risen to heights in the corporate world were held up as examples of success. I tried to get them to honor graduates who were members of Catholic communities working for justice and peace, but that doesn't produce money. I learned that universities are basically trade schools for corporate life. They had abandoned the whole business of liberal arts education and of trying to put you in touch with great values and the great ideas of the past, to make you think and reflect, and they did away with philosophy courses. It was all marketing.

CP - When you came to the Lower East Side and saw drugs being sold openly on the street what was your reaction? It must have been startling and certainly the block where you are was a famous drug location. (Avenue B and 7th Street).

GK - Well I wasn't that unaware of the huge drug problem in the United States and in New York.

CP - But this wasn't just a problem. During the late '70s to mid '90s the Lower East Side was an out and out open-air drug supermarket.

GK - There was a conflict on Seventh Street where drugs were woven directly into the fabric of people's lives and some people thought that good.

CP - When PS 20 attached a sign: "This is a drug free zone — Drugs can not be sold within 500 feet of the school" thirty feet from a drug location and drug sales took place feet from a police car, I was shocked. "The Laundromat" on your block, 7th and Ave B was run by JR, ask any junkie about his brand "bag in a bag" and they could tell you location, who ran it, who worked there, name of the head guy, situation on

the block, hours open, how good the dope was, and not only that the bags had a brand name stamped on them like chiclets or lifesavers.

GK - You came from where?

CP - I came from Western Canada.

GK - I grew up in New York City so I had some sense of the vastness of the drug problem. Also I was arrested several times in connection with Vietnam so I wasn't that surprised, but I remember being somewhat shocked by a cop guarding Tompkins Square Park a few feet from a drug line on 7th Street. I told him, "that's a drug line and you should do something." He said that's not my job I'm assigned to stand *here*. Call City Hall.

CP - Elsa videotaped a man at the UN who was the head of the world drug organization who said that Hong Kong was central to international drug cartels who met there to sell product and launder money through international banks. The fear was that after China took over Hong Kong in 1997 their operations would split into fractions.

GK - Peck who wrote the "Road Less Traveled" hit the nail right on the head with the demonic nature of lies, in fact it's no accident that the Scriptures call Satan the Father of All Lies. Lies and drugs goes hand in hand-not only the ones who sell but the ones who are addicted. They'll tell you lies to the degree that they don't even know that they're lying anymore.

CP - One thing I discovered in documenting a lot of junkies is that they don't all lie and they're not all immoral. Not totally worthless people and some of them really have a value system, they will only go so far, unlike the business with the government and the police. At Easter when you marched people from your parish around the neighborhood with a police car escort, you used to stop in front of the Laundromat pointing and saying, "This is a drug location."

GK - We did the stations of the cross, not specifically to name the Laundromat. We did one of the mobile stations also because they're all related. The two things that we've touched upon that are traditionally biblical words is the lie and greed. Greed in theology is one of the seven capital sins meaning that they hinge and several other sins flow from that whole sense of greed. It is rampant, we lived in such an atmosphere of greed that greed is not even recognized as such.

CP - For a while I was involved with protesting the Beth Israel methadone clinic on Avenue A because it was directly across the street from the Cardinal Spellman School head start program. The school was not opposed to a clinic, several parents of children who attended were drug addicts. Not a case of "not in my backyard" it was just don't put it *directly* across the street. Methadone clinics normally have hanging out, selling spit-backs and the culture that comes with drug rehab and the school didn't want that culture in their face.

A Radical Political and Social History of the Lower East Side

Eventually these meetings evolved into discussions of neighborhood drug locations. P.O. Ritchie Johnson, who was the Ninth Precinct Community Affairs Officer, attended our meetings as would several block associations who would give drug location information in full detail to P.O. Johnson who took extensive notes. But nothing ever happened. So suddenly we became aware, whether it was conspiracy, innuendo or guessing, that without question P.O. Johnson knew of all the drug locations in the Ninth Precinct. If kids in grade one in P.S. 20 were asked who sells drugs on your block they could tell you. It was not a mystery.

After the 1988 police riot when the community became involved with the homeless situation, "Tent City" in Tompkins Square Park. I think it was certainly an important part of New York City history and you were an instrumental character in that. What was there about that you found interesting or important?

GK - Well, it was very tricky because nobody wants to say the park is an appropriate place for people to sleep, but the fact is that they were chasing people from all over the city, from places like shopping centers, like Fifth Avenue and chasing them out of subway stations. When someone is homeless, where do they go? The Lower East Side had traditionally been one of the more inclusive communities because of all the different immigrant groups that came there and some how had worked out an arrangement of peaceful coexistence, so it is an appropriate place for people who are displaced. Where are they supposed to go? So they wound up on the Lower East Side. And my position basically was that the central issue here was a housing issue. Everyone will admit that there is a crisis in affordable housing and yet they cannot see or admit that this the primary reason for homelessness. We have a situation with housing now that's even progressively worse, they call it affordable housing but you have to be making $50,000 a year to qualify. This excluded a whole bunch of people who are often a very difficult population to work with and there is no provision to deal with them. You can't simply put up housing for people who are in the zero to $25,000 income range because there are a lot of social problems.

CP - When I was a kid $25,000 used to be a lot of money, but not anymore.

GK - A lot of people in Yonkers are living three or four families in small apartments in old buildings and combining their income just to pay the rent, so it's a crisis.

CP - The police down here specifically told people loitering in Penn and other stations to go to Tompkins Square Park because "they will accommodate you and it's a great place to be" and there was also Diane and others who supplied food at the park. Diane's food was gourmet, so good that people who were not homeless also came from all over the city, even from as far away as Staten Island and Yonkers. I spoke to Diane about this and told her that I had no opposition to her and feeding the homeless but why not divide it into three or four different locations like the Bowery, 23rd Street, and Tompkins Square Park. She said, "No I'm bringing it all down here. It turned out that the gourmet food came from City Harvest and when Malcolm Forbes died he requested that any money given on his behalf should go to City Harvest.

Father George Kuhn - Interview by Clayton Patterson

GK - There is so much secrecy in government that it breeds conspiracy theories. And I no longer think they are theories but that there is some legitimacy to it. I remember returning from my three-month sabbatical program in California. Coming back I drove on the Southern route near Fort Hood, Texas. I stopped in a diner for breakfast where there was a lot of military people from Fort Hood but they were all in uniforms of different countries. I stopped one guy who was speaking English, a German, and I asked him what is happening here? He said we are doing joint exercises in urban guerrilla warfare.

It was the first time I heard that term, either in April or May of 1995 and now we know what urban guerrilla warfare is all about, not only in Iraq but in preparation for dealing with large numbers of people at some point. How does the government keep a balance to pacify people and just throw them enough to keep them quiet. Where is that line? The government, of course, doesn't walk across that line because then they have to call the troops into the cities. On our way down here today there were people in military fatigues with rifles.

CP - You can go to Macy's now or in the subways and find military guys with submachine guns.

I believe the Tompkins Square Riot wasn't looked at citywide but at a federal level. And I think the tapes had something to do with that. The tapes clearly showed lack of military ability in the Police Department during the riot. I also know they used Tompkins Square to reorganize and militarize the police. In 1988 the cops were not controllable. I saw Captain Fry physically pushing — not protesters, but the police — saying "form a line." It took until 1992-93 to form a razor sharp military organization within the NYPD. However since 911 that sharpness is starting to diminish and there has gotten to be an arrogance again in the police department. They are getting soft and slacking off. You see cops driving around smoking cigars, making illegal U-turns, going through red lights. That means the discipline factor has diminished again because of arrogance, but in the mid 90s NYPD was an absolutely razor sharp troop that was in absolute control.

About two years ago there was a small incident at Tompkins Square where a protester burned a flag and the cops went crazy. Cops aren't supposed to go crazy. They are supposed to follow orders but they ran up on the sidewalk, over motorcycles and were arresting people in really vicious ways. I asked a cop "Who's in charge?" and the cop said, "you are!" I thought ahhh. They've lost it again.

So what were your thoughts about Tompkins Square in the 80s, the tent city era? What did you think about that?

GK - It just highlighted the social problems in our country to see so many people in the park, and there were talented people there, and as you know a lot of Vietnam veterans were also there. It was kind of a microcosm of homeless who were there for different reasons. But what was nice, in one sense, in the midst of this darkness was that I used to have the kids from school, the kids whose parents would let them, bring food to the park, and the homeless always said "God bless you." Of course there were some parents who forbade their

A Radical Political and Social History of the Lower East Side

children to do this because they were afraid. St. Brigid's had many school lunch programs and all unused food are supposed to thrown away so we got the people who worked in the program to put the unused food in a marked black garbage bag that they put it out as trash and I would go and pick it up. They would cover what they had to do and I covered what I had to do, and so we had lots of food. That was one of the compromises that happened with Deputy Inspector Julian when four priests went to the Fourth Street Squat "ABC Community Center" that had been under police siege for several days. [The "ABC Community Center" was an abandoned school on 4th St. that community activists began to fix up for community use after throwing out the prostitutes and drug addicts].

But, of course, the city had other plans so rather than to send in the police to throw them out they put the police there to surround it and no one was allowed to go in or out. Father Pat Malone, the Baptist minister from Graffiti Church, Bob Wallenberg from Trinity Lutheran and I elected to bring in food and water. Joseph Papp and Judith Malina came as support persons. We knew we were risking arrest but we figured we would get the food in any way. At the barricade Julian said "Father if you go over that line we will have to arrest you, I'm sorry, just following orders." I said, "I understand this is nothing about you, I understand what it is to follow orders, but I'm following orders too. To give food to the hungry and drink to the thirsty. I hope you don't hold this against me. I respect you, so do what you have to do, and I'll do what I have to do." This was live on WBAI which I did not know until later.

So I told the other ministers, let's just take a symbolic bag of food so we don't loose it all. When we started to cross the barricade, Julian called me over and said ,"It's dangerous for my men, they have been throwing sand bags and I will not risk my men to go in there, but you will be arrested when you come out." I read between the lines and what he was doing was like Thomas More who went as far as he could with the law and with his orders but found a way to follow both the law and at the same time make allowances for his beliefs. So Julian was following his orders to arrest people but he allowed me to follow my orders to bring food and drink and arrest after. So we put all the food in plastic crates and they were hoisted up with pulleys. We came out and were arrested. I felt sorry for the cops because there was the crowd who chanted "Shame, shame," and "Look who you are arresting," and "Look there's a drug sale, look at what you're doing." And so it was a wonderful action and I was happy that there was no violence. It has been one of my concerns and I do not want to be involved in anything where there is violence. The crowd knew what was going on and I remember asking them "Please no violence," and there wasn't. But those cops got the message and when they put us in the van they kept saying "We hate to do this, but what am I supposed to do?"

So they took us to the Ninth Precinct and give us desk appearance tickets. They were very apologetic and offered us coffee so Father Pat told them a joke about four cops who arrested priests and when they got to the Pearly Gates Peter said "You've been arresting religious leaders," and the cops said to Saint Peter "You want a cup of coffee?" Peter said, "Take your coffee and go to Hell."

CP - Tell me about when you testified at the trial of the Mayday 29.

Father George Kuhn - Interview by Clayton Patterson

GK - They had built up a case by having loads of police officers there and lie one after the other and they painted the crowd as terrible people with no ounce of goodness in them at all, vicious people, the dregs of society, so it threw some dust in their case before the jury when I was called as a character witness. I identified myself as pastor of the archdiocese from St. Brigid's and testified as to the integrity of the program that day and to the people involved in it who were very concerned about the loss of housing and what was happening in the Lower East Side and how people were losing their homes. The organizers were called Resist to Exist, basically very spiritual, where there is no resistance there's no holiness. I felt very comfortable and I was a speaker at the event. I thought it was well-planned so I was happy to speak there. That threw up some dust and confusion at the trial. I wasn't there for the summation but I know the prosecution summarized by saying if you acquit these people it means you are saying that every cop on that stand lied.

CP - At the beginning you weren't going to swear on the Bible.

GK - I know that from the sermon on the Mount in Matthew 5 you are told not to take oaths and this is one of those areas where a lot of Christians and even theologians don't pay too much attention. But it is a very clear teaching: when you say yes, mean yes; if you mean no, say no. Everything else comes from evil. So I was not going to take an oath, not only for that reason and also because all the cops swore to tell the truth and it didn't mean anything. This is the age of the lie. There was a Sister I know who was called to be a juror and in the voir dire the Judge asked, "If someone swore to tell the truth would you believe them because they took the oath?" She said, "I would be inclined to believe them." Everybody including the Judge laughed and she was dismissed.

Postscript:

In July 1988 Father George spent 10 days traveling through El Salvador where he heard horror stories about the National Police who were essentially assassins. With this still in his mind he found himself as a benevolent party to the August 1988 Tompkins Square Park Police Riot where 400 and more NYPD officers beat passersby in the streets and inside private property. *New Common Good*, a weekly paper, wrote a thank you to Father George for his leadership: "He was on the streets during the riot, and may very well have been the voice that ended the violence that night and he has been running ever since, providing information and bringing people together through meetings in the church school basement."

The large basement hall in the school had multiple uses: As a meeting hall for specific community concerns from 1988-95, like the reaction to the 1988 police riot, CCRB briefings, political stances, and neighborhood problems. It was also used on weekends to house 10-15 homeless men at night, or used for its original purpose, as a school lunchroom and auditorium. Father George regulated hall usage so no events overlapped, including keeping it clean.

A Radical Political and Social History of the Lower East Side

Father George's goal was simple, his mission was "to practice the gospel of Jesus, so if Jesus said to feed the poor and the political climate is anti-poor, then the gospel has political implications." (*New York Times* 12.11.94)

In 1991 Father George hung a huge cloth banner across the front of St Brigid's protesting the Gulf War for which he was criticized by the usual factions in the community.

Then there were problems caused by the local establishment, including politician Antonio Pagan who took it upon himself to go after Father George personally as in a letter to Cardinal O'Connor in 1992 where he accused Father George of defending the rights of junkies, prostitutes, and criminals, of supporting a proposed AIDS treatment center that was to be built near the school and for firing members of the school staff whose actions were not in accordance with the best interests of the school. When Father George arranged for a Seventh Street block fair, a frequent event on any block in the Lower East Side that usually hired the same company to cater the event, he was again accused, in a letter citing complaints of excessive noise and of employing members of the Mafia.

This accusation is almost laughable because the drug spot on Seventh Street and B, "The Laundromat" had been selling drugs unimpeded for years. Soon after the Mollen Commission Report became public, the Feds finally shut "The Laundromat" permanently.

Antonio Pagan's unhappy tenure as member of the City Council ended soon after he demanded officers arrest Margarita Lopez during a heated public discussion at Cooper Union. M. Lopez went on to serve two terms in the City Council, replacing Pagan.

Chapter 16

Anarchist Art from the Lower East Side
By Richard Kostelanetz

In his practical work for the masses, the revolutionary easily forgets — and sometimes likes to forget — that the real goal is not work but sexual play and life in all its forms, from orgasm to the highest accomplishments. — Wilhelm Reich, *The Mass Psychology of Fascism* (1946)

Works of art with anarchist themes and anarchist forms is not the same as art containing anarchist slogans. The latter includes certain poems by Kenneth Rexroth, Jackson Mac Low, or even Jenny Holzer, who writes phrases that can be understood, or interpreted, as anarchist but are formally no different from newspaper headlines, which are not art — just newspaper headlines, even if enlarged, as she does them. Another artful masterpiece written by an anarchist is Emma Goldman's *Living My Life* (1930), which finally conveys not anarchist themes but the story of individual accomplishment over severe adversities. Instead, let us consider art that is distinctly anarchist in plot, anarchist in image, and anarchist in form, much of it emerging from New York's Lower East Side, where Goldman lived for a while incidentally.

An example of the first familiar to us all is Henry Miller's multi-volume novel, which portrays self-liberation from society and the discovery of an instinctual self that cannot be socialized by outside forces, whether those be institutions, bureaucracies, employers, or marriage. I speak from personal experience, having read Miller while in college and completing an honors thesis on his work in 1962, just as his once-banned books were becoming commonly available in America; for his book(s) certainly affected my continued resistance to all those socializing antagonists.

A less familiar example of anarchist plot appears in Clayton Patterson's great videotape about the Tompkins Square Riot of 1988. Using an early portable video camera, held on his hip, and the natural lighting of a hot summer New York night, Patterson portrays the police attempt to disrupt a people's protest against the closing of a Lower East Side park that had become the last refuge of Manhattan's homeless. As more and more cops come, Patterson's camera portrays them looking anxiously at one another, visually revealing the truth that officials later made public — that the policemen did not know what they were supposed to do. After many taunting screams and some violent exchanges, all intimately portrayed in Patterson's footage, a tall man in civilian clothes arrives, surveys the scene, and with a flick of his head instructs the police to retreat back into the buses that take them home. The film ends with the anarchist image of people retaking the park as the sun comes up.

Another unfamiliar example of anarchist plot is Lee Baxandall's play *Potsy* (1963), written on St. Mark's Place and first produced upstairs on Second Avenue. It tells of the local power monopoly's attempt to electrify an outhouse over its owner's objections. In collusion with the state, which has no doubt authorized that all man-made constructions be electrically serviced, Consolidated, Incorporated, intimidates a reluctant customer. In response, Baxandall's protagonist Potsy lays his body on the pot, so to speak:

Pay yet some attention, workmen. Loka! Piszok Baika loka! Brudy! Mykja mykja! Skita. Cacones cacones. Alhorre zulla szenny! Szenny! Saasta bagla gaika, vaika. Lort, plehna. Lort lort lort lort lort lort! Kunya suka zurullo! Suka! (The gestures grow more anguished.) Szar ulosteet! Oosee oosee oosee cacones! Sprosnosc meco- nio. Mykjaa dynga cacones camara. Plasta! Kot kot kak kak, aolach! Szeku, cuch cach cauch, oosee oosee. Caakaaaaaaaaaaaaaah! Track smuts. Aolach! Inneir, teyl fegradh schijt, mon. Gaorr, salachar. Orenlighet orenlighet orenlighet, cac cac! Bee- Emmm. Oosee, oosee, oosee, ooseeeee - gamees! Porcheria porcheria porcheria porcheria! Bouse crotte etron selles, gavno, crottin. Selles scheiss ficate, guano. Gavnoh sporchezza! Gavnoh! Plot plop dump gamees! Gamees gamees gamees gamees! Feung feung, cacaaaah! Pez. Inmundicia. [Etc.]

Though Baxandall thought himself a Marxist at the time, even compiling a bibliography of Marxist esthetics (and later editing an anthology of mostly Marxist esthetics, *Radical Perspectives in the Arts* [1972]), it seemed to me clear at the time that the thrust of Potsy was anarchist, much as the pervasive politics of the LES was anarchist (rather than "social- ist"), affirming that no society can legitimately invade a human being's throne. So I was scarcely surprised that Baxandall went on to write guides to nude beaches, which is, need- less to say, another kind of outhouse that authoritarians and their ally the state want to shut down. (It's surprising that we never had one in the LES, considering how common they are in Northern European parks.)

An example of art with anarchist images is the Living Theatre's *Paradise Now* (1968). It is structured as a series of challenges to the audience, in which the performers scream slogans that are not ends in themselves but provocations designed to make the audience respond. "I'm not allowed to travel without a passport." "I'm not allowed to smoke marijuana." When they scream, "I'm not allowed to take my clothes off," some spectators respond by undress- ing and others not, creating an image in which some are liberated and others not. A second anarchist image so vivid in my head has audience members leaping off the stage into the crossed arms of several men. Both nudity and leaping into the air are images of liberation, which is what the paradise of *Paradise Now* is all about. (The leaping image resembles a famous Yves Klein photograph of himself, but without the context that, for the Living Theatre, makes leaping so distinctly political) It is indicative that when the Internal Revenue Service closed the Living Theatre in the fall of 1963, it was rehearsing a produc- tion of Baxandall's *Potsy*! During the 1990s, the LT had a theater east of Avenue A.

The master of anarchist form was John Cage, who lived around 1950 on the intersection of Grand and Monroe Streets, deep in the (very lower) Lower (far east) East Side. From early in his career he made sound pieces without climaxes, without definite beginnings and ends, without boundaries. Another characteristic is that they were performed by individuals func- tioning as equals. Looking back over his entire work, to the beginning of his career in the

1930s, you'll find him never employing a conductor who makes interpretative decisions. (His conductors, instead, merely keep time, not even beat.) Nor does Cage allow solo performers to stand out from the background group.

His pieces are customarily characterized as chaotic, but in their chaos is their politics. On the floor of *HPSCHD*, performed in a humongous basketball arena, were seven amplified harpsichordists each with different scores. Two had different collages of harpsichord music from Mozart to the present; three had differently fixed versions of Mozart's "Introduction to the Composition of Waltzes by Means of Dice." One more harpsichordist played "computer printout for twelve-tone gamut," while the last keyboard operator had nothing more specific than blanket instruction to play any Mozart he wished. Around the arena Cage distributed 52 tape machines, each playing tapes of computer-composed sound in 52 different scales (ranging from 5 tones to an octave to 56 tones). With so many disparate sound sources the result could only be microtonal din. If you listen to the recording made of this piece, that is what you hear. For the original performance Cage added a profusion of images from both slides and film. What is portrayed in this and in other Cage pieces is individuals working together and apart, each acting on his or her own authority, in concert with others, all without a conductor. In these respects, *HPSCHD* and other Cagean pieces become models of an anarchist society.

He was always anarchist. When Cage was first invited to write music to accompany a text, back in the early 1940s, the writer he first approached was Henry Miller. Since Miller's obscenity proved problematic, Cage chose another writer whose politics were likewise anarchist, Kenneth Patchen; and when setting writer's texts, Cage frequently favored the poetry of E. E. Cummings, who lived most of his life on Patchin Place in the Village, whose politics were, to my mind, mostly anarchist as well. Consider not only *The Enormous Room* (1922), which is easily available, but the prose masterpiece that has long been out of print, *Eimi* (1933), which is a critical report of Cummings's 1931 trip to Russia. In the recently published collection of letters between Cage and Pierre Boulez in the late 1940s is Cage's charming proposal for "a society called Capitalists, Inc. (so that we will not be accused of being Communists). Everyone who joins has to show that he has destroyed not less than 100 disks of music or one sound recording device; also everyone who joins automatically becomes President." Making every member a king, Capitalists, Inc., would, of course, be another anarchist community reflective of the Lower East Side, not only around 1950, when Cage wrote, but decades later.

Richard Kostelanetz
PO Box 444, Prince St.
New York, NY 10012-0008
website: www.richardkostelanetz.com
art gallery: www.minusspace.com

Chapter 17

"Some Habitation Attitudes and Practices on
New York City's Lower East Side, 1982 to 2002"
    By Eric Miller

This essay seeks to portray and discuss some habitation attitudes and practices of people
on New York City's Lower East Side, from 1982 to 2002. Before getting to the heart of the
matter, which will be a guided tour of a six-mile walk I used to take on the Lower East Side
and vicinity, please permit me to give a bit of background about myself. My briefly telling
of some prior and subsequent experiences might help to contextualize my points, give some
sense of where I am coming from, and perhaps support my view that, as well as being an
observer of the neighborhood culture I describe, I am also in my own way a practitioner of
some aspects of that culture.

This essay is being written in Internet browsing centres in the small city of Nagarcoil, in
the state of Tamil Nadu, in south India. Nearby is a mountainous forest area where I am
engaged in a two-year doctoral research project regarding the language and verbal arts of
the Kani people, an aboriginal tribe. I am a Ph.D. candidate in Folklore at the University of
Pennsylvania, Philadelphia, where I did coursework in the winters of 1998-9, 1999-0, and
2000-1. Since 2002 —that is, for the past year —I have been out of the USA, in India.

The Kani people are members of the African-Indo-Pacific migratory group. Members of this
group were, it seems, the first modern humans to inhabit this entire part of the world.
Now they tend to live in mountain areas, where it is sometimes said they have gone to
escape from the more-recently-arrived inhabitants. Some tribal people in India have similar
housing and cultural issues that some bohemians had in the East Village in the '80s and
'90s-such as being faced with the constant threat of eviction from homesteads that have
uncertain legal standing. The Kani people I am visiting with, however, are fortunate in
that they are recognized as having the right to live where they are living, which is in a
mountain forest region adjacent to a vast wilderness, into which they can travel whenever
they wish.

Growing up in midtown Manhattan, a child of two editors of arts-related magazines, I
enjoyed a comfortable and very culturally-rich life. In our apartment, however, I at times
felt trapped in my room, cut off from the other people of the city. I tell this story from
the privileged perspective of one who loves shared and outdoor living, but who has, when I
have desired it, been able to have my own space in NYC, however small.

While attending Oberlin College in Ohio, I lived for a time in the hippie dorm: co-ed floors,
co-ed bathrooms, and organic vegetarian kitchen. As in many dorms, a long central hallway
connected the rooms on each floor. One night I slept on our hallway floor. This was not
really roughing it: room and hallway floors were carpeted, and I had sheets and a blanket. I

just loved the social activity in our dorm — people dropping in and out of each other's rooms day and night — and I made this gesture to express that I did not want to miss any of the fun. I dropped out of college and, with backpack and sleeping bag, hitchhiked, zigzagging across the country a number of times.

It was not until I returned to New York — where I slowly and intermittently at NYU completed my B.A. and did my M.A. — that I found a place and cultural situation that was as a stimulating and exciting as hitchhiking: the East Village, which became my physical and spiritual home. Although I had attended high school nearby (Stuyvesant, in the old building on 15th St., between 1st and 2nd Aves.), during my high school years (the early '70s) I did not visit the East Village very much, nor was I particularly aware of its existence. For some reason, it seems I needed to shelter myself from the East Village during this stage of my life.

In the early '80s, however, I was ready, and I immensely enjoyed 'the city that never sleeps,' especially the all-night and perpetually-open spots in Lower Manhattan. Around every New Year's Eve there was a 72-hour continuous reading of Gertrude Stein's epic novel, *The Making of Americans* (at the Paula Cooper Gallery, a half-block south of the East Village, in Soho, on Wooster Street): one year I stayed for the entire reading. On New Year's Eves there was also an all-day-and-all-night poetry reading (at St. Mark's Church, on 2nd Ave., near 10th St.). The 'Korean groceries,' with their vegetable and fruit shelves stretching out onto the sidewalks, were always open, as were numerous other shops. And of course, there were many after-hour bars, clubs, hang-outs, etc., in the East Village and its surroundings: one often saw people who seemed to be on their way home from such places at around 9 am. The presence of these all-night and perpetually-open spots began, in some small way, to satisfy my yearning for togetherness.

Most of the small amount of money I made in the '80s and early '90s was earned through video documentation of performances (which I did alongside my video business partner, Diane Dunbar). I also did a bit of documentation of parades and other public events, but usually this did not pay, and I didn't contribute very much to public access cable TV shows. My energy for creative/unpaid/community work and play primarily went into creating video art events.[1]

In short, I was not in the league of people like Clayton, Rik Little, and others, who were constantly videotaping the neighborhood, including clashes with the authorities in regard to the authorities restricting and closing down living spaces. Nonetheless, I brought a documenter's, as well as an artist's, eye to the neighborhood.

The East Village, which comprises the far northern section of the Lower East Side, can be said to be bordered by 14th Street to the north and Houston St. to the south; and Broadway to the west and the East River to the east. Some people say that the East Village's official western border is Third Ave. (also known as the Bowery), but to many people the East Village includes the area out to Broadway. Following this latter definition then, the East Village's nine avenues (running north-south), from west to east, are: Broadway; Fourth Avenue; Third Avenue; Second Avenue; First Avenue; Avenue A; Avenue B; Avenue C; and Avenue D. Alphabet City is the eastern half of this area — from Avenue A to Avenue D (and on to the river).

128 In the early '80s, I lived on Fifth Street, between Avenues A and B. It was not until some years later, however, when I was living on 2nd St., between Second and Third Avenues, that I developed the habit of talking the following walk: I would walk eastward through the East Village, through Alphabet City, to the East River. Then I would walk southward along Lower Manhattan's east coast, down to under the Brooklyn Bridge, and westward along the island's southern coast. Then I would begin up the west coast, on Battery Park City's promenade along the Hudson River, usually to the World Financial Center. From there, I would make my way back towards the East Village, usually either by subway (from under the World Trade Center towers), or by walk (up to Chambers Street, and then eastward through Chinatown — where there were a number of 24-hour restaurants, by the way).

As I would walk, these are some of the things and people that I would see and think about:

Usually, first I would walk to Ray's Newsstand (on Avenue A, between Seventh Street and Eighth Street [also known as St. Mark's Place]). There I would look around for, and say hello to, friends and acquaintances, and would most likely have a small chocolate egg cream (seltzer, milk, and just a little chocolate syrup), for sixty cents. Ray's — open 24 hours, of course — was the center and anchor of the neighborhood. As mentioned, Ray's was on Avenue A, the neighborhood's main strip. It was across the street from Tompkins Square Park (henceforth TSP), which lies within the area, Avenues A to B, and Seventh to 10th Street. Clayton tells me that Ray is from Turkey. It was often difficult for me to get a straight answer about such things from Ray: he was very fond of joking around. Ray hired Polish young women to help him operate the store. It seems these women might have been related to the Polish people who owned the restaurant next door, and who were also Ray's landlord.

What really marked Ray's as a special place was that almost every night, weather permitting, six or seven people, mostly guys, would be standing on the sidewalk in front of Ray's, talking, late into the night. They would greet passersby, many of whom were their friends. People would be coming to Ray's at all hours, emerging from their apartments, their work projects or whatever, for coffee, egg creams, and other supplies, and perhaps for a brief social interaction — just like how office-workers are said to gather at the water-cooler. People in various altered states of consciousness, and demented people, were also often floating through the scene. In short, it was a casual, ongoing, outdoor party.

One of the men who stood in front of Ray's night after night, Sidewalk Bob, tended to act as a social manager, a host. He would often introduce people to each other, and he could tell you all about almost any subject. Sidewalk Bob looked like (my fantasy of) Benjamin Franklin, in his late forties. He usually had a tiny earphone in one ear, with which he was listening to police radio reports, and he was always ready to dash off to the scene of a crime. Sidewalk Bob always seemed to have a camera in hand, but I don't recall ever seeing any of his photographs. In this way, he was different from Clayton, in that the front window of Clayton's storefront (which was just south of the East Village) was almost always filled with recent photos of neighborhood people and events.

Another Bob, Povercide Bob, could also often be found stationed on the sidewalk near Ray's. Povercide Bob seemingly always had with him a shopping wagon full of his belongings, including a stack of photocopied handwritten fliers detailing the authorities' efforts to destroy the people and his own ideas about how the people could defend themselves. Povercide Bob was perhaps in his late fifties. His white hair was usually cut very short, to a crew cut. A USA flag was often draped over his shopping wagon. Povercide Bob almost had the air of a military man, a drill sergeant. However, his mission was to regale anyone who would listen regarding how the people who operate the multi-national corporations, the government, the CIA, and the military were killing the rest of us — committing "povercide" against us. He had no doubt regarding all of the conspiracy theories: all of the assassinations were the work of president-approved or rogue CIA operatives. One solution he had to peoples' economic woes was to add six zeroes to everyone's bank accounts. This proposal ignored the fact that many poor people do not have bank accounts, but you get the idea. This proposal was part put-on, part serious, and I found it quite amusing and intriguing. I was never sure where Povercide Bob slept at night: it seems that for a while, at least, he had an apartment.

In those days it was often somewhat of a political statement to not have a conventional apartment, to not be paying rent, to be living if not outside the law, then certainly outside the system. Squatters however, were not just outside the system: they were trying to transform the system, and to build other systems. It must also be remembered that East Village squatters were members of the international and historical squatter community, and also, in many cases, of other anarchy-oriented communities. For the entire nation, the East Village— along with, in a less concentrated way, the San Francisco area — were the places that people who did not want to join the system could go to join each other. Runaways from all over the country converged on Avenue A, as was attested to by the fliers concerning their missing teenagers that anxious parents posted in Avenue A laundromats.

In the East Village of the '80s and early '90s, many people lived in interstitial spaces. This was possible in those days in part because there were so many abandoned and crumbling buildings, and unused or under-used lots, especially between Avenues A and D. One would come upon people sleeping on staircase landings, and roofs; in sheltered sidewalk areas, alleys, and self-storage rooms; and at deserted construction sites: in short, along the edges of civilized, constructed society, in no-man's-lands, in unfinished, semi-wild, contested, up-for-grabs, in-flux, uncertain, unlabeled, unclassified, ambiguous, and unclaimed places. Sleeping and camping in such places is quite common in many areas of the developing world, but it has not been so in most of the USA in recent years. Maybe it was in the 'hobo jungles' of the 1930s.

One of the people who did die perhaps of a form of povercide was Merlin. After two of the squats he was living in were shut down by the authorities, Merlin decided to camp out on the street. And that is what he did. For almost a year in the early '90s, Merlin lived on the sidewalk, on the east side of Avenue A, just south of Sixth Street. The building on this street was a Con Ed electrical station, and thus was not residential or commercial; Merlin camped against the side of this building. He had blankets for protection against the cold,

A Radical Political and Social History of the Lower East Side

and a tarp for protection against the rain. People would come by and chat, sit for a while, give him food, etc. Finally, he died. The problem involved an internal organ, I believe. It was a mystery to me why the police permitted him to live there for so long. Many people were chased away from similar spots. Perhaps it was because Merlin was so good-natured and polite. It seemed he was always smiling. A saintly smile.

Merlin's corner was a-block-and-a-half south of Ray's, on the other side (the east side) of Avenue A. There were cafes on Avenue A with outdoor tables on the northeast corner of Sixth Street (across the street northward from Merlin's corner), and on the southwest corner of Seventh Street. These outdoor restaurant seats added to the 'outdoor-life' nature of the area: but there is a marked difference between *paying to temporarily sit* (something one may do in someone else's space), and *lying down for as long as one wants without paying* (something one may do in one's own space, or in free space).

Jim the Mosaic Man sometimes dropped by Ray's at night, although he was really more of a day person. Jim's long white hair was usually pulled back in a ponytail.[2] Jim frequently lived at his work places: that is, if he was hired to do a large mosaic on and/or in a building that was in the process of being built, he would, if possible, move in and live at the construction site, sometimes for months. Other times, Jim received nearby living space in exchange for the mosaic work, or other work, he was doing. He seemingly never paid rent.

During sunlight hours, Lawrence might also be around Ray's. Lawrence said he was from Montana. Lawrence was quite tall, over six-and-a-half feet. He had the quality of (my fantasy of) an Old Testament prophet. He was often furious at activity that was going on in the park across the street. One thing that really incensed him was guys going about bare-chested. He felt that this was insulting and offensive to women, of whom he considered himself very protective. He had a philosophy regarding boy and girl natures. The spiritual and emotional qualities of colors were also important parts of Lawrence's philosophy. He would often stalk up and down the sidewalk in front of Ray's, shouting to others, or muttering to himself, about peoples' bad behavior. Away from the park activity that he objected to, however, he tended to be very quiet. Actually, people like Lawrence, who do a lot of camping out alone, are quiet much of the time. Lawrence has a fine sense of humor, and is warm, gentle, sensitive, sweet, and sentimental. Lawrence was one of those people who would disappear for months at a time. One did not know if they had gone home, to jail, to a hospital, etc. But in time they would return.

A few doors uptown from Ray's there was a diner with a large front window. Almost every night, from the sidewalk, through that window, one could see the same group of middle-aged people —some looked like old-time comedians, labor organizers, professors, etc. They would be sitting there, talking, for hours.

There was a mix of old East Village culture and the new computer technology. I remember once visiting the home of a computer worker in Alphabet City. This was in the early days of the Internet, in the early 90s. His space was unusually large: lots of stuff was piled up in the darkness on either side of the pathway that led to the far end of the large room. When we reached the far end of the space, I was amazed to see four large monitors, with accompanying keyboards and computers — all piled up and side-by-side, in full operation! I never learned what he was doing with these computers: website design, software development, hacking, etc.? Such was a typical mysterious East Village computer set-up and lifestyle: a combination of mess and brilliance. There were many people with one-of-a-kind worldviews, people who were at times unbalanced, creative, driven, urgent, obsessive, grandiose, awesome, on-the-edge, delightful, funny, stimulating, mad, and desperate.

Many New Yorkers keep a lot of stuff, too much stuff, in their apartments: this is a story unto itself. Perhaps some do it to compensate for the smallness, the limitedness, of their spaces. Sometimes there is barely enough room to open the doors and walk around. Sometimes, as in the case described in the preceding paragraph, there is a pathway along which one can walk, from one end of the space to the other. In short, many New Yorkers, East Villagers included, are 'pack-rats.' This is perhaps one aspect of a larger condition: New Yorkers are, after all, famous for their (psychological, as well as spatial) boundary issues: confusion, or perhaps ambiguity, over where one thing ends and the next begins — me, you; inside, outside; etc.

In the '80s, many people in the neighborhood survived largely on SSI (social security insurance), SSD (social security disability), veterans' benefits, or other types of government checks. For some people, it was a struggle to maintain a mailing address to which their monthly checks could be sent. Having received the check, typically people would cash it at a local check-cashing shop. By the '90s, some 'together' people in this situation had a bank account into which the monthly payments could be placed electronically, and then be accessed with an ATM card.

It seemed to me that at the end of each month there was a certain tension in the air, which at the beginning of the next month was replaced by a certain excitement and joy, as people who had received their payments could, however briefly, once again spend extravagantly. In the late '90s, however, many people were taken off the SSI and SSD programs, and *work-for-welfare* (also known as *workfare*) was introduced. People receiving welfare benefits would be seen, in uniform, picking up garbage in the park.

On Friday nights from time to time there were speak outs at the entrance to TSP, at the northeast corner of Seventh Street and Avenue A. At these speak outs, people of the neighborhood defined for themselves what they felt was the news of the day, and of course they commented upon this news. The speaker would sometimes stand on a plastic milk crate. Povercide Bob would often speak at the speak outs, but actually every day was speak out day for people like him. John the Communist was a longtime squatter and squatter organizer. John, with his long brown hair parted in the center, was often one of the most eloquent speakers at the speak outs. Speakers would often relate local governmental and law enforcement actions — especially their restrictions in regard to, and closings of, squats, community centers, parks, and gardens — to national and international occurrences and trends, including the development of the prison-industrial-military-complex.

At the height of the TSP camping scene (in 1988, before the midnight curfew was imposed, or enforced), hundreds of people were camping out there, in and around the band shell, the grassy areas, etc. I recall that there was one young African-American man who would often

A Radical Political and Social History of the Lower East Side

be carving wood, working on sculptures that exhibited traditional African as well as modern art styles. This living situation may not have been viable, but it was intellectually and artistically stimulating for the neighborhood in general. One reason that the situation was less sanitary than it could have been was that the public restrooms were often not open.

Lack of access to restrooms never seemed to bother the 'crusties,' as they were known. In the years following the imposition of the park curfew, crusties would often sleep in packs in the park together during the day. When they woke up they would sit around in a circle, leaning on each other, holding a council. Sometimes they lived in squats. They had a uniform of sorts: they all seemed to wear cloths that were green and brown. Earth colors. Perhaps it was just that their cloths were colored with dirt. As they would not wash their cloths or bodies for long periods of time, they developed a distinctive odor. Their look and smell were, it seems, badges of honor and identity among them. They just were not going to buy into the system. They wouldn't even go in for fancy tattoos: a number of them had homemade designs on their faces, made with permanent black markers. As most of the squats were closed down and many of the squatters left town or blended into the rest of the city population, it seems the crusties did too. By 2002, crusties no longer roamed the East Village in large numbers.

For years, Jamaican and other West Indian men often played soccer in the afternoons in the band shell area of TSP. This has dwindled. Spontaneous drum circles, especially composed of Hispanic people, used to occur in various places in the park. This has also dwindled, as more and more Hispanic people have been forced by high rents to leave the area; and also perhaps because they simply did not feel the park was theirs anymore, culturally speaking.

One factor that contributed to the dwindling of life in the park was the busting of people for smoking marijuana there. At first just tickets were given, but by the late-90s people were routinely handcuffed, taken in, put through the system, and held at least overnight. The police generally lived in the suburbs and often seemed to view East Village people as weirdoes and jerks. Once I overheard an undercover policeman say with a smirk to a young person he was arresting: "You know you can't smoke pot in the park. Do that at home." To do things like smoking marijuana in one's home, behind closed doors, is a middle-class, suburban approach: many East Villagers wanted to do such things out-of-doors, in nature, and with each other.

By 2002, although it was now certainly simpler on certain practical levels for children and their guardians to make use of the park's playground areas, the park was much less the social and cultural center that it had been years earlier. The imposition of the midnight curfew in 1988 had marked the beginning of the end of the East Village's unique outdoor lifestyle and culture.

On my way to the river, I often walked along Ninth Street from Avenue B to Avenue C so as to pass by La Plaza Cultural. This was a garden and amphitheatre area, with huge willow trees, and other trees. The beautiful scenes of nature were in dramatic visual contrast to the many ruins of buildings in the area. CHARAS, the community arts center in an old public school building, was also on this block. CHARAS was evicted a few years ago, and La

Plaza Cultural has been fenced off so that although one can always see it, one can only enter the space when its managers have opened the lock on the gate.

WBAI radio-99.5 fm-was also an important part of the cultural milieu of the period. WBAI featured a lot of talk, much more so than the other Pacifica stations. People from the East Village often used to speak on WBAI, especially on Bob Fass' late-night program. In the late '90s, when WBAI was commandeered by Pacifica's national board, numerous WBAI people were locked out of the station office and/or fired. This national board was eventually reconstituted and some of its policies were rescinded, but I don't know how things are developing at WBAI these days.

Bob Fass' program on WBAI, and the scene outside Ray's Newsstand, were for many years central to the neighborhood's public sphere, unlike the sham public sphere of television (with the exception of certain public access cable TV programs), and the very limited and unsatisfying public sphere that was available via the Internet.

To reach the East River, one had to cross over the East Side Highway on the walk-bridge either at Seventh or 10th Street. (The 10th St. walk-bridge was removed in 2002, making access to the East River Park more difficult for many people) Usually, I would take the Seventh Street walk-bridge.

The East River Park is located between the East Side Highway and the river. This park is not very wide —only wide enough for a ball field. In the years before encampments were removed all over the city in the mid-90s, there was a sizeable colony of people living in one section of the East River Park, between two of the ball fields. I was told that the people of this group had HIV/AIDS. It was like a lepers' colony, a community of outcasts, literally living on the edge of society, with no further to go other than into the East River. I heard that some of these people were learning reiki and other forms of health maintenance, and healing. I remember seeing these people and thinking, "What a tragic shame it is that sometimes it takes something like getting HIV/AIDS to get people to the point of learning methods of improving health, and of practicing them together."

Having reached the East River, I would walk through the East River Park and proceed in a southerly direction on the promenade along the water's edge. In 2000, from 12th Street down to around Delancey St., a ten-foot high wire-mesh fence was erected along the eastern edge of the East River Park. This fence blocked access to the 10-yard-wide promenade along the water. The word was that the concrete promenade was in danger of eroding and falling into the river. However, no work schedule or projected completion date were ever included in the notices that were put up, and I never saw repair work being done. Many local residents saw the construction of this fence as one more instance of the Giuliani (mayoral) administration's predilection for control and restriction of public movement. This fence made me feel claustrophobic, hemmed in: for one thing, one could no longer imagine freely jumping into the river and swimming to Queens on the far side.

Down near Grand Street there was a deserted open-air amphitheatre. Only the massive stage and backstage areas were covered by a roof: there was a great deal of trash in these areas.

A Radical Political and Social History of the Lower East Side

There were also holes in the fence, and signs, such as mattresses, of people living inside in cleared-away spaces. In the late '90s, the city reclaimed this amphitheatre, and with the assistance of a non-profit arts group — cleaned it up, and fenced it off thoroughly. Under the Brooklyn Bridge (on the Manhattan side), there was a genuine beach — complete with sand, pebbles, rocks, and driftwood — running approximately 200 yards. This was one of two beaches that I was aware of on the Lower Manhattan coastline (the other was beside the East River, near 20th Street). At these beaches in the early and mid-'80s, numerous people lived just above the littoral zone (the shore area between high and low tide watermarks). Here, at the top of the beach, they built encampments, using tarps and found materials of all sorts. Some of these makeshift homes looked like rural huts, or caves (if they were adjacent to walls), and had a mythic, primeval, and haunting quality to them. In ancient days, whalebones were perhaps used in the construction of such homes. Much riverside camping also occurred on the Brooklyn side of the East River, in under-used industrial areas, and in areas that would eventually become parks. By the late '90s, the beach encampments were long gone, at least on the Manhattan side, but I am happy to report that the beach area was permitted to remain under the Manhattan side of the Brooklyn Bridge. One could still walk on that beach in 2002.

Beyond the Brooklyn Bridge, I would come to the Fulton St. Fish Market — in fascinating full swing at four in the morning in those days, now relocated. And then, as I would proceed westward, I would enter the 'sanitized zone': beginning with the tourist mall area which is the South Street Seaport; and following that, the Wall Street area. I would pass the Staten Island Ferry terminal, often wishing I could take a ferry to some far, far away, wild and adventurous place! But, shaking myself from the daydream, I would usually head back northward on the west coast of Manhattan Island, walking up the Battery Park City promenade, along the Hudson River. This promenade, being part of the very upscale Battery Park City neighborhood, was always beautifully kept: it was patrolled by Parks Department guards, unlike the East River Park riverside promenade, which was patrolled by police.

Then, near the northern end of the promenade, I would come upon the World Financial Center, which faced the river. The WFC was a huge building with a massive glass-enclosed atrium, with palm trees and picnic tables inside. This style of architecture, like domed cities, produces space that is, in a sense, a mixture of inside and outside: that is, the enclosed space, with its sunlight and vegetation, almost seems like it is outdoors. Many homeless people slept here, sitting at the picnic tables, until the space was closed at night in the mid-90s (previously, it had been open 24-hours). Finally, I would return toward the East Village, either by subway (the E train stopped under the nearby World Trade Center towers), or by walk, via Chinatown.

If I still had more energy after this six-mile walk, I might head back to Ray's, to see who was still there, and perhaps to have another small chocolate egg cream. There certainly were nights when some of the same people would be out there both before and after my coastline walk.

In summary:

In 2002, East Village streets were filled with people who had been attracted by the neighborhood's artistic and bohemian flavor. College students, for example, were present in ever-increasing numbers. But much of the actual artistic activity had vanished. Where were the people on the streets going? To bars, to drink? If they had dared to sit on the sidewalks, the police would likely have ordered them to move. Aside from TSP, which was closed at midnight, one could for the most part only exist in public if one were in transit, or sitting someplace for a price. This is why it was so important that people had been standing in front of Ray's, talking. They had not been there to consume anything, but rather to produce and to share. They had not been on their way to anyplace else. They had arrived. They were at the center of things. Other people came by to see and visit with them.

But by 2002, the above-described scene around Ray's had dwindled. Many nights, the old regulars were not there, even in good weather. Ray talked about having to close down due to his rent being raised astronomically. When the restaurant on the corner was refashioned (from a Polish diner to a 'hip' bar), this was an ominous signal of the end of the old ethnic and personal style of the neighborhood.

What had happened? A combination of things: First and foremost, there had been an increase in public-space management by the police and by city authorities in general. Regulations of all sorts had been tightened up and enforced. (This was prior to 9/11; the situation became only more extreme after that date.) It had become increasingly difficulty to get, and to continue getting, SSI, SSD, and welfare. Rents had risen greatly, and rent-control protections had been weakened. Many gardens had been confiscated by the city. Artists could no longer afford outdoor lots — or, in many cases, indoor studios. With fewer performers and painters present, there were fewer performance spaces and galleries; for in the old days, in the mid-80s, Lower East Side performers had performed primarily for other performers. There had been a real community of artists, living and working in close proximity to each other.

By 2002, a global evolutionary trend was also affecting the situation: there were just fewer and fewer people engaged in the old-fashioned physical activities of performance, dance, theater, painting, and sculpture. Instead, more and more people — including artistically-oriented individuals — were spending much of their time working with computers, using computers as their primary medium. Due in part to the state of computer technology at the time, this meant that many people were now working indoors, and alone. Working with computers and the Internet also made it increasingly difficult to function outside the mainstream economic and legal systems, without, for examples, a credit card and bank account, for such things are often needed for dependable and high-quality electrical, telephone, and Internet connections.

Over the past 20 years, a number of social and cultural shifts have occurred in the East Village. The numbers of Hispanic and Eastern-European people, artistic people, 'progressive' people, and poor people have diminished. It is not clear to what extent this has been willed and planned, but city authorities are well aware of the East Village's historical role as a national and international center of radical thought and action, and it seems that some of

A Radical Political and Social History of the Lower East Side

them have been only too happy to see some of the East Village's traditional people and culture dispersed. It also seems that some politicians may have been guided by landlords and real estate owners in this process. Nomadic and independent-minded people everywhere tend to have a difficult time in civilizations, as civic authorities naturally tend to seek to establish pervasive administrative grids.

One could see the old East Village being transformed with every locally owned store that closed, and with every huge 'convenience store' (Duane Reade, etc.) that opened in its place. One type of product that the convenience stores specialize in selling is processed and preserved foods that have very long shelf lives. These convenience stores are like huge truck stops, helping to reduce neighborhoods to non-neighborhoods. There are ways to promote local arts and crafts — even in this era of national and international franchises — but sadly, it seems that such ways have not been developed and applied in the East Village very much to date.

It is a shame that the residents of the East Village and city authorities have not found many ways to work together to channel East Villagers' vibrant energy and creativity into productive projects. I have always felt that there should be arts, health, spirituality, community building, and other types of workshops (perhaps with the use of folding tables), on the sidewalks of Avenue A. (especially between Seventh Street and St. Mark's Place), every single afternoon and evening (weather permitting).

It should be noted that the squats, most of which were in Alphabet City, were no utopias. Stories abounded about nasty behavior by squatters toward each other, about how squatters had been forced out, or victimized by each other in other ways. Neither should one romanticize the outdoor living that occurred in and around the East Village near the end of the twentieth century. Every animal likes to have a quiet, safe, comfortable place she or he can retreat to and relax in, and many people living outdoors in the East Village did not have this. Many people had no choice but to put up with uncertain and difficult living conditions if they wanted to stay in the East Village, near each other, in this cultural milieu. Many people grew to depend on each other, for they were undergoing an ordeal together. Some people may not have had much, but at least they had each other — and the outdoors, including some precious parks and gardens. There was a sense — however evanescent and illusionary — of everybody in the neighborhood being in this together.

Yes, many East Village street people were a little unbalanced and short-tempered, and many of them could turn on you very quickly and surprisingly. But this did not happen too often or seriously, at least in my experience. The point is, there was a community of independent thinkers who would hang out together. What is a community anyway? What is a neighborhood? Common styles, customs, inclinations, ways of seeing and doing things. In the case of the East Village, it was a special neighborhood: an art-making and experimental-thinking capital of the nation and of the world, going back to the '60s, the '30s, and earlier. For many people, it was a place to meet people, get high, and listen to music. A place to enjoy 'wine, women, and song' (or the equivalents). A place for variants of those near-universally-sought-after complementary pleasures: intoxicants, love and sex, and art. And, of course, for many generations the Lower East Side has been an interface between the rest of the USA to the west, and to the east, the rest of the world.

A common chant when spaces would be closed down, torn down, or restricted, was, "US out of the Lower East Side!" The Lower East Side was the only place where many people felt comfortable in those days: for such individuals, the prospect of going north of 14th Street, beyond the 'liberated zone,' was daunting. There was a feeling that, on some level, East Villagers were a separate people (with mystical links to like-minded individuals of all places and times). NYC in general is different from most of the rest of the USA. Most USA people don't care very much for much of NYC's people and culture: note the still-popular Christian preachers who hailed the 9/11 incidents as divine punishment of New Yorkers.

In the '80s and early '90s, there was a sense in the East Village that here, just as at Woodstock, people were in the process of making a new culture, a utopian civilization, of making history. In that East Village, there were many social connections to the Woodstock scene: in a sense, the East Village and Woodstock were sister art colonies. (The town of Woodstock is less than a three-hour drive from New York City) Of course "Woodstock," the rock concert and social experiment, actually occurred in Bethel, some miles away from Woodstock, but the town of Woodstock has been, and remains, an important arts center, and many people of the old East Village had connections to this and countless other arts colonies and individuals around the world.

There were also many connections to the rainbow gathering scene. There are numerous legends regarding how rainbow gatherings began. One is that a few years after Woodstock, in the early '70s, some people wanted to gather annually in the Woodstock spirit. Thus they meet in national parks around each 4th of July for a week or so. Electricity and money are done without. People cook, lead workshops, make music, and just enjoy nature and each other. There are also smaller regional gatherings, and gatherings outside the USA. Many rainbow gathering people stay in touch throughout the year, and chances are if one visits an organic food store or restaurant in most USA cities, one can find rainbow gathering people. Many rainbow gathering people used to live in the vicinity of Ray's. The old East Village almost seemed to be on the verge of being a perpetual Woodstock, a perpetual rainbow gathering. This was especially so on the days when Jerry the Peddler and other squatters would facilitate cultural festivals in TSP.

I have written most of this essay in the past tense because many of the things and people described herein no longer exist on the Lower East Side, although many still do. Because I have been out of the country for a year, I do not know exactly what remains, and how things have changed. There are some positive developments: Lach has built the music room, known as The Fort, of the Sidewalk Café into a major cultural institution, featuring what he calls "anti-folk music" (this is on the northeast corner of Sixth Street and Avenue A, just uptown, across the street, from Merlin's corner). North of First Street, on the west side of Third Avenue, the Bowery Poetry Space and DV (Digital Video) Dojo are facilitating wonderful poetry and computer-video work, respectively. Some gardens survive. The Federation of East Village Artists has come into being. A few years ago the city permitted a small number of the remaining squats in Alphabet City to go legit: that is, residents of the squats were

A Radical Political and Social History of the Lower East Side

allowed to purchase the properties from the city. I am most interested to learn how this experiment is working out.

However, friends tell me via e-mail that the old cultural life of the East Village has dwindled drastically in the year I have been away, and that I will be shocked when I return. Although I hope to visit and interact with the people of the East Village perpetually, I am planning to settle in Chennai, the capital of the south Indian state of Tamil Nadu. Chennai, formerly called Madras, faces Singapore, and seems to be a good spot from which to collaborate on artistic, academic, telecommunication, and other projects with people around the world. There is still a strong sense of wilderness in this part of the world.

The speak outs, the conversations in front of Ray's and those in TSP: these were public sphere activities that are very rare in modern society. Certainly, I have never found so much public sphere space, discussion, and socializing in any other part of NYC, or in any other USA city. I wish Ray's, and the sidewalk in front of Ray's, could be recognized as an historic site, as a cultural treasure. There is not another spot like it in the world (although there is much more street life in places like India than in the USA). While living in the USA, I, for one, only felt truly at home, at peace, centered, and in the bosom of the public sphere, when I was standing in front of Ray's.

No matter where I am — even in the mountain forests of south India — in the evenings I sometimes get the urge to get up, get out of my personal space, and wander over to Ray's, to see who is around, say hello, and discuss the day's news.

Endnotes:

1. (Regarding these activities, please see my article, "Live Video as Performance on New York City's Lower East Side in the 1980s," pp. 261-6, in *Captured: A Film/Video History of the Lower East Side*, edited by Clayton Patterson and published by the Federation of East Village Artists in NY in 2003; and also posted at http://ccat.sas.upenn.edu/~emiller/video_history.html).

2. He was often full of the blarney, and was often up in arms about something or other. Jim made tile mosaics in the neighborhood, both indoors and out. (An essay I have written about Jim's mosaic work, "Festive Art in a Festive Neighborhood: Street Mosaics in the East Village," is posted http://ccat.sas.upenn.edu/~emiller/mosaics_paper.html).

SECTION TWO - HOUSING/SQUATS

Chapter 1

The Struggle for Space
10 Years of Turf Battling on the Lower East Side
        By Sarah Ferguson

June 2005 -"It's one minute before midnight. The park is now closed." The tin voice bleated from the loudspeaker of a squad car slowly circling Tompkins Square's winding paths, disrupting a few amorous couples on benches, a pair of dog walkers, some drunks dozing in the surprisingly crisp summer air. But aside from a rather well dressed couple who wondered aloud, "Why do they have to close the park on such a beautiful night?" there was little objection. A clump of college kids in artsy punk attire clustered at the exit, checked cell phones, debated which bar or party to try out next. But the real punks, the crusty alcoholic travelers, had already retired to the East River to drink their spare-changed beer unfettered by police. That motley rabble of squatters and hippies, anarchist bike messengers, homeless agitators and soap-boxing radicals who'd once made this park their crucible and crusade, had long since moved on.

The cops padlocked the gates and called it a night.

There was a time when closing Tompkins Square was unthinkable. In 1988, when police attempted to impose a 1 a.m. curfew, it sparked a bloody riot. But for more than 150 years prior to that (aside from a 15-year span following the Civil War when the park was requisitioned as a military parade ground), Tompkins Square was considered a "people's park" a community living room, recreational arena, and radical stomping ground that stayed open.

From the "bread riots" of 1857 and 1874 and the draft riot of 1863, Tompkins Square earned a rep as a stage for politicking and social strife, a legacy that continued through the 1960s and '70s, when the park became a mecca for downtown bohemia, with smoke-ins and love-ins and antiwar rallies organized by the Diggers and Yippies, and free concerts with the Grateful Dead, Janis Joplin, Jimi Hendrix, Charles Mingus and Sun Ra. In one infamous incident on Memorial Day in 1967, police brutally rousted and arrested a group of hippies and Puerto Ricans who were strumming guitars and beating congas, in defiance of the "Keep Off the Grass" signs. (There were 38 arrests and dozens of injuries.) A judge dismissed the charges, stating, "This court will not deny equal protection to the unwashed, unshod, unkempt, and uninhibited."[1]

Ambling through the park now, with its verdant lawns and gardens tended with the help of volunteers sponsored by corporate interests, it's hard to fathom that legacy. It's hard to comprehend a time when neighborhood people —squatters, tenement dwellers, politicos and lunatic poets — would put their bodies on the line to clash with the blue meanies over the right to occupy a four-block-square patch of earth. Or that punks from New Jersey and Long Island would actually commute to take part in the Friday and Saturday-night bottle throwing and street bonfires that became, from 1988 to 1991, something of a neighborhood rite.

142

In this post-9/11 moment, with the geography of oppression blown open as far as the mind can see, it's sometimes hard to remember how a turf war over a scrappy piece of green in the middle of New York City could have so captivated a movement, become its locus and spiritual center, with the battle cry of "Free the land!"

Memory intercepts hollowed-out refrain of conga drums, "Pigs outa da park . . ." a police siren echoing like graffiti bleeding through freshly painted walls.

TOTAL WAR FOR LIVING SPACE

What's changed is the notion that this was OUR space to be defended. The squatting and political movement that rose up in and around Tompkins Square from roughly 1985 to 1995 was in many ways the last generation of activists to conceive of the Lower East Side as oppositional space.

The battle over Tompkins Square grew out of a much larger and decades-old struggle to preserve the multiethnic, working-class nature of the neighborhood against the forces of "urban renewal" and gentrification. For the squatters, homeless activists, artists, and social renegades who agitated there, defending the park was part of a much more ambitious gambit to liberate space, to wrest control of the city's abandoned buildings and rubble-strewn lots and create a new kind of community operating outside the realm of property law.

The act of squatting city-owned buildings, of exempting them from the cycle of speculation, was not a symbolic protest but an eminently hands-on assault on the bedrock of New York capitalism— real estate— which offered tangible results: You got a cheap place to live and consort with fellow radicals making art and ragging on the system.

In this context, Tompkins Square served as both a living symbol of the neighborhood's dissent and a physical locus for organizing and agitating against the homogenizing tide of wealth and redevelopment.

"The idea of space — of organizing around space — came from the negative, from the idea that the government was actively moving to spatially *deconcentrate* inner city areas," says former squatter and activist Frank Morales. "It became an operative understanding, part of the analysis of areas like the South Bronx and Lower East Side."

A radical Episcopal priest who had helped a group successfully homestead a couple of buildings in the South Bronx, Morales arrived on the Lower East Side in 1985 with a stack of federal housing documents relating to the Kerner Commission Report on the riots that ripped through America's inner cities during the late 1960s. While generally thought of as a rather benevolent attempt to remedy the country's deepening racial divide (the report famously warned the U.S. was "moving toward two societies, one black, one white — separate and unequal"), the Kerner Report's authors also made some controversial recommendations for restoring order in urban areas. In order to alleviate poverty and the growing hostility toward mainstream society by minorities living in these overcrowded "slums," the report recommended policies to encourage "substantial Negro movement out of the ghettos," and into the white-dominated suburbs.[2]

Subsequent documents from the Department of Housing and Urban Development (HUD) and Kerner Commission consultant Anthony Downs referred to a policy of "spatial deconcentration" — essentially deconcentrating the poor from the inner cities by withholding funds and services to these areas in order to make way for more middle-class development. Whether or not "Spatial D" itself was ever instituted as public policy remains unclear; the documentation seemed vague at best. But when Yolanda Ward, the activist who'd sought to expose this conspiracy, was shot to death on a Washington, DC street in 1985, it reconfirmed the sense among urban radicals that the government was actively engaged in a war on the poor. [3]

Published in the radical graphic zine *World War 3 Illustrated* in 1986[4], this theory of spatial deconcentration was central to the perspective of the more militant squatter activists. Coming out of the fiscal crisis, when the Beame and Koch administrations cut services to poor neighborhoods like the Lower East Side and the South Bronx and whole blocks of tenements were burned to the ground in arson fires, it was easy to see why. Less conspiratorial minds might be tempted to cast the city's actions during that period as more indicative of depraved neglect by an institutionally racist bureaucracy with no money and nothing to be gained from helping the poor. (Daniel Patrick Moynihan had famously advocated a policy of "benign neglect"; Abe Beame's housing czar Roger Starr came up with the term "planned shrinkage.") But for community agitators like Morales, this was a concerted plot to clear the poor and neutralize urban dissent involving the police, the military, and the Federal Emergency Management Agency (FEMA)[5] acting in concert with city planners and real estate developers. And the subsequent, obscene speculation on the abandoned and dilapidated housing stock of the East Village in the 1980s and early '90s, followed by the city's paramilitary evictions of squatters and homeless, would serve as proof of the conspiracy:

"We saw the taking of buildings as part of a counterattack in this spatial war, so to speak," Morales explains. "From then on, the notion of space — seizing territory as a defensive strategy against this onslaught to remove and push [poor people] out of the area — became the center of what we were talking about. The idea of building communities of resistance was precisely that. It was hands-on ideology, not abstract but ultimately practical. We were resisting this effort to remove us from these areas."

The strategy, Morales explains, "was both affirmative   taking buildings or making gardens to create free space, to extend the space where there was no speculation; and defensive — defending the squats that had already been taken, and thereby slowing the real estate pressures around you, which in turn helped preserve the low rent housing in the area."
The notion of free space also harkened back to the Diggers of the 1960s (themselves a throwback to the 17th century squatter movement in England) and Proudhon's old anarchist adage, "property is theft." It was also a reaction to the stultification of the traditional left and the evisceration of the workplace as a field for social struggle. In contrast to marching in the streets, squatting was direct action that could boast of more than symbolic gains: To take a building and make a home in one of the richest cities in the world. To make that

building a stage for political dissent and an anti-consumption lifestyle, thumbing your nose at the system and the market theocrats who served Mammon.

Flyers circulating in the neighborhood spoke of "Total War for Living Space." And indeed, the battle over the squats and Tompkins Square took on mythic overtones, with activists casting the fight to "free the land" as a guerrilla struggle against the rightwing ideological assault of the Reagan administration, or in solidarity with the uprisings of landless peasants in Latin America. That stance gave this otherwise local struggle its radical cachet, attracting punks and activists from across the U.S. and Europe, along with the usual parasitic elements of the sectarian left seeking to capitalize off the latest social unrest.

Of course, many minorities and long-term Lower East Siders saw the squatters and Tompkins Square agitators less as defenders of the neighborhood and more as interlopers on their turf. (The LES has never been kind to newcomers, and it had seen all manner of idealism before.)

THE MYTHOS OF TOMPKINS SQUARE

This conception of the Lower East Side as a kind of final frontier for urban struggle drew from the area's radical history — a culture of dissent that dates back to the neighborhood's formation as an immigrant entry point and working class slum, home to socialists, anarchists, feminists and numerous competing ethnic groups vying for space. Tompkins Square played a key role in the creation of that ethos. When it was constructed in 1834, city officials expected the park to attract wealthy families to the area, like those already occupying elegant townhouses to the west of Second Avenue. But the expansion of the wealthy district was halted by the economic depression of 1837. Instead, the neighborhood surrounding the park was soon filled with German and Irish immigrants drawn to work in the local shipyards, known as the Dry Dock, along the East River.[6]

Living conditions in the overcrowded tenements were abysmal and grew worse during the economic crunch of 1857, when many were thrown out of work. For the first of many times, Tompkins Square was transformed into a field of protest, as unemployed Dry Dock workers demonstrated to demand that the city provide jobs in public projects such as the construction of Central Park, then underway. Park benches were torn apart for bonfires. A *New York Times* headline read: "THE UNEMPLOYED: Great Gatherings in Tompkins Square and the Park. U.S. Troops Guard the Custom House."

City Hall responded to these disturbances by having the park completely renovated in 1859. But this effort to impose a new standard of decorum was short-lived. Large-scale rioting erupted in Tompkins Square and across the city in 1863 to protest the Civil War draft (beyond not wanting to fight for "negroes," many poor whites were pissed that the rich could get out of the draft by paying $300).[7] Three years later, the State legislature had the whole park razed and transformed into a drill ground for the New York State militia. The heavy military presence in the area did little to cool neighborhood agitators — from feminists advocating women's suffrage to anarchists and socialists urging working class revolution, or organizing rent strikes and boycotts for cheaper food.

Tensions exploded in January 1874, in the wake of the financial "panic" of 1873, when police brutally shut down a 10,000-strong rally of workers and unemployed in Tompkins Square, clubbing both demonstrators and bystanders in a melee that labor leader Samuel Gompers described as "an orgy of brutality."[8] Accounts of the event eerily presage the Tompkins Square riot of 1988. Without warning, police on horseback surrounded the square and suddenly charged into the crowd from all sides with their nightsticks swinging. "Women and children went screaming in all directions. Many of them were trampled underfoot in the stampede for the gates. In the streets, bystanders were ridden down and mercilessly clubbed by mounted officers."[9] Newspaper reports demonized the demonstrators as "riotous communists" raising the specter of the "red flag" over Manhattan. But this brutal attack on the working class also served to radicalize and alienate the local populace from the city at large, setting off a dynamic of militant Lower East Siders resisting City Hall that would repeat for generations to come.

Six months after the 1874 riot, some 3,000 people gathered in Tompkins Square and resolved that the park should always remain "open to the people for their free assembly." Local residents campaigned for the removal of the military, and in 1878, the whole park was finally reinstated for public use.[10]

It's worth reviewing this early history because it helps account for the degree of political and economic exceptionalism that evolved on the Lower East Side — the way the neighborhood seemed to function for so many decades as an island unto itself. Despite the area's relatively easy proximity to the downtown financial district, efforts by New York's ruling class to transform the neighborhood into a Wall Street bedroom were repeatedly confounded by a combination of community resistance and economic downturns. In 1929, the Rockefeller-sponsored Regional Plan Association came up with an ambitious scheme to raze large blocks of tenements to erect a Second Avenue speedway, "high-class" high-rises, modern shops, even a yacht basin on the East River. The plan met heavy neighborhood opposition from tenant and labor groups, but was largely sunk by the arrival of the Great Depression. Similarly, a 1956 urban renewal plan by Robert Moses that would have mowed down whole blocks of tenements between East Ninth Street and Delancey Street was defeated by a decade of intense political organizing by the Cooper Square Committee, combined with the ongoing exodus of the middle classes to the suburbs, which drew government and investment capital out of the inner cities.[11]

Instead, other waves of immigrants — Puerto Ricans and Dominicans, and African Americans fleeing poverty in the South — flooded the Lower East Side, retrenching the perception of the area as an "ethnic slum." As social geographer Neil Smith writes, "In the postwar period, disinvestment and abandonment, demolition and public warehousing, were the major tactics of a virulent antiurbanism that converted the Lower East Side into something of a free-fire zone."[12]

Cheap rents drew beatniks and artists from the Greenwich Village in the '50s, then the hippies of the '60s, along with all manner of radical factions from the Diggers to the Young Lords, Black Panthers, free-loving communalists, Kerista sex cultists, dervishing Hare Krishnas, and Up Against the Wall Motherfuckers. The radicalized, offbeat tenor of the neighborhood, combined with the deepening squalor and crime wrought by the influx of heroin, speed and crack cocaine in the '60s, '70s, and '80s, gave the Lower East Side its reputation as an "outlaw" zone.

With the arrival of artists in the early '80s sprouting renegade galleries and performance spaces in the area's bottomed-out storefronts, that outlaw flavor became chic. Many of these new artists were white and middle class, staking out a new frontier against the soul-less consumerism of the suburbs and frightening Cold War posturing of the Reagan administration. They reveled in the clash of their freewheeling, downscale bohemia thriving in the shadow of the corporate titans that ruled midtown and Wall Street. But their mediagenic spectacle made them pilot fish for gentrification, as both speculators and City Hall rushed to capitalize on the notion of the "East Village" as the new hipster SoHo.[13]

In 1981, for example, Mayor Ed Koch proposed auctioning off vacant buildings to developers to create artist co-ops. But the plan was fiercely opposed by local housing groups and many artists themselves when it was learned that the co-ops, publicly financed as low and moderate-income housing, would sell for $50,000 and could be flipped at market rates after only three years. Members of the Lower East Side Joint Planning Council (JPC) — a coalition of more than 30 housing and community groups, many of them closely aligned with the Cooper Square Committee — tacked up signs on the abandoned tenements proclaiming: "This Land Is Ours. Property of the People of the Lower East Side: Speculators Keep Out!" (One of these signs still proudly adorns "C Squat" at 155 Avenue C), and the plan was voted down by the Board of Estimate in 1983.[14]

HOMESTEADERS TAKE OVER

Many of the members of the JPC were themselves pioneers in the first wave of home-steading on the Lower East Side that began in the mid 1970s. While there had been sporadic efforts at squatting in previous decades (books like Ed Sanders' *Tales of Beatnik Glory* and William Kotzwinkle's *The Fan Man* are rife with scenes of hippie crash pads), the notion of people using "sweat equity" to fully renovate buildings for low-income housing took root in the '70s, led by neighborhood residents and tenants of in-rem buildings who refused to leave during the onslaught of fires and abandonment that swept the area during the fiscal crisis, along with some inspired social activists drawn to the urban battle zone. At the time their efforts were quite celebrated. In 1976, *CBS Evening News with Walter Cronkite* featured a report on the 11th Street Movement, a group of homesteaders who took over several abandoned buildings on East 11th Street, presenting the group as pioneers in the fight against urban despair.

The group was founded by local residents and activists such as Michael Friedberg, a maverick from South Africa, who teamed up with Interfaith Adopt-a-Building, a newly formed, citywide sweat equity group. By today's standards, their project to create a kind of self-sufficient commune in the East Village seems wildly idealistic. At 519 East 11th, the homesteaders installed an African fish farm in the basement, along with solar panels and a windmill on the roof, and at one point even succeeded in forcing Con Edison to buy the excess electricity it generated. (The scheme admittedly didn't last long; the windmill is still there but never functioned all that well and has been dormant for years.) They also transformed a series of drug-infested lots on East 12th Street into a community garden called El Sol Brillante — one of the few such green spaces in New York City that is cooperatively owned by local residents.[15]

Impressed by the success of the 11th Street Movement and similar projects in the South Bronx and East Harlem, President Jimmy Carter authorized a National Urban Homesteading Demonstration Program in 1977, which funneled federal monies into homesteading projects, generally through established community organizations such as Adopt-A-Building and UHAB (the Urban Homesteading Assistance Board). Others eschewed the red tape and bureaucracy of these schemes in favor of a more "self-help"-minded approach, such as A Better Way, a group of local activists and tenants who took over four tenements on East Sixth Street. In fact, it was in part to quell a rash of unauthorized building occupations across the city by both tenants and activist groups like ACORN and Banana Kelly (in the Bronx) that the city launched its own homesteading program in 1980. The program, which was fairly informal in its early years, granted groups title and financial assistance to renovate buildings that the city otherwise might have torn down.

In the early days, one homesteader remembers, a group could form a tenant association to rehab a building and actually get the city to deliver materials. "We would just go into these buildings and start gutting them out to kind of stake our claim, then back that up by putting in an application for the city [homesteading] program or to get funding from the federal government or state," says Howard Brandstein, executive director of the Sixth Street Community Center, who helped homestead numerous buildings on the Lower East Side through Adopt-a-Building and RAIN (Rehabilitation in Action for Improvement of Neighborhoods), a local sweat-equity group funded by the Lower East Side Catholic Area Conference (LESCAC). "We'd tell the city we were applying for funding, and the city would give us provisional site control. The city just didn't care. The neighborhood wasn't worth anything back then," Brandstein says.

At one point, homesteaders could qualify for $45,000 per unit or more in city and state and federal funding to renovate buildings.[16] Brandstein estimates more than 30 buildings were homesteaded on the Lower East Side by various groups. Many of those homesteaders went on to become members of the local community board, such as Margarita Lopez, who was subsequently elected to represent the neighborhood on the City Council; others became successful artists such as composers Butch Morris and Jemeel Moondoc, and actor Luis Guzman.

But many others were left out in the cold. Reagan dumped the federal homesteading program along with all of Carter's "green renewal" efforts as soon as he took office, and the city's housing department became increasingly restrictive about approving buildings, eventually canceling its program in 1986 as real estate values across the city surged.
City officials now insist that homesteading was never "practical" enough to be considered a viable means of creating low-income housing. For all those buildings that succeeded, many others dissolved in internal disputes or as people drifted off. In fact, many of the truly

needy homesteaders became fed up with the refusal of the city and its sanctioned housing groups to allow people to live in the buildings until they were fully renovated.

Local housing advocates also became disillusioned with homesteading as a means to create low-income housing—especially as market pressures in the neighborhood intensified. Brandstein reflects: "Homesteading was inherently more of an anarchist structure of self-government in each building. It was a very elaborate model, but it didn't hold together in terms of the forces that were tearing people apart on the Lower East Side. There was no longer a political conception in the neighborhood to keep building this cooperative structure . . . People would start exploiting the situation—behaving like owners and trying to get out of the resale restrictions. A lot of buildings were ending up in conflict. Also, there weren't enough people with skills; we weren't drawing a critical mass of people. And the buildings themselves needed support structures so they didn't fall into this kind of capitalist thinking. So we came up with a scheme for a land trust," whereby the tenements would be owned as low-income co-ops, but the land would be held by a community land trust.

The problem, in the eyes of Brandstein and other JPCites, was that homesteading alone could not check the wave of gentrification that by the mid-80s was threatening to subsume the remaining undeveloped properties on the Lower East Side. Neighborhood housing advocates turned their attentions to fighting off Koch's plans to auction off large numbers of empty buildings to private developers. That fight led to the infamous 50-50 cross subsidy plan, whereby the city agreed to allow the remaining in-rem buildings to be renovated for low and moderate-income housing in exchange for the ability to sell off vacant lots for market-rate development.[17]

Negotiated by members of the JPC and Community Board 3 and finally approved in 1987, the cross-subsidy plan was considered a triumph of localism over the city's real-estate-friendly housing bureaucracy. (Housing cross-subsidies were a relatively novel concept at the time). The problem, of course, was where to get the money to renovate the buildings for low-income people? The feds weren't giving much of anything, and following the stock market crash of 1987, the city wasn't either.

SQUATTERS MOVE IN

In the meantime, a new generation of activists was already taking over buildings on the Lower East Side, and pushing a more radical notion of homesteading than the community groups that came before them. There have been so many misconceptions of who the squatters were, and in fact their collective identity has always been hard to define. Some were locals who sought official sanction and title to buildings, but found that the city had cancelled its homesteading program—or were refused entry, such as the residents occupying three tenements on East Seventh Street between Avenues C and D, which were taken over by a mixture of original tenants and squatters in the early 1970s. Others were radicals who wanted no part of "the system." Many squatted from necessity, or to sustain their downwardly mobile art careers. Others because they wanted the freedom to create their own homes and live outside the "rent slave" housing market. Or to demonstrate with their own hands the criminality of a housing bureaucracy that could leave so many without homes. There was never any single reason if you pressed.

Their outsider status was reinforced by the state's refusal to recognize sweat equity as a means of creating housing any longer. That refusal helped define a more radical and desperate population. Anyone willing to live with perpetual threat of eviction had to be something of a rebel—whether you called yourself a homesteader or a squatter.

Still, within the squatting scene there were two somewhat overlapping philosophies: those who considered themselves homesteaders using self-help to create homes, with the ultimate aim of forcing the city to give them title to the property, and those who squatted in defiance of property laws, believing housing should be "free" (or at least free to those who worked to reclaim it.)

David Boyle epitomized the former philosophy. A former Police Academy recruit and New School university student, Boyle helped found the 13th Street Homesteading Coalition, which took over six buildings on 13th between Avenues A and B in the mid-1980s. Boyle says he got the idea to squat the buildings from Sarah Farley, a former civil rights organizer from the South who had squatted a building on East Sixth Street in the '70s (it later burned down) and ran a group called LAND (Local Action for Neighborhood Development) out of the thrift shop on the ground floor.

"Sarah told me to work on building gardens in the [empty] lots, which I did at Sixth Street," notes Boyle, who helped found the Sixth Street and Avenue B Community Garden. "And then she said to start taking over buildings." Boyle says he and Rolando Politti, an Italian artist who immigrated to the Lower East Side in 1980, initially tried to join the fractious mix of homesteaders on East Seventh Street between C and D but were put off by the infighting.[18] They then opened a building on East Third Street, which got taken over by Mickey Cesar, the infamous "Pope of Dope" pot dealer. They also made a stab at clearing out a nascent squat on East Fifth Street, which Boyle says was already occupied by several homeless drunks and a couple of street peddlers who objected to their efforts to remove their junk.[19]

Then Farley directed Boyle, Politti, and a young activist named Marissa DeDominici to the swath of unoccupied tenements on East 13th Street.

"We were like gung-ho Sandinista Marxists at that point," says Boyle. "We were interested in doing something new. Our inspiration was the Mondragon cooperatives led by the Basque separatists in Spain [during the 1950s]. Rather than pursuing some kind of military program, the Mondragons believe the best way to obtain independence was to control the land and industry. So we thought we were going to be setting up some sort of cooperative economy on the Lower East Side. And the first step was giving value to people's labor, so the sweat equity thing really dovetailed into that. We actually printed up our own money with some labor guy's face on it that we used as receipts. If you couldn't pay your rent money to the building, which was then like $75 or $100 a month, you could pay it with labor notes." According to Boyle, this system functioned fairly efficiently for about a year, with roughly 60 members. "With everyone paying $75 to $100, we had a couple thousand a month to spend

A Radical Political and Social History of the Lower East Side

on the buildings, which meant we were able to pay outside contractors to do some big $8,000-job, like run an electrical line from the street. We had a real commonweal going. We were moving toward being a part of RAIN, toward becoming legal homesteaders. But we had a more adventurous model than RAIN because we were living in the buildings while we renovated them."

Living in the buildings while you renovated was a major sticking point in negotiations with the city. While many early homesteaders got away with inhabiting the spaces they worked on, by the early '80s, that wasn't an option in the eyes of city bureaucrats and the housing groups that funneled people into its legal homesteading program.

"The city really went nuclear against you when you moved people into a building, because that meant you were taking it over," says Boyle. "The city didn't want people to live there. That meant you were squatting, and the city wouldn't deal with squatters. When home-steading groups like RAIN and Adopt-a-Building went in and started working on a building, they did it without city permission. But they didn't go so far as to say, we have this build-ing. It was more like, we've invested energy in it. Whereas our position was, we have it."

Nevertheless, Boyle says initially there was some crossover between the two camps. "Groups like RAIN and Adopt-a-Building were really building a constituency more than they were taking over buildings," Boyle maintains. "The people in their groups who came to work days at a particular building weren't necessarily the people who moved into it. We showed up and worked on some of RAIN's buildings, and they helped us a bit, too." (In fact, Boyle says he helped initiate the JPC scheme to put up signs on abandoned tenements declaring them "Property of the People of the Lower East Side" in direct response to all the "For Sale" signs that the city was tacking up. They fashioned the signs from the tin the city had used to board up the vacant buildings, and spray painted them at one of the 13th Street squats.)

In order to get around the fact that the city would not negotiate with squatters, Boyle and some of the other 13th Street homesteaders formed their own not-for-profit group, Outstanding Renewal Enterprises (ORE). "The idea was to have an entity that the city could deal with, because they wouldn't deal with us," Boyle explains. As a legal not-for-profit, ORE was allowed to join the Joint Planning Council. The group got grants to start the Lower East Side's first recycling program and was instrumental with other members of the JPC in helping found the Lower East Side People's Credit Union. Although ORE and the 13th Street homesteaders initially won approval from the local community board for a couple of their buildings, Boyle says the group's drive to become a legal homestead unraveled because of internal disputes.

"We got a couple of bad apples in there who took apart the program by going for rent strikes against us," Boyle says. "We were moving toward becoming a part of RAIN, and some people didn't want to go that way. I think they figured that once we were part of RAIN, they couldn't get away with not paying rent, so it was easier to take us out. So they initiated this campaign of rumor-mongering and scandal, and then RAIN wouldn't take us in."

By that time, the 13th Street buildings had attracted other squatters who felt housing should be free. They clashed with Boyle and the other ORE members' efforts to impose rules and structure. "I was pretty Stalinist at the time," Boyle concedes. "I felt that if we were trying to produce some kind of small utopian thing, you had to work, produce some kind of money, and contribute to the collective. But these other people didn't want any part of `the system,' and at that point, we were a system [in the buildings]. So they spent all their energy resisting us," he says.

Others involved at the time would no doubt object vociferously to Boyle's version of events. [20] What's always been fascinating about the squats is the intensity of competing personalities, ideals and objectives within them. For all its conflicts, the 13th Street scene became a seedpod for other squatting efforts and art projects, such as the Shuttle Theatre in the ground floor of 537 East 13th Street, which became a venue for Living Theatre plays, jazz improvs and performances by local and traveling artists like Baba Olatunji.

OCCUPIED TERRITORIES

Another corridor of squats evolved on East Eighth Street between Avenues B and C when Michael Shenker, a musician and self-taught electrician (who had also been inspired by Sarah Farley), opened up an empty tenement at 319 East Eighth Street in the spring of 1984 with his girlfriend Natasha and some other people from the neighborhood who were seeking cheap housing. One of them, a Jamaican-American woman named Tya Scott, split from 319 and opened up her own building across the street at 316 East Eighth Street with her sons and their extended families. (Tya kept her distance from the rest of the squatting scene and conceived of herself more as a property owner.)

Later that fall, some activists traveling with the Rock Against Reagan tour returned from the Republican Convention in Dallas and broke into the back of 327-29 East Eighth Street. According to Yippie Jerry "the Peddler" Wade, the building was more of a crash pad until "English" Steve Harrington and Cathy Thompson arrived, fresh from the squatting scene in Europe and looking to put in practice the revolutionary ideals and squatting skills they'd learned there. Wade says he helped sledgehammer open the front door with Harrington and Cathy Thompson in December 1984. They were soon joined by Frank Morales, who had returned to the Lower East Side in 1985 seeking to apply the model of homesteading he'd learned in the Bronx.

The intersection of radical idealism at 327-29 proved to be a fertile mix. "We didn't really become organized as `squatters' until we opened up 327-29," says Wade, who had earlier taken over another abandoned building at 643 East 11th Street. "We were still arguing about the use of the word squatting, and whether we should be squatters or homesteaders. Most people wanted to call it homesteading. They kept saying 'squatting is something you do when you take a shit.' But we weren't homesteaders. We didn't qualify for any of the [homesteading] programs, and most of those programs wouldn't want us anyway, even if we did [laughs]. Then English Steve and Cathy came and started using the term squatting left and right, and we kind of went with it from there."

Recalls Harrington:

> We were the anarchist squatters, so we had no intention of going legal.
> Becoming legal would have been too much dealing with the system. We'd been
> squatting in Europe, where you just didn't consider that, where becoming legal
> was up there with informing on your neighbor. It was too much. That's how we
> thought of it back then.

According to Morales, 327 became a pit stop for activists and folks traveling the underground circuit — including folksinger Michelle Shocked, who squatted there for a summer
and held hootenannies in the ground-floor community room. "327 was a mothership on the
block," he recalls. "People from all over the world were coming there —from Brixton, Latin
America, different parts of the US, Italy, lots of film crews. Wherever people were squatting,
they would hear about squatting in New York and they just showed up there. Between 1985
and '87, we had all kinds of things going on there. It was really great . . . Soon after that,
two or three other buildings were opened up on the block. So Eighth Street became the initial jumping-off point, and little by little, we moved out to [other squats] in the neighborhood."

Admittedly, the other squats that opened on Eighth Street remained rather marginal. Across
the street at 336-38 East Eighth Street, Momma Lee, a spirited middle-aged woman,
presided over a kind of collective crash pad for punk rockers, transients, druggies and
numerous dogs inside a cavernous double-barreled tenement that never seemed to get
worked on much. Dwight, a former shelter resident, led the squat next door and ran all-
night punk fests in an abandoned garage down the block dubbed the People's Warehouse.
318 was occupied by several former street dwellers along with Ralphie and his hardcore
punk crew, Squatter Rot.

But the Eighth Street scene was significant because it marked the emergence of a more militant, youthful and openly contentious squatting movement. Not only did they openly defy
the city by taking over the buildings, they went against the older housing advocates in the
neighborhood, who already had their dibs on some of those tenements.

"Eighth Street violated the peace treaty we had with LESCAC and the JPC," says Josh
Whalen, a writer and defacto squatter (he lived in a rent strike building for 20 years). "We
had divided the territory among us like rival gangs, and everyone knew it was hands off
Eighth Street."

Other squats cropped up on East Ninth Street, Avenue C, Third Street, Tenth Street, Fourth
Street, Sixth Street, Fifth Street —fueled by the arrival of young punks and activists funnel-
ing though the old Yippie headquarters at Number 9 Bleecker Street, the Anarchist
Switchboard on East Ninth Street, or the Rock Against Racism concert network (which was
founded in England by squatter-friendly punk bands like The Clash), as well as young artists
looking to make their mark in New York. Not all were newcomers of course. Bullet Space
squat on East Third Street was founded in 1986 by Andrew and Paul Castrucci, twin brothers
who had been priced out of their art gallery on Avenue B, and some members of the

Rivington School art gang, who operated a rather anarchic metal-sculpture "garden" on an abandoned lot on the corner of Rivington and Forsyth streets. The new arrivals dovetailed with the older activists, street dwellers, and local residents pushed out of their rental apartments to create an eclectic, dissentious mix.

More than just building housing, squatting was seen as an extension for other arenas of social activism. There was an early crossover between homesteading and the Central America solidarity movement. Activists who had been traveling to war-torn Nicaragua and El Salvador in the 1980s to build housing and schools decided to turn their attention to fixing some of the bombed-out buildings in places like the Lower East Side, Brooklyn, and the Bronx. Some of the early members of 209 East Seventh Street "homestead," for instance, were members of the Nicaragua Construction Brigade.

The growth of squatting also coincided with the surge in activism around homelessness, which, as the crisis mushroomed in 1980s, became something of an "in" cause. Indeed, the more activist-oriented squatters such as Morales, English Steve, Thompson, and Alfredo Gonzalez actively sought to recruit homeless people into the squatting movement by giving workshops in city shelters through groups such as the Valentines Day Committee.

"We were organizing against the forced relocation of poor people into the shelters," explains Morales, "and we saw squatting as an antidote to that." In the process, they also sought to convert housing advocates who remained skeptical of squatting as a means to create viable homes for low-income people. At the time, Morales says, 'Most of the housing people on the left didn't want to touch squatting."

The squatters even advertised for new recruits on the back pages of the *Village Voice* ("Need a Home? Squat . . .") and on the WBAI radio show *Listeners' Action*, which was then functioning as a kind of citizen-led homeless relief project in conjunction with the food pantry at the Cathedral of St. John the Divine.

Recalls Morales:

> We got on the radio and said 'show up at Seventh and B on Saturday morning if you want to work,' and like 50 people from the tri-state area would show up, mostly because they wanted to volunteer to help out. People would come, old and young, experienced and not, and actually volunteer to shovel rubble or scrape paint. This one guy came in and organized a crew of welders and construction workers to replace the entire stairs in one squat on East Eighth Street. They just showed up one day, and after a month of weekends working on it, it was done.

A key factor in the expansion of the squatting scene was the creation of Eviction Watch, an activist phone tree used to fend off eviction efforts by local police, as well as attacks by competing housing groups and drug dealers. In a movement without any centralized structure, Eviction Watch became an important tool for networking within the squats and with supporters in the community. They also set up a communal kitchen in the ground floor of

537 East 13th Street to feed people using food culled from dumpsters or donated from local restaurants, which meant that squatters who didn't have kitchens could go cadge a meal when they needed to.

"There was a level of self-organization in the beginning, and for a while, a kind of organic connection," says Morales. "We weren't just inhabiting space, we were actually changing the environment, working it, in a `freedom in action' kind of way."

YOUR HOUSE IS MINE

At the height of the movement in 1988-1989, there were about two-dozen squatted buildings on the Lower East Side, and probably two dozen more in East Harlem, Washington Heights, and the South Bronx. While the squats uptown were more cohesively working class and rooted in their communities of color, the scene on the Lower East Side was more countercultural and provocative, as rendered in the iconic flyers that plastered the nabe, from John the Communist's predictions of imminent martial law to Missing Foundation screeds like "The Party's Over," "Your House Is Mine," and "1988 = 1933."

However hyperbolic, such rhetoric reflected how severe gentrification had become on the Lower East Side. By the winter of 1984, small cockroach-infested apartments that rented for $400 a month were suddenly, with minor renovations, going for $1200 and up — thanks in large part to the NYPD's "Operation Pressure Point," when scores of officers rounded up an astounding 14,000 drug suspects over 18 months. Stripped of its most violent and brazen drug trade, Alphabet City went from being one of the poorest areas in the city to one of the most "up and coming." Increasing numbers of elderly and Latinos were driven from their rent-controlled units through a combination of illegal buyouts, harassment, and denial of services as landlords emptied buildings in order to drive up their resale value. Whole buildings were warehoused vacant while the streets became flooded with homeless people — refugees of the crack epidemic, the closing of state mental hospitals, Reagan-era crackdowns on welfare and social services, and an insane rental market that meant one slip and you were out the door.[21]

The more militant squatters saw themselves as establishing a kind of beachhead against gentrification — their presence brought neighboring property values down — and agitated inside the park with rallies and smoke-ins and punk concerts, along with frequent marches to the local offices of the city's Department of Housing Preservation and Development (HPD). Influenced by the theory of Spatial D and the transfer of authority over homeless shelters to FEMA, John "the Communist" Potak and several others formed the Emergency Coalition Against Martial Law and began protesting everything from police brutality and AIDS to the shelter system while calling for mass rent strikes. Indeed, Jerry Wade says he and Potak fantasized about building an American version of the Christiania Free State, the countercultural mecca built by Danish squatters who took over an area of deserted army barracks in Copenhagen.[22]

"John and I had always wanted to attract radical hippies," says Wade of his throwback idealism. "There was a real conscious effort to bring in hippies, but by that time, there just wasn't enough hippies around anymore in the neighborhood, so we settled for punks. We used to recruit people off Avenue A."

But aside from a few tussles with local precinct cops, the anti-police-state rhetoric remained more of a paranoid gloss on the scene than any real guiding ethos. Beyond the diehard radicals, most folks were more DIY (do it yourself) than ardently anarchist, too busy scrapping to make a living, make art and build their homes than to seek out confrontations with police.

"A RIOT IS NOW IN PROGRESS IN TOMPKINS SQUARE"[23]

That changed with the police riot of August 6, 1988. On that night, John the Communist's and Missing Foundation's predictions of imminent martial law appeared to come true as more than 400 cops stormed through Tompkins Square and its surrounding streets, brutally clubbing protesters and bystanders indiscriminately. It was almost as if the neighborhood's history was caught on repeat, things accelerated out of control so quickly, subsuming the immediate triggers — gentrification, displacement, the effort to clamp down on the area's anything-goes counterculture — into this volatile, epochal event that would resonate for years to come.

The ostensible cause of the riot was the imposition of a 1 a.m. curfew in Tompkins Square in response to neighboring residents' complaints about rowdy revelers spilling out of the bars along Avenue A and holding late-night "concerts" inside the park. But underlying that were growing tensions over the way gentrification was undermining the multicultural base of the neighborhood. The previous summer, a plan by the Parks department to close Tompkins Square temporarily to make repairs and discourage revelers was rejected by the local community board after some complained it was a city plot to promote real estate speculation. So when the curfew cropped up unexpectedly in the midst of a powerful heat wave in 1988, it put even local dog-walkers on edge.

Activists, squatters among them, saw the curfew as another effort to tame the Lower East Side for a wealthier class of people. The militants were apoplectic. This was an invasion of their turf, an effort by the police and real estate developers to assert control over the "people's" park, to remake its rough, unsocialized edges into something more akin to Union Square.

Some of these squatters and activists had fought to save Adam Purple's renowned Garden of Eden from the city's bulldozers and were involved in a campaign to preserve La Plaza Cultural, a community-tilled park on East Ninth Street, which was then slated to become a senior citizen home.

They put out leaflets calling on the community to resist. But the reaction of both the cops and the community went beyond even the most paranoid militants' wet dreams, as the battle raged in the streets till dawn with a fury not seen in decades. No doubt most of the thuggery came from the police, who were clearly spoiling for a fight after being forced to retreat from the park the previous weekend. On July 30, when a small contingent of 9th Precinct

A Radical Political and Social History of the Lower East Side

police arrived to break up a midnight rally called to oppose the curfew, they were beaten back by a hail of bottles. Five police were injured in scuffles, including one who suffered a broken wrist, and four people were charged with felonies, among them Jerry Wade, who had helped spark the melee by spraying a line of police with a can of shaken beer.[24]

In the following days, Wade and other local agitators recall that cops driving on patrol would slow down to threaten, "We're gonna get you guys on Saturday night."

"It was almost like a gang fight," says Morales. "Everyone knew there was gonna be a showdown on Saturday night."

Still, no one expected that police would arrive with their badges covered, fully prepared to bust heads, or that they would be called out in such provocative numbers — including about 30 mounted police on horseback, sharpshooters on neighboring rooftops, a mobile command post, and a helicopter that swooped menacingly over the crowds. (Fifty-three people were injured over the course of the night, including 14 cops, 31 were arrested, and 121 complaints of police brutality and excessive force were lodged.)

Although Mayor Koch and Police Commissioner Ben Ward initially sought to blame the riot on "skinheads and degenerates from Scarsdale," most in the crowd that night were simply locals who liked to hang out in the park or folks spilling out of nearby bars and restaurants on a hot Saturday night. By staging such a massive display of force and brutally charging the crowd, the police managed to galvanize large numbers of local residents and bystanders who joined the militants blocking traffic along Avenue A chanting "Pigs Go Home!"

But if the riot had not been planned, there's no question that some in the crowd helped escalate the confrontation by setting off M-80 firecrackers and chucking bottles at police. There had already been an informal campaign of "property devaluation" by some on the scene. Random acts, like leaving a quarter stick of dynamite under a parked cop car to blow out the windows, were not unheard of back then. The week before the riot, cops and local landlords were set on edge by leaflets plastered on doorways the night before the riot, vowing to "burn down" the houses of all those who supported the curfew. An absurd threat, no doubt, but provocative nonetheless.

Although the riot was not led by squatters and anarchists, it helped propel their cause into the limelight. Media crews swarmed into the neighborhood seeking to uncover the "shadowy" world east of Avenue A, and many returned with sympathetic if sensationalized portraits of the scrappy folks who'd turned rubble-filled tenements into homes. And, as in the 1874 park riot, the 1988 riot also helped radicalize the surrounding community, which now felt itself under assault from City Hall. Suddenly residents of the Christodora House — the luxury condominium building on Avenue B and Ninth Street that had become a hated symbol of gentrification — were visiting the park with care packages for the homeless. Rudolf Piper, the owner of the Tunnel nightclub in Chelsea who'd gotten battered by the cops during the riot, appeared on news broadcasts denouncing "yuppie" invaders.

Boosted by swelling numbers of supporters, the more militant squatters and agitators stepped up their resistance in the park. "We decided to squat the park," says Morales of the campaign they led to encourage and defend the growing homeless encampment in Tompkins Square. "It was a conscious effort to reconfigure the nature of the park, and also make this more than symbolic protest against the lack of housing and horrible conditions in the shelters," Morales says.

John the Communist and Jerry the Peddler erected a teepee on one of the central greens emblazoned with the slogan, "Free the Land!" They and others promoted the park encampment as both a refuge for the homeless and a kind of firewall against further gentrification east of Avenue A. Protesting in the park, they believed, would draw heat away from their buildings.

In retrospect, Morales concedes this notion of staging a long-term encampment in the park was not sustainable — especially as the city began referring more and more homeless people, evicted from other parks and public spaces, to Tompkins Square. "It created an untenable situation for us. It was a contradiction," Morales says of the tent city that would swell to nearly 400 people. And many squatters steered away from the park battle, seeing it as a distraction from the hard work they needed to accomplish in their buildings. But initially there was a lot of support on the Lower East Side for the "hands off the homeless" stance. For a brief window of time (1988-1991), Tompkins Square was redefined, locally and even nationally, as a "symbol of resistance to gentrification."

WAR IN THE NEIGHBORHOOD

But while the park riot helped win support for the squatters' cause, it also amped the level of confrontation with police, setting off a cycle of increasingly militarized battles as the city moved in to divest this population of "thieves and troublemakers" from its buildings.

The first casualty was Tya Scott's squat on East Eighth Street, which the city condemned after a bulldozer "accidentally" nicked the front façade while clearing the remains of an abandoned tenement next door. What began as a rush-job demolition turned into a six-hour standoff as supporters, mobilized by Eviction Watch, rushed to Tya's building in the early hours of April 1, 1989. I can recall a mob of about 20 squatters and incensed locals rushing at the plywood construction fence wielding a police barricade as a battering ram, storming past the astonished beat cops posted to defend the demolition crew like a horde of crazed Vikings.

The fight over 319 East Eighth Street — when the city used a fire in the building as a pretext for eviction — was even more *Escape From New York*. In my notes of the period, I find this effort to account for the police presence assembled on May 9, 1989:

95 cops on Avenue B
30 cops at 8th and C
33 cops at 9th and C
33 cops at 7th and B
13 mounted police at 9th and C
5 police with dogs at 9th and B

A Radical Political and Social History of the Lower East Side

3? sharpshooters on rooftops, guarding lot on 7th
1 busload of cops at 8th (about 30 inside), 2 empty police busses on C
3 police media vans

In fact, more than 400 police were dispatched to maintain a complete cordon around two city blocks for five days as the demolition crew worked round the clock, using high-powered klieg lights that lit up the block like a movie set, as a giant wrecking ball slammed into the building, sending up giant plumes of dust. The massive police overkill and expense (the demolition costs alone were estimated at $600,000) prompted cries of outrage from no less than Catholic Archbishop John Cardinal O'Connor, Episcopal Archbishop Michael Kendall, and Manhattan Borough President David Dinkins. The scene was easily cast as a David and Goliath narrative of squatters struggling to create homes versus the city bureaucrats intent on crushing them.

Just two weeks earlier, the squatters at 319 had managed to subvert the city's demolition plans. There was the grand heroism of Willie, a gay man who moved to 319 after being made homeless by AIDS. He sauntered past the police lines and scaled the fire escape to reclaim the building, dumping bottles of fermented piss from the roof that sent the cops and demolition workers running for cover. Then a ragtag crew led by Morales lassoed the construction scaffolding and yanked it down, as city officials looked on in disbelief.

Despite the unorthodox tactics, this mediagenic victory earned the squatters some popular support, as well as the help of some architects from the Pratt Institute, who argued the building could be saved. So when the city imposed a state of virtual martial law on the neighborhood, with police occupying neighboring rooftops for days and forcing residents to show ID to enter their own buildings, it had even co-op owners voicing conspiracy theories.

Looking at my notes of the street protests, what's striking is how radical the sentiments expressed by local residents were. Standing on the police barricades, with bottles flying and M-80s exploding in the distance, I interviewed a man who lived at a recently co-oped building at 323 East Eighth Street who said his bedroom had been damaged by the demolition at 319. A nurse at Beth Israel hospital, he was trying to reason with the cops. "I'm sick of private capital getting everything it wants, and what makes America great getting screwed," he responded when asked why he was out there demonstrating. "The thing that makes New York such a great place is the variety of lifestyles. It's a beautiful garden, and they want to tear it down and make it into a homogenous, climate-controlled, plastic-turfed lawn."

Famed attorney William Kunstler, who was then defending the squatters, declared: "There are seeds of rebellion here, people pushed to their outer limits. What could be more compelling than homeless people taking over an abandoned building?"

Kunstler's law partner, Ron Kuby, was even more emphatic: "A thousand years of property law says the buildings are for the owners. There's no common law for squatters in the U.S. But if you get a mass movement, the laws will follow. We saw that in the Civil Rights movement."

PYRRHIC VICTORY?

Ron Kuby's prediction did not come true. But back then the riots and street protests really felt like mini epics. The activists were emboldened by the neighborhood's history — even if within the Lower East Side there were often profound disputes between squatters and community housing groups that tended to split along generational lines. The folks who had helped squat the Christodora House in the late '60s with the Black Panthers and Young Lords, and who took over an abandoned school in 1979 to create the CHARAS/El Bohio community center on East Ninth Street, now saw this new generation of squatters as irresponsible, revolutionary wannabes playing a game in a place where the stakes were too high. The competition for cheap housing was fierce. What gave some twenty-something artist or college drop-out the right to cop a crash pad and rumble with the police when there were whole families doubled and tripled up in the projects with no place to go? The squatters wasted buildings, they said. They passed out with their candles lit and let their houses burn down. They were parasites dancing amid the truly urban poor.

For the squatters, the housing advocates were pimps and sell-outs who'd traded in their radical roots for careers spent grappling with a bureaucracy intent on dispensing crumbs at best. Their answer to the housing crisis was the 50/50 plan — a compromise that squatters said would only fuel gentrification and displacement by sanctioning new market rate housing next to low income rehabs.

Yet the two fronts reinforced each other, despite their differences. The housing advocates on the Lower East Side had always operated to the left of the baseline politic that governed the rest of Manhattan. That changed with the 1991 election to the City Council of Antonio Pagan, a neo-con Democrat who upset the longtime liberal incumbent Miriam Friedlander. Pagan became a darling of the Manhattan Institute, a conservative think tank, for seeking to curb the excesses of New York liberalism that the Lower East Side had come to epitomize. Backed by the police union, he rode to power on a campaign to evict the homeless from the park, roust the anarchists and squatters, and stop letting the area be a "dumping ground" for social services. His election coincided with the dramatic closing of the park for a two-year renovation that would permanently clear the homeless shanties and establish the 12 a.m. curfew that remains in place today.

This final reclamation of Tompkins Square pretty much closed the book on the park's legacy as a cauldron of unrest. It was followed by paramilitary eviction assaults on five East 13th Street squats, spearheaded by Pagan, who pitted "lazy" squatters against a scheme to use low-income tax credits to renovate the buildings for more "deserving" poor. In 1995, the city went so far as to send in sharpshooters and an armored personnel carrier to evict the squatters, who welded themselves inside the buildings. (Most were booted out then, though a lawsuit allowed residents to remain in three of the buildings until 1996, when the police again forcefully evicted everyone, and the buildings were gutted.)

The use of tax credits to produce low-income housing reflects the triumph of market-based strategies for urban renewal over the old state-sponsored model of subsidized housing — not to mention any lingering idealism about grassroots sweat equity. While Pagan lambasted the 13th Street homesteaders as privileged troublemakers who "treat the whole neighborhood as a radical Romper Room," the not-for-profit organization he directed, Lower East Side Coalition Housing Development, made out quite nicely: LESCHD owns and manages the former 13th Street squats as low and moderate-income housing. (After leaving office, Pagan returned to LESCHD as a "staff analyst.")

Would Pagan's and City Hall's campaign to evict the squats have been so successful had the activists not spent so much time — and political capital — fighting to defend Tompkins Square and the homeless encampment there? There's no question that the increasingly squalid conditions brought by hundreds of needy people occupying the playgrounds and lawns without proper sanitation and services — combined with the park warriors' often inanely provocative efforts to recreate the 1988 police riot — undermined community support. Looking back, even hardliners like Morales and Harrington concede that the squatters involved in the park cause could have made more concrete gains by focusing on upgrading their buildings rather than scrapping with police. "We were so integrated with the issues of genocide and racism in the shelters, we couldn't separate it," says Morales of the social struggle around the park.

"If the squat scene hadn't happened, the park battle wouldn't have happened," concludes Harrington. "It was part of what we were about, bringing people in off the streets and into the squats. So the homeless situation in the park was part and parcel with the whole squatting movement."

Indeed, the 1988 riot and subsequent park battles helped inspire Tent City, a group of former park dwellers, who marched on Washington to demand housing and attempted their own building takeovers on the Lower East Side. [See Section Three, Chapter 2, "Tent City" by Ron Casanova.]

But the effort to integrate street people, many with drug and alcohol problems, into the often anarchic and contentious world of squatting proved far more difficult to achieve. "Most of the [street] people who came through and did okay would clean up their act and then move on," says Harrington. "They really didn't want to stay living in the buildings. Others we took in — quite often I think we did them a disservice. We were so radical then, we never believed in getting people services, and some of these people really did need that. They had real substance abuse or mental health problems, or I mean, some of them couldn't even really read and yet we weren't really prepared to deal with that. It was like, grab a hammer and start building a wall, and they just couldn't fucking do it. They'd hang around getting fucked up. And then they'd steal a camera or something, and we'd throw them out."

GOING LEGAL

Still, the fact that people would even attempt such a social experiment is significant. The years of costly park battles and squat evictions undoubtedly helped convince the city to legalize 11 of the dozen remaining Lower East Side squats, which are now in the process of becoming low-income co-ops.[25]

These squatters are the survivors, the ones that managed through a combination of luck and hard-won experience, to hold their ground. That the Giuliani administration in its final year in office would ever agree to grant them title to their buildings is a reflection of how diligently many worked to restore the buildings and rehab their living spaces—some of which now look better than your average co-op. Bloomberg officials, who finalized the deal in September 2002, said they were motivated by the fact that the squatting scene had "matured" over the years and had come to include a more racially diverse population of families and people with stable jobs—blithely overlooking the fact that many were the same rabblerousers the city had fought with for so many years. They'd simply grown up a bit. But legal observers say the city must have also realized that if it moved to evict these squatters in court, it would have risked losing and thereby codifying the right to take adverse possession of city properties in a way that could have dramatically expanded the rights of squatters elsewhere in the city.

But while the city has ceded them the buildings for a dollar apiece, the squatters must bring them up to code without any of the government grants afforded to the homesteaders of the '80s, let alone the hefty tax breaks that for-profit developers receive for setting aside a portion of their apartments to low-income people. And the squatters are not allowed to sell or rent their spaces for profit. So in a sense, they are being charged with creating permanent low-income housing, without any of the subsidies that both developers and not-for-profit housing groups normally receive.

The 11 buildings have formed a new coalition to negotiate with UHAB, which is overseeing the financing and renovation process. But outside of that formal unity, these days the "squatters'" fights are largely internal. They are reconciling their space within the system, trading in free rent for the promise of security, while battling to keep the banks, contractors and UHAB from driving up their mortgages. While UHAB initially pledged to keep the monthly maintenance charges low—$300 to $750 depending on apartment size—many fear mounting rehab costs will become a mechanism for pushing the poor and more dysfunctional out.

Meanwhile, fights have emerged as the now legal homesteaders struggle to come to terms with what real ownership of their spaces means. If one person doesn't pay, who does?

In the same vein, many of the neighborhood's community gardens, which were started on squatted land, have won preservation. They are now working to set up bylaws and boards of governance, contending with insurance liabilities—all the formalizing elements that constitute property ownership.

A Radical Political and Social History of the Lower East Side

Meanwhile, a new urban renewal plan is reshaping the community, this one spearheaded by the Cooper Square Committee. The same progressive housing group that defeated Robert Moses' scheme to mow down blocks of tenements for upscale housing has just leveled the old Cuando community center on the corner of Second Avenue and Houston Street, along with four historic loft buildings on the Bowery — including a former brothel and saloon occupied by feminist author Kate Millet. These properties were sacrificed to make way for 700-units of new housing, just 25 percent of which will be dedicated to low and moderate income people. The rest of the housing, which includes a 14-story housing complex on the corner of Houston and Bowery, will be luxury apartments, including 200,000 square feet set aside for commercial space, where a Whole Foods is slated to open.

There are still a few countercultural venues left in the nabe, such as ABC No Rio, Bluestockings bookstore, and the more avowedly lefty May Day Books, housed at the Theater for the New City on First Avenue. There's also an effort to resuscitate the East Village's "legacy of counterculture" via the HOWL! Festival, a week-long celebration of the arts — though one wonders whether this effort will only succeed in reinforcing the kind of hackneyed nostalgia and countercultural boutiquing that have overtaken places like Woodstock, rendering radicalism a tourist attraction, detached from its roots.

But the notion of organizing around space as a locus for political struggle no longer applies. Political organizing these days centers on the war, the media, the corporate colonization of the globe. The players and battles are far-flung and transitory by nature. There are still local struggles, such as the campaign to block a proposed 23-story luxury tower on Houston Street by local residents who fear it will inundate the area and hasten gentrification, or the ongoing effort to reclaim the old CHARAS/El Bohio community center on East Ninth Street, where the new owner has proposed building a 19-story dorm. (In an ironic twist, these days the folks petitioning in Tompkins Square are residents of the Christodora House, including penthouse owner Michael Rosen, who developed the swank Red Square apartment complex on Houston Street in the late '80s, and who now speaks earnestly about the need to preserve the "sanctity" of neighborhood against high-rise incursions.)

Still, these are defensive, rear-guard tactics. The idea of taking or reclaiming property and using that as a base for further social agitation is gone. Unlike the young idealists of the '60s, '70s, and '80s, it seems unlikely that the current crop of newcomers to the Lower East Side would align themselves with any neighborhood-wide struggle against gentrification.[26] The East Village's identity has already been subsumed into the grid of Manhattan real estate. It's no longer an island of diversity or cultural resistance but an "entertainment district" (to use City Hall's phrase) — a trendy theme park of bars, restaurants, and chic boutiques whose shifting aesthetics look more to LA, Tokyo, Paris, or Berlin rather than anything indigenously Loisaida, whatever that is. (The neighborhood was always such a concatenation of cultures and influences, it becomes harder to pin down what that essential Loisaida spirit ever was.)

The atomization of social struggle on the Lower East Side reflects the splintering of communities and workplaces brought on by globalization. For relative "old-timers" like me, there is a sense that the spirit of the Lower East Side has been hollowed out, deconcentrated. The old romance of the East Village as a harbor for outcasts, fuck-ups, and artists was defeated by the militaristic incursions of the Giuliani administration, followed by the ethos of market efficiency embodied in the Bloomberg administration, for whom even smoking cigarettes in a bar or catching a nap on the subway is considered a ticketable offense.

Bohemias are predicated on cheap rents and free time, the time to mix it up with people from all races and classes and transgress social barriers, and so reinvent one's relationship to the world. Without cheap rents, there is no free time. Kids working four jobs to pay for a cramped bedroom in a $2400 a month, Ikea-furnished apartment don't have the luxury of such free-floating interaction. Starbucks becomes their living room, Barnes and Noble their library, the bars a field for networking and self-promotion and/or an escape from the get-ahead grind. Fighting the system is a waste of time; the struggle now is to have a stake in it.

Many of the old-guard rebels and rads are now raising families or have escaped to upstate or Vermont, places where free minutes don't only come with cell phone plans. But those of us who lived through this period of social upheaval in the neighborhood need to remember and celebrate the idealism, however flawed, that fueled the movement to "liberate" and defend the Lower East Side. The idea that people have a right to housing provides a check to the dehumanizing market fundamentalism of our times.

"It was liminal space," says David Boyle, reflecting on the bombed-out landscape that he encountered on the Lower East Side in the early '80s. "The property was neither here nor there. It wasn't quite controlled by the government or contested by the landlords who walked away from it. That's the space in which change takes place, the kind of space that's important for revolutionary ideas to come forward.

"Back then, the Lower East Side was an incubator, but it didn't last. It was already becoming a constrictive environment," Boyle continues. "If you're gonna change the world, you're not going to change it by hanging out on the Lower East Side and talking to the same people, because the Lower East Side is not the world. In fact it sort of has an entropy about it."

Author's Note: This essay began as an effort to reassess why the battles over Tompkins Square Park mattered, given that there's so little battling over it now. That inquiry led inevitably to the struggles by various groups to claim turf on the Lower East Side, from the early homesteaders who took over abandoned tenements and founded community gardens in forsaken lots, to the squatters, who did the same but were rendered outlaws when the city cancelled its homesteading program. This remains an incomplete survey of a complex social movement that evolved over time. Left out are the voices of the many quiet doers and artists, women and mothers, professionals and laborers whose hard work succeeded in preserving the buildings. I leave that exploration to another chapter.

A Radical Political and Social History of the Lower East Side

Endnotes:

164

1. Quoted by Bill Weinberg in "Tompkins Square Park and the Lower East Side Legacy of Rebellion," *Downtown*, February 14, 1990.

2. Report of the National Advisory Commission on Civil Disorders (New York: Bantam Books, 1968), chapters 16-17.

3. Three men were in fact arrested and convicted for Ward's murder, which prosecutors deemed a street robbery gone awry. The shooter was sentenced to 15-years to life, and his two accomplices pled guilty to charges of manslaughter and robbery for their role, and for robbing someone else a block away just prior to Ward's killing. Nevertheless, Ward's friends and supporters in the housing movement, who conducted their own widely publicized investigation of the case, continued to insist that she had been assassinated for her work, noting that she had been harassed and received phone calls threatening her with bodily harm. [See: "3 SE Men Plead Guilty to Murder of Housing Activist," by Al Kamen, *Washington Post*, November 17, 1981; "Man Gets Jail in Activist's Death," by Al Kamen and Benjamin Weiser, Washington Post, March 10, 1982.]

4. *World War 3 Illustrated*, No. 6, 1986

5. Much was made out of the fact that in 1987, the Federal Emergency Management Agency (FEMA)— which was established in 1979 to oversee domestic security and relief in the event of natural and nuclear disasters and/or wartime emergencies — was also put in charge of administering federal homeless relief efforts established by the Stewart McKinney Act of 1987, which codified the right to shelter. Former military bases and prisons were retrofitted as homeless shelters, prompting fears of new federal "Bantustans" for the poor.

6. This historical overview draws heavily from Bill Weinberg's "Tompkins Square Park and the Lower East Side Legacy of Rebellion," cited earlier, as well as Marci Reaven and Jeanne Houck, "A History of Tompkins Square Park," published in From *Urban Village to East Village*, Janet L. Abu-Lughod, ed. (Cambridge: Blackwell Press, 1994), pp. 81-98.

7. Mario Maffi, *Gateway to the Promised Land: Ethnic Cultures on New York's Lower East Side*, (Amsterdam Monographs in American Studies, 1994), p. 33.

8. Christopher Mele, *The Selling of the Lower East Side: Culture, Real Estate, and Resistance in New York City* (University of Minnesota Press, 2000), p. 58.

9. Philip Foner, *The Labor Movement in the United States, Vol. 1* (New York: International Publishers, 1978), p. 448. Quoted by Neil Smith, *The New Urban Frontier: Gentrification and the Revanchist City* (New York: Routledge, 1996), p. 11. See also Raven and Houck.

10. Reaven and Houck, pp. 87-88.

11. See Mele, chapter 3 and Smith, chapter 1.

12. Smith, p. 21.

13. The name "East Village" was first promoted by real estate interests during the 1960s in an effort to reinvent the area north of Houston Street as a fashionable destination, and disassociate it from the image of the Lower East Side as a working class slum.

14. Rosalyn Deutsche and Cara Gendel Ryan, "The Fine Art of Gentrification," in *The Portable Lower East Side*, Volume 4, Number 1, Spring 1987; online at http: www.abcnorio.org/about/history/fine_art.html

15. Ronald Lawson, "Tenant Responses to the Urban Housing Crisis, 1970-1984," *The Tenant Movement in New York City, 1904-1984* (Rutgers University Press, 1986); online at http://www.tenant.net/Community/history/hist05b.html. John Kalish, "Urban Agriculture is Working in the Middle of Manhattan," *The Aquarian*, June 25, 1980.

16. Interviews with Carol Abrams, spokesperson for the Department of Housing, Preservation and Development August 22, 2002; and Howard Brandstein, who besides being a homesteader was the former director of the Home Ownership Project for Catholic Charities, Archdiocese of New York.

17. According to Val Orselli, executive director of the Cooper Square Mutual Housing Association and a former member of the JPC, the JPC and CB3 forced the city to provide funds upfront to do the low-income rehabs first. The 1000 new units of market-rate units were never built. "We purposely selected the sites for that market-rate housing that were next to low income housing. So they never happened. We did not know at the time that that would make them that unattractive, but that's what happened." (Interview with Orselli, May 2004)

18. According to East 7th Street residents, those buildings were then being run by a "Ma Barker-type" woman and her drug-dealing sons.

19. This is Boyle's version of the story. According to Jimmy Stewart, a street peddler and electrician who first moved into the Fifth Street squat in 1982, what he and his partner "Web" objected to was Boyle's effort to "take over" the building. (Interview with Stewart, June 14, 2004.)

20. Brandstein recalls that RAIN rejected the 13th Street squatters because they were for the most part white — a common if somewhat exaggerated allegation made by housing advocates, who tended to overlook minority participation. Other 13th Street squatters say they rejected ORE and Boyle's leadership because they viewed him as a "takeover artist" out to establish ownership of the buildings for himself, or because they did not believe going with RAIN would give them control of their buildings.

21. According to Census figures, 14.5 percent of the Latino population on the Lower East Side left between 1980 and 1990.

22. It would be wrong to overplay ECAMA's following; for the most part the group was a front for John the Communist's one-man propaganda machine and offered a caricature of resistance to oppression. But JTC was expert at showing up at all the demonstrations with big, brightly painted banners and stacks of flyers bearing a mix of angry denunciations of the police collaged with clippings of the latest government atrocity against the poor.

23. This was the headline used in the 1874 edition of the *New York Graphic*, cited in Andrew Castrucci's *Your House Is Mine*, Bullet Space Collective, 1993.

24. That same night, Wade and several other activists had been invited to appear with rabid talk show host Morton Downey at Downey's nightclub act in midtown. They arrived at the park around midnight, drunk, pumped and bearing several cases of beer.

25. One other longstanding homestead on East 7th Street refused to enter into the deal and hence remains in legal limbo.

26. This chapter was written before the current movement to rezone the Lower East Side to limit high-rise incursions. It remains to be seen how well residents will unite around that.

Chapter 2

Homelessness, Madness, the Power Elites and Final Battles of the East Village
By Seth Farber, Ph.D

The East Village in the late 1980s was on the cusp of major changes — on the eve of destruction, as it later became clear. The East Village had been born a long time ago: In the 1960s the Lower East Side became the site of a new bohemia, as the hippie movement emerged unexpectedly out of the womb of American middle class society. A generation of pubescent and post-pubescent refugees from the comfortable but spiritually vacuous bardo of American suburbia found asylum in hippie havens, collective "crash pads" and assorted living arrangements in the cheap rental district on Manhattan's Lower East Side. The neighborhood was newly christened the "East Village," as distinguished from Manhattan's West Side Greenwich Village, the legendary home of previous generations of bohemians.

From all over America, "hippies" and "freaks" — in the jargon of the times — alienated from the wasteland of American materialism, revolted by the burgeoning power of the American military industrial complex and its cult of war and violence, made the pilgrimage to the East Village — the new Mecca of the 1960s counter-culture. Many stayed: The allure of a sense of community, a spiritual homeland for society's discontented idealists and cynics, a neighborhood where kinsfolk lived and "hung out" together, where misfits and rebels could finally feel they belonged somewhere — compensated for some of the inconveniences that arose from living in an area populated mostly by the urban poor, primarily of Spanish descent. Perhaps the most ubiquitous and unnerving inconvenience was the necessity of securing one's apartment with double and triple locks, lest it be broken into and ransacked by any of the plethora of junkies who lived in the East Village. (This was not always successful, as many of the thieves were quite proficient and found various means to gain entry). More worrisome was the risk of being mugged in the street, or even — particularly if one came home alone early in the AM — of having one's throat slit by a native gang-member or junkie who had no particular sympathy for the children of privilege who had moved into their territory.

My own experiences visiting the East Village as a high school student were at best fulfilling, and at worst benign. I went to meetings of the new left college student radicals at NYU, and worked in a storefront set up by NYU members of Students for a Democratic Society (SDS) to serve and "radicalize" the local Hispanic community. And although I stayed out until after midnight and my slight build did not deter prospective muggers, none of the junkies who robbed me ever assaulted me. One mugger — upon my request — even gave me 25 cent subway fare to get home after he had taken all the money I had on me — probably about $15. My parents' efforts to get me to return home earlier in the evening were futile — in my mind I was making the revolution.

The East Village remained a relatively low rent quasi-bohemia even in the late 1970s when the 1960s counter-culture had faded across most of the country, and the era of the Yuppie had begun. Even in the mid-80s when I returned from graduate school in San Francisco, the East Village still had a counter-cultural allure. But by then most of the junkies had been cleared out by the police and a process of gentrification was in its incipient stages. But rents were still cheap east of Avenue A, and students and aspiring artists who worked part time as waiters or copy editors or lived on modest parental allowances, as well as hangers — on from the 1960s, still experienced community in the East Village, still hung out in coffee-houses discussing Marx and Foucault and Fassbinder, still watched their backs late at night; and those who lived between Avenue B and Avenue C in the 1990s still joked that they lived between life and death.

Homelessness and the gentrification of the East Village (heretofore referred to alternately as the LES and the Lower East Side) and other low rent neighborhoods and were two sides of the same coin. The housing policies that led to high rents and gentrification also led to homelessness — to evictions and to a paucity of housing for all but the very rich and for Young Urban Professionals or Young Upwardly Mobile Professionals — Yuppies. The "urban removal" housing policies (euphemistically termed "urban renewal") designed by real estate interests could not have been implemented without the connivance and sanction of the successive mayors and governments of NYC. Yet the public came to believe the propaganda that was promulgated by vested interests and journalists in order to shift the blame of homelessness onto the victims themselves. According to this mythology, homelessness was a product of mental illness, and more specifically the policy of "deinstitutionalization," transferring the mentally ill from the state mental hospitals to "the community."

In actuality, homelessness in American cities, and specifically New York, in the 1990s was a manifestation of a housing crisis that had nothing to do with "mental illness" or psychiatry — except to the degree that the psychiatric industry tried to turn this problem to its own advantage by cornering the market on "services" for the homeless (redefined as the mentally ill) and helped to propagate the ideology that obscured the social/political roots of homelessness.

It is true that former mental patients were among those homeless people who began to appear on the streets of the East Village and other sections of New York in the late 1980s, but they constituted only a small percentage of the homeless, and certainly could not account for the epidemic of homelessness that swept New York in the 1990s. Most importantly the emptying of the state mental hospitals took place almost entirely in the 1960s and 1970s, decades before homelessness became a social epidemic. The housing crisis and homelessness was not caused by "mental illness" or by deinstitutionalization. They were caused by the social policies adopted by city governments that abandoned the poor and the lower and middle classes and catered to real estate interests: rich landlords, and affluent Yuppies. Contrary to the propaganda, homelessness was not a psychiatric problem, but a social policy problem.

The rational solution to homelessness was not to throw the homeless ("back") into state mental hospitals (as if most of them had come from there in the first place) as former liberal

A Radical Political and Social History of the Lower East Side

Peter Hamill urged in the 1990s, an interpretation that mirrored that of prominent neo-conservatives. The rational — and humane — solution, which was never implemented, was/is to provide persons rendered homeless with affordable housing and decent jobs.

Deinstitutionalization

It was expected that the process of "deinstitutionalization" which began in the early 1960s would lead to the integration of mental patients who had previously been warehoused in state psychiatric institutions into the community at large. But deinstitutionalization was only the first step; the next, more important step was what John McKnight aptly called "recommunalization." At least that is what the advocates of deinstitutionalization promised in the 1960s — and the idealists among them genuinely believed. As John McKnight wrote in *The Careless Society*:

> Those who seek to institute the community vision . . . see a society where those who were once labeled, exiled, treated, counseled, advised, and protected are, instead, incorporated into community, where their contributions, capacities, gifts, and fallibilities will allow a network of relationships involving work, recreation, friendship, support, and the political power of being a citizen. (McKnight, 1995, p.169)

As it turned out, former patients remained segregated from the community not in psychiatrically supervised institutions, but in smaller, privately-run institutions such as half-way houses, board-and-care homes and single room occupancy hotels (SROs). Maverick psychiatrist Thomas Szasz put it well: "Deinstitutionalization is simply a new fashion in mental health care, consisting of storing unwanted persons in dwellings, not called mental hospitals but nevertheless treating them as if they were mental patients who required lifelong psychiatric supervision." (Szasz, 1994. p. 171). He wrote that "deinstitutionalization" was actually "transinstitutionalization": "Individuals formerly in mental hospitals have been relocated in dwellings that are de facto psychiatric facilities but are not called 'mental' or 'hospitals.' Neither the patients' mental conditioning nor their functioning has improved." In 1984 the historian Andrew Scull commented that "it is only an illusion that those who are placed in boarding or family care homes are in the community. These facilities are for the most part like small, long-term state hospital wards, isolated from the community." (cited in Farber, 247)

The community mental health system was supposed to provide therapy, vocational training, education and rehabilitation — the essential supplements required in order to enable former patients to make the transition to non-institutionalized life. But it soon became clear that it was not meeting this challenge. As Scull noted, "little effort is directed toward social and vocational rehabilitation. One is overcome by the depressing atmosphere, not because of the physical appearance of the boarding home, but because of the passivity, inactivity and isolation of the residents." The "mentally ill" had time on their hands but the system provided them nowhere to go, other than custodial "day-treatment" programs, where many of them spent their days segregated with fellow "deviants" and engaged in productive activities like stuffing envelopes and drawing pictures with crayons. A small percentage of them wandered the streets talking to themselves and attracting the attention of passers-by and journalists. The new community health care system — the out-patient clinics and day treatments centers — had not delivered on its promise to integrate patients into the community, and the newspapers were filled with analysis of what went wrong.

Family Therapy-The Promise Betrayed

In 1984, after I had received my doctorate from a graduate school in California, I took a class in family therapy, and discovered that "systems theory" — the theoretical underpinning of most family therapy approaches — constituted a new paradigm, an entirely new way of understanding "mental illness," or more precisely (to use the new operative construct) "dysfunctional" behavior. The masters, the VIPs, in the family therapy field were able to work with difficult cases and frequently "cure" them in a matter of months! These were the people traditional therapists would have dismissed as incurable, or at best in need of years of therapy in order to overcome their psychological defects. These were the kind of people one found in NYC in the 1990s wandering the streets talking to themselves. If these individuals and their families had been treated with family therapy they never would have ended up in the mental health system in the first place.

In 1985, I applied to study hands-on family therapy with the family therapy impresario, psychiatrist Salvador Minuchin. I was accepted and moved back to my hometown, New York City. Minuchin was the creator of his own distinctive variant of family therapy — "structural family therapy" — which like most family therapies was based on systems theory. When historians write about critics of the myth of mental illness, they invariably single out R.D. Laing and Thomas Szasz. They don't mention Salvador Minuchin, although he also rejected the concept of mental illness. From Minuchin's perspective, there were no mentally ill individuals, there were only dysfunctional families. Pathology did not reside inside a person's mind or brain, but was characteristic of certain patterns of family interaction.

For example, in one common kind of dysfunctional family, an "enmeshed" family, parents who are frightened of the natural process of family-life cycle typically attempt to stifle the growing independence of their adolescent children. A teenager might respond to this situation by "acting out," or acting crazy. (In family therapy there is a fine line between acting crazy and being, or becoming, crazy). The parents are quick to define this behavior as "mental illness." and to take the young person for professional help, thus unwillingly initiating a scapegoating process. The therapist plays an integral part in the scapegoating process by "diagnosing" (i.e. authorizing) the "identified patient" as a genuine patient, i.e as mentally ill. The identified patient internalizes the authorities' construct of her as mentally ill-incompetent. This is often the first stage in a sequence of events that results in the troubled youngster being hospitalized for mental illness, which in itself becomes an initiation into a lifetime career as a chronic mental patient. Minuchin and other family therapists had identified the iatrogenic nature of the mental health system, and they developed alternative family therapy interventions that could prevent or reverse this process.

A Radical Political and Social History of the Lower East Side

Minuchin's techniques relied largely on extricating the "identified patient" from the sick role and encouraging her to act more competently. As she does this, she begins to see herself as a competent person and prepares to meet the often difficult tasks of adulthood in society, rather than shirking these challenges and hiding in the role of a chronic mental patient. Minuchin also taught the other family members to accept their responsibility for the family's dysfunctionality — instead of scapegoating the "sick one" — and to change their own patterns of interacting with each other.

After I spent a year studying with Minuchin, I spent another year training bi-monthly in family therapy with family therapy pioneer Jay Haley, and his brilliant young partner, Cloe Madanes. Jay's innovative work doing therapy with young "schizophrenics" and their families was well known in the field. He was adamantly opposed to the use of anti-psychotic drugs because of their disabling effects (discussed below). I was also working that year in a clinic in New Jersey. I was experiencing considerable success applying family therapy techniques to the largely working class clientele: I was often able in a few sessions to solve problems that I used to think would require years of therapy. I was saving persons from being labeled "mentally ill" and spending their lives in psychiatric facilities.

Despite my success as a family therapist, I was asked to leave the clinic in New Jersey after one year because I had enraged the psychiatrist by encouraging clients to wean themselves off of psychiatric drugs. I spent two years looking for a job in the New York area but I could not find a single one where my orientation and skills as a family therapist were not considered a problem, rather than an asset. (All of the clinics practiced traditional individually-oriented psychotherapy based on the mental illness model.)

Transinstitutionalization and Neuroleptic Drugs

Deinstitutionalization might have succeeded in integrating "the mentally ill" into their families, and/or communities. But mental health professionals would have had to base their interventions upon the premise that psychotics were *not* permanently disabled. They would have had to resist the various pressures to define identified patients as chronically mentally ill. This did not happen. I should add that it *had* happened in the past on a number of occasions — but therapists were not interested in learning from success.

The controversial psychiatrist R.D. Laing had proclaimed in the 1960s that "mental illness," in particular "schizophrenia," was a spiritual death-rebirth process that when allowed to run its course contributed to the individual's depth and religious insight. In the 1960s, Laing had established an asylum for mad people in England based on his ideas, but it was poorly organized and rather an embarrassment outside of Laing's personal fold. On the other hand, psychiatrist Loren Mosher, an associate of Laing, established a Laingian-style asylum that constituted a benchmark for alternative approaches. Mosher was the director of Schizophrenia Studies at the National Institute of Mental Health (NIMH) when he founded Soteria House in the early 1970s in California. Mosher managed to get NIMH funding for the program and the research, which demonstrated that the results for treatment of schizophrenics without drugs based on Laing's revolutionary idea about psychosis were far superior to that of the control group of hospitalized (and medicated) patients. A two year follow-up showed that the Soteria patients were far less likely to have relapsed, and far more likely to be attending school or holding a job (Whitaker, 222). Despite the high quality of the Soteria project research (or perhaps because of it) its funding was cut in 1977, and Mosher was pushed out of NIMH by 1980. Soteria Project was not unique — other less well-known experiments produced similar results, but they were all essentially ignored.

In virtually all psychiatric residential homes, patients were induced —wittingly or not —to assume the roles of chronic mental patients. Furthermore patients were invariably maintained on "anti-psychotic medications," neuroleptic drugs that kept them in a stuporous state, prevented higher level cortical functioning, and accentuated their physical and behavioral abnormalities All of these effects impeded their integration into the community. Over time, these drugs frequently caused permanent neurological disorders such as tardive dyskinesia (TD), an irreversible movement disorder characterized by uncontrollable (and often disfiguring) spasms, tics and/or writhing contortions of the face, arms and legs. The newer class of anti-psychotics introduced in the mid-1990s are also disabling and damaging to the body and mind, although they are tend to produce less conspicuous disfiguration; see Whitaker.

The side effects caused by neuroleptics are typically assumed to be symptoms of mental illness. As Robert Whitaker noted in *Mad in America*, "All of the traits that we have come to associate with schizophrenia —the awkward gait, the jerking arm movements, the vacant facial expressions, the sleepiness, the lack of initiative —are symptoms due, at least in large part, to a drug induced deficiency in dopamine transmission. . . . Our perceptions of how those ill with schizophrenia think, behave and look are all perceptions of people altered by medication." The madman whom society shuns is the creation of psychiatry.

Due to the skillful marketing of neuroleptics as wonder drugs, the pharmaceutical companies, with the assistance of psychiatry, made billions of dollars. The partnership with the drug companies enabled psychiatrists to boost their own fortunes and to consolidate their power. The American Psychiatric Association had been in financial trouble in the early 1970s as a result of competition with non-medical professionals who charged lower fees. But in 1980 the APA decided to seek the financial assistance from the drug companies. As psychiatrist Peter Breggin observed in *Toxic Psychiatry*, "floodgates of drug company influence were opened and . . . would grow wider each year . . . Whatever function APA had ever filled as a professional organization was now superseded by its function as a political advocate for the advancement of psychiatric and pharmaceutical business interests. Continually reiterated is the conviction that only a medical or biological image can enable psychiatry to compete economically."

In the 1990s, the pharmaceutical companies, psychiatry and National Alliance for the Mentally Ill (NAMI), an organization for the families of the "mentally ill" (funded by the drug companies), joined in an unholy alliance and launched an all-out effort to convince the public that deinstitutionalization had failed, ostensibly because mentally ill patients were too irrational to take the anti-psychotic medications that made them better. The solution, they argued, was out-patient commitment laws —forced drugging. The effort succeeded. By the late 1990s, almost every state had out-patient commitment laws.

The Movement Against Coercive Therapy

Shortly after I was asked to leave the clinic in New Jersey, I met George Ebert, an activist in the mental patients liberation movement. I had reached a dead end with my work as a family therapist. Family therapy had itself changed — most family therapists had abandoned the revolutionary ideas discussed above. Rather than fighting to change the system, as Minuchin and Haley had advocated, they abandoned the bedrock principles upon which family therapy was based so that they would be accepted as team players in an increasingly lucrative psychiatric-pharmaceutical industrial complex. Family therapists' hunger for status and acceptance as a mental health specialty was greater than their desire to help their clients change and "grow." Family therapy had lost its own raison d'etre. Minuchin and Haley remained icons in the family therapy field but one could not follow their methods and survive in the public mental health sector.

With the help of George Ebert, and a few other former mental patients, including Judith Greenberg (a founder in 1971 of the first — now defunct — Mental Patients Liberation Front), and with the guidance of radical psychiatrist Ron Leifer, and feminist social critic Kate Millet (also a former patient and author of The *Loony Bin Trip*), I formed the organization which, after a period of gestation, became in 1991 the Network Against Coercive Psychiatry.

Kate Millett, the renowned author and feminist, a long time East Village resident, did not live in a squat, but she did spend years battling her landlord in court in order to retain her apartment. She eventually won.

At this point, I had begun to think of social activism as a variation on the kind of inter- ventions I had previously made as a family therapist. That is, my goal as a public speaker and writer was to convey to former patients the same message I had as a family therapist: "You are not really patients. You are competent persons."

My first breakthrough was when I managed to interest Geraldo Rivera in doing a show on women and madness in 1989, which included Kate Millett, feminist therapist Phyllis Chesler, and Rae Unzicker, a leader in the patients liberation movement. The phone did not stop ringing for weeks. People called me to ask for advice, or to thank me for giving them hope. Many called to tell me that they themselves had been labeled "schizophrenic" and managed to get out of the system, off of drugs, and to reclaim their lives. In 1993, my first book was published, with a foreword by Thomas Szasz, the famous psychiatric iconoclast and author of numerous books, including The *Myth of Mental Illness* (1960). My book was titled *Madness, Heresy* and the *Rumor of Angels: The Revolt Against the Mental Health System* (Open Court).

I tried unsuccessfully to get funding for the Network Against Coercive Psychiatry. I went a few times with some ex-patient activists to the state capital in Albany to talk to legislators and to the Commissioner of Mental Health about various plans to "improve" the mental health system. One time I was accompanied by Professor James Mancuso, a psychologist and critic of the idea of mental illness, co-author of the seminal 1980 book *Schizophrenia: Medical Diagnosis or Moral Verdict*. The plan that George Ebert, Rosary Marinara (a former patient and patients rights advocate) and I favored was getting state subsidies to open up "half-way houses/ detoxification centers" where patients would be helped to wean themselves off of anti-psychotic drugs. The authorities listened politely, and then ignored us.

173

The East Village-Defending the Homeland

In the late 1980s and early 1990s, people were resisting the relentless march of progress and big business and fighting to preserve democracy, to maintain community. During this period the East Village or LES was a site of contestation between the urban counter-culture on the one hand and real estate interests, Yuppies and City Government, on the other hand In 1990, I met Clayton Patterson, a community activist, a video artist and a chronicler of the struggle to resist the gentrification of the East Village and LES. I would stop by his apartment from time to time to visit and chat. I told him about the battles against the psychiatric establishment and he would update me on the struggle of the "lower classes" to retain their rightful turf on the LES. When residents were evicted from their apartments a few hundred of them took over several abandoned buildings on the LES and turned them into squats —until the police under Mayor Giuliani ordered all but one token building evacuated so that real estate developers could move in.

These squats were experiments in collective living. People who were evicted from their apartments or homeless in some way now had a place to live. Clayton and I both knew through different channels a number of people who lived in the squats who were former mental patients — "psychiatric survivors" to use the term preferred by the radicals in the 1990s. (The more moderate and conservative wings of the patients' rights movement referred to themselves as mental health "consumers.") Some of them were evicted from apartments and some had fled from halfway houses where they had been forced to take psychiatric drugs. Now they were in squats. They had successfully de-institutionalized themselves: They were living in the *community*, not in segregated residences supervised by psychiatric personnel. They participated in community life instead of watching from the margins, stupefied by psychiatric drugs. One mutual friend of ours who lived in a squat was a young African American psychiatric survivor named Carla Cubitt, who, a few years later, gained a reputation in New York art circles as a talented painter and sculptor. Another squatter and psychiatric survivor, Cassanda Mele, was a talented poet who later became a mother and school teacher.

Kate Millett, a long time East Village resident, did not live in a squat but she did spend years battling her landlord in court in order to retain her apartment. She eventually won. It was from her East Village loft that Kate helped to plan the battle against forced-psychiatry. Kate was the godmother in the 1990s of the mental patients liberation movement. Another East Village resident was the world-renowned American poet Allen Ginsberg. Ginsberg was also a former mental patient whose first great poem, "Howl," (1956) celebrated the sensitivity and spiritual ardor of mental patients and other social pariahs ("I saw the best minds of my generation destroyed by madness . . . angelheaded hipsters burning for the ancient heavenly connection to the starry dynamo in the machinery of night"). Ginsberg retained throughout his life a sympathy and affinity for the outsider and the underdog — due in part to the suffering he had experienced as a child watching his mother, Naomi, destroyed by

A Radical Political and Social History of the Lower East Side

madness, and by the mental health system. Ginsberg, who lived in a five-floor walk-up on the LES, considered the neighborhood his home and never left it even when his finances permitted more bourgeois lodgings. He frequently allowed homeless poets, former mental patients and various down-and-out hipsters to "crash" in his apartment.

Louise Wahl was a 70-year-old former mental patient who was involved in Project Release, a support group of former patients that encouraged patients to wean themselves away from psychiatry. Unfortunately many had nowhere to go but halfway houses where they were forced to take psychiatric drugs. Some of the more fortunate ex-patients had found cheap apartments or SRO rooms in the East Village in an earlier era. Now it was hard enough to get into a halfway house as opposed to a city shelter. Not only were the shelters dangerous places where boarders were subjected to the risk of violence but they were also besieged by teams of city workers who would visit the shelters regularly and try to force the sheltered homeless to take psychiatric drugs, or cart them away to psychiatric wards. Louise introduced me to Harriet Nesbitt, also a friend of Clayton's, who had founded an organization called Mothers for More Half-Way Houses. Harriet agreed with me that the half-way houses should not force residents to take psychiatric drugs. But her lobbying efforts for genuine half-way houses, for affordable housing for the "mentally ill," were in vain. Legislators met with her, listened politely and then ignored her.

The housing crisis continued to worsen. The squats, even before they were closed down, did not provide enough space to accommodate all the people who were victims of the housing crisis. Then the streets themselves became the last refuge from the NYC shelters for many of the victims of urban removal. When former LES residents lost their apartments, some of them moved into Tompkins Square Park, home of the 1960s hippies and a symbol of the counter-culture. When Mayor Koch announced in the late 1980s that homeless persons could no longer sleep in Tompkins Square Park, there were numerous battles between baton wielding policemen, many on horseback, ordered to take over the park, and East Village residents who regarded the park as theirs and fought for the right of the homeless (many former residents and neighbors) to sleep in the park. These scenes were captured on videotape by Clayton, and were used as evidence in several police brutality suits. They were the last valiant battles fought by the indigenous people of the East Village but the City won, the Yuppie settlers moved in, and the East Village finally lost its identity as a home of the counter-culture.

Homelessness and the Medicalization of Social Problems

The psychiatric establishment was quick to jump on homelessness and define it as a psychiatric problem. In fact, psychiatric ideologues claimed that homelessness was a product of the resistance to psychiatry treatment by the mentally ill and their instigation by radical psychiatrists like Szasz and Laing, and by the civil liberties lobby which, in the late 1960s, had successfully established safeguards — rarely observed — against arbitrary, involuntary psychiatric confinement. Mental health professionals and journalists argued that homelessness was a product of deinstitutionalization — a ludicrous theory, as mentioned above, since homelessness emerged 20 years after the state hospitals were emptied. Neo-conservative pundits generalized this theory and claimed that *both* homelessness and the growing problems of the mentally ill were caused by the 1960s counter-culture — its revolt against authority, its alleged contempt for rationality and the virtues of the middle-class life style and its romanticization of mental illness. Neo-conservatives and the psychiatric establishment made common cause in the 1990s in an effort to exterminate the lingering remnants of the counter-culture of the 1960s. From this perspective, the gentrification of the East Village in New York City and the evacuation of its indigenous population represented a decisive and heroic triumph of authority and progress over pagan savages unwilling to recognize the necessary constraints of civilized existence.

The establishment raged against the antinomian intellectuals who "romanticized" the mentally ill as if they were noble savages instead of poor victims of psychiatric disorders. Deinstitutionalization has failed, they announced — it was a misguided venture in the first place, a product of the 1960s counterculture and its refusal to accept the reality of mental illness, a denial of the verdict of science itself which, psychiatrists and their ideologues claimed, had proven "schizophrenia" was a brain disorder. Look what these trouble-makers have now wrought: "Madness in the streets!" shrieked the psychiatric establishment and their allies. And indeed *Madness in the Streets* was the title of a popular 1990 book by the neo-conservative ideologues Rael Jean Isaac and Virginia Armat. The authors chafed at any constraints placed on the power of psychiatrists.

Like Isaac and Armat, neo-conservative Myron Magnet, whom George W. later hailed as his mentor, blamed the 1960s counter-culture for a legacy of dangerous libertarianism and civil liberties legislation which, he argued, were the causes of homelessness. Look what this irrational insistence on freedom at all costs and the rejection of psychiatric authority has done to the mentally ill, Magnet scolded, as if the mental illness had caused thousands of people to abandon their comfortable homes. And as if Laing, Szasz, and the critics of psychiatric methods had not presented an alternative to forced psychiatry — recommunalization. Magnet pontificated: "Is it not a deplorable notion that it is freedom to be left enslaved to madness. . . that it is freedom to rave and defecate on the streets, to be untreated and afraid?" The mentally ill have "a right to involuntary treatment." Completely obscured by this demagoguery is the fact that the homeless, including the "mentally ill," needed housing, education, vocational training, and jobs, not forced stupefying psychiatric drugs and "psychiatric services." The "mentally ill" may have needed other services as well to assist their recommunalization — but while coercive drugging might have made the mentally ill less conspicuous and compliant (and therefore, no doubt, secretly satisfying Magnet), it could only further degrade their quality of life. But the good faith of psychiatry was beyond doubt for Magnet, Hamill, and Armat.

Let me reiterate: Homelessness was not caused by "mental illness"! The mentally ill (with a few exceptions, probably) had not "abandoned" their residences in the 1980s and taken to the streets. There were a small number of patients in the 1980s who were released from state mental hospitals into homeless shelters. But the emptying of the state mental hospitals took place almost entirely in the 1960s and early 1970s, before homelessness became a social epidemic. The cause of homelessness was poverty, not insanity. The "homelessly mentally ill" was merely a modern term for the indigent insane, "who are homeless because they are indigent not because they are insane" (Szasz, 92, my emphasis) — that is, they are homeless because they do not have the funds to afford the dwindling share of low income housing in urban areas like NYC. Former mental patients constitute only a minority of the homeless, a minority (albeit substantial) of poor people. (Johnson, 145)

The poor were victims of the gentrification process that occurred in the 1980s and 1990s — long after deinstitutionalization had occurred — combined with the reduction in housing assistance initiated by the Reagan Administration in 1983. As Ann Braden Johnson, a social worker for the mentally ill, observed, "each year about 2.5 million people are involuntarily displaced from their homes by gentrification, economic development schemes, eviction or inflated rent. Another half-million housing units of low-rent dwellings are lost each year to arson, co-op or condo conversion, abandonment, demolition and inflation" (Johnson, 138). In New York City, the number of persons living in SRO units declined from about 100,000 in 1965 to less than 20,000 in 1986 (Szasz, 94).

As a consequence of the destruction of low-income housing and the reductions in the welfare rolls, homelessness soared. In 1987, there were about half a million persons homeless on any one night in the country, whereas by 2000 the number had increased to over 2.3 million. In New York City, Giuliani's cutbacks in the city's housing capital budget aggrandized the problem. By the summer of 2001, the number of homeless families in city shelters had risen higher than ever before. By the end of 2001, the Coalition for the Homeless reported that 29,000 persons were in shelters on any night, more than at any time in the city's history.

Yet by the end of the millennium the homeless were also less visible than ever before. Psychiatry had enlisted the media in its campaign against "madness in the streets," which undermined sympathy for the homeless by sensationalizing and dwelling upon several instances of violent crimes committed by criminally deranged homeless persons — a very small subset of former mental patients who, according to a study by the MacArthur Foundation, were no more violent than an equivalent population of non-mental patients, i.e. "normal people." As the Lower East Side was transformed by real estate developers from a low rent haven for bohemians and artists to a high rent district for urban yuppies, new homeless shelters and transitional residences for "the mentally ill" were built in peripheral areas of the city. In these "urban reservations" (Parenti, 106) the homeless, mental patients, the poor and other pariahs were domiciled far away from the public view. This new policy was a far cry from the policy of deinstitutionalization (as originally conceived) with its ideal of community integration: It was reminiscent of the era when the poor and the mad were warehoused in state institutions — out of sight, out of mind.

Psychiatry had succeeded in painting homelessness as a mental health problem by "blaming the victims" (the identified patients and culprits) and claiming that the homeless consisted largely of mentally ill persons who refused to take their medication, became crazy — and often violent — and abandoned their homes. Once the public had been convinced of this psychiatric version of reality, the obstacles to enacting out-patient commitment laws were eliminated. Here was the magic solution to homelessness, and all social ills: All we have to do is renounce the misguided 1960s critique of psychiatric power and eliminate all obstacles to total psychiatric control over the mentally ill. In the 1990s almost all states had enacted out-patient commitment laws (i.e. forced drugging), even though they conflicted with the higher courts rulings that patients had a constitutional right — unless proven incompetent or dangerous — to refuse psychiatric drugs. In New York State, out-patient commitment finally passed in 1999 despite the existence of a strong patients' rights lobby.

The psychiatric interpretation of homelessness obscured its real causes — the policies that led to the eviction of hundreds of thousands of poor people (including former patients) from the SROs and other low-income rentals that were demolished or converted into high-income housing. Social problems now appear as mental health problems that can be solved with psychiatric drugs, and the implementation of social engineering by mental health professionals. Psychiatry thus serves to protect the status quo and to disguise the operations of a social system that has led to an increasing economic polarization between rich and poor, and that continually reproduces the social pathologies of poverty and homelessness.

The Triumph of the Mental Health Establishment

I do not believe the ideal of deinstitutionalization was flawed. It was a product in part of the idealism and communitarian vision of the 1960s. The problem, as I see it, was in the defeat of the 1960s counter-culture, not in its alleged triumph. Had the insights of Szasz and Laing, Goffman (1961), Minuchin and other family therapists, all products to varying degrees of the cultural ferment of the 1960s, been applied to the problem of mental health after deinstitutionalization, then the "mentally ill" would have disappeared as such; they would have been integrated into their communities — they would not have taken on permanent identities as chronic mental patients. But how could this project have succeeded when affordable housing was being eliminated for all but the rich and the lucky (who were grandfathered in under rent control)? Homelessness was blamed on the mad, on society's pariahs, but they were only the most visible face of homelessness. I repeat: homelessness was caused by housing policies implemented by the city government at the behest of the real estate interests. Psychiatry jumped on the bandwagon, claimed homelessness was caused by mental illness, and demanded — and received — the power to force the homeless (those they could capture) to submit to their power, and be forced on drugs and placed in sub-standard residences for the mentally ill.

In Ken Kesey's 1962 novel, *One Flew Over the Cuckoo's Nest*, the mad house where McMurphy finds himself is a microcosm of American society in the 1950s: Each individual is viewed by those at the top of the hierarchy — "the Combine" — as a fungible element that must be suppressed or eliminated and replaced if it becomes an obstacle to the efficient functioning of the social machine which has no raison' d'etre other than its own existence. In the book, as in the movie, one of the heroes is eventually lobotomized and the other, Chief Bromden, escapes the mad house — but the Combine retains its control. In the 1960s through the 1980s, the East Village was a symbol of the victory of the human spirit over the social machine — over the Combine. In the 1990s the Establishment decided it had to be destroyed. As Ken Kesey would have said, the Combine was challenged, but it deflected the threats to its power, maintained its control and suppressed again — for the time being — the revolt of the human spirit against the Machine.

A Radical Political and Social History of the Lower East Side

References:

"Tardive Dyskinesia: *A Task Force Report of the American Psychiatric Association*." American Psychiatric Association (1992).

Bockoven, J. S. *Moral Treatment in American Psychiatry*. New York: Springer,1963.

Boyle, Mary. *Schizophrenia: A Scientific Delusion?* London and New York: Routledge, 1990.

Breggin, P.R. P*sychiatric Drugs: Hazards to the Brain*. New York: Springer, 1983.

Breggin, *P.R. Toxic Psychiatry*. New York: St Martin's, 1991.

Breggin, Peter. *Brain Disabling Treatments in Psychiatry*. New York: Springer, 1997.
Cohen, David. "Biological Basis of Schizophrenia." *Social Work*. 1989, 255-7

Cohen, David. "Neuroleptic Drug Treatment of Schizophrenia." *Journal of Mind and Behavior*, 5 (1994): 139-156.

Cohen, David, and Michael McCubbin, M. *"The Political Economy of Tardive Dyskinesia."* *Journal of Mind and Behavior*, 11 (1990): 455-474.

Farber, Seth. *Madness, Heresy and the Rumor of Angels*. Chicago: Open Court, 1993.

Haley, J. *Leaving Home*. New York: McGraw Hill, 1983.

Hamill, Peter. "How to Save the Homeless and Ourselves." *New York Magazine*, 20 Sept 1993: 34-9.

Isaac, Rael Jean, and Virginia Armat. *Madness in the Streets*. New York: Free Press, 1990.

Johnson, Ann Bredan. *Out of Bedlam*. New York: Basic Books, 1990.

Karon, Bertram. *"Psychotherapy Versus Medication for Schizophrenia." The Limits of Biological Treatments for Psychological Distress*. Ed. S. Fisher and R.P .Greenberg. Hillsdale N. J.: Lawrence Erlbaum Associates, 1989.

Magnet, Myron. *The Dream and the Nightmare: The Sixties' Legacy to the Underclass*. New York: William Morrow, 1993.

Minuchin, Slavador and Joel Elizur. *Institutionalizing Madness*. New York: Basic Books, 1989.

Mosher, Loren, and Lorenzo Burti. C*ommunity Mental Health*. New York: Norton, 1989.

McCubbin, Michael. "Deinstitutionalization: The Illusion of Disillusion." *Journal of Mind and Behavior.* 15 (1994): 35-53.

McKnight, John. *The Careless Society*. New York: Basic Books, 1995.

Oaks, David. *Pushing Back the Pushers*. Dendron,1997.

Parenti, Christian. *Lockdown America*. New York: Verso, 1999.

Policy Research Associates. *"Research Study of the New York City Involuntary Outpatient Commitment Pilot Program."* New York City: Department of Mental Health, 1998.

Scull, Andrew. *"Deinstitutionalization: Cycles of Despair."* Journal of Mind and Behavior. 15 (1990): 301-311.

Szasz, Thomas. *Psychiatric Slavery*. New York: Free Press, 1997.

Szasz, Thomas. *Insanity: The Idea and its Consequences*. New York: John Wiley and Sons, 1987.

Szasz, Thomas. *Cruel Compassion*. New York: John Wiley and Sons, 1994.

Valenstein, Elliot. *Blaming the Brain*. New York: Free Press, 1998.

Whitaker, Robert. *Mad in America*. Cambridge, Mass: Perseus Publishing, 2002.

Chapter 3

Writing the RFP
By Joanne Edelman

After many weeks of carrying sheetrock up three steep flights of stairs, unsuccessful plumbing attempts and the lack of services (that even poor people who live in the civilized world have grown to expect — running hot and cold water, electricity etc.), I began to fully realize the strange world that we inhabited. The world outside the Rainbow Co-op had little to no effect on us. We did not have to follow the rules of an ordinary co-op, condo or rental because we were squatters and were making up the rules as we went along. Nothing was taken for granted. Some tenants paid on a monthly basis and some did not. The members of the Rainbow Co-op really didn't have to pay their rent (or as we liked to refer to it — maintenance — as if we actually owned the place) because all of us were living in the building illegally. We were living on the honor system and we all know how that works. It doesn't.

The Rainbow people worked together fixing up each other's apartments and even this endeavor was very unfair since only a few members had skills and fewer still had tools.

When speaking to my mother, I described my apartment as "unfinished." "Oh so you don't have a tile bath?" she replied. How could I tell her that we didn't even have a bath as of yet and were running across the hall to my neighbor's "unfinished" apartment to bathe and wash the dishes in her shower stall. My husband learned his plumbing skills from a Readers Digest Manuel. We were so pleased after installing the tub, sink and toilet to find that there were only 20 leaks. Another triumph.

It wasn't all bad. Once we had facilities, life became more civilized and we could settle down to the writing of the Request For Proposal (RFP). (The RFP was a document that all Homesteaders had to fill out to prove to the city that they knew what it took to own and operate a building). An organization had to be allowed by the city to fill out an RFP. We were thrilled at the prospect of having this document in our possession. But before I get to that comedy of errors (right down to the coffee stain on the city's reply to our RFP), I must tell you how we actually got Con Ed to give us lights. We simply bribed the Con Ed guy. None of us had ever bribed anyone before. Who do you ask for advice in these matters? Do you ask the squatters next door even though they hate you? We did. Their advice: ask the Con Ed man (who was later fired by Con Ed and even worse) if you could take him to lunch and if he said yes, ask him how much the lunch would cost. Our Con Ed guy replied that the lunch would be around $500. It was so easy.

We now had lights (at a commercial rate — higher than a residential rate) and it was all legal, unless you factor in the fact that we had to bribe a Con Ed supervisor. And we now had water. That was much easier because it was done through a licensed plumber who didn't need to see a lease and who filed his own permits through the city. No bribe was necessary, but when our neighbors in 272 East Seventh Street saw the plumber, they called the police on us. The police looked at the plumber's license and left us alone.

Joanne Edelman

Here is how the city screwed up. There was no cross-referencing for permits. Even though the plumber was working on a city-owned building that was taken over by the Rainbow Co-op, the city could not stop the process because he was a licensed plumber. Of course the city could not even prove that it was the building's rightful owner because no one could find the Certificate of Occupancy.

So we cleaned the sheetrock dust off our kitchen tables, opened many bottles of bourbon and prepared to fill out the most important document we had.

The RFP was very long and complicated. We really did not know many of the answers and so we just made them up. If anyone really read the entire document they would have been justified in just throwing it away — no one would have blamed them at all. Not even us.

Well we did it. We completed the document to the best of our ability. A woman who was eight months pregnant delivered the document to city officials by hand. Hillary Porter rode to City Hall on a unicycle and my husband ran alongside her. At first they were both on the unicycle, but some part of his body started to hurt, and he eventually jumped off and ran. It was the quickest way to get to City Hall. No one even considered taking a cab — that was not an option. Everything we did was outside of the norm.

Why then were they cycling and running? Because they were trying to make the deadline. Why did we wait so long to start working on the RFP? Because the city gave us permission to fill it out about four days before it was due. They knew that it could not be filled in properly in that amount of time. Was it a conspiracy against us? We thought so and so we got all fired up and kept drinking the bourbon just to spite them.

Of course we were denied. This is where the coffee-stained letter comes into the story. The minute we received the denial someone spilled coffee over the one piece of communication that we had from the city — it was the most important piece of paper we had.

You can imagine our surprise when we were denied — not because of the idiocy of how we filled out the document, but because we had too many apartments listed. How could we have made such a mistake? That was an easy problem to fix. Take two of the small apartments and make them into one apartment. Done! Now are we in? We were trying to make the leap from being squatters to being in the Homesteading Program, or the TIL Program. We believed that even though we were denied, we were closer to having legal status. We now had proof that the city knew we were living there. They mistakenly mailed the letter to us at 274 E 7th Street. They could no longer say that they didn't know we were living there. They sent us a letter, therefore acknowledging our presence and residency in a formal way.

We were not your usual squatters. We never broke into an abandoned building; we had services and we had a letter from the city addressed to our building (proof that they knew we lived there) stating that the only thing wrong with the proposal was the *number* of apartments. This letter officially became the "coffee-stained letter from the city."

We knew we were close to legality. That was 20 years ago and just this year, the city has given the Rainbow Co-op the right to pursue legal ownership.

Chapter 4

Leaving the Building (or Then I went Home and Made Lunch)
By Joanne Edelman

My 9-year-old son, Joshua, had a friend over for the night. We had since moved from a dark first-floor apartment to a larger apartment, on the third floor, in the front of the our building. We put in new floors, ceilings, windows, a stove, a refrigerator, a washer/dryer and a dishwasher. I acquired some of these by giving private exercise classes to a woman who instead of paying me per class added them all up and bought me appliances from Sears.

So the place was looking great. Joshua's former baby-sitter, a friend from Canada, passionately believed that bright yellow curtains would make our squat at 274 East Seventh Street beautiful. She was right. Life was good in the Rainbow Co-op.

Except for this one family on the top floor.

The husband was an exceptionally good-looking man who served in Vietnam. The wife was a nurse who worked part-time. They had a beautiful baby daughter who they sometimes tied to the high chair when they went out. He called himself Mozambique. She was Linda. Mozambique used to beat up Linda on a regular basis. After many failed attempts by the women in the building to convince her to get help, we decided to call the police when we heard the next beating. When the police arrived Linda and Mozambique said that all was fine and they did not know what we were talking about.

The police knew our building quite well by now. They made many visits. They were kind and patient, arrogant and shitty to us. Their advice to us was to move to Brooklyn or Queens or New Jersey, but to definitely get the hell off of East Seventh Street. Who knew that one day it would become fashionable to live on East Seventh Street. Between Avenues C and D. Certainly not the police.

We had a lovely tenant who took over our first floor apartment and who was very friendly and helpful. He was from Eritrea. He loved our son. (Later, after my husband, Bill, and I separated, he took care of Joe, my second son, in the morning while I was giving private exercise classes to rich people on the Upper East Side). He spent many nights with us just talking about his country and the building. We were always "talking about the building." He was fiercely loyal to my husband and so when Mozambique threatened Bill with bodily harm, Tess took off his slippers and, in his bathrobe, holding a pole of some sort (could have been a broom handle) over his head, chased Mozambique down the center of East Seventh Street. What a day that was! It was warm and sunny and many of the tenants of East Seventh Street were outside sitting on the stoops. And there they were, Tess running down the middle of the street, trying to attack Mozambique with a warrior-like weapon.

Joanne Edelman

After the Rainbow Co-opers corralled Tess, he went into his apartment and, unbeknownst to us, grabbed a machete and ran up the stairs to try another attempt at doing away with Mozambique. My apartment door was opened and I ran out to try to help the group stop Tess. As the men were holding him, I grabbed the machete and pulled it out of his hands.

I turned around quickly and carried it into my apartment to hide it.

Right then my son Joshua asked me to make tuna fish for lunch. I did. I made tuna fish for Aliah and Josh right after I pulled the machete out of Tess's hands.

Then I received a call from Aliah's mother, Shelley, who asked me if Bill and I would be interested in applying for an apartment in a legal homestead building on East Tenth Street. I sat down and looked at the machete that I was hiding and then I looked at the little boys eating their tuna sandwiches and without even asking Bill I said yes. I told her that I would be at their next building meeting and apply for the available apartment.

I was done with the Rainbow Co-op. I wanted to have another child, but not there. As it turned out I did have another boy on East Seventh Street.

My two sons and I moved to 367 East Tenth Street when Joe, my younger son, was about 6 years old. My first marriage was over and I was heading into my second marriage when we moved in. Joe fell down the stairs and broke his wrist during the move, but nothing could dampen the incredible feeling of elation about getting out of the Rainbow Co-op.

Chapter 5

A Tenant's Story
By JoAnn Wypijewski

The neighborhood was decked out with Dominican markets when I moved in twenty-five years ago. There were vegetable stalls and bodegas and, in easy view from my kitchen window five flights up, a curious little candy store that children never seemed to frequent — which was not so curious after all, because jawbreakers and licorice straps were in scant supply there, and then only as dingy props which the loose-legged men who came and went cared nothing for either. Warm evenings on the block old ladies would settle into plastic lawn chairs to gossip, Italian here, Spanish there; and on summer weekends the smooth-strutting fellow with the white hair and dark glasses, a man I didn't realize was at the center of the local drug business until many years later, after he'd returned from jail, would mix it up with the sidewalk musicians who for a time were fixtures out by the candy store. They played salsa and merengue late into those weekend nights. It was something I came to regard as an unremarkable feature of the bohemian package of the street, wonderful and annoying, unlike the midnight car alarms which were just annoying, and eminently remarkable as signals that the place we loved was disappearing.

The familiar arc of this kind of story would now have me catalogue what was lost, but we know that too painfully already. And it's best not to go all romantic. In dreams I'd like to think that the drunks and druggies found happy endings, that the couple across the street whose domestic conflict erupted one night in pushing and shoving and sent her fleeing up First Avenue in her slip, with him in pursuit, cursing and waving a gun, achieved a separate peace as well. Maybe, but maybe not. I do know, though, that some things were saved, that it's at least as important to remember what was saved as what was lost, and here is where GOLES (Good Old Lower East Side) comes into the story.

There are the big things: the Sirovich Senior Center, Children's Liberation Day Care, the Ottendorfer Library, the Theater for a New City (though let's not get started on what became of its air rights), the community gardens, Tompkins Square Park (though let's not get started on what became of the bandshell) etc. Neighborhood fights — some grand, some modest, some more successful than others — were necessary to save all of those, and GOLES was in the fight. But we ought to train an eye, too, on the smaller things which actually aren't small at all. There are the invisible things, which are invisible only because they haven't been converted into luxury condos: the thousands of apartments saved, the thousands of evictions prevented over the years of almost unceasing economic violence upon our neighborhood; the resistance in the face of arson, warehousing, harassment. The shredding of the safety net, and consecutive city administrations that regard the moneyed classes as the only legitimate claimants on Manhattan housing.

184

I count myself among that lucky, resistant throng that has GOLES to thank for quite a lot. I live on the corner of 13th Street and First Avenue, in the same apartment I have always lived in. Back in February of 1979 my roommate and I, college girlfriends fresh to the city, had never seen a proper lease and knew nothing of housing law; we thought nothing, therefore, of signing a single piece of paper that enumerated no rights, no obligations, that didn't even come with a carbon copy. A year later the "landlord" presented a similar single sheet that provided no option for more than a one-year renewal — and that stipulated a new rent almost 10 percent higher than the old one — even though, after the usual acrimony, the Rent Stabilization Board had just settled on a percentage that was considerably lower. We signed that piece of paper too, and then decided to look into it.

I don't remember how I heard of GOLES, but I remember the first conversation I had with its founder, the wily, lovable, righteously angry and frequently irascible Floyd Feldman. "If you have this problem, chances are other people in the building have it too," he said. "Talk to your neighbors, get yourselves together, call a meeting and I'll come to see how we can help you." He was more right than even he knew; we organized our one building, but as we eventually found out, people in about a hundred apartments sprinkled throughout the neighborhood had the same problem. Our "landlord" wasn't a landlord at all, but a middle-man who rented batches of apartments at low rates with long leases, fixed them up a bit, put his name or the name of his paramour, his secretary, any close relative or business associate on the standard lease, and then "sublet" the places to poor, young, usually transient people for double the rent. He had done this for years, and had a little storefront on 6th Street where the unsuspecting handed over their money. The city had no sublet law at the time, so strictly speaking this was not illegal. But since the piece of paper we signed was also worthless in terms of securing for us any legal rights to the apartment, it made a joke of housing law and of every tenant protection that did and does exist.

After about a year of action we won, and for those hundred or so other Lower East Side tenants, whom we didn't know and who didn't know us, it was like Christmas in July. One day they opened the mail to find a check representing all that they had overpaid, plus a new standard lease with the real landlord, at half the rent. It was my first direct organizational experience, beyond mass petition-signing and protest-going, and my first victory. When our case then became the basis of the New York City sublet law, I learned that victory is often tempered by compromise somewhere down the line. And when the middle-man, put out of his middle-man business by us, really struck it rich in the legitimately venal real estate boom of the 1980s, I was reminded again of capitalism's cunningly accommodative nature, and the necessity of resistant vigilance.

Every tenant who has worked with GOLES over the years has a particular story. Mine never really ended. Floyd convinced me to volunteer at the office (which was then high up a narrow staircase in a building on Great Jones Street) and later join the board, on which I have served an improbable twenty-two years. Like the toniest downtown clubs, that first office was seemingly anonymous, and yet, also as with the clubs, people always found it. Those were the years when "Rent Strike" banners hung from dozens of Lower East Side buildings, when the assumed benefit of collective struggle was still part of the Zeitgeist. It takes looking back to realize how much the political ground has shifted. Floyd founded GOLES in 1977.

A Radical Political and Social History of the Lower East Side

The experience of the anti-war and civil rights movements was still fresh. The modern women's liberation and gay liberation movements were in their salad days. The housing rights movement was part of the hundred flowers that bloomed in community organizing throughout the country. Floyd had had this theory of tenant organizing as a kind of chain reaction — from building to block to neighborhood to city. Back then it didn't even seem utopian, so much was it part of what was in the air-conditioning system of the culture. I remember testifying at a City Council hearing on the populist necessity of community gardens, and remember hearing Floyd talk about tenants seizing abandoned, city-owned properties long before the squatters' rebellion and garden defense reached their zenith. Thinking about it now, it's clear that in that post-sixties period the side of the people was strongest when it seemed the least dramatic; down the road, drama would belong to the side with the biggest guns — literally — to the backlash, with its justification, however unjust, of law and order.

I can't here provide the full GOLES chronology, or even the full account of things saved. Individual memories will have to fill in the blanks. But for me the organization's treasure is what it was from the beginning, the faith in a collective consciousness, now the more remarkable because the more rare. Moving into its second quarter-century, GOLES occupies a storefront whose rent has just doubled, putting the organization in the same precarious position as tenants and small businesses whose survival spells the difference between the neighborhood as home and the neighborhood as "destination." We have a thrift store, where business is as tough as it is for the local copy shop, the local Italian grocer, the self-employed writer or graphic artist or clothing maker who in that long-ago crafted a bohemian life and is determined to keep it. We have helped bring to life an historic alliance between poor people and union workers, specifically public housing residents and the building trades, striving to turn vulnerability into strength. We have a staff that knows what it means to live in public housing, to live in a squat, to navigate the city's welfare labyrinth, to experience America as an immigrant, to be defiant when everything around a person seems to say, "Give it up." We have a board that knows what it means to be homeless, to succeed despite the slings and arrows, to fight for the organization, to be grateful. These are hard times but not the worst of times: GOLES is still with the people, preserving the spirit that insists, "No, we will not be ground down."

The other night at a meeting in Lower Manhattan to discuss spending priorities in post-9/11 rebuilding, one of our tenant leaders, Marie Christopher, made the case as plain as day: the people need housing, the people need jobs, the people need education. They don't need a train tunnel to nowhere or any more private enrichment dressed up as a public good. The crowd exploded in applause. Listening to her, I thought, how terribly amazing that these things need to be argued in the twenty-first century. The fact that they do indicates the distance we have to travel; that the clear, strong voice for truth, justice, and common happiness makes itself known and felt without apology or concession. That's the stuff of all our efforts, and all our honoring.

Chapter 6

DLA Statement
Squatting on East Seventh Street
        By Daniel Edelman

I have been a lawyer since 1969, over 34 years ago, and have predominantly done work involving tenants, defendants, employees and other people who have been the victim of discrimination, unjust treatment, etc. I am writing this story to let you know how I remember meeting the Rainbow Collective, a group of people with different backgrounds, origins and status who lived in a building on East Seventh Street.
I don't remember how the group came to me but over about a 20-year stretch I was called upon to deal with the powers that be on behalf of the Rainbow Collective in courts, on the streets, in politicians' offices, before the Department of Housing and Preservation Development, and finally to facilitate the entry of Rainbow into a self-help program sponsored by the city when they finally received status.

But for the longest time Rainbow Collective did not receive status because they were squatters. The Koch, Dinkins and Giuliani administrations would not recognize their existence because they didn't want to encourage other members of the larger New York City community to squat and take over abandoned buildings, fix them up, make them safe and thereby create affordable and reasonable housing for themselves and their families without buying the building or paying anything to the city as landlord.

But what really happened was that I was able to meet Joanne, Beverly, Bernard, Angela, Angel and a whole lot of other people who asked me to help them facilitate the kinds of things that it would take to run a building without having legal title to it which meant getting rid of the junkies, collecting rent, convincing HPD and the Department of Buildings people that the buildings were safe and sanitary and sound, providing services like heat, hot water, electric, gas and the like, all of which was done without any authority or money, in the best and most generous spirits.

I remember being called on an emergency basis to come down and represent some squatters in court who the landlord was trying to evict and have criminally arrested because of a situation on East Seventh Street. Apparently, one of the tenants, Beverly, had paid a rent check to the former landlord who had let the building go in foreclosure which meant that she hadn't paid the real estate taxes. When either the old landlord or the City of New York took the title to the building back for failure to pay taxes and tried to evict and arrest Beverly, we presented this one check which showed that she had a legal right to be in the building and the criminal proceeding was dismissed. But it was a very long and involved process over 20 years involving countless hours, actually hundreds of hours, spent for little or no money in fees before we got it together.

187

A Radical Political and Social History of the Lower East Side

I do remember some interesting points which had to do with how we got the police department to allow us to use self-help and get the junkies out of the building when we didn't have legal authority to do what we needed to do and that involved an interesting visit to the police station and some definite danger issues.

Remember we also formed a tenant's association and helped the building to develop and pass bylaws and they fought back all attempts to evict them informally or formally without the benefit of the law.

But the thing that I remember the best is when the City of New York decided that the buildings were unsafe and sent the city managers to inspect the building with a representative of the Commissioner of Real Estate and many other important city officials who wanted them out because the Rainbow Collective was squatters and an embarrassment to the City, which didn't want to be perceived as coddling the squatters.

People from the city came down and I came down armed with my business cards (which said that "my lawyer can beat up your lawyer") and a number of lollipops including "Get Out of Jail Free" cards from the monopoly set because I always believed that lollipops, "Get Out of Jail Free" cards and "my lawyer can beat up your lawyer" cards would be sufficient to deal with any problem that existed throughout my travels as a lawyer. But in any event, I had just completed a transaction with one of the commissioners whereupon the city agreed to sell real estate to a building that was occupied by tenants who were artists in Soho, and, in the course of negotiating with the city, I had built a relationship with one of the commissioners who was sympathetic that the former landlord of that building had tried to punch me out in the elevator. When this guy came in knowing the combative nature of this, I basically told him that the building was safe and that he could come into the building and observe with his people and make a determination and, if he believed that it was not safe, I would take steps to make it safe and, if he believed it was safe, then he would leave us alone.

In any event, a very cold day in January one year when the city was coming in, we gave them the cards and the lollipops and, in the best Kojak imitation I could do, I showed him around the building and, as they left, he indicated to me that it was safe as long as I said "who loves you babe." This is my strongest recollection of what we did for the building at East Seventh Street where the Rainbow Collective lives on. I could tell you of other times that we went with the Commissioner of HPD and other city officials who said that there would never be squatters recognized by his or her dead body, but that is another story for another time.

Chapter 7

Cooper Square
By Chris Brandt

There was a meeting of a committee associated with Cooper Square recently. The subject was garbage. Low-income neighborhoods like the Lower East Side produce more garbage for city pick-ups than do wealthy ones where people go out to eat most nights and where their garbage is disposed of by private carters contracted by restaurants and businesses. Yet the city sends its sanitation trucks into the wealthy neighborhoods more than twice as frequently than into the poorer ones. The question before the committee was what to do about the accumulation of garbage — and the accompanying rat population.

We decided on five steps. We'd write to our councilwoman, Margarita Lopez, and ask her to pressure the Bloomberg administration to pick up trash four times a week instead of the current two. We'd write directly to Mayor Bloomberg. We'd circulate a petition to all our tenants and around the Lower East Side and enlist other LES advocacy groups in the effort, making it clear that we are fighting to get more frequent pick-ups throughout the community, not just on our blocks. We'd try to educate our own tenants about ways we ourselves can decrease the volume of garbage. "And if the city doesn't respond," said Frances Goldin, who was chairing the meeting, "we'll take lots of bags of garbage and plenty of rats and dump them on the steps of City Hall."

One of the people attending the meeting was a recently hired Cooper Square MHA staff member who grew up in another country. His eyes grew large at Frances' statement. "Are you allowed to do that?" he asked, disbelief and wonder at the strange ways of Americans written on his face. "Allowed?" said another member of the group. "We're not going to ask permission." "But won't that get us in trouble?" continued the staff member. There was a lot of good-natured laughter around the table, and someone said, "Sure! Some of us will probably get arrested too, if it comes to that." And Frances explained, "It's bad publicity for Mr. Bloomberg if it becomes a public issue that the rich are treated so much better than the poor."

And that in a nutshell is the history of Cooper Square — the polite (at first), then combative, but always humorous determination by a low-income community not to be shunted aside in the interests of the rich.

It all began back in the late '50s with a plan by the Wagner administration, led by Robert "Terminator" Moses, to condemn large swaths of the Cooper Square area under the Slum Clearance program. Modern co-op housing was to be built in place of 60 and 70-year-old tenements. The old buildings were crumbling walk-ups with tubs in the kitchen, and many still had communal toilets in the hallways outside the apartments. Something did need to be done; the problem was that the city was making no provision for the people who lived in

190

the old apartments. Moses' plan would have displaced 2,100 families, 3,000 men in furnished rooms and flophouses, and over 500 businesses; they would simply have to leave and find new housing elsewhere, most likely in outlying areas of the outer boroughs, and this would mean the destruction of an old, vibrant community. In its place the city planned 2,900 units of new housing, at higher rents and a buy-in price that was affordable to only 7% of the area's residents.

So a group of people, led mostly by women, began to meet in 1959 to oppose the city's plan and offer an alternative that would both meet the housing needs and preserve the historic community. They included Thelma Burdick, the Director of Church of All Nations Settlement House; Esther Rand, the founder of Met Council on Housing; Helen DeMott, an artist and tenant; and the same Frances Goldin who remains so combative today. They were joined by others, notably the sociologist Staughton Lynd and the city planner Walter Thabit. They named themselves the Cooper Square Community Development Committee and Businessmen's Association (CSC), and began preparing an alternate proposal that would avoid the displacement of tenants, keep the neighborhood at a human scale, and improve the lot of the homeless and those on fixed incomes.

Many of the Committee members were veterans of political struggles of the '50s; some were quite radical socialists. The Chairwoman, Thelma Burdick, who was loved and respected throughout the community for her work with children and the homeless (they were called "bums" then) from her base at Church of All Nations, was not. She approached the city government with the naïve faith of an idealistic Midwesterner; she'd been raised in Nebraska. But she quickly learned that such faith was often misplaced, like the promises of the pols she began by trusting. She never lost her calm politeness, but she grew tough as nails under her white-gloved exterior. "Thank you very much for your promises," she'd say. "Will you write us a letter to that effect?" To the pols' replies that they'd already promised, she'd answer, "Yes, but sometimes those promises have a way of getting lost, so please put it in writing."

The committee knew it was in for a fight, but none of them knew how long and hard the fight would be: How many city administrations would have to come and go before Mayor David Dinkins would finally sign a memorandum of understanding that had enough legal force to tie Mayor Giuliani's hands and force the city to comply; how many changes and compromises would have to be made along the way; how internal squabbles within the committee would twice nearly send it to an early extinction; or how the neighborhood itself would change under the relentless attack of the gentrifiers.

It has taken 45 years, but Cooper Square is finally within sight of achieving a large part of the goal it set itself that half-century ago:

- The Thelma Burdick apartments, 146 units of low-income housing on Stanton Street between Chrystie and the Bowery, opened in 1984.

- The JASA (Jewish Association Services for the Aged) building-150 units housing for the elderly and disabled at Third Avenue and Fifth Street — was part of the Cooper Square urban renewal plan.

- The world's first homeless co-op was founded in the abandoned "Cube" building on First Street and Second Avenue — 22 beautifully renovated units entirely occupied by formerly homeless families, opened in 1985.

- 21 tenement buildings on Third and Fourth Streets and on Second Avenue have been gut-rehabbed and renovated inside and out. These buildings are administered and maintained by a Mutual Housing Association (MHA) spun off by the CSC; they are owned by the MHA (that is, by the tenants themselves, who own shares in the association), and the land they stand on is owned by a Community Land Trust which was created to keep the MHA honest and which is answerable to both the tenants and to the larger Lower East Side community.

- A new 54-unit supportive housing facility with social service facilities is going up at Second Street and Second Avenue, to replace and improve on the SRO the city tore down at First Street.

- And finally, the new construction on either side of Houston Street between the Bowery and Second Avenue — Chrystie Street is in development. It will provide over 175 units of low-income and some 400 units of market-rate housing and will include 150,000 square feet of new retail space and a 30,000 square-foot community center with basketball court/gymnasium, swimming pool, meeting rooms and activities for youth. The community center is the final piece; it replaces the settlement house we lost when the Church of All Nations was abandoned, and it will, with the guarantee of continued mixed-income housing, provide an anchor for a neighborhood that has been threatened all too often with dissolution by runaway real estate development and short-sighted city policies.

Those are some of the facts, but they alone don't tell the story; for it's a story of the people who, through tenacious organizing and fierce determination, made it so that the city shall be of, by and for the people who live here, rather than for profit or sale. And they almost always achieved this with humor. (The two internal battles got rather unfunny.)

The public battles with the city were backed up by tough negotiating, but serious as they were, they were also theatrical, and fun. There was the time in 1965 when the *Village Voice* reported that State Assemblyman Louis DiSalvio had a private arrangement with Robert Moses; he would soft-pedal his opposition to Moses' plan for a Broome Street Expressway (which would have turned large parts of the neighborhood into an off-ramp for Long Island commuters) in return for middle-income housing at Houston Street (which was to be the centerpiece of the committee's low-income alternate plan.) Cooper Square members picketed the Assemblyman's liquor store on the Bowery with guitars and specially written songs. There was the "Cooper Square On The Warpath" campaign, in which residents dressed up in Native American headdresses and built tepees along Houston Street to dramatize the need for housing; one man in full Indian regalia carried a long-stemmed pipe and a sign that read: "Jason [R. Nathan, Chair of the Housing and Redevelopment Board]: You sign treaty, we smoke peace pipe." Or the time in 1978, after years of frustration, when residents used cardboard cartons to erect a "building," again dramatizing both the ever greater need for new housing and the city's string of broken promises.

A Radical Political and Social History of the Lower East Side

There were the quieter moments of drama as well. Once a bus was chartered to go to Washington and picket HUD. Some members of the delegation were enthusiastic picketers; others did not like picketing but did it anyway, lending their bodies if not their voices to the cause. No one even bothered to ask Thelma Burdick to march; she was too proper, too ladylike, and though she recognized their necessity she truly did not like such public manifestations. In the midst of the picket, Walter Thabit (one of the silent ones) whispered to Frances Goldin (one of the loud ones), "Look over there." And there was Burdick, neatly dressed and with white gloves as usual, carrying a picket sign and marching.

Always of course, there were arrests; at demonstrations and once at a City Hall hearing when the city had procrastinated beyond all patience, and committee members refused to give up the microphone until there was some sort of resolution. The colorful demonstrations caught the public imagination, and the willingness to go to jail forced the city's hand.

And through it all, Cooper Square grew. When the city suddenly withdrew all funding in 1979, members who had been paying $1 a year in dues pledged monthly contributions until alternate sources of funding could be found. The committee weathered the loss of a development partner because of excessive political correctness by some of its members, and later the threat of a takeover by Roberto Napoleon and his gang of thugs. Some members, formerly homeless and without prospects, after they had settled in Cooper Square apartments, became a new generation of leaders. Sons and daughters of tenants born here grew up and became active members of the committee. Over and over Cooper Square nurtured leadership from society's discarded humans. Once there was criticism from within that we allowed too many marginal and crazy people to stay; we should get rid of them because "there are places for people like that." The answer shot back without hesitation: "Yes, and this is one of those places." This faith has been amply rewarded. Many current board members would never have had a chance to be leaders in a "normal" setting. Now they sit in meetings with movers and shakers and are not awed. When the first renovations turned out to have major flaws, such as a lack of sound attenuation, several tenants who had experience in construction work formed a committee to work with the contractors and make sure the best standards of quality were met. As a result the renovations improved with each building done.

A combination of individual initiative and collective action has always informed Cooper Square; once, someone redid the lyrics to "The Battle Hymn of the Republic" —"The ball game's almost over, but it's now our turn to pitch. We must have action now" — and seventy pickets sang it during a 14-hour picket at Gracie Mansion in 1964. More recently, at two a.m. one morning in the later nineties, two board members were passing one of the buildings then under renovation when they heard sounds of demolition from within. They entered the dark building and found workers breaking up the concrete stairs. The men with the hammers were undocumented immigrants, poorly supervised, being made to work ridiculously late hours in inadequate light, and it turned out, paid less than minimum wage. The board members put a stop to the work, and the committee exposed the contractor and made sure that work and safety conditions and pay met minimum standards from then on.

Chapter 8

Frank Morales
Interviewed by Aaron Jaffe in the
Odessa coffee shop, Avenue A, Lower East Side

Q: What is your background and how did you get involved in the squatter movement?

Frank Morales: I was born and raised here on the Lower East Side. I grew up in the Jacob Riis projects. In 1978, I was working in the South Bronx and we got involved in squatting up there at that time, in 1979. We took a few buildings, which became legal homesteads after a while. These days, the city is normalizing relations with squatted buildings here on the Lower East Side. Well, they always said, "We don't negotiate with squatters." Over the years, individual buildings have made various attempts to strike a deal with HPD [the city's department of Housing Preservation and Development], particularly after the latest attack on one of the squats by police. And they always get the same line: "We don't negotiate with squatters. You want to talk to us, you have to leave the building." And we say, "Yeah right, we'll leave the building and you'll surround it with tanks and we'll never get it back." Back in '79, we took some buildings in the Bronx. We'd been in the building a year and some people from HPD came, and they were essentially run off the block by people in the neighborhood. They were just young guys —and what did they know?

They had been sent to the South Bronx to check on some buildings where, you know, suspicious things had taken place. People had gone and knocked out the cinder blocks and gone in. So, consequently, we wound up going down to Maiden Lane around 1980 to sit down with some of these people and in the course of one meeting with a dozen or so people from the Bronx and these buildings, they pulled out a full set of leases — sweat-equity leases-passed them around the table and we all signed them. At that meeting, we became legal squatters. We became legal homesteaders. We walked into the meeting squatters, and we were normalized in one sit-down.

Q: Why was it easier to do in the South Bronx than it was down here?

FM: I have no idea, because the problems some of the people are having uptown are similar to the ones we've had for years. And there's a group of buildings in the Bronx you might have heard about through Inner City Press and Matthew Lee — people who are now hopefully gonna get the same kind of deal that the buildings down here received. In terms of precedent, it was never the case that the city would not negotiate right then and there with people who were occupying the buildings. Maybe they had no design on those buildings. I mean this was the late '70s. There was a lot of burning going on. So maybe they didn't really give a hoot about 'em and figured "What the hell?" I don't know. But it was about then that I became familiar with Yolanda Ward's work. Through her and people she was associated with in Washington, D.C., we were able to get all these documents relating to this thing called

193

A Radical Political and Social History of the Lower East Side

"spatial deconcentration." Yolanda Ward was a black woman, 22 years old, part of a group known as the Grassroots Unity Conference. I got the stuff they had essentially expropriated from various HUD offices around the country, which referred to a program called spatial deconcentration. The Conference subsequently became aware of a federally sponsored effort to spatially deconcentrate — that is, remove — black people from the inner cities.

This grew out of the riot commission studies in 1968, particularly by Anthony Downs, who authored the housing section of the Kerner Commission report. In Chapter 17, Downs writes about this process. It's like, "by 2005, the inner cities will become ungovernable. We need an outflow, a migratory outflow." Roger Starr, at the turn of the '70s and early '80s in New York City put it in terms of "planned shrinkage." It's the same basic concept. In the cities of the U.S., there were 109 "riots" in 1967. So by '68, there was a real concern that the demographics were becoming dangerous from the point of view of "white America." The Kerner Commission report was seen as sort of benign, the "we live in two separate Americas" idea. But behind the scenes was a kind of counterinsurgency apparatus dealing with the urban centers and the troublesome poor. "We're congested in these cities and there are these riots, and the Young Lords and the Black Panthers and all this is taking place." So by 1980, the plan to spatially deconcentrate cities is in operation. By 1980, places like the Bronx had been burning for several years, since the middle '70s. And in city after city across the country the same thing was happening. You know, the organized Left would put it in terms of profit motive and insurance scams: the economy does not provide housing for poor people because it's not profitable. But what Yolanda Ward pointed to were the social control motives behind decimating these urban centers. It was impossible to dis-empower people, disorganize people and disenfranchise people, without attacking the base. Attacking the base, namely housing, is the plan of counterinsurgency people like Anthony Downs, who has a police affiliation on his resume. It became clear that there were other motives behind the creation of places like the South Bronx, as sort of war zones. The war-zone metaphor was not such a stretch when one discovered that the phrase "spatial decon-centration" utilized in HUD manuals was actually lifted from Pentagon manuals. It's part of military tactics and strategy that somehow wound up in the context of housing. In 1980, when I got this information through the conference people in Washington, our analysis of the housing crisis in the early '80s was that the government didn't want to spend any money on affordable housing, on low-income housing. It's become patently clear that their basic assumption was: "The government's not here to serve the people. That's big govern-ment. We don't want big government. We want government that oppresses the poor." All the rhetoric that came out of this period, and the attack on welfare, was "Get the govern-ment off the backs of the people," which is code for cutting services. Because the '60s were typified by throwing money at the poor. Welfare boomed from '64 to '68. Food stamps boomed. It was throwing money at the problem.

Q: How much of the situation in the South Bronx was created by running highways through the area?

FM: I think that set the stage for it. The whole issue of land, and how it is utilized and speculation on land — that's the general basis for the housing question. Speculating means that someone else is always looking at, analyzing and figuring out ways they can make

Frank Morales Interviewed by Aaron Jaffe

more money on land, on your home, wherever you happen to be. Essentially, you're expendable. Even if you "own" that thing, there's eminent domain. People owned those houses in the Bronx [that were demolished to make highways]. But through eminent domain, the city would come in and take you out. They made you an offer, like the farmers in the Midwest. And as long as it's legal to speculate on land, we'll always have these kinds of crises within a social system that does not want to put money into low-income housing for economic and political reasons.

There was a change from the late '60s, where allowing for certain wherewithal on the part of poor people, whether it's through education and so on, came to be seen as a dangerous approach. If you read The Crisis of Democracy, for instance, authored by Samuel Huntington — he recently wrote The Clash of Civilizations about Islam and the West — he authored this report for the Trilateral Commission in '75. He lays it right out. It's essentially a blueprint for counterrevolution. He says too much education for black people leads to greater political participation. How do you shrink political participation? Limit education. This is the report that closes with the line, "therefore, there are potential desirable limits to the indefinite extension of political democracy." We've been dealing with this strategy laid down in 1975 ever since. There's been cutbacks in education because, as Frederick Douglass said, teach a slave to read, and you're creating a dangerous situation. You know, talking to the master. And that's essentially Huntington's point. The '60s War on Poverty was creating ungovernable — that's the phrase they used — situations. Huntington refers to it as "an excess of democracy." The distemper of the '60s led to this perception of an excess of democracy. This led up to the '70s and the attack on housing and this attack on housing we saw as a political attack. It was rooted in certain economic requirements. Now government is not set up to serve the people, but to stay out of everything and let the market forces dominate. So squatting, the reclamation of hundreds of abandoned buildings in places like the South Bronx and the Lower East Side, was seen as a defensive strategy to deal with the offensive that was taking place on the part of the state against the poor.

Q: But your strategy worked in the Bronx. You walked into HPD and walked out with what you wanted. What did the city say when you tried this on the Lower East Side?

FM: When they would respond to us, which was rare, they would say that we were criminals, that we didn't deserve to be negotiated with. Even this latest deal, in 2001, we never talked directly to HPD. UHAB [the Urban Homesteading Assistance Board], a nonprofit group, was the go-between. They did the negotiating. Dinkins, his first day in office was asked at a press conference, "What about the squatters?" and he said, "They're criminals." I mean, this has been the thing from the beginning. We started taking buildings down here between '85 and '90, and we lost a few over the ensuing decade. We held onto 11, the buildings that have been normalized.

But it was clear even in '85 that the abandonment was a political attack on a certain sector of the community. When the military attacks an area, and we're talking about this in Iraq right now, the problem is what the Pentagon calls consolidating your hold on the land after you topple whoever. Consolidating their hold on the Lower East Side was gonna be a whole lot easier, given that you're 10 minutes away from Wall Street. It's an area that can be spruced up and gentrified. In '85, we were moving quickly to try and beat that flow, saying the only way to forestall this massive kind of gentrification that was coming was to take as many buildings as we could.

Q: When you grew up here, the area was working poor. When did buildings start to get abandoned? How long did they sit abandoned, and what effect did the city's policy to get out of the housing business play in shaping the housing conflict?

FM: Small owners, the Jewish people and the Irish and the old Italians, the ones who owned their one or two buildings or whatever, they were squeezed out through various means of disinvestment. An owner who'd had a building since the '30s or before couldn't get refinancing from their local bank where they'd gotten refinanced for 40 years. It wasn't like suddenly everyone decided to go out and buy a box of matches and burn the places down to get insurance money. They were forced out through a very clear method. Another method was to create an agency known as the Office of Housing Preservation and Development. The displacement and the abandonment really starts getting heavy around 1970. Lots of drugs and all that kind of thing. It was the post '60s period where people were asking what the hell we're gonna do about these cities, and then mysteriously, every-thing starts to burn. Things start burning, the police are looking the other way when on every other street corner around here there's massive amounts of drugs. It was allowed to happen in certain areas, in Harlem, in the South Bronx, in areas where poor people lived. You didn't see people selling heroin at the corner of Park and 67th Street.

In the late '70s, HPD was set up as a housing agency but also as a quasi-legal agency which called individual owners — long-term ma and pa store thing or whatever — into Housing Court, because they didn't pay the increase in the water thing or this other tax. If they couldn't make the payments, the building went *in rem*. The whole *in rem* process was the means by which HPD became the second-largest landlord in New York City, next to the New York City Public Housing Authority. They took buildings through legal means in the courts away from small owners. HPD was set up as a repository, for the *in rem* process, which we always argued was illegal. They just basically ripped off the buildings from people who'd been in there 40 or 50 years. It's a crime. The in rem process is a sham. It was a slick maneuver to deprive hundreds of thousands of working-class people of their housing through legal means. That's why we always claimed we weren't squatting. These buildings were abandoned and people need housing. We owned them as much as the HPD did.

Q: Was there a plan at HPD for how long they wanted to hold these buildings and what they wanted to happen to them?

FM: Some individuals who were working there probably knew that HPD had at most a 15-20 year life span, that they were basically set up to broker buildings from small owners to larger owners and derive what they could for their own pockets bureaucratically and in between. Basically, they were set up to be the repository for hundreds of thousands of units that the government knew was coming, because of the process I discussed — a process set in motion throughout the country. HPD was set up to take these buildings. The "left," the progressives within HPD, set up an Alternative Management Division, literally the alternative management within HPD. That division created a sweat-equity lease possibility, so that in the early '80s, up to '85, you could get a lease to do homesteading, which is what we did in the Bronx.

We were able to go to Maiden Lane. They sat us down and in one meeting, they gave us a lease, in 1980. By 1985, we were doing the same kinds of things down here, where I'm from. We'd go to HPD at that point and say we'd like to apply for a sweat-equity lease for this building. It's falling down, no one's doing anything with it. We have a group of people, skilled. We can do it. We have some financing. But the city, HPD phased out any kind of homesteading or sweat-equity approaches, any kind of legal approaches to doing sweat equity in exchange for a lease or moderate rent about 1985. I remember the last RFP ["Request for Proposals"] that HPD offered for homesteading was around '85 or '86. You know, in the RFP they put the word out to various housing organizations in the city, local community groups that would like to apply for a homesteading lease in their neighborhood. What you did is get a group together, look around and see what buildings were abandoned and apply for that address. Since '85 or '86, 12,000 applications were received. The head of urban homesteading at HPD told me this.

This is the working class of the city who couldn't afford the escalating rents and understood that hey, we can use some muscle here and make some housing. The city took six buildings out of 12,000 groups, and then that was the end of it. So then we started squatting the buildings.

Q: What was the city doing with these buildings?

FM: Nothing. We would go to them, literally, in this neighborhood here, with roofs gone in some of these buildings that were sitting empty since '68, '69, '70, '71, when the fires hit. And by '85, '86, we were saying we'll put the tarp on the building. We'll cap it for you. We'll do this for your building. We won't go in. We won't take it, but we're concerned about the deterioration of the housing stock in the neighborhood. They wouldn't cap them themselves. They would just allow them to deteriorate. They didn't manage. They managed to hold on to the land. It was basically land banking. Our argument at the time, in 1985, was that there were 100,000 abandoned units, abandoned apartments, according to the most conservative estimate. Now these were not warehoused apartments — meaning two or three units in a building that remain unoccupied. There were 40,000 of those. These were abandoned units. You figure there's anywhere from 20 to 30 units per building, so it's a few hundred buildings. And there was no legal way in which people could sweat-equity them. They cut the leases off. So there was no other way to do it.

Q: What was the incentive to let the buildings deteriorate while holding the land, rather than just tearing them down right away?

FM: There were competing sectors within HPD, those whose interest was in some sort of private management program and others who were more into the nonprofit sector. There was a kind of competition going on. You'd get some sort of "good work" depending on what sector you were dealing with. The Alternative Management Division within HPD is constantly fight-

A Radical Political and Social History of the Lower East Side

ing these developments for their own self-interest, obviously, but also because they're progressives. And they would often contact some of us and have us go do their pickets in front of HPD. HPD employees picketing HPD so they could keep that program going. But HPD essentially killed tenant interim-lease programs, which was the only program that offered any sort of sweat-equity lease at that point. Essentially HPD was the holding agent for 100,000 units that were abandoned to the city. By the late '80s, it was time for speculators and real-estate people to sit down with HPD. They were at what they called the "tipping point" in real-estate jargon, which means we've gotten rid of enough blacks and Latinos and now we can invest here. The tipping point had been achieved, although there was a bit of a rollback after the Tompkins Square confrontation down here in '88, as noted in some of the financial magazines. The investment climate was not suitable. Some of us were engaged in a campaign of dissuasion. It was clear at that point that what HPD had been set up to do, it was going to do in an accelerated way. It had been very lethargic over the years, now they became hyper-efficient, turning these buildings over to favored real-estate interests, and phasing out.

Q: Was there a watershed moment when you and your people down here said, "It's time"?

FM: We came on in 1985, because we took two buildings in the Bronx and we lived in those buildings until '83, '84, and we came down to the Lower East Side specifically to continue. It wasn't like we decided to do it when we came down here. We came specifically to do it.

Q: What kind of people were squatting buildings then? For you, it was a political movement . . .

FM: It wasn't really political. Yet I do it in a political context, because most of the people who study the housing question reduce it to an economic analysis. We were saying from the very beginning that the reason that there were places like the South Bronx was that there were political requirements of the elite in America. That was the analysis that we brought. It had less to do with economic realities — "We can't build housing here in America because we don't have the money, but we can spend millions on one more missile." That's a bunch of bullshit. In terms of the grassroots aspects of it, I started working in the South Bronx, and what we were most decidedly about was keeping people off the street. By the mid-'80s, there was this whole reality of homelessness, and homeless people. This didn't exist in the '60s. Nobody had ever heard of a homeless person in America. There were, like, the hobos and the bums. It was a different culture. But now blacks and Latinos were living on the street. Many were mentally imbalanced because it's hard to be on the streets for any period of time and keep your sanity. And they were dying young. As the United Hospital Fund pointed out a few years back, it's a 10 to 15 year less life span for males if you're homeless. We were going to the shelters and dealing with that, linking up to the shelters and taking buildings and stuff like that.

In the Bronx, it was 100% Latino and some blacks, and in the section where I was working, it was pretty much all Latino. We came down here because of the eclectic nature of the Lower East Side — that kind of eclectic thing. The difference being that by the time of the

Frank Morales Interviewed by Aaron Jaffe

Tompkins Square confrontation of '88, it was world news. Everyone knew. We weren't media-savvy, but the media found us. I can't tell you how many video interviews I've done. There was a lot of hype, so that wherever there was a squatter movement around the country, they came here. During the first few years, from '85, '86, 327 East Eighth Street was the "mother-ship" of the early scene, with a few other buildings on Eighth street. There were people from Berlin. There were people from England. There was an African squatter. Lower East Side people. It was very politicized, it was very culturally active. It was a real scene. We had our celebrities. Michelle Shocked lived with us at 327. It was really very vibrant and exciting, and I don't want to sound trite, but one of the exciting aspects about it, was that people knew what they were doing was clearly illegal. Going into an abandoned building, working collectively with people you didn't even know before, creating a home for yourself, and then realizing you weren't going to get thrown out — it dawned on people, Hey, I didn't have to work that job. I didn't have to pay this heavy rent. It was like freedom, you know.

Q: The city knew what you were doing?

FM: The city knew. We put out various manuals on the ABCs of squatting. By the time we put on the front door, put a number on the front door and a mailbox, we'd already been in there for six months. Then we'd send HPD a certified letter from the building, saying we were now in occupation of this building and just wanted to let you know. That constituted an adverse-possession claim. Adverse possession being that the owner knows that you're there and refuses for whatever reason or doesn't for whatever reason to evict you. It constitutes a kind of de facto acquiescence to your being there. Once we were there, we sent HPD a certified letter. We knew they got it. We knew they knew we were there. Every day that passed, we actually accrued more status in the building. There was receipt of mail. We received mail there right away, before we even had the door on, people would meet the mailman on the corner and get the mail for that address.

We'd get Con Edison to set up a public account. Even though Con Edison had orders from various mayors not to deal with us, Norman Siegel from the ACLU argued that we could pay the bill. We had our rights and we wanted the account, and they had to do it. We forced them to do it. We received this documentation and we were basically establishing residency. We basically said, "Look, we live here. We're homesteaders." "Are you legal?" "Well, we're negotiating with the city right now." The cops basically played it off. Barring any direct order from above, the street cops on a personal level were usually 100% with us. "I really wish I could do this in my neighborhood. Me and my friends applied last year to be home-steaders, but they turned us down." It was a working-class thing, so they would just leave us be. But that was essentially how we did it because the point was, once you established residency, maybe not from the legal perspective, but you've made the claim that you're a resident, then you need to be evicted legally. That's essentially what we were pushing for. If you have to evict us, you have to evict us legally, because we want to go to court and argue our case.

It would not be unusual in the early days, in '86, '87, where we'd be in the building, working or whatever, and suddenly there'd be some cops in the front and some bureaucrat from HPD and they'd say, "According to our papers, this building is empty. This is an abandoned building." And we'd say, "Well, it's obviously not abandoned. We've got mail here dating two months back. Where've you been? We live here. We're working on the building. You haven't been doing shit. I remember two months ago when we came to you to ask for a tarp, to put a tarp on this roof, and you said no, we couldn't do that. Ask the community if we're doing good work here. What have you been doing for the seven years it's been abandoned? Nothing." We had what was called an eviction-watch network, which was basically a phone tree, but it was broken down into groups, different sectors, so that you could call and get like five video people to show up right away and put cameras in the face of these guys. Pete [Missing] was involved in some of those aspects — not the video cameras, but some other aspects of defending against eviction.

The same thing would happen over and over again. Because we were in legal limbo, they didn't know quite how to deal with us. In New York City, there's what is known as a 30-day law. If you could show that you were receiving mail and you resided in a place for 30 days, you're not a trespasser anymore. You have to be evicted legally, even if you don't have a lease or a shred of paper or nothing. If you have a letter that shows this is your address that's dated 30 days ago, they can't just come in at the pulling of a gun and push you out. And inevitably, they'd come back from their phone call and say, "Alright boys, let's get out of here." The bureaucrat would be fit to be tied. "You've got to do something," And the cop would say, "I can't do nothing." But we basically strung them out like that and they got a bit hesitant of showing up like that because we got really efficient at bringing 100 people to the building at 7:30 in the morning. It was really important that each of the buildings supported one another. And that was what the Eviction Watch thing was. We would have collective meetings, where we would share tools and stuff like that, although we stressed that each building was autonomous. There was no central direction. Each of the buildings made their own decisions about who they brought into the building, how they worked, how much money they collected. There were various ones, like myself, who would try to do broader kinds of dictums, put the shit out there, like "Let's not try to get evicted. Let's try not to let hard drugs in the building." And stuff like that. "You want to kill yourself, kill yourself, but don't sell hard drugs in the building."

Q: Can you tell me more on the nature of the squatters?

FM: It was very eclectic. 16-year-old runaways, a lot of runaway kids in the early days. I remember that at times there was a real sense that we had to do some kind of counseling. Some of the older ones took it on to help depressed kids, who wanted to kill themselves, run away from home. We had cops who said, "Have you seen this girl?" and that kind of thing, from California, the Midwest, so you had that. You had a lot of ideological squatters, like people from Berlin and England and places like that. Black American people, Salvadorians, people who were fleeing death squads in El Salvador. A handful of intellectuals, artists looking for a space to do their art. Homeless people form shelters, some who are still in the buildings today . . . The Eviction Watch methodology was we'd get together in order to defend each other, but the rest of the time, we'd act autonomously in our own buildings. We created a — I wouldn't say elite — but executive function. There were four or five or six or seven people who spent a little more time thinking about the overall picture.

Q: Some of you were more oriented toward that kind of thing?

Frank Morales Interviewed by Aaron Jaffe

FM: Yeah. Others were more oriented, probably quite rightly, toward fixing the roof, saying, "All you guys want to do is sit around and jerk off and talk about the evils of this or that and you don't want to do any work." It was a healthy tension, different types of people and that's what it required — people with different kinds of interests and skills, and people generally moved on the basis of needs and desires. Some people said, "Hey, I need a place to live. Hey, I'll get down with anything you guys are doing." We tried to get people to be involved in protests — that was what it was about. We weren't about just making homes for people to just have a home, and forget about the world, have a middle-class existence and forget about the world. People lived in illegality for 20 years, and what does that mean? And what did it mean for the people who sacrificed to get those buildings going, some of whom aren't here anymore, who died? If we could create whole neighborhoods that were squatted, we could create communities of resistance that we could impact in terms of the tenants, the people who were paying rent, and begin to do some cross-fertilization, because there's no reason for people to be paying $1,500 a month, $2,000 for buildings that have been paid for 40 years ago. They're just being ripped off royally.

The whole housing thing is an obscenity and we were watching it. We were working in our buildings over these years but we could see people coming into Avenue C paying so much — one family gets pushed out and they're paying $300 and suddenly, it's 1,200 bucks for some student at NYU who turns around and gets their stereo ripped off because there are people in the neighborhood who are strung out and are preying on suckers like them. It was sad, and even now, people are coming in and paying these ridiculous rents. I was talking to these guys the other day who are paying that kind of rent, $2,500 for some little studio and they split it up and pay half their monthly earnings. Sure, they're working. They've got money. But they're still paying 50% of their income to rent. And I said, "Why don't you go to the movies." and they said "We can't afford to go to the movies. I'm just paying my rent. It's basically all I've got money for. I live, I pay my rent, but I don't have a whole lot extra, but I want to live down here." And he's literally living in a building on Eighth Street that we squatted years ago, but we lost it to a fire and they kept it and renovated it. What if they and the whole block went on rent strike and said, "You know, if one block in this neighborhood went on a rent strike, if you guys talk to each other, like unity, you know, a dozen buildings, and you all decided, 'We're gonna go on a rent strike in our building, how about you?'" And the whole block went on rent strike, right, and what this means is that they call a press conference one afternoon. A lot of press was gonna cover it. This was middle, upper middle class people going on strike. What's this, right? They wouldn't actually have to withhold their rent. By the time they had this press conference, they could say, "Well, by the end of the month."

Let's say they had it tomorrow, they'd say, "By Halloween, we're gonna stop paying rent. Next month, we're not paying." They wouldn't have to do it because the landlord would negotiate. That's how quick they'd get a reaction. It's all they'd have to do. "Look, we're interested in paying $1,000 a month rent. We think that's fair. But we think $2,200 for these apartments? We want a rollback." It would be this kind of moderate demand put forth on the part of a dozen buildings of middle and upper middle class people in this neighborhood with a press conference and a little bit of political support behind them, they would

A Radical Political and Social History of the Lower East Side

win without a problem. Because there's no way that these lawyers are gonna send marshals for all these people. It's just not gonna happen.

Q: Let me take you back. In '85, '86 down here, how many buildings were being squatted? How many abandoned buildings there were, and what was the ultimate goal at that time for the squatter movement? Was it normalization? Was it for the city to come in and start building affordable housing? And then let's move on to what the Tompkins Square Park riot meant as a watershed date for all this.

FM: As far as the goal goes, my goal at that point was to instigate a squatter takeover around the city. It was to, basically, light the fuse and create a movement, because it could not be contained by police or any marshals. There's a couple of different ways to look at it. First of all, down here we wound up taking around 20 buildings, and we now have 11. So, over the course of that time, we lost some to fire — we lost four on 13th Street in one fell swoop — it was that kind of thing. And there were 50 or 60 abandoned buildings down here. Maybe more. Maybe 100. A good amount, but it's a small neighborhood. Our goal wasn't to, as far as I recall, seek any kind of legal arrangement with HPD, mainly because we didn't think it was possible politically, and we didn't think they'd go for it, and frankly, I don't think people really wanted it. Most people felt that HPD was illegitimate, that it was a sham, a front for real-estate land-bankers.

But people are still there. We were never quite sure how long we were gonna be there. I think some people had that kind of long-term goal thing going, that at some point we would own the buildings and they'd be ours and so on. I never did, because I think if you kind of get caught up in that, it becomes your dominant thing. I, for instance, lived in a number of different buildings because my interest was really to open them up, get some groups going and just kind of move on. We weren't really involved in that sort of thinking. From my perspective, it was really about occupying and consolidating as many buildings as possible as a defensive strategy against what I considered to be a genocidal assault on poor people, particularly against the shelter system. The clearest recollection I have as far as what goals were at that point was just to spread it. We didn't have any long-term goals in terms of legalization. We would fantasize that HPD would collapse and we once had this goal of planting this big squatter symbol at the top of the Empire State Building and igniting this takeover. It seemed so simple. If 100 people started squatting in East New York and 100 people started squatting in the Bronx and 100 people started squatting on the Lower East Side, in storefronts and so forth, and had any kind of level of coordination, it couldn't be stopped.

In the individual cases, they'd be negotiating. They being the landlords, the city, HPD, whoever it was that was keeping the people away from the buildings. They would negotiate in a second because they'd want to limit it. That's one of the reasons for the process now. The move to normalize the situation now is an attempt to contain it. The whole squatter scene — the whole idea of people creating housing for themselves through their own means — is a global phenomenon, and I don't mean a global phenomenon on a small scale. Three-quarters of all the housing that poor people live in around the world . . . No city, whether it's Nairobi or South Asia or Latin America, the various cities around the world, and I've studied this through the U.N., is doing any better than New York at providing low-income housing. It's not New York that sucks. It's basically like this all around the world.

Seventy-five percent of poor people around the world create their own housing. Most poor people throughout the world make their own houses. Basically, what we're looking at in the U.S. in the long-term process is a situation where more and more people are going to become disenfranchised and they're not going to have a house and they're gonna do what people do all around the world, which is to seize abandoned land, generally on the periphery of cities, so here it's in East New York or parts of the Bronx. Mind you, the technological ability to repress and isolate and incarcerate and detain is much more pronounced here. Nothing exists anywhere in the world like the shelter system here. The shelter system is essentially low-intensity detention. It looks like a prison, with video cameras and cots. AIDS and TB rates are twice what they are on the street.

In the early days, we didn't have any long-term goals of being legalized or normalized, or any of that sort of thing. We felt that this needed to be done as a defensive measure. We called it "community self-defense." There was an assault taking place on communities that we could articulate, that you could show, that you could prove that there was no good faith on the part of HPD, locally.

You want to try to do sweat-equity — look, here's this competitive program. And they're in their soup over the fact that they can't take more leases. There's 12,000 groups that wanna do this and they say no. So that's why we're doing it this way, because in a sense we are trying to force them to renegotiate. We always did. We always thought HPD would cave in. "We need sweat-equity leases. We demand the right to do what we're already doing."

As far as the left goes, we would often interact with various sectors of the left. Whether it's the housing movement or the political left, whoever that might be, from The Nation to various sectarian parties to the various leftist groups, and none of them wanted to deal with us, probably because we were autonomous. In other words, we didn't buy the party line, necessarily, in terms of the housing organizations, like MET Council, who were coming out of a Communist Party line, which is that the benevolent state should provide the housing. Their only problem with HPD is that it wasn't run by Communists. Because if it were run by Communists, they would be doing the right thing and they would be making housing for poor people. But nobody argued that the federal government's outlay for low-income housing was shrinking, shrinking, shrinking, and from the Reagan era on, now. Down to zero. Now, where's the money for poor peoples' housing? It's not there. It should be an obscenity morally, just in and of itself, because A) there are a lot of poor people that live in the U.S., B) they have to live somewhere, and C) the government doesn't spend a dime on affordable low-income housing.

Q: It would seem that what you were doing would be in line with a Republican position. You weren't asking for handout. You were going to do the work yourselves . . .

FM: We would do little surveys. We would go up and down the subways and what we were doing was advocating for people to send money. We would call it squatter material aid. You could send a check, and you'd have to trust us that it would be used for squatter materials for the buildings. We used various schemes-I mean the buildings didn't erect themselves. There was a lot of money raised to put them together. Some of the buildings had no central stairs. We're not just talking about screwing in light bulbs here. We're talking major demolition in a lot of these buildings. A lot of work had to be done. We'd had a thing through WBAI for years, a couple of years called Listeners' Action. And the whole idea was to get the listeners to be active. It struck us that the best way to be active was I'd get on the radio with Paul Norman, who had a show Saturday mornings and I'd say we were meeting on Sunday morning on the corner of Seventh Street and Avenue B down here on the Lower East Side. All of you at the sound of my voice that want to help us renovate some buildings for homeless people, under-housed people, people who are just frustrated at having to pay those rents, show up. Bring some tools and come. You can help us. We advise you that this is not legally sanctioned. Some people would say it's illegal, but we think it's a morally correct position. Plus, it's a necessity for some people. They're not gonna live in the street. We've got to build . . . 50 people would show up! From Jersey, from Scarsdale, from Brooklyn and they'd all show up. And we'd work together.

Q: This is all still pre-Tompkins Square?

FM: Right.

Q: In the summer of 1988, when the big night of Tompkins Square Park happened, did you know it was a watershed moment? How did the police action fit in with what the squatter movement was doing? When you woke up the day after the riot, how did you know things had changed?

FM: First of all, I have to stress that there isn't really any squatter movement per se, because it's not a centralized thing. What happened leading up to that was that people started . . . the squatter ethos began to take hold. By '88, people started to really understand what we were about, because we started to make people aware through public education, a constant flow of propaganda, for instance, the slogan "Gentrification is Genocide," which was a bit harsh. We had a dozen people who are now making pretty good money doing their art, everybody from Eric Drooker, Seth Tobocman, various people; they were all basically doing propaganda for squatters, and being squatters.

The word was out, and people were really beginning to take notice. It was becoming generalized, such that homeless people were beginning to set up encampments in the park. We were doing workshops in the shelters. The city was counterattacking by making it impossible for us to get into the shelters. They installed video cameras in the shelters. The whole shelter thing became politicized at that time because homeless people started to organize. It was a union of homeless people that was organized. The vice president was myself, a squatter. The agenda of that union was to seize abandoned buildings. So that was extremely dangerous from the point of view of the state. This was exactly what they didn't want because squatting, understood in terms of seizing private property to meet one's needs, particularly abandoned private property, is poison to the state, in terms of controlling the

Frank Morales Interviewed by Aaron Jaffe

population so they can't organize around food, shelter, clothing, health, education, union rights, whatever. When you're shunted from place to place, you can't do much organizing.

So it started to really take hold. It was becoming a threat. The situation in the park was basically an attempt to break that base, which was being developed in the community. They had made, as I said, continued attempts from '85 through '88 to dislodge us from our buildings through a shrewd kind of counter-organizing, basically. We were able to defend ourselves right up through '88. The occupation of the park by homeless people was after '88. The situation before '88 was that we, collectively, used the Tompkins Square Park and the bandshell as a staging area for a lot of political meetings, rallies, large gatherings. It was basically our outdoor office. Some of us became very adept at getting permits, which were very easy to get in those days. Now, they're impossible to get. We were basically booked in there all summer long. And you can imagine. We had large shows, very political shows, hundreds of people, tables of literature and it was like the outdoor organizing, basically. And we were linking up to the buildings. We were having giant food fests. People would get food. It was dangerous, from the point of view of the powers that be. So, they wanted to attack our ability to be in the park and organize the park, particularly overnight, over 24 hours. We'd have shows that would go late, people would be hanging out, reading, all kinds of things.

Right-wing elements in the community — Antonio Pagan and some of these other politicians tried to force a resolution through the community board at its June twenty-something meeting — its last meeting of the summer, to take back the park. It was voted down, and the community board voted against trying to impose a curfew on the park, because the arguments were bogus, keeping the neighbors awake. It was bullshit, Everybody knew what it was about.

At the end of July — mind you, the community board has already disbanded for the summer — certain figures on the community board met with the Manhattan South police department. We got the minutes of this meeting and they basically laid out a plan to attack the park outside the community board, so it was extralegal, in a classic sense. There was no sanctioning, other than a few right-wing elements who were liaisoning with the police department. So the police department couldn't turn around and say, "Well, we were asked by the community." So this went down. We knew it went down, and that the police were gonna come, so we knew they were coming. So the week before August 6 and 7th, July 31st and right around then, they had a tryout, they came in and tried to displace us out of the park. There were a bunch of people in there, playing guitars, and they came in. But they made the mistake of coming in with only 20 or 30 cops, and they were basically run out.

One of the people in the park said "It's like the Vietnamese said let a thousand flowers bloom and let 1,000 bottles fly." So they were pissed. About midweek, we get up one morning, and through each of the entrances to the park, we saw "Curfew at midnight." It was just scrawled with yellow paint, there wasn't a professional sign person. Each of the entrances had this thing painted on the ground. We were like, "Who painted it?" because it looked like a two-year-old had done it. Basically, this woman who had been at the Manhattan South meeting came to us with the minutes of the meeting. She said they were holding up our flyers, saying they were gonna get this one, they were gonna get that one.

A Radical Political and Social History of the Lower East Side

All week long, the cops were riding around in their police cars and if you and I were walking down the street they'd slow down and say "We're gonna fuck you up on Saturday night."

That's what led up to it. So Saturday night, we put out a flyer, asserting the right to assemble, the freedom to be in our park at night. The park had never been curfewed in its history — the site of many years of protests and Lower East Side history and all that. We printed up 20 flyers, because we were all just so spent that we didn't really have enough time to really get the word out. So there was essentially very little public notification. Through word of mouth, hundreds of people showed up. Because I was somewhere else, we didn't get to the park until around 11 o'clock that night and we walked to the bandshell and I thought there was a concert going on. There were hundreds of people in there and the general vibe was "We're waiting in here. Let them try to throw us out."

They surrounded the park and then all hell broke loose. What happened was, that fray was over in a half hour's time. They're swinging, and they grab a few, and everybody's running here and there, like chaos, right? And the cops proceeded to bring in more troops and then they started marching up and down St. Mark's as far as Second Avenue beating people. I mean, it was like a police riot. They went nuts. They went crazy. You know, the people who were in the park, the activists, the ones who came knowing they're gonna have to be moved out of there, they were already gone. So it went, essentially, till four in the morning, five in the morning, more cops showed up in the course of the night.

They just kept coming. And they were just hitting everybody in sight. I don't know if they were given some kind of orders, like "hit everybody in sight." There were something like 300 complaints, and those were 300 people who had certain beliefs and said "I'm going to complain. Maybe they'll do something." For every one, there's another one who says, "Well, they ain't gonna do shit anyway." Three hundred people complained, and they probably beat up close to 1,000 people. Smacked, hit, for no reason at all. There was story after story after story of someone getting out of a cab at three in the morning coming home from uptown and they live on Second Avenue and they're getting out of a cab and they get jumped by the police. I mean, Odessa, all the various places here, the management was standing out in the street, all these bars around were going "Come in here. Come in here." And they were letting people come into their stores, closing the doors and locking them with the people holding the door shut. The cops were hitting the doors. The bars, the same thing. They were shutting their doors and the cops were like taking their clubs and beating the doors and there were old ladies — it was like World War II — old ladies were throwing flower pots down on the police.

It was like they just attacked the entire neighborhood. There was a helicopter hovering 40 feet above Avenue A. It was like a war game. It was very, very calculated. The guys had no badges, or they taped over their badges. The way that things broke down was that. And so they basically dug their own grave. The next day, Koch had to get on the air and say, "We're really sorry." And they rescinded the curfew, they said, "We're not gonna do it." So for us, it was a great victory. We beat the curfew. We beat it back. So in the next year, that's when people started moving into the park. People were like, "Well, we held the park. Now, we're gonna . . . squat the park." So, for about a year's time, maybe a little less than that, eight

Frank Morales Interviewed by Aaron Jaffe

months, there was this very interesting, quasi-Woodstock homeless encampment thing. There were its dark sides, but people would bring food . . . At one point, there were about 300 people living in the park.

Q: Given the choice between living in the park and squatting a building, it would seem like there'd be no choice. Squat the building.

FM: We would try to move as many people as we could, but we didn't have enough space. Our thing was, we had to open up new buildings. A couple opened up on Houston, which were called "test squats." People built tents and lean-tos and different kinds of things in the park. So there was that process, which was very interesting. One day, I saw all these homeless guys coming in and I said, "Where'd you come in from?" "We were over on the Lower West Side, in a park over there. And the Parks Department said we couldn't sleep in that park anymore. But they said 'You can go sleep in Tompkins Square.'" And we learned later that the Parks Department was officially ordering all their parks to clean up the homeless problem and send everybody to us. So they basically created an untenable situation for us. Because the right wing, at that point, were saying things like "There are needles in with the children's swings" and Antonio Pagan would be on the cover of the *New York Post*. And so, it became untenable.

We put so many people in the building and it was at that point, when even our supporters—who put the branch here between the squatting and the people who are renovating the buildings—said the park is going a little far, I can't even take my kids there anymore. For years, the community's been wanting the park to be renovated. They wanted new swings, and they were never going to get it.

So, suddenly, a $10 million project was OK'd to renovate the park. Of course, it'll necessitate closing the park for two years. You could really see the handwriting on the wall. So they came in and swept everybody out, closed the park, literally with guards, around '89. And that was how it all evolved, and as a side matter, they took out the bandshell, because they knew they couldn't maintain that. So now the bandshell's gone. You try to get a permit to do a show, you've got to come up with a thousand bucks. Now, it's a crime to have political assembly in there. If you go there and have a speak-out without a permit, you can be arrested. We've come a long way now toward a repressive environment. But I think a part of it, in terms of the work I've done since then, was a kind of war-game exercise to deal specifically with civil disturbance. You look at it now, from beyond the '60s, it was the first large civil disturbance confrontation leading into the '90s.

Q: So 1990 comes and the park is closed and you and your people retreat back into your squats. What's the mindset then, compared with, say, 1986?

FM: For most people, I think the mindset was "Let's work on our buildings." There's still a crew that's quite active externally-involved not only in politics, but also doing the squatter thing, working with homeless people, going to shelters, trying to connect up with people who are doing squatting in other parts of the city or general tenants working with people around town. The thing was located here but we were pretty much located all over the city.

A Radical Political and Social History of the Lower East Side

We were doing workshops for Brooklyn Legal Aid on squatting. They didn't have any concrete experience on which to base their legal strategy, so they were very interested in this 30-day law stuff. "They actually left? You showed them a letter?" "Yeah, they left." For them, it was an uncharted area, and we'd do workshops at shelters around the city, with housing groups, pushing housing organizations and other groups to look at this, you know, advocate this kind of thing.

At that point, there was no one willing to deal with it. No one on the left. You can search *The Nation*, for instance, for an article about squatting and you won't find it. To me, it's like, shocking, because I'm trying to be objective about it, and I don't think I'm like so immersed in it, but you have a situation, particularly now, where these buildings are still there . . . There's talk about revolution and there's the actual revolution. The reality of it is really the primary datum. These buildings are there. They exist. And now people are reminded about them because now they're normalized. There's no analysis in The Nation and places like that. It's like they're like, "Well, we really don't know how to evaluate this, so we're not going to look." To me, that's like, cowardice.

We saw that all the way through. We couldn't get a positive word out of, you know, MET Council, or any of these groups. Privately, some of the individuals were like, "Hey, you got a place for me? I'm really looking . . ." But as far as their line, we'd get the absurd thing like, "Hey, you guys are taking heat off the system to provide the housing." And we'd say, well, no, we're putting pressure on the system so that when you guys go in to negotiate for affordable housing, they'll listen to you. You ever hear of good cop/bad cop? You know what I mean? You try to work these kinds of discussions. To naught. We pulled all the fucking angles, the housing question . . . and we got basically no support. What we got was from working-class people, even a Republican ethic. When we'd have those work days I mentioned, that we'd call for over the radio, I remember one of the buildings we were working in was Sulzberger's wife's, from the Times. She looked to be about 60 years old. I think Ochs was there with her. Two matrons, and there scraping a wall in an abandoned building with us. And one says to the other, "You know, this is really amazing." And the other one says, "Yeah, but isn't this illegal?" And the other one says back to her, "Yeah, but that's OK."

Mind you, these are law-and-order Republicans . . . By all accounts, these women were law-and-order people. They couldn't give a shit about whether it was legal or not when they were there because they were just immersed in it, and they just did it. People who could just relate to it — the building's falling down, these guys are working on it. I don't give a hell what these guys are calling themselves or whether they wear A's on their shirts or Q's on their shirts, I don't give a shit. It just sounds like a good idea. They're doing a good job. So, it was those people. The ideological left? Forget it. Deadbeats. The young anarchist kids — fine, but let's face it, it's anarchist in name, but there isn't a depth of experience there. But, you know, they would get down with it. And, you know, obviously, people who needed a place. But a lot of homeless people and poor people are so shell-shocked or dependent. I just assumed that if I went to the Bronx to talk to the people up there, that people would jump on it, but even a cot in an AIDS and TB-infested shelter where you were surveyed 24 hours of the day was in some senses better than taking a chance on an aban-

Frank Morales Interviewed by Aaron Jaffe

doned building, where you might have John Law to deal with at some point and maybe you had a record and such and such . . . That to me was a bit of a rude awakening, I realized you had to be tough to deal with it. The winters could be cold without central heating. You know, it requires a certain kind of individual, although it was a diverse bunch of individuals. Some people really just enjoy the experience, or they have a problem, like me, with paying $1,000 a month for some apartment in a building that I know, intellectually, was paid for 40 years ago. Just putting money in somebody's pocket. It's arbitrary.

Q: It's 1990, 1991 and it's obvious that the rules of the game had changed. How have things changed, especially with normalization? Things don't seem nearly as volatile.

FM: Before '88, we had some serious battles. In '89, we had a battle at 319 East Eighth Street, where we lost the building there. We had a fire. I was living in the building at the time and people were burning out. It was pretty heavy. I can't recreate it right now. It was a lot of informers. I would be walking down the street and two guys would be walking by me on either side of me, both bumping me in the shoulder. You know. Boomp boomp. And keep walking. I thought, "What the fuck is up with these guys?" And they wouldn't say anything. I found out they were cops, and they basically were just fucking with me. Or a cop would come up to me and say, "Don't you ever sleep?" And I'd say, "No. I don't ever sleep." And they'd say, "Well, pretty soon, you're gonna be asleep." Shit like that. And other people were getting it. It was real. [Norman] Siegel knew, because he had seen a document from the police department, of 22 undercovers assigned just to Tompkins Square. And they were pretty obvious. Some of these guys were just thug-oriented, and they would let you know who they were and they were content to just rough you up, if they could.

They'd let you know that if they could get you in an alley, they'd really rough you up. Between that and the fires, it was rough. When there were some quiet periods, people just took the opportunity to concentrate on working on their buildings. They'd rationalize it, well more than rationalize it, justify it by saying, "We didn't fight in the streets, blah, blah, blah, but meanwhile, the roof is still leaking. What kind of squatters are we? We can't even reno-vate our own houses." So there was a lot more just concentrating on the renovation work, because squatting—there's a lot of politics involved, but if it's anything, it's hands-on con-structing, about learning how to do it if you don't already know how to do it, and working collectively.

Because one person can't change a roof beam. It's too heavy. There's no way around it. They have to work together. And something costs money, so you have to get all this money. So all this process of making a home for yourself was to be all-consuming. You could eat up two years just doing that. And if you're working full-time, then it's even more time. So, I think, there was a lot of that. We would be working on the buildings, but we'd also have a bit of a break. We'd have a rest. "They're gonna lay off us a while." Then '94 rolls around and we really weren't prepared for that, in terms of the fate of the community and the whole squat-ter scene being mobilized. There were some internal contradictions. We had some people on 14th Street, who I don't know if they actually were working with the police or being paid by some police elements or whatever or concretely interfacing with HPD and giving them infor-mation about other people in the 13th Street scene. It was overt. It wasn't speculation. We knew, and they admit it. And HPD officials admit they had people. "Well, where did you get that information about so and so?" "Well, we got it from this guy." And these were people who lived in the buildings, and they were overtly working against us. They've since left.

So there were those kinds of things and then one afternoon, or one day, the Times had a front-page piece, in the lower right-hand corner. It was a little piece way on the bottom. "New York Plans to Evict Squatters." This is '94, so after this period of quiescence, all of a sudden, out of the blue. "Wow, we thought they'd leave us alone forever" and this kind of thing, but it was this woman, Evelyn Nieves from the *New York Times*, who tipped us, basically. She had heard and wanted to let us know. I subsequently talked to her and she said that the best way to do it was to put a story there and it would kind of fuck up Giuliani's plans to move more discreetly with it.

So what we did was we immediately sued — the buildings on 13th Street consolidated into one entity —and sued the city for title just to block this eviction we knew was coming down. And it worked, so we bought a couple of years, or whatever it was. We bought some time and went to court. The court thing was a subchapter that was very interesting, because we all got to testify and there was a long proceeding with Judge Wilk and we had to sit there and listen to all these HPD bureaucrats talk about how the buildings were abandoned. And Judge Wilk would say these buildings haven't been abandoned since the mid-'80s. It wasn't quite like the Chicago 7 trial, but it was on that order. It was a fuckin' riot, man, the way we deconstructed all their shit. It wasn't hard, and we had the backup. We gave Wilk 10 years worth of receipts, in 15 buildings, and he was impressed. We said, "We're arguing for the title of these buildings. This is how much money we put in, and this is what they failed to do." We had it going. And then, through some legal loophole.

Q: They swooped in?

FM: Yeah. The night that it came in, literally the next morning, we went to court. And we actually won. But the buildings had already been hit.

Q: You've got title to 11 buildings now. What's the situation going forward?

FM: As far as the 11 buildings go now, I think that people will have to be aware it's a different type of a struggle. The struggle now will be against the inevitable pricing out of poor people, the kind of "middle-classization" of the squats, which I think is a danger. Particularly if they come with all these loans and you really need to do this work and you really need to do that. So basically, the byword is going to be vigilance in terms of maintaining control over the buildings. In other words, don't assume something, that they're doing is a favor. They're not doing us a favor. We basically renovated these buildings with our sweat and our own money, so, you know, they could cough up some cash. Give us the material aid and be gone. As far as any kind of legal recognitions and so forth and so on, it doesn't mean a whole lot. If, functionally, it means it keeps the police from coming in and throwing us out, then that's fine. What I think, politically, we have that anyway, because at this point, now, it would be hard for them to turn right around and come in and do what they've done. But it's not out of the question. They could do eminent domain tomorrow.

Frank Morales Interviewed by Aaron Jaffe

Some legal owner could come around. The whole process by which the buildings were turned over to the tenants as low-income co-ops under HDFC has never really been tested in court. The whole shit is so new. It could happen next year that some judge could say "It isn't legal for the city to give these buildings to these squatters. No, no, no, no. We're giving 'em to Trump. Thank you, bye bye."

If people just maintain the struggle and keep the priorities in line, nobody gets evicted off this thing, for economic reasons. Just be careful not to take loans that put you in a hole. When you have to go to five, six, seven, eight, $1,000 a month rent, where people used to pay two or three hundred dollars. Some people really can't afford more than that. You have to displace them. That would be it. Plus, I think the most important thing is that people have to remember that the authority — this is related to the idea of controlling the building — the people who live there control it. If you deal with outside bureaucracies, there are those within the buildings, when a conflict arrives they look to the outside authorities to make decisions relative to the group. It shifts the whole focus of the group from being its own authority to something outside. And that can really be insidious. It can create splits in the group — this one's busy calling one, another's calling a different bureaucrat.

People start playing games like that and it could be troublesome. I think people have to realize it's a struggle of a different sort. On another level. People are now discussing this and that's what signifies to people around the city and other poor people and other people working on buildings is that this is doable. They don't need to know anything else, and people here get lost in all the sort of details and history of the scene and their own personal lives, so they miss the point. The point is that the word on the street right now is they gave the buildings to squatters. That's the word on the streets. Those of us now who go up to Harlem and to East New York or the South Bronx tell them there's a lot more light for people to do this now, let alone legally. The legal precedents are irrelevant. They know this. They know that they're taking a chance. They're in a bind right now. Why they went and made a move like this at this point is anyone's guess. My guess is that politically, it's a way to contain it. Maybe they think it's a way to get rid of this whole history. But I know that there are people, including myself, who see this as a golden opportunity. As this one friend of mine said the other day, "This squatter victory represents the beginning of the end of the housing crisis in New York City," which is sort of a grandiose statement. But what he was saying is that if people get a hold of what this signifies, this can be done —physically, in terms of tactics and strategies of renovating buildings, for $10,000 an apartment as opposed to HPD's figure of $100,000 an apartment. It physically can be done. We've shown that it can be done. It exists objectively as a model that groups can do this. Because a lot of people don't think this can be done, think that people don't have skills. They're just not aware— they don't know what it takes to wire and plumb and sheetrock an apartment. They just don't understand it. HPD says $100,000 a unit. Some of us just laugh at it. We can do a whole building for that. They don't know that they're ripping the city and everybody else off. The public's getting ripped off on this and that's what we have to get across to people.

What I've been hearing from groups around the city is "Oh, we heard you got it. That's great." The word is, hey, they gave those buildings up to squatters. Let's look at this. See, so it's much more acceptable now to people who were already leaning that way. But now it

A Radical Political and Social History of the Lower East Side

becomes much more palatable. So we need to build on that. So we can't basically sit back. Now is really the time to get out there and to foment some similar kinds of movements in other parts of the city. Because, as I said, it doesn't matter if they know what it is we're planning. If you get 100 people moving here, 100 people moving there, they can't cover it. What it'll do in terms of the housing movement is it'll create more opportunities. They city will then create more sweat-equity options. They're always going to try to co-opt it as a way to contain it. That's the smart thing. If they see a lot of people start to squat, they'll say, "This is the way you can do it, and we'll even give you a free boiler. You don't have to be in those cold buildings with those squatters." That's how sweat equity got started. In the '60s and '70s, Young Lords started squatting in East Harlem. Operation Move-In. This is a world-wide thing. Most people around the world make their own housing. Poor people. The analysts understand this quite well, and now the homeless population is back where it was in '85, actually more. It's more visible now. To me, we're in a better position now than we were in '85. From a legal point of view, way better. People can get in there now and the city can't say "We don't legalize squatters." Now's the time to get out there and be a squatter. Now's the time to get the housing movement to look at this, even though they're all sticks in the mud. So that's what I would say.

Chapter 9

Squatting On The Lower East Side
       Written by Fly with research assistance from
          RAP, Kurt Allerslev and Steven Englander

I arrived in the Lower East Side of NYC for the first time in 1988. At the time I was more
nomadic than I am these days so I didn't officially live here until 1990. I chose to squat out
of necessity for a decent place to live with people who I respected. At that time the LES
squat scene was much more visible than it is today and there were more squatted buildings.
In case you are unfamiliar with the term 'squatting,' it basically means occupying a building
(or 'property') without the consent of the owner. Officially the city of New York housing
department (HPD) considers itself the owner of these occupied buildings. The Lower East
Side squatters would argue otherwise. They believe that renovating many of these buildings
at their own expense and acting as owners 'openly and notoriously' for over a decade should
legally entitle them to the buildings according to the statute of 'adverse possession' which
originated in English Common Law.

I'm sure that people have been squatting in NYC since it was first established but the only
'movements' I am familiar with are the more recent ones. In the Lower East Side the squatting community has developed somewhat along the same lines as a homesteading movement
— with the idea of long term occupation and permanent housing at the forefront. Because of
this, the LES style of squatting is a little different than the more transient squatting methods of travelers or the more communal aspects of the European squats.

Some Background:

In the late '70s there was a wave of building abandonment. Many of the buildings in the LES
were taken into REM (Real Estate Management) by the city at which time any tenants were
'relocated.' Most of these buildings were then systematically stripped of any building materials of any value and then were left to deteriorate —periodically occupied by drug dealers or
used as shooting galleries —until they collapsed or were destroyed by fire. A friend of mine
who was around back then said that in the early '80s "junkies falling off rooftops became
such a common occurrence that you would always have to look up when you walked under a
city owned consolidated building."

The city did not have the money or the interest to rehabilitate so many buildings in what
was then considered an undesirable area. Instead, what happened was a federal plan referred
to as 'spatial deconcentration' in which the area was allowed to deteriorate to a point that
living there became unbearable and people would be forced to leave. In this way the authorities hoped to get rid of the poor inner-city minorities that they had come to fear after the
riots of the '60s. Then real-estate speculators could move in and acquire properties for very
little money hopefully to renovate them for future exploitation. But the future was a long

A Radical Political and Social History of the Lower East Side

way off and at that time the Lower East Side was turning into a war zone ruled by drugs and gangs. As a result people decided to take the matter into their own hands. The city had instituted a homesteading program by which local groups could organize to fix up a building and they could then buy it for $1. There was a widespread movement to take back the housing. A highlight of that campaign was the "this land is ours" action when all the organized Lower East Side housing groups banded together and tagged 100 city owned buildings in the area and proclaimed "This Land is Ours: Property of the People of the Lower East Side Not For Sale!" Unfortunately the homesteading program was discontinued soon after its inception, probably due to the overwhelming response by those seeking affordable housing. The administration was perhaps afraid of losing control of so much property.

The building where I have lived since 1992 is a serious home-in-stead style squat —meaning that we are interested in renovating the building as a long term commitment. The building itself, just up the street from Tompkins Square Park, was originally built in 1899, and, after a typical LES tenement history, was abandoned, vacated and eventually squatted in 1985. The biggest crisis was a major fire in 1990 that gutted the east wing of the building and destroyed the roof. It was amazing that people got back into the building! By the time I got involved in 1992 the roof had been replaced. I started working up on the sixth floor replacing joists and doing masonry work. I could see all the way down to the first floor. I was eventually granted a space in the building to renovate as my own apartment. This space had no floor or ceiling, the windows were all just gaping holes in the wall and the walls themselves were bare brick in need of extensive repairs. I had to learn to do everything in order to build this place every step of the way. The highlights were: when I actually had a floor(!); the first window I put in was also exciting — all materials scavenged and the frame built out of police barricades (we used to joke about how we should call a demonstration when we needed to install windows cuz the barricades make such good frames). I learned all the nifty squatter construction techniques based on how to make do with what you can find. Framing out my walls, and running the BX cable (I learned how to do all my own wiring) was also exciting.

Being involved in this whole process, learning the steps of building a habitable space, really makes you appreciate and respect your surroundings. You are not helpless and waiting for a landlord or super to fix something for you and you can suddenly see how much time and money is wasted making repairs that are actually simple; you can see how useless 'landlords' are and you can judge the quality of repair work done by professionals against your own (you would be surprised how sloppy many professionals are). The knowledge of how to build and maintain my own living space gave me a sense of calm in the midst of chaos. I figured even if the city threw us out and I lost everything I at least now had 'the knowledge' and I would be able to do it all again somewhere else. Thinking like that can be encouraging or depressing.

On the other hand it takes more dedication and responsibility (and at times insanity) to live this way since you do have to learn how to do everything for yourself which can be difficult and time-consuming, especially when it is winter and you have no heat. It can also be a problem if you don't get along with some of the people in your building — when you have to live with someone you don't trust. And what if someone starts getting really violent? Or threatening the safety of the building? The politics of squatters evicting squatters can get incredibly messy. In my building there have been two such removals of violent and threatening individuals, and both times it took months of stress to get them out, and then months of stress as they attempted to enlist city agencies to get the rest of us evicted since if they "can't live here then no one should" — yeah right. It's not easy to maintain a positive group dynamic when you live in stress.

Everybody wants to live for 'free,' but not everyone is able to handle the responsibilities, stress and rough conditions that go along with it. A new squat can be really raw; no electricity, no plumbing, and sometimes no roof or stairs, etc. The amount of time and money required (some materials cannot be scavenged) can make squatting seem like a full-time job. And although we don't pay 'rent' we do pay 'house dues' every month —an essential minimum to cover general maintenance and emergencies. For example, a couple of years ago we had to pay a contractor $3000 to dig up the street and fix a broken water main after being contacted by the Environmental Protection Agency (EPA) and told that our water main was the cause of the whole street being constantly flooded. Well after all that, it turned out to not be our water main and we had to file a claim with the city to get the money back. We still have not heard a response from them. However, if we had not acted on the matter, our water would have been shut off and it would have been very difficult to get it turned back on.

Today, in 1999, the building is full of very dedicated people — five families and lots of kids, including Felix, who was actually born in the building over 3 years ago. Everyone is interested in trying to buy the building. After putting so much sweat and money and love into this place we don't want to lose it. In 1999 our house will be 100 years old. We would like to establish it as a historical site. We feel that we are the owners/caretakers of this building, which was abandoned and left for dead by the city.

Of course the Giuliani administration — with its relentless Disney-ification and gentrification of the entire island of Manhattan — might have different ideas. In the past few years, one of the favorite tactics of the city in dealing with, not only squats, but low-income housing as well, is to respond to minor violations in a building by vacating the tenants and tearing the building down. This has happened on numerous occasions. Some of the more notorious examples are Fifth Street Squat, an SRO on Second Ave and East First Street and the Stanton Street low-income residential building.

In the case of Fifth Street —on February 9, 1997, there was a small fire that did not do any structural damage (although the Fire Department took their time responding to it). The OEM (Office of Emergency Management) officer came to the site and without even entering the building he issued a demolition order. The squatters were not allowed back in to retrieve any of their personal belongings. Early the next morning the demolition crane was already in place and although there was a court order to halt the demolition, the city continued with it and ignored any subsequent court orders that were issued that day and the next. Brad managed to stall them for a few hours by climbing back into the building and escaping police detection for a few hours. When it became clear that they would continue to demolish the

A Radical Political and Social History of the Lower East Side

building even though they couldn't find him he emerged from his hiding place in fear for his life. The destruction continued around the clock complete with police harassment, high-powered lights at night, noise, shaking buildings and billowing clouds of toxic dust. The EPA even admitted that the site had been "taken out of their jurisdiction by the city." About ten windows were smashed out of the building next door, and an eight-foot hole bunched in a wall. The former residents had all their possessions buried in the rubble. Jason tried to stop one of the trucks from carting off the rubble — in which all his DJ equipment was buried — and he was arrested. Kurt tried calling 911 to tell them to send someone to stop these police from breaking the law; eventually they just hung up on him. The whole street was barricaded for days. As of 1999, the former residents of 537 are still waiting for a decision regarding the charges of contempt of court filed against the city for willfully disobeying the judge's stay of demolition. Once this case is resolved the residents still have the option of filing a civil suit against the city for the damages done to their possessions.

About four months after the demolition of Fifth Street, the city struck again. The SRO (Single Room Occupancy) building on the corner of Second Avenue and First Street was city owned and (mis)managed. Due to sloppy renovations, the showers were not properly drained and leaked through the floors. When one day a piece of plaster from the ceiling underneath one of these areas rotted enough to fall, the OEM was called in, the residents evacuated and the building quickly and summarily demolished. The residents were easily dispersed by the city.

The third building, on the corner of Stanton and Clinton, was privately owned with rent-controlled apartments, and once again, because of a minor problem, the whole building was immediately evacuated and torn down. Some of the residents were very old, some families with young kids — Mark Zero, a film and video artist lost his life's work. Staying with him at the time was Rockets Redglare, an old school underground demi-celebrity who lost a huge archive of punk memorabilia including original pictures of Sid and Nancy, etc. Residents were not allowed to retrieve anything from the building — not even their pets; they were assured by city officials that the animals would escape on their own.

These examples are just to illustrate the tactics now being adopted by the city administration. If Giuliani treats legal residents with this much disrespect, you can imagine the anxiety and instability most squatters feel. The city definitely doesn't want to give us a chance to go to court and try to fight legally — that would take too long and there is the chance of it losing. The squats on East 13th Street went through years of legal proceedings before they were finally spectacularly and illegally evicted. It took several evictions spaced out over a year. The first one, in the spring of 1995, involved hundreds of riot police closing off the area in a four block radius. There were police snipers on nearby rooftops, swat teams, helicopters and they even drove a tank down the street — it was originally from the Vietnam War and now painted blue and white. Later that summer on July Fourth, Independence Day, a group of squatters managed to retake one of the buildings on 13th Street even though there was a police guard stationed outside. That turned into a spectacular event as the squatters, wearing hats and masks, danced around on the roof waving to the police helicopters and the cheering neighborhood. The best part was that they were then able to escape before the police could break back into the building. The police were pretty pissed off at this very public display of their incompetence and so they raided a party in the adjacent building and made some random arrests. They charged a few people with ridiculous things like attempted murder (because they were allegedly throwing bricks off the roof). The charge was later dropped.

The final eviction of the remaining buildings took place in August of 1996. It happened on a cold and very rainy night so there weren't many people around. Technically this was also an illegal eviction because the squatters were still undergoing legal proceedings regarding their right to occupy these buildings. It seems that Giuliani has no patience for the time involved in legal proceedings, preferring instead to rely on the dirtiest tricks and the power of his demolition equipment.

Of course there are also success stories like ABC No Rio, the community arts center, also the infamous home to the notorious Saturday afternoon all-ages punk and hardcore matinee. No Rio was initially established as a result of an action that took place on New Years Day in 1980 when the artist group Co-Lab squatted an abandoned building on Delancey Street to protest the city's real estate policies. The city evicted them in what became an embarrassing media spectacle. In order to fix their image, the city then granted the building at 156 Rivington to the group. Since then it has been a constant battle to keep the city from taking the building back. I first got involved with No Rio in 1989 and I squatted a space there in 1990 for about six months and it was crazy. The city was always trying to get in, and, if they did, they would immediately start punching holes in the walls or doing any damage they could so that they could then declare the building to be unsafe. Eventually they broke into my space one weekend when I was away in DC and stole all my stuff and put a big new deadbolt lock on the door. I remember hanging out the window from the third floor on a chain ladder trying to break the shatter proof windows and when that failed it took me about three hours to break through the lock. I never did get my stuff back from them. They wanted $500 or some such idiotic amount for a stack of books, tapes, journals and some ratty old clothes.

The latest crises brought No Rio the closest to eviction it has ever come, but truly, at the last minute, the building was saved. This was mostly due to a small group of dedicated individuals who organized protests and put themselves on the line. The final successful action was when they managed to storm the offices of H.P.D. They could have been arrested, but the Commissioner said OK lets discuss this. The deal that resulted was that the ABC No Rio collective could buy the building for a dollar, but they would be responsible for all the renovations. This may sound simple but it basically means we have to raise a shit-load of money —at least $150,000, which means $50,000 per year for the next three years. ABC No Rio has been an incredible resource, providing a space for punk and hardcore shows, a base for the NYC chapter of Food Not Bombs, a place for unknown artists to show their work, a zone library, silkscreen workshop, darkroom, computer room, a place for political groups to meet such as Zapatista's Support Network and Eviction Watch. Basically it's an essential part of our community here in the LES and an essential part of the punk community in general. So send some spare change or better yet put on a benefit in your town. Write or call for more

information and updates ABC No Rio, 156 Rivington Street NYC, NY 10002 U.S.A. Tel: 212 254-3697.
There are way too many stories I could tell — I've left out millions of gory details.

The squats in the Lower East Side are truly ingrained in the neighborhood and it's the whole neighborhood that is being gentrified. Actually it's the whole island of Manhattan that Guiliani wants to turn into a big night-club with the police as the bouncers. The real estate (over) developers need space and so gradually buildings are being torn down, gardens are being bulldozed and the squats, being a very visible target, are all in a vulnerable position. What are we doing? A lot. One thing we are not doing is leaving.

Chapter 10

St. Brigid's Church
119 Avenue B and East 8th Street, New York, NY
By Carolyn Ratcliffe

St. Brigid's Church sits on the southeast corner of East Eighth Street and Avenue B. It has overlooked Tompkins Square Park almost since it's erection. St. Brigid's was built in 1848 by the Irish Americans living in the Dry Dock area of New York City (now referred to as the East Village by developers, the Lower East Side by old time residents). Most of them worked in the shipping and related industries that flourished along the banks of the East River. They built the clipper ships that brought great wealth to the United States and its merchants.

Patrick C. Keely, a well-known Irish-American architect, designed the church and oversaw its construction. It was built in a record 15 months. Keely, who designed over 600 churches throughout the United States, used the faces of the Irish shipwrights he had hired as carpenters and masons to represent the 12 apostles in the interior church decorations. He placed their faces between the pilasters beneath the gothic arches of the clearstory. Keely himself carved the organ case and the ornate wooden reredos that decorated the nave of the church.[1]

The church was constructed just as the potato famine in Ireland became a major motivating force in the mass immigration of millions of Irish people, fleeing starvation and death, into New York City. It became known as a "Famine Church," a mecca for the recent immigrants to find help along the way with food, clothing, shelter and a job. St. Brigid's history is unique in this aspect. It was the major center for the newly arrived immigrants during the late 1840s and '50s as the blight swept through Ireland, taking between 500,000 to 1,000,000 lives. Another 2,000,000 people left Ireland to escape the "An Gorta Mór" or the Great Hunger.

The history of St. Brigid's is closely intertwined with that of the Lower East Side. For 158 years it has overlooked the park with a benign grace, while military maneuvers, riots, and demonstrations transpired in the park and surrounding area. It is actually older than Old St. Patrick's on Mulberry Street, which burned and was rebuilt in about 1860. St. Brigid's is the 20th oldest church in Manhattan according to research done by Barry Moreno, a librarian at the National Park Service at Ellis Island, and one of the oldest libraries on the Lower East Side.

The fate of this important historical architectural treasure (it was found to meet the criteria for the State and National Historic Registers by the New York State Office of Parks, Recreation and Historic Preservation in July of 2005) presently hangs in the balance, waiting for a decision from New York State Supreme Court Judge Barbra Kapnick to determine whether or not it will remain. Cardinal Egan has decreed that the church must be demolished because it developed a crack along the back northeast wall in 2001. Even though the parishioners raised $103,000 to help defray the cost of the repairs to the church, and had obtained a bid for $275,000 to do the repairs, the cardinal states that it would cost millions and wants to demolish the church. In a taped interview with Diane Williams last year, he said that a parish of 165 people was nothing. As of yet, he states that no decision has been made as to how the property will be used, once the church is demolished. Parishioners and other concerned neighbors have hired an attorney, Harry Kresky, to pursue the matter, and they've taken the diocese to court to stop the demolition and demand the return of the church to the parishioners. We are presently waiting for a decision to be rendered by Judge Barbara Kapnick who heard the case on August 30, 2005. An appeal is planned if her decision is unfavorable to the parishioners.

1   "The History of St. Brigid's Parish in the City of New York under the Administration of the Reverend Patrick J. McSweeny, 1877-1907," by Reverend Patrick D. O'Flaherty, dissertation toward the Master of Arts degree, Fordham University, May 15th, 1952; St. Brigid's article, by Father Barry Bossa, Keely Society newsletter, no date; "Patrick Keely, Architect," by Katharine Zeltner, Common Bond, Volume 15, No. 3/Spring 2000; Keely Society website, administered by Edward H. Furey; Cathedral of the Holy Cross website, administered by the Archdiocese of Boston.

Chapter 11

Zoning: What Is It Good For? The Committee For Zoning Inaction
By Richard Kusack - Founder

On January 24th 2006, The Committee For Zoning Inaction presented an Appeal before the NYC Board of Standards and Appeal (BSA) concerning the Department of Buildings (DOD) "final determination" which allowed the New York Law School (NYLS) to occupy the "Half-Dorm" at 81 East Third Street (between First and Second Avenue). The building has been a heated issue for the community since the developer skirted the requirements of having an educational institution affiliated with the project prior to the issuance of any new building application. The requirement of institutional affiliation is typical of the DOB procedure for Community Facility development in order for a project to receive approval.

At issue for the community with the "Half-Dorm is the misuse of the process of developing a Community Facility (CF) Dormitory; in addition, there are several specific violations of the Zoning Resolution pertaining to Use Groups 2 & 3; (Open Space and Backyard Requirements). For the record, the building on East Third Street has been known as the "Half-Dorm" since it is a hybrid; part dormitory and part residential use. This distinction matters because each use group impacts different zoning requirements.

We have to ask: why is it necessary for private citizens to drag the DOB into compliance? The purpose of governmental agencies is to safeguard the community and the public. The Committee For Zoning Inaction (CZI) was formed specifically to respond to the inaction the DOB showed to the East Village community regarding the development at 81 East 3rd Street. The Community Facility issue is actually a larger one impacting the entire New York Metropolitan Area. The "Half-Dorm" and the way that it has been developed ignores the community interest and the intent of the Zoning Resolution.

Currently, zoning is a front burner topic in the East Village and the LES below Houston Street where currently "mixed-use" hotels are breaking the scale of the neighborhood and taking advantage of the extra zoning density below Houston Street. What many people are concerned with is the eventual conversion of these hotels to residential housing. This is what is now occurring with many building throughout Manhattan (take the Plaza Hotel for instance). This "technique" would eventually allow the owner of the property to effectively develop a residential property (when "converted") that would generally twice exceed the current permissible residential density and height restrictions.

This "Trojan Use" reference is one of the issues pertaining to "The Half Dorm" on East Third Street. The other issue as previously mentioned is how the developer ignored the CF zoning requirements in the first place. Community Facilities dormitories have always required a lease 221

A Radical Political and Social History of the Lower East Side

in place prior to the granting of a New Building Application for the development of a dormitory. This has been the DOB's guiding policy for many years.

The DOB's top technical expert (Fatima Amer, P.E.) made this clear in an industry presentation before the New York Society of Architects in a DOB Technical Forum (#12) during the fall of 2004. Why was it ignored on East Third Street?

The developer in an apparent "bait and switch" filed two New Building Applications for the 81 East 3rd Street. The first application, amended with a PAA (or Post Approval Amendment) for a Community Facility was somehow approved but with major zoning questions unanswered in the review process such as: "Where is the Community Facility"?

The second new building application, filed some seven months later after initial approval was "self-certified" by its engineer (whose financial interest was never disclosed raising separate ethical issues). This self-certificated application allowed for undetected errors because the application was never reviewed by the DOB.

We view the developer's tactics as an attempt to obscure their intention in a deceptive manner. The developer told the community that they were building a 6-story building; the permits posted on the sidewalk bridge indicated as such. They pulled the "bait and switch" in July of 2004. (Currently, there are no punitive penalties for architects who overtly violate the zoning resolution with egregious self-certified filings.)

We have raised the question "why and for what legitimate reason" did the developer and engineer of 81 E. Third Street file a "self certified" NB application for a smaller six story building when they had an "approved" application for a 13-story dorm building?

The CZI pointed out in its 5 page letter and "Technical Memo" to the Department of Buildings prior to the DOB's Technical Compliance Unit (TCU) Audit of the developer's plans in November of 2004 that the original comments of the examiner in October of 2002, asked one major question: where is the Community Facility? (The above referenced memo is part of the documents submitted in CZI's Appeal before the BSA).

We would like to point out that the DOB's TCU found 17 major violations including "no lease in place" as is required by the Zoning Resolution. We contend that the objections of the original examiner were never "cured" but somehow the PAA was erroneously approved. In our view this has never been explained and it requires an explanation. We still want the answer.

Backing this position up is the CHARAS decision by the BSA in August of 2005. On page one, the DOB's objections sited "Substantiate Dormitory Use (UG3)" This use is permitted for "College or School Student" housing only as per Z.R. (Floors 3-19 indicate Residential Apartments layout)." At 81 E. Third Street no educational use was ever affiliated nor substantiated with the property at the start; in fact, we believe that never in the history of granting a CF bonus was a PAA used to approve a CF Dormitory. Tell us if we're wrong.

We ask for a consistent application of the Zoning Resolution; of policy and of the rules. We ask that the BSA as an administrative oversight agency to reverse the DOB's "final determination" regarding 81 East 3rd Street so that the Zoning Resolution is correctly interpreted and implemented. The public trust is at stake.

It is an abuse of discretion for DOB to ignore the clear statutory language of the Zoning Resolution by failing to give effect to the terms "college and school"(educational institution). The DOB has allowed the developer of 81 East 3rd Street to more than double the FAR (floor area); the height and the number of dwelling units in the building at 81 E. Third Street. This could lead to inappropriate potential windfall profit for the developer and an inappropriate building for Manhattan and the East Village. The DOB appears to have applied the rules inconsistently and arbitrarily especially in light of the CHARAS decision.

In addition, the tenant (The New York Law School) has appeared to act as an "enabler" for their own apparent gain in a distressed sale situation where the developer had to find an after-the-fact bone-fide educational institution to occupy the speculative dormitory at 81 E. Third Street. Similarly, at the St. Anne's site in the East Village, NYU is taking advantage of a controversial air-rights transfer from the US Postal Service to a development they are interested in occupying Our educational institutions should be model citizens leading the letter and spirit of the law to a higher standard. This does not seem to be the case at all.

Additionally, what sticks out as a sore thumb in the development process for the "Half-Dorm" is that the DOB approved the Certificate of Occupancy (CO) of 81 E 3rd Street for both residential use (Use Group 2) and dormitory use (Use Group 3). The Community Facility bonus (double the area) only applies to a Use Group 3 designation. How is the community protected if the "restrictive declaration" in the deed does not apply to the "residential" portion (Use Group 2) of the "Half-Dorm"? Other questions arise.

At the January hearing the BSA Board questioned the developer's attorney and Counsel for the DOB on this point; they asked for additional submissions regarding FAR calculations and whether it exceeds the permissible amount of space; additionally, does the property meet the ZR pertaining to OPEN SPACE (which is required for residential use and not a dormitory) as well as the violations we pointed out with regard to BACKYARD Requirements. Before the BSA we set forth the following; and this will be submitted in writing in our next submission to the BSA before the March 2006 hearing.

1. In fact, no one DENIES that "open space" is REQUIRED for the residential floor area.

2. The issue is this: the so-called "open space" provided at the rear of the building as approved by DOB simply DOES NOT COMPLY with the relevant definition for "open space" as set forth under Section 12-10 ZR.

Under the definition, "open space" must be both accessible to and usable by the residents of the building. We continued that . . . .

3. DOB's approval ignores Section 12-10 ZR's definition entirely.

A Radical Political and Social History of the Lower East Side

4. The definitions of Section 12-10 ZR are part and parcel of the substantive law of the Zoning Resolution, and the DOB cannot choose to ignore its definitions.

Part of the problem surrounding the process in developing the building is that the DOB has ignored its own rules and the Zoning Resolution. The CHARAS decision (609 East 9th Street) went on to make very clear distinctions between Use Group 2 and Use Group 3. Manhattan Commissioner Osorio writes (4/21/05) to the petitioner's attorney in the CF dormitory case (PS 64 CHARAS):

> As you know, the Department (DOB) requires an institutional nexus in order for construction to be classified as a dormitory. This is necessary to distinguish a "student dormitory" which is a community facility use and entitled to extra floors, from other types of housing that are classified as Use Group 2, including buildings that house students, and that are not eligible for additional bulk. To reflect the nexus, the Department asks for either a deed or a lease from a school.

We want to emphasize the point that Manhattan DOB Commissioner Osorio is referring to a project on East Ninth Street (CHARAS) which has yet to file their new building application and the DOB is asking for a lease to be in place in order to distinguish between Use Group 2 and Use Group 3. Commissioner Osorio continues in her letter:

> Where the two uses appear very similar on plan, yet result in very different zoning benefits (such as the Use Group 2 residences and Use Group 3 dormitory), it is incumbent upon the Department to ask for documentation to substantiate the particular community facility use . . . (she continues in her letter) . . . it is not sufficient to justify deviating from the Department's general requirement that a dormitory use be substantiated prior to permit.

We believe that the developer of the "Half-Dorm" will not be able to meet the requirements of the Zoning Resolution; something will have to be modified or the issue will be ignored politically.

In passing, another matter of interest impacting this development is the recently developed "rules" written by the DOB regarding the development of Community Facility Dormitories. The "rules" were promulgated by the irregularities pertaining to 81 East Third Street. This has indirectly helped save CHARAS (for the time being) from the wrecking ball and the proposed monstrous 23-story dormitory. The Committee For Zoning Inaction pointed out these matters in numerous memos and letters to the DOB; they are also on the record as part of public testimony in the hearings on rule 51-01.

CHARAS has been a "hot spot" for the East Village Community for many years and the subject of much division within the community. The EVCC and local politicians have campaigned to save the property and restore it to Community Art related uses. The property was "auctioned" at the end of the Giuliani administration and has remained vacant; it is a potential landmark but it is subject to a deed restriction for a Community Facility. The developer has tried to build a "speculative" CF without a lease in place and have been stopped in their tracks. The case will probably go through the legal system.

While we agree with the DOB rules that a development of this nature requires an "institutional nexus" substantiated "either by deed or lease" prior to permit in order for the construction to be classified as a CF why aren't these rules applied to the "Half-Dorm"? We also take issue with the length of lease as recently defined by the DOB. The DOB would allow a ten-year term to satisfy their "rule"; we think that the standard really implies "ownership" and/or a lease term of longer than twenty years. We have recently made a legislative move towards the City Counsel for a remedy.

The "straw that broke" the fix-it/patch it up method used by the DOB with regard to the Half Dorm was the discovery by the CZI's that NYLS lease for 81 East 3rd Street actually does not meet the 10 year "term" requirement "threshold."

It is bad enough that the DOB has extended to the developer extra time and every consideration to fulfill after the fact "lease" requirement which has infuriated the local community; however, adding insult to injury is that the developer/DOB have papered over the threshold lease term requirement by issuing a lease document with hollowed out provisions. The lease term does not meet anyone's definition of the required ten-year term (due to the existence of a Termination Clause) let alone a standards body such as FASB (Financial Accounting Standards Board).

On the surface we find a ten-year term for NYLS; however, the "Termination Clauses" will enable the school to terminate the lease at anytime up until 2010 rendering the lease inadequate. On page 46 Article 34 from the Tenant's Termination Notice:

> Notwithstanding anything contrary contained herein, provided not Event of Default then exists, Tenant shall have the right, at any time prior to July 31, 2009, to give irrevocable written notice that the Tenant has elected to terminate this Lease, effective as on July 31, 2010 (the Termination Date).

To our knowledge, neer in the history of Community Facility development has a building such as the "Half-Dorm" been granted such wide abuse of the Zoning Resolution. The lease in place standard has been violated; several sets of plans were filed simultaneously violating the DOB's own procedures; plans were approved with major violations; the DOB granted both a Use Group 2 (residential apartments) and Use Group 3 (dormitory) status; no 'institutional nexus" has ever been substantiated or affiliated from inception.

The DOB admits that there was an error in not having a lease in place prior to approval of a New Building Application for the "Half-Dorm." . . . but it was "harmless" they claim! The East Village has been harmed and we are looking for a remedy.

The development abuse at 81 East Third Street is not an isolated instance. Fortunately, we must realize that this threat can undermine the community in not so subtle ways and we must meet it with the proper resolve. Just down the block at 4 E Third Street on the corner

A Radical Political and Social History of the Lower East Side

of Bowery (The Alien v Predator Building); a building formerly "proposed" as a Community Facility which morphed into a hotel has significant Zoning Resolution violations and excessive FAR violations. The way we meet these two struggles will make an impact. The tremors of "Take-it-down!" still resonate from some protests held in front of the building. Will the Civitas experience in the early 90s be revisited and duplicated? Will a rezoning of the area eventually occur?

Many groups and individuals have emerged to help in the various struggles from CHARAS to the "Half-Dorm" such as the GVSHP (The Greenwich Village Society For Historic Preservation); the EVCC; The Cooper Square Committee; the involvement of CB #3 board members and key individuals such as Kevin Shea and of course The Committee For Zoning Inaction.

It is difficult to gauge at this point regarding the "Half-Dorm" whether the BSA will require a change of the CO; the destruction of the back portion of the building which violates the zoning or perhaps the complete removal of the upper stories of the building. This is probably doubtful without a full legal challenge by the community. We'll have to see whether the resolve is there; whether a deeper effort will be made by the community. So, what's it been good for? Well, absolutely something!

Chapter 12

The Soul War for the East Village
By Roland Legiardi-Laura

Walking back home from a screening of Antonioni's The Passenger, an iconic work of '70s 'alienation cinema', my dear friend Natalya suddenly blurted out that she didn't know why she was still bothering to live in the East Village. "I don't go to parties or out to restaurants, or to bars or clubs, or even cafés. I don't go shopping at cute little boutiques and most of the art around here seems so self-indulgent." She's a thoughtful, intelligent woman, a working architect, feisty, utterly independent, a screenwriter and a filmmaker — The kind of person that you might guess would refuse to live anywhere but in the East Village — The kind of person the East Village needs to retain in order to lay claim to a future as rich and meaningful as its past.

Her comments were very troubling. I have lived in the same place in this neighborhood since 1978 and it was precisely because of people like Natalya that I first found this community compelling and real. If people like her can no longer justify living in a neighborhood that the rest of the world lauds as a bubbling ethnic broth, the center of edginess, creativity, progressive politics, and constant catalytic flux, then perhaps those of us who smugly feel we have found the last slice of eccentric Nirvana need to take a closer look. Just what is really going on in our beloved bastion of highbrow lowlife? What's left of the poetry, politics, passion, proud poverty, and unbending tradition of struggle that seeded a community so unique it has been the subject of novels, plays, poems, films, and even a frightening clone of itself erected in the Las Vegas desert.

It is in the spirit of such an inquiry that I shall try to piece together a reflective 'state of the union' progress report on the East Village.

But first, a bit of required historical background is in order:

The East Village ca.:

15,005 B.C.-The 1000-foot-thick ice-sheet covering much of our neighborhood begins to melt leaving a marshy wetland in the area of Tompkins Square Park.

1605 A.D.-The Lenape, the dominant tribe on Manahatta, use the area for a seasonal hunting and fishing ground.

1705-Much of the East Village is divided up into farmland. Mostly farmed by the Dutch, some 'half-free' slaves, and a smattering of English. The lion's share of the land belongs to the Stuyvesant and Fish families.

A Radical Political and Social History of the Lower East Side

1805-Farms have begun to give way to streets as the city boundary works its way up the island. The traditional compass drawn east-west streets laid out by the Dutch are overlaid with a grid following the axis of Manhattan. The beginnings of the boat building and tanning industries appear along the local shores of the East Village.

1905-The East Village has become the northernmost edge of the crowded teeming tenement community known as the Lower East Side. It is called Kleine Deutschland because so many of the residents are from Germany. Over the next 100 years successive waves of Eastern European Jews, Irish, Italians, Czechs, Hungarians, Poles, Ukrainians, and Puerto Ricans move into the neighborhood.

2005-*The East Village is on the cusp of its biggest transition since the late 1960s, when wholesale property abandonment, redlining, population decline, and a surge in drug trafficking combined with the post beat-hip, and political movements, transformed the neighborhood from an ethnic poor and working class enclave to a center of counter culture and social struggle. Since then the change has been sometimes gradual, sometimes cataclysmic. The soul-war to preserve the essentially unique communal and creative qualities of the East Village comes down to three battlefronts: Gentrification, Trendification, and Chainification. At stake is not just the piece of ground that many fondly call Loisaida but something potentially global in impact, along the lines of a Jane Jacobs dream: A national model for a community that is self-sustaining, humane, balanced, and alive.*

Below is a brief summary of the most significant challenges, as I see them, confronting the East Village:

1. Zoning - Without question the most important issue confronting our community today. We have a rare historic opportunity. And if the often contentious, political forces in the East Village find a way to take advantage of it, the rampant development-construction of high-rises, luxury towers and the eroding of the traditional built environment of our neighborhood-could be brought to a screeching halt. Most significantly this could happen soon! The City Planning Commission, under the leadership of Amanda Burden, has indicated both in word and deed that they understand that the rezoning of Loisaida is long overdue. The recent rezoning victory in the far West Village, spearheaded by Andrew Berman and the Greenwich Village Society For Historic Preservation, has created a model and a precedent. But as ever, the situation is complex in the East Village — Community Board 3 has drafted a set of principles calling for an overall height restriction of roughly 5-6 stories. This would retain the existing built character of the area and prevent the abuse of the Community Facility height bonus granted to builders who can prove they are constructing something that will serve the community — all good and necessary given the *Attack Of The Giant Towers* that is currently underway. But the sticking point in internal CB3 committee negotiations is the key issue of inclusionary (affordable) housing. Some members of the board don't want to sacrifice this principle for the sake of fast-tracking the normally cumbersome rezoning process. The planning commission, for its part, has indicated a willingness to move forward quickly. At the November 2005 meeting of the CB3 Zoning Committee, members agreed to seek a prompt meeting with the Planning Commission to discuss the options. The ball right now is in the hands of CB3. If they can't navigate through this issue efficiently, the East

Village could soon resemble a field of sprouting phalluses. Closely connected to zoning are a number of specific battles: 81 East Third Street and 4 East Third Street are sites that have been developed under the aegis of the Community Facility Bonus. The buildings have already been built, but the local residents, led by Richard Kusack and Kevin Shea have challenged the developers, claiming that the structures are not in compliance with city's building code. If successful in their challenges, the owners could be required to slice off the upper floors of their buildings. These are important test cases and Mr. Kusack has filed a Board of Standards and Appeals request for 81 East Third Street.[1]

2. Preservation/Landmarking - Just as important to the character and soul of the neighborhood as zoning, is the battle to landmark and preserve our history as expressed by architecture. With only six buildings landmarked east of Second Avenue, the community is sorely under-designated. Two important buildings that must be saved not only because of their architectural, cultural, and historical merit but because of what they mean to the current and future life of Loisaida are Old PS 64, former home of CHARAS/El Bohio and St. Brigid's Church.

The neighborhood won a significant victory when, on October 18th, the Landmarks Preservation Committee agreed to calendar a designation hearing for PS 64. The 100-year-old school building easily meets all the criteria for designation. However, the commission needs to be reminded just how much this building means to our community. They must prioritize and set a date for the designation hearing. In light of recent reversals of Landmark designations at the City Council level, our work is not nearly over. The East Village Community Coalition (EVCC), including folks like Aaron Sosnick, Michael Rosen, Dominique Camacho, Nicola Baker and David Leslie, has led the charge to designate. Local residents will need to follow through and make strong showings both at the Landmark's Commission and in the City Council Chambers when the hearings occur.

Saving PS 64 also represents an immense opportunity for the East Village.

At present we have no full service cultural/community center. St Marks Church, under the inspired leadership of reverend Julio Torres has tried to pick up the slack but is limited by space and long-term obligations. A vision for PS 64 with its 135,000 square feet could, if well planned and executed, allow the structure to reemerge as one of the most important cultural centers in the city. Unfortunately, Gregg Singer, the owner for the past six years, has failed to develop a plan that meets the needs of the community, or the requirements of the City. Without divine intervention, it appears that Mr. Singer will be obliged to one day pass on this property to a more benign steward.[2]

The other endangered building is St. Brigid's Church. After 148 years of spiritual service to the Roman Catholic community of the East Village, it appears that the divinely-inspired New York Archdiocese has determined the building has no future other than to generate a good price on the auction block. Anchoring the northern end of an entire block of church-owned property fronting on Tompkins Square Park, it is easy to see why the Archdiocese might want to demolish and sell this venerable bit of our history. Plagued with a dwindling flock and huge bills generated by the plethora of scandals confronting the church, the property represents a potential windfall. The parishioners of St. Brigid's beg to differ however. They have taken the Archdiocese to court to prevent demolition and to demand redress of a promise to restore the building. As of August 30th, when Justice Barbara Kapnick heard the arguments, the future of the building has been put on hold. The next phase of the struggle will begin when Justice Kapnick renders her decision. Until then there is a standing court injunction preventing the Archdiocese from swinging the wrecking ball.[3]

In both of these cases the community has spoken and expressed its will. These are hopeful signs that the East Village still has the heart to stand up and fight for what it believes in. We seem to be engaged in a house-to-house struggle to preserve the essential character of our neighborhood. The challenge ahead is to effectively link the individual issues.

Another more broad-based way to preserve the built character and history of our community is to create small landmark districts. They can be just a block long or several square blocks in scope. The process is time consuming but the end result is a protective netting for whole clusters of buildings. The area around Tompkins Square Park — Seventh Street between Avenues C and D and Second Street between First and Second Avenues — all have the potential to become such districts. The advantage of this method over down-zoning is that it also protects an area from low-rise devastation, i.e. staying within height restrictions but still managing to create new unappealing and unacceptable structures that maximize square footage allowances. The disadvantage is that there are probably only a few spots in the neighborhood which could qualify.

3. Housing - Basically this has been the back-story in every other struggle in our community. Urban pioneers, gentrifiers, yuppies, immigrants, workers, the homeless, subsidized tenants, students, squatters, anarchists, and artists all need a place to sleep. The East Village up to about 10 years ago provided a pretty good balance supporting the needs of those mentioned above. But in the last decade the balance has shifted steadily toward those who are more well-to-do. And now it threatens to accelerate to warp speed. No one wants to live in a neighborhood just made up of rich people — not even rich people. And no one believes that living under a cardboard box is quaint and romantic. Effective models for mixed income housing abound. We must protect the poor and the homeless. On my block alone, dozens of homeless camp out under the scaffolds at night. The work needs to be done by our politicians and our community board. It is a long-term challenge, there are no quick or easy fixes and thoughtful plans need to be evolved.

Homage should be paid to the squatters whose movement stretches back more than twenty years. Of the two-dozen or so buildings that were squatted, eleven remain. After a sometimes very brutal and confrontational struggle, a settlement was finally reached and the residents of those eleven buildings are in the final stages of negotiating legal and permanent ownership of their homes. A piece of East Village history was written in this struggle. At a time when city policy seemed to favor abandonment and demolition of sound structures, these intrepid urban guerillas put successive municipal administrations on notice that common folks were ready and able to take matters into their own hands.

4. Bar and Restaurant Proliferation, Chain Store Creep and the Sidewalk Economy - A Dunkin' Donuts just opened on Sixth Street and First Avenue, where a laundromat used to be. It opened right next to the long suffering but apparently immortal McDonalds. There is another Dunkin' Donuts six blocks further up on First, and another across from St. Mark's Church. Starbucks has bracketed Astor Place and sits diagonally across from Veselka's. Bank branches, after being conspicuously absent for decades, are filling prime retail space along Avenue A. Is Wal-Mart far behind?

Two weeks ago the good citizens of Loisaida convened a town-hall meeting in the Angel Orensanz Center — a former synagogue, now a performance space — to decry the rampant howling nightmare that has become nightlife in the East Village. Police commanders were put on the hot-seat, the State Liquor Authority vilified, and politicians put on notice that if something wasn't done and done soon, the pitchforks and torches would be passed out and there would be hell to pay. What has happened to the old East Village, where people didn't wake up until nine p.m. and breakfast was served at the Kiev 24 hours a day? Have we all just gotten older and crankier and less tolerant or is there a problem here? The answer unfortunately is that there is indeed a big problem, brought about perhaps by the natural evolution of a neighborhood from one that is poor, abandoned and dangerous, to an ultra-chic destination spot. Tourists, bar-hoppers, boutique shoppers, people who saw the play and will see the film Rent, those who need to feel 'cool,' have all been hypnotically drawn to our homeland. The economic stakes have been ratcheted up. With new luxury towers, like the Gwathmey "squiggle" rising on Astor Place and the Avalon Chrystie on Houston, my bet is that there is plenty of money to support this new playground.[4]

Reverend Billy calls the impending global doom we are facing, "The Shopocalypse." What can we do to slow this grinding ice-sheet we are facing? How can a few yokels armed with pitch-forks fend off the monster? It's going to take a concerted effort, discipline, and a bit of luck. Luck will come our way if the real-estate bubble bursts soon. Discipline needs to be shown by boycotting the chain stores and offending bars, lobbying, picketing if necessary, only buying locally. We can't build a moat around the East Village, but we can band together and show people that we mean business — their business will suffer unless changes are made. I'm not sure if it's time yet to start planting vegetables in our backyards and local gardens but stranger things have happened so I'm tossing out a handful of seeds and pray-ing for rain.

5. Gardens - A Garden District-Parks-The Greening of the East Village. There are 42 public gardens in the East Village, down from a high of about 70 in the mid-1980s. The bat-tles fought to save the gardens from the encroaching developers culminated in the agree-ment signed by the city and New York State Attorney General, Elliot Spitzer. The gardens were given a fixed amount of time to comply with a set of city regulations: i.e., regular community hours, open membership, etc. In return the gardens would be brought under the control of the NYC Department of Parks and protected. Roughly 35 of the gardens are now under Parks; three others are controlled by The Trust For Public Land; another three have been brought under the aegis of Bette Midler's New York Restoration Project; and the last garden is its own private trust. This all sounds well and good but the agreement signed by the state and city runs out in 2007. As long as the Dept. of Parks is run by a pro-garden administration, and this one is, and as long as the city sees no better use for the lands, the gardens will continue to be safe. But further protections can be afforded. The gardens can become 'mapped parkland' and they can be officially 'designated' parks by Albany. These conditions would make it much harder, almost impossible in fact, for the gardens to be turned over for other uses.

The gardens and the gardeners need to band together and insure that they become fully protected. Mapping is a costly process and there is some sense out there that the city would prefer it if the gardens retain their current status and preserve the widest option for municipal use determination. A small but steadfast organization, the East Village Parks Conservancy has made it a part of their mission to assist the gardens in organizing a mapping and designation campaign. The only problem is that the gardeners are a wonderfully individualistic and independent group . . .

The gardens of the East Village together make up one of the most unique and precious urban landscapes in the country. Per square acre, the East Village has more public garden space than any other neighborhood in the United States. The EVPC is also developing a plan to have the East Village designated as the nation's first urban garden district. It is an ambitious plan but preserving and respecting these green lungs, these oases of quiet and contemplation, is without question a key part of preserving the essential and unique quality of our community. Go EVPC!

The parks in our neighborhood are looking quite good these days. The Parks Department, perennially under funded, has creatively found ways to allot resources, build partnerships with the community, and nurture these most important local patches of earth. Tompkins Square now has a full-time gardener assigned to it. Each year, the parks are scoured for traces of Dutch Elm disease and Asian Long-horned Beetle infestation. There has been quite a flap lately about trees being cut down in East River Park. But the Parks Dept. reacted quickly and the new plan with inlet coves and additional plantings should ultimately be a welcome renovation that the whole neighborhood will enjoy.

We have much to be thankful for regarding our green spaces. But much to watch out for: It is critical that the East Village develop a policy to 'green' itself. Con Edison has proven itself insensitive and lethal in our neighborhood. The additional service now being provided by the enlarged 14th Street plant may yield greater instances of asthma and other pollutant driven illnesses. Alternative energy sources, and sustainability are no longer optional — they have become necessities. A big part of keeping our community independent and vital will be determined by how we respond to this set of challenges.

6. Cultural Life - Most of the cultural institutions of the East Village seem to be stable at the moment. St Mark's Church, The Anthology Film Archives, The Nuyorican Poets Café, The Bowery Poetry Club, PS 122, Theater For The New City, and Tribes are all more or less intact and functioning. CBGB's will soon be leaving its longtime Bowery home. A new location will be found and one can only hope that the spirit of punk will live on. The post-9/11 world shook many of these organizations and severely tightened their already limited resources. But they still stand and represent what is certainly one of the most culturally open and vibrant places in the world. However, our cultural eco-system is fragile and there is still considerable work to be done to insure that the creative core of the East Village thrives.

There is no formal link between the arts and the youth of this community.

A number of the groups mentioned serve young people, but not in a particularly assertive or organized way. If we don't make a concerted effort to bring the arts into the lives of our children, the fate of this neighborhood as a creative cauldron is sealed. The problem is that we don't have enough space to do this effectively and the will is not there just yet. This, of course, is where a place like PS 64 could add immensely — with after-school programs, and an alternative high school dedicated to the arts through internship and mentorship. There are nearly 2,500 kids in this neighborhood of high school age and we don't have one high school that serves them. Bard High School, which is south of Houston, is a special Early College Acceptance program and takes kids from all over the city. So most of our children have to leave the community to attend school. I digress, but the point is that for the arts to remain vital our youth must be engaged, period.

And for celebrating the counterculture we have created and protecting the artists who make it we have FEVA, The Federation of East Village Artists. After more than three years of hard work, three HOWL! Festivals, innumerable events, meetings, memos and e-mails, the dreamers are waking up to reality. A tremendous amount of money has been spent; the important work of artists' health insurance and artists' housing are no closer to realization; and the centerpiece of the effort to date, The HOWL! Festival, has come under a cloud of criticism — claims of selling out to corporate interests, misallocation of funds and autocratic control of the process have been leveled. The Board of FEVA, at first slow to react, has now begun to focus on the work ahead. I am hopeful that what we are witnessing will be a productive period of assessment and rededication rather than recrimination and dissolution . . . But only *The Shadow* knows for sure . . . We could sure use an efficient and potent FEVA. A visionary organization in this neighborhood that could see beyond its own nose would be a boon. If FEVA fails it would be a shame but I imagine another organization will take up the cause.

In the end, for me the question Natalya posed — "Why am I still living here?" — is still the most poignant. The best answer I can give comes from the people I know who live around me. They are my friends and they are in my life everyday:

I have
    A friend who struggles to build labyrinths and create a sustainable urban lifestyle.
    Another friend who writes about the looming planetary change of consciousness,
    Another who struggles to organize the undocumented and immigrant workers.
    Another whose PhD thesis is on theater in Cuba.
Another couple who have taken poor neighborhood kids into their comfortable home and raised them as their own.
    Another, a boxer and performance artist, who fought and won the effort to keep street fairs away from Avenue A.
    Another who runs a toy store with the most magical of toys.

Another who gives his wealth away selflessly.
Another who practices trumpet everyday.
Another whose home is a menagerie for lost animals.
Another who composes the wildest avant-garde music.
Another who has been on rent strike for 16 years.
Another who makes wonderful hand made films.
Another who creates the most brilliant theater pieces.
Another couple who struggle to teach yoga as a path to life and wisdom.
Another who takes photos of the horrors of war.

I have poor friends and rich friends who live in this community and struggle every day to make it a better place — this is why I still live here. Selfishness has not yet triumphed in the East Village and the spirit of struggle is alive.

Endnotes

The following updates were written as of Oct. 1st, 2006:

1. The rezoning plans for much of the East Village/Loisaida have made considerable progress and it is believed that the process should be complete by the end of 2007, limiting the heights of all new construction, providing inclusionary housing FAR bonuses on certain Avenues and wide streets, and closing the Community Facility bonus loophole.

2. On June 20th, The Landmarks Commission voted unanimously to designate PS64 a landmark. This vote was unanimously upheld by a vote of the City Council on Sept. 13th. However, the owner, through a permit issued prior to the beginning of the Landmarking process, retained the right to strip the façade of the building and is currently doing so, claiming that this defacing (permitted under the architectural terms 'repair and restoration') will help his case to reverse the designation. The owner earlier this year lost his legal case against the Board of Standards and Appeals, requesting permission to construct a dormitory on the site. It is not known whether he is appealing that loss. For further updates please go to: www.evccnyc.org.

3. The original legal complaint was essentially rejected by Justice Kapnick, and further lost on appeal, however, The Archdiocese began demolition on St. Brigid's in late July, destroying most of the 130 year-old hand-painted windows, however an amended complaint filed by the legal firm Holland & Knight LLP, along with Harry Kresky is now again before Justice Kapnick who is expected to rule in the near future. For further information please go to: www.savestbrigid.com.

4. On September 6th, The State Liquor Authority imposed a four-month moratorium on all new liquor licenses for bars, clubs and cabarets subject to the 500-foot rule.

A version of this article first appeared in *The Villager*, Nov. 30-Dec. 6, 2005. Volume 75, Number 28, p. 23.

Chapter 13

Tenants of 47 East Third Street Fight Mass Eviction Attempt
By David Pultz

Since the Summer of 2003, East Village tenants at 47 East Third Street have been waging a legal battle against mass eviction with landlords who claim to want to turn their 15 unit apartment building into a mansion for themselves. The landlords are using a loophole under the rent stabilization law for "owner use" in an attempt to empty out the entire 11,600 square foot, 60-room building. The tenants believe this action is a scam and an illegal assault on affordable housing in New York City.

The landlords, Alistair and Catherine Economakis own or control some two-dozen apartment buildings in New York City through Granite International Management in Brooklyn. The company is owned by Ms. Economakis' father, Peter Yatrakis. The couple currently live on an entire floor of a family owned brownstone in the toney Cobble Hill section of Brooklyn. In legal documents, the landlord makes claim to want to turn the 105-year-old tenement at 47 East Third Street into a single family residence with five bedrooms, six bathrooms, a gym with shower, a library, a nanny suite and a two-story living room with an overhanging walkway. The Economakis family acquired the building in 2001 at drastically below market price by taking advantage of a city tax lien against the tenement, then bringing the building through a bankruptcy proceeding, and finally transferring it from a family-controlled company to themselves as individual owners.

Owner occupancy law can allow owners in need of a place to live the right to refuse to renew a tenant's lease and acquire "one or more" apartments for themselves. The mass eviction underway at 47 East Third Street is one of the first buildings in which a landlord has attempted to use this loophole to claim an entire tenement for personal use. Residents at 47 East Third Street and their supporters believe the real goal is to remove the building from rent stabilization and charge market-rate rents, or to sell the emptied building. The law for owner use states that owners must live in any recovered apartments for a minimum of three years before being able to re-rent or sell the unit. Unfortunately, the state or city does not keep track of abuses of this provision, and the law provides few legal remedies to the evicted tenant, and virtually no penalties to the landlord, if abuses—such as a landlord not moving in at all—should occur. In any event, the tenants strongly believe the entire action by the landlord is entirely illegal and contrary to the intention of the law.

The tenants at 47 East Third Street are, by and large, middle to moderate-income working people. Many of them have lived in the building more than 10 years, and some nearly 30 years. In the fall of 2004 the case was brought to the New York State Supreme Court, where Justice Paul Feinman imposed an injunction that temporarily barred further eviction proceedings against tenants with expiring leases. With great expense to themselves the residents, from the beginning, formed a tenant association, hired an attorney and have bravely

A Radical Political and Social History of the Lower East Side

fought this scam. They expect to see the case eventually brought into the State Appellate Court.

The case has also drawn significant media attention, with articles appearing in *The Villager, The Independent,* and *The New York Daily News*; and on June 26, 2005, the cover story for the *New York Times* Real Estate section. The tenants also organized a rally on June 25, 2005 in front of their building, drawing many supporters and politicians, as well as coverage by local television outlets.

Congressman Jerrold Nadler states, "The owner-occupancy provision was never intended to enable landlords to pursue such ruthless mass evictions. I commend and support the tireless efforts of the residents of 47 East Third Street to save their homes. This is not just their fight: a victory for them will be a victory for thousands of other rent-regulated residents throughout the city who are at risk of losing their homes through this loophole in the law." Community Board 3 in the East Village calls the landlords' mansion plan, "an obviously contrived plan," and State Assembly member Deborah Glick adds in support, "At a time when the city is struggling to keep working-class and middle-class New Yorkers from being forced out of the neighborhoods that they helped to build, mass evictions, such as this one, run counter to preserving a sense of community. I am proud to stand with the tenants of 47 East Third Street in their fight to save their homes and neighborhood and preserve affordable housing for all New Yorkers."

Chapter 14

Timetable
   By Laura Zelasnic

" It's not late, it's early."

1799. Lets say the story begins here. It could begin in 1651 when Stuyvesant took the land or it could begin in the prehistoric mist when the Lenni/Lenapes sat in longhouses practicing concensus democracy. Or it could begin back even farther all the way to the very beginning of time. But this is as good a place to start as any. St. Mark's Church appears way out in the country on Stuyesant's farm. A truncated landmark, the steeple appeared in 1828.

1807. Daniel D. Tompkins, who had inherited land along the East River through the Stuyvesant family, is elected Governor of New York. In his last year in office, 1817, he signs an emancipation proclamation which will make slavery illegal in New York State in 1827.

1834. Tompkins dies. His family donates the land which will become Tompkins Square Park (see 1850).

1832. Seabury Tredwell, a hardware importer, builds his family a townhouse on 29 E. 4th St., an elegant neighborhood filled with pleasure gardens. Now known as the Merchant's House, it remains untouched through all of the changes in the area until Gertrude Tredwell dies in 1933. In 1936 it opens as a museum.

1834. NYU begins construction on its first permanent building around Washington Square. They realize that putting the convicts at Sing-Sing to work dressing stone is cheaper than buying on the open market from free artisans. There is a riot. Some people have their houses attacked. They were put down by the 27th Regiment who camped in the park for some days. Then back to work, the convicts that is.

1849. By this time the Tredwell neighborhood had added some legitimate theatre to the mix. It seems there was a production of MacBeth on. MacReady, an Englishman, had been putting Forrest, the homegrown American, down in the press. This was supposed to sell tickets. Instead it inflamed nativist elements. The Order of United Americans had already hooted MacReady off the stage and closed one show. Now he was at it again. 20,000 people rioted on Lafayette Place between 4th and Third. The Seventh Regiment swung in. When the smoke cleared there were 31 people dead and more wounded. MacReady snuck out of town.

1854. Mercantile Library at Astor Place. McSorley opens his Alehouse (see 1970)

A Radical Political and Social History of the Lower East Side

1850. Tompkins Square Park opens.

1857. Police riot, Gang Riots, and Bread Riot and then on July 4-5, the Bowery Boys and the Dead Rabbits go at it in the Five Points area. From the diary of George Templeton Strong . . . .

> . . . the Old Police being disbanded and the New Police as yet inexperienced and imperfectly organized, we are in an insecure and unsettled state at present . . . . It seems to have been a battle between Irish Blackguardsmen and Native Bowery Blackguardsmen, the belligerents afterwards making common cause against the police and uniting to resist their common enemy.

Along Ave A that summer, there were bonfires and speeches. Then a riot for bread among unemployed workers that lasted days. A public works program building Central Park was instituted to employ them.

1859. Central Park opens. Cooper Union established to provide free education to workers.

1862. A.T. Stewart builds a department store on Astor Place (see 1956).

1863. Draft Riots.

1865. More than 15,000 dark airless tenements in lower Manhattan housing over 500,000 miserable souls.

1866. Seventh Regiment takes over Tompkins Square Park as a parade ground.

1871. The Paris Commune.

1872. Charles Loring Brace writes in *The Dangerous Classes of New York*, that in this tenement district "congregate some of the worst of the destitute population of the city — vagrants, beggars, nondescript thieves, broken down drunken vagabonds who manage as yet to keep out of the station houses, and the lowest and most bungling of the 'sharpers'.

1874. The [First]Tompkins Square Massacre. As 7000 men and women gather in Tompkins Square on Jan 13, organized by the International Working Association led by Karl Marx (not present) they listen to speeches about the First International. Mounted police charge the crowd injuring hundreds. Police commissioner Abram Duryee, "It was the most glorious sight I have ever seen . . . ." The park is closed in 1877. Three regiments of the National Guard are posted there.

1878. Tompkins Square reopened as a public park.

1879. Tenement Act of 1879, requiring light and air in every room creates the architecture of the dumbbell tenement.

1888. A delicatessen opens at Ludlow and E. Houston. In 1912 it will be named Katz's. The Temperance Fountain appears in Tompkins Square Park donated by the Moderation Society and paid for by a patent medicine salesman named Cogswell from San Francisco. Among other activities, the Moderations Society gave bouquets of flowers to the poor to brighten up their lives. Blizzard of '88- 20 in. of snow, 100 dead. After this power lines will be buried.

1898. Great consolidation. Five boroughs join to form New York City.

1899. Hebrew Actors Union founded at 31 E. 7th St.

1900. International Ladies Garment Workers Union founded at Labor Lyceum, 64 E. 4th St.

1903. Williamsburg Bridge opens.

1904. General Slocum disaster. Overnight the German population moves out to be replaced by Jewish, Slavic, African and Irish immigrants. Tompkins Square Branch Library built as part of the Carnegie library system opens to serve them. A new school, P.S. 64, is built to educate their children. (see 1964, 1998, hopefully 2006).

1907. Apr 17. 11,747 people processed through Ellis Island, highest number of immigrants in a single day. J.P. Morgan bails out the overextended NYC government with $30 million loan.

1909. Women's strike. A three month strike of shirtwaist makers, mostly teenage immigrant girls, against Lower East Side sweatshops. This is also known as the Uprising of the 20,000. It was settled in Feb., 1910 with better wages, working conditions and hours. (See 1911).

1910. Yonah Schimmel's Knishes opens at 137 E. Houston St.

1911. Mar 25. Fire at the Triangle Shirtwaist Company fire in the Asch Building, corner of Greene and Washington Place kills 146 women. Now something will be done about working conditions.

1912. The Modern School, an anarchist education experiment is established. The Armory Show in 69th Regimental Armory building at 25th and Lexington introduces modern art to the U.S.

1914. Overcrowding in public schools forces the city to turn away 70,000 immigrant children.

1916. Margaret Sanger arrested for distributing birth control information.

1917. U.S. enters WWI. There is tremendous opposition to the draft. The Espionage is passes which makes it illegal to 'undermine' the war effort. This is followed by the Sedition

A Radical Political and Social History of the Lower East Side

Act of 1918, allowing the Post Office to confiscate socialist literature. *"The Masses"* magazine is put on trial and closed down. Emma Goldman is arrested for opposing the draft (see 1919). Eugene V. Debs, Socialist is sentenced to jail for 10 years for counseling against the draft. 15,000 Blacks march down 5th Ave. in protest against E. St. Louis race riots. Leon Trotsky is living at 77 St. Marks Place, reporting for Novy Mir. After the revolution he returns to Russia.

1918. Flu epidemic kills 20 million worldwide. Meyer Lansky, 16, arrested for assault on Ludlow St. (see 2002).

1919. Palmer Raids. Emma Goldman and Alexander Berkman arrested at the Modern School, 104 E. 12th St., tried and deported to Russia. The New School for Social Research founded by Charles Beard, Thorsten Veblen, John Dewey and others opens. So does Ratners. The mayor convenes a "Committee on Rent Profiteering."

1920. Women get the vote. Prohibition. "Emergency Rent Laws" are passed giving tenants protection against huge rent increases. Attempted assassination of J.P. Morgan at St. George's Church. Successful bombing of J.P. Morgan Bank on Wall St.

1921. The Little Red Schoolhouse opens at 535 E. 16th St.

1923. New York population is 30% Jewish. It's the heyday of Yiddish Broadway on Second Ave. In 1926 the Yiddish Art Theatre will open on 2nd Ave. and 10th St.

1924. Tong War in Chinatown.

1925. New Immigration laws favor "Nordic" peoples. Africans and Asians barred. Southern and Eastern Europeans restricted. Robert Moses enters public life as president of the Long Island State Park Commission.

1927. American Communist Party moves from Chicago to 35 E. 12th St. Herbert Asbury publishes *"Gangs of New York."*

1928. Christodora House opens as a 17 story "skyscraper settlement house" at 147 Ave. B. Ageloff Towers is built to lure the affluent to LES. Strand Bookshop founded on 8th St.

1929. Oct. 29. Stock market crash. All rent regulations repealed. 7 blocks of tenements between Chrystie and Forsyth and Canal and Houston are destroyed for model apartments that were never built. Later this will becomes Sarah Delano Roosevelt Park. Tammany Hall dedicates new clubhouse at 4th Ave. and 17th St.

1930s. The word Smack for heroin originates on LES from Schmecker, the Yiddish word for taste. 17% of the City's population is of Italian descent. 50,000 people march at Communist Party rally at Union Square. Police ride into crowd swinging clubs.

1931. 100,000 people evicted because they cannot pay their rent. Street peddlers banned. Whitney Museum opens on 8th St.

1933. "Hard Luck Town," a shantytown on E. 9th and E. River houses 450 people. Chinese Hand Laundry Alliance of New York founded. It wins revocation of law closing Chinese laundries.

1934. Knickerbockers Village (see 1953). Prohibition ends. Fiorello LaGuardia is elected to his first of three terms as mayor.

1935. Franklin Roosevelt (Dem.) The New Deal.

1941. Robert Moses attempts to destroy Castle Clinton and Battery Park for bridge between Brooklyn and Manhattan. Instead the Brooklyn-Battery Tunnel is built. The historic preservation movement is born.

1943. Carlo Tresca assassinated by Carmine Galante outside his office at 2 W. 15th St. Mass migration of blacks from South to Harlem. Rent control established as an emergency wartime measure.

1944. White flight. GI bill and low cost mortgages = Levittown.

1947. Stuyvesant Town and Cooper Village built by Metropolitan Life Insurance Co. for returning G.I .s and their new families. Except blacks. "Cold War." House Un-American Activities Committee fights it in the theaters and bookshops of America. Robinson joins Brooklyn Dodgers.

1949. Jacob Riis Houses. Death of a Salesman opens.

1950.   Birdland opens on Broadway with Charlie Parker playing. Parker lives at 151 Ave B until 1954. Robert Moses appointed to head "Slum Clearance Committee."

1951. Stuyvesant Town forced to admit African-Americans. Dashiel Hammett goes to jail for refusing to divulge the location of 6 people arrested for being Communists.

1952. Nov 23. Peretz Square 1st Ave bet. E Houston and 1st St. is dedicated.

1953. The peak year of Puerto Rican immigration —over 58,000 in one year. This is the first mass migration by airplane. They have been recruited to work as cheap labor in factories. Allen Ginsberg and William Burroughs share an apt. on 7th between B &C. Julius and Ethel Rosenberg of Knickerbocker Village executed for spying for USSR.

1954. Army-McCarthy hearings. Abe Lebewohl (see 1996) opens the Second Avenue Deli (see 2005). He installs a sidewalk "Walkway of Yiddish Actors" honoring the stars of Yiddish Second Avenue Broadway (see 1923) in front of the restaurant. Joseph Papp stages his first

A Radical Political and Social History of the Lower East Side

season of Shakespeare at the East River Amphitheatre. Puerto Rican Nationalists led by Lolita Lebron open gunfire during a session of Congress.

1955. 29% of the city is African-American or Puerto Rican. The Mitchell-Lama Act is passed in the New York State Legislature. In exchange for real property tax exemptions and subsidized loans, 269 buildings with 105,000 apartments will be built (see 1991). Jerome Robbins and Arthur Laurents begin discussing the idea that will become West Side Story by Leonard Bernstein and Stephen Sondheim with Robbins as choreographer in 1957. The AFL and the CIO merge. The last segment of the Third Avenue El from Chatham Sq., near City Hall to just below 149th Street in the Bronx is torn down beginning May 12, 1955. June 15. Judith Malina, Julian Beck and others are arrested for refusing to take shelter during an "Air Raid" drill. Plans are announced for a Second Avenue subway. The *Village Voice* appears. Joan Mitchell advises David Amram to move to the Lower East Side. She calls it an island within an island.

1956. Federal Highway funds and Robert Moses widen E. Houston St. (see 1958). The East Village is detached from the traditional Lower East Side. Blocks of tenements bull-dozed. East of A, the Lower East Side Neighborhood Assn. (LENA) is formed. They will create Mobilization for Youth (see 1961). An African-American art scene is flourishing in the neighborhood. Galerie Fantastique owned by Ted Joan opens at 108 St. Marks Place. George Nelson Preston will open the Artist's Studio at 48 E. 3rd St. The sound track is jazz — The Five Spot with Thelonius Monk, Slugs at 242 E. 3rd. The Strand moves to Broadway & E. 12th St. The old A.T. Stewart dept. store on Astor Place burns and is replaced by a white brick apartment building. Allen Ginsberg publishes "*Howl*."

1957. Norman Mailer published "*The White Negro*." Jack Kerouac published "*On the Road*." His picture is taken on E. 11th St. Baruch Houses.

1958. The West Village Committee led by Jane Jacobs successfully thwarts Robert Mose's proposal for Washington Square Park — a curved and sunken four-lane highway through the middle with a pedestrian bridge in the center. In a few months it will be closed to all traffic.

1959. Cooper Square Committee is founded to fight a plan to demolish blocks of tenements between Delancey and E. 9th that would displace over 7,000 people (see 2004). This has been called the peak year of gang activity. Frank O'Hara moves far east on 9th St. Allan Kaprow produces "*18 Happenings in Six Parts at the Reuben Gallery on 4th Ave.*" "*Pull My Daisy*" by Robert Frank filmed in Alfred Leslie's loft on 4th Ave.

1960. Feb 7. First mention of the term East Village in the *New York Times*. WBAI is on the air.

LaMama Theater, 74 A E. 4th St. 10th St. Coffee House. War Resistor's League purchases building at 339 Lafayette St. after being raided at their former HQ near City Hall.

"For Two Cents Plain," Harry Golden's best-selling memoir of Jewish Lower East Side. Seward Park Houses. The *Village Voice* names the area east of B 'Apeland'. Heroin is for sale in an open market at Ave C. and Fifth St. And everything that goes with it. Decline of NY waterfront as container ships are routed to Port Elizabeth.

1961. Claes Oldenburg opens STORE at 107 E. 2nd St. Diane di Prima publishes *"The Floating Bear"* from 309 E. Houston St. Apr. 9. Police crackdown on folksingers in Washington Square Park. John Mitchell of the Gaslight leads protesters into the Judson Church. Folkies win in court. Cabaret Law is extended to coffee houses which have poetry readings. No poetry without a License. Known as the Coffee House Law. Apr. 11 Bob Dylan performs in NYC, opening for John Lee Hooker. First U.S. military arrives in Viet Nam.

1962. Estimates that $600 million in goods are lost annually due to theft by heroin addicts. Naked Lunch is published. Poetry coffee houses along Ave. B: The Annex, Mazur's and Stanley's. Stanley's closes in 1966. New York Poet's Theater at 85 E. 4th St. Shakespeare in the Park moves from East River Park to Central Park. Velvet Underground. International Typographical Union strike closes 9 NYC newspapers for 114 days. Mobilization for Youth a program for counseling delinquent youth developed by LENA receives federal funds.

1964. Jan. 1. First New Years Day Poetry Marathon at St. Marks Poetry Project. Jackson MacLow arrested at Cafe Le Metro, 149 Second Ave., for reading poetry without a License. Jonas Mekas and Ken Jacobs arrested for screening *"Flaming Creatures"* at the Bridge Theater on St. Marks. The film is banned in New York State. Free Speech Movement begins in Berkeley. Chatham Towers rise at 170 Park Row.

1965. Feb. 21 Malcolm X assassinated. Riots in all major American cities. Peace-Eye Books opens at 338 E. 10th St. The Fugs debut at the opening party at Stanley's. Real Great Society (now CHARAS) builds domes with Buckminster Fuller in vacant lot, corner 9th St. and Ave. C. Sun Ra has a steady Monday night gig at Slugs. Landmarks Preservation Commission established in NYC on the grave of Penn Station. First loft conversions in SoHo. Blackout.

1966. "New York is a Fun City." — John Lindsay. Heroin use on LES is 38.6 per thousand residents compared with citywide average of 22.9. Bernard Rosenthal's Alamo is installed at Astor Place as a temporary piece. Andy Warhol stages "Exploding Plastic Inevitable" at DOM soon to be Electric Circus. Bandshell erected in Tompkins Square Park. Abbie Hoffman leads first anti-Viet Nam march kicking off from Tompkins Square Park. Peace Eye Books raided and closed. Psychedelicatessen raided and closed. Peace-Eye will reopen at 147 Ave. A. International Society for Krishna Consciousness (Hare Krishnas) founded in Tompkins Square Park. Timothy Leary founds League for Spiritual Discovery with LSD and marijuana to be legalized as religious sacraments.

1967. Jan. 1. The Yippies founded in Abby Hoffman's apt. at 30 St. Mark's Place. The Summer of Love. Popularization of the word "hippie." 50,000 march in D.C. The Fugs and Ginsberg attempt to levitate/exorcise the Pentagon. 70,000 march in NYC. Smoke-in at Tompkins Square Park busted. The "Groovy Murders," James Hutchinson and Linda Fitzpatrick

A Radical Political and Social History of the Lower East Side

found bludgeoned at 169 Ave. B, lead to newspaper phrase — "generation gap." Muhammad Ali stripped of his title for refusing induction. Secret funding from CIA revealed for 30 organizations in education, law, religion, journalism and labor. Race riots in Newark, Detroit and 125 other cities. University of the Streets founded at 7th and Ave. A. Village East Towers rise on Ave. C, a Mitchell-Lama project.

1968. Murder rate in NYC has doubled since 1960. Lillian Wald Houses. In March the Filmore East opens. It will close in 1971. Columbia University student strike. Martin Luther King assassinated. Robert Kennedy assassinated. Riots in Harlem. Black Panther Party opens an office in NYC. Two month teachers strike promotes decentralization of schools and community school boards (see 2002). Lower East Side Print Shop founded to provide activities for children. Later this becomes one of the founding organizations of Seven Loaves. Yippies nominate a pig for president at Democratic National Convention in Chicago. Police riot leading to trial of Chicago 7.

1969. Stonewall riots launches gay rights movement. Sam Melville of 69 E. 2nd St., bombs Army Induction Center on Whitehall St., Marine Midland Bank, General Motors Building, RCA Building and Chase Manhattan Bank "in support of the NLF, legalized marijuana, love, Cuba, legalized abortion, and all the American revolutionaries and GIs who are winning the war against the Pentagon. Nixon, surrender now!" Sentenced to 18 years, he died in the 1971 Attica uprising. The Attorney General calls for repression of "ideological criminals." The Weather Underground bombs Criminal Courts Building. It is said that Redlining of LES began this year. There was definitely an unchecked heroin epidemic. Yuri Kapralov remembered that residents of E. 7th St. between B and C petition for police protection from robberies but there was no response. Young Lords founded. And. Man walks on moon. Woodstock.

1970. Redlining. In addition, a policy of "Spatial Deconcentration" instituted through Daniel Moynihan's policy of "Benign Neglect" is promoted as a way of emptying the inner-city of minorities, so that it can be rebuilt for the middle classes. An epidemic of fires, ad hoc and disorganized squatting in buildings abandoned by landlords who can no longer get insurance. Lowe's Ave. B movie theater becomes American Nursing Home.

1971. New York Times published article on graffiti artist Taki 183. Weather Underground blow themselves up in a townhouse on W. 11th St. Women allowed into McSorley's. In NYC protesters in the Wall St. area are attacked by hard-hats and Wall St. white collar workers. Adam Clayton Powell loses his seat to Charles Rangel after redistricting.

New York is now the "Big Apple." A.I.R. zoning exception in SoHo. Interfaith-Adopt-a-Building established (see 2005). Rockefeller signs legislation to move rent-controlled apartments to market rate as residents die or move out. 421-A program offers tax breaks to developers who build market rate housing in low income neighborhoods. Young Lords lead evicted tenants back into their buildings in the Times Square area — Operation Move-In. Filmore East closes. Castelli opens on W. Broadway. Viet Nam Vets against the War return their medals. Women's Equality March on 5th Ave. Attica.

1972. Between 1972-1975 there is a 25% reduction of police and fire service. Gregory Foster and Rocco Laurie, two cops, are gunned down at 11th & B. A communication is received from the George Jackson Squad of the Black Liberation Army. By 1973 eighty-three neighborhood tenant organizations existed in New York City, sixty-seven of which had been founded since 1969. Over one hundred service centers funded by the federal Office of Economic Opportunity also claimed to serve tenants. Read *"Mau Mauing the Flak Catchers"* by Tom Wolfe (1970). On his own, Adam Purple moves to 184 Forsyth St. He begins the Garden of Eden in the rubble of a burned tenement across from his building. Eventually it will encompass 5 lots and have 45 fruit and nut trees along with countless flowers and herbs (see 1986). United Graffiti Artists formed to promote graffiti as an art form.

1973. SoHo is designated a historic district. First Community Garden and Farm founded on a vacant lot on Bowery & Houston by Liz Christy and the Green Guerrillas. CBGB's opens (see 2005). Kenkelaba House founded on the Bowery by Joe Overstreet and Corinne Jennings (see 1978). West Side Highway collapses near Gansevoort Market. Ground broken for World Trade Center. Abortion legalized. Seward Park Extension. Watergate hearings. Last U.S. troops leave Viet Nam War. AIM occupation at Wounded Knee. Arab Oil Embargo. Worldwide economic depression. Universal Zulu Nation founded on Nov. 12 — the birth of Hip-Hop. The Nuyorican Poets Cafe began as a living room salon in the East Village apartment of writer and poet, Miguel Algarin.

1974. NYC faces bankruptcy. City workforce slashed, frozen wages, and a restructured the budget. More New Yorkers die of Methadone poisoning than from heroin overdoses. Yuri Kapralov writes his memoir of the East Village. *"Short Eyes"* by Miguel Piñero. Bimbo Rivas coins the term for the area east of Ave. B — "Loisaida," Spanglish for Lower East Side. Norman Mailer writes *"Faith of Graffiti."* Waterside Plaza built with 421-A tax breaks. Catholic Workers move to 55 E. 3rd St. Jewish Daily Forward building sold.

1975. FORD TO CITY: DROP DEAD. Massive national unemployment and inflation. 1.2 million New Yorkers on Welfare. 13,000 fires in the South Bronx. Nuyorican Poet's Café moves to an old Irish Bar, "The Sunshine Café" on E. 6th St. In 1980 they will purchase an "in-rem" building at 236 E. 6th St. *"BAD"* by Andy Warhol and Paul Morrissey about a family of Puerto Rican heroin dealers glamorizes drugs. Section 8 housing for blocks E. Houston, Stanton, Bridge and Pitt Sts. Christodora House sold at Public Auction for $62,000. Battery Park City breaks ground. FALN bombing of Fraunces Tavern. 50,000 gather in Central Park to celebrate end of Viet Nam War. Blackout.

1976. Abe Beame's Commissioner of Housing publishes an article advocating "planned shrinkage" "Planned shrinkage is the recognition that the golden door to full participation in American life and the American economy is no longer to be found in New York." At that time, New York City had a population of 7.5 million. Starr decreed that, "New York would continue to be a world city [sic] even with fewer than 5 million people. This led to only one conclusion: forcibly killing or expelling one-third of the city's population." Zoning allows landlords to charge 1000% more for space used for offices than those used for manufacturing. City loses more manufacturing jobs. CUNY begins to charge tuition. La Plaza Cultural is cleared, designed and planted by Chino Garcia (of CHARAS/El Bohio), Slimma Williams and

A Radical Political and Social History of the Lower East Side

Liz Christy. 519 E. 11th St. taken over by residents who install windmills and solar panels for power. "*Punk*" magazine by Leggs McNeil, John Holstrom and Ged Dunn. Lady Carpenters founded at 19 St. Marks to train women in construction trades. This will become All-Crafts Center (see 2003).

1977. The Summer of Sam. Blank Generation, Richard Hell and the Voidoids. Jul 15. Blackout with extensive looting. 1,000 fires burn, 3,776 people arrested in the largest mass arrest in city history. Revised City Charter creates 59 Community Boards. Con-Ed loses its battle with 519 E. 11th St. They must buy excess power generated by its windmill. Manic Panic opens at 33 St. Marks. "Everything for Everybody" buys 131 Ave. B. Mickey Melendez and former Young Lord Party members take over Statue of Liberty and cover it with the Puerto Rican flag. Confucius Plaza opens.

1978. Ed (Pooper Scooper) Koch is mayor. Federal Government loans NYC 1.65 billion dollars — CETA Program employs artists; Governmental Green Thumb program for community gardens begins. Interfaith Adopt-a-Building is active. Kenkelaba Gallery moves to Second St. and Ave. B. Carter imposes wage-price guidelines. "*Delirious New York*" by Rem Koolhass forsees Manhattan as a theme park. Nova Convention at Entermedia Theater.

1979. Tenant Interim Lease Program (TIL) established by city to enable tenants in city-owned buildings to operate their buildings. RAIN founded and begins to operate 641 E. 11th St. and 606 E. 4th St. Anthology Film Archives opens at 32-34 Second Ave. P.S. 122 founded by Charles Moulton in an abandoned school. Armando Perez, Chino Garcia, Robert Nazario, known as CHARAS and the Seven Loafs, found El Bohio in P.S. 64, the abandoned school on E. 9th St. Rockefeller drug laws. Iranian oil crisis allows fuel surcharges to rent stabilized buildings. Lines at gas stations. Iran hostage crisis. Three Mile Island Nuclear accident.

1980. NYC population is 7,071,649 — lowest since 1930. Real Estate Show. ABC No Rio founded. Transit strike lasting 11 days. High Line closes. Oct. 3 Leak at Indian Point Nuclear Facility. Dec. 8 John Lennon murdered.

1981. City puts together a Homesteading Program for vacant buildings. Reagan frees the hostages and fires air traffic controllers. First AIDS cases reported. Jack Henry Abbott shoots Richard Adan in Binibon. Binibon closes. Fun Gallery and 51X.

1982. Cooper Square Committee builds low-income high rise on 4th and Bowery. Barracks style shelters are opened to contain growing homeless population. LESCAC (Lower East Side Catholic Area Conference) formed to create low cost housing. Other organizations active at this time: LAND, ITS TIME, LEAP. First residents move into Battery Park City. "*The Message*" by Grandmaster Flash and the Furious Five. 1 million people protest for end to nuclear arms and power at Central Park.

1983. Pat Hearn Gallery opens on Ave. B & 6th. 8BC opens at 337 E. 8th. Sold in 1985. Mar. 14 "1,112 Dead and Counting," Larry Kramer's AIDS wakeup call in "*Native.*" Klaus Nomi dead of AIDS. Proposal for 51 units on E. 8th between B&C and Forsyth St. for artists housing (AHOP) is defeated. 30 housing groups have joined together as JPC (Joint Planning Council) to fight this on grounds of race. Trump Tower. Office building boom in Lower Manhattan. Graffiti artist Michael Griffith beaten to death by police.

1984. *"Bright Lights Big City,"* Jay McInerney. *Wall St. Journal* announces that the art scene had moved to E. Village. Jan. 17 Operation Pressure Point closes open-air drug market at Ave. B & 2nd St. Cop on every corner. 3000 arrests in 3 months. Community Land Trusts established. LESCAC (Lower East Side Catholic Area Conference) purchases 17 buildings which are sold to tenants. May. Eleanor Bumpers killed by police during an eviction. Dec. Bernhard Goetz shoots 4 muggers on an IRT train.

1985. Christodora house sold for $3.5 million. St. Mark's Baths and other gay bathhouses closed by NYC Dept. of Health in response to AIDS. *"Desperately Seeking Susan"* opens wide. Zeckendorf Towers on Union Square. Grand Central Station bars homeless people. Murders rise after six-year decline

1986. Koch announces massive city-financed housing program — the "Cross-Subsidy" program. Kalikow family buys 10 buildings in LES. Joint Planning Council (JPC), opposed to "Cross-Subsidy" program. Joint Planning Council march on City Hall "This Land is Ours." Adam Purple's Garden destroyed. Jan 17. Theater for the New City moves to 1st Ave. Retail Market (see 1998). They were evicted from their original location across from St. Mark's church. NYU builds skyscraper Alumni Hall on 3rd & 10th St. Street Research Group — State Police undercover as drug addicts. NYC homeless population reaches 4000. A dozen Koch administration officials exposed for corruption. Donald Manes, Queens Borough President commits suicide. Crack arrives.

1987. Oct. 19 Stock Market crash. Civilians allowed on Civilian Complaint Board Jun 23. 50/50 Cross-Subsidy Plan is finalized. 5, 662 vacant buildings in the city. Temple of the Rainbow Kitchen serves 300-500 meals per day at 9th and C. Pueblo Nuevo tenants organize to fight drug dealers. June 21. Sen. Alfonse D'Amato channels $1.5 million in U.S. government funds to LES Catholic Conference for rehabilitation of 66 Ave. C. BASTA formed to pressure the city to close the E. 3rd St. Shelter. Antonio Pagan finds his base. Grand St. Coops cited for racist policies. Board of Ed. Inspector General reports that over the last 16 yrs. School Districts 1 & 3 have lost millions of dollars with excessive hiring of personnel and other expenses (see 1968). East Village galleries move out. Han Haacke's first one man show canceled by Guggenheim over piece about Harry Shapolsky's real estate dealings.

1988. Summer. Tompkins Square Neighborhood Association led by Antonio Pagan pressures CB3 to remove homeless (see 1991). Mayor announces curfew in all city parks. Aug 6-7 Tompkins Square Park Anti-Curfew Protest. Police riot. Christodora House attacked. 147 civil complaints. Aug. 10 March on the 9th Precinct. Curfew lifted for Tompkins Square Park. Miguel Piñero dies. *"Slaves of New York"* begins filming. Lower East Side Tenement Museum opens. Homeless encampment at City Hall lasts for 50 days. Jun. 12 60,000 march for nuclear disarmament. Tawana Brawley case. Yussef Hawkins murdered in racial attack in Bensonhurst. Jun. 12 60,000 march for nuclear disarmament. 17,800 homeless in New York

A Radical Political and Social History of the Lower East Side

City. 4 million dollar a year cocaine empire of Alejandro "The Man" Lopez cracked at 507 East 11th St.

1989. Jan. 27 East Village Scene declared "dead" by *Village Voice*. May 2 Frank Morales' squat, 319 E. 8th St. demolished. Jul. 5 Tent City destroyed by police. Homeless evicted from Tompkins Square Park in a 3 day battle. Squatters erect flag tents. Aug. 19 Con-Ed explosion on Park Ave. South. Aug. 31 Day of Outrage. Tompkins Square Task Force, comprised of citizens is set up to investigate police activities. They recommend that more civilians be allowed on the Civilian Complaint Review Board. In 1993 the Civilian Complaint Review Board became entirely civilian. Sept. 12 attempted demolition of Umbrella House. Oct. 6. Housing NOW marches on D.C. Oct. 26 Police attack & occupy ABC Community Center on 4th & A. Dec. 14 Tompkins Square Park Tent City demolished.

1990. *Time Magazine* features New York in a story called "New York: The Rotting Apple." Homicides peak at 2, 263. David Dinkins is the mayor. Meier Kahane, founder of the Jewish Defense League, assassinated in a Manhattan hotel by El Sayid Nosair, an Arab terrorist. Nosair is acquitted (see 1993). March 15. Fire at 7th St. Squat. Apr. 5. CB 3 votes not to have a curfew at Tompkins Square Park. May 1. Squatter May Day. Police turn out the lights at Spy v. Spy concert in the bandshell. Riot. 12 arrested. May 23. 90 Wall Street March. May 31 TAP protest Tompkins Square Park closing. Oct. 6 Rage On-Housing Now Demonstration. Tompkins Square Park exhibit at Municipal Art Society. Daniel Rakowitz murders Monika Beerle. Accused of serving body parts to the homeless in Tompkins Square Park.

1991. Antonio Pagan, director of Lower East Side Coalition Housing Development (LESCHD) wins City Council seat from Miriam Friedlander — without support from the Joint Planning Council. Pagan has financial support of developers and contractors. He is building low-cost housing that will be able to be sold at market rate. He labels squatters "yuppie gentrifiers disguising themselves in revolutionary garb to get free rent." By early '90s 32 buildings on LES were squatted. Dinkins vows to remove squatters from all city-owned buildings. LESCHD attempted to get squat buildings. Pagan elected with financial support of real estate developers and contractors. The Mitchell-Lama Act is amended to make some buildings easier to buy out and turn into market rate. Reconstruction of Williamsburg Bridge begins. May 27. Riot on Ave. A. May 31. Riot during "Housing is a Human Right" concert. Tompkins Square Park ordered closed for "renovations." The Bandshell is demolished (see 1966). Hands around the Park protest of its closing. Followed by Art Around the Park sponsored by restaurants and real estate offices. Followed by the first double-decker tour buses. Jun 3. Housing Conference at All-Crafts Center (see 1976, 2003). Jul 11. Rage On women's march. Aug. Crown Heights Riot. Sept 18. Squat eviction on 3rd St. Oct. 12 Squat protest. Nov. 10 Squatter's Ball. Dec. 14 Homeless evicted from the park. Dec 22. Homeless march on Union Square. Shantytown on E. 6th St. bulldozed. Last remnants of Adam Purple's garden bulldozed..

1992. Cooper Union dorm at 9th St. and 3rd Ave breaks the height barrier and wins an award. Tompkins Square Park reopens with curfew. Jan 6. Keith Thompson funeral. Followed by the Mark Fisher funeral procession. And Jon Greenburg's open casket funeral in

Tompkins Square Park. Shantytown with landmark teepee under Manhattan Bridge torched. The squat at Houston and Clinton St. collapses. Pest Squat evicted.

1993. Commercial real estate slump. City unemployment rate reaches 13.8 percent. Terrorist bomb at World Trade Center kills 6. El Sayid Nosair (see 1990) implicated and receives life sentence. G.G. Allin's last performance — Gas Station, 2 & B. 150 low-income Latino families squatting at 670 and 675 E. 170th St. are evicted by 200 cops. Shantytown at 4th & D burns. Loss of Satan's Sinner Nomads HQ. Steve Cannon starts Tribes Gallery. Father Pat arrested for Brinks robbery to aid IRA. In 1994 he will be sentenced and spend almost 4 years in prison.

1994. Giuliani Time. First Republican mayor since 1965. May 30 17 arrested in Tompkins Square Park. Sept. 5 Squatters Day on E. 13th St. — attempt to gain positive publicity for squat movement. The Inside Out Show. Nov. Squatters sue to gain possession of 535-545 E. 13th St. City-ordered inspection of squats. Restraining order preventing evictions of 537, 539, 541 545, E. 13th St. Nov 28 Glass House evicted.

1995. Workfare program initiated. Capitol punishment reinstituted in New York. Feb. 643 E. 9th St. burns to the ground. Apr. 541 & 545 E. 13th ordered evicted because of imminent collapse. Restraining order. May 25. Restraining order lifted. City attempts to give building to LESCHD chaired by Antonio Pagan. May 31. 541 and 545 E. 13th St. evicted. Sign goes up "Affordable Housing for New Yorkers." Buildings will revert to market rate. Jun 3. Protests. Injunction against eviction. Sept. Police raid party at Plaza Cultural garden. Oct. 11. Hellraiser heroin brand on Ludlow St. busted by DEA. Eliza Izquierdo dead from horrendous abuse and city neglect. Child Welfare Administration overhauled. Pope celebrates mass in Giant Stadium.

1996. Feb 16. Occupation of B'Nai Moses, 317 E. 8th St. Aug. 8 13th St. injunction overturned. Aug 13. Police occupation of 13th St. between A & B. Riot cops and armored tank. 535, 537 and 539 E. 13th St. squats demolished for "low income housing." Aug 14. Siege of Glass House, attempt to reoccupy the building. 30 arrested in protest in Tompkins Square. Sept. 11. Housing march on City Hall. Minimum wage raised to $5.15. Plaque honoring Jack Kerouac dedicated at 133-01 Crossbay Blvd., Queens.

1997. Jan. City owns 1,325 vacant buildings. Census figures show the East Village has a 64,756 population with a median household income of $34,201. Feb. Fire at 537-539 E. 5th St. Squatters evicted by the Fire Department. Buildings demolished. Mar. 4 Abe Lebewohl of the Second Avenue Deli shot and killed in a daylight robbery. Case never solved (see 2006). April 5. Allen Ginsberg dies. Giuliani bans firecrackers for Chinese New Years and July 4 celebrations. U.S. Labor Dept. investigates sweatshops in Chinatown. Police raid apartment in Brooklyn and capture terrorists planning to bomb NYC subways. Dec. 30 Mendez Garden protest. Theater for the New City and NYC Economic Development Corp. sell air rights over 2-story city market that has housed it since 1986. (See 2001). "Rent" debuts.

A Radical Political and Social History of the Lower East Side

1998. Giuliani reinauguration is disrupted by community garden protesters. On 5 January, protesters block traffic in front of the offices of the New York City Partnership. Jan 24. 172 Stanton St. bulldozed. March. Three gardens sold off. April. Transfer of 741 Green Thumb Gardens to HPD. There are more that 11,000 truly vacant lots in the city. Mar. 31 Police Brutality protest. July 20. In a city auction at 1 Police Plaza, disrupted by the release of hundreds of crickets, CHARAS/El Bohio is put on the block and sold to Greg Singer. CHARAS occupied. CUNY ends open admissions.

1999. Armando Perez murdered in Queens. Jan. 10 HPD announces auction of 112 community gardens." Jan. 15 Grand St. Garage collapses. Feb. 4. Amadou Diallo shot down by cops. Al Sharpton leads protest across Brooklyn Bridge. Feb. 24 Community Garden protests at City Hall. Apr. 11. Reclaim the Streets protest on Ave. A blocks traffic for hours. Apr. 27. Dos Blocos eviction (713 E. 9th St.). Building sold to private developer for $285,000. 13 of 22 residents charged with "obstruction of governmental administration." May 5. 62 people arrested doing Civil Disobedience at Chambers St. and West Side Highway. Giuliani: "This is a free-market economy. The era of communism is over. May 11. Trust for Public Land and New York Restoration Project buy many gardens, spending $4 million dollars. Aug. 40,000 gather in Central Park to hear Dali Lama. Giuliani administration begins negotiations with the squats through UHAB.

2000. Feb. 15. El Jardin de Esperanza on E. 7th St. bulldozed. Protest catches attention of Attorney General Elliot Spitzer. He issues an injunction against further sale of community gardens.

2001. A deal structured with the city's Economic Development Corp. results in a 17-story luxury residential tower atop Theater for New City, 155 First Ave. Greg Singer evicts CHARAS/El Bohio from E. 9th St. Jun 26. The Squat Settlement. 11 out of 12 remaining squats opt in. They are: 292 E. 3rd St. aka Bullet Space; 719 E. 6th St.; 209 E. 7th St.; 274 E. 7th St. aka Rainbow Coop; 278 E. 7th St.; 733 E. 9th St. aka Serenity; 377 E. 10th St.; 544 E. 13th St.; 7-Second Ave.; 21-23 Ave. C aka Umbrella House and 155 Ave. C aka C Squat. 272 E. 7th stays out of the deal. Sept. 11. World Trade Center mass murder

2002. Mayor Michael Bloomberg Jul. 21 Con Ed explosion at 14th St. plant. Blackout. School decentralization declared a failure. Local school boards closed. (see 1968, 1987). Sep 18. Sept. Eliot Spitzer settles suit against NYC. Many Green Thumb gardens become Parks Dept. leases. Sep 29. Ratner's closes.

2003. Faux-historical condos with chain restaurants in the bottom replace the All-Crafts-Center-Electric Circus-DOM. Aug. 21-26 First Howl Festival opens with Allen Ginsberg Poetry Festival. New York Public Library closed Mondays.

2004. Aug. 1800 jailed in a week of protests around the Republican National Convention. Times-Up and Greene Dragon open things with a wild revolutionary bike ride from Central Park to Webster Hall. Who's War?

Laura Zelasnic

2005. NYU dorm at 81 E. 3rd St. opens as a community facility, 7 stories higher than zoning law allows. NYU plans a 17-story dorm on 12th St. and 3rd Ave. Residents of 47 E. 3rd St. fight eviction as new landlord claims the whole building as a one family residence. Residents of 528 E. 11th St. and 390 E. 8th battle Interfaith-Adopt-A-Building over self-management CBGB's fights and loses eviction case. Housing Activists march on Battery Park City: Where are the 24,000 units of low income housing that the developers were supposed to deliver in exchange for the tax breaks and government bond issues?

2006. 2nd Ave. Deli closed. Residents of 47 E. 3rd St. win permanent injunction against landlord converting it to one family residence. The LES has changed it will never be what it was before.

Chapter 15

Poems
Housing, Preservation, & Development
    By Tom Savage for Shari Woodard

"My landlord's lawyer aspires
To be a phony but, in fact,
He can't even get that far
Just like his boss would like
To think himself a Mafia don
But remains just an ex-tailor
From Brooklyn who terrifies
His tenants but can't even force
Us to move from his collapsing
Building, full of junkies and dealers
Who, like his lawyer with the limp
That gets worse when he's looking to
A judge or jury for sympathy, are
Also in the landlord's employ.

"When we found out our rights
And stopped paying rent he found
He couldn't evict and began threatening
To burn the building down. I contacted
'Arson Watch' care of the NY Police
So when a mysterious fire damaged
The building next door also in
This landlord's possession, he claimed
To the Fire Dept. that he no longer
Owned the place but was back here
The next day to find out if his efforts
Had finally succeeded in driving out
Any of his rent controlled tenants
Or had merely interfered with the flow
Of business in cocaine and crack
Out of which he attempts to make up
For the rents he will never see again

1986

This poem was first published in the book "*Housing, Preservation, & Development:Poems by Tom Savage,*" New York, Cheap Review Press, 1988.84 pgs.

Chapter 16

Poems By Will Sales - Art by Mac McGill

Drawing by Mac McGill

Will Sales Poems

Scattered through the graveyard
of wasted city blocks,
are the snaggletoothed hollow-eyed shells
of abandoned buildings,
standing like old wounded animals,
waiting to die.

Drawing by Mac McGill

Drawing by Mac McGill

Drawing by Mac McGill

Drawing by Mac McGill

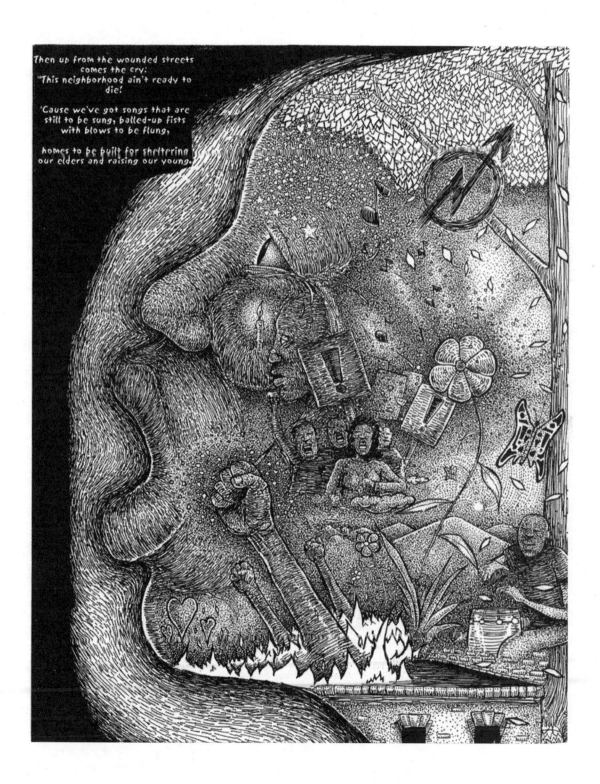

Drawing by Mac McGill

Will Sales Poems

So sing your death song in some
other tounge
and do your death dance on someone else's stage.

No! This neighborhood ain't ready
to give up the ghost.

We're planning on living our lives
to the very utmost.
To live, not die,
To live.

Drawing by Mac McGill

A Radical Political and Social History of the Lower East Side

Photographs By Clayton Patterson

261

Tompkins Square: Chino Garcia, Dan Biele of the Diggers, Robert Boardman Vaughn, Fred Good, of the Real Society, 1967

From left to right: R. Buckminster Fuller and Fred Good at the University of the Streets, 1968

Fred Good, Angelo Giordani of the Real Great Society East Harlem Branch, Chino Garcia and Angelo Gonzalez in the foreground Harvard, 1966

Photographs from Fred Good archives

Homeless sleeping on the corner of
Houston and 1st Street, 1988

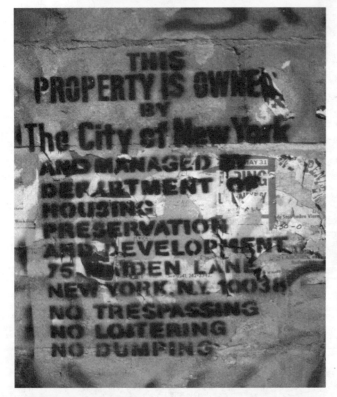

A stencil on Ludlow Street, one of the many
abandoned city owned properties, 1988

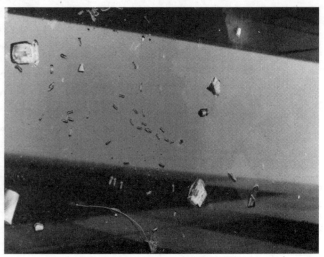

empty crack vials by entrance to 100
Center Street Criminal Courthouse, 1989

THE NEW YORK TIMES, WEDNESDAY, SEPTEMBER 7, 1988

Man Jailed for Refusing To Give Up Melee Tape

By CONTANCE L. HAYS

Defying a court order and disclaiming professional legal help, a Manhattan artist refused again yesterday to surrender his videotape of police officers and demonstrators clashing in Tompkins Square Park and was jailed for contempt.

The artist, Clayton Patterson, 39 years old, of 161 Essex Street on the Lower East Side, was led from the courtroom in handcuffs after acting Justice Richard B. Lowe 3d of State Supreme Court pronounced him guilty of civil contempt and ordered him to jail for at least 90 days.

A dozen supporters of Mr. Patterson attending the hearing, at State Supreme Court in Manhattan, broke into applause and shouted, "Free Clayton

The four-hour tape, which was viewed last month by The New York Times, shows police officers striking demonstrators with nightsticks and some officers wearing badges with their numbers concealed.

Just before a hearing on the charge began Thursday afternoon, Mr. Patterson dismissed Mr. Maddox and said he wanted to represent himself. Judge Lowe adjourned the hearing until yesterday, released Mr. Patterson on his own recognizance and appointed a lawyer for him, saying he did not want to proceed otherwise.

Mr. Patterson told the judge yesterday, however, that he did not want his court-appointed lawyer, Gerry Rosen, to represent him. At one point, when Mr. Rosen whispered, "They're going to toss you in jail," Mr. Patterson interrupted him, saying, "Excuse me. You're not wanted here. And I'm not interested, for the 100th time, in what it is you have to say."

Action 'Hampers' Investigation

After questioning the defendant, the judge said he was satisfied that Mr. Patterson understood what he was taking on in becoming his own lawyer. Mr. Patterson is a sculptor and painter and an embroiderer of hats. He and his wife, Elsa Rensaa, run a hat store, Clayton Hats, at 161 Essex Street.

The Manhattan District Attorney, Robert M. Morgenthau, said in a statement yesterday that Mr. Patterson's action "hampers the grand jury's efforts to investigate allegations of illegal police conduct." At least one copy of the tape exists, Mr. Patterson has said, but it is not known where it is.

In an impassioned statement to the court, Mr. Patterson told the court that he was not going to turn over the videotape because of his concerns about

The New York Times/Wei Wei Ai

Clayton Patterson, who has refused to surrender his videotape of the Tompkins Square confrontation, before he was sentenced yesterday to 90 days in jail for civil contempt.

conditions in New York City, ranging from crime to homelessness.

"It's my belief that in America, there's a certain time to stand up for your rights," he said, when asked by Judge Lowe why he would not produce the tape. "It's my belief that it is wrong for the police to beat up and maim and kill people. It's wrong for the drug dealers never to go to jail and for there to be large amounts of illegal activities. It's wrong for the Mayor to separate himself from his constituents. It's wrong for the District Attorney never to effectively prosecute the police, and it's wrong to have blocks of empty buildings and the streets filled with homeless people."

He concluded, "This is not a racial issue, but an issue that involves everyone in this city. I think my going to jail works as a statement towards that."

When asked by Judge Lowe yesterday whether his refusal to turn over the videotape was a publicity stunt, Mr. Patterson denied it.

His arguments did not convince the judge. "I don't think the law is adequately served by making martyrs out of people who want to be martyrs," Judge Lowe said in delivering his verdict. "I also don't think the law is served when the law is flouted."

Mr. Patterson was sent to a special section of the Bronx House of Detention for Men for 90 days.

The defendant is protesting crime in the city.

Patterson!" and "This court is in contempt!"

Mr. Patterson's videotape of the Tompkins Square incident on the night of Aug. 6 was subpoenaed last month by a Manhattan grand jury investigating allegations of police brutality and misconduct.

Maddox Was Dismissed

Mr. Patterson was arrested last Thursday after his lawyer at the time, Alton H. Maddox, filed a letter telling the grand jury that the tape had been given to a Michigan Congressman, John Conyers, chairman of the House Subcommittee on Criminal Justice.

Why Does The
Government Own All
Of The Abandoned
Property? 1989

Principals of the NYC, Black owned newspapers and activists, Rev. Al Sharpton (not visible), C Vernon Mason (right glasses), Tawana Brawley (left front) Alton Maddox, (left standing glasses) families of victims killed by NYPD, and Clayton Patterson (TSP police brutality representative) have a special meeting with Congressman John Conyers in Washington DC, 1989

A Radical Political and Social History of the Lower East Side

Joel Myers (left) and Money Tree (right) of Tent City holding banner, 1989

Tent City residents, Larry (left), Terry Taylor (right) protest luxury Christodora, 1989

A Radical Political and Social History of the Lower East Side

cooking facilities in TSP
(Tompkins Square Park),
1989

Joel Myers and Clayton Patterson took over Henry Stern's Park Commissioners office. After several hours, negotiated with police and worked out a compromise. No arrests, 1989

A Radical Political and Social History of the Lower East Side

TSP band shell 1989

TSP. Eviction of homeless, Tent City — they burn their tents and belongings —
scorched earth. Activists protest, 1989

Police Administrative Court

TSP Help Center, 1989

A Radical Political and Social History of the Lower East Side

TSP Residents Sleeping, 1989

TSP Tents on the 10th Street side of the park, normally a children's area, 1989

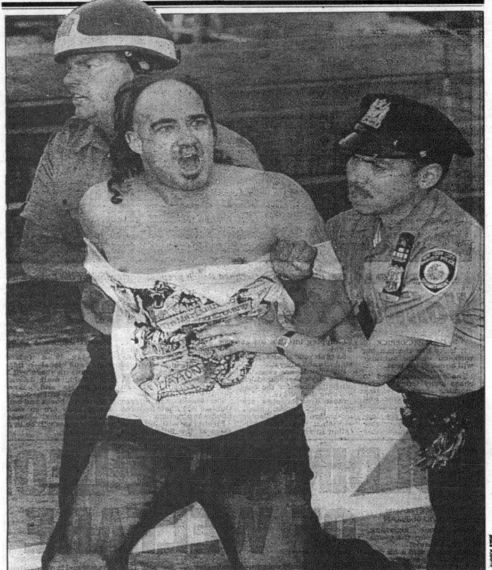

POST 09.02.89

Cops bust activist fotog at riot

This is Clayton Patterson, the controversial Tompkins Square Park activist, as he was arrested and led away during Thursday's violent march to protest the murder of Yusuf Hawkins.

Patterson was taken into custody at the Brooklyn Bridge and charged with assault. He was issued a desk appearance and later released.

The 40-year-old activist who works as a Lower East Side hat designer and amateur filmmaker, is no stranger to controversy.

Last summer, Patterson videotaped the bloody Tompkins Square riot in which numerous cops were charged by local residents with police brutality.

The tape showed some cops viciously bashing protesters — and some of the cops' shield numbers could be seen covered with black tape in violation of department rules.

But Patterson refused to turn over the tape — believed to be the most graphic one made — to a Manhattan grand jury probing 121 police brutality complaints.

Patterson was jailed for several days on civil contempt charges as a result.

An eventual legal tug of war over the four-hour tape ended when a state supreme court judge ordered it shown in its entirety to the grand jury.

Partially as a result of that tape, several cops were eventually charged with criminal assault.

Other cops involved in wrongdoing have been disciplined by the department.

Bill Hoffmann

B'Bridge, 9/2/89, courtesy of the New York Post

A Radical Political and Social History of the Lower East Side

60 Center Street
Court House,
1990

Family Court building.   Black marble exterior gives the building a menacing
max lockdown prison from the future, 1990

Housing in A Human Right day in TSP, 1990

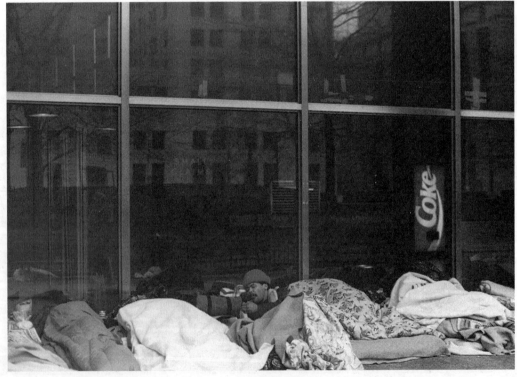

Homeless sleeping by 111 Center Street NYC Civil Court, 1990

A Radical Political and Social History of the Lower East Side

People's Camp on 4th Street between Ave. B & C, 1990 (another homeless camp), support camp across the street from squatted ABC Community Center

Number 2 homeless camp on 4th Street between B & C, 1990

A Radical Political and Social History of the Lower East Side

Rage On warehoused apartment demo, corner of 10th Street and Ave. B, 1990

ACT UP demo outside 7th Precinct supporting those arrested, 1990

A Radical Political and Social History of the Lower East Side

Red Square commercial stores for rent, 1990

New York is burning graffiti — over bus stop poster of NYC Mayor David Dinkins, 1991

Antonio Pagan for City Council endorsements, 1991

Park is fenced off and closed for one year. City orders tearing down of band shell
because homeless were sleeping in the band shell, 1991

A Radical Political and Social History of the Lower East Side

Dinkinsville camp on 8th Street (former lot of Tya Scott's squat. Demolished by city April 1st 1989)

Dinkinsville camp on 8th Street, 5:00 a.m. cops coming -- scorched earth (former the lot of Tya Scott's squat. Demolished by city April 1st 1989)

A Radical Political and Social History of the Lower East Side

Bottle Squad, 4:00 a.m.,
Ave. A & St. Marks, 1991

Hands Around the Park, 1991

A Radical Political and Social History of the Lower East Side

Judges Bench 100 Center Street, 1991

Williamsburg Bridge 1991

Jon Greenburg died of AIDS. Political funeral TSP, 1992

Moes Discount Center, between 7th & 8th Street — only case of looting, 1991

A Radical Political and Social History of the Lower East Side

100 Center Street waiting for court, 1992

Carmen's Garden with Carmen (poem Carmen's Garden), 1994

A Radical Political and Social History of the Lower East Side

Barbara Henry, Member of Tent City memorial in TSP, 1995

Bathrooms in Family Court, 1995

A Radical Political and Social History of the Lower East Side

Chino Garcia speaking at rally to save Charas. Armando Perez in doorway
entrance to Charas (PS 64), 1996

Police get organized before entering block to evict people in buildings on 13th Street, 1996

284

Police bring in armored vehicle to help with the eviction, 1996

13th Street protester under car, police turn over car, 1996

A Radical Political and Social History of the Lower East Side

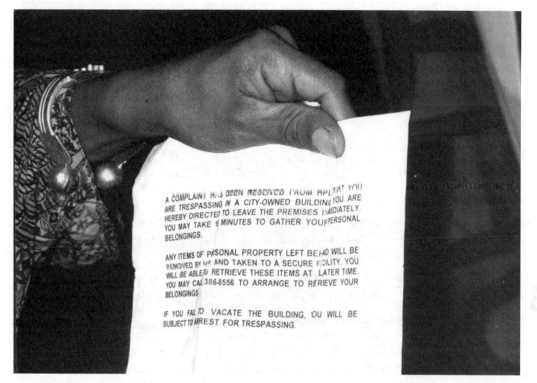

Eviction order 13th Street squat resident, 1996

Squatters evicted from 5th Street, 1997

172 Stanton bricks fell off back wall. Tenants wait on street for several hours. They were told that they could go back in the building. Mayor Giuliani ordered demolition of the building. No one was allowed to get any belongings; pets, ID's, nothing, 1998

Clayton Patterson choked by NYPD, 1 Police Plaza, NYPD Headquarters, 1998

What's Extell going to do with your building?

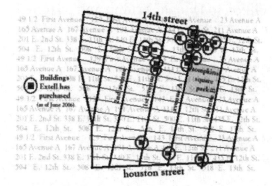

Dear Neighbors,

Within the last five months, the Extell Development Corporation has purchased 17 rent-regulated buildings – including yours – in the East Village/Lower East Side for an astounding price of $72 million dollars.

Based on their past development practices (*see fact sheet on reverse side*) we, as a tenants' rights organization, are very concerned about their plans for your building.

We expect that Extell will try, through various means, to empty out these buildings of existing tenants - both rent regulated and deregulated. A meeting of East Village/Lower East Side Extell Tenants was held on June 26th, 2006. At that meeting it was decided to bring the concerns of the tenants to the attention of the local Community Board. Please join us at the Board's upcoming meeting, where they will discuss the Extell issue, among others:

Community Board #3 Housing Meeting

Tuesday, July 18, 2006 @ 6:30pm
333 Bowery (Kenton Hall)
Between 2nd and 3rd Streets.

For more information, call the Cooper Square Committee:

FACTS ABOUT EXTELL DEVELOPMENT CORP.

Extell Development and its funding partner, The Carlyle Group, "a global investing conglomerate with ties to powerful politicians", have purchased large swaths of NYC real estate for luxury development, including the following:

- Paid $1.8 billion to Donald Trump and a Hong Kong Consortium in 2005 for riverside property on the west side

- Launched a twin skyscraper project —the Ariel— on the upper west side between 99 and 100th Streets

- Developed a 500 unit condo— The Orion— at 350 West 42nd Street, converted the Stanhope Hotel on Fifth Avenue to co-ops that are being offered for $10 million or more

- Purchased approximately 250 Manhattan buildings, for hundreds of millions of dollars since January, 2006

- Purchased 4 buildings on West End Avenue that it plans to demolish for a new residential construction

- Filed a demolition application with the NYS Division of Housing and Community Renewal (DHCR) for a building on E. 17th Street in late May, 2006

This is only a partial listing of Extell's vast and growing real estate holdings and activities as of June, 2006.

Community Board #3 will meet and discuss this issue on Tuesday, July 18th – see reverse side for details.

Planned Shrinkage is almost over and the gold rush to
fill the vacuum is going full speed ahead, 2006

SECTION THREE - TOMPKINS SQUARE

Chapter 1

A Short History of the Tomkiins Square Neighborhood Revolt:
1988 to 1991
By A. Kronstadt

This is a brief history of a political uprising, conveniently forgotten by all officially recognized historians and political commentators in New York City and elsewhere, that occurred in
the Lower East Side of Manhattan during the last phase of the old liberal New York 12 to 14
years prior to the date of this writing (completed in 2003). I was a participant in those
events and am writing from memory, and some more detail will be provided in a longer
account of the history that will be written at a later date. I am going to be somewhat parsi-
monious with the use of names — this may seem strange in this age of gossip, but I do not
feel that it is responsible for me to mention the names of all of the people with whom I
shared these experiences; I wish to heal the rifts within my community instead of pointing
the finger or factionalizing. I refer to us all collectively as "the activists"; we were all
responsible, each in our own way, for both the successes and failures of our movement. One
day perhaps, when I get around to writing the longer account of all this, I will mention the
names of the principals and their roles in making the events of the Tompkins Square revolt
happen. At that time, I imagine, this history will read much more like a novel because we
each contributed to the growth and decline of the Lower East Side political revolt according
to our own psychological proclivities. But this short summary is probably the first attempt
to document these events all in one place, and though it be sketchy, it is worth the writing,
even if all it does is provoke other people to write more detailed accounts. Let this work be
an expression of the fact that I still believe in the fundamental principles of the Tompkins
Square rebellion. I believe that in 2006 the best solution to the moral rigor mortis that has
overtaken New York City is yet another grass-roots rebellion on the same scale.

The Tompkins Square Park Neighborhood Revolt, and I am calling it that only because I have
to call it something, occurred in the late 1980s and early 1990s. I will not put an exact date
upon the beginning of the Revolt because, in a sense, the rebellion began when the first
bohemian artist set foot in downtown Manhattan, many decades ago, and because in another sense, the Revolt still goes on as long there are people like myself and others who dwell
in the neighborhood, writing articles for publications like *The Shadow*, analyzing the urban
malaise which reigns in New York City. But names and dates aside, it did happen. It was a
rebellion, leading in some cases to exchanges of blows between citizens of New York City
and the police, a rebellion akin to Shay's Revolt and the Whiskey Rebellion of early U.S.
history and, more directly to the political antics of the Yippies and SDS in the sixties and
seventies, with which many of us identified. The Revolt was local and relied on spontaneity,
word of mouth, and gatherings of people in the public square, namely Tompkins Square Park,
and these are the things that were both the beauty and the downfall of the Revolt.

A Radical Political and Social History of the Lower East Side

This eminently American revolt was about nothing more than American democracy, even though all of us had a huge contempt for patriotism as it had been force fed to us in America's schools and spoon fed by the media. You see, two very undemocratic things were happening in American society — among the myriad of other undemocratic things that were also happening — which affected the counterculture community in the Lower East Side of Manhattan very deeply, more so than it did other categories of people. One was the conscious decision of government officials at all levels to pursue policies of gentrification, intended to make cities run more like businesses in the age of Reaganite pro-business policies. The key feature of gentrification was a dramatic increase in the amount of money that people would have to pay for living space and working space, which had remained relatively reasonable in the Lower East Side ever since the Great Depression and the liberal administration of Fiorello H. LaGuardia, who had maintained fairly strict pro-tenant policies of rent regulation (even as he sold out certain other parts of the city for complete demolition). Gentrification had a human face, albeit a not too pretty one, in that of Mayor Edward I. Koch. Earlier in his career Koch had been regarded as an extreme liberal, but in line with the new order put in place by the Reagan Revolution, he eagerly took up the task of making New York's down-at-the-heels neighborhoods pay for themselves by means of a fearsome raise-the-rent policy. Apartments that rented for 150 dollars a month in 1977 (when Koch was elected mayor) were renting for seven hundred a month by 1983, two years into the Reagan administration. The "liberal" city and state authorities authorized a bevy of loopholes in rent laws: co-op conversions, major capital improvements, and vacancy increases, which enabled landlords to charge astronomical rents that the people who already lived in the neighborhood could simply not afford.

Gentrification went hand in hand with other policies of the City and State authorities such as catering to the industries of Finance, Insurance, and Real Estate (F.I.R.E. — to remind us of the great wave of landlord arson that the Lower East Side suffered during the Koch administration) at the expense of other branches of the economy. Manufacturing and transport, unable to make the kind of efficient use of real estate that the new order demanded, were left to wither, unable to pay for needed space. Yuppies poured in and filled the apartments that the neighborhood folk, be they Puerto Rican, Slavic, Jewish, beatnik, hippie, punk, or conceptual artist, had been priced out of. In the bohemian/ethnic vs. yuppie/mainstream dichotomy, one can see the central conflict of our story. The word "yuppie" would play a prominent part in the discourse of the Tompkins Square Neighborhood Revolt because we perceived the young upper middle class and rich boys and girls moving into the neighborhood in an adversarial manner. Many of us had been through co-op conversions in which groups of yuppies bought into a building and put the apartments up for sale at prices that we could never hope to come up with, and in which the threat of eviction and displacement from the neighborhood was ever present. Developers would hire private detectives to spy on tenants and rent apartments to drug-addicted thugs to drive out the old residents of buildings. Gentrification was also accompanied by a great deal of landlord arson, which not only allowed building owners to collect large insurance payments but enabled them to sell the fire-damaged buildings vacant to developers for gut renovation and rental at astronomical rates.

A. Kronstadt

The Tompkins Square Revolt was also a revolt against the first inklings of the police regime that was to come to maturity under Rudolph Giuliani a few years later, but which was first tried out under Koch. Ed Koch was among the first U.S. politicians to start using the term Quality of Life to describe a focus upon the prosecution and punishment of petty violations such as public drinking and pot smoking. Certain ideologues had been pushing the Quality of Life slogan as a means of selling to urban liberals some of the objectives of the Reaganite culture wars — including a crackdown on drugs, pornography, prostitution, and slackerly behavior such as hanging out on the street. While conservatives had long wanted the cops to start busting the perverts, druggies, and bums, the liberals, being slicker people, needed a slicker justification. According to the Quality of Lifers, punishing those who violate certain rules of middle-class appropriateness helps improve the Quality of Life of the community by letting the decent people reclaim public spaces, and makes it a better place for mothers and children. Quality of Life-ism is a very Hillary Clinton-like form of fascism with a human face. There are indeed "feminist" Quality of Life ideologues who claim that any venues that attract primarily men, in particular prostitution and porno zones and areas with lots of bars, are bad for society and need to be shut down, or as in the case of old Times Square, torn down and replaced with a gentrified "family venue." Koch's Quality of Life crusade was inseparably bound up with his desire to gentrify Manhattan, and was little applied to other boroughs. His stated desire was to bring more well-to-do people into the city and thereby raise the price paid for real estate, and he could not do this in a place where the poor, vulgar slobs ruled the streets and made noise.

One of the first inklings of Koch's new Quality of Life regime was the crackdown on pot smoking, initiated in 1982 in Washington Square Park, an old gathering spot for Lower Manhattan nonconformists located in Greenwich Village. A midnight curfew was imposed upon Washington Square Park in 1987 with the support of Koch and local Democratic politicians. Tompkins Square Park on the other hand remained relatively free of this regime through the end of the eighties, and remained a haven for bohemian freaks, ranging from artists to drug addicts, and especially for homeless Lower East Side people who were priced out of housing during the big real estate shakeouts of the early eighties. Falling somewhat into both categories were the squatters, who had taken over endless rows of abandoned buildings just east of the park, for whom the park was a collective backyard. The freaks, squatters, and homeless mingled with neighborhood people around the Tompkins Square Park bandshell at political events in defense of the Sandinistas of Nicaragua and at punk concerts put on by squatter impresarios.

This is really where our part of the story begins. In 1988, people who might best be described as Quality of Lifers organized some of the people living in the blocks around Tompkins Square Park into an association to demand that a curfew be placed on Tompkins Square Park, thereby putting an end to the noise that emanated from the park at night. Officials of the Koch administration backed them and, in July of that year, the police began driving around the park at midnight shouting over their PA system that the park was closed, and that everyone had to leave. Apparently, the City bureaucrats were not aware that it was only a small, vocal group of people who actually wanted the park closed at night, and that a much larger group of people were outraged about the curfew, immediately identifying it with the hated gentrification policies of the Koch administration. The squatters, some of whom were highly politicized, took the initiative of putting out flyers encouraging people to violate the curfew, and then organized concerts at the bandshell that brought the atomized counterculture together around this issue where gentrification and the police state converged.

I was not present at the Tompkins Square police riot of 1988, having returned from Europe the day after it happened, and will leave the details to Clayton Patterson and others who risked serious injury to document that event. In a nutshell, on July 31, 1988, an anti-curfew rally and concert took place in the park where there was a minor skirmish with cops. Over the next week, a massive campaign took place via wheat pasting (that sticky precursor to e-mail) to announce a rally for Saturday night, August 6, 1988. A vastly larger number of people showed up for the rally than the police imagined, and the cops could do nothing as some seven hundred people assembled in the interior of the park. Convinced that members of the crowd intended to resist the curfew, police prepared for retaking the park by setting up their command center inside the park near the bandshell. But as curfew time approached, the throng unexpectedly exited the park onto Avenue A, separating the police who were supposed to hold the crowd in check from the brain trust that was supposed to command them. This threw the cops into confusion, and, adding to it all, one of the top commanders, Inspector Darcy, drove back to the station house at this point to use the toilet, leaving the inexperienced Captain McNamara to look after the situation. In the absence of better instructions, cops started pushing and shoving demonstrators on the avenue, some of whom pushed and shoved back, and bottles were thrown from the crowd. A confusing "10-85 Tompkins Square Park forthwith" command was issued to police cars all over Manhattan and Brooklyn, and hundreds of cops flooded the area, with no central leader and no orders. Demonstrators surged through the streets and cops began beating up demonstrators, people who looked like demonstrators, and people who were accidentally in the vicinity of demonstrators, including residents trying to flee into their houses. It was not until early the next morning that Koch administration officials realized the travesty that was going on, withdrew the police, and lifted the park curfew, both on Tompkins Square Park and Washington Square Park.

At this time the City's real estate values were faltering under the influence of the stock market crash of 1987. Ed Koch was in a tailspin; even his health was suffering, as he was reported to be having a series of mini-strokes. Koch was on his way out and it was only poetic justice that he should be humiliated by a ragtag band of radicals representing those most directly threatened by his gentrification and quality of life policies. All at once, a political movement had been forged in the Lower East Side that included a diverse group of people who had little else in common but that they felt targeted by the lofty plans of Koch and the gentrifiers.

The Tompkins Square movement was composed, as described in the *Village Voice* shortly after the riot, of "kitchen table cabals" and groups of people worked on their own projects which all tended to serve the common objective of getting people to assemble at events, in Tompkins Square Park and elsewhere, that reached critical mass and showed that there was opposition to gentrification in the city. The agitation would culminate in the big events in Tompkins Square Park, the concert every Memorial Day, Squatter Mayday, and innumerable

A. Kronstadt

smaller demonstrations and rallies. If you want to understand the Tompkins Square political movement, do not think of the Communist Party or any kind of military or guerilla movement. The Tompkins Square movement was a kind of bohemia cum political movement that embraced loud music and mind-altering substances, and considered these things elements, or perhaps better stated, sacraments, of political resistance. While we were not a party in the sense of the Communist Party, one of our objectives was to organize "parties" in the other, more fun sense of the word, that would reach a sufficiently critical mass of determined people to discourage the cops from breaking them up. The marijuana smoke-ins, held in Washington Square Park at the time that the Tompkins Square movement was in full swing, were our events as much as any of the countless political rallies that we sponsored in Tompkins Square Park. The people who frequented these events were the movement, period --nobody needed a membership card and nobody needed to do anything that they didn't want to.

The first events that ensued after the riot of Aug. 6-7, 1988, were the weekly demonstrations to roll back the curfew in Washington Square Park, which ran from August 13, 1988, through early December of that year. Koch reneged on repealing the curfew in Washington Square Park, and the police car announcing the curfew reappeared on August 13. On that evening a huge, nonviolent demonstration, larger than the one on the night of August 6, assembled in Tompkins Square Park and marched up St. Mark's Place and into the West Village, only to be barred from entering Washington Square Park by a massive show of police force. Many people in the Lower East Side who were sympathetic to the Tompkins Square movement did not approve of the decision by the most active of the activists to take the struggle into the West Village, which was a middle class neighborhood and the place where the idea of enforcing park curfews originated. But for months on end, groups of Tompkins Square political activists would assemble in Washington Square Park every Saturday night at 8:00 and face off against phalanxes of hostile police who greatly outnumbered them. People were arrested by the dozens and roughed up by Lt. McKenna, chief enforcer of the new regime in Washington Square. The demonstrations had a high profile because they took place on Saturday night at the crossroads of Greenwich Village. Although ineffective in stopping the hated curfew from being enforced, the demonstrations at least showed the city bureaucrats that its shift to enhanced enforcement of petty laws in the name of "quality of life" would meet with some form of resistance. For weeks the demonstrations drew hundreds of people and ended in head-on mass refusals to leave the park when the sound truck came around at midnight, with consequent mass arrests in which dozens of people were kept in jail for forty hours and longer. As the fall progressed, the demonstrations became smaller in size, but were accompanied by non-violent guerilla actions in which barricades used by the cops to enforce the curfew were removed and carried blocks away, and graffiti was sprayed encouraging people to resist the curfew. The Washington Square demonstrations, however, showed a pattern that would be seen with other forms of intense, repetitive protest in which numbers would dwindle with time. The ultimate success of the quality of life regime under Giuliani came from recognition of this and other weaknesses of spontaneous mass protest by police strategists who now, fifteen years later, successfully herd and control demonstrations using lessons learned from the Tompkins Square protest movement.

A Radical Political and Social History of the Lower East Side

While the Washington Square protest effort was burning out, however, developments were taking place back in the Lower East Side that would lay the groundwork for the subsequent year of exciting events. Tompkins Square activists began to target Community Board 3, a fake grass roots council, many of whose members were political appointees of the Koch Administration, and which had rubberstamped the park curfew in July. The cowardly CB3 members who had voted for, or who at least failed to oppose, the curfew were now mortified at being, at least indirectly, the authors of one of the worst orgies of police brutality in New York history. They quickly flip-flopped in the wake of the bloody police riot, and many of them now claimed to oppose the curfew, although the dominant "quality of lifer" faction on CB3 wanted to re-impose it. While CB3 issued any number of toothless resolutions calling for investigations into the riot, the majority faction of these "liberal" Democrats was one hundred percent down with Koch, particularly on issues related to gentrification. Their job was to put their seal of approval, in the phony name of the community, on projects that were intended to further a land grab by developers. The biggest of these involved the some three hundred abandoned buildings between Fourteenth and Houston Streets, at the time. Some of these projects were disguised as low-income housing, indeed the "50/50 plan" supported by the liberal housing organizations and community preservation groups that dominated CB3 was intended to sell half of the city-owned abandoned buildings, most of them confiscated for back taxes, for market-rate development, and to develop the other half as affordable, though nevertheless expensive, housing; in a sense this was a part of the Reaganite policy of "trickle-down" economics. But the fly in the ointment was turning out to be the squatters, who now occupied a good 10% of the abandoned buildings between Houston and 14th. The squatters were indeed a cross-section of the people who were being displaced from the Lower East Side by the rising rent — marginal artists, perennial hippie freaks and the like — and commanded support from many others who were not squatters but who were in overlapping social categories and who felt threatened by the rising tide of yuppification. Just as one group of people had taken on police repression in Washington Square Park as its issue, another group of "Tompkins Square Activists," not completely separate but not exactly the same group of people, began following CB3 around (it met in different places) and throwing it into chaos every time it tried to hold one of its perfunctory hearings to rubber-stamp a development project that would involve the eviction of squatters. By the end of 1988, a noisy peanut gallery of Tompkins Square Activists had become a fixture at CB3 meetings and was having an effect upon its functioning, especially in terms of its rulings on real estate and land use. The successes of the activists in disrupting CB3's nefarious machinations earned them the enmity of local poverty pimps such as Antonio Pagan (he called us "master intimidators"), who stood to make millions developing squatted buildings into low-income housing that would revert to "market rate" after six years, whereupon the apartments would be rented for profit to yuppies.

Since I have used the L-word several times already, let me say a word about the liberals of the Lower East Side. Most of the liberal Democratic activists on Community Board 3 and among the local elected officials supported or failed to do anything to stop the curfew from being imposed on Tompkins Square Park. Like most New York City liberals, they bought the arguments of the "quality of lifers" who advocated a curtailment of freedom in the interests of "family communities" and higher real estate values, and wanted to see Tompkins Square turned into a quiet, yuppie park. As I have said, many of these liberal Democratic politicians and neighborhood activists were also involved in plans to rehabilitate buildings that would involve evictions of squatters and their replacement with politically connected tenants. This is why "liberal" was almost as much a dirty word among the Tompkins Square Activists as among Staten Island conservatives. The activists had no compunctions about smoking marijuana and lighting fire crackers under chairs at Community Board 3 meetings and, at one point, seizing the microphone from its chairwoman Ann Johnson, who, incidentally, was not all that liberal. We Tompkins Square Activists proudly wore the label of radical, as opposed to liberal, because we knew that the liberal regime was coming to an end and that all of the liberals were getting ready to sell out our homes and our liberties and line up behind whatever fuehrer the real estate interests wanted to put into power, as they did a few years later when Giuliani was elected.

In summary, then, the Tompkins Square Activists were radical, as opposed to liberal, and were riled by two main issues:

(1) Gentrification, which we fought in part by supporting the right of squatters to reclaim abandoned buildings as housing and by highlighting the homeless problem through supporting and comforting our homeless fellow citizens;

(2) No Police State, a political slogan opposing park curfews, quality of life crusades, anti-homeless sweeps, and other aspects of the embryonic Giuliani mentality that was gestating in the years before Giuliani.

Aside from that, there was little other structured political ideology. Many of the Tompkins Square Activists wore other political labels like anarchist or communist, or even liberal in some cases, although their association with us caused them to be ostracized by the mainstream liberals. We were vilified by some communist groups, such as the pro-Soviet Workers World Party, even as others, such as the Maoist Revolutionary Communist Party or RCP, participated in our events and were even accepted as hard-core Tompkins Square activists. The term Tompkins Square *Anarchists* was also used to describe us, and the name was never totally inappropriate because we did include a large contingent of politically aware anarchists, and our No Police State slogan was a classical anarchist battle cry with which even the most anti-intellectual drunk punk could identify. The anarchist label was also justified by the fact that two anarchist organizing centers —the Anarchist Switchboard on 9th St. between 1st and 2nd, which was also a kind of flophouse, and later, Sabotage Books, on St. Mark's Place between 1st Avenue and the park, were the closest things to "headquarters" that the Tompkins Square Activists had. Activists or anarchists, however, we could work together, and the tight cohesion and sense of camaraderie that held together big groups of us in confrontation with the police was our greatest strength. The movement relied on spontaneity, with all its assets and liabilities. We used to tell each other "the cops are our best organizers," because we were at our best, our noblest when we were defending ourselves against some kind of police attack. The problem with spontaneity, however, is that your adversaries are always trying to figure out your patterns and eventually they will have your number.

A Radical Political and Social History of the Lower East Side

The winter of 1988-1989 was a cold one, and, because the Koch administration had re-imposed the curfews, to a greater or lesser degree, on every city park except Tompkins Square Park, many more homeless people joined the contingent of those who had long been sleeping in Tompkins. Two phenomena characterized that period in New York City history: one was the economic doldrums following the stock market crash of 1987, and the other was the epidemic of crack addiction, which by 1988 had reached its peak. These were both factors that contributed to a massive spike in homelessness, building on a trend that started in the early years after Ronald Reagan was elected President of the U.S. When combined with gentrification and insanely inflated rents, homelessness took on diversity in terms of ethnicity and former economic status that defied the stereotype of the Bowery bum with which New York had long been familiar. In the park, homeless people would huddle around wood fires lit in 55-gallon drums, and sleep on benches with the fire barrels situated a few feet away, to avoid hypothermia. The police, again feeling out aspects of the new "quality of life" approach to law enforcement, would go around extinguishing these fires and leaving the park denizens to freeze, or more likely, to build another fire after the cops were gone. In most cases, the police would not precisely extinguish the fire, i.e., with a fire extinguisher, but would simply kick the barrel over in a gesture of meanness and create a hazardous shower of sparks. One frigid night in mid-December of 1988, a man in his sixties named Eddie Rutter was asleep on a bench when a policeman knocked over his fire barrel. Perhaps even before he became aware that his primitive source of heat was gone, Eddie Rutter was dead of hypothermia. The weekend after this happened a large demonstration was organized through wheat pasting and word of mouth that attracted many more people than the usual core of activists to Tompkins Square Park. We all gathered around fire barrels, smoking pot, playing drums, and sharing food and beer with people who lived in the park. This event marked the re-opening of the Tompkins Square Neighborhood Revolt after the Washington Square protests had run their course. During the festivities, two cop cars that moved in to intimidate by shining their lights were slightly damaged, one having a can of paint poured over it and the other dented by a protester's bare fist.

The gathering for Eddie Rutter was the largest event in the park since the days following the riot, and was the first spark in a chain reaction of political activism that would continue unabated over the next two years. Each Tompkins Square event, brought together through word of mouth and wheat pasting, sometimes but not always accompanied by chaotic meetings at the Anarchist Switchboard, would result in networking and the exchanging of phone numbers that would enhance organizing of future events, be they demonstrations, concerts, or parties, and this is the way the movement grew and attracted talent. A cadre of artists, rhetoric writers, and guerrilla wheat pasters assembled at kitchen tables throughout the neighborhood. The personal computer, then in its XT and DOS stage, without modems or e-mail, was drafted into service, generating a continual stream of leaflets dripping with political invective against gentrification and the police state, accompanied by often lurid artwork illustrating the same themes. The flyers were then plastered onto the walls of the Lower East Side by four-six person postering crews (two to put them up, two-four as lookouts) that did their work between 1 and 5 AM. Some of our rhetoric bordered on conspiracy theory —I will not dwell on the Emergency Coalition Against Martial Law, one of several independent kitchen table cabals, whose leaflets spoke of plans drafted by none other than Lt. Col. Oliver North to have the Federal Emergency Management Agency

A. Kronstadt

round up political dissidents and other deviants. The propaganda on the lamp posts, mailboxes, and side walls of buildings developed a following and, as in nineteenth century Paris, people awoke eager to see what news the walls would bring them. Some of the posters announced events and others were just about ideas. The sticky postering glue, purchased at hardware stores in the form of a dry carbohydrate in a yellow bag and whose legal use was for affixing wallpaper, became one of the bonds that held the movement together.

The atmosphere at Tompkins Square events was a mesmerizing mix of the primitive and the futuristic. Fire, in some form, was always in evidence, and attempts by the police to extinguish the fires that bonded us together, even in the coldest weather, were often the things that touched off confrontations with the City authorities. There are still indentations in the asphalt pavement on Avenue A that are the result of bonfires that had been built there during protests starting with the Tompkins Square riot of 1988 and continuing through 1991, when the full extent of repression was brought down upon us. The fire became a kind of focus, or hearth, for the temporarily liberated zone, and was a statement that we preferred prehistoric freedom to the yuppie utopia. Starting with the Eddie Rutter demonstration in 1988, and continuing through the repeated clashes over squats and the park in 1989, the ability to build a fire and to congregate around it, for survival, for a sense of solidarity with those who were forced to build fires to survive, was a political issue on a level with any other.

The organizing continued throughout the winter of '88-'89, and plans were made for large-scale events during the radical spring to follow. During this time, meetings took place in the Anarchist Switchboard, a cellar on East Ninth Street which, as fellow veteran Tompkins Square activist Jerry the Peddler ironically remarked, lacked not only a switchboard but a telephone. On the broken-down couches, squeezed in among the snoozing street punks, we congregated and smoked large quantities of free marijuana provided by the pope of dope, Micky Cesar, who in his own way was a Tompkins Square Activist and provided the movement with much creative stimulation both herbal and otherwise. The fact that the Switchboard was also a flophouse where a number of homeless people from Tompkins Square Park drank beer and crashed actually made these meetings more effective and involved homeless people in organizing Tompkins Square events. It was during this time that activists and people around the Switchboard began regularly cooking and serving free food, donated and dumpster-dived, to people living in Tompkins Square Park.

In late winter of '89, the NYPD, worried about the bad publicity from the August 6 riot and the amount of organizing going on in the neighborhood, appointed Deputy Inspector Michael Julian, a young, new breed of cop with a Kennedy-like demeanor, to be the commanding officer of the Ninth Precinct, thus replacing Captain McNamara, the cop who called in the "10-85 Tompkins Square forthwith" command at the Aug. 6 demonstration and thereby unleashed a wild mob of police upon the neighborhood. Shortly after his appointment, Julian took questions from members of an audience that packed the cafeteria of St. Brigid's Roman Catholic Church, adjacent to Tompkins Square Park, and even implied, in not so many words, that the police would overlook the discreet consumption of beer and marijuana in the park and that some of the overt harassment of the homeless would be lessened.

A Radical Political and Social History of the Lower East Side

On April 1, 1989, the New York City Department of Housing Preservation and Development moved in to evict a city-owned building at 316 E. Eighth Street, near Avenue B, which was occupied by the family of Tya Scott, one of the pioneers of Lower East Side squatting. This was the first test of the ability of the young movement to respond to an emergency, since there was no time for any wheat pasting, even though the attack was not completely unexpected. A grapevine of telephone numbers existed among the activists and, since the squat under attack was located so close to the park, dozens of people who just happened to be there rushed to the nearest phones to activate the communications network. A crowd of over one hundred people assembled in the middle of the afternoon, but a SWAT team had broken through the back wall of the building and the eviction was well underway before a critical mass had formed. As the demolition crew moved in, the crowd crossed the street to the edge of the park and one of the first "mini-riots" broke out, in which squatter activists started stoning the front doors of the Christodora building, an architecturally prominent older building that had functioned as a hippie flophouse years ago but was now one of the most notorious yuppie condos. During the course of the mini-riot, Inspector Julian appeared in his dashing trench-coat and tackled one of the rock throwers, a man much older than himself who had really only thrown a symbolic rock, falling right on top of him as the rioter went down, a comical performance that delighted the many neighborhood photographers who had followed the activist grapevine to the scene.[1]

Around the time of the Aug. 6, 1988 riot, various reporters from the local press became interested in the Tompkins Square scene, and the movement was written up. The Washington Square demonstrations appeared in the *New York Times* only once, in an article in which Lieutenant McKenna was quoted as saying that most of us were under the influence of alcohol or marijuana, which was not far from the truth. A parenthetical note here is that it takes one to know one; McKenna was notorious for his binges and for the fact that he tippled in and out of uniform. He was once seen terrorizing Tent City residents in Tompkins Square Park riding, bareheaded, on a borrowed Parks Department motorcycle whooping and hollering through the park to impress a group of skinhead girls who had befriended him at an Avenue A bar where the Tompkins Square cops hung out. Perhaps more interested in transmitting our side of the story to the world were reporters Donna Ladd and Sarah Ferguson, who traveled with us and the cops during the long strange trip, as well as writers who came from within the movement itself, most notably the staff of the *Shadow*. Although we heaped abuse upon many of the reporters who covered us, we were also grateful for the coverage. And thus it was that the mini-riot outside the Christodora House, which ensued upon the eviction of Tya Scott's building, was well covered in local newspapers including Ladd's *Downtown Resident*, and the *Village Voice*, where Ferguson covered the Tompkins Square beat. They wrote some good stuff about us, and they also wrote some trash, and were equally flattered and insulted by us. After the eviction of Tya Scott's building we received a brief write-up in the Metro section of the *New York Times*, including a photo of demonstrators facing off against cops, with a wrecking crane in the background, one of many such photos that would be published in a variety of newspapers over the next several years.

Not so well appreciated was the lurid reportage of CBS's Mike Taibbi, who blamed the social-rejectionist industrial band Missing Foundation (MF) for the August 6 riot, claiming that the riot was planned in advance as a kind of real-life performance. In addition to being a band, MF was one of the kitchen table cabals which met to stir up the neighborhood in those days. MF's trademark, an upside-down champagne glass representing "the party's over" for the eighties and yuppiedom, was a common icon for Tompkins Square graffiti and flyers, and was to us sort of what the hammer and sickle was to the commies. Taibbi's report included talk of Satanism and footage of altars with melted black candles — all very amusing to the central core of us Tompkins Square activists, mostly devout atheists with a few practicing Christians and Jews. We brought the Tompkins Square scene uptown to CBS headquarters in the winter of '88, with some fifty of us up on West 59th Street to protest Taibbi's account of the riot. In those days we did not mind protesting on cold nights, even in obscure parts of the city, to represent obscure issues that we had to explain to passersby starting from the beginning. I think that this had to do mostly with a sense of camaraderie and enjoyment of one another's company as much as any specific political program.

In the spring, meetings were held at the Anarchist Switchboard and in various living rooms through the neighborhood for a series of concerts-cum-political rallies in Tompkins Square Park, running over a period of several days, and which would be accompanied by protest events in far-flung parts of town. Spring was beginning to send pheromones into the air and attract the new bohemia to the now legendary Tompkins Square Park where the freaks had beaten back the forces of repression. The first Resist to Exist concert was to be a vast carnival of the Lower East Side counterculture and a celebration of the wave of "glasnost" that was set in motion by the defeat of the Tompkins Square curfew. The events occurred with little police interference and there were no confrontations; attendance at the events leading up to and including the gala Squatter Mayday on May 1, 1989 was in the thousands. For days, the bandshell was draped with banners reading "No Police State" and bearing the infamous upside down champagne glass, as performers ranging from punk and hippie bands to Nuyorican poets took the stage. It is hard to picture such a thing today, but there was a feeling in the air like there was a new kind of '60s just getting started and that the Lower East Side was again becoming the center of nonconformist culture.

On April 24, 1989, dozens of Tompkins Square activists accompanied by homeless people from Tompkins Square Park attended, or rather, invaded a public hearing on the new Parks Department rules for imposing a Quality of Life regime on New York City parks, which included a rule prohibiting gatherings of more than 20 people in parks without a permit, a rule which was aimed directly at us and which, when successfully implemented years later under Giuliani, was a useful tool for mopping up the remaining resistance. Our chanting, accompanied at points by the throwing of eggs and unfurling of a huge banner, drove Parks Commissioner Henry Stern from the podium and delayed the implementation of the new rules for several years.

On April 20, 1989, a fire seriously damaged the squat at 319 E. Eighth Street, located between Avenues B and C. It is widely believed that the fire was the result of arson by some neighborhood tough guys who had once been allowed by the squatters to build a pigeon coop on the roof, but who were expelled from the building after they started dealing drugs there. The fire department prevented the flames from spreading to the condominium next door, but did little to prevent 319 E. Eighth St. itself from burning. Over the following week, the City's Department of Housing Preservation and Development (HPD; called "Housing

302

Prevention and Destruction" by the squatters) gradually dismantled the interior of the building with a crane, and on the morning of April 27, contractors hired by HPD starting building a scaffold for the demolition itself. The demolition crew came protected by only a small number of police, unaware that several of the former residents of the squat had re-entered the building, and that the grapevine had once again been activated and people were on their way not only to demonstrate but to actively disrupt the demolition.

One of the squatters re-entered his apartment and retrieved the bucket that he used as a makeshift toilet, dumping its fermenting yellow-brown contents from his fire escape on to the heads of the demolition workers, who promptly fled the scene as demonstrators destroyed the scaffolding that they had put up. The squatters planned to retake their building and rehabilitate it as they had done when they took it over, abandoned and fire damaged, years before. One of our lawyers, Ron Kuby, went to court and got a temporary restraining order to halt demolition. The building continued to be occupied and there was a standoff for several days, during which time the big Squatter Mayday concert took place and hundreds of people became aware of the fact that the building was occupied and that the squatters were preparing to resist.

The clash over Tya Scott's building and the stoning of the Christodora had only been a taste of the action that was to be seen when HPD came to demolish 319 E. Eighth on the afternoon of May 2, 1989, even as Kuby was returning from court with a fresh restraining order. There were clashes all day between police and protesters as police finally established a perimeter sealing off the block and the demolition workers filtered back in. The crowd became angry — as darkness fell, police barricades were knocked over and bottles were thrown after people learned that the restraining order was being ignored and the demolition had commenced once again. Cops were chasing people through the park, and the chant of "Pigs Out of the Park," one of the flagship slogans of the Tompkins Square riot of 1988, was revived. There were eighteen arrests, and the usual reports of injuries among the police. The following day, after the building had been successfully demolished, there was a retaliatory strike — an evicted squatter took a piece of cinder block and attacked the plate glass windows of the Gap at St. Mark's Place and 2nd Avenue, a notorious symbol of gentrification, causing hundreds of dollars worth of damage. The successful evictions of Tya Scott's building and the 319 E. Eighth St. squat made a serious dent in the massive squatter scene on Eight Street and touched off a wave of paranoia in the squatter community that fed into the activism during the subsequent spring, summer and fall of 1989.[2]

The spring of 1989 was a great growth period for the Tompkins Square movement. America was seeing the beginning of a new phase of mass counterculture — there were a lot of musicians around and gutter punks flocked to the streets of the Lower East Side in numbers not seen since the seventies. The Tompkins Square movement was an institution and an outgrowth of the new street culture. The events at the Tompkins Square bandshell that were organized by the Tompkins Square activists were a serious venue for the music of the late 1980s counterculture — in those days, the city granted permits that went on for as long as seven hours for musical events, and that even extended to more than one day. The bandshell had been built in 1967, by a more liberal and democratic New York, as a means of promoting understanding between rockers and Latinos in the Lower East Side. The budding dreadlock and grunge culture during the eighties took to organizing concerts in the bandshell, which had been neglected in the 1970s and became little more than a graffiti wall. These concerts included the original Squatter Mayday, and bands such as Millions of Dead Cops, also known as Millions of Damned Christians, would bring in hundreds of people. One thing that people who have grown up under the despotism now in force in the city often are not aware of is that in those days, the police usually did not bother people for drinking beer or smoking marijuana at concerts in parks. And there were no riots or mass violence, people danced, there was a mosh pit, it was one big party; until of course the tide changed and cops started enforcing the new Quality of Life regime.

On June 25, 1989, a large contingent of Tompkins Square Activists participated in the Gay Pride Parade and stayed for the festivities on the piers. As the party was winding down, some of the Tompkins Square people noticed that there was a great deal of leftover food — some 400 hot dogs and an equal number of rolls — and got permission to take it back to Tompkins Square Park. In the park, homeless people and gutter punks built stone barbecue pits and held a massive weenie-roast which fed not only the park dwellers and the activists but neighbors and passers by. Though our vegan and animal rights friends took issue, these hot dogs became the focus for a great scene of fraternization between the homeless of Tompkins Square Park and the rest of the neighborhood. Armloads of forty-ounce bottles of beer, paid for by visitors to the barbecue, were passed around. To some of the non-homeless people, having a drink around a fire with homeless people was their way of saying: you are not the 'other,' a homeless alcoholic, but you are like me with the same weakness for pleasure. The party did not end on that one night, and bringing food to the park became a whole Lower East Side "thing" that went far beyond the core of activists and brought in a whole new crowd. Tompkins Square Park, which had long had a reputation for being dark and threatening, was now all lit up and the place to be. The solidarity made the people who lived in the park more comfortable and, in addition to the fires, more and more tents started to be built in different parts of the park. This was the beginning of Tent City and the true golden age of Tompkins Square activism.

The police response to this people's takeover of Tompkins Square Park consisted of alternating tolerance and repression which, willy nilly, was very much in line with the anarchists thinking that the police are the best organizers. You would have the regular cops going around, who would know the names of all the homeless people and establish relationships with some of them to obtain information about the kind of activism that was going on. Then, suddenly, there would be some kind of raid, which was usually coordinated at a level higher than that of Inspector Julian's liberal Ninth Precinct and which involved the blue meanies of the Manhattan South Task Force (MSTF). All at once, Inspector Gelfand's MSTF forces would sweep through the park accompanied by Parks Enforcement Officers who would have the actual job of tearing down the tents and throwing people's stuff into the back of the garbage truck. There would then be a quiet return of the tents. This went on through June and July. Park-based homeless activists were agitating both independently and in conjunction with the core of Tompkins Square activists, and many heretofore uninvolved people from the neighborhood were bringing food to be cooked in the park on a regular basis. On July 5, 1989, cops completely evacuated the park and the Parks Enforcement guys dumped everything that people couldn't carry with them into garbage trucks. The grapevine was again activated and a crowd of hundreds joined the homeless clutching their belongings on

Avenue A. Another riot broke out, comparable in scale to the riot over 319 E. Eighth St., as demonstrators tore apart police barricades and cops held the surging crowd back from retaking the park. Bottles and firecrackers were thrown and there were over a dozen arrests.

Yet, the tents began to return as soon as the cops were gone. A showdown was planned for Saturday, July 8, and a call went out for plastic, sticks, and string to be used for "symbolic tents," since the police and Parks Department vowed to have no further tolerance for tents. Eight hundred people had gathered in the park by two on that sunny afternoon when the Parks Department workers and police came to tear down the "symbolic tents." Squatters, homeless people, and visitors to the park linked arms in circles around groups of tents in the dirt areas of the park, which had also been outfitted with a labyrinth of metal wires, rising to about knee level, to slow the advance of the cops and park workers. The scuffles were intended to be symbolic and there were a lot of cameras shooting footage of the cossacks pushing their way through the crowds of people who were singing the pacifist anthem "We Shall Overcome," and scrimmaging against them as if on a football field, with the plastic and string tents finally being ripped to pieces by the Parks Department workers. This was one of the high points of the Tompkins Square movement in terms of its ability to attract those who were not hard-core Lower East Side political fighters. By the end of July, Tent City had become a symbol of the homeless problem, that evil by-product of the Reagan/Koch success story, and people from all over the city were visiting Tompkins Square Park, bringing with them food as well as alcoholic and herbal refreshment and listening to the stories of the homeless. Even some of the yuppies whom we were wont to vilify came and offered help: several people responding to a call for firewood arrived with expensive store-bought logs of the kind that they burn in the fireplaces of condos.

The media attention turned favorable and expanded beyond the local press. These were the glory days, and it is fitting to mention a few other things that happened during the summer and fall of '89, when the whole world was watching and the neighborhood was full of nonconformists and street people. The Anarchist Switchboard, still a combination organizing center and flophouse, was going through a crisis. It had been founded by academic anarchists who continued paying the rent even as they turned their noses up at the scene which gathered there. Things were getting a little bit too real at the Switchboard; as the Lower East Side anarchist movement gained notoriety, the space came under attack by right-wing skinheads, many of them friendly with the Ninth Precinct cops who patrolled Tompkins Square Park. On July 4, 1989, some of the anarchists joined with the Revolutionary Communist Party for a "flag burning festival" in Washington Square Park, where a fight with skinheads broke out and a member of our contingent was beaten to the pavement and had his head split open, right under the nose of Lt. McKenna. The skinheads then proceeded to the Anarchist Switchboard and beat up some of the slackers there who tried to deny them entry, and during a subsequent march of a hundred anarchists through the streets, an American flag was torn off its pole in front of the Veterans of Foreign Wars hall on Ninth Street.

The July 4 skinhead attack on the Switchboard caused the academic backers to get cold feet, and when the person who had his name on the lease decided to withdraw from the project, the Anarchist Switchboard was shut down by the landlord. Some of the activists immediately started looking for another rented space; at that time, storefronts, though expensive, were not absolutely out of the reach of funky projects like this. However, the gutter punks and hard core squatters compensated for the loss of the Switchboard by squatting a long-abandoned public school on East 4th Street between Avenues B and C, which was given the name of ABC Community Center and which was big enough to accommodate not only the people who used to sleep at the Switchboard, but a good portion of the "summer punk" scene who had rolled into the city and who formed the periphery of the Tompkins Square movement. Those in search of a legal, rented space located a storefront on Saint Mark's Place between First Ave. and Avenue A, a block west of Tompkins Square Park in the more yuppified part of the neighborhood, not far from the former Switchboard. They began outfitting it as an anarchist bookstore, which they called Sabotage Books.

The collective that ran Sabotage Books consisted of the most hardcore Tompkins Square activists in combination with some "mainstream," or purely intellectual anarchists, and there was a lot of tension. The Sabotage bookstore collective was one of the few institutions of the Tompkins Square movement that was not based on spontaneity; it had weekly meetings that ran on the ridiculous principle of consensus, where a single destructive person can stop anything from going forward, and was therefore doomed to failure. However, many good things came out of the Sabotage space itself during the nine months of its existence. Sabotage, although little suited for the purpose, became a kitchen where food was cooked and brought to Tompkins Square Park at night, and the shower in the back was made available to homeless people whom we knew from the park. The storefront was also a venue for mass meetings and parties, and the first computer and printer that were collectively owned by the movement were installed there. At one point early in 1990, Sabotage received an anonymous bomb threat. Instead of evacuating the place, which would have given the (probably crank) caller something to gloat over, we sent out word through the grapevine that a quarter-pound of pot had been spread out on the counter of Sabotage and a "bomb threat party" was in progress. Within an hour the store was packed with revelers, some of whom had never been inside Sabotage before. It was the fact that we were all together that kept us from being intimidated, just as the fact that we were not intimidated kept us all together.

By late summer/fall of 1989, although the big demonstrations around Tent City had somewhat died down, the tents remained and the cops seemed to be tolerating the situation if only to avoid provoking a renewed wave of activism. The core activists were devoting more attention to getting ABC Community Center and Sabotage off the ground than to activities in the park, and this was having a bad effect upon the alliances with homeless organizers that had been forged over the course of the summer. Inspector Julian's ostensible policy of tolerance was more method than madness, since the cops were starting to realize that the thing we responded to best was a police attack, and that a big confrontation with mass arrests was exactly the thing that we needed to galvanize us. Furthermore, Koch was soon going to be out of the picture — David Dinkins was the choice for Democratic mayoral contender in the primaries of Sept. 1989, to face off against Rudolph Giuliani — and one way or another it would be a new ball game. Either a black mayor or a law-and-order white racist mayor, and City officials felt it was no time to take drastic initiatives one way or the other.

A Radical Political and Social History of the Lower East Side

During August there were continued clashes over attempts to close down the bathrooms in Tompkins Square Park at night, which were essential to preventing tent city from becoming an environmental disaster, and the Parks Department temporarily capitulated, apparently in accordance with efforts to stabilize the situation and avoid confrontations. A concert and rally to celebrate the first anniversary of the August 6, 1988 riot was followed by a sit-in on Avenue A; this led to six arrests, including several for pelting a police car with eggs. Homeless activists took the initiative of camping out in U.N. Plaza, where they had been denied a permit, resulting in a number of police raids in late August and early September right within view of an encampment of Chinese students supporting the Tiananmen Square occupation that was going on in Beijing at the time. The connection between the Tompkins Square and Tiananmen Square uprisings was not lost upon the activists-both were mass liberations of public space and rebellions against authoritarianism and most of us, even those who had a general sympathy for communism, identified with the Chinese students.

On September 11, 1989, HPD and the police made an unsuccessful attempt to evict Umbrella House, a squat on Avenue C near East Third Street which also served as space for an artists' collective. The pretext had been the collapse of a neighboring building. Again, the grapevine made it possible for a large group of people to gather very quickly and prevent the cops from erecting barricades. Cops invaded Umbrella House, committing various acts of vandalism including the destruction of artwork, but were unsuccessful in evacuating the building. Inspector Julian was forced to agree to halt the eviction and allow Umbrella House to remain occupied even as the demolition of the building next door continued.

On October 26, 1989, HPD and cops moved in to evict ABC Community Center and thereby set off the biggest and most concerted riot up to that point in the history of the Tompkins Square uprising. The wave of cops that attempted to enter the reconverted school was met with ferocious resistance that included bags of rubble and cement hurled from the roof, which, intentionally or not, failed to hit any of the cops. As the afternoon progressed, a huge crowd gathered at the intersection of Fourth Street and Avenue B. Large M80 firecrackers were used as weapons against the police, a dangerous practice that not all of us approved of, and there was a case of collateral damage in which *Village Voice* reporter Sarah Ferguson almost lost an eye. Her reporting in the *Voice* on this and subsequent demonstrations was somewhat less than flattering; at one point she came two inches short of telling us all to go get a life, but, after all, who could blame her.

There were reports of injuries among the police and 43 arrests among the protesters. For the first time, some of the demonstrators were ordered held on bail and were shipped to Riker's Island before being ultimately released, but no felony trials resulted from the ABC riot. Most of the arrests were for linking arms and resisting attempts to clear the streets and put out the bonfires that had been set on the pavement. They were never able to build a case against anyone for throwing objects from the roof. A wave of agitation spread through the neighborhood over the next couple of months and any fears that the incipient cold weather would put an end to the momentum were unfounded. In the days after the ABC riot, spontaneous demonstrations drawing in some cases hundreds of people wound their way through Alphabet City and up St. Mark's Place. The official theme would be to protest the eviction of ABC Community Center. The characteristic banners made by Tompkins

A. Kronstadt

Square activists, made out of an old bed sheet, or several bed sheets attached to one another, carried dripping, spray painted slogans such as No Police State and Hands Off the Homeless. The demonstrations would invariably end up in Tompkins Square Park, with fraternization and fire barrels.

I would estimate that during the spring, summer, fall, and winter of 1989, very close to one hundred demonstrations, rallies, concerts, and spontaneous interventions were hosted by "the movement," including people around the Switchboard and Sabotage Books, as well as the Tent City organizers and local mavericks. This was the glory year for the Tompkins Square crowd. If you wanted to pinpoint an apex in terms of community support and internal cohesion for the scene and its movers and shakers, you would have to say that it was during the wave of Tent City rallies in July and August. Here we were able to mobilize the greatest number of regular people, who recognized and resented the social trends that led to homelessness, who hated gentrification, but who saw the squats as somewhat of an issue between the squatters and the government and who would never participate in any of the anarchist trashing expeditions that accompanied events like the eviction of ABC Community Center. The unfortunate thing about high points is that things tend to go downhill from there. Although the Tompkins Square riot of August 6, 1988, and the first squatter and Tent City confrontations galvanized the troops and gave us all a sense of solidarity and heroism, continued reliance on spontaneity and the police as the best organizers resulted in a lack of direction. It would have been better, in my opinion, if at the height of our influence in mid-to-late '89 we had put down some roots in local politics, some sort of anti-gentrification alternative to the Democratic political machine.

It is necessary to understand this original sin of "spontaneism" when we talk of the declining phase of the scene in 1990 and 1991. I am not going to condemn the "riot" as a means of protesting evil or promoting social change, it is no more immoral than the everyday violence of law and order in which evictions are carried out like clockwork and homeless people are driven from doorway to doorway at the point of a billy club. On all of these occasions in 1989 and 1990, we did not assemble with the purpose of engaging in violence, we assembled with the purpose of being together. But we responded to incursions upon our rights by City Hall just as American patriots responded to George III: it was like the Boston Massacre, when a bunch of independent-minded Americans pelted the British with snowballs, and the redcoats responded with bullets.

In early November 1989 an incident took place in which one of the key Tompkins Square activists, during one of our many rallies during that time, insisted on stoking up a very large fire, not in a fire barrel but right on the blacktop just inside the Avenue A and St. Mark's entrance, which did some minor damage to a bench and a tree branch. Vandalizing fixtures inside the park was anathema to a great many activists and the homeless people who lived there, and most of those attending the rally moved over to the bandshell, leaving the pyromaniac and his few minions alone with their inferno. This was the first sign of a schism in the core of Tompkins Square activists, and one that would only widen over the next year and a half. The cops used the bonfire incident as yet another pretext for cracking down on fire barrels in the park, and the winter of '89-'90 saw a series of lawsuits on the part of homeless advocates and counter-suits by city lawyers on the subject of the right of people to use fire barrels to survive the cold. On December 10, a detachment of activists broke through the back entrance of the shut down ABC Community Center, where the police had let down their guard, and declared the place to be liberated again. The reoccupation took place just as a huge number of members of the AIDS (Acquired Immune Deficiency Syndrome) activist group ACT UP (AIDS Coalition to Unleash Power) converged on Tompkins Square Park after holding a raucous demonstration outside St. Patrick's Cathedral, thereby diverting the attention of the cops.

Nobody in the scene expected ABC to be retaken, and because members of the Revolutionary Communist Party were prominent in the initial occupying crew, some activists, particularly the anarchists, were convinced that this was an RCP plot to divert the energies of the movement. However, those backing the re-occupiers could always contend that they were giving a focus to a movement that seemed to have lost direction after the big Tent City battles. The reoccupied ABC and the vacant lot across 4th Street became the focus of the movement during the winter of 1989-1990. It is amazing that the police could not figure out that the activists were freely coming and going through the back entrance of the abandoned school, squeezing under a bent piece of fence in the parking lot of the still-functioning school around the corner. People were even bringing armloads of firewood in through the back without being noticed. I personally overheard a police captain guarding the front of the school speculating that we had built a tunnel, Viet Cong style, into the basement of ABC.

If the second ABC occupation accomplished anything, it was that it brought the moderate political forces together around a seemingly safe symbolic issue, since nobody expected the occupation to last very long. On December 13, Father George Kuhn, pastor of St. Brigid's Church near the park, was arrested when he delivered a shipment of food and water to those inside the building. On December 14, police carried out another mass evacuation and raid in Tompkins Square Park, destroying all of the tents and grinding everyone's possessions up in garbage trucks. The media declared the end of Tent City, although the homeless did return to the park and the tents went up again, in a more low-key fashion. Some people who had been evicted from the park now moved into ABC. But the enhanced media attention in the wake of the park raid made the re-occupied ABC a political venue; a Catholic Mass was held outside the former school by Father Kuhn and local priests on December 17, and on December 18, a group of celebrities including Broadway producer Joseph Papp and actors Kevin Klein and Tracey Ullman delivered food to the people inside ABC, in full view of the police, without being arrested.

One reason why the City did not raid ABC Community Center as quickly as everyone expected was that there was about to be a change of regime at City Hall. David Dinkins, New York's first African-American Mayor, had been elected in November of 1989 and was to assume office at the beginning of January, and the lame duck members of the Koch administration had no pressing reason to stick their necks out. They did not intervene in any way when the activists threw a big New Year's Eve bash inside ABC at which a performance by Missing Foundation was the main attraction. In January of 1990, Dinkins' people started out with the velvet glove, inviting ABC supporters to a meeting that was brokered by Local 1199, a politically liberal union with which Dinkins had a close relationship. There, Dinkins

A. Kronstadt

aide Michael Kharfen offered the occupiers a 500-foot row of city owned storefronts as headquarters for homeless organizing. The ABC occupiers, meanwhile, made public their intention
to restore ABC's original function as a school, offering GED preparation, exercise, art, creative writing, political education, and special sessions for senior citizens. However, at dawn
on January 24, the velvet glove was replaced with the iron fist as one hundred cops
descended on ABC, simultaneously breaking through the front and rear walls with the aid of
blow torches, and through the roof. Some of the occupiers fled without being arrested, but
the cops used dogs to round up 10 people inside the building who were hauled off.

Following the second ABC eviction, the Tompkins Square scene was in a funny position. The
Dinkins Administration, perceived by liberal New Yorkers as a breath of fresh air after twelve
years of Koch, had to take some sort of position on the Tompkins Square problem. It was
obvious that the key group of activists, particularly those based at Sabotage Books, did not
expect the new regime to compromise with the movement, and they regarded it as a sacri-
lege to suggest that we should made any concessions to the City government just because
the liberals were back in the saddle. We would continue to attack the City bureaucrats, even
though, with the liberal black mayor, it was no longer "politically correct" to do that.
However, some of the neighborhood's so-called liberals, quality-of-lifers from the Democratic
Party machine who now had their own local rag called *Lower East Side News*, were now taking the offensive again and demanding that Tent City be removed and the park "returned to
the community." By the end of January we were already well on the bad side of the Dinkins
Administration, and these right-wingers were the ones being welcomed at City Hall. The
movement had once again lost direction; in the winter of 1990 there was less activism
around the park than a year earlier and, although the neighborhood crawled with freaks and
bohemians whose favorite gathering place was the sidewalk in front of Sabotage Books, they
were not organically connected to the things that were going on in the park. The events
that were being organized at Sabotage had a more directly anarchist motivation and flavor
than events from a year earlier; they were being planned in advance and flyers, rather than
the grapevine, were the prime organizing tools. When the anarchists held their "Bash the
Rich" demonstration in the park on the anniversary of the eviction of Tya Scott's building,
which included a scavenger hunt against yuppie buildings and during which a drunken anarchist burned a hole in Inspector Julian's trench-coat, most of the homeless people did not
want anything to do with it. They considered things like this provocations that would get
homeless people in trouble and bring excessive numbers of hostile cops into the park.

In order to revive the spirit of 1989 and take advantage of the spring pheromones, the gang
at Sabotage, in March of 1990, began putting together plans for a second Resist to Exist
festival, on an even larger scale than the previous year. As a means of presenting, in particular, the anarchist political point of view, but also that of the Tompkins Square political
movement as a whole, the first Resist to Exist had served the purpose of establishing a pole,
a tangible institution of the Lower East Side anarchist/squatter scene such that people from
around the city could participate and acquire a political identity. After all, we owned no real
estate like a church or a corporation, and in order to exist as a socially relevant entity one
must have a place that people can come to. So, permits and money were gathered for a
four-day concert that would build up to Squatter Mayday, 1990. While Sabotage Books was
humming with organizing activity — postering runs were going out every night plastering the

A Radical Political and Social History of the Lower East Side

neighborhood with solicitations for performers and volunteers to make the Resist to Exist concert happen — the neighborhood continued to hear rumors of site control over squat buildings being transferred to this or that agency, and of renewed plans to slap a curfew upon Tompkins Square Park. The core activists like myself were participating in dozens of relatively small demonstrations, but the political momentum during March, April, and early May of 1990 was nowhere near what it was in 1989. The problem was that people were waiting for some kind of attack — eviction of a squat or an attempt to re-impose the curfew — instead of taking measures to organize something.

During this same period of time, the intelligent Inspector Julian, and the rest of the cops, were thinking strategically while we were not. They were observing the way our people spontaneously reacted to things, and were thinking about what the cops did wrong in 1988 and 1989. Some in our ranks saw Inspector Julian's liberalism with regard to beer and pot, and when it suited him even to tents and fire barrels, as a sign of weakness. He, on the other hand, saw himself as giving us enough rope to hang ourselves. A crowd, which forms on the basis of spontaneous reaction, has no mind and can be manipulated. The thing that was preventing the police from doing what they would do today, namely deny us the right to assemble at all was the political climate which, in these years following the stock market crash of 1987, had turned against big real estate and gentrification. Julian was looking for the right moment to manipulate us into pulling the political rug out from under ourselves, and he succeeded in doing this on May 1, 1990.

Here is what happened at the May Day riot of 1990[3]: The Resist to Exist concert in the Tompkins Square bandshell continued for three days. The first three days were incident-free and on each night the organizers voluntarily shut the amplifiers down at the moment when the sound permit expired, which varied from 8:00 to 9:00 from day to day. On May 1, the concert started a little late, partially as a result of one of the organizers being arrested that morning for sleeping in a tent in the park. As the 9:00 curfew approached, the party was still well underway and there was one more performer waiting in the wings. It was common in those days for people in the audience to climb on the stage and dance, especially at the end of a long and successful event, and there were at least a dozen people doing this just before nine. The last performer got on stage, and the organizers were expecting the cops to have the common sense to wait the few minutes for him to finish his act, which would have ended at about 9:10. At a minute after 9, however, Sergeant Marron of the 9th Precinct climbed the stairs of the stage, told some random people who were not the organizers that the show was over, and engaged in a shoving match with people who stood in his way. Julian was standing right in the back with a phalanx of cops, as if he knew in advance that Marron's clumsy method of shutting down the concert would cause a riot since the Inspector had been observing us long enough to know our crowd dynamics. It was a deliberate move on Julian's part; had he simply been interested in ending the concert, he could have flipped a switch to cut off the electricity in the Parks Department office at the other end of the park, where a large contingent of police were already stationed. Julian was carrying out an experiment in which would see whether he could preemptively cause a disturbance under circumstances where the rioters would get no sympathy from the press or the public and where some of the arrests could result, as had not heretofore happened, in felony convictions.

A. Kronstadt

The cops advanced, mounted the stage in droves, and started hitting people with their clubs as three hundred concert participants looked on. Within minutes there was a fracas in which several cops were hit squarely in the head with bottles, while the organizers of Resist to Exist, some of them with their faces dripping blood, were hauled away in cop cars. The crowd regrouped outside the park and one more Tompkins Square riot raged far into the night. People swarmed through the streets and up St. Mark's Place, then back to Avenue A where the biggest bonfire in the history of the movement was built — this is the one that caused the scars that can still be seen on the blacktop on Avenue A between Seventh Street and St. Mark's Place. When the riot cops busted up the crowd around the fire, there was a surge up Avenue B and another attack on the Christodora building. A contingent of cops arrived to defend the Christodora, but they were pelted by a barrage of debris so dense that it was they, and not the crowd, that were forced to retreat. The crowd was chased through the park by the helmeted riot cops and a reporter from *USA Today* was beaten unconscious by the police, who were running around like wild men hitting stragglers.

The press the next day treated this as a riot by common criminals. Restoring order in Tompkins Square Park was now on the agenda of the Dinkins administration, which had heretofore treated the situation with kid gloves. On a rainy afternoon the following week, a contingent of high-ranking police brass showed up in the park, pointing in different directions and jotting things down on maps. That Friday, the park was flooded with a small army of police, at least forty of them in the four-square block park at any given time, arresting people for the slightest violation of any arcane park rule, even for sitting on the back of a bench rather than the seat. Lieutenant McKenna, the scourge of Washington Square Park, was coordinating it all. It was a little taste of Giuliani in the days of Dinkins. The movement held a "speakout" on the corner of St. Mark's Place and Avenue A that week. Cops shined spotlights into the crowd and made arrests on its margins. A cop car regularly showed up at Sabotage Books and dispersed the groups of punks that hung around the front, again using bright spotlights. For the entire summer, ample police patrols were instituted up and down the streets around the park to make alcohol and pot busts, even of people sitting on the steps of their own buildings, and to break up groups of people hanging around. Old neighborhood residents compared the repression to that which followed the heyday of hippiedom, in 1968, when people were arrested for sitting on their own stoops.

So this was what life was going to be like under the liberal Dinkins administration. Although there was no immediate move to evict the homeless people from the park, many of the homeless blamed the activists for the enhanced police repression, and the solidarity of the year before began to ebb. Fingers were pointed in various directions, defensiveness set in and, as often happens in time of great repression, paranoia caused people to turn on one another. In June and July of 1990, there was a split in the collective that ran Sabotage Books. The person who had his name on the lease wanted nothing more to do with the core activists, and eventually canceled the lease and left the movement with no indoor organizing center. The Tompkins Square movement, although still intact and combative, was now in a much less favorable situation. Just as the heat came down in the park and it became more difficult for members of the scene to interact there, the activists were now driven back to their kitchen tables to organize. The posters continued to appear on the walls, but it was now a rearguard action. Most of the propaganda now was reacting to the repression in the neighborhood: the continual expansion of police authority was becoming the exclusive issue; we no longer had time for the more joyful, playful anarchism of the previous year.

In spite of the repression and bad morale, the Tompkins Square scene hung together during the months following the Mayday riot. The movement had never before had as many of its most enthusiastic organizers facing felony charges, and although the Mayday defendants had a core of people who rallied around them, the continual court appearances and need to plan out a defense drained their energies. Concerts and rallies continued to happen in 1990, with much larger police presence, and the focus turned to more global issues including the threat of a Persian Gulf War. During Operations Desert Shield and Desert Storm, mammoth demonstrations swept through Manhattan and anarchists from our scene pioneered tactics of "unarresting" cohorts who were grabbed by the police, as well as breakaway marches and trashing expeditions that are now being used by anti-globalization activists at every gathering of international finance. Some of our antiwar speakouts in Tompkins Square Park were attacked by right-wing skinheads and there were vast disagreements on the subject of the war within the homeless encampment which included many Vietnam veterans. At the big anti-war demonstrations, the police knew our faces and would send groups of undercover cops to follow us around. The Workers World Party, a stodgy Communist group that organized some of the anti-war rallies in late '90 and early '91, saw the Tompkins Square Anarchists as their mortal enemy. At one demonstration a phalanx of their parade marshals attempted to rip down our banner and there was a shoving match between us and the commies reminiscent of the kind that more often transpired between us and the police. The most enduring legacy of the Tompkins Square scene, although we cannot claim exclusive credit as its originators, is this style of anarchist street fighting seen later at meetings of the international capitalist thieves from Seattle to Genoa.

In early 1991, just after the end of this first Persian Gulf War, the Tompkins Square activists were planning to start a coalition to organize events around the Democratic National Convention, which was to take place in Madison Square Garden the following year. There were bad vibes around the park; the repression worsened as Inspector Julian, who had outlived his usefulness, was replaced by a series of more ordinary, hairy-knuckled commanders. Rumor had it that the city was planning to close down the park and carry out a full-scale renovation; this was what the quality-of-lifers, now personified by poverty pimp and future City Councilman Antonio Pagan, had been demanding ever since the Mayday riot. The movement had acquired a new indoor space, Mayday Books on Seventh Street between Avenues B and C. The scene there was more subdued: a wild party that we had thrown on the day Mayday Books opened got us on the bad side of the drug dealers who controlled the block, and we had to be careful not to aggravate the situation. At one of our meetings to plan the coalition for the Democratic Convention, an argument broke out among several key activists who had been the closest of friends and comrades since the early days of the Tompkins Square Movement, and this led to a political schism. It was on this forgotten date that the end of the movement as I have described it in the preceding pages took place.

Since I regard the Memorial Day riot of May 31, 1991, as denouement, while others go so far as to call it the day the movement died, it is not necessary to treat it at length.

A. Kronstadt

Concerts were still taking place in the park even amid the repression and the rumor that the City was going to shut Tompkins Square Park down. On Memorial Day, the concert that was traditionally put together by the hippie pacifist wing of the Tompkins Square Activists went off in a peaceful fashion, until about a half hour before it was scheduled to end. At that point, a highly familiar person whom this writer and many others had never trusted as a source of accurate information came running into the crowd standing by the bandshell shouting "Police brutality on Avenue A," and was followed back to Avenue A by a group of fifty or so people from the concert. It was learned that a young man who hung around with certain members of the scene had just been grabbed by cops off of a line of people waiting to receive food from a local soup kitchen, whereupon he was jacked up against the cop car and arrested. Many different versions of the event filtered back to the bandshell, suggesting that no one really knew what happened, but even before the concert had begun to shut down, there was a clash between some punks and the police, and bottles were thrown.

One of our hotheads, cut adrift in the abovementioned schism, decided to lead a traditional charge on the Christodora, and got some people to follow him as he ran up to the door of that establishment and tried to bash it in with a cardboard pole. I do not often quote Karl Marx anymore, but there is a saying by him that goes something like "history repeats itself, the first time as tragedy and the second time as farce." The Tompkins Square riot of August 6-7, 1988 was a spontaneous response to a very palpable, transparent attack upon democracy that a broad swath of the movement could understand. All of the confrontations of 1989, peaceful and not so peaceful, shared this model. The Mayday riot of May 1, 1990, while the police started it, concerned an insult dealt to the scene itself, i.e., the police rushing our stage, and it was less easy for the community to understand why it happened. Finally, there was the Memorial Day riot which started on the basis of a rumor and was stoked up by the bravado of a group of activists who were, let us put it bluntly, pissed off at another group of activists. A bonfire was built in the street, as always, and volleys of bottles were thrown at the cops. However, as the thing progressed, people whom we had never seen before were throwing bottles at occupied buildings around the park, and someone else showed up with a crowbar and ripped the gating off the front of a discount store on Avenue A, prompting a spree of looting. These were things that had never before happened at any of our events, and reflected a combination of the decay of the scene and frustration at the continual repression.

The response from the Dinkins Administration was swift. At dawn on June 3, 1991, while activists camped out overnight in the park knowing that the end was near, six hundred police marched into Tompkins Square Park, drove out the crowd and arrested everyone who refused to move. They then erected enormous cyclone fences and posted cops around the periphery of the park at two-meter intervals. Large demonstrations took place in the subsequent days and weeks, but the police controlled things by implementing Giuliani tactics pre-Giuliani: all those arrested were now being held in the system for three days. The park would remain closed until late summer, 1992, during which city officials were to implement renovations as well as an ambitious program to change the "use patterns" of the park via aggressive policing. The lid had been clamped upon the cauldron.

A Radical Political and Social History of the Lower East Side

In 1991 the City bureaucracy delivered a one-two punch against the Tompkins Square movement in the form of the closing of the park and a criminal trial of the key activists arrested during and after the May Day Riot of 1990. The City's plans to punish the activists did not succeed, although the three month trial during late 1991 and early 1992, one of the longest in New York State Supreme Court history, sapped the strength of those who had made the events of 1989 happen. In the end, a New York City jury acquitted the organizers of Resist to Exist 1990 of charges of riot, incitement to riot, and assault on police officers. Another member of the scene, less involved with organizing the concert, was convicted of misdemeanor incitement to riot; he was sentenced to the maximum, a year in upstate prison, the sacrificial lamb for the frustrated forces of repression.

I am going to end this story here because there is no point going into detail about the declining phase of the Tompkins Square scene; it is clear enough from the last several paragraphs why it took place. Some of my old comrades will no doubt be angry because I have spoken ill of the Memorial Day riot, which, undeniably, was a righteous community response to police brutality. Indeed, they have a point when they contend that, given the possibility of responses such as that which happened on May 31, 1991, Giuliani would never have been able to impose his kind of police regime on the city. But, for the education of future activists, certain things must be said about the events of that night which reflect upon the inadequacies of the Tompkins Square scene. Spontaneity was both the life and the death of our movement, and although we were able to attract a large periphery of rightfully angry people, because we relied on the uncontrolled, the unplanned, we were not able to crystallize them out of their entropy.

Even with all of its faults, however, the Tompkins Square movement was justified and righteous. The only thing for which I condemn myself and the people whom I worked and played with, day and night, from 1988 through 1991, is for failing to make the changes that we believed in happen. It is because we did not form a viable political alternative to Giuliani-ism and gentrification that these evils have prospered, and New York's creativity and freedom are threatened with extinction. But the very fact that anyone resisted at all, just like the fact that some of us continue to resist, each in our own way, is what redeems this city and has stopped things from becoming as bad as they could be.

1. A detailed account of the eviction of 316 E. Eighth St. and the confrontation that follows can be found in Issue No. 2 of the *Shadow* ("Domino Effect: Another Homestead Building Bites the Dust").

2. Readers interested in the full stories behind the disruption of the hearing on park rules, as well as the squat eviction and ensuing riot at 319 East Eighth Street should refer to Issue No. 3 of the *Shadow* ("HPD Strikes Again").

3. And those seeking more detail, as well as dramatic photography, should consult Issue no. 11 of the *Shadow* ("Pigs Riot")

Chapter 2

Excerpts From Each One Teach One: Up and Out of Poverty,
Memoirs of a Street Activist
By Ron Casanova & Steven Blackburn

TENT CITY

At two in the morning on August 6, 1988, I was standing in Tompkins Square Park near the entrance on Avenue B, across the street from a bar and a liquor store, holding a Bible in my hands, watching a riot between police and people in the park.

I always seemed to come back to Tompkins Square Park. That night I stood watching over some of the homeless people who wanted no part of the clash and who were trying to sleep on benches behind the band shell. Right then I didn't even care if I was part of the world. At that time I was experiencing inner turmoil. I don't remember exactly, but I believe I was either contemplating leaving the Bowery Mission or had just left it.

A writer named Sarah Ferguson, who lived in the neighborhood, asked me that night why this group of homeless people was outside the circle of violence.

"We just want to be left alone," I told her.

The police had told us to stay where we were in the park so we weren't caught in the beatings. It felt like we were in a bubble that the raging violence couldn't touch. Later I painted a picture of that night which I titled "Shadow of Protection."

In the end, a lot of people got beat up in that action. 121 complaints of police brutality got filed, although not one of the officers was ever convicted or punished, mainly because the court system would not admit that police brutality had occurred unless fellow officers said it had. And the officers were not talking.

Rather than put myself through the Bowery Mission program any longer, I withdrew. Hurting, disappointed in my life and the world, I went out of control. I returned to my old ways of drinking and wildness, living in abandoned buildings and in Tompkins Square Park. Once again alcohol was in control of me, not the other way around. Though I did not commit any crimes or do needle drugs during that period, I was wild, reacting against the strictness and the unfairness of the Mission.

After I left the Bowery Mission, I went back to Shanty Town for a little while, but by that time it was ruled by a homeless gentleman who was controlling people in the camp through alcohol, through drugs. With him it was all about power, but power just for him. That was not my cup of tea, so I went back to living in Tompkins Square Park.

A Radical Political and Social History of the Lower East Side

I'll give credit to a Christian crew out of Jersey. I forget the name of the organization, but they used to come down there to Tompkins Square Park to try to talk religion to us, and they always brought us food. They'd come down every Saturday to sing their Gospel songs, pass out their tracts and feed hundreds of people. They served the best food, so a lot of homeless from Queens and the Bronx came down on Saturdays to eat. Though the feeding was good, it brought all kinds of people, and not all the homeless were very friendly. Sometimes they were very angry, sometimes they would steal, sometimes there would be a fight.

Because of my recent experience at the Bowery Mission, I myself was feeling anger toward Christians at that time. In the beginning when the Christians from Jersey would come I would tell them "Please, leave me alone, I'm sick," or "I need a drink," or "I want to get high."

They were smart, however. They learned not to keep shoving their religion down our throats. They did not stop coming and showing their concern for us just because we refused to listen to their Christianity. What convinced me of their sincerity is that they came back despite our refusal. Because of their humanistic ideals, they still fed and clothed and listened to us.

For a time I moved in with some squatters at a building on Ninth Street between B and C. While I was there, somebody from the Bowery Mission tracked me down because they had something for me, which came as a surprise: a good-sized wooden cross. All the time I was at the Bowery Mission I had been after the Mennonites to build me some wagons for hauling food around the streets to help feed people, and here instead they sent a cross. But I guess I must have smiled when I saw that cross because it had been put together for me by the Mennonite kids as a class project, and I had a fondness for those kids. As it happened, one of the squatters in the building was a black-haired Mennonite minister named Frank, who had a blonde wife and baby, so I donated the cross for the room in our building we had set up half as a kitchen, half as a meditation room.

That winter it got very cold, even for New York City. One night in about the middle of December 1988, my Polish brother, Ed Rutter, went to sleep on a park bench in Tompkins Square Park. Even in the winter, Eddie wouldn't go in a city-run shelter because he was afraid of getting hurt or robbed there. That night he had an overcoat, two blankets and a bottle to keep him warm. Another homeless man, Elliot Lopez, helped Eddie over to a bench next to where Lopez bad built a fire in one of the park's metal trashcans. During the night, a police officer kicked the trashcan over.

"No fires allowed in the park," the policeman said.

And the mercury just kept falling. It got down to five degrees that night.

By morning, Eddie had frozen to death. Lopez said Eddie's hand was reaching out to the scattered, cold ashes where the fire had been. Later when I heard what had happened, it made me angry, but scared too. I thought of my own plight. I was almost 44 years old and

Ron Casanova and Steven Blackburn

without a secure place to live. I could end up like Eddie. But for the time being, all I did was drink until I forgot to be scared.

Unfortunately, at the squatters' building we had problems sometimes with the Puerto Rican brothers and sisters in the neighborhood because they considered squatters to be hippies, and they did not like the idea of all these hippies moving into their block. So most of the neighbors there did not like us. They were the Latino rich; they were only into their cars and didn't think about the problems of people with no place to live. Partly because of that animosity, I quit living there and returned to the park.

It seems to me that it was around my birthday in 1989 when I ran across my old friend Red Wolf. I was sitting on a bench in Tompkins Square Park and he came by. We had not seen each other in ages.

"Hey, man, what's up?" he asked.

"Ain't nothin' to, it," I said. "I left the Bowery Mission a while back, and right now I need a place to stay."

Red Wolf was on his way out of the city, but he pulled a tent out of his knapsack and gave it to me. I pitched the tent in Tompkins Square Park close to Ninth Street and Avenue A.

Next day, Red Wolf was back. He ended up not leaving town, so we shared his tent. We were there about a day and a half when a friend of ours, a fellow named Spider, pitched a tent next to us. Next thing I knew, my good friend Gypsy showed up and set his tent up as well. Within that week we must have had anywhere from five to ten different tents in this one area of the park, and a number of the people in them had been part of the Casanovas. I felt a sense of security being with people I knew —a comradeship.

All kinds of people came to the park whether they lived there or not: African Americans, old Polish people and Ukrainians; Cubans, long-haired hippies and spike-haired punk rockers; Puerto Ricans playing jibaro music, skin-heads in steel-toed army boots, Jamaican rastas with dreadlocks. People walked their dogs while skate-boarders shot past concentrating chess players and heavy metal bands. Reeboks were squeaking as pick-up teams played basketball while mothers walked their infants in strollers. But something different was happening this time. People who were coming to sleep in the park began to act aware of themselves as a community. I felt happy because it reminded me of the Village in the old days.

People just kept coming. The police themselves, all over New York, began telling homeless people in the subways and doorways of the Bronx, Brooklyn and Queens to go down to Tompkins Square Park. We had an influx of people coming in, pitching tents and building shacks. The park became a sanctuary. I guess the cops and the neighborhood liked it that way because while we were in the park we were not sleeping in their doorways. We were not blocking any businesses. At the time we did not realize that we would soon have to fight to live in the park. We did not know that we would have to fight to survive. And the police had helped to set up the situation.

A Radical Political and Social History of the Lower East Side

But June 1989 was fantastic. We were a festive combination of squatters, anarchists, activists and mostly just homeless people. Some people slept in the band shell, some people slept beneath the flat roof of the brick pavilion that was between the restrooms. We had a lot of homemade lean-to type tents made out of clear plastic, stretched over wooden frames, and pitched side by side on the hard-packed dirt underneath the park trees near the benches. They were about the size of pup tents. Refrigerator-box cardboard walls for some, store-bought tents for others. People slept covered by blanket and sheets, or some had sleeping bags. We were getting a lot of clothes donations, which we hung up on fences for anybody who needed them and could use them. Beside each one of the tents we had campfires, and there was one communal campfire where we fed people who were hungry. People in the neighborhood would go out and buy or collect food and bring it for our kitchen. The word got out that we were feeding the homeless and anybody was welcome.

I had seen people living in the streets since I was young. The general plight of the homeless did not really affect me back then; I only worried about myself. But by that summer of 1989, things had changed very drastically from the way they had been. I had never seen so many homeless people.

We had a veteran living in the park, another drinker, who we called Old Man John. Old Man John was disabled mentally; he couldn't live with his family, and his sisters couldn't take him —he couldn't live with anybody. In fact, he was a thorn in my side because he was a very aggravating person.

Old Man John was a coffee fanatic. He made sure we had coffee. If there wasn't coffee at the crack of dawn, I was the first person he would come to.

"Cas! Where's the coffee? Where's the coffee? Where's the coffee?"

I guess I had the patience of Job in those days to keep from kicking his ass. But he did not want to live in an institution, and I understood that. So I would get up and take the coffee pot somebody had donated and start boiling the water on the fire. We strained out coffee the best we could.

Old Man John also wrote poetry of a sort. He would jot down sentences, fragments of thought. A woman from the neighborhood used to put out a paper printed in Jersey called *Voices From the Street*. She somehow got John to write out one of his poems and she edited it down and printed it in her paper. Unfortunately, I lost my copy in one of the police raids that were to come.

Soon we had a lot of churches supporting us. One day some people we knew from Long Island brought a van full of food from a gourmet store. We had something like 18 boxes of groceries. We bagged them individually and passed out the bags to people who came by and needed the food.

Everybody and anybody could eat with us. At first we would be cooking on fires outside the tents. We did not have a stove. Then the Parks Department warned us that no fires were allowed in the park, so when we finished cooking a meal, we put out the fire. For a while the authorities left us alone. Eventually, however, they started messing with us again, saying no fires in the park. They brought in the Police Department and the Fire Department to try to get our camp fires extinguished. But that plan backfired. As it turned out, the police and firefighters went all over the park checking these fires. The Police Department said there was nothing wrong with them. They were safe fires. The Fire Department also said they were safe fires.

Not happy at all with this result, the Parks Department went to court about it. This time it didn't go our way.

"Put them out," the court ruled. So we moved our cooking inside of a tent where we made ourselves a big stove out of bricks. Pretty soon we lucked out and got us a cook, a black dude by the name of Artie Wilson. He first came to the park because some of his friends had come to Tompkins Square from different institutional shelters. When we saw that Artie could cook, we got to know him very well. He became our official cook. Artie liked cooking for the people who came.

"People are here for various reasons," I remember Artie saying. "How you wind up in the park, you don't want to remember, but you are here, so we have to deal with it from there."

On that brick stove, Artie prepared food three to four times a day and fed several hundred people at each meal, and did a very good job of it. Our regular meal times were morning, afternoon and maybe about five o'clock in the evening. The neighborhood anarchists helped with the food. They worked out of a bookstore called Sabotage, which closed at four in the afternoon. Afterwards, they would come to the park and drop off chickens and vegetables. The anarchists liked to wear dark clothes, a lot of black, and they smoked cigarettes continuously. Frank, a Latino anarchist, dressed all in black and wore a beret. He had a narrow face and whiskers on his chin. Frank was very intense.

"We're facing a fascist police order in this city," Frank said one time. "It's out to attack and kill blacks and Latinos especially, but really it's indiscriminate in terms of poor people in general."

Artie would cook the chicken and vegetables the anarchists brought. Later at night the squatters would come by with more food and so we would eat again. The late crowd. We would pretty much feed people throughout the night because people would come at various times.

Neighborhood people would come down with their instruments and play music. One night a guy brought his portable xylophone and played while we sat smoking reefer and drinking beer and talking. On every bench you could see people sitting, conversing, politicizing. They were all comfortable here. It was a beautiful atmosphere.

I noticed a tall, slim woman talking with some people. I went over and introduced myself. She said her name was Karen Margolis, and she was an activist. Back in the 1950s, when she

A Radical Political and Social History of the Lower East Side

was only eight years old, she had gone on a CORE (Congress of Racial Equality) Freedom Ride. Later she worked against U.S. involvement in Vietnam, and in the '80s she opposed U.S. intervention in Central America. Until recently Karen had taught school in New York.

I expressed my interest in getting to know her. Well, that night she left with the married couple she had come with, but in the days to come she became one of the neighborhood people who would come around bringing food.

Early in the morning Karen would be one of the first supporters to come to the park. She would come wake me, always bringing me something to eat. She was a lot of fun to wake up to. In the freshness of the morning, Karen and I would sit and drink coffee and talk, and as the summer days passed, I learned about her. Karen had lived for a year on the Upper West Side with a dude she said "turned into the fiancé from hell." Karen told me that after she had gotten pregnant, her fiancé had become physically and mentally abusive. So Karen left him and spent a few months with a friend. Eventually she took the shelter route, moving into a shelter and going on welfare. She was 39 at the time.

In those days, Mayor Koch had a program for pregnant women — Karen was able to get into a low-income tenant co-op in the East Village. While Karen was living there, she had her son, and she named him Ethan.

"The name means 'strong'," she told me. "It's such a beautiful name."

Our community grew, and we soon gave it the name of "Tent City." Things were happening fast. Tent City did not happen as a planned organization. There was no revolution, no movement there. It started as a place where people came because they needed a place to stay. We had no place to stay, so we went to the park and pitched a tent. It was people of like minds, comfortable with each other, sharing their space in the park. Tent City was open to anyone and everyone who rejected the city's so-called solutions to homelessness. We had a slogan: "No Housing, No Peace." Now that did not mean that we wanted a violent confrontation with the authorities. That meant we were not going to allow ourselves to be quietly put out of sight in jails or dangerous shelters. That is no solution — that is burial.

Some of the squatters and anarchists and other activists from the neighborhood who were already in the antipoverty movement started talking to us about how to deal with the authorities. There were several groups and they all had plans and ideas. I would just pick out which one sounded the best and make suggestions along those lines to the Tent City residents. Usually they agreed.

Something was happening in Tompkins Square Park, All our lives we had accepted poverty as a way of life, whatever the reason. People had accepted welfare as a way of life. Now we were doing things for ourselves. Outside the entrance to the park, we set up a table with information about Tent City, poverty, homelessness, and social services people could get. We began educating people about the politics of poverty, During the day, while most people from our park community would go looking for work or do their hustle to bring some money in, I would sit there in the camp and paint. That was my hustle. I would keep an eye on peoples' clothes and property while doing my art.

I would stretch a t-shirt over a section of cardboard and slant it off my knees as I sat up against a tree painting. Then we would sell the shirts at the table we had set up. That summer I painted and sold a lot of t-shirts showing scenes from Tent City and Tompkins Square Park.

Because I had been living in the area off and on since the mid-'60s, I had a lot of friends in the street, a lot of people who knew me. Sometimes they and the more curious people from the neighborhood would come by the park to find out what Tent City was about.

"Why are you living in the park?" they would ask me.

I would explain that most of us in the park were single people, and we could not afford to rent. If you were to rent a room in Manhattan, you would be paying something like $200 a week. First of all, if you could even find a room in that low a price range, the place would be roach-infested and filthy. You were lucky if you got a window, You were lucky if nobody broke into your room.

Let's say you are working and getting paid the minimum wage of 1996. You cannot even afford that rent. Do the math. For the sake of discussion, let's say you're getting paid one and a half times the minimum wage; hell, round it off to $6.50 an hour. You might be able to make rent, if taxes don't take too much. But then where do you get the money to eat? What happens if you get sick? If you have kids, what about child care? How do you get your laundry taken care of? What about transportation? Utilities? And on and on and on and on. The minimum wage needs to be tripled.

"Why don't you homeless go into the shelters?" some people would come by and ask me.

"Have you ever been to a shelter?" I would answer. "Have you ever been to the shelter on Wards Island? Go to Wards Island; I would tell such people. "Then take a walk through Tompkins Square Park to see the difference."

People in Tompkins Square had their problems, but they also kept their own kind of dignity, which you will not find among the fearful inmates of a shelter. The homeless of Tompkins Square remained individuals, refusing to become the beaten?down penitents that too many of the shelters want, demand, and make.

Kids did not live with us much at the park, although kids would come down there to visit a parent who was living in the park. Some of these kids came with their grandparents or some other relative.

Despite the fact that a lot of the shelters are terrible, there are reasons some people go there, even though they may not want to. Being homeless is hard on couples. If you really love a person, you don't want them sleeping on the ground and worrying about where they are going to eat. A homeless family living on the streets has an added problem: the welfare system or the courts will take away the kids if they catch up with that family. So if there is a homeless family that does not want to go into a shelter, they have to dodge the law so they can keep their kids with them. Some of the family people I have met in the streets are responsible parents. For example, they try to stay in one area so the kids can go to school, and if the kids get sick they take them to a clinic or hospital. But it is much more difficult to stay out of the shelter system if you have children or a loved one with you. Some families who do go into the shelter system don't want to, but they do it for the sake of their kids.

One of the biggest problems we experienced at Tent City was that the Parks Department would lock the public restrooms every day at 4 p.m. That made things difficult. At that time, counting Tent City and the other folks who were not part of our camp, you had anywhere from 300 to 325 people living in the park, including some women and children, and no bathroom after four o'clock. Of course that meant that you would get a bad smell in some areas. We preferred the restroom to using the trees and the grass. We did not want to go to the bathroom outside, but we were left with no choice.

Late that month, the police told us to move to the other side of the park. We told them we did not want to move. Finally, Deputy Inspector Michael Julian, of the 9th Precinct, came in person. Julian was tall, slim, and fairly good-looking. He had come into power under the banner of Bush's "kinder, gentler" phrase. But he was very condescending. He came over to us and told us we had to move to the Avenue B side of Tompkins Square Park.

"We'll leave you guys alone in this park if you go down to Avenue B and pitch your tents," he told us.

I said, "Hey, you gotta be crazy."

I told him we refused to go because that side of the park was drug-infested. That was where the people who did the drugs hung out, and we did not want to be bothered with that. We did not want anything to do with hard drugs. Imagine a situation with over 300 people living in the park at one time, and a little bit more than half were doing needle drugs. There were also people from the neighborhood who came to the park to buy needle drugs. In every section of the park except ours, they were dealing heroin and cocaine. We had created our own security force in Tent City, and we would kick out people who were doing heroin or coke.

Besides the hard drug situation, we had strategic reasons for not wanting to be bunched together into one crowd with everybody who was living in the park. Not all the people living in the park got along with each other. We had an ongoing feud with the punk rockers who lived in another part of the park. More importantly, though, we were aware that a park curfew law was going into effect starting July 5th. We were aware that the parks department police were going to come and get us.

Ron Casanova and Steven Blackburn

"There is no way you are going to put us in one bundle,' we told Julian. "We don't intend to make it easy for you, and we have no intention of leaving."

So we stayed where we were and Julian and the city officials stayed where they were — for the time being. Their stated reason for wanting us out of the park was bogus. They said they were concerned about the drug problems in the park. Drugs had been rampant in the park for years and the police ignored it. Now suddenly they were concerned.

One part of the problem was that since the police were sending any and all homeless people to the park, drug use in the park naturally increased. But the truth of the matter is, if it weren't for the fact that Tent City existed in Tompkins Square Park, they would not have done anything about the drugs. Once we started making noise about poverty and homelessness, the cops started putting it in the paper that the homeless people in the park were all drug addicts. Later, they told the *New York Times* that we had been living there for only a week, as if that lie could justify what they eventually did.

On Wednesday, the fifth of July, 1989, we waited.

Police were gathering, but nothing overt was happening yet. Over at Washington Square Park, a lot of skinheads had been burning American flags, demonstrating against anybody living in Tompkins Square Park. Then they left Washington Square Park, marching to Tompkins Square Park. They came into the park raising hell, trying to scare all of us out.

I was sitting in front of my tent with Red Wolf. We were just sitting there on one side of the benches, the skinheads and their crowd on the other side of the benches. As long as the skinheads stayed on their side and didn't come to our tents, we were going to leave it alone. But Red Wolf and I sat ready with our pieces of pipe. Instead of trying to calm down these skinheads, or walk them out, the cops just watched.

We passed the word around that the skinheads were coming. There were a lot of people who were scared. It was bad enough we were going to get taken by the cops, but we were not going to let anybody else do it. Everybody started coming out from their tents, and even the punk rockers came over carrying sticks and pipes. They were with us.

We were ready to do business.

The skinheads were surrounded. They were confronted by the homeless residents of the park, as well as activists and people from the neighborhood who were coming to our aid. That's when the cops started dispersing the crowd. As it turned out, most of the skinheads, seeing the crowd of homeless people with clubs and bats, realized they were not going to be able to do what they wanted, so they backed off. So we had a rest that day.

At nine that evening the police force came.

More than 250 police in riot gear with long billy clubs advanced on the park, with about a dozen Parks Department police. Helmeted police on horses; helicopters loudly chopping over-

A Radical Political and Social History of the Lower East Side

head. The police told all non-homeless people to leave the park. But by that time we had almost 200 supporters from the area.

At 9:30, three green Parks Department garbage trucks rumbled into the park. The line of police pushed us back, while the Parks Department workers came in tearing and ransacking, knocking down our handmade shelters with sledgehammers and axes and throwing food, clothes, and IDs into the garbage trucks.

The cops were already hip to the idea that Tent City contained the noise-makers and the ones that were going to give them the problem. They cleared out all the other shacks and tents in the park before they came to the Tent City area. This was Inspector Julian's "kinder, gentler" way — the same as all the rest: dragging off homeless people.

"Out of the park and into the street!" people were chanting. "No police state!"

This was my first time being involved in anything this heavy. As I watched, I was scared, but I was angry too. I had no intention of leaving because my blood was in that neighborhood. One of my daughters had been born on Ludlow Street nearby. My Polish friend had died on a bench there, frozen to death. All my life I had tried to escape New York and make a life. I had worked in New Jersey, Wisconsin and Florida. But by the night the cops came in, I was at the point where I didn't want to go anywhere else anymore. I no longer wanted to escape New York. This time I would not stand apart from what was happening.

When the cops were coming to tear down all the tents, Red Wolf and I stayed, as did some of the punk rockers and some concerned citizens from Jersey who were willing to stay there and maybe get their heads beat in. I decided I was going to sit there by my tent, and they would have to pick me up and take me away. An inspector or captain kept coming up to me.

"Take your stuff and leave," he would say.

"I'm not going to leave:' I kept telling him.

At last he said, "If you don't do it, we're going to have to come in and people are going to get hurt."

That was a good method because I did not want any blood on my hands, especially the blood of people we were trying to help. I did not want anybody to get hurt. So I told the guys to come on and we split.

One of our Tent City residents, a black man named Keith Thompson, was sitting on the ground crying, with one arm over his suitcase and his other clutching a garbage bag of his belongings. Armed police stood guard with their arms crossed or hands on their guns, making sure that no one stopped the Parks Department workers from trashing the belongings of the homeless. I watched as real litter got left in the park while the Parks Department workers threw everything some of us had including ID, medication, and clothing — into the mouths of those big green trash trucks.

That is the moment I became an activist, when I saw the destruction. I realized that the government or powers-that-be could do that at any given time. Now it became personal. As it turned out, we ended up going out onto Avenue A and Seventh Street that night. That's where the real demonstration was going to take place.

Up from the Wounded Streets

That night, after the cops kicked us out of Tompkins Square Park, we gravitated toward 7th Street and Avenue A, the site of the bloody confrontation that people in the neighborhood were having with the police. The cops barricaded all park entrances and made sure their forces were numerous enough that nobody could get back into the park.

In response, over 400 neighborhood supporters, housing activists, squatters, and homeless proceeded to block the streets so that no cars were getting through all night long. The intersection at A and Seventh was filled with people. More than 30 plainclothes officers were helping to arrest people. We ended up starting a bonfire in the middle of the block between Seventh and Eighth Street on Avenue A. Somebody set an American flag on fire. Firecrackers were set off under cars. Some people threw bottles and eggs at the police. Thirty-one people were arrested and others got beat up by the police or the skinheads. It seemed as if the cops did not care who they hit. They were indiscriminate. People came out of buildings, who knows, maybe just to try to get to the store, and they were attacked by police. It was a very bloody incident.

A fire truck pulled up. The firemen came with the intention of using the fire hose on us, but at first they didn't do anything. They just stood there and watched. By that time we had been there almost eight hours. Eventually Inspector Julian decided it was time to stop the fire and get the people out of the street. So they put out our bonfire, and we started another one.

Finally the authorities decided they had had enough of us being in the streets, so they let us back into the park. Everybody who still had any of their stuff brought it back in. But the police had destroyed most of the tents.

When they tore down our tents that night, I realized for the first time just how much they really didn't give a damn about me. When they tore down my tent they were tearing down part of my heart. They took out everything, my clothes, my identification. If I had not held onto my birth certificate, I would have had no ID. When they took away people's ID, then those people in effect became homeless criminals. Because when they take that away, even though you might not realize it at the time, your identity is gone. Go look for a job without an ID. If you don't have ID when you apply for work today, they tell you to go get a green card. I was born and raised in the United States, but do you know how hard it is to get a green card with two federal arrests?

A Radical Political and Social History of the Lower East Side

The cops came back about four o'clock the next morning. By that time the only people they had to confront were the people staying in the park, not the supporters from the neighborhood, who had gone home. When they came this time it was myself, Red Wolf, Spider, and a few others. They came in and ushered us out of the park. Then they tore down everything. It started raining the next day.

The cops and Parks Department had destroyed our tents, but neighborhood people brought materials for us to rebuild. We had a unity going with the neighborhood to where we had a backup of supplies. I have been told that during the Depression in the 1930s residents of this same neighborhood used to defy evictions by helping people carry their belongings back into apartments after the cops left. This time they started going to the hardware stores and buying heavy-duty plastic, wood, and hammers for us.

Miriam Friedlander, a city council member, made a big public statement July 6th, complaining that the community had not been consulted about the raid and demanding that the city replace the possessions of the homeless that had been destroyed.

She also called for them "to immediately rehab all city-owned buildings in the Lower East Side for low-income housing, and . . . cease harassment of the homeless." That sounded good for the moment, but that's the last I ever heard of that demand of hers.

The same day as the Friedlander statement, the New York Supreme Court ruled that the city could not prevent real estate speculators from demolishing or converting SROs — single-room occupancy housing — into condominiums. Although that type of hotel shelter is not my favorite, the ruling showed the attitude of too many of the powers-that-be toward the homeless. Even Mayor Koch was quoted in the *New York Times* as saying that the ruling was a "devastating blow" to the effort to keep homelessness from spreading.

An example of this problem of gentrification was the Christodora House, a 16-story settlement house building in the Tompkins Square area which had once been used as a city welfare office and then kept empty for a long time until it was yuppified, renovated into expensive condominiums for rich people.

At 1:30 in the afternoon that Saturday, July 8th, people marched past the Christodora House carrying a banner "HOUSING-NOT CONDOS." That was more laid-back than it had been in the spring, when the anarchists heaved cinder blocks through the Art Deco entrance as they shouted, "Die, yuppie scum!"

Police patrol cars, paddy wagons and green garbage trucks lined Tenth Street between Avenues A and B. The people marched on to the Ninth Precinct station on Fifth Street to protest the raid on the Tompkins Square Park homeless. They carried a banner that had "NO CURFEW, NO EVICTIONS" painted on it, and posters that said "STOP WAREHOUSING APARTMENTS."

At the park, about 200 homeless and our neighborhood supporters held hands and linked arms around the new shelters we had built. A big painted banner strung up between two

Ron Casanova and Steven Blackburn

trees said "NO HOUSING, NO PEACE/SQUATTERS RIGHTS NOW." When six o'clock rolled around, about 70 cops in riot gear, along with Parks Department workers, who we called "Green Meanies" because of their green uniforms and general attitude, ripped apart our plastic tents. And again we put them back up. At 8:45 that night the cops swept through the park and cut down six tents. One person got arrested for playing a radio without a license. Interestingly enough, I got the feeling that some of the police did not like being part of pushing people out of the park.

We hung on to our place in the park. Somebody came up with the idea to evict Henry J. Stern, the Parks Commissioner from his home. It was the consensus among the various groups: yeah, let's do it. So I designed and painted a t-shirt for the occasion, and it was presented to Stern outside his office as he was coming down the stairs.

On July 12th, we marched to the home of Henry J. Stern, who lived at 510 East 84th Street, and placed an eviction notice on his door. About a hundred police blocked off the street between York Avenue and East End Avenue. We marched on to Gracie Mansion, which is where the mayor of New York lives. At Mayor Koch's the police tried to get us surrounded, but we broke away, split up and scattered, with police after us. We knew the back alleys and thereby mostly eluded them, regrouping to march past the United Nations on our way back to Tompkins Square.

That night we celebrated in Tompkins Square Park, enjoying music and food, while a few police officers kept an eye on us. Somebody offered them a taste of some donated caviar on crackers and stuffed mushrooms, but they declined to eat with us.

Without exaggerating, I would say we were raided ten to twelve times that season. We could expect the cops any time, but usually when they did come it was when the people in the neighborhood were asleep or at work. Sometimes the authorities would leave the rest of the homeless in the park alone, coming specifically to Tent City to harass us.

"Why do you come to us?" I asked one of the Parks Department workers.

"Because we were told to come to you guys first," he said.

Each time the cops came for us, the neighborhood came back stronger after the cops left. The neighborhood people were becoming more involved. Food would come in and clothing would come in. From our table in the park we sold "Tent City" buttons, passed out flyers and collected food, clothing and medical supplies for the homeless in the park,

We had a lot of community support on the Lower East Side: organizations such as Emmaus Haus for women, run by Father David Kirk; Homeward Bound; St. Augustine Church down near Grant; Trinity Church, downtown between Avenues B and C, which had been feeding homeless people for years; and a church called Graffiti Church, on 7th Street, which was another organization that had consistently fed the homeless. There was also Diane, a lady who for three or four years had been coming out to the park feeding people on Saturdays, Mondays, and Wednesdays. She had an abundance of food and connections. I had first met

A Radical Political and Social History of the Lower East Side

Diane several years earlier, before I had joined the Bowery Mission. It was snowing that Thanksgiving. She came down to the park with a busload of food — Thanksgiving dinners. She just brought it to us in the park and set it out. We had Thanksgiving Dinner for three days.

These groups of people and others like the squatters and the anarchists, as well as people who just lived in the area, came through for us. They were for real. Every time we ran out of equipment, they brought in more equipment for us to rebuild. The police would tear down, we would build up; they'd tear down, we'd build up. Tear 'em down, build 'em up. People were going to the hardware store all day long. The hardware store got rich that summer.

Not everybody who was homeless and in the park was in agreement on how to deal with our situation. Our side of the park held the activists. The rest of the park wanted nothing to do with us because we were making too much political noise. They felt like we were destroying their harmony with what they had in the park. In reality, they had next to nothing, but they did not want to lose even that little bit,

I understood how they felt. I myself had been one of the people who was, if not content, afraid to make any changes, afraid to make any noise, content to be on that bench because I could see no other place to go. Afraid to lose that spot.

After we had been raided about the second or third time in July, we received a visit from some people from Philadelphia who came specifically to meet us. They told us of something called a "National Survival Summit" that was coming up in Philadelphia. One of the people who talked to us was Leona Smith, a dignified black lady, a former homeless person and the president of an organization called the National Union of the Homeless, We were told that she and another homeless person named Chris Sprowd had started the Union of the Homeless themselves, and that 90 percent of the board was made up of homeless or once-homeless people. The Union had a shelter run by homeless people.

These facts made some difference to me. While I still did not like shelters, the fact that these folks had homeless people in control of it was a different story altogether.

A brother named Willie Baptist, wearing a baseball cap, also talked with us. Willie was a very articulate dude. He called himself a "political educator" and said he was also a member of the Union of the Homeless, and of another organization called Up and Out of Poverty.

All that afternoon we talked and talked and talked about the homeless situation and the differences from the way it had been in years past. Talked about if anything had changed in the past few years about homeless people.

"Nothing has changed," I said.

Ron Casanova and Steven Blackburn

"That's not true," somebody else said. "Think about it. There were homeless people before and a lot of them fought their situation, but you didn't have the struggle then the way you have it now."

I realized that was true. In 1989 one-bedroom apartments in the neighborhood, on Avenue A, were commonly costing $1,200 a month. Prices kept going up. Even the Cherry Tavern, the down-to-earth Polish bar I used to frequent, had started going yuppie, trying to appeal to the rich. (The Cherry Tavern would end up closing down anyway.) The consensus of our talk with these folks from Philadelphia was that there were more people who were homeless, but there were also more people involved with the homeless struggle than there had ever been before. That much progress had happened.

For Leona and the others to come talk with us was a reinforcement of our resolve. Before they came, we thought we were alone in our fight. All we knew was that we were hurting, we were fighting to survive. Now it seemed that there were other people who were fighting the same fight.

We had a Tent City meeting to discuss the so-called summit. One of our people, a fellow named Justice Robles, felt it was a good idea.

"Our government," he said, "would rather see us under the ground than lying on top of the ground. They would rather have us buried underneath Tompkins Square than sleeping on top of it."

Somebody mentioned my name as a candidate for attending the Philadelphia conference.

"I don't want to leave the park," I said. I still thought my plight was only in Tompkins Square Park. That was where the immediate battle was, where people were going to jail.

"Cas, we want you to speak for the homeless living in the park," somebody said. At that time I still did not fully understand my position, but Karen Margolis and a majority of the Tent City homeless finally convinced me that it might be a good idea for me to go and represent them, to speak for the homeless of Tent City. There was something in the air and Tent City wanted to be part of it.

I still wasn't very happy as the contingency from Tent City traveled to the survival summit in a van driven by David Green and Shigemi, who were with an organization called Homeward Bound, one of the sponsors of the event. But now I was curious. Leona had told me that there were going to be Indians —Native Americans —at this meeting, as well as coal miners and other organizations fighting against poverty. My curiosity, more than anything, got me to the summit.

I went with two other homeless people from the park, Justice Robles and a black woman named Darleen Bryant, who liked her nickname of "Mama." That night the organizers put us up, along with other summit participants, in nice student quarters at St. Joseph's College in Philadelphia, two to a room. It was decent, and that impressed me.

A Radical Political and Social History of the Lower East Side

The next day, the three-day conference, organized by the National Welfare Rights Union and the National Union of the Homeless, began in the auditorium at St. Joseph's College. I do not think I can truly put into words the emotions I felt when I walked in there to that conference and saw all those people. The vitality of the struggle against poverty struck me. This was the first time I had ever seen so many people, and such a variety of people, together for the same purpose of doing something about their plight themselves. I couldn't help but get caught up in the enthusiasm. About 50 people from 30 to 40 states showed up, representing people from various races, young and old, from all walks of life, all different organizations, not only the Union of the Homeless and Welfare Rights, but also others such as Up and Out of Poverty. You had the American Indian Movement and coal miners concerned about black lung and welfare rights activists and kids against drugs. Maybe more women than men.

Then, when people started getting up and talking, it was as if I was speaking. It was phenomenal to see other people's struggles, hear their fights and ideas and get inspired at this unity. Nearly everyone who stood up and spoke touched me and my life and the life that we were living in New York. It was as if we were all living the same life, but in different places. It almost freaked me out. It sure woke me up. It was the best thing that could have happened to me.

I liked the name of the group from Minneapolis, which was called Up and Out of Poverty, and was led by a woman named Cheri Honkala. I thought that was a good banner to be under because this issue of poverty encompassed all the other issues we were dealing with.

Then I heard Leona Smith speak. She was wearing a black collared t-shirt and a dress. I found her to be a forceful, earnest speaker, and she emphasized her points with her index finger. I could see the emotion in her talk and realized that she was a person who deeply cared about other people. She herself had experienced being homeless in the streets. She was a very strong go-getter, vibrant not only in organizing, but also in getting out and talking to the politicians. But it was more than that— she was not just a talker; she had been to jail for what she believes in.

I learned that Union of the Homeless also had a school where they taught political science as it pertained to their lives and the future of their kids. They had a program called Dignity Housing. They would take people out of shelters and put them in a house. The only obligation for the people in the house was for them to go to school, learn a trade, and/or get a job. And they had to put time back into the Dignity Housing Program — put back some of what they got.

All things considered, Union of the Homeless impressed me quite a bit. They were changing the situation. Instead of "advocates" being in control, the homeless themselves were gaining control of their own destinies.

After Leona spoke, a heavyset black sister in glasses, wearing a yellow baseball cap and a red sweatshirt, led the group in a cheer:

"What are we going to do?" she asked.
"Fight!"

Tent City made an agreement with Leona Smith and Union of the Homeless to have our own homeless convention in Washington, D.C., and take part in a "CD" or civil disobedience in Washington on the sixth of October, the day before a big nationwide protest rally against homelessness. We were intent on taking over the HUD building.

On about the third day of the summit I finally got to speak. I was bearded, with a moderate Afro, wearing a black t-shirt with a few buttons up near the neck. Justice and Darleen and I introduced the fact that Tompkins Square Park Tent City intended to build tents out of American flags. As I spoke I rapped my hand with a rolled-up agenda, explaining how we thought if we used the American flag as a symbol of protection, that would prevent the cops from destroying our tents.

The response to our plan at the summit was tremendous, it impressed me. People were jumping out of their chairs and clapping hands and cheering. Our announcement went over so grand and gloriously that I thought, oh well, it looks like I'm in this for a while.

What enthused me the most about the Summit was the reinforcement of the realization that if I wanted to get my life straightened out, I could not depend on anyone else to do it for me.

We were doing for ourselves in Tompkins Square Park. There were no real alternatives. All we knew was that we needed housing and we needed jobs, but we had no idea of how to get them. By then we were thinking in terms of organizing politically, but we did not know exactly how to go about it. And before going to the summit I thought we were alone in these troubles. My job for the homeless of Tompkins Square Park had been to go to the Survival Summit and find out what was happening with other people like us. What the Summit did for me was to give me more courage, knowing that Tent City was not alone, that things were happening all over the country, and there were people all over doing the same things we were doing. So it kind of built me up. It started waking up my consciousness.

On Saturday, July 22, 1989, the day that the flags were scheduled to go up in Tent City, we were still at the summit. I wanted to get back to New York so bad that I put pressure on Darleen and Justice.

"Come on, let's go," I said. Darleen and I ended up leaving Justice at the conference.

We came back into Tent City with just enough daylight to see our tent made out of American flags. A rope had been strung between two trees, and then four flags — big flags, about seven or eight feet by four or five feet — had been attached to the rope side by side, the blue fields of stars up near the rope and the red and white stripes angling out, fastened to the ground. A gathering of people sat on the ground beneath the shelter of this tent. A couple of other people were walking around holding a banner somebody had painted: "KOCH VS HOMELESS." The area was beautiful. We even had an art festival going. People were there in

A Radical Political and Social History of the Lower East Side

the park with their art. People were eating and it was a festive day. People were everywhere. It seemed like the Fourth of July, like our own independence day.

When it started getting dark, the Parks Department came and told us we would have to break down the structures. Of course, we were not about to take them down, so the Green Meanies backed off for the night.
In the warm, humid dawn 20 cops in riot gear formed a line standing shoulder to shoulder, facing our line of homeless. Behind the cops a dozen or so Green Meanies waited.

For the moment I almost believed they would respect the symbolic refuge we were claiming by using the flags.

Then the cops moved in, fighting us, tearing down all the flags. There was a tug-of-war between the police and us for the flags. Though we gave them a struggle, by 7 a.m. the helmeted cops had folded up our flags and taken them away.

I had come back from the Summit politicized, which now influenced my strategizing. On July 25th we got a flyer typed up. A well-educated black man named Thomas was our press-man, our computer whiz, our brain. Thomas had parents he could have moved in with, but he stayed downtown, he stayed working with us in the streets. Although he liked computers, he preferred to work in a socially conscious atmosphere.

Thomas put out our flyers, printed our newsletters and did our press releases. In the July 25th flyer we noted that, "We now are organizing, educating, and feeding one another without institutions to guide us to: drugs, alcohol, TB, AIDS, and Criminal Ways of Thinking." It was signed by me as chief representative, a dude named James Naphier as chief of security, and Chris Henry as Public Relations for what we called C.H.S., or "Creating Housing Somewhere."

Our lawyer found out that the police had taken our flags to somewhere in Long Island. I guess they were figuring we had neither the money nor the support to go all the way out there and get the flags back. Fortunately, we had a receipt for them. We got a ride out to Long Island from a lawyer friend of Chris Henry and his lady, Barbara Henry. Chris was one of the founders of Tent City and a member of the Tent City board of directors. Barbara was our secretary. We went with a couple of supporters who had given up the money for the flags in the first place, and we got the flags back on July 31st.

The day we got the flags back, we put up the flag tent again. Since the parks department had still refused to agree to our proposal to keep the bathrooms open on a 24-hour basis and were still officially outlawing any temporary structures in the park, we also proceeded to build another eight shelters.

The police and the Parks Department left us alone at first, probably because we had such a big turnout of supporters. We were told that we had until 6 a.m. before the authorities would come in.

Ron Casanova and Steven Blackburn

But this time the attack came just before midnight. Most of our supporters and the curious had drifted away as 40 to 60 police in riot gear came against us, along with about 40 Green Meanies and a couple of dozen maintenance people. This time they threw all the flags except one in a garbage truck, along with all our food and clothes and property. That showed us how much the flag meant as a symbol of protection.

The last flag we managed to get away from them. We had a tug-of-war, yanked it over the fence and got away with it.

Nearly a week later, on the night of August 6, 1989, a year after that first big police riot, the homeless of Tompkins Square Park were again forced out of the park. We were told by Inspector Julian and some of his task force that around four or five o'clock in the morning they would be coming in to take everything again. So we were on vigil, waiting.

At the brick, flat-roofed pavilion between the restrooms, people were sleeping. A Green Meanie came over and politely said, "We're getting ready to clean up this area. Could you get all your personal belongings, please?"

They had more than one team of Parks Department workers. One guy from the Parks Department talked with me. He was a heavyset young white dude.

"We're going to clean the entire park, section by section, starting here," he said.

"What about the tents?" I asked. I was a little bit hoarse that morning. I had a butterfly bandage on my right cheek from the previous encounter with the authorities.

"You'll just have to take them down while we do the cleanup' " he said. "We're not looking to confiscate. What we're asking is that everything be physically moved off the benches because we're going to clean the park,"

"You're saying that we have to take everything outside the park?" I asked.

"If you take it outside of the park, that's even better while we do the cleanup. We've got a 40-man crew here simply to clean the park."

"Why can't we just pick everything up," I asked. "put them on the benches and get it out of your way?"

"Because we're going to clean around the benches, in the benches, down the benches. Everything's going to get cleaned."

My friends and I talked over what to do.

"They want us out of the park," somebody said.

"We could stop traffic," Chris said,

A Radical Political and Social History of the Lower East Side

"All right," somebody else agreed. I turned to the Green Meanies a little ways off from us.

"You're not going to like what we do," I said. "We'll take it out, but you're not going to like it."

We went around informing the other residents of the park of the situation and what we intended. We started gathering what little we had in the way of possessions.

"What's most important?" a guy asked. "The food or the blankets?"

"The food."

It was August. In the winter the answer would have been different.

"The food," I said, "because right now we're going to be sleeping on the street."

Ultimately we held on to all that we could and tried to keep the Green Meanies from trashing the rest. When we saw them filling their garbage trucks with our belongings, tossing them into the backs of those trucks, we could not help getting agitated and provoked, and calling them names.

I went up and grabbed a metal cabinet out of the back of the garbage truck. At first they tried to stop me, but then the black Parks Department man wearing glasses and a blue t-shirt stopped them.

"All right," he said. "Is it yours? Take it out of here:'

So we moved out of the park early that morning, but we put whatever bedding we managed to salvage out right in the street, blocking traffic. People just lay down in the street on their pads. I myself was sitting in the middle of the street on Avenue A on my spread-out sleeping bag near a Parks Department dump truck. One of the homeless had put up a sign "THIS IS OUR LAND" Somebody else had made a sign that said:

NO

NIGHT-STICKING

GLASS THROWING
BEAT-UPS, BY ANYONE!

I was mad. I started drinking beer and got even angrier. I was standing in the street with a bullhorn in one hand and a brown-bagged quart in the other.

"No housing, no peace!" I shouted. "It don't make no difference what anybody says. Just remember what we're here for. Fuck what anybody else says! We're here to get homes, food, clothing . . . "

Ron Casanova and Steven Blackburn

Not my most persuasive speaking engagement, but I was feeling frustrated. Still, no traffic was getting by, so I was not the only frustrated one.

That night people kept demonstrating. There was singing and lots of yelling. Cops chased down demonstrators and broke up the protest.

"It's over," one cop kept saying. "It's over. It's over."

People were videotaping the proceedings, and at a paddy wagon one plainclothes cop can be seen growling at the cameraman in Nith LaCroix's video *First Anniversary Tompkins Square Riot Demonstration*.

"Take a walk, asshole," he says.

Next morning the sergeant of police came to us in his crisp, white, short-sleeved shirt. It went like this:

"You're welcome in the park," he said.

"They told us to get out," we said.

"Your complaint was you were asked to leave the park," said the sergeant. "Now you're invited back into the park, so I wish you would just vacate the street, so the people can get back to work."

"But we were told to vacate the park."

"Okay," he said. "You're welcome back into the park. Right now you're obstructing traffic. You're welcome to go back in the park right now, all right? You're welcome to go back in and keep your stuff!'

That's the way it went. We were stubborn. We had still more battles with the cops, fighting with them almost continuously the rest of the summer and into the autumn. But we were still in the park.

Chapter 3

May Day!
The Tompkins Square Park May Day Riot of 1990
By Ellen Moynihan

Sandwiched in between the better-known riots of August 6th & 7th, 1988 and Memorial Day 1991, there occurred an upheaval in Tompkins Square Park just as pivotal, every bit as politically motivated, and as strong a fiber in the historical tapestry of Lower East Side resistance.

The May Day Riot of 1990 exploded at the tail end of a four-day-long festival in the park called Resist to Exist/Fourth Annual Squatter May Day, which consisted of live music, art-making, poetry, free food and info-sharing. Ironically, the event was organized with a peaceful, unifying goal; the flyer read: "Our idea is to bring everyone in the community together so that we can talk together and hopefully, break down the barriers that may currently be separating us . . . We hope that this Park Festival will help foster greater understanding between all of us who call Loisaida home." While the festival no doubt achieved some of its goal through the intended means of art and cooking, another way the community was brought together that evening resulted in the injury of 28 police officers and the arrest of 29 civilians, who came to be known as "The May Day 29." For some arrestees, that night also resulted in a four-month long criminal trial, and for one, incarceration.

May Day is a history-laden date. The American Federation of Organized Trades and Labor Unions led a strike in demand of an eight-hour workday on that date in 1886 (which resulted in Chicago's Haymarket Riot). May 1st was many unions', including The International Workingmen's Association's, date of choice for Labor Day in the United States. However, the adoption of May Day by communists, socialists, and anarchists as a day of celebration and demonstration caused then-president Grover Cleveland to deny that date as a state-observed labor holiday. Instead, it was officially relegated to September.

The first of May was also when tenement dwellers' leases typically expired in 1800s New York City. This created a mass migration of families in search of affordable housing on May 1 of each year, with their possessions in pushcarts and children in tow. It occurred most notably in the slums of the Lower East Side.

The May Day tradition of the struggle for an affordable place to live, an unwillingness to be stepped on by the powers that be, and general vociferousness came together in its own particular brand that night in Tompkins Square.

Tompkins Square Park at that time was the only home to some 200 people who called their settlement "Tent City." They had had their tents torn down and had been kicked out by the police numerous times by May 1990. Eddie Rutter, a well-known member of the park's homeless community, died there in December 1988 when police officers had extinguished a trashcan fire he had been sleeping next to. The following morning, friends found his frozen, lifeless body next to the knocked-over can.

Longtime residents of the neighborhood had watched as the blight, drug trade and economic climate of the 1970s manifested itself in property devaluation, which resulted in an epidemic of landlord-sanctioned arson of buildings that were deemed more valuable vacant (for the insurance money) than occupied by tenants. They continued to watch as the drug trade became more overt, transforming the streets where they lived into an open-air bazaar of sorts, while the police failed to take any real action. Squatters began moving into some of the abandoned properties and fixing them up, in some cases transforming former high-traffic areas of drug use into decent places to live, and in at least in a few cases, community centers.

The 1980s brought with it a new day for the Lower East Side. An influx of money to the neighborhood first made its mark on places like the Christodora building. The Christodora, located on Avenue B between 9th and 10th Streets, had originally been a settlement house for immigrants, donated by the Christodora nuns, then a community center. It was purchased, developed and finally re-opened in 1986. As luxury housing. Brooke Shields had reportedly purchased the penthouse apartment as a Manhattan pied-a-terre for when her work brought her to New York. The symbolization of a former place of assistance to the poor and disenfranchised transformed into a perceived haven for yuppies was not lost on the park denizens and others in the neighborhood. Nor was the juxtaposition of that symbol with the realities of many in the Lower East Side —the homeless living in the park, the squatters dealing with the daily threat of eviction, people struggling in SROs or tenements. Indeed, the Christodora was intended by developers to be a symbol —of the tip of the financial iceberg they imagined as a new, profitable face for the Lower East Side. And people responded to it as such — the 1988 riot, acknowledged by the city as having been a police-instigated riot, culminated in protesters smashing in the windows of the building, while chanting "Die Yuppie Scum."

But even with this precedent, by all accounts, the previous three days of the Resist to Exist festival had gone smoothly. Lori Sbordone Rizzo, the organizer of the event, recalled:

> We got the permits for the show, and paid the deposit for the clean-up fee, and everything. We were just trying to put on a neighborhood concert! We'd been there for four days, and we were raising a lot of issues about the homeless. I mean, that was really my thing, the homeless people in the park, so I was hitting that point over and over again from the stage. And the homeless people had taken chances coming up on the stage, and we let them say whatever they wanted. I even invited the cops on stage! And we were giving away food, and we had a party here for four days. This happened at the last second.

Inspector Michael Julian, from the 9th precinct, testified at the subsequent trial that the scene around 7:00 that night had been "orderly, festive."

A Radical Political and Social History of the Lower East Side

The show, attended by between 300-500 people, was to conclude at 9:00. However, due to technical difficulties, many of the bands had been going on stage late and it became apparent that a few minutes more would be needed for the final band, Spy-vs-Spy, to finish their set. Lori had a secured a promise from Mike Jordan of the Parks Department to allow the show to run until 9:10 PM.

A few minutes before 9:00, Baby Monroe, the singer of Spy-vs-Spy, was singing, incorporating a chant of 'No housing, no peace' into the lyrics. Also onstage were several people dancing, including Lori and Kenny Tolia, who had been one of the main organizers of the first two Squatter May Days, as well as the protest against the park curfew in 1988 that had resulted in the riot that year.

At 9:00, Sergeant Marron walked onto the stage, accompanied by Officers Flynn and Hernandez, and declared that the show was over. When informed by Lori that they had been allotted an extra ten minutes, Marron disagreed, and made a move towards the rear of the bandshell to shut down the power. Kenny, who was also arrested that night, remembered the minutes before the eruption of violence. "Lori had asked them if they could run a few minutes over the permit, and they had said OK, and to a certain extent the whole thing was a set-up, knowing that there would be a reaction from the crowd. I mean, you have to look at the whole history down here."

There were likely few people at the 4th Annual Squatter May Day who weren't aware of that history. Everyone was conscious of the fact that riots of the recent past had resulted in widespread police brutality, with what seems like no recourse from the Citizen Complaint Review Board. In between Marron and the power switch were about twenty people, and as they began to see what was happening, more people began to climb onto the stage, and more cops began to push their way through the crowd towards the bandshell. Baby Monroe was still singing, Spy-vs.-Spy still playing, people still dancing. Then someone in the crowd threw a bottle onto the stage.

The police immediately flew into action; billy clubs swung at those on the stage, handcuffs clicked around wrists and the drumkit was kicked in. Bottles began flying from all over, as people were beaten and arrested by the police. On the mike, Baby Monroe tried to calm the crowd down, to no avail.

Long after the first of the arrestees were led out of the park and into custody, the riot continued in and around Tompkins. Hundreds of people marched to the 9th precinct, demanding the release of those being held. When the police refused, the crowd turned back towards St. Marks Place, where a bonfire was lit at Avenue A, and trash thrown into the streets. The riot finally ended around 2:00 AM, with another attack on the Christodora.

Lori and Kenny's perspective, however, was not of rioting. Onstage when the first bottle sailed through the air, they were among the first ones beaten and arrested.

"The riot started with an obvious, in front of everybody, incident of police brutality, right there on the stage. People had been beaten up and brutalized [before] by the police, and no complaints were ever substantiated, and no police ever had to suffer any consequences as a result of this. And then in 1990, they beat me up on the stage, and Kenny, and the rest of us, pretty blatantly, in front of all those people," Lori recalls.

"There's a picture of the riot, and it looks like a tackle in football, with a bunch of cops, and you can see my feet sticking out," remembers Kenny. For many people, although angered by what had taken place at Tompkins, the night was soon a memory. For others, though, the true implications of May Day hadn't even begun. When the trial finally started in November of 1991, of the 29 people arrested only eleven people had been indicted. Four of them pled guilty to a lesser charge, and another jumped bail and left the country. The remaining six either indignantly refused the 'out' of copping a plea, which would have required them to publicly admit responsibility for actions they hadn't taken, or were not offered that option. Those who stood trial were Lori Sbordone Rizzo, charged with Riot in the First Degree and Incitement to Riot; John Potok, charged with Riot in the First Degree and Possession of a Weapon (an empty bottle); Kenny Tolia, charged with Riot in the First Degree and Incitement to Riot; Anthony Baldini, charged with Riot in the First Degree and Possession of a Weapon (also an empty bottle); Rob Miller, charged with Riot in the First Degree and Assault on an Officer (with a full bottle), and Tom Gembka, originally charged with Disorderly Conduct, but eventually with Riot in the First Degree and Assault in the Second Degree. Gembka had not even been in the park; he had been on his way to shoot a game of pool when he saw the police and protesters squaring off outside the Christodora. He remarked to an officer something along the lines of "If you would all just go home, we wouldn't have any problems in this neighborhood," and was immediately chased down and arrested. Later, the arresting officers maintained that he was the one responsible for injuries suffered by Officer Mike Kelly, who had had a bottle thrown at him hours earlier, when Gembka had been at home. In addition to the felony charges, Kelly sued him for $1.2 million for his injuries.

It was a risk going to trial but the defendants believed that standing up and denying the false charges was a key statement of resistance, even if it meant the possibility of losing their cases. Lori, Kenny, and John were identified as the three major players in the events of the evening, while the others were seen as participating in what they had started.

From the beginning, there was a widespread feeling that some of the arrests had been strategic on the part of the police. Most of the defendants had been guilty of no more than being present when the riot began, but some of them were longtime activists in the neighborhood, known by the police for being involved in protests, marches and demonstrations for years.

Lori remembers the eventual arrest of John Potak, better known as John the Communist: "John, they didn't even arrest him for May Day until about a week later. He went out to pick up groceries, and didn't come back for three days. We had no idea where he was. And they hurt him. They said while he was holding his banner, he threw a bottle. Which was ridiculous. Because the thing about John was, he never let anybody, except Maria, his girl-friend, carry his banner, and no one claims that he was with Maria when he was holding his banner. So, somehow or another, he was holding the banner with both hands, dropped the

A Radical Political and Social History of the Lower East Side

thing, pulled a bottle out of his bag, threw it at the police, and then grabbed the banner again. Interesting move, but. . . And then they didn't catch him until a week later. And they fucked him up in jail. They had him high-cuffed, hanging by his wrists. He came out like a wreck. I've never seen anyone come out of jail so bad. He was a wreck." Additionally, when he was released, John said he had been beaten, threatened, and had "stupid" written on his face in black marker while he was handcuffed.

Kenny's understanding of why he was arrested had more to do with who he was than what he did: "That's the weird thing—I was an activist down here who was central to a lot of this stuff, but *not* that night. That night, I was just dancing on the stage, pretty much. But the thing is, once they realized the different people they had caught up in their net . . . . they had a thing with me. Mayor Koch had mentioned me and Frank Morales and Jerry the Peddler in the days right after the '88 riots, You know: 'We have our eyes on these people', but Julian, when he was on the stand claimed never to have heard of me. But we were central to a lot of what went on, so . . . they had a bone to pick with me from '88."

The trial proved to go on longer than anyone had originally expected. Four days a week, every week for four months, the lawyers, defendants, judge and jury sat in Criminal Court, hearing evidence of the night in question. Notable liberal attorneys, Susan Tipograph and Ron Kuby among them, were representing the defendants. There were rallies held in support of those on trial, including one held at lunchtime outside the courthouse during the first week, which had begun as a press conference and ended in a sea of chants, "Fuck the Police!" among them. "We said 'Fuck the Police' like we said 'Hi, how are you,'" recalls Lori.

Frustrating for the defendants was the insistence of the prosecutor, Assistant District Attorney Dan Connolly, to isolate the night of May 1, 1990 from any prior incidents in the park. The other riots in Tompkins Square had created a historical and political context that could not lie separate from May Day. The case was a political one, but the climate of the neighborhood, precedence of police-activist animosity and even the nature of some of the issues—homelessness and squatting—that were being raised at Resist to Exist were all deemed inadmissible as evidence. The May Day 1990 riot case was being tried as if it had occurred in a vacuum.

Rob Miller's case was slightly different than the rest of the co-defendants. He was charged with Riot in the First Degree and Assault on an Officer, accused of throwing a full bottle of beer at Officer Peter Smeding and knocking him unconscious. But although present at Tompkins for the 4th Annual Squatter May Day, he wasn't particularly politically active. He had been drunk that night, and that was his main motivation for throwing the bottle. He'd had a confession beaten out of him in the back of a paddy wagon, so that, along with the double felony charge, was putting him in danger of a long prison term. He ended up pleading guilty to Assault, and receiving 500 hours of community service and five years of probation.

If there was ever any doubt that the case wasn't a political one, Judge Richard Failla himself cleared that up. After Rob Miller's sentencing, the Judge told Miller's lawyer the only reason he didn't consider jail time for his client was because all that was behind his actions was drunkenness, and so was clearly not one of the 'major players' in the case, or a harborer of agitation, and thus not a continuing threat.

A key piece of evidence for the defense arrived during the first week of the trial. It was a videotape of the riot, anonymously delivered to William Kunstler and Ron Kuby's office by a woman who never identified herself. The tape clearly showed Spy-vs-Spy playing, people dancing, Kenny and Lori on the stage, and then the police approaching. The tape also showed Lori, Kenny and others being beaten by officers as bottles crashed around them. What was not on the tape was anything to substantiate the Incitement to Riot charges they were facing. However, there was a gap of indeterminate length in the middle of the footage, which may have been the result of the camera operator losing his or her balance as people began to push and shove at the outbreak of violence. The prosecution initially argued that the tape not be allowed into evidence, saying that the gap was essentially undetectable. When it was admitted as an exhibit, the Assistant District Attorney later tried to portray the gap in the tape as being long enough for Lori and Kenny to have given speeches, whipping the crowd into a frenzy and calling them to action against the police. This gap in the footage, and implied actions, were to become the bulk of the prosecution's case.

Closing arguments were delivered on January 27, 1991, nearly nine months after the night in question. Jury deliberations took over a week, during which time the members were sequestered in a hotel and the defendants, their lawyers, and the Judge attended court each day to wait for their verdicts. A positive sign for the defense came in the form of a some-what familiar slogan: a court officer reported to Susan Tipograph that one morning, while waiting for their bus to the courthouse, the jury began to spontaneously chant "Whose fuckin' bus? Our fuckin' bus!" an appropriation of the "Whose fuckin' park? Our fuckin' park!" chant that had often been quoted in testimony.

When the verdicts were finally reached in February, the results were mixed. Tom Gembka's case ended in a mistrial, and the other four pushed for a partial verdict. Anthony Baldini was convicted of both charges, John the Communist and Lori were both acquitted of their charges, and Kenny was acquitted of Riot in the first degree, but found guilty of Incitement to Riot. The imaginary speeches given by Kenny during the gap in the videotape, and sub-stantiated by testimony from over a dozen officers, were enough to sway the begrudging jury.

Having grown fond of the defendants over four months, the jury asked to meet them after the verdicts were handed down, and some members admitted to Kenny that they hadn't wanted to convict him. Others congratulated Lori and John on their acquittals, and expressed concern for the beatings they had seen occur on the videotape at the hands of the police. They also showed off the sweatshirts they'd had printed with the legend: Part 38-The Greatest Jurors In The World.

On April 6, Kenny was sentenced. Judge Failla cited the letters he had received in support of Kenny, including six from jury members saying they did not wish to see him go to jail, and many of which mentioned his new wife and child. He then drew analogies between Kenny and Officer Kevin Flynn, who was the most severely injured on May 1st 1990. He

A Radical Political and Social History of the Lower East Side

noted that Kenny and Officer Flynn were the same age, and that while Kenny had a new family, Flynn would be unable to bear children or return to a beat, and instead would feel the effects of the reckless activity allegedly instigated by Kenny for the rest of his life.

Failla then sentenced Kenny to the maximum allowable time in prison — one year — and he was instantly led to the first prison of several he was to stay in.

"I was on Riker's Island, and then I went up to Riverview in Ogdensberg, New York, which is as far north as you can be and still be in the state, about an eleven hour drive. And then I was shipped back to the jailboat on the East River, and after that I was sent to the jailboat on Riker's Island. I was moved around so much because somebody like me, someone who's been arrested for Incitement to Riot, is not someone you'd want to keep in your cellblock for very long. And when I was in jail, the guys had great respect for me and took care of me. I mean, it was hard not to . . . when you're talking about what you're in for, I'd tell them I put 28 cops in the hospital, which is pretty much what the judge said when he sentenced me."

Kenny's application for a vegetarian diet in prison was denied on the grounds that as an anarchist, he had no religious basis for his request, and special diets were allowed only for adherents to organized religions. The other inmates gladly traded their portions of vegetables for his servings of meat. When Judge Failla charged the paperwork processing fee for prison to his account at Riverview, overdrawing it by $90, the other inmates bought extra food to share with him, a rarity in prison.

There was plenty of support for Kenny on the outside as well, on an international level. The anarchist network Neither East Nor West launched a campaign demanding his release from prison, with petitions signed in Scotland, Brazil, and Sweden, among other places. Demonstrations were held at U.S. Embassies in Mexico City, Minsk, and most notably, Warsaw, where 34 protesters were arrested by the anti-terrorist brigade.

Kenny was eventually released after serving eight months.

These days, of course, Tompkins Square is a different place. The park was closed for over a year in June 1991 for repairs, close on the heels of the Memorial Day riot. Some of the differences can be called progress, and some can be attributed to the capitalistic forces of gentrification. There's now a formal dog run, the playground area is safer, and the gates get locked promptly at midnight. Instead of a campfire and tents, a more likely sight is young professionals toting shopping bags from nearby boutiques. The bandshell is long gone. Lori noted that the renovations eradicated most of the community-style seating, with benches facing each other, in favor of more solitary design of several stand-alone benches. Plenty of people who live in the neighborhood don't know the riots ever even happened. So why were they significant?

"I mean, people were taking the law into their own hands, I think that's what was so scary about 1990, I think that's why they spent a million dollars to try to put us in jail. It was insurrection." Says Lori.

Kenny remembers: "Well, the cops reacted to it like they would to a real political movement, and it was. It was a threat. Anarchists are always out there telling people 'rebel' and 'protest' and 'assert yourself,' but it's only at certain times that people listen . . . and so what was really a bad situation for them was not that we were doing the same thing that we had always done, but that the whole neighborhood pretty much turned out to support the stuff we were saying. That was the amazing thing and what was so threatening to them ultimately."

Chapter 4

Tompkins Square Park Riot
By Police Officer John Mellon

In the summer of 1988, Tompkins Square Park, sitting on over ten acres of land and located on Avenues A and B between 7th and 10th streets, was the Lower East Side's biggest symbol of anti-gentrification. It became a haven for, and symbolized the slow but steady displacement of, the homeless, squatters, drug-pushers, Marxist ideologues, liberals and anarchists/ punk rockers. Tensions between these groups and outsiders, which included older park residents, came to a head during that hot summer. Local residents, yuppies or not, complained about late night park noise. They also feared anonymous leaflets that called for the destruction of homes belonging to anyone supporting a police proposal for a 1:00 am-to-sunrise park curfew. On July 11, despite Community Board 3's lack of support for a curfew, 9th Precinct Commanding Officer Captain Gerard McNamara announced the police department's intention to enforce the curfew. As noted by author Janet Abu-Lughod, "even after the order was issued, the regulation was applied inconsistently. The police continued to tolerate the homeless in the park after closing hour. Given this ambiguous situation, there seemed to be no urgency to mobilize the community against the closing." (p. 238)

Over the next few weeks, an organized protest, in the form of a concert at the park, was planned for the night of July 31st. Shortly after midnight on August 1st, 9th Precinct police officers responded to noise complaints emanating from the park where about 300 people assembled to protest the 1:00 am curfew imposed by the police. Five police officers were injured from thrown bottles. Grossly outnumbered, the police withdrew. However, four men were arrested on charges including reckless endangerment and inciting to riot. Angry organizers called for another protest at 11:00 pm the following Saturday, August 6th. *New York Times* reporter Todd S. Purdum recalled that, "On Friday, August 5, Captain McNamara asked Patrick J. Pomposello, Manhattan Borough Parks Commissioner, for permission to tap Tompkins Square Park power lines to supply electricity to a park command post. That evening, about 100 police officers evicted the park's occupants, except for the homeless, without incident." (p. 1)

By 11:00 pm on August 6th, about 86 officers on foot, a dozen mounted officers and Captain McNamara, were at the park (Purdum, 1988). According to video shot on the scene by Clayton Patterson, at about 11:30 pm loud chants of "take down the park," "no police state," "it's our fuckin' park," and "hell no we won't go," were heard, and banners that read, "gentrification is class war, fight back" and "1988-1933, revolt" (a reference to Hitler's assumption of power in Germany) were seen. Powerful M-80 firecrackers, sounding like gunshots, were also heard. Purdum said that, "by just after 12:30 am, most protesters had left the park and the police sealed it. But Dean Kuipers, a reporter for *Downtown* magazine, said some remained inside. During the next 15 minutes, the first bottles were thrown from the back of the crowd blocking traffic. Officers waded into it to arrest one

man and put him in a patrol car. In the Patterson film, this arrest was at Avenue A and East
Eighth Street.

When the crowd tried to surround the patrol car, mounted officers moved in to block them.
Physical confrontations between the police and protesters began. Purdum further notes that,
"at 12:45 am, police computer records show, Capt. McNamara called for reinforcements from
Manhattan North and Brooklyn North Task Forces. At 12:53 am, he called for emergency
service units, and three minutes later called for officers to close off Avenue A."

At this point, Capt. McNamara can be seen on Mr. Patterson's film with a bullhorn saying,
"Clear the streets," and "Get off the sidewalk." Demonstrators blocked traffic at the intersection of Avenue A and St. Mark's Place as officers were hit with bottles. Now the police
retreated south towards Seventh Street and reformed. According to McFadden, "at about
12:55 am, the phalanx, led by the mounted officers, charged northward toward the crowd,
who broke and ran into St. Mark's Place and farther north on Avenue A." Other protesters,
however, regrouped at Avenue A and Sixth Street, where a large portion of Patterson's film
takes place. Aviation was seen hovering low over the park and chants of "Chicago 1968,"
and "We want the park," were heard. At one point a couple of officers were seen taking
their nightsticks to the body of a man who, after the beating, is left on the ground. Mr.
Patterson approached the man, now on his feet, but bleeding and dazed and asked, "Where
are you?" The man responded, "I'm Russian." About halfway through the film (about 1:00
am), Mr. Patterson greeted a black male and asked him how he was doing. The man
responded, "I don't believe this captain can get a hold of this situation." Mr. Patterson then
asked him if this was a racial issue. The man said, "It's not a race issue, but close near
there." Purdum further noted that "at 1:00 am, police transmissions from the scene reported
a few injured officers, and at 1:03 am, noted that Capt. McNamara and Chief Thomas J.
Darcy, were on the scene. At 1:09 am, highway units were summoned to the scene, and at
1:11 am, the Brooklyn South Task Force." Throughout the night, about four hundred officers
were called in to reinforce the scene.

Other incidents of sporadic police brutality were seen during Patterson's film. For example,
shortly before 3:00 am, the film shows a heavyset man being kicked and clubbed by officers
who pulled him to his feet by his hair while an unidentified plain clothes officer with a captain's shield on his shirt stood nearby. The officers did not appear to arrest the man. On
the other hand, there were officers who were physically provoked by the protesters.
According to Lt. Paul Putkowski of the 61st Precinct, who was a 1st Precinct police officer
working the original detail on the night of August 6th, he was standing on post off the
northwest corner of Avenue A and 6th Street when he was hit twice in the left leg by small
rocks thrown from an unknown location. Interestingly enough, Lt. Putkowski recalls feeling
somewhat invigorated to be involved in such a big event, but at the same time a bit scared
of the unknown. He compared the experience to a roller coaster ride. The riot had brought
back memories of when his dad, a former NYPD detective, told him about the Harlem riots of
the mid and late-1960s of which he was a part. Besides police, protesters, and bystanders
present for this historic event, however, there were also reporters and members of the clergy.
One priest in particular, Father Kennington, was seen in Patterson's film listening to protesters' complaints and relaying their messages to Capt. McNamara and Chief Darcy.

A Radical Political and Social History of the Lower East Side

In chapter 11 of her book, Abu-Lughod writes,

> . . . the tensions are noticeably defused by the arrival, in elegant civilian
> clothes, of the head of Metropolitan Police south, who takes command. Does he
> order the police to leave? It's hard to know, but the mounted police inexplicably
> turn their horses around and retreat north on Avenue A. The demonstrators
> sneer and slowly advance after them, applauding and shouting, 'every night!'
> People feel they have triumphed. (p. 244)

Shortly after re-entering the park from Avenue A, this same group revitalized by the retreating police, was seen on Mr. Patterson's film in symbolic fashion throwing police barriers into, and large tree plants out of, the lobby of The Christodora House, a tall newly converted luxury co-op building. Shouts of, "Die yuppie scum," were heard throughout the destruction. Abu-Lughod further notes that, "the last act in this night's drama makes the meaning of the events crystal clear. The demonstrators post their banner, 'Gentrification is class war' on the facade of The Christodora House — the deeply resented emblem of neighborhood change. The 'riot' is over." (p. 245)

By 6:00 am, the last of the protesters dispersed. The total count of injured included over fifty civilians and eighteen police officers. There were over 100 charges of police brutality. There were nine arrests including charges of assault, riot, reckless endangerment, resisting arrest and disorderly conduct. Mayor Koch ordered the park to remain open during the night for the time being.

Clearly, solid police leadership was almost non-existent both in preparation for and in response to the Tompkins Square Park Police Riot. In defining the requirements of good leadership, writer Andre Swanson wrote, "leadership requires that a person have an appreciation of the importance of influencing the outcome of events and the desire to play a key role in that process. This need for impact must be greater than either the need for personal achievement or the need to be liked by others." Capt. McNamara, having been the Commanding Officer of the 9th Precinct where Tompkins Square Park was located, was the focus of failed leadership in the aftermath of the riot. In July, 1988, he took some preventive steps in trying to stop future park protests. For example, a meeting was held at the Manhattan South Headquarters with Chief Darcy as the host. However, neither representatives from the Parks Department nor the 9th Precinct's Community Board #3 were asked to attend. Here, by not inviting all the parties concerned, Capt. McNamara lacked problem solving skills and insight to the real issue of gentrification. It is evident throughout the 1988 *New York Times*' articles and Abu-Lughod's book that Capt. McNamara saw the ongoing Tompkins Square Park disturbance more as a quality of life issue than a deep rooted socioeconomic one.

Capt. McNamara had position power and assigned leadership because of his rank and place as commanding officer of the 9th Precinct. However, it is clear in watching Patterson's film that the first detail of officers on the scene the night of the riot arrived, as Lt. Putkowski puts it, "in a pell mell where officers asked themselves, 'Why are we here?'" (P. Putkowski, personal interview, September 23, 2004). Obviously, Capt. McNamara used poor planning in not addressing the troops about the police department's purpose or goal that night. For that manner, he also failed to communicate well with his lieutenants and sergeants. Patterson remembered one Task Force sergeant in particular, who, when asked, "Who's in charge here?" stated, "You are." This meant that this sergeant in particular had no confidence in himself or his higher ups. Patterson agreed. Capt. McNamara seemed to have no influence over the officers beneath him on the day of the riot in achieving a common goal. This meant that there was little or no communication between officers of all ranks on the scene and also between police supervisors and the demonstrators. According to Lt. Putkowski, he was on three different detail rosters that night. The third roster he was on was a 1st Precinct roster. This showed how unorganized the detail was from the beginning (P. Putkowski, personal interview, September 23, 2004)

Leadership was clearly absent throughout the riot. This laissez-faire leadership technique took a hands-off-let-things-ride approach. According to writer Peter G. Northouse, this non-leadership style, "abdicates responsibility, delays decisions, gives no feedback, and makes little effort to help followers satisfy their needs. There is no exchange with followers or any attempt to help them grow." (p.179) Capt. McNamara personified this non-leadership approach by making few command decisions during the riot. His hands-off-let-things-ride approach showed that he had no long-range plan on how to deal with the protest that had gotten out of control. His approach was passive in dealing with subordinates. According to Swanson, this laissez-faire style says leaders make "no attempt to appraise or regulate a course of events." (p.137)

Rather than being one of the 'reform oriented' "college boys" Swanson speaks of, Capt. McNamara showed more 'tradition oriented' behavior in refusing to create leadership goals (Swanson, 1988). Even when he did give orders like telling people to clear the streets and seconds later to clear the sidewalk, they seemed contradictory or futile. At one point early in the protest, he gave an order for mounted police to disperse a group that had sat down in the middle of the street on Avenue A, but he never closed traffic on Avenue A.

It seemed as if Capt. McNamara came to the detail with no proactive or offensive strategies in place, but rather chose to let the protesters and poorly supervised police officers dictate the tone of the event. For example, the temporary headquarters was set up inside the park, where the initial protest had taken place and where the largest number of protesters had been. This command post area location could have gotten ugly, but the protest moved out-side the park where there were few, if any, intimidating police vehicles present. Secondly, every time a police officer put his hands on someone there was no supervision around to take control of the situation or verify any possible arrest situation. Arrests, in general, were sporadic and arbitrary. Thirdly, rooftops were not secure until aviation was called in, and the film showed that the helicopters, flying very low, riled the protesters further.

Another theory related to the overall atmosphere of the officers present at the protest was the contingency theory. This theory is characterized by the situational variables of leader-member relations and task structure (Northouse, 2004). Since the atmosphere or attitude of most of the officers around Tompkins Square Park on August 6-7 was negative, as shown by Lt's Putkowski's descriptive 'pell-mell' statement, and since officers' task requirements were

A Radical Political and Social History of the Lower East Side

not clearly spelled out, the contingency theory shows that the framework for effectively matching the leader, Capt. McNamara, and the situation, an anti-gentrification riot, was doomed from the start.

I do not think it is fair to fully blame Capt. McNamara for the failures of the NYPD that night, even though he and Chief Darcy were used as scapegoats by the police department. It is common practice for the NYPD to want to blame someone for major police incidents gone wrong. According to Purdum, "In an unusually harsh preliminary evaluation, Police Commissioner Benjamin Ward has already admitted that poor planning and tactical errors led the police to lose control of the situation, and he has questioned why mid-level commanders did not consult higher ones sooner." (p. 1) Similarly, Paul Derienzo writes, "Chief of Department Robert Johnston, the highest ranking uniformed officer in the city, said after the riot that he had no knowledge of events as they unfolded in Tompkins Square Park on August 6th and 7th "(p. 1)

Interestingly, Mr. Michael Julian, Capt. McNamara's replacement as commanding officer of the 9th Precinct, and a former chief of personnel, stated in an e-mail that Capt. McNamara was an aide to Chief of Department Robert Johnston, and that Chief Johnston and Capt. McNamara were "enamored with new gadgets to control crime and disorder" and that McNamara relished the Emergency Services unit gear.

According to Mr. Julian, when Capt. McNamara got to the 9th Precinct he effectively used department resources to shut down the most notorious drug spot in the city known as "the rock." Mr. Julian also stated that on another occasion, a Jewish radical named Mr. Levy, fired shots from his apartment on Bleecker Street at an acquaintance on the street. Capt. McNamara, ranking supervisor on the scene, sealed the block, brought a tank in on a flatbed and ultimately gained the surrender of Mr. Levy (Julian, Michael ,"personal communication," October 4, 2004). Using Mr. Julian's examples, it is clear that Capt. McNamara had proven leadership qualities. It took some time to understand, but Mr. Patterson's next comment is well taken. He said that Capt. McNamara and, to a certain extent, Chief Darcy, "ate the onion on the night of the riot," but it was not fair to totally blame them because they could have been any other captain and chief working that night. In other words, it was the culture/climate of Tompkins Square Park and its gentrification, in the mid to late-1980s, that the NYPD did not understand (C. Patterson, personal interview, September, 18, 2004). The police department knew that it had failed to intervene as a peacekeeper in maintaining order during the riot. Ultimately, the two police officers at the protest with the highest assigned leadership, Capt. McNamara and Deputy Chief Darcy, were disciplined for failing to properly coordinate assignments and failing to notify top police officials of the riot until the worst was over. Capt. McNamara was transferred and Deputy Chief Darcy retired shortly after the riot.

In short, the New York City Police Department was neither prepared to deal with the complex nature of the roots of the riot nor the riot itself. The event became the first large scale New York City riot since the Blackout Riots of 1977. In 1988 the NYPD was considered to be a young and inexperienced department. On the nights of August 6th and 7th, 1988, in particular, Officer McKinley recalled that, "Most of the officers who arrived at the scene had received only three hours of training on basic formations for crowd control. Few had ever been confronted with such violent antagonism from a crowd."

The Tompkins Square Park Police Riot of 1988 was an unfortunate historical event for the NYPD and the residents of New York City living on the Lower East Side. Based on the circumstances of the events leading up to the protest, if Capt. McNamara had used skills and situational leadership in his approach to dealing with the ongoing protests, then the outcome of the August 6th and 7th riots might have been better. So, it was possible that Capt. McNamara and others lacked the technical and conceptual skills needed to lead their officers through the riot.

According to M.D. Mumford's theory on how motivation affects leadership, perhaps they lacked motivation because they didn't have sufficient knowledge on the issue at hand: gentrification (Northouse, 2004). At a time in the history of Tompkins Square Park when so many issues involving gentrification had come together at once, the NYPD was thrown in the mix without rehearsal or preparation.

The riot itself proved to be a catalyst for change for the department from a classic one to a para-military one. In this sense, the riot was, as Mr. Patterson said, "The worst and the best thing for the NYPD." (C. Patterson, personal interview, September 18, 2004). The department was forced to evaluate its training and tactics and how to better handle large-scale protests and potential riots.

In my opinion the NYPD has learned how to better prepare itself for potential riot situations by using the Tompkins Square Park Police Riot as a model. I do not believe that history will repeat itself in a similar riot in Tompkins Square Park because so many steps were taken by the police department to correct what went wrong. The Dinkins administration closed the park for a year for major renovations. This closing and subsequent re-opening proved beneficial to all, police and citizens alike.

Chapter 5

Lower East Side Class War and the Subversive
Media Spectacle
        By Joshua Rothenberger

In the summer of 1988, the forces of gentrification, homelessness, drugs, and community politics culminated in what could be considered New York's last 'urban revolution.' A police-enforced curfew in the Lower East Side's Tompkins Square Park forced hundreds of homeless back out onto the streets and effectively ended the park's function as a neighborhood locus of cultural exchange. On Saturday, August 6th, the homeless, local residents, activists, artists, anarchists, communists, and various marginalized groups joined together to protest the curfew as well as the fast-growing problem of gentrification in the Lower East Side. What began that night as a botched attempt at crowd containment soon escalated to senseless beatings. According to one *Village Voice* reporter, "the police were radiating hysteria."[1] On this night, Clayton Patterson, a Lower East Side artist, captured over three and a half hours of the protest and ensuing violence on video. *The Tompkins Square Park Police Riot* is an astoundingly comprehensive look at a specific instance of cultural, political, and economic upheaval. By exposing himself to police aggression, Patterson's camera is not merely a passive eye, but rather an active agent in the fight against the corporate seizure of one of Manhattan's oldest immigrant residential neighborhoods. *The Tompkins Square Park Police Riot* is an unmediated and un-doctored look at the physical realities of violent social transformation, an essential anecdote to any historical narrative of New York City.

* * * * *

While the term "police riot" accurately describes the diegetic action in Patterson's video, local activist Joel Meyers argues that it "can be misleading in that it seems to imply that a night of spontaneous violence, rioting and 'wilding' on the part of certain police officers was the length and breadth of the entire event," and thus "distracts from any deeper significance." Meyers sees the strategy of police violence that night as received "from at least the top of the NYC government." (Minority Report 2) Meanwhile, in mainstream newspapers the blame had fallen almost solely on the shoulders of 'rookie cops' and 'inefficient police tactics.'[2] "Melee," was originally used to describe the night's events. Such rhetoric should not be seen as impassive, but rather as a rhetorical defense of police violence that night, a shared understanding that when things 'get out of control' a policeman must do whatever it takes to restore order. The term "police riot" was reluctantly pronounced by Mayor Edward Koch and Police Commissioner Benjamin Ward after an embarrassing abundance of photo and video evidence emerged and forced the city's government to back down from their initial diagnosis. In a sense, then, Patterson's video performed a forced-baptism on the whole event, transforming it from a taxonomy of ruling class ignorance ('scuffle' or 'melee') to a form of nomenclature that directly served the protesters' needs and drew attention to the irregularity of police operations that night ('riot').

Joshua Rothenberger

* * * * *

Mass media communicates to its audience through images that mean on the surface, that are isolated from any sort of social or contextual system of meaning (even if the 'stories' attached to such images rely on social context to derive their meanings). The preservation of this myth — that the image's meaning is self-contained and its consequences self-present-is the most essential characteristic to any form of successful mediation on behalf of the status quo. *Ruling ideas are most effectively communicated when made manifest through images that mask the hand of the mediator.* This is admittedly an obvious point, and one that has been made repeatedly since the beginnings of media analysis. Yet, it would be an oversimplification to theorize the effectiveness with which ruling class interests are promulgated In the mass media as a series of isolated attempts at concealing the processes and politics of mediation (in other words, the audience's 'mystification' does not necessarily depend on an editor's ability to cut the images a certain way). Rather, the myth of self-presence relies heavily on a culture of self-presence, and the self-contained meaning derives its poignancy from a web of images that claim self-containment. In the oft-quoted words of Guy DeBord:

"The spectacle presents itself as something enormously positive, indisputable and inaccessible. It says nothing more than "whatever appears is good, and whatever is good appears." The attitude it requires in principal is this passive acceptance, which in fact it has already obtained by its method of appearing without reply, by its monopoly of appearance." (65)

The myths that surround (that is to say the ideology embedded in) the independent or subversive media image is something quite different. The process by which the independent media image communicates is wholly contextual, and therefore always biased. Truth, in this sense, is always *a posteriori*. The subversive image has forsaken any claim to ubiquity and instead begs the mainstream audience for mere conditional acceptance. For this reason, the audience should be skeptical when asked to worship the independent image outside of the specific 'reactionary' argument that resurrected it. Here, the mediator is always visible, in fact cannot be hidden, for the image's very status as oppositional is brought about by mediation, and while the images may be 'real,' reality has, at the very least, been organized into the form of a counter-argument.

Patterson's video plays into neither set of presuppositions. Throughout the three hours and thirty-three minutes duration of the original video, the only moments of temporal disjunction occurred when the camera was turned off for precautionary reasons (to replace a battery or tape). The spectatorial experience here lies totally outside of editing techniques of any kind, whether they be the slick, self-presence associated with mainstream news montage or the rhetorical tidiness of alternative visual arguments. What is communicated first and foremost is that the filmmaker is a 'bystander' who used his camera to record 'what happened that night.' Patterson's non-filmmaker status reinforces the fact that such shocking acts of police violence occurred in open view and merits guarded optimism regarding a fast-growing technological capacity of the public to monitor official uses, and abuses, of power. As we will see, such "non-cinema" aesthetics allowed the video to transcend a preaching to the converted status within the left and infiltrate the corporate/state hegemony of mainstream media.

A Radical Political and Social History of the Lower East Side

*****

Neil Smith has shown how the mainstream visual media worked to silence opposition against the Lower East Side resistance by depicting the neighborhood as "Indian Country." (Bird 93) Local news programs displayed their 'objective' interest in the conflict by running 'background stories' on the Lower East Side, exposés that painted the whole neighborhood as bohemian, transgressive, and dangerous. Such representations effectively erased the large amount of Puerto Rican, Eastern European, and Black working-class families that comprised the largest portion of the neighborhood's population at the time[3], instead casting the neighborhood either as 'white bohemian playground' or as 'unruly Other badly in need of a large-scale crack down.' The flurry of such network propaganda culminated in the now famous exposé on a potential Lower East Side cult conspiracy lead by the CBGB's-bred punk rock quartet Missing Foundation. Reporter Mike Taibbi attempted to link the band to uprisings like the Tompkins Square Park melee and general deviant behavior that continued to proliferate in the region.

The *New York Post* seems to have been most directly tied to the pro-gentrification movement. "Antonio Pagan seems to have owned Peter S. Kalikow and the *New York Post*," argues community activist Fran Luck, whose research shows that the *Post* had a number of affiliates who owned property in and around Tompkins Square Park.[4] This alliance manifested itself in a series of right-wing propagandist headlines before, during, and following the August 6th police riots. The brand of conservative 'objectivism' that governed the policies and practices of the *Post* during this time are reflected in some of the less than objective headlines of the time: "Foul Play in the Lower East Side," "Just One Small Victory over the Derelict Army," and "A Bunch of Young Bums Stealing Tompkins Square Park." In many ways, the *New York Post* was the most friendly media outlet to the pro-gentrification movement, and was used copiously to promulgate a "soft on" gentrification sentiment amongst New Yorkers. Such propaganda became all the more necessary after the reckless actions of the NYPD on August 6th foregrounded the social contradictions embedded in the city's move to displace thousands under the guise of "redevelopment" or "revitalization."

Such representations were necessary if class war was to be waged against certain vulnerable segments of the city's population without serious impediment. In addition to journalistic media, various feature films of the time depicted the Lower East Side as a happy bohemia that drew caché whites to its tenement buildings with cheap prices and used 'cutting-edge' art galleries, 'independent' boutiques, and 'posh' bars to keep them there. Films like *9½ Weeks* and *Slaves of New York* used ethnic diversity and low-income retro/vintage decor to create an altruistic Lower East Side that existed solely to provide middle class whites with fabulous 'arty' jobs and exhilarating sexual escapades. *Desperately Seeking Susan*, on the other hand, uses the Lower East Side to define a bona fide urban princess protagonist in opposition to her staid, middle-upper class Jersey counterpart. Yet the self-sacrifice of this naturalized land of bohemia wins in the end, as the two women, in the words of Gabriel Esperdy, "join forces in friendship and mutual understanding, an outcome which hardly reflected the reality of the East Village in the mid to late 1980s." (*Parallax* 138)

*****

Patterson's video contains none of the truth-establishing devices commonly found in documentary or newsreel video. Instead, reality is presented through the absence of a voice-of-god telling us what to think about the images presented, of in-the-know talking heads 'objectively' guiding us toward a very specific history, of archival footage as proof that what such talking heads say is 'factual,' of extra-diegetic music to evoke mood, and of cutting for the sake of montage effects. Because of the spontaneity of the police riots, Patterson had no time to plan, shot-list, or even fully charge his camera battery. The camera is fast-moving and at times sways the audience to dizziness. What is forsaken in aesthetic polish is more than salvaged by the illusory ubiquity of the camera's eye. At times it seems that Patterson is in two places at once, and his instinct for both beguiling images of brute violence and foreboding periods of calm create the ultimate portrayal of a Tompkins Square Park "non-cinema man"[5] at a specific historical intersection.

*****

The first crucial cinematic moment occurs when Patterson's camera finds policemen equipping themselves with riot gear. As we slowly pan across the faces of officers on horseback, the camera performs a true cinematic physiognomic interpretation, exposing a trepidation and uncertainty amongst the police force and foreshadowing the chaos that would erupt shortly thereafter. We hear shotgun blasts . . . not just firecrackers off camera, amongst chants like "It's our fuckin' park!" and "No police state!" The party-like energy amongst the protesters is growing and some bottles are flung. More police cars have arrived at the Avenue A and Seventh Street entrance, and a loudspeaker voice fills the tense air: "Clear the Streets!" Yet before the unruly crowd has much chance to flee, the cops stampede the crowd, creating a pandemonious mélange of nightsticks, helicopter spotlights, flailing horse hooves, and blood. While we see many members of the crowd scattering to the boundaries of the frame, the camera seems particularly apt at conveying the terror of being a straggler. We see a man receive several blows as punishment for lagging behind. The camera approaches and he reveals his bloody face to us, deliriously muttering, "I am Russian." A voice can be heard off screen saying, "Sir, when you get some good footage, I'd get outta here."

In *Film and the Anarchist Imagination*, Richard Porton reads Patterson's role in the riots as "neither a leader nor a bystander but part of the struggle." Certainly this sentiment is conveyed during the most extreme scenes of violence and chaos, where Patterson must forsake attempts at cinematographic precision and instead run for safety, thus destroying the artifice of detached observation. At the same time, however, Patterson's role in the struggle is not quite the same as those around him: he is a 'man with a movie camera' and in a sense cannot help but to filter his interactions with fellow protesters through that lens. This is acknowledged interdiegetically in a variety of ways, though most poignantly in arguments over Patterson's right to film. At one point Patterson is confronted by what appears to be a fellow protestor, who asks the documentarian, "You got a press card? Why are you taking pictures?" Patterson doesn't hesitate to retort (and in fact 'loses his cool,' signified by the camera drifting clumsily out of focus): "It's not illegal." The comment comes off as somewhat ironic following shots of politically disinterested bar-hoppers being cornered and

A Radical Political and Social History of the Lower East Side

beaten by storm trooper-esque, riot-gear-clad policemen. Later Patterson attempts to film a girl (presumably not a protestor but a passerby who got caught in the bloodbath) who has been badly wounded. While the girl is far too insensible to order Patterson's camera away, her friends and those helping her scream at the cameraman to "stop taking her picture!" Moments pass and Patterson is able to continue filming without impedance, the caretakers too distracted by the profusion of blood. Then Patterson is again bombarded with vicious insults, "Coward!" and "Rabble rouser!" The novelty of the video camera—still a rather new form of technology in 1988—is apparent in such shots. Aside from the antiquated language used in reference to the camera ("Stop taking pictures!"), clearly the public captured in *Tompkins Square Park Police Riots* is not wholly comfortable with its presence or the contradictory potentials it poses.

Equally provocative are the shots depicting 'downtime': the moments following one burst of violence and in anticipation of the next. Here the camera drifts in and out, apparition-like, of emotionally charged 'what's at stake?' discussions between some half-cocked punks and a priest; of morale speeches given by a local activist before a small crowd of Puerto Ricans and Blacks; of ideological debates between a club owner and a middle-aged immigrant mother of three. "If they'd attack drug areas like they attack this park we'd have a better city!" The unscripted, adrenaline-imbued dialogue then is the film's best and only exegetic device. Rather than inundate the spectator with tables, charts, archived footage, and disinterested critical testimonials, contextualization is achieved through a colloquial and spontaneous dialogic exploration of latent (but significant) political and social issues surrounding the visible, spectacular brutality. The word of mouth history is sometimes, to the film's credit, misinformed and contradictory and creates a frame of multifarious historical meanings representative of the very "anarchic" forms of resistance practiced by the film's subjects—oppressed individuals of strikingly disparate social, economic, and ethnic background. "Who's in charge?" / "They'd never do that on a fuckin' drug block!"/ "Who's responsible?" / "This is a real estate conflict" / "What's the truth here?" / "If we give in tonight, they have us" / "This is gonna be a media circus" / "This is dangerous, there are some people here who really want this . . . we call them 'anarchists'" / "They have to leave first" / "Nobody throw a bottle" / "Every night, every night!" / "The Park at least diffuses tension" / "Tompkins Square Park is not the problem."

*****

Richard Porton rightly claims that Patterson has "fulfilled Hans Magnus Enzensberger's prognostication that the 'new media' have the potential to be deployed as a 'means of production' not merely means of consumption" (225). Patterson's will/mania to document everything he could in effect "produced" a story that otherwise would have been written out of the media archive before it had a chance to be museumified.[6] This is evidenced by the sudden massive proliferation of mainstream press coverage on the event after Patterson's video was screened for the *New York Times* and by various news stations. Patterson's video rendered the socio-economic contradictions and militaristic recklessness irrepressible, a sentiment echoed by Paul Garrin, a video artist who also filmed the event for twenty minutes: "The footage created the story. The story didn't exist for them until the video tapes emerged."[7] Patterson's video was used in multiple court cases against the city and provided strong evidence for the forced resignation of at least half a dozen police officers. *The Tompkins Square Park Police Riot* must be considered alongside the *Rodney King Video* in terms of its potential for exposing injustices within the dominant order. The weight of the video is evidenced by the fact that since the August 6th protest, Patterson has been jailed, attacked, and has had his apartment illicitly searched multiple times.

The Tompkins Square Park Police Riots served as a particularly useful tool in mounting an opposition to the closing of the park and the further subjugation of the homeless. In the weeks following the August 6th incident, the video rapidly muscled its way into the role of mediator, a role usually filled by the mainstream media editors and producers. Todd Purdum and Howard French's article in the *New York Times* and Eric Shawn's feature story on Channel 11 provided a mainstream stage for Patterson's shocking footage, and soon after it became a necessary visual component for any news piece on the riot and police brutality in general. It stands as one of the most successful attempts at challenging mainstream media hegemony. Here the grassroots media gained a dominant voice (albeit temporarily) in the reconstruction of the events and 'truths' that took place on a particularly crucial night in the struggle against state-sanctioned disenfranchisement.

* * * * *

What, then, can we say of the filmic text at hand in terms of its relationship to those specific contradictions in the economic and political fabric of the state? How does *The Tompkins Square Park Police Riots* work as a subversive text in relation to such historical 'fissure' (to use Gramsci's language) in the ruling class stranglehold on the media's truth-telling capacities? I think it is useful to look at Patterson's alternative media intervention in terms of what Michel Foucault called "governmentality." In his re-reading of Machiavelli's *The Prince*, Foucault shows how the institutions used to strengthen the monarch's claim to material transcendence were disrupted during the base shift from feudalism to capitalism, rendering *The Prince* a mere arranger or organizer of the social rather than "the embodiment of immanent rule" (Miller 14). The processes and contradictions that arise here can be seen as the replacing of the feudal subject's quotidian crisis ("how shall I be governed?") with that of an emerging capitalist era ("how shall I govern myself?"). It is in this antagonism that the need for a police force arises, a mediator between the 'freedom' of the individual and the necessary limits of that freedom in the interest of the governing state.

The Tompkins Square Park Police Riots offers us a specific moment in history where the limits of self-governance can be seen as incongruent with the needs of the ruling class, and thus the responsibility of re-articulating this relationship according to the terms of the latter party fell on the shoulders of the mediating institution — the police force. This is echoed in Joel Meyers and Clayton Patterson's "Minority Report," a document drafted and presented to the federal authorities during the weeks of NYPD investigation following the riot:

"The police riot is often blamed by official sources and media on inexperienced, panicked or over-zealous rookie cops, insufficiently supervised. But these same sources at the same time claim to be unable to establish the identity of the cops present. Videotapes of the police riot show many faces well over thirty years old. The "rookie" explanation is also contradicted

A Radical Political and Social History of the Lower East Side

by TSPTF testimony of CCRB member William Kuntz and Assistant D. A. Jonathan Fried, who claim that many police identification photos are largely useless because they are upward of five years old. More than adequate supervision was provided by "at least forty supervisors ranging in rank from sergeant to deputy chief," according to the CCRB Final Report issued in April 1989." (4)

Police brutality, while certainly a significant problem in and of itself, became the stand-in for a more insidious, pervasive type of warfare that was, to some extent, mandated by larger shifts in the late capitalist mode of production. The rapid changes in the U.S. workforce beginning in the late '70s and accelerating through the '80s have been well documented, and it is commonly asserted that such cultural and economic reconstruction was felt most drastically in New York City during this time.[8] The redevelopment necessary to accommodate New York's vast increase in white-collar presence and the gradual erasure of the blue collar created a manic level of social polarization and community conflict in the '80s.

This is most evident in the newly christened "East Village" and "Alphabet City" (trendier names to mask their recent past as immigrant tenement enclaves and working class ghettos) where the "gentrification frontier" is capitalized by institutional investors — such as non-local commercial banks and real-estate companies — from *outside* the community (Abu-Lughod 336-351). Communal spaces, like Tompkins Square Park, become the physical site of such contestation. On the night of August 6th, the cultural politics and recreational interests of long-time Lower East Side residents clashed with the interests of penetrating alien investors who had poured money into the neighborhood in hopes of creating a more lucrative business venture (which, for all intents and purposes, meant converting it to what Fran Luck called, "The bedroom of Wall Street").[9]

Furthermore, such ruling class pressures to 'revitalize' the neighborhood necessitated a reformulation of Tompkins Square Park's spatial politics, namely an eradication of the "we're here, we're homeless, deal with it" spectacle that occupied the southern third of the premises.[10] While both city and state governments are traditionally thought to be responsible for the basic rights of their citizens (housing, public recreational space, protection from drugs and disease), clearly this was not the case in 1980s New York City. The imposed agendas of gentrification and lower class eradication rendered such "basic rights" responsibilities merely contingent upon capital growth prospects.

It is here that *The Tompkins Square Park Police Riots* makes its most profound intervention. In a sense Patterson supplies us with a visual aid in understanding Foucault's proposal that "a society's 'threshold of modernity' has been reached when the life of the species is wagered on its political strategies." At times the camera seems to depict war as it has been learned ("showed" or "taught"?) to us through movies: the terror apparent on the faces of those under attack and, at times, those preparing to administer the attack speak most overtly to the fact that some facet of 'the system' has failed badly. Indeed the actions captured would strike anyone as 'atypical' and even 'unthinkable.' Patterson's video teaches us that the reproduction of the social is never a seamless process, never occurs without noise or interference, and on this particular occasion resulted in a violent, reckless attack against normal people 'like you and me' by the very institution that is put forth to protect 'us.' This

sentiment is echoed by Richard Porton's analysis of the video as "an example of media pedagogy that transcends the boundaries of the classroom."

* * * * *

Patterson's video serves as the centerpiece of a short but potent outgrowth of independent
media texts surfacing between the years of 1988-1992 in response to the police riot and
subsequent conflicts over free speech, real-estate policies, police violence, and governmentality. This era presents us with a rare case in which forms of independent media were able
to infiltrate the ruling class hegemony of mass media images and provide a significant voice
in the public's reconstruction of the event. Such subversive media was embodied by, but not
limited to Patterson's video-document of the event. Patterson and Meyers' "Minority Report,"
cited earlier in this paper, can be seen as a more traditional form of independent media in
that it attempts to construct an alternate history and factual analysis, and use it to argue
against the dominant version.

The document itself is clumsily structured, especially given its intentions of exposing the
contradictions of the state to members of its constituent institutions. Yet, the primary aim
here is to open the floodgates of repressed "truth," and thus the structure correlates well as
a series of disjunctive interpretations of various acts of police, government, and real estate
investor injustice. The same logic seems to have informed a vast majority of anti-State propaganda posters. These posters, usually very heavy on text with a slapdash approach to
graphic design, spoke to the utter hybridity in the anti-gentrification and 'free the park'
movements. Some of these posters concentrated solely on "Class War" and haphazardly
attempted to link larger social phenomenon (such as President Bush's "Gulf War") to the
State's oppression of working class Lower East Siders. Others crashed merrily through the
'taste' barrier, ranting and raving about government-endorsed genocide of the homeless via
AIDS vaccinations and food tampering, while paying little mind to theoretical fecundity. The
goal it seems was to blanket Lower Manhattan in oppositional text and image, whether that
be a socialist, anarcho-punk, conspiracy theorist, etc.

Additionally, graffiti was used all over the pubic spaces of the Lower East Side to comment
on the state's repression of free speech, its commandeering of social space, and it's oppression of the homeless and long-time lower class residents. Stencil artists fought against the
attempted closing of the park by covering its perimeters with signs in an official font:
"NYPD RIOT ZONE." (Bird 93). Paul Garrin used his footage of the event in an art installation that fostered an awareness of the police riot and surrounding issues amongst
Manhattan's gallery intelligentsia. While some forms of independent media obviously had a
greater impact on the status quo than others, all of the above vehicles worked in unison to
transfer authorship of media spectacle from the disembodied, detached dominant classes to
those directly and materially effected by Lower East Side gentrification and homelessness.
The politics that fueled all forms of alternative media intervention can hardly be linked to
one distinct political agenda. Rather the resistance to gentrification and institutional violence (both latent and manifest) in this case can be considered an "anarchic" response to a
particularly messy case of state authoritarianism.

A Radical Political and Social History of the Lower East Side

The Tompkins Square Park Police Riots illustrates this in various ways, through Patterson's own narrative of self-emancipation via the technology of digital video, and also by capturing protesters of widely varying political creeds fighting, hand-in-hand, against policemen. Certainly there is work to be done on how forms of subversive media like the propaganda posters, the "Minority Report," and graffiti assisted in keeping the park open without curfew for four more years, as well as to combat certain state-sanctioned forms of disenfranchisement.

Works Cited:

Abu-Lughod, Janet. "The Battle for Tompkins Square Park." *From Urban Village to East Village: The Battle for New York's Lower East Side*. Ed. Janet Abu-Lughod. Cambridge: Blackwell Publishers, 1994. 233-267.

Esperdy, Gabrielle. "Slouching Back to the East Village: Social and Spatial Meaning in Urban Landscape." *Parallax*. Issue 5. 1997. 137-168.

Miller, Toby. *Technologies of Truth: Cultural Citizenship and the Popular Media*. Minneapolis: University of Minnesota Press, 1998.

Porton, Richard. *Film and the Anarchist Imagination*. New York: Verso, 1999.

Smith, Neil. "Homeless/Global: Scaling Places." *Mapping the Futures: Local Cultures, Global Change*. Ed. Jon Bird et al. London: Routledge, 1993. 87-119.

Endnotes:

1. C. Carr. "Nightclubbing. Reports from the Tompkins Square Park Riot." *Village Voice*, August 16, 1988. Pg. 10.

2. Purdum, Todd S. "Lessons of '60s Forgotten in Park Riot." *New York Times*, August 11, 1988, p. B4.

3. See Abu-Lughod's chapter "Welcome to the Neighborhood," in *From Urban Village to East Village*.

4. Operation Class War. VHS. *Paper Tiger TV*. 1994.

5. *"Non-cinema Man"* is what Alfred Hitchcock called the "man who is not doing things primarily for the camera" (Miller 187).

6. This goal could not have been realized without the help of Patterson's assistant Elsa Rensaa. Rensaa ran nearly half a mile on at least four occasions to store used tapes and recharge batteries. This point is particularly important because prior analysis of the film have failed to take into account the importance of such non-cinematic tasks. Given the nature of the film-all endeavor, Rensaa's assistance could very well lead the critic to reconsider authorial treatment of Tompkins Square Park Police Riots, which up to now has situated the video as one of the great feats of one-man documentary production.

7. Operation Class War. VHS. Paper Tiger TV. 1994.

8. See Neil Smith's "Homeless/Global" in Bird et al, and Rosalyn Deutsche's essay "Krysztof Wodiczko's homeless projection and the site of urban revitalization" in *Overexposed* (ed. Carol Squires).

9. Operation Class War. VHS. *Paper Tiger TV*. 1994.

10. See Esperdy *"Slouching Back to the East Village."*

Chapter 6

Tompkins Square Park: 1989-1991
By Chief Michael Julian

"What are you going to do about IT!!" She barked, pointing over her shoulder at the park house restroom a few feet away. I was focused on another homeless woman, propped against the wall, blood trickling down her thigh and pooling at her feet. The interrogator repeated: "What are you going to do about that baby in the sink!"

An image flashed before me —bloody hangar on the floor, aborted fetus in the sink. I sent a rookie into the restroom. She could learn from a nasty dose of Tompkins Square reality. I had reached my limit of this failed social experiment — three hundred people camped on patches of grass, stretched across park benches, and billeted in the bandshell or the toilets. They were loosely organized into separate camps: heroin junkies to the south, crack addicts to the north, and alcoholics in the center, mostly harmless to everyone but themselves. Homeless advocates had created an enclave of self-destruction.

"Did I hear right?" Father George Kuhn asked. "Did a baby die?" He had rushed right over from St. Brigid's on Avenue B where he cared for the underclass and the unborn. He soberly talked about the misery and the death. The park was a killer. A guy froze to death over the winter before they protected themselves with blankets and tents. The Parks Department wanted to continue the no-blanket rule to maintain some order in the park. To me, the community board's decision to lift the citywide curfew and allow the homeless to sleep in the park included a right to put something between a body and the cold concrete. I would have the cops assigned to the park enforce the criminal laws, not the park aesthetics.

My demurral was followed quickly by an accumulation of structures in an expanding encampment that did not stop the dying. Another guy burned to death in his makeshift tent. Without protection they froze, with protection they burned. Proselytizers flooded the park with soup kitchen salves. The homeless were lured en masse.

To the police in the 9th precinct covering Alphabet City and the Lower East Side, this park qualified for a circle in a 20th century version of Dante's *Inferno*. Dazed homeless men, many with open sores and tattered clothing, roamed the park and nearby streets. Junkies sharing needles spread AIDS, tuberculosis, hepatitis and other diseases.

Behind the bandshell off 7th Street, human waste poured out the doors and surrounded the portable rest rooms. In an ill-advised effort to eliminate the stench, someone took a match to the fiberglass porta-johns. Plastic and human waste melted into an amorphous and odious mess. While most citizens and civil servants avoided the area, the addicts were oblivi- ous. They appreciated a safe respite to shoot up no matter how foul. Had the junkies con-

A Radical Political and Social History of the Lower East Side

fined their activities to the bandshell, families might have coexisted. But needles were regularly discarded in the sandboxes and grassy areas. We carved out needle-free playgrounds, but it was a small concession for a meager group of brave women and their babies.

1

The "homeless" dominated the social issues in the late 1980s. The media and social activists pounded the city for allegedly abandoning its huddled masses. Into the fray entered a new breed of squatters who adopted the homeless and a phrase "No Housing, No Peace." Taking sides with a sympathetic underclass masked their self-interest in occupying abandoned buildings.

Many of these new squatters were more interested in sloganeering and slingshots than sweat equity. If they didn't get their way, they attacked the cops and harassed anyone who criticized their tactics. Behind an empty chant they handcuffed and tortured the Lower East Side for three years. Their charade accelerated the market forces that left the Lower East Side nearly uninhabitable by people of modest means.

Brevity is the beauty and the bane of slogans. It leaves no room for intelligent discourse on whether psychologically damaged and drug dependent people have the simple skills to maintain an apartment. To listen to the "No Housing" rhetoric you would not know that tens of thousands of public housing units had been built in the past five years or that one of the largest enclaves of public housing existed a stone's throw from the park. Being on the receiving end of rocks and bottles, I had a clearer understanding of "No Peace."

The new squatters had one thing right. In the '60s the landlords abandoned the tenements east of Avenue A to the river. The city foreclosed on the tax delinquents and left the buildings vacant. Hundreds of heroin dealers filled the void, setting up shop in the abandoned buildings. The city's addicts lined up around the block in broad daylight to buy their fix. Rents plummeted, triggering arson for insurance payouts. The city razed the burned out hulks leaving a landscape pockmarked with abandoned lots.

Homesteaders stepped in to stop the destruction. These pioneering tradesman and artists successfully drove out some of the drug dealers and addicts. They reclaimed some of the abandoned housing stock before it burned to the ground. They built community gardens on the empty lots and carved islands of peace in the chaos.

In the late '80s young runaways and dropouts, interested in crashing not renovating, began to occupy the less salvageable abandoned tenements. The long and peaceful legacy of the talented homesteaders was lost in the ensuing melees with the police.

One of my saddest encounters was with a wizened homesteader named Mr. Walls whose estranged son was a police officer who worked for me in Washington Heights. The son was embarrassed to acknowledge his father because squatters were attacking the police and destroying the neighborhood. He did not understand that this new group of destructive squatters had little in common with the homesteaders like his father who peacefully reclaimed abandoned housing stock, built communities, and obtained government approval for their efforts.

361

2

The Lower East Side is a neighborhood proud of its tolerance and diversity. But the extreme activists share one emotion —antipathy towards the government, the police, and anyone in the community who dares disagree with them. While their strident rhetoric attacks anyone with a differing viewpoint, their myopia provides a welcome mat for psychotic and malevo-lent loners.

Daniel Rakowitz, a soft-spoken Texan with long blond locks, was one of the flock. He dealt pot and carried a rooster. When we met in Tompkins Square Park, he thrust the bird inches from my face and whispered "we're going to cut the cops heads off!" I dismissed it as more "street theater." When his roommate disappeared in August 1989, he gave detectives a chilling account of drawing, butchering and boiling her. He opened a Port Authority locker where they recovered her remains, a skull and human bones stuffed into a five-gallon can.

But it wasn't always this way. Tompkins Square Park sat on the edge of Alphabet City. Widely used by residents, it had been spared the violence that befell more ominous streets to the east through the 70s and 80s. The park deteriorated after a simple miscalculation and overreaction by the police.

One August weekend in 1988 the police acted on community complaints about noise and disorder in the park and along Avenue A. They evicted the revelers on Friday night without incident. Next Saturday evening, a small group staged a protest at an intersection outside the park. The police came well prepared with the latest riot regalia. They sent police horses into the intersection to move the crowd. Unfortunately, the protesters didn't back up like law-abiding citizens. Emboldened by the show of force, they attacked the horses and ran through the streets with the cops in pursuit — for six hours!

The police responded by calling for helicopters to sweep low over the rooftops in search of any bottle throwers. With searchlights illuminating the street action and tenement bed-rooms, residents poured from their steaming apartments into the streets. To the police rein-forcements arriving from as far away as the Bronx and Coney Island, everyone in the street looked like a participant. For some it was an all-night party. For the poorly supervised police force it was an all-night disaster with over a hundred complaints of brutality, months of negative media coverage, and six officers indicted.

With no major media working on a normal summer Sunday morning this would have passed with little fanfare or interest. But a new avocation, videographer, was born that night. Clayton Patterson, a video artist, and Paul Garrin, a video camera owner, filmed the festivi-ties and the force. Long before the Rodney King video and its progeny, we were treated to weeks of the same police officer swinging his baton at a pair of legs on top of a van repeating over and over "Get down! Get down!" A hungry press and an outraged public buried the fact that the baton never struck the man.

3

Pressured by the emotion of the moment, the community board voted to keep the park open — for the homeless. During the entire August 6 conflagration, homeless people slept peacefully in and around the bandshell, the extent of their occupation of the park at the time. Though the riot had nothing to do with them, the media and history record this event as a battle between the police and the homeless.

I was appointed commander of the 9th precinct in March 1989 in time for the spring influx of local nihilists and New Jersey new jacks who enjoyed provoking the police.

What started as an effort to contain the excesses of the party people became a fight for the homeless. At encampments throughout Manhattan, activists recruited the homeless to relocate. Communities all over the city gratefully released their burden to Tompkins Square Park.

Theft around the neighborhood went off the charts. A horde of homeless addicts needed cash for their daily heroin fix or hourly crack hit. The Alphabet City drug outlets provided an endless array of points of sale. The park homeless blended with the historical homeless living in Bowery shelters a few blocks west of the park. Twenty-four hours a day they engaged in a destructive ritual: breaking into cars to steal contents, laying the contents on the sidewalks for sale, using the proceeds to buy crack from other homeless street dealers, smoking the crack in residential doorways, and roaming the streets with a drug induced courage and urge to break into the next car and repeat the cycle.

In the evening, bicycle thieves from Central Park, burglars from the five boroughs, and car boosters with valuable bounty presented their treasures on Second Avenue near St Mark's Place. Neighborhood residents partook of the discount shopping and victims came from around the city to inspect the goods and buy back their property. Shelter and park residents were regularly caught with stolen golf clubs, luggage, clothing, music CDs and assorted car contents.

A police officer could watch a peddler sell an item and within 15 minutes catch him breaking into a car. With police resources at a low point, an all out offensive against petty thieves would have left the community unprotected. A steady uniformed presence to move the peddlers could have prevented the activity, but the cops lacked the initiative and were more interested in arrest overtime pay. This was the secret side to the Lower East Side saga — the local police force was demoralized by the constant verbal and physical attacks. When I arrived I found many of them working for themselves, not the community.

The 9th precinct led the city in arrests for possession of a crack pipe or a dime bag. The officers learned to manipulate the system for the highest overtime in the city. Out of nearly 30,000 city police officers, five of the top ten overtime earners were in the 9th precinct.

Robberies, assaults, grand thefts and other felonies were commonplace, but occupied with the petty offenders, the officers apprehended few of the felons.

4

I confronted the top overtime earner who had low-level drug arrests almost daily. When I asked him to focus on violent crime, he responded sarcastically, "I see it, I make it" and returned to the precinct five minutes later with an arrest for a crack pipe. The city sent me to the 9th precinct to deal with anarchists. They didn't tell me that they wore blue uniforms as well as Mohawks.

I noticed that he wrote in most of his reports that the defendants dropped the drugs to the ground when he approached them. "Dropsy" cases are often cover stories for illegal searches. I suspected violations of the search and seizure laws, as well as a pattern of felony perjury. I ordered him to submit all of his activity logs for me to submit to the prosecutor. I added the familiar words: "I see it, I make it!" The officer showed up the next day, announced that he would not be making any more minor arrests, and asked to be transferred.

There was another malcontent who paced the floor clenching his teeth and pounding his nightstick into his palm when I spoke to the platoon about how to respond professionally if antagonized by cop-baiters. After the roll call he announced that he was "moving to Florida where a cop can be a cop and no-one questions his motives or actions." I told him that Florida sounded like a dangerous place. If he wanted a place where people in authority didn't have to account for their actions, he would be better off further south in a Latin American dictatorship. I transferred him the following week. I could deal with time bombs in the street, but not in the station house.

Police work molds young idealists into sober realists. There is a limit to how much of the world can be saved and how little of the world will appreciate it. The best officers thrive on small doses of good for children, the elderly, the infirm and other needy cases. The worst officers allow the realism to fester into cynicism. The so-called "Blue Wall of Silence" and the "Us-versus-Them" pack mentality is no more than human nature and self-preservation in a job where nothing is what it seems and nothing is what people tell you it is. The job comes with enormous lawful power-to detain, arrest or use force. In the hands of a cynic, those powers are easily abused.

I had to void some bad arrests, but the worst was the arrest of Helen DeMott. She was an artist with a mathematical mind, carefully sketching the lines of interacting ocean waves and filling the patterns with brilliant blues. Frail and over 70, she enjoyed walking her dog and dispensing advice in the park. She asked for a dog run and we agreed to overlook unleashed dogs in a plot of dirt near the Avenue B side of the park. A few weeks later I found her shackled to a steam pipe in the precinct cellblock. Her wrists were rubbed raw against the tight thin steel.

When the cuffs were removed she explained that she was not caught up in an earlier sweep of the 10th Street drug dealers. Her offense was asking a cop for his badge number. It seems there was a dog fight in the park, a rookie cop broke it up, Helen offered her advice on which dog was the initial aggressor, the cop resented her attempt to influence his objective analysis, she asked for his shield number, he covered his shield with his hand, she reached up to pull his hand away. Bing, bang, bing, she was handcuffed to the park fence. A challenge to authority mishandled by a poorly trained and influenced police officer.

The rookie explained to me what he learned in the police academy: "you touch a cop, you get arrested." I asked him if he could think of any other way to deal with an elderly woman who asked for his shield number. He repeated, "you touch a cop, you get arrested." He had learned the language of the station house cynic before he had the experience to be cynical. He resigned the following week to join a Long Island police department. In a poorly veiled attack, he said that the Long Island commanding officers would "back him up."

When I left the precinct to work in the management and planning division, I proposed more intelligent handcuffs, using secure but soft material. Taking 15th century torture devices out of the hands of angry police officers would reduce injuries and lawsuits, not to mention taking an affirmative step to improve the image of the police. But the proposal landed in the hands of a think-tank commander who laughed away the idea of "fur" handcuffs. As time passes, we will either see the metal handcuffs replaced by a kinder and gentler device or, more likely, more front-page exposés of back room abuses.

My highest priority was preventing another outburst of unwarranted police violence. On the first day in the precinct I moved the commander's office from the second to the first floor just inside the front door where I could see every arrest brought in to the station house. I observed hundreds of arrested suspects, some illegally arrested and released, but I never saw one prisoner beaten. The cops knew that if they lost their temper, they might lose their job. I'd rather be respected than feared, but any strategy that prevents police brutality is acceptable.

The office location wasn't popular with the cops but it helped the community. They could walk into the precinct and meet me without being swept aside by the desk officer. One day Rev. Kuhn visited to report a beating in the back seat of a police car and the back room of the station house. A frank young man accompanied the priest to tell his story.

A few days earlier, he had been arrested for throwing a rock at police officers guarding the scene of a squatter eviction. He complained that while his hands were cuffed behind his back one of the officers struck him in the chest with his two-way radio. I asked him if the officer had been hit by the rock. He said, "no, he was angry because during the ride to the station house I kicked him in the back of his head as hard as I could with the heel of my boot. The cop turned and hit me with his radio."

6

I asked the Roman Catholic priest if he understood quid pro quo. Rev Kuhn accepted the cop's sudden reaction, but added that the desk sergeant should not have allowed an angry officer to drag him to the back room, knock him down and kick him.

I took the complaint. Force against a shackled prisoner is never acceptable even if deserved. The key is to anticipate and prevent excessive force, not justify it when it happens. Whenever an officer at a demonstration was spat on, punched, hit with paint, eggs or other objects, or emotionally affected by some instigation, I sent him on a break and replaced him with an officer who was not personally involved. It helped reduce retaliatory force. Several years later in another part of the city, Abner Louima punched and angered a police officer. Had the police department adopted this "relief" policy, the understandably emotional officer would not have been in a position to sodomize the prisoner with a broomstick.

My tolerance for street theater and police critics stood until I was challenged by Police Officer Richie Johnson, an imposing 6' 4, 300-pound black veteran. I momentarily wavered out of respect, not fear. For 25 years, Richie patrolled the blocks of Alphabet City, Avenue A to Avenue D, 14th Street to Houston Street. He walked on foot at night while drug dealers murdered fifty people a year on his beat. He witnessed five police officers bleed to death on those streets from gunshots and a stabbing. Yet he was the most caring officer in the precinct. Several times during major disturbances he walked away from me to take the arm of a frightened elderly person or a woman with small children to escort them to safer areas.

He had little tolerance for the childish but dangerous pranks of outside agitators. He knew that the explanation, it is all just street theater, was a lie. In the 1970s the Black Panthers had a headquarters near the park. They pronounced breakfast programs for the poor and death to the cops. The words turned real when they shot to death two young uniformed police officers as they walked on Avenue B and 11th Street. Richie was not going to get fooled again.

He was a man of action who did not agree with my notion that it is futile to engage in confrontation without clear and winnable goals. I couldn't see the point in taking the possessions of the homeless in the park when they could just bring in more the next day. To me it was foolhardy to bust down the doors of illegal squats when the squatters would only reoccupy them as soon as we left the area. Until the city or landlords were ready and willing to close the park or renovate the buildings, we could not win a running war with police baiters.

He saw that the squatters did not attack police officers routinely patrolling the streets. The worst and most protracted violence occurred when the overhead police commanders ordered hundreds of cops into the area. Many officers practiced a military strategy involving massive shows of force. Whenever they decided to clear structures from the park or evict squatters, they amassed over 250 police officers in riot gear. The police presence attracted more agitators and prolonged the police occupation for days.

We usually encountered less resistance when we provided notice to the park residents of impending removals of their structures. Over one weekend, we advised them that Monday was clean up day. As I led ten officers into the park, the structures burst into flames along with park benches and bushes. Providing prior notice allowed the homeless advocates to distribute fuel and matches. We cleaned up what was left, leaving the homeless and the community with useless ashes in place of cherished benches. It was another example of how idiotic activists could act. On the positive side there was no other violence because we had only ten police officers for the activists to annoy.

Despite this experience I continued to prefer small teams of officers to battalions of police officers descending on the park. But I couldn't control the overhead command. The next time that structures built up to the boiling point, the overhead command called out the army.

The politically active but peaceful Tent City group erected a makeshift tent from a sheet to display their defiance. The commanders bit. They called for 20 cops to form a double line. In half-step they moved towards the sheet, pulled it down in a frenzy of resistance, and backed out. A minute later another sheet went up. The 20 cops re-grouped and re-entered the area in half-steps, batons at the ready. They won a tug of war and removed the second sheet. In a Buster Keaton-like scene, as the police slowly retreated, another sheet went up.

The commanders gave up on the sheet, but found another pressing need to enter the Tent City area. Some of the people were sitting on a horizontal section of a blue police barrier. As a commander began forming a new group of 20 officers to rescue the barrier, I walked up to the fence and asked one of the organizers, Casanova, if he would surrender the barrier. With the help of other Tent City denizens, he passed it over the fence. There were alternatives to confrontation even in this bastion of belligerence.

Besides advocating the benefits of restraint, I sought to reduce conflict by communicating with the most strident critics. Just days after my assignment to the 9th, the activists scheduled a meeting in the basement of St Brigid's Church. The overhead commander ordered me to cancel the meeting because in his view "the anarchists will disrupt the meeting and no good could come from it." I disobeyed the order and sealed my fate. I would never receive a recommendation for promotion from this commander, but open communication would prove its value and prevent violence in the ensuing years.

With over a hundred activists in attendance, Reverend Kuhn and Norman Seigel of the NY Civil Liberties Union facilitated a productive discussion about the homeless, the peddlers, and the squatters. The audience was inquisitive and receptive. I learned what made them tick and what ticked them off. Several of them worked with me over the next two years to avoid violence. The only disruption was from "Mosaic Man" Jim Power who repeatedly blurted out support for the police and pranced back and forth in front of the room berating the activists. They waited politely for his tirade to subside and continued with the meeting. This was a crowd seriously interested in hearing all sides.

Trust was even more valuable than communication. I made a commitment to stand by promises in the face of provocation. It was useful to adopt ground rules acceptable to all sides. By providing notice of what action I would take under what circumstances, I could avoid surprise attacks and the reverberations fueled by distrust.

Trust was essential when dealing with volatile squatter evictions. Based on an unrelated statute, I would not provide police support for an eviction if the squatters could prove residency for more than 30 days. I would, however, evict squatters if a landlord or the city produced a court order indicating that notice had been provided. The city agencies opposed any concession to trespassers. That was typical of agencies that did not have to face the violent consequences of forced evictions that much of the community considered heavy-handed.

When the city tried to evict the occupants of Umbrella House at 21 Avenue C, the squatters produced mail postmarked to the building over 60 days earlier. A week before, I had arrested the mail recipient for trashing a symbol of gentrification, the Christodora building, in retaliation for the city demolition of a squatters' building. I swallowed hard and refused to participate in the eviction. The city workers hurriedly packed their demolition gear and left the scene.

It was the only practical solution. With the city unprepared to renovate the building or properly seal it, the squatters would have re-entered the building the same night while many police officers and residents injured in the battle healed their wounds in local hospitals. Then they would have sent me in to do it all over again. I had no interest in déjà vu evictions.

Over the two years, in every instance of a less than 30-day occupancy, the squatters left without incident. Likewise, when I presented a court order to squatters with a longer occupancy, they walked away without protest.

A year later the city staged cranes to make a second attempt to demolish Umbrella House. I intervened with the assistance of friends at City Hall who sensed the danger. Today, anti-police squatters lawfully occupy the building. Uniformed police officers walk past Umbrella House every day without incident or injury.

"Policing light" tactics, however, did not work with nihilists, malcontents and outsiders bent on chaos and destruction. They blended in with concerned activists. Because they were anti-police, the serious activists lacked the will to ostracize the hate-mongers. The police lacked the ability to distinguish those committed to reform from those committed to war.

The best example of the failure of activists to separate themselves from the nihilists was the demise of the Anarchist Switchboard on 9th Street, apparently a place to study the option of anarchy. The academic anarchists called me one evening to maintain the peace while they shut down the office because a new breed of anarchists made it impossible to operate. It wasn't that they applied a strict definition. Rather, they were refugees from suburban homes fed up with parental constraints. They fled to the Lower East Side where they expected no behavioral limitations. No rules soon led to no Anarchist Switchboard.

I wonder what would have happened if we all joined together to ostracize these obstructionists. Without their disruptions, we could then have bickered but resolved issues that couldn't be addressed with all the violence. It seems futile to seek conciliation with people unwilling to contribute or concede.

A group of squatters and homeless had one plan to create something positive, the "ABC Community Center" on 4th Street. In dramatic fashion they occupied an old public school with a vision to house every conceivable social services program known to man. The city had a less creative but highly important plan, earmarking the building as a home for the elderly.

We evicted the squatters twice using a small team of four police officers. After the second eviction, the city agreed to post unarmed guards outside, but the occupants soon returned through the rear of the building. They posted notices of a grand opening party for Christmas Eve. I shut down the entrance in the late afternoon to stop the flow of people attending the affair. Those who couldn't enter, lit a barrel fire in the street.

With the temperature in the teens, we all warmed ourselves around the fire as Christmas Eve passed into Christmas Day. Shortly after midnight, bottle rockets were shot from the building in our direction and we cleared the block. They could have their abandoned school for another day.

In subsequent days, the press gathered outside to hear the occupants' proclamations and plans. Food was passed to the barricaded occupants while celebrity photo ops were staged outside. The city ordered us back in to evict them. My executive officer walked into an ambush. Heavy bags of concrete were dropped from the roof, crashing inches from him and the officers. We had no idea that they had recruited ex-cons to share the space. Police reinforcements were called, hundreds of squatters filled the street, and a stand off ensued.

By nightfall, bonfires were lit in nearby intersections, rocks and bottles were thrown, people were injured, and arrests were made. To avoid further violence, we agreed to allow all occupants to leave, unless they were identified as the people who dropped the concrete. When they walked out, they had changed clothing and the police officers could not make an identification. They got away with attempted murder.

9

369

There were activists who repeatedly staged events with the purpose of attacking the police. Videographers were always nearby to catch the use of police force, unauthorized or excessive, on video. Nearly every weekend and often during the week they could always find a reason to march through the streets, block intersections and ultimately require the police to use force.

In May, 1990, our thin trust was shattered. Activists obtained permits for a 4-day concert from noon till 7 pm. On the prior three nights, they unplugged at 7 pm but continued to play drums and kept neighbors awake until dawn. Despite their irresponsibility, on the fourth day of the concert, the Parks Department extended the permit from 7 pm to 9 pm. They didn't consult me and now I had to shut down the concert in the dark. More ominous were warnings from that stage that the audience should be ready to fight the police tonight!

I placed plainclothes cops on both sides of the crowd and staged the disorder-trained Manhattan Task Force a block away from the park. With three officers who regularly worked in the park we approached the stage shortly after 9 pm. We left our batons and helmets at the park house to avoid the message that we were looking for trouble.

The activists on stage called to the crowd. They surged forward, hurling rocks and bottles. The police reinforcements were unable to stem the hail of missiles until many cops were hurt. We left the park with several arrests and wounded officers in the hope that the violence would subside. Shortly later they emerged and ran through the streets, lighting fires and overturning trash. The destruction continued for several hours. There were no reports of the police using excessive force.

I might have chalked this up to another excess by a violent minority. But at a community meeting the following week, several activists who regularly communicated with me, angrily accused the police of starting the riot. Despite video evidence to the contrary, they described a fictional account of helmeted cops wielding batons storming the stage. Their lies, more than the violence, shattered the foundation of our tenuous partnership.

For a time after the incident, I questioned my decision, wondering if I had waited whether the music would have stopped and the course of park history and my beliefs would be different. In retrospect, I realize that the people committed to violence would not have let me walk away that night unscathed.

In time, the rhetoric wore thin and the novelty wore off. Residents tired of riots without reason and the hideous condition of their park. The spring of 1991 once again brought rockers from their suburban homes to the Avenue A clubs. While bottles were thrown, the police stood their ground and contained the aggressors. In the cover of darkness behind the demonstrators, a few opportunists looted a store. By curbing their anger and holstering their batons, the police allowed the rest of the city to see that the park was no more than a mosh pit.

The city closed the park for complete renovation. There were unsuccessful attempts to storm the police barricades, but the activists were too small in number, they lacked the old fire and moral conviction, and the police contained their emotion.

When the park closed, rents soared. The activists claim the area has lost its edge. The newcomers embrace what they see as a vibrant and permissive part of the world. The new arrivals have jobs, some money and little interest in hurling bottles and rocks at police officers. They are also less inclined to criticize, complain or look skeptically and closely at government policy. Something gained, something lost.

Wiser residents know that the park would never have deteriorated without the excesses of the police but would never have been renovated without the excesses of the activists.

I left the precinct in 1991 to coordinate the community policing effort for the city, to try to get police officers to care about their communities. I still live just north of 14th Street and Avenue B, but I've never returned to the park.

After the birth of my first child, my wife told me she found a little park with a clean playground and tranquil winding paths. It took me a few minutes to understand that she was describing Tompkins Square Park. I won't ruin her Shangri-la by sharing the stories, the videos, or the news clips. I'm glad that she never saw the horror, but sad that she never met the diverse group who tried to find a better way, peacefully, from Rev. Kuhn to Casanova to Mr. Walls to Richie Johnson. They and hundreds more who cared can claim some responsibility for the urban oasis that is Tompkins Square Park today.

Chapter 7

Looking Back On The Tompkins Square War
By Bill Weinberg

The journalism I did for the East Village weekly *Downtown* on the struggle for Tompkins Square from 1988 to 1991 was all on a typewriter. That was in the days before digital editions. *Downtown* has folded, the neighborhood has changed, and I felt like a whole slice of local history was going down an Orwellian memory hole as yellowing pages returned to dust.

Now that three of these articles are being included in an anthology, I ask myself if they are of value for anyone beyond anarchist nostalgists and neighborhood history buffs. Reading the stuff over some fifteen years later is inevitably a painful exercise. I'd like to think my writing has improved. But worse than stilted prose is the earnest weight I gave pronouncements from the handful of motley anarchists who repeatedly made trouble in the park. The provincialism that can persist in this most globalized of cities is really funny. The drama playing out on the patch of concrete and asphalt circumscribed by 14th Street, Third Avenue/Bowery, Delancey Street and the East River took on an earth-shaking importance among the neighborhood anarchists, and some local journalists were infected by the bug.

On the other hand, even the most obsessively, annoyingly apocalyptic of these anarchists have to an extent been vindicated by history. Their warnings of an impending police state and martial law seem almost prophetic in the wake of the post-9-11 sweeps of Muslim immigrants, the establishment of the Homeland Security Department and a Pentagon Northern Command for domestic operations. The modernization of the NYPD began in the wake of the Tompkins Square riot of August 6, 1988 and continues today in the appointment of David Cohen, a 35-year CIA veteran, to head a new counter-terrorism desk at the Intelligence Division (the old "Red Squad"). There is some truth to the perception that Tompkins Square was a sort of social laboratory of the new security state.

In any case, I have resisted the temptation to re-write. Apart from some very limited editing for clarity, these articles appear as they did in *Downtown*. They are presented as historical documents. I am aware that they will seem over-long by today's bite-sized standards, and I admit that I probably did need a more aggressive editor.

Another thing to strike me as I re-read these relics is how the physical and psychic shape of the neighborhood has changed. Tompkins Square was closed for nearly two years after the police sealed it off in June 1991. For two summers, the Lower East Side was without a park — aside from out-of-the-way East River Park flanking the waterfront across the FDR Drive. The bandshell was demolished. When the park re-opened, not only was a curfew imposed, but a *midnight* curfew — an hour earlier than the one the city tried to impose in 1988, and was forced to rescind following the riot.

A Radical Political and Social History of the Lower East Side

Rents have soared. The gentrification which I described as having halted west of Avenue C in 1990 now extends nearly to Avenue D — where it runs into the impenetrable wall of the Jacob Riis and Lillian Wald public housing projects. But there is fear that even these will be cleared of low-income tenants and razed or redesigned for a new class in years to come. The 9th Precinct has moved from the old station house on 5th Street east of First Avenue to a new, huge complex at 8th Street and C — perfectly situated for policing (or pacifying) this last working-class bastion in the neighborhood. The mural across Avenue C at the community garden called La Plaza Cultural — depicting global revolutionary struggles from Nicaragua to Angola, sloganizing *"La Lucha Continua"*— has long since been painted over. (The Plaza itself survives.)

The neighborhood eateries have overwhelmingly gone upscale. The remaining wholesome, family-run, inexpensive ones are now more likely to be Puerto Rican, Dominican, Mexican or even Indo-Pakistani than Jewish, Polish or Ukrainian. The open-air cocaine-and-heroin supermarket which was Alphabet City in the '80s was first pushed south of Houston Street by police pressure, and then cleared out completely. The homeless, who were ubiquitous in the neighborhood in the '80s and early '90s, have largely disappeared. Sometimes I wonder what happened to them all.

Some squatters have been evicted — most notoriously in the May 1995 raid on 13th Street, in which the NYPD brought out an armored personnel carrier. But the surviving squatters have largely become legal homeowners under a deal worked out with the city in 2002.

The most serious activist struggle in the neighborhood since the contest for the park has been over city plans to bulldoze community gardens to make way for housing developments — a struggle also being played out in Harlem, Mott Haven and elsewhere in the city. Several activists were arrested after locking down with chains when police moved against the Esperanza Garden on 7th Street between B and C in February 2000. Emulating the tactics of Earth First! tree-huggers out west, these new activists (and their fellow spirits in groups such as Reclaim the Streets and Times Up!), have an ecstatic ethic that contrasts with the chronically dour and black-clad aesthetic of the old Tompkins Square anarchists. Rather than throw-a-bottle-and-run, they are willing to U-lock their necks to a fence grate and wait for the police. They have also forged real alliances with Puerto Rican community leaders in a way the old guard never did.

Similar arrests preceded the December 2001 eviction of the CHARAS community center on 9th Street, which had been a key point of cross-fertilization for white and Puerto Rican artists and activists. The old school building which had housed CHARAS since the legendary Bimbo Rivas and Chino Garcia first reclaimed it from abandonment in the 1970s now sits empty, sold by the city to a new owner who proposes to raze it for a 23-story dormitory. Another CHARAS founder (and strong opponent of the general development blitz), local Democratic district leader Armando Perez, was slain under mysterious circumstances in Queens in 1999, and La Plaza Cultural has been re-named in his honor. The Nuyorican Poets Café on 3rd Street, the neighborhood's proudest legacy of Latin bohemia, is still going strong — but as a private (if non-profit) business, not a community center.

The ABC No Rio and Soto Velez community centers south of Houston still survive. The former is largely the domain of white punks, while the latter is currently debilitated by a bitter split between Latino thespians and white artists. Both are vital institutions, just a block apart; neither provide the kind of much-needed cultural exchange that took place at CHARAS. The Rites of Spring parade each May, winding through the community gardens with elaborate floats and costumes, is another testimony to the survival of alternative culture in the neighborhood. And if the neighborhood sees far fewer riots these days, it now actually has two anarchist bookstores --- Mayday Books, which operates out of the Theater for the New City on First Avenue, and Bluestockings, a few blocks south on Allen Street. Another anarchist project, a pirate micro-transmitter dubbed "Steal this Radio," broadcast from a clandestine location in the neighborhood for a few years in the mid-'90s before it was closed by FCC threats.

The division of the old Lower East Side City Council district into two gerrymandered entities designed to dilute working-class voting power was approved and took effect. The conservative Antonio Pagan rode a backlash against the anarchists to become the first councilman for the new district encompassing the conflict zone in 1992. But he was succeeded in 1998 by Margarita Lopez, his nemesis and now the most progressive member of the City Council --- although even she has been accused of conniving with the authorities to sell out community gardens.

In 2001, for the first time in the city's history, one Republican mayor, Rudolph Giuliani, was followed by another, Michael Bloomberg. The Democratic machine, with its corruption and populism alike, is in decline — and New York City is becoming more like the rest of the United States. This is evidenced (for instance) by a proliferation of suburban-type corporate chain stores, even a K-Mart on Astor Place.

Local history is important to localites, if nothing else. Even now, the Lower East Side's legacy of rebellion has not been completely erased. I'll note one happy irony. When I first started hanging out in the neighborhood in the '80s (I grew up in Queens, and had been living in Brooklyn before moving to the East Village in '89), the old-timers told me I had missed everything --- that it was all over after the 1967 Tompkins Square riot, the cutting-edge alternative scene had been destroyed by rising rents and cultural repression. I answered back that the 'hood still had a vibrancy and fighting spirit unequaled elsewhere in the city. Today I find myself telling the young ecstaticists that they've missed everything, that it's all been over since the police closed the park in 1991. And they give me the same reply that I gave the old-timers back in the '80s --- almost word for word. It's Yogi Berra's deja vu all over again.

Cultural erasure isn't as easy as it looks, even in this age of lightning-fast change. In a 1972 essay entitled "Persistence of Place," the germinal ecologist René Dubos, a transplant to New York from rural France, noted how remnants of an organic human past survive even in the ultra-developed cityscape: "The activities of modern man rarely obliterate the marks left on the land by the work of his ancient ancestors . . . An erratic cow path in what was then called New Amsterdam became Broadway, which still meanders through the gridiron pattern of New York City . . ."

374   I take some comfort in that whenever I use Broadway as a short-cut across the grid heading downtown on my bicycle. Deviationism, it seems, can be a very tenacious virus.

East Village, NYC, April 21, 2004

Tompkins Square Park and the Lower East Side
Legacy of Rebellion
By Bill Weinberg

The city planners who have been attempting for the past decade to turn the Lower East Side into a high-rent yuppie playground have not achieved their aims. Throughout the '80s, one could see the gentrification moving east block by block — Second Avenue, First Avenue, Avenue A, Avenue B. But before it reached Avenue C, something went awry. It had something to do with soaring rents and yuppie ambitions leveling off in the wake of the October 1987 stock market crash. It had something to do with the mounting resistance to the east-wards-creeping gentrification from squatters and others in the community. The tension exploded decisively in the violence of the Tompkins Square Park riot on the night of August 6, 1988.

The ostensible issue which sparked the riot was the 1 a.m. curfew which then-Mayor Ed Koch had slapped on the park. In the wake of the riot the curfew was repealed, and today Tompkins Square remains the only park in the city with no curfew. The city has also drawn up plans to reconstruct areas of the park. Critics contend that this is being done in an effort to facilitate gentrification and head off resistance, and have succeeded in getting the city to substantially modify its plans. But there is still opposition even to the new limited recon-struction, mostly from the most militant and radical squatters.

How many of the players in this drama are even aware of how many parallels it has in the history of the community going back well over a century? Perhaps the briefest explanation as to why the city planners bent on utterly transforming the character of the neighborhood have met so many obstacles is this: history is coming back to haunt them.

In 1811, when much of Manhattan island was still farmland, the city planners adopted a grid system for the expanding urban area south of what is now 14th Street. Streets intersected avenues to form blocks, allowing for orderly development. What had been the public hanging grounds was turned into Washington Square Park. And a marshy and disease-plagued area to the east was slated to become another park which would be named after Daniel D. Tompkins.

The naming was almost prophetic of the park's future as a hotbed of agitation in a working class neighborhood, because Tompkins was seen as a champion of the common people. The son of a Revolutionary War patriot, he defended New York City in the war of 1812. As gover-nor of New York State between 1807 and 1816 he sought to liberalize the criminal code and relieve the poor from an undue share of duty in the state militia — and succeeded in abol-ishing slavery in the state, although the abolition did not take effect until 1827. He also fought for decent treatment of the Indians. He would go on to become vice president of the republic under James Monroe.

A Radical Political and Social History of the Lower East Side

Tompkins Square Park was completed in 1834, and it was anticipated that it would be used by the wealthy. The map of lower Manhattan neighborhoods was considerably different back then. The now-fashionable Greenwich Village was a poor Black area, while the area between Second Avenue and Lafayette — today a bleak terrain of warehouses and gas stations which gentrifiers are attempting to make fashionable with an incursion of upscale eateries and a name-change to "NoHo" — was then one of the swankiest parts of the city. Elegant town-houses were built by prominent families such as the Astors, Vanderbilts, and Delanos. The ritzy real estate development was expanding east from this area and was expected to move into the area of the new Tompkins Square.

Fate had other plans. The expansion of the wealthy district was suddenly halted by an economic depression of 1837. Instead, Irish and German immigrants moved into the area around Tompkins Square. The area became known as Dry Dock, as it was populated by workers employed by the shipbuilding industry along the East River as the economy recovered. Recovery brought work, at least, but living conditions in Dry Dock were abysmal, with large families crammed into small, unventilated rooms. Dry Dock won a reputation as a total slum.

With the next economic crunch, in 1857, the Dry Dock residents were thrown out of work and for the first of many times Tompkins Square Park was transformed into a forum for public debate and protest. Unemployed Dry Dock workers demonstrated in the park for the city government to provide jobs in public projects, such as the construction of Central Park which was then underway. Park benches were torn apart for bonfires. A *New York Times* headline read: 'THE UNEMPLOYED. Great Gatherings in Tompkins Square and the Park. U.S. Troops Guard the Custom House."

It was in response to these disturbances that the city government had the park completely renovated in 1859.

Riots were common in this era, and were virtually an accepted part of the political process through which parties and ethnic groups vied for power. The national guard was called in to contain a melee involving Irish workers at Astor Place in 1849. Irish Catholic immigrants supported the Democratic Tammany Hall political machine which was consolidating power under the legendary Bill "Boss" Tweed. This consolidation of power was in turn resisted by the fiercely anti-Catholic and anti-immigrant "Know-Nothings," a political party and secret society of the radical right which hired a gang of thugs known as the Bowery Boys to do their dirty work.

One serious point of conflict which would eventually plunge the city into the worst bloodshed it had ever witnessed was the abolition of slavery. Abolition was supported by the Tammany machine and bitterly opposed by such right-wing Protestant groups and the Know-Nothings and Orangemen, who regularly duked it out in the streets with the machine's own hired thugs.

The issue also led to violence in Black districts such as Greenwich Village. In an 1837 incident, a crowd of Blacks rescued a captured runaway slave who was claimed by a doctor in Baltimore and beat the judge who was hearing the case.

These tensions exploded into a city-wide orgy of violence in 1863 after President Abraham Lincoln instated military conscription for the first time in the nation's history in response to the secession of the Confederacy. State militias had long used a *de facto* conscription based on exploiting the economic pressure on the poor, but it was only with the Civil War that the federal government resorted to an official draft to raise an army.

In the wake of the Vietnam debacle, draft resistance is today seen as politically progressive, a tool in the more general struggle against injustice and oppression. Things were considerably different in 1863. The outrage which led to a general uprising in New York City was the outrage of anti-abolitionists and racists aghast at the thought of "fighting for Negroes."

The rioting centered around several locations throughout the city, including Tompkins Square, Times Square and Central Park. Pro-abolitionist publisher Horace Greeley was besieged in the offices of his own paper, the *Tribune*. Both the *Tribune* building and City Hall were protected by artillery and turned into virtual fortresses. Draft offices were burned and a Black orphanage was pillaged. The Black neighborhood of Greenwich Village was invaded by marauding white mobs and Blacks were beaten, burned and lynched all over the city. Historians would later term the episode a "Black pogrom." The New York state national guard was called out and state militias were brought in from as far as Michigan to quell the uprising. A reliable body count has never been arrived at, but the death toll was easily in the hundreds.[1]

In the wake of this bloodletting, the authorities once again moved to make changes in Tompkins Square Park. But this time the changes were far more drastic. In 1866, the New York state legislature voted to raze the park of "all trees and other obstructions" as part of a militarization of the entire area. The empty space which had been Tompkins Square Park was transformed into a drill ground for the 7th Regiment of the New York State militia, while a weapons armory was established at the nearby Cooper Union. This bleak transformation was completed when "Boss" Tweed, in his official capacity as Public Works Commissioner (and his unofficial capacity as political powerhouse of the Tammany machine) had the barren square paved over with concrete. The concrete shortly broke up into jagged rocks and craters after a harsh winter or two, making the former park even more grim and foreboding.

Unrest was not to emerge again until the 1870s. By then industrialism was rapidly expanding, coal, oil and railroad barons were building fortunes, and smokestacks were starting to blacken the sky. The changing economy coupled with a severe financial crash in 1873 transformed the posh Lafayette Street area into a deserted realm of warehouses, while the Tompkins Square area to the east, then known as "Little Germany," once again became a hotbed of agitation, despite the heavy military presence in the community. Ideologies of every sort contended in the streets, from early feminists advocating women's suffrage to teetotalers advocating prohibition of liquor to left-wing anarchists and socialists advocating a

A Radical Political and Social History of the Lower East Side

working class revolution. The community was starting to eye the big, vacant drill ground which had once been Tompkins Square Park with growing impatience.

The breaking point came in 1874. The winter was one of the harshest in memory and thousands throughout the city were on the verge of starvation. Unemployed workers held meetings at many places throughout the city appealing for public relief, but none came. Finally, it was agreed to hold a single massive demonstration on Jan. 13, which would march on City Hall after assembling in the Tompkins Square drill grounds. The city government gave the march organizers a permit to assemble in the square and hold the demonstration — but the permit was revoked the very night before the event was to take place, on the grounds that the gathering "threatened public peace." By then it was too late to inform the multitudes throughout the city that the event was prohibited. On the next day 10,000 workers and their families from all over New York converged on Tompkins Square.

Without warning, police on horseback surrounded the square and suddenly charged into the crowd from all sides with their nightsticks swinging savagely. Fleeing men, women and children were chased down and beaten as they attempted to escape into the streets. Dozen of bystanders were also beaten and trampled under hooves. According to one account, "the blood of many stained the streets." A headline following the fracas would read: "THE RED FLAG IN NEW YORK — RIOTOUS COMMUNIST WORKINGMEN DRIVEN FROM TOMPKINS SQUARE BY THE MOUNTED POLICE, JANUARY 13."

This forgotten episode in American history was actually to have a far-reaching, if little recognized, impact. One of the workers in attendance that day was a young labor organizer in New York's Cigarmakers' Union by the name of Samuel Gompers. The young Gompers escaped serious harm by ducking into a cellar. But what he witnessed that day was to have a lasting impact on his life. While many were radicalized by the police violence, it had the opposite effect on Gompers, convincing him that radical and extreme politics would never accomplish more than provoking violent repression. Seeming to accept the city government's rationale for revoking the permit — the allegation that the march was sponsored by professional "radical agitators" rather than actual workers — Gompers would later write: "I saw how professions of radicalism and sensationalism concentrated all the forces of society against a labor movement and nullified in advance normal, necessary activity."

Gompers, of course, would go on to found the American Federation of Labor, which would wage a battle for control of organized labor in the U.S. against more radical unions such as the American Railway Union led by the socialist Eugene Debs and the Industrial Workers of the World ("Wobblies") led by communists and anarchists.

While the Wobblies sought to organize an international general strike which would collectivize world industry and overthrow the bosses, Gompers' American Federation of Labor merely sought to wrest better wages and working conditions from the bosses without challenging their actual position. Accused by the Wobblies of timidity, the American Federation of Labor would also be accused by African American leaders W.E.B DuBois and Booker T. Washington of discrimination against Black workers.

Following the repression of the Wobblies in the first decades of the twentieth century, the American Federation of Labor would eclipse its more radical rivals and eventually merge with the Congress of Industrial Organizations to form the AFL-CIO, which remains the monolithic mainstay of organized labor in the U.S. today. However, the struggle continues in the developing nations of Asia and Latin America, where AFL-CIO-sponsored unions, often with the aid of the CIA, are seeking to displace more militant and revolutionary unions. The labor struggle being waged today in El Salvador has roots in an 1874 riot in Tompkins Square.

Little Germany was not beaten into submission by the police violence of that January day. On the contrary, Tompkins Square was once again turned in to a public forum for all of New York City. In 1877, another demonstration filled the square, this one in support of the USA's first national labor strike, called to wrest the eight-hour-day from the railroad barons.

The residents of Little Germany launched an activist campaign to turn Tompkins Square back in to a park again. Local mothers circulated a petition which appealed on behalf of their children who had no place to play. Mass meetings were held in the square and sympathetic press coverage was won. Finally the city government ceded to a compromise — Tompkins Square was to be half military drill ground and half park. Frederick Law Olmsted, who had designed Central Park and Brooklyn's Prospect Park, was called in. With his usual visionary scope, he conceived the park half of Tompkins Square as an enchanted garden out of a fairy tale, which would serve as an escape from the tensions and ugliness of the local environs.

But the city government's commitment to the project was half-hearted. Construction was stalled midway, resulting in an even bigger mess, the budget was mysteriously eaten up, and the newspapers screamed scandal. This reflected high-level power plays in the city government. Olmsted had been appointed parks commissioner by the Tammany machine following his rise to national fame as the mastermind of Central Park in the 1850s, but by the 1870s was growing increasingly impatient with that machine as he saw his beloved parks falling into disrepair due to official corruption. Olmsted and a group of idealists around him pushed to make the city more livable, while the corrupt Tammany-controlled city government dragged its heels. This conflict finally resulted in Olmsted's ouster as parks commissioner.

But community activism for the greening of Tompkins Square and other such "breathing spaces" in the slums was not deterred. (One prominent activist in this struggle was Bernhard Cohen, whose grandson would completely reshape New York City in the twentieth century — Robert Moses). In fact, furious community residents demanded that the drill grounds be eliminated completely and the entire square be turned back into a park. In 1878, a new design by landscaper Julius Munckwitz was adopted and the 7th Regiment left for good. On Sept. 4 of the following year, 10,000 gathered to listen to dignitaries make speeches and German bands perform in a celebration of the re-opening for the park.

The economic recovery in the 1880s prompted a new wave of immigrants fleeing poverty and persecution in Europe. While the first waves had brought Germans in the 1830s and Irish in the 1840s, this new wave beginning in the 1880s brought Italians, Slavs, Hungarians, Poles, Russians, Ukrainians and Eastern European Jews. Thousands of them poured into the area, prompting the by-then-prosperous Little Germany to move uptown. With all of Manhattan

A Radical Political and Social History of the Lower East Side

island being rapidly urbanized by then, the area became known by the name which is still used today, the Lower East Side.

The new immigrants kept alive the area's activist tradition, and Tompkins Square continued to metamorphize. In 1888, the Moderation Society, a social reform movement with wealthy backers advocating teetotalism, erected the Temperance Fountain in the park. In 1898, an Outdoor Recreation League was established to build playgrounds in the park.

The wave of immigration was felt throughout the city and the map of Manhattan island was reshaped. Chinatown was established as thousands of Chinese arrived via California. Between 1890 and 1914, well over a million Jews fleeing the pogroms of Eastern Europe arrived. The immigrants would keep coming until strict federal limits were imposed in the 1920s. Tenement housing to accommodate the booming numbers sprung up everywhere, as did the sweatshops of the textile industry which viciously exploited the labor of the new arrivals desperate to survive in the strange new world.

Living and working conditions were inhuman, prompting a wave of social reform move-ments. Danish immigrant and muckraking *New York Sun* reporter Jacob Riis sparked a move-ment for housing reform. A 1911 fire at the Triangle Shirt Waist Factory a block east of Washington Square killed 145, mostly immigrant working women, and strengthened organ-ized labor's fight for more humane workplace conditions.

Meanwhile, Irish and Italian gangs used threats and actual violence to push the African American community from Greenwich Village up to Chelsea, and then up to Harlem.

Harsh as conditions were in the new city, most immigrants were fleeing even harsher condi-tions in Europe, and many brought with them a commitment to revolutionary social change. Radical ideologies exploded on the Lower East Side in those years. The famous anarchist Emma Goldman, a Jewish immigrant from Russia, lived on 13th Street between First and Second Avenues in the 1890s and frequently orated in Union Square, resulting in her imprisonment on charges of "inciting a riot" in 1893. Her lover and comrade Alexander Berkman was at the time serving a much longer prison sentence for the attempted assassi-nation of Henry Frick, overseer at a Carnegie steel plant in Pennsylvania who had brought in hired thugs and Pinkerton rent-a-cops to break a strike. When another prominent anar-chist comrade, German immigrant Johann Most, criticized the attempted assassination, he was literally *horsewhipped* by Goldman onstage at Cooper Union.

Goldman and Most would both be arrested after a lone Polish immigrant anarchist named Leon Czolgosz assassinated President William McKinley in Buffalo in 1901, even though nei-ther of them were involved. Goldman, a feminist as well as an anarchist, would also serve time in prison for distributing information on birth control, which was then illegal. She would finally be deported for advocating draft resistance in World War I.

In 1900 the famous Russian aristocrat-turned-anarchist Peter Kropotkin spoke to the assem-bled multitudes at Cooper Union in a tour of the U.S. Between 1917 and 1919, an anarchist Modern School based on the ideas of the martyred Spanish anarchist educator Francisco

Ferrer operated out of a building on St. Marks Place. And in 1927, police set up machine guns around Union Square to contain a demonstration after the execution of Nicola Sacco and Bartolomeo Vanzetti, two Italian immigrant anarchists in Massachusetts who were framed for murder.[2]

This era also saw the establishment of settlement houses, humanitarian efforts which provided rock-bottom rents for struggling young immigrants, especially those involved in social reform, music, theatre and art. Under the leadership of Lillian Wald, these settlement houses began to dot New York's low-income areas. One was established in a 16-story building on 9th Street across Avenue B from Tompkins Square Park — the Christodora. It provided health and dental services, free birth control, a swimming pool, English classes and cultural events for 150 young artists and social workers. Among them were Ira and George Gershwin, who gave their first musical performance there in 1914 and would go on to compose such classics as *Porgy & Bess* and *Rhapsody in Blue*. The Christodora would be taken over by the city government in 1947 for use by several social welfare agencies.

Despite (or perhaps, in part, because of) the terrible conditions endured by the immigrants, New York became the center of massive industrial and financial empires in the 50 years following the depression of the 1870s, and the leaders of the capitalist world were universally convinced that such economic disasters were a thing of the past. The stock market crash of 1929 was devastating evidence that they were wrong.

The skeletons of new buildings were left incomplete all over the city, factories were shut down, and thousands were thrown out of work and forced to turn to self-help to survive. One dramatic example of this was the conversion of part of Tompkins Square Park into a farm garden for children. Thousands of neighborhood kids each got a 4-by-4 plot to work, and the crop was divided equally at the end of the harvest. Many more kids were turned away for want of space.

It was during the Depression that Dorothy Day founded the Catholic Worker movement, which ran soup kitchens in the neighborhood and advocated non-violent resistance to social injustice.

The Depression also shook up city politics. In 1933, the reform-minded Republican Fiorello LaGuardia was elected for the first of three terms as mayor and finally broke the back of the Tammany machine. One of his first acts was to appoint a commissioner to the newly-unified Parks Department — Robert Moses. Moses became an expert at directing federal funds to reshape the city in the gargantuan development projects that he envisioned. President Franklin D. Roosevelt founded the Works Progress Administration to provide employment in such public sector efforts as electrifying the countryside with new hydro-dams and power plants, and Moses immediately appropriated these funds for the reconstruction of New York City's parks.

Moses' plans for the parks were typical of his obsession with mega-scale planning and complete insensitivity to local neighborhood character. For the convenience of maintenance by a single centralized Parks Department, he had a standardized design applied to parks through-

A Radical Political and Social History of the Lower East Side

out the city, with mass produced play equipment park furniture, paved surfaces and chain-link fences. The streamlined operation made for a more efficient city bureaucracy, but also resulted in a uniformity which would have appalled the aesthetic sense of a Frederick Law Olmsted.

Under Moses' plan, a total renovation of Tompkins Square Park began and the current park design was implemented, with a road aligned with 9th Street separating the concrete "active use area" (for handball, softball and basketball) from the grassy "passive use area" (for strolling, relaxing). The conversion was completed in 1942, mere weeks after Japan bombed Pearl Harbor.

A familiar figure in the area then was folksinger Woody Guthrie, who frequently sang at McSorley's Tavern on 7th Street in the early days of World War II, before he shipped out to Italy in the Merchant Marines with his friend and fellow folksinger Cisco Houston.

The next wave of immigrants arrived in the 1950s and 1960s. In an ironic cycle of city history, just as the Irish had been met with racist contempt by many Germans, just as the Italians, Jews and Slavs had been met with racist contempt by many Irish and Germans, this new group was met with racist contempt by many Irish, Germans, Italians, Jews and Slavs. They were Puerto Ricans and African Americans fleeing poverty and squalor just as the previous immigrant waves had. Subsequent smaller waves of Latin Americans would arrive in the area later, in the 1970s and 1980s — from the Dominican Republic, Colombia, and even a few from Central America seeking refuge from death squad terror. They would rename the area "Loisaida," a Latino-ization of "Lower East Side."

When the economy proved incapable of meeting the aspirations of these new immigrants and the neighborhood once again became know as a slum, liberal bureaucrats stepped in with "urban renewal projects." The public housing developments named after Lillian Wald and Jacob Riis between Avenue D and FDR Drive were built. While boringly uniform and standardized, these are not nearly as chillingly impersonal as many such developments else-where in the city.

> *Ain't a chick in the world*
> *Half as groovy as she,*
> *My swingin' little goddess*
> *from Avenue D*
> *Slum Goddess from the Lower East Side!*
> -The Fugs

With the cultural explosion of the 1960s, the Lower East Side became a Mecca for teenage runaways from across the nation and a hippie subculture based on drug experimentation and loose communal living blossomed, much as in San Francisco's Haight-Ashbury district. But the Lower East Side scene was more of an underground milieu, never attracting the media limelight that the parallel scene in San Francisco did. This was a strange new breed of immigrant — not fleeing squalor overseas in search of a better life in America but fleeing spiritual impoverishment in middle America in search of liberation through willingly accepted squalor.

In the 1950s, the beatniks had settled in Greenwich Village to the west. In the 1960s, as Greenwich Village rents began to rise, hipsters were forced east into the cheaper tenements of the Lower East Side. The Lower East Side above Houston Street became known for the first time as the East Village. Strange new groups proliferated, from the ascetic Hare Krishnas who danced in Tompkins Square Park and peddled their devotion to a Hindu god with free food, to the pacifistic Diggers who took their name from a 17th Century peasant squatter movement in England and ran a "Free Store" on East 10th Street, to the radical Yippies who sought to politicize the counter-culture and harness its creativity to protest the war in Vietnam.[3]

Underground and alternative newspapers like *The Rat* and the *East Village Other* ran astrology columns and reported on the latest sex positions. A psychedelic rock club called the Electric Circus opened on St. Marks Place, while more famous names such as the Jefferson Airplane and Janis Joplin played at Bill Graham's Fillmore East on Second Avenue. Free concerts in Tompkins Square Park featured local acid rock bands such as the Fugs (featuring [then] current *Downtown* cartoonist Tuli Kupferberg) and the official Yippie songsters David Peel and the Lower East Side band (who would play with John Lennon when the Beatle moved to New York in the early 1970s). In fact, the bandshell in the park was completed in 1966 — just in time to accommodate this explosion.

But the explosion also led to increased tension in the park and the neighborhood. Friction had already existed between the Puerto Ricans, African Americans and older immigrants. The arrival of the hippies added an unpredictable new element to the increasingly uneasy mix. And the new tensions were reflected in increased police harassment.

In one incident, Yippie leaders Paul Krassner and Abbie Hoffman were in a Lower East Side crash pad high on LSD when they received a phone call informing them that a group of young Blacks had been busted for smoking marijuana in Tompkins Square. They immediately rushed down to the local 9th Precinct house, where Hoffman, out to prove that there could be solidarity between hippies and Blacks, insisted that the police arrest him as well. When the cops repeatedly refused to comply, Hoffman pressed the point by smashing his boot-clad foot into a glass trophy case inside the station house. The Yippie finally got his wish and finished that particular acid trip behind bars.

A more violent incident took place Memorial Day of 1967. A group of hippies and Puerto Ricans were in the park strumming guitars and beating on congas. Complaints about the noise brought the police to the park to break up the group. However, met with linked arms and defiant chants, they started grabbing guitars and swinging their night sticks, and a melee ensued. Thirty-eight were arrested for disorderly conduct, but the judge dismissed the charges, saying: "This court will not deny equal protection to the unwashed, unshod, unkempt and uninhibited."

A Radical Political and Social History of the Lower East Side

One city official would 20 years later tell historian Jonathan Soffer in an interview: "It was precisely at this point when that which was left of the flower children began to fade into something much more real. That is, the children saw the world as they wanted it to be. But at Tompkins Square that day, they saw the world as it was and lost their innocence. And it was a pity for all of us."

Things did indeed start to change after that. The politics got harsher as the Yippies and the Diggers gave way to openly revolutionary groups like the Provos, the Up Against the Wall Motherfuckers, and the Black Panthers, and violent confrontation with the police became more frequent. "People drugs" like marijuana and LSD gave way to "death drugs" like heroin and speed.[4]

The Christodora, which had been decaying and vacant under City ownership for several years, was squatted by radical groups including the Diggers, the Black Panthers, and the Puerto Rican Young Lords until the City finally offered it to them as a community center. The experiment lasted for a few years, but bickering between the groups and lack of funds led to the building's abandonment in 1973.

There were other attempts at squatting as well. A "Squatters' Park" which had been created on a vacant lot at 10th Street and 3rd Avenue was destroyed by landlords in 1970 and fence-cutting at the site subsequently became a local pastime. 1970 also saw nationwide May Day strikes in which New York University campus buildings around Washington Square were occupied.

Meanwhile, the War Resisters League purchased a building at Lafayette and Bleecker which even today houses the headquarters of so many anti-war groups that activists facetiously call it the "Peace Pentagon."

But the radical scene on the Lower East Side rapidly disintegrated in the 1970s. Cocaine and heroin addiction escalated to epidemic proportions. As century-old tenements decayed, landlords found it cheaper to abandon them to the City than to maintain them. The flames of landlord-sponsored arson which were then engulfing the South Bronx flickered ominously on the Lower East Side.

By the 1980s, the "Alphabet City" area between Avenues A and D had become an open marketplace for heroin and coke, with junkies descending from all over the metropolitan area to feed their habits. Violent crime rose alarmingly. The community which had been the Lower East Side/Loisaida seemed to be coming apart at the seams.[5]

New York City's economy was changing following the severe fiscal crisis of the 1970s. Labor-intensive industries had closed shop, leaving the factory zones across the East River in Brooklyn and Queens deserted ghost towns, while the City wooed new capital-intensive interests of finance and media. Much of the working class had been effectively disenfranchised of any stake in the economy, and the ranks of the homeless swelled. Already marginal areas such as the Lower East Side were hardest hit.

Drugs, arson, inhumanly mega-scale housing projects and Robert Moses' neighborhood-crushing Cross-Bronx Expressway had already pushed the South Bronx to the point where city planners deemed it irredeemable, and it was left to rot.[6] A different fate, however, was designed for the Lower East Side, with its easy access to Midtown and Wall Street. It was to be redesigned for the new elite class which was to drive the city's new economy — the "yuppies."

In the 1980s, real estate values soared, driving up rents and leading to an appalling explosion of the homeless population. The Christodora, which had been sold by the City to a private developer for $62,500 in 1975, was sold to its current owner Harry Skydell for $1.3 million in 1983. Skydell resold it for $3 million the following year, and has since regained a sizeable interest in it and had it co-oped. The swimming pool and other facilities which served poor artists and activists in the 1920s is now serving the high-income class.

A new art scene unfolded in the area, as struggling young artists who could no longer afford the soaring rents in SoHo fled to the East Village. Ironically, once the artists had settled in the area, it became more fashionable and the rents soared there as well.

But the surreal contradiction of decaying slum tenements on the same block as luxury co-ops led to the reemergence of unrest and resistance. In 1986, City bulldozers destroyed the "Garden of Eden," a squatter garden created in a vacant lot south of Houston Street by an eccentric visionary named Adam Purple, to clear the way for a low-income housing project. The struggle to save the Garden of Eden had divided community activists, pitting those who believed in working through the liberal bureaucracy of public housing developers against utopians and radicals.[7] As AIDS, crack and displacement tore at the fabric of the community, squatters took over the abandoned City-owned tenements, setting the stage for the struggle which climaxed with the cataclysmic police riot in Tompkins Square Park in the summer of 1988.

The developers so utterly bent on completely transforming the character of the neighborhood have a struggle ahead of them. They will have to erase a century-and-a-half of history. The current controversy over the partial reconstruction of Tompkins Square Park has historical parallels going back to the 1830s. The squatters are not, as ex-Mayor Ed Koch, chief architect of the new New York City, would have us believe, a movement with no roots in the community.

The squatter movement and the Sabotage bookstore on St. Marks point to the re-emergence of anarchism in the 1980s, and the squatter paper *The Shadow* is in the tradition of *The Rat* and Emma Goldman's paper *Mother Earth*. A surviving remnant of the Yippies still operate out of their dank warehouse on Bleecker Street, and are playing for influence in the squatter movement along with other fringe groups such as the doctrinaire Mao-worshippers of the Revolutionary Communist Party. Even the Hare Krishnas still dance in Tompkins Square and give free food to the homeless. The Catholic Worker also gives food from their house on East 3rd Street. A mural at La Plaza Cultural, the unofficial citizen-created park at 9th Street and Avenue C, sloganizes: *"La Lucha Continua."*

A Radical Political and Social History of the Lower East Side

In the words of the immortal Yogi Berra, it ain't over till it's over.

HEARTFELT THANKS TO: The recent Municipal Arts Society exhibit by curators Marcy Reaven and Dian Mitchell entitled "*Tompkins Square: Past & Present — 150 Years of a Park and Its Community*," and Bob Palmer's Walking Tour of Radical New York.

Bibliography:

Caro, Robert, *The Power Broker: Robert Moses and the Fall of New York*
Chasen, Robert, *Samuel Gompers: Leader of American Labor*
Cook, Adrian, *The Armies of the Streets: The New York City Draft Riots of 1863*
Goldman, Emma, *Living My Life*
Joll, James, *The Anarchists*
Josephson, Matthew, *The Robber Barons: The Great American Capitalists*
Zinn, Howard, *A People's History of the United States*

(*Downtown* newspaper, Feb. 14, 1990)
NOTE: Footnotes added in 2004

Endnotes:

1. In his excellent book *Low Life: Lures and Snares of Old New York*, Luc Sante estimates up to 1,000 rioters killed by the national guard, and about 100 Blacks killed by the rioters, along with fifty guardsmen. The depiction in the popular movie *Gangs of New York* of the city being shelled from a gunboat in the harbor, however, is pure fiction.

2.   Those who wish to literally follow in the footsteps of Emma Goldman and her contemporaries are directed to the pedestrian-friendly *Radical Walking Tours of New York City* by Bruce Kayton — who still schleps his devotees around to such near-forgotten attractions as the one-time headquarters of Marx's First International, site of a new housing development near Sara Delano Roosevelt Park south of Houston Street.

3.   Bhaktivedanta Swami Prabhupada, founder of the Krishna Consciousness movement, established his first toehold in America on the Lower East Side in 1966. The Diggers' charismatic leader Emmett Grogan paints a vivid picture of life in the neighborhood in this era in his memoir *Ringolevio: A Life Played for Keeps*. So does Yippie leader Abbie Hoffman in his own *Soon to be a Major Motion Picture*. Both Grogan and Hoffman would meet their demise in drug-related deaths, probable suicides, after the counter-culture crash-landed.

4.   Some have argued, of course, that the flooding of inner cities with heroin at this historical juncture was an intentional government strategy to defuse revolutionary currents. The brutal impacts of the transition in available street drugs are vividly described by Martin A. Lee and Bruce Shlain in their book *Acid Dreams: The Complete Social History of LSD*. Meanwhile, Alfred W. McCoy's classic *The Politics of Heroin in Southeast Asia* documents how CIA involvement in the heroin trade from Vietnam and Laos peaked at precisely this moment.

5.   One now-global subculture spawned in the neighborhood in this era self-consciously took its aesthetic from the atmosphere of decay — the punks. The decrepit Bowery nightspot CBGB's (for country, bluegrass, blues — a holdover from the folkie days) switched to the raucous noise of The Ramones, Television and Patti Smith in the mid-'70s. Joey Ramone, the seminal group's Queens-born frontman, died in 2001, and the corner of Bowery and Second Street has been officially renamed Joey Ramone Place — the clearest evidence that punk has been defanged. The once-underground CBGB's is now an international tourist attraction.

6.   This callous policy of encouraging neighborhood decline by radically reducing essential services (especially fire-fighting) was put in the most blatant terms imaginable. City Housing Commissioner (and future *New York Times* editorial board member) Roger Starr called it "planned shrinkage" in 1976. In 1970, Nixon White House urban affairs advisor (and future New York senator) Daniel Moynihan coined the term "benign neglect." A generation later, the strategy is revealed as a largely successful bid to push an expendable and potentially troublesome population out of the urban center and make way for a new class.

7.   There was also a depressing racial context to the struggle over the Garden of Eden, with most (not all) of its proponents white "hippies" and radicals, and most of the opponents Puerto Rican residents who needed housing for their families. Margarita Lopez, now the neighborhood's City Council member, was a key campaigner against the garden. It was obviously a divide-and-conquer ploy, because there were plenty of vacant lots in the neighborhood where housing could be built. The new development on the site today, near Eldridge and Stanton, is low-rise and relatively human-scale — but numbingly sterile and (of course) bristling with surveillance cameras. It is the cultural antithesis of Adam's intricate spiral garden, which— with its productive fruit trees and corn stalks — was living embodiment of the ethic of "building the new society in the vacant lots of the old."

'Anarchy' Versus 'Police State'?
The Stakes Get Higher In The Battle Of Tompkins Square Park
By Bill Weinberg

Anarchism — a political theory holding all forms of governmental authority to be unnecessary and undesirable and advocating a society based on voluntary cooperation and free association between individuals and groups.

Anarchy — 1. a: absence of government b: a state of lawlessness or political disorder due to the absence of governmental authority c: a utopian society made up of individuals who have no government and enjoy complete freedom 2. absence of order.

Nihilism — 1. A viewpoint that traditional values and beliefs are unfounded and that existence is senseless and useless 2. A doctrine or belief that conditions in the social organization are so bad as to make destruction desirable for its own sake independent of any constructive program.

Police State — a political unit characterized by repressive governmental control of political, economic, and social life usually by arbitrary exercise of power by police in place of regular operation of administrative and judicial organs of the government according to publicly known legal procedures. (*Webster's*)

The April 23 edition of *Crain's New York Business* quoted Deputy Inspector Michael Julian, commander of the Lower East Side's Ninth Precinct, as pinpointing the unrest in the community on "a contingent of anarchists, nihilists, and revolutionaries." A week later, Tompkins Square Park, a key flashpoint in the conflicts which are tearing at the community, exploded yet again. It was the most serious violence around the park since the notorious riot of the night of August 6, 1988 — and the felony charges which have been leveled against demonstrators represent a serious escalation of the ongoing battle for the fate of that particular block-square patch of greenery.

Local self-declared anarchists and revolutionaries see Tompkins Square as a buffer zone between the gentrification creeping east from Avenue A and the realm of abandoned City-owned buildings, many of which have been taken over by squatters (anarchists among their ranks), between Avenues B and C. Between C and D, Puerto Ricans, Dominicans, and Central Americans struggle to keep their homes against the waves of rising rent and drug-related violence, largely uninvolved in the conflicts which periodically erupt around the park a few blocks to the west. The 1988 riot had been sparked by resistance to the curfew which then-Mayor Ed Koch had attempted to impose on the park. In the aftermath of the riot, the curfew was lifted — after witnessing the cataclysmic police violence of that fateful night, virtually nobody in the community was willing to vocally support closing the park at 1 a.m.

every night. Tompkins Square remains the only park in New York City with no curfew, and the local squatters and radicals consider that an important victory.

But in the ensuing two years, voices supporting a curfew have emerged in the community again. There have also been what the anarchists view as defeats —most notably the police eviction of Tent City, the homeless shantytown which had been assembled in the park on Dec 14, 1989. So the anarchists and their supporters have increased their wariness, vigilance — and commitment to resist any moves by the City which could be construed as a step back towards curfew.

This is the subtext of the violence which erupted on the night of May 1, 1990. A four-day "Resist 2 Exist" celebration at the Tompkins Square bandshell, featuring live bands and free food — largely organized out of Sabotage, the collectively-run anarchist bookstore on St. Marks Place — ended on the night of May Day.

Organizers claim that in their initial contacts with the City Parks Department they had been led to believe that they would be given a sound permit until 10 p.m. and went on to schedule enough bands to fill that time slot. However, when they actually received the permit it had been filled out to expire at 9. They cut the length of each band's set, but when 9 o'clock rolled around, the crowd was still shaking to the heavy funk groove of Spy vs Spy.

One event organizer, Lori Rizzo, claims that she at this point started to negotiate with one of the Parks Department enforcement officers who was on hand. She requested 20 minutes — he agreed to 10. But before the 10 minutes were up, Deputy Inspector Julian and several other Ninth Precinct officers had approached the stage in an effort to break up the party. Bottles were thrown at the stage, a melee ensued, and two of the organizers — Lori Rizzo and Mary Shero — were arrested on the spot. Manhattan South Task Force riot police who had been waiting along 7th Street responded as the fighting spilled out of the park.

Battles with the police continued late into the night. They spanned as far west and Third Avenue (when a group of demonstrators led a march there through St. Marks Place, overturning trash cans and dumpsters all along the way, only to be turned back by a phalanx of police before they could proceed into the intersection) and as far east as Avenue B (where a barrage of bottles was launched at police guarding that favorite target of local unrest, the luxury Christodora condominiums). At one point, a fire truck had to be called in to quench a bonfire which raged in the middle of Avenue A

In addition to battles with the police, anarchists were also at one point fighting right-wing skinheads who attacked them after they burned an American flag in the park.

By the time it was over, 27 demonstrators had been arrested. According to the police, 28 cops had been wounded, five "seriously." A professional photographer had also been wounded. But perhaps the most unprecedented development is that of the 27 arrested, all but two have been charged with felonies — mostly inciting to riot and assaulting an officer. Unless the felony charges are dropped, there will be grand jury investigations and the accused could face lengthy prison sentences. "Unprecedented" is also the word used by Deputy Inspector

A Radical Political and Social History of the Lower East Side

Michael Julian to describe the level of violence with which the police were met on the night of May 1.

One thing can be said for Deputy Inspector Julian: both his supporters and his detractors agree that he is a "good cop"— although for his squatter/anarchist detractors, the assumption is that a "good cop" is merely a tool, either witting or unwitting, of the "bad cop" who is waiting in the wings to clamp down after the "good cop" has played his assigned role of getting the intended victims to lower their guard. Julian was assigned to the Ninth Precinct in the wake of the 1988 riot to replace the unpopular Gerald McNamara. Since then, Julian has been widely credited with defusing tensions in the community and heading off potential violence.

After the May Day riot, rumors abounded in the Lower East Side squatter/anarchist milieu that Julian had been transferred out of the Ninth Precinct and that his second in command, Lieutenant James Sullivan, had replaced him as the Ninth's commanding officer. The next day's report of the riot on the WBAI news referred to Julian as "former" commander, and Sullivan — not Julian — was widely believed to have been calling the shots during the street-fighting. Perceived as an "old guard" Irish cop and rumored to have cut his teeth as a rookie in the Lower East Side street-fighting of the late 1960s, Sullivan symbolized the "bad cop" to Julian's "good cop" for many local anarchists and their sympathizers, and his supposed ascendance to the top post at the local precinct was read as an ominous signal.

Although Sullivan would not return my phone calls, everybody I spoke to at the Ninth Precinct vigorously denies the rumor — especially Julian.

"You don't transfer somebody out in June or July in the Ninth Precinct," says Julian. He says the force considers the Ninth to be one of the most challenging precincts in the city, and the summer to be the most volatile time. Sullivan has never commanded a precinct before, and the commander of the Ninth is usually replaced with someone with previous experience as a precinct commander (although Julian himself is an exception to this rule). Finally, Julian says that Sullivan has already decided to retire from the force before the summer. Julian emphasizes that he will be commanding the Ninth at least through the summer of '90.

Julian claims that he usually deals with disturbances in Tompkins Square with only around 10 uniformed cops, plus a small contingent of plainclothes to pick off bottle-throwers. He claims that he had only seven uniformed cops (including himself) in the park on the night of May 1. After hearing somebody exhort into a microphone from the stage "Everybody be prepared to break the law — tonight we're gonna resist," he says that he called in the Manhattan South Task Force riot police. But he says that he kept them on stand-by outside the park on Seventh Street, rather than risking confrontation by bringing them into the park.

He says that he and his six fellow officers approached the stage at 9:06 to tell the organizers to end the show after that song, but figures onstage called for "resistance." Julian says that Sgt. Steve Marron told him that he heard Lori Rizzo respond by saying "Fuck you, we're not stopping."

The next thing he knew, says Julian, "bottles were flying all over." He says that he and Sgt. Marron were both hit, and that Officer Kevin Flynn was at that point actually knocked out cold by a flying bottle. "The violence was unprecedented," says the commander. "Cops got hit right in the face with bottles."

He acknowledges how several cops approaching the stage mid-song may have escalated the situation. But he says that the level of reaction completely took him by surprise — and that much of it may have been instigated by outside agitators. "I understand how what we did might have sparked violence — although that doesn't excuse the violence at all. But there were some people who were here for the violence, people from outside the area who were quick to throw bottles. People I had never seen before threw bottles. One cop was knocked unconscious by an English citizen with a Mohawk haircut. Of the 27 arrests, there were 25 we didn't know. The only ones we knew were Jerry [the Peddler] and Lori."

Lori Rizzo tells a different story. A Bronx native and five-year resident of the Lower East Side, Rizzo characterizes herself as a longtime activist. "I was against the Vietnam War at 9, I picketed for striking farmworkers at 12. I was vice president of student government at Hunter College. In '83 I was active in the South Africa divestment movement at Hunter." Today she is a member of the Sabotage bookstore collective, and was a key organizer of the Resist 2 Exist concert.

Rizzo acknowledges that before 9, speakers on the stage were urging "resisting enough to let Spy Vs. Spy finish their set." She also says that she saw around 50 uniformed police in Tompkins Square in the minutes before the riot started at nine. (When informed of this allegation, Julian said, "Did you ask her what kind of drugs she was on?") Despite this intimidating presence, Rizzo said she negotiated for the extra 10 minutes with Parks Department Officer Michael Jordan.

Just after nine, Rizzo claims that she was dancing onstage when a bottle hit the wall behind her. Then Sgt. Marron and several other cops "jumped onstage." Rizzo was "knocked down with night sticks from behind." A foot was shoved in her back as she was beaten with nightsticks. Mary Shero and other organizers were also beaten. Bottles were shattering all around her. Her face was pushed perilously close to broken glass on the floor. She pulled her cap down over her face to keep from getting cut as the cop standing over her said "Keep your face down, bitch." Contrary to Sgt. Marron's alleged assertion to Julian, Rizzo claims that she had had no verbal interchange with the police before they attacked her.

Rizzo says that she and Shero were taken to the Ninth Precinct, but as an angry group of demonstrators marched on the precinct house they were quickly put in a van and transferred to the Seventh, on the other side of Houston Street. She was still demanding to know what she was being charged with and who her arresting officer was.

A Radical Political and Social History of the Lower East Side

Hours later, Julian, Marron and Inspector Elson Gelfand, commander of the Manhattan South Task Force, arrived at the Seventh Precinct and pointed out Rizzo and Shero as organizers, according to Rizzo. Rizzo found out what she was being charged with just before her transfer to Central Booking at 7 a.m. — felony riot and assault on Sgt. Marron. She was released on the afternoon of May 3 after demands for $30,000 bail had been dropped.

Rizzo says that she is innocent and will fight the charges. She believes that the Ninth Precinct wanted a riot, and thinks that police provocateurs may have thrown the first bottles. "To me it looked like Julian was behind it. He could have let the band finish the last song, but instead he was saying 'Shut the sound down, it's 9 p.m.' I think Julian and Sullivan were calling the shots all the way."

But why would the Ninth Precinct have wanted a riot?

We had had a really excellent park festival. There was all kinds of music and everyone had a good time. The misconception that anarchy equals violence was negated. The cops didn't like that. Also, what the cops did was a step towards a curfew. A 9 o'clock sound cut-off is almost like a curfew. They interrupted four days of really positive music by storming the stage in a very brutal act of violence. If they could have gotten away with that, then why not have a curfew? That's the next step. But they didn't get away with it. Twenty-five of them went to the hospital. If the march on St. Marks, the attack on the Christodora hadn't happened, they would have gotten away with it. But since they didn't, they won't be so enthusiastic about busting heads because they know we'll fight back. In a lot of neighborhoods, people just would have said 'Oh well, it's terrible that the cops shut down the stage, but what can you do?' But not in this neighborhood. I have no regrets.

Rizzo speculates on how the police will react to the resistance they met in the park on May 1. "Next time, they'll have to either back off or escalate. I think they'll escalate. I overheard cops talking in the Seventh Precinct about using tear gas, fire hoses, calling Julian a wimp. I heard one Italian cop at the Seventh say 'Look what they did in South Korea — they turned water cannons on 'em. They know how to take care of the rioters there.' The heat will be turned up if Julian is replaced. But if they think this neighborhood is just going to collapse. I think they're wrong."

One local anarchist who asked to remain anonymous concurs: "Every level they can escalate, WE can escalate — all the way to the end. Next time we'll throw more than bottles. If they want to escalate it all the way to firing into crowds, we can escalate it to that level too. We will protect this neighborhood by any means necessary."

Mary Shero is not as stridently political as Rizzo. A Lower East Side native who recently returned to the area after 10 years out west and currently a squatter, she got involved in the Resist 2 Exist concert more out of a love of live music than a commitment to the struggle for Tompkins Square.

"There's more that I want to do with my life than defend a bunch of asphalt on the Lower East Side. I like music and electronic power. I love speaker cabinets, and I'm half deaf no doubt, but they're the things that make life worth living for me." Shero also places the blame for the Mayday violence squarely with the police. "If Spy vs. Spy could've played out the set, there would have been no trouble. The police did the wrong thing."

But did the demonstrators do the right thing by responding violently? "It didn't make me feel good to hear about people getting hurt — either cops or demonstrators. But I have to be honest — I was glad that it didn't go down quietly, because it was so outrageous. There was no cooperation or respect from the police."

Ron Kuby is the attorney who along with his partner Bill Kunstler is representing the demonstrators arrested at the Mayday riot. The Kuby-Kunstler team is notorious for its defense of political radicals. While Kunstler's experience goes back to the Chicago 7 trial of 1968, the Attica prison uprising of 1971 and the Wounded Knee occupation of 1973, Kuby has gotten Lower East Side anarchists out of trouble on several occasions in recent years. What he finds most disturbing about the Mayday riots is that nearly all of those arrested were charged with felonies. As Kuby sees it, this represents the breaking of a *de facto* truce which had existed between radicals and police on the Lower East Side.

It had been understood that there was unrest in the community and that both police and demonstrators would get hurt in skirmishes from time to time, but that no felonies would result, nobody would do serious prison time. Now that has changed, and Kuby is outraged by what he sees as a double standard. He says that apart from one who had needed several stitches, most of the cops injured in the Mayday riot had merely suffered "basketball injuries." Demonstrators had been far more seriously hurt during the 1988 riot.

"Why didn't a single police officer get indicted for felony in the 1988 riot?" asks Kuby.

> Maybe if there was some justice, people wouldn't feel that the only justice they can claim is by throwing a bottle. What happened makes everybody's life more dangerous — the people and the cops. If the court system attempts to do with the law what the police do with billy clubs, you're gonna see some fierce resistance. The police are sometimes seen as the reluctant enforcers of bad policy rather than an enemy in themselves. That could change if these felony indictments go down. People could come to see the police as the enemy and raise the level of confrontation.

What is the likelihood of the felony charges sticking? "It's hard to convict people in New York of assault on a police officer, because the police have such a loathsome record of brutality and torture. Larry Davis was acquitted."

Which side does Kuby believe is responsible for starting the riot? "Quite frankly, nobody covered themselves in glory on the night of May 1. Neither the cops nor the demonstrators. Standing at the rear of a crowd and throwing a rock at a policeman is not the world's greatest political strategy. To respond to police brutality with similar spontaneous violence —

A Radical Political and Social History of the Lower East Side

well, I don't condemn it, I understand why people do it. But I just don't think it's that productive."

What of the rumors that Julian is slated to be replaced? "Julian has saved lives, offset a lot of violence. To transfer him out now would be beyond the customary folly of the NYPD."

Yet, Kuby expresses some ambivalence about Julian remaining in command.

> A part of me would just as soon have them remove the velvet glove, and not have someone who is thoughtful and sensitive, who talks about the First Amendment and the rights of demonstrators. That way the lines of confrontation are much clearer. People can forget that the police are the tools of the rich and powerful and will ultimately follow their orders at the end of the day. It's a contradiction between my belief in protracted struggle and my humanitarian feelings of not wanting to see people get hurt, especially people I like. It would be best if the DA dropped the felonies and cooled everyone out for the summer.

Lower East Side anarchists believe that American society is drifting towards a police state and that pockets of unrest such as their own community are a testing ground for repressive tactics which will eventually be unleashed on society at large. In their view, AIDS, gentrification and crack are a form of genocide, and police-state tactics — cloaked in the so-called "War on Drugs"—will be used to squash the resistance to that genocide. Tompkins Square is contested turf, a battleground in the ongoing struggle between the forces of genocide and the forces of resistance. In such a world view, an act as seemingly innocent as interrupting a rock concert takes on highly charged political meaning.

Conservative elements (in this context, "conservative" often means what mainstream America would call "liberal") in the neighborhood and on the local Community Board 3 are pushing for reinstating a curfew in Tompkins Square, and the Parks Department is alleged to be considering compromise measures such as closing down the bandshell. The day before the Mayday riot, Parks Commissioner Betsy Gotbaum had an interchange with a local resident over the airwaves of WNYC Radio, which local anarchists viewed as ominous.

A community resident had called into Brian Lehrer's talk show "On The Line" which featured an interview with the Parks Commissioner that morning, to complain about the rock music blasting from the Resist 2 Exist concert and about the condition in Tompkins Square in general. Gotbaum sympathized:

> We are looking very carefully at the situation in Tompkins Square Park. You had an awful time this Saturday night. We were down there at 3 o'clock in the morning, and people could not sleep. It was terrible. We are looking very closely at it, we are going to try to do something. Unfortunately, the community is so divided about what it wants done that every time we try to do something we get a barrage of letters telling us not to do that. So we are looking at it very carefully. We are going to take some action in Tompkins Square Park, but at this

point I'm not sure exactly what it's going to be. But I hope you'll be pleased with it.

The statement, was of course, a pretty typical, noncommittal bureaucratic song and dance. But some of the more paranoid local anarchists started wondering just what kind of "action" the parks commissioner was considering. And following the next night's crackdown on the concert, many began to smell a conspiracy.

Reached for comment two days after the riot, this is what Gotbaum had to say:

> I was outraged by what happened May 1. We are making coordinated citywide effort to find a solution — not just the Parks Department, but also DOT [Department of Transportation], NYPD [Police Department], HRA [Human Resources Administration]. We will not do anything without first talking to the community to see how they feel. But the community Board vote on a park curfew was split 14 to 14.

What about rumors that closing the bandshell is under consideration? "We will consider turning off the lights around the bandshell area earlier if people insist on ruining the park for everyone else by not following our regulations. I don't think anyone can fault us for that. We are also looking very carefully at any group who applies for a permit. We will not grant a permit and then get burned the way we did this time. They negotiated an extra two hours out of us. Our position was that people had to get up for work the next morning. They screwed us, they took advantage. From now on, we are going to be discriminating. I can assure you that if Spy vs Spy comes back to apply for a permit, we won't give it to them."

The Saturday night noise Gotbaum referred to on the radio, which extended many hours after the sound permit had expired, was reportedly the handiwork of the Missing Foundation. After the electric sound had been turned off, the MF and their cohorts began banging on garbage cans and sheet metal in an improvisational — and loud — "industrial music" jam.

Ostensibly a hardcore rock band, the MF are major political players in the Lower East Side anarchist milieu. Misunderstood and sensationalized by the media, they have been referred to in the *New York Times* as a "shadowy organization" and by CBS infotainer Mike Taibbi as a Satanist "cult of rage."

While they probably have little to do with Satanism, the MF are definitely angry. In fact, the shade of difference between anarchism and nihilism is arguably absent from the MF. Describing the band's philosophy to *Downtown* reporter Randi Hoffman last year, MF lead singer Peter Missing said: "Industrial civilization is on the brink of collapse and a police state will rise from the ashes. This is a realist kind of thing. Other people are singing about flowers and relationships. We're not about entertainment."

One thing which the MF is about is vandalism. The band's logo — a crude representation of an upside-down champagne glass with the contents spilling out — is scrawled in spray paint and magic marker on walls throughout the Lower East Side and elsewhere in the city. The implication of the logo is that "the party's over" — that the yuppie extravagance is about to be rudely interrupted, either by class warfare or the prophesized police state which will arise in response to it.

To an extent, the MF really is a "cult" because an underground network of vandals and graffitists have adopted the logo. Rather like the "silent agitator" logos of the old radical trade union the Industrial Workers of the World, which were pasted to factory walls as a warning to the bosses and overseers, the MF logo is seen as a menacing signal to real estate interests that no property is safe. Sometimes the logo is accompanied by a slogan, such as "WE WILL NOT ACT CIVILIZED IN THIS FUCKING CITY." After then 1988 riot, MF adopted the slogan, "1988=1933." This was a reference to the 1933 Reichstag fire which brought the Nazis to power in Germany.

The seemingly random nature of the graffiti, vandalism and hurled bottles of MF and their fellow travelers has earned them a reputation for irrational destruction — especially among the liberal housing activists of the established community groups which make up the Lower East Side Joint Planning Council. Like their squatter and anarchist rivals, the Joint Planning Council groups see themselves as on the frontlines of combating homelessness. The two camps accuse each other of being self-deluded and ineffective.

Many of the Joint Planning Council groups got their start in the successful struggle to head off a plan which was being pushed in the late '50s by mega-developer Robert Moses which would have razed tenements from Ninth Street to Delancy between Bowery and Second Avenue, and displaced 2,400 tenants to create housing for a wealthier class. The Joint Planning Council continues to push for low-income housing in the area through negotiations with the city and federal agencies, and the housing projects are overseen and administered by the Council's member organizations. The fact that the City-appointed Community Boards in the area are largely staffed by supporters of the Joint Planning Council's projects is viewed as measure of the organization's political success. The view that such mainstream housing advocates take of the squatter/anarchist scene was effectively summed up in a recent article in *City Limits*, the New York community affairs magazine.

In the Lower East Side, longtime community activists who have battled the city for years have reached a tenuous agreement for community development — but local squatters have branded it as a sellout. Behind the rhetoric is naked self-interest: some of the sites for housing are now occupied by the same squatters who are protesting the plan.

These squatters, who consider governments and bureaucracy untrustworthy by nature, are reluctant to even negotiate with local and city leaders. Their action may be in keeping with anarchist ideology, but they are rejecting the will of a broad based coalition that includes minority, tenant and labor groups that back the community development plan. And while many of the squatters may chant a robust 'No Housing, No Peace' they've done little more than carve out rudimentary shelter. It's the coalition that's created some 3,000 apartments.

The "community development plan" in question is the so-called "50-50 Plan," the result of long negotiation between the City and the Joint Planning Council. It takes its name from the intended strategy of turning 50 percent of the abandoned City-owned properties on the Lower East Side over to real estate developers for co-op and condo conversions, the tax revenues from which are to be spent converting the other fifty percent into low income housing. The City Limits article failed to explain why the local squatters consider the 50-50 plan a "sell-out."

For starters, countless reams of newsprint have been expended in the Lower East Side anarchist newspaper *The Shadow* detailing precisely how sites slated to be developed for low-income housing by the 50-50 Plan are mired deep in the corruption scandals at the federal Department of Housing and Urban Development. But, more importantly, the 50-50 Plan is predicated on funding from upscale real estate development — the very same force which is fueling rent hikes and driving tenants out of their homes. By the time the cumbersome wheels of bureaucracy have succeeded in turning the slated 50 percent into low-income housing (if, in fact, this ever comes to pass at all), the problem of homelessness and its attendant plagues of crack and AIDS will have worsened still more.

As the squatters and anarchists see it, the 50-50 plan will only accelerate the tailspin of hopelessness into which the Lower East Side has been descending. They are outraged that the plan is being used as a means of legitimizing the paradoxical state of affairs in which people live in the streets and the shelters and the park while abandoned City-owned buildings sit vacant. Taking over those buildings is not merely "carving out rudimentary shelter" — it is a living example of a direct-action strategy against homelessness, in the anarchist tradition of "propaganda of the deed."

But the anarchists aren't resisting the plan merely by squatting the empty buildings. The more nihilist-oriented among their ranks, such as the MF followers, are accused of "senseless violence." Deputy Inspector Julian actually used that phrase, but his sentiment echoes that of many on the Joint Planning Council in this regard.

Whether or not the nihilist violence is justified, it is, perhaps, unfair to call it "senseless." There is a political strategy behind it, if a crude and facile one. By keeping a minimum level of unrest, unsightliness and downright danger in the neighborhood, the nihilists are slowing down the process of gentrification, which can only thrive in an environment which is perceived as safe and fashionable by the new wealthier class that the developers are attempting to woo. In the nihilist equation, more flying bottles translates into fewer homeless. It is a form of direct action to lower property values. This attitude can be summed up in the graffiti to which graces many lower Manhattan walls: "MUG A YUPPIE."

This strategy may allow justifiably angry people to blow off steam, and even have a measure of political effectiveness. But at best it is a stop-gap measure. At worst, it is counterproductive, alienating potential sympathizers from the squatter cause.

A case in point is Mike Hirsch. Hirsch is a photographer for Gamma-Liason who was injured by the police in the Mayday riot. At around 1:30 a.m. the cops were fighting against a barrage of hurled bottles to clear Avenue B in front of the Christodora, using their nightsticks to push the demonstrators back into the park. Hirsch moved in to get shots of the scuffles

A Radical Political and Social History of the Lower East Side

on the edge of the park, and was told by a cop to "get out of here." He showed the cop his press pass but the officer responded with "I told you to get out of here." Hirsch held up the press pass again, and the cop charged at him. He ran for it, but didn't quite make it over a park bench which barred his way. The nightstick rammed into his kidney. Hirsch folded over the bench, in pain and unable to catch his breath, then slumped to the ground. Within a half hour he was on a stretcher, being loaded into an ambulance.

Hirsch said he was still in "a lot of pain" when I spoke to him three days after the riot. He was awaiting the results of kidney and urine tests to find out if there is any permanent damage. He said he was speaking to a lawyer and that a colleague has a photo of the cop.

A victim of police brutality, Hirsch has few kind words for the demonstrators. "I don't like this Tompkins Square Park situation. I think it's just a bunch of troublemakers. I don't know what these anarchists want. Was it necessary to start a riot because they couldn't play past nine? We live in a civilized society, and you have to follow certain rules. Without them you "have anarchy. Right?"

A two-year neighborhood resident who characterizes his politics as "liberal Democrat," Hirsch says he doesn't "necessarily think the police were wrong. The cop who hit me was very wrong. But I can't blame the police for trying to break that thing up. I don't think the anarchists are really concerned about the neighborhood. I can't relate to them at all. All of their concerns center around one park in a small area of Manhattan which they're only a part of because they're illegally living in City-owned buildings. A lot of them are young. Where do they expect to be 10 years from now?"

The slogan which the anarchists used to publicize the Resist 2 Exist concert was lifted from the Paris uprising of 1968: "ALL POWER TO THE IMAGINATION." Yet even some local anarchist sympathizers feel that the response to the police on the night of May 1 was singularly unimaginative.

Sarah Ferguson is a Lower East Side journalist who has covered many local skirmishes (including the Mayday riot) for the *Village Voice*. Despite the fact that in one such skirmish she was hurt when an M-80 firecracker thrown by a protester exploded near her eye, she has sympathies with the squatters and anarchists, and many of her Voice pieces have portrayed them in a positive light.

But in the wake of the Mayday riot, Ferguson had this to say: "The throw-a-bottle-and-run trick has been going on for two years now. It was fun when it started but it's getting old. The cops have figured it out. What would happen if next time the cops started acting up everyone took off their clothes? What if everyone just sat down? Anarchism is not just an abdication of authority, but a greater reverence for personal responsibility."

Another source of contention has been between the anarchists and the Tent City organization of homeless park-dwellers. The anarchists have organized militant support for the right of Tent City to remain in the park, and have fought with the police on occasions when the City has attempted to evict the shantytown. But there have also been accusations that the anarchists stir up trouble in the park and can then retreat to their squats and apartments, leaving the park homeless to deal with the resultant heightened police harassment. Some anarchists claim that this kind of insensitivity is actually more frequently perpetuated by the Revolutionary Communist Party, a Maoist group which is attempting to ride piggy-back on the squatter and homeless struggles.

There are class and race overtones to this issue — most of the Tent City activists are Black and all of them are either currently or formerly homeless, while most of the anarchists and squatters are white and more than a few of them come from middle-class families. Yet, one thing that can be said for the Lower East Side struggle is that it has a clear class consciousness — "rabble" versus "yuppies" while the conflicts in other city neighborhoods have degenerated into racial battles — Italian versus Black, Black versus Korean, Black versus Jewish.

Tent City is a member organization of the National Union of the Homeless. Many members participated in New Exodus, the homeless walk from New York City to Washington D.C. for the big housing rally last year. Upon returning to the Lower East Side, Tent City activists took over the abandoned East Fourth Street public school, which was then renamed the ABC Community Center. Evicted from the building by the police in October, Tent City returned their focus to the defense of the Tompkins Square shantytown. That shantytown was evicted from the park in December. (That same day, the ABC Center was retaken, but this time the key group in the occupation appears to have been the Revolutionary Communist Party.)

Artie Wilson is a Tent City activist who has been living on the Lower East Side for two years. Before that, he was in the HRA shelter system. A Black Panther veteran from Jamaica, Queens, Wilson's manner is soft-spoken but deadly serious. He describes Tent City as an organization made of homeless people trying to get changes made in the system which will get people out of the park and into homes. People who can still get their lives back together, get a roof over their heads and get back into a daily routine.

Wilson says that the park encampment is a better vehicle for doing that than the City shelters. "It's less of a hassle to live in the park than the shelters. There's a curfew in the shelters, and if you break any of their rules, they'll put you back out on the streets anyway." In addition, he sees the HRA bureaucracy which pays so many City salaries as having no interest in actually eliminating homelessness. "The shelter system is designed to perpetuate homelessness as a viable business."

On the night of the Mayday riot, Wilson had just returned from Philadelphia where he had been participating in a nationally coordinated take-over of empty buildings by the National Union of the Homeless. He arrived in the park just as the riot was starting. "The police initiated the action. It didn't have to go down like it did. After four days of festivities, the police couldn't wait another 10 minutes? I spoke to Inspector Julian and he tried to explain it away, but if you go up onstage and try to shut it down, you know how these people will react. It was pouring gasoline on a fire."

A Radical Political and Social History of the Lower East Side

What was Tent City's role in the riot? "Our people had nothing to do with the riot, but a few of our people got hurt. A former Tent City person got his arm broke. The police were randomly grabbing people from the crowd and slamming them."

Wilson does see this as part of an ongoing pattern. "The anarchists and squatters come into the park to make a statement to the police, to the public. One police tactic is to try to divide the anarchists from the people in the community, the people in the park, by coming down on the park people when they can't come down on the anarchists."

Wilson says that he sees the anarchists as allies. "Their basic statement is they're tired of the gentrification which is just like a tidal wave moving through here with no regard for human life. I may not agree with all their tactics, but sometimes you gotta react. The police come in with intimidating tactics, either you get intimidated or you fight back.

Tompkins Square Park is a demilitarized zone. If they push the people out of the park, they're gonna push a lot of people out of Loisaida, Alphabet City. But the activists of the area, including Tent City and the anarchists, have slowed them down. We may not agree with the anarchists' ideology, but the bottom line is that the rich are getting richer and the poor are getting poorer. Where we agree is that the system is at fault for perpetuating this kind of neighborhood geno-cide for the sake of the dollar.

The City could come up with some kind of compromise for the people in this area. What they could do — which will *not* happen — is to cease selling out buildings to the real estate interests and turn over these buildings which have been sitting here abandoned for 10, 15, 20 years to the area's homeless. But being that the City has such a deficit, they're gonna reach and grab for every dollar they can get. It seems like a lost cause. But it's never really lost. This is a microcosm of an overall system which places profit before people. Sometimes you just gotta fight the power. Against overwhelming odds, you gotta fight it.

(*Downtown*, May 23, 1990)

Tompkins Square Park as Police State
Demolition Underway; Battle Rages in Courts and Streets!
By Bill Weinberg

A decisive turning point has been reached in the conflicts which have been tearing at the Lower East Side for the past several years. The anarchists and nihilists who have regularly mixed it up with the local constabulary in the streets around Tompkins Square Park continually raise the specter of Nazi Germany in their propaganda: the City-run homeless shelters are "death camps"; a "police state" is impending. Less extreme elements in the community have attacked this propaganda as alarmist. But on the night of May 27, a Memorial Day rock concert in Tompkins Square organized by local squatters and housing advocates, exploded into violence as the crowd reacted to police harassment of one of the several homeless who had taken up residence in the park. For the first time in over a year, the anarchists occupied Avenue A, blocking traffic, overturning garbage cans and lighting bonfires in the middle of the street.

This was nothing that East Village residents hadn't seen many times before — but this time there was a new twist. As the melee reached a climax just before a drenching thunderstorm struck, a shop was looted. In all of the disturbances on the Lower East Side in recent years, it was the first time that this had happened — and it wasn't even an overpriced trendy "yuppie" joint, of which there are now so many on Avenue A. It was an unassuming convenience store owned by Pakistani immigrants.

Even the anarchist sympathizers immediately admitted that the looting had been a major *faux pas*. But at the time few suspected the magnitude of the political fallout. Only a week later it would be evident that with the shattered glass of that Avenue A convenience store, the Lower East Side's long-awaited Reichstag fire had finally arrived.

One week later, early on the morning of June 3, police moved in, sealed off the entire park behind barricades, and ejected the homeless and their local supporters who had been camping out there. The park remained off limits to the community, and within two days the earthmovers and backhoes had arrived and started tearing up the turf and asphalt, demolishing the benches and chess tables.

If the anarchist accusations of "genocide" can still be called premature and alarmist, the same can no longer be said for the accusation of "police state," at least as far as the Tompkins Square area is concerned. My dictionary describes "police state" as "a political unit characterized by . . . arbitrary exercise of power by police in place of regular operation of administrative and judicial organs of the government according to publicly known legal procedures." Even the liberals in the community, who have long reviled the anarchists as immature and adventurist, are saying that the Dinkins Administration's action in Tompkins Square smacks of a police state.

A Radical Political and Social History of the Lower East Side

According to NYC's new City Charter, local community boards must be advised of major reconstruction in city parks, and their input sought. Public hearings must be held. At the emergency meeting of the local Community Board Three (CB3) Parks Committee called for the evening of June 3 at a public building on Eldridge Street, the board members and neighborhood politicians expressed their outrage that City Hall had gone over their heads — and read the riot act to the lone representative from the mayor's office who had been sent in a futile effort to pacify the high emotions.

CB3, Friedlander Outraged

Michael Kharfen of the Mayor's Community Assistance Unit told the assembled CB3 members and the angry audience of community residents that there would be "no changes in the configurations of the park," and "no removal of trees." There would be "restoration and reconstruction of the lawn areas." The bandshell is to be removed and "replaced with a mobile sound system," and there will be a "general reconstruction of passage ways." Kharfen asserted that the funds for this renovation are "already in the city budget — no other projects will be affected," and that the plans had been drawn up with "the cooperation of various community organizations."

Such organizations, claimed Kharfen, were also involved in the Administration's plans for the homeless who had been booted from Tompkins Square that morning — plans which were intended "not to remove people, but provide them with services." He stated that 30 homeless people from the park had been "reached" through the city's "outreach program" and offered space either in shelters run by the city's Human Resources Administration (HRA) or community organizations.

Asked by CB3 member Sandy Anderson whether the Mayor's office had made any effort to reach the Community Board before implementing these plans, Kharfen replied "We did not," but asserted that "we had been talking for years with many members of the CB."

Asked by Anderson whether there were plans to provide permanent housing for the homeless removed from the park, and whether they would be placed in the very HRA shelters they had previously refused to enter, Kharfen replied "If they do not wish to be placed in a shelter, we will respect this. No individual has been placed in permanent housing."

CB3 member Donna Ellaby, a key figure in the housing advocacy group GOLES (Good Old Lower East Side) chided Kharfen: "I think it's outrageous that the mayor just comes down here and invades our neighborhood. We want this bandshell — we fought to have it here in '86. Where do you get off putting in a mobile sound system?"

Noting that previous CB3 resolutions had called for only piecemeal renovation in the park and no demolition of the bandshell, GOLES activist Mike Farrin asserted that "the Community Board's wishes for park design have been entirely ignored."

Asked by this reporter which "community organizations" and "community shelters" were involved in relocating the Tompkins Square shanty-dwellers, Kharfen mentioned the Little

Mission of Charity on St. Mark's Place, and BRC Human Services and the Manhattan Bowery Corporation on the Bowery. Asked when the park would be reopened to the public, Kharfen stated, "We expect the construction period will last a little over a year."

Local City Council member Miriam Friedlander also got her licks in at the sullen and increasingly dejected Kharfen: "Both the Borough President and I are absolutely outraged that there was no effort to respond to our repeated efforts to find out what was planned for the park. The Mayor's action was anticommunity. When you know you are going to do something drastic, bring in police, tell the community — not consult with, but tell — that their park is off limits — that's anticommunity."

Friedlander stated that the CB3 Parks Committee should demand to see the plans. She protested the slated demolition of the bandshell, and expressed skepticism at Kharfen's claim that no trees would be cut. For the first time at any CB3 meeting in recent memory, the councilperson was unanimously and enthusiastically cheered.

An aide from Manhattan Borough President Ruth Messinger's office read a statement from Messinger, which was also met with applause. "We in government now seem increasingly relegated to criminalizing the people we fail, and playing to a thirst, often fueled by the media, for the appearance of a solution. While such short-term actions might have symbolic or cathartic appeal, they solve nothing. Tompkins Square Park might benefit cosmetically by this action, but the conditions that brought people to the park, our failure as a city and a nation to deal with the underlying problems of housing, jobs, healthcare, and drug treatment, will continue to create new Tompkins Square Parks throughout the City."

A homeless man and onetime Tompkins Square resident who goes by the name of Chris and worked to register Lower East Side homeless folks to vote for David Dinkins in the last mayoral election said: "We worked real hard to get homeless people to vote. We were crossed. That was the first time I ever voted, and I'll never vote again. You can have your voter registration card and your Homeless Voter '89!"

A tense moment occurred when attorney Stan Cohen, who frequently represents neighborhood squatters and radicals, stated that "the hallmark of a free society is when public meetings are held it will not be under the watchful eye of plainclothes police," and fingered a stocky and quiet man at the back of the room. Called upon by the audience to come clean, the man finally admitted to being an undercover cop

Aside from Kharfen, the only person to speak in favor of the park action was the representative from the notoriously conservative State Assemblyman Steven Sanders' office, who said that "this was the only way to return the park to the people" — only to be met with jeers and taunts of "Orwellian!"

The New Political Configuration

Even longtime CB3 member Frances Goldin, a harsh critic of the local anarchists, said live on the airwaves of WBAI Radio on the night of June 8: "Right now, if you go to Tompkins

A Radical Political and Social History of the Lower East Side

Square Park, it looks like Nazi Germany. Every three feet there's a cop surrounding the entire six-block park."

But it isn't just the opponents of the park seizure who are using World War II analogies. Another CB3 member, Antonio Pagan, told *Newsday* on the day the cops sealed off the park: "I now know how a Frenchman felt in World War II when liberation troops came in . . . I've been whistling 'The Marseillaise' all day." For Pagan, the new fascists are not the police who, on orders from City Hall, are trampling the City's own democratic process, but "the pseudo-anarchist squatters . . . who are living out their revolutionary fantasies in the park."

The WWII analogy may have more to say about the politics of the Lower East Side than either side in the debate realize. With the rise of fascism in Europe, the left closed ranks with the establishment in the democratic countries against the new threat of the totalitarian ultra-right. Communists and anarchists in Britain and America ceased to see Churchill and Roosevelt as enemies. These differences were put on hold in the name of anti-fascist solidarity for the duration of the war.

A similar dynamic seems to be at work on the Lower East Side in the wake of the Tompkins Square closing. Longtime enemies — the anarchists and squatters versus the liberal elements in CB3 and the Joint Planning Council (JPC), a coalition of housing advocacy groups — are closing ranks against the new threat. The squatter/anarchist scene had long despised the liberal CB3/JPC figures as sellouts, because they were willing to compromise with the conservatives in the neighborhood on such issues as park renovations and squatter evictions. Now that the conservative elements have gone unilateral, undermining the established political process by resorting to a police action, the liberal elements are miffed. They are demanding, with their former radical opponents, that the park be reopened. A de facto alliance is emerging, even if neither party to this new alliance will yet admit to it publicly.

The liberal element in the CB3/JPC is generally seen as revolving around the leadership of Frances Goldin of the Cooper Square Community Development Committee, one of the oldest housing advocacy groups in the nation, which led the fight to save the Lower East Side from a Robert Moses development scheme which would have demolished much of the neighborhood in the '50s. Cooper Square-controlled city-subsidized buildings on East 4th Street house such neighborhood institutions as the Good Food Coop, the Meadowsweet Herbal Apothecary, and even the offices of CB3.

The conservative element in the CB3/JPC is generally seen as revolving around the leadership of Pagan of Lower East Side Coalition Housing Development (LESCHD), one of the many housing advocacy groups built on the model of Cooper Square. Other neighborhood groups perceived as being in Pagan's camp include BASTA (Before Another Shelter Tears us Apart), which has agitated to get HRA homeless shelters out of the Lower East Side, and the Democratic Action Club, which has pressured to kick the homeless encampment out of Tompkins Square.

Last fall, when Pagan and his fellow conservatives unveiled a plan to build low-income housing on various city properties currently inhabited by squatters, Goldin and her fellow liberals gave the scheme official CB3 approval. This won them the wrath of the squatters, who not only saw the plan as a ruse to justify their eviction, but also pointed out that under the plan LESCHD and the other developers would be able to convert the properties to high-rent or condominium dwellings, or sell out to the highest bidder, after 15 years. To compensate for the lack of City and federal funds, the projects would be underwritten by private corporate investment brokered by two nonprofit groups, the Enterprise Foundation and the Local Initiatives Support Coalition (LISC). Although the liberals were roundly condemned by the radicals upon the approval of the LISC/Enterprise plan, as it became known, few realized just how strained the CB3/JPC coalition had become.

Earlier this year, the CB3/JPC fractured over the issue of the redrawing of the City Council districts mandated by the new City Charter approved by voters in 1989 (see *Downtown*, May 29-June 5, 1991). The council district now represented by the liberal Friedlander includes both the predominantly minority and low-income Chinatown and the predominantly minority and low-income Lower East Side. The new district lines which have just been approved by the Dinkins-appointed Redistricting Commission would separate these two neighborhoods, and critics charge gerrymandering. One new district would link Chinatown to the predominantly white and yuppified Tribeca, while another would link the Lower East Side to the predominantly white and upper class Gramercy Park. In an almost eerie twist of irony, Tompkins Square would fall into the same district as a park which can only be considered its polar opposite — Gramercy Park is tightly controlled by the upscale private apartment buildings which surround it, and can only be entered by those elite tenants who have a key to the park's tall cast-iron gate.

The principal proponent of the Lower East Side/Gramercy Park district is Antonio Pagan, who is believed to have his eye on the City Council seat which would be created. The chief proponent of the Chinatown/Tribeca district is Asian-Americans for Equality (AAFE), which, with Pagan's LESCHD, hopes to gain control of local City properties under the LISC/Enterprise plan. Both of these new districts are opposed by Lower East Siders for a Multiracial District, who charge that the proposed lines would effectively disenfranchise both the Lower East Side and Chinatown by linking both communities to more affluent neighborhoods, and by replacing a predominantly minority district with two predominantly white districts. When the Redistricting Commission granted a final okay to the new district lines on June 3, the same day the police sealed off Tompkins Square, it was met with angry chants from the Multiracial District advocates. "SAVE THE LOWER EAST SIDE! DON'T TEAR US APART!"

If LISC/Enterprise had caused internal conflict within CB3/JPC, and the redistricting controversy had led to a split within CB3/JPC, with the seizure of Tompkins Square the split has become open and official. The liberal majority in CB3/JPC has broken ranks with the conservative minority. And the neighborhood freaks and radicals who have traditionally heaped verbal abuse on the Community Board and Friedlander are now cheering them.

Arguably, the stakes are higher than they have ever been since Robert Moses launched his attack on the Lower East Side over 30 years ago. It is easy to believe that if the LISC/Enterprise plan, the new council district lines, and the "renovation" of Tompkins Square are all allowed to remain unchallenged, within a year the neighborhood will be unrecognizable — streamlined, sanitized, sterilized, and spit-shined, the squatters evicted, the homeless whisked off to HRA shelters where they will be conveniently out of sight and mind, political power consolidated in the hands of the conservative anti-homeless, pro-development faction. If the current pattern of police overreach proves typical of this new order, it does not bode well for the neighborhood's centuries-old tradition of tolerance, cultural diversity, and dissent.

The LISC/Enterprise plan is at the moment apparently stalled due to a lack of private investment — and perhaps the threat of squatter resistance. The new district lines have to be approved by the federal Justice Department to assure that they comply with the Voting Rights Act of 1965, and may be stalled by court challenges after federal approval. Whether Tompkins Square will remain closed for a year and rebuilt depends upon how effectively the residents of the Lower East Side can organize to fight City Hall, halt the demolition now underway, and get the park back open.

The Face of the New Tompkins Square

The paper trail establishing that CB3 is dead set against the City's unilateral action in Tompkins Square is clear. Koch Administration proposals for razing the bandshell and redesigning the park's layout had been axed by the Community Board in 1986. Limited and piecemeal renovation of the basketball and handball courts and playgrounds had been approved. In the wake of the cataclysmic Tompkins Square riot of 1988, a veritable orgy of police violence unleashed on a demonstration against the park's recently announced 1 a.m. curfew, CB3 voted that "Tompkins Square be kept open 24 hours 7 days a week." After the police evicted a homeless shantytown from the park in July 1989, CB3, "recognizing that homelessness is today a dire social emergency," voted to demand "that the homeless in Tompkins Square Park be allowed to use blankets, mattresses, and plastic sheeting or other materials to protect them from the elements," and that "the Tompkins Square Park bandshell, when not in use for public events, be made available to the homeless." All of these resolutions have now been rendered void by the police action.

While Michael Kharfen initially stated that the park would be reopened in a year, the city subsequently revised the figure to 18 months. Kharfen's claims that no trees would be cut have also been met with skepticism, especially since the 1986 plan proposed by then Mayor Ed Koch, based on the Union Square renovation plan which had then just been completed, called for clearing the park of many shaded areas.

Even if no trees are actually felled, the noise, vibrations and exhaust fumes from the demolition are likely to have a negative impact on the fragile oasis of greenery in the concrete jungle.

Norman Stotz of NYC Audubon Society states that "house sparrows and starlings are cavity-nesters and might be dwelling in the bandshell. This isn't a legal issue, because they are non-native species, which are not protected by law in New York State. But there might be a robin or a blue jay nesting in the trees. Constant disturbance could cause the adult birds to leave the nest — and the eggs need brooding or they won't survive."

In addition, says Stotz, any greenspace in New York City may provide temporary habitat to northbound migratory birds such as vireos and warblers at this time of year.

With the exception of bandshell repairs, all of the renovation plans approved by CB3 are already complete. Those areas which had already been renovated — the handball and basketball courts north of the pathway aligned with 9th Street, and the kiddie playgrounds — remain open. Despite organized protests by local tots and parents on the avenues surrounding the park, children still have to walk through police barricades to enter the playgrounds. The dog run near Avenue B has also been opened. The rest of the park has been cordoned off, with a high chicken-wire fence being erected around the perimeter. Police surveillance is omnipresent.

As I write (Sunday, June 9), earthmovers have made a mess of much of the park, but demolition of the bandshell has not yet begun. Destruction of the bandshell would be seen as a serious defeat by many in the community. It was erected in the '60s when neighborhood tensions were escalating between East European, Jewish, and Latino immigrants, African Americans, and hippies. The bandshell was seen as a peace gesture, allowing each of the groups a forum for cultural expression. It has continued to serve that function into the '90s. It is regularly used not only for squatter rock concerts, but for all-day reggae gigs featuring topnotch local talent from the neighborhood's growing Caribbean community, and Labor Day weekend brings transvestite performers from all over the East Coast for the annual Wigstock festival.

Administration plans to replace the bandshell with a "state of the art mobile stage and sound system" are dismissed by critics. With the city descending into a budgetary abyss, it is hard to believe that the sound system will ever materialize. Even if it did, such an easily removable sound system places obvious limits on First Amendment rights, critics contend — a mobile stage can be conveniently wheeled away on one pretext or another when its use is sought by those with unpopular political views.

Kharfen says that the $2.3 million slated for the Tompkins Square redevelopment "was allocated in '84. The budget lines are sufficient to cover the cost for the project that we're doing, and no funds will be diverted from other projects."

When Kharfen spouted that line at the June 3 CB3 Parks Committee, he was chastised by Friedlander for duplicitous numbers juggling and told that "of course other projects will be affected."

Where to the Homeless?

Dave Tompkins is a homeless man who takes his name from the park where he dwelt for two years. He also served on CB3's Tompkins Square Task Force, which was established after the 1988 riot. He says that before the June 3 eviction, he stayed up for 30 hours trying to negotiate with Kharfen and Deputy Mayor Bill Lynch, who had been sent down to the park by Dinkins to head off resistance. But Dave says that Lynch told him "I'm not here to negoti-

A Radical Political and Social History of the Lower East Side

ate." He says he was particularly disgusted when Lynch, who is a black man, "tried to appeal to my color by saying, 'We're all brothers.'"

Tompkins says that the park renovation is "all politics. The bandshell is acoustically sound — I've worked as a stagehand and I know. This has happened before — after the riots in the Civil War, the park was razed and was a pit of rubble for several years. If there's trouble in the park, there's something wrong in the city, even the nation, which needs to be addressed. The riot in '67 was a reflection of the strife over Vietnam."

Such a seasoned and philosophical view is especially disarming from a man who has braved the elements and community hostility rather than face the disease, mobility restrictions and institutionalized violence of the HRA shelter system. The Tompkins Square homeless encampment was one of the thorniest issues surrounding the park. Even Frances Goldin and the CB3/JPC liberal camp eventually conceded that the encampment would have to be removed. Only the anarchists and the homeless themselves remained uncompromising in their defense of the shantytown — and there was even friction between these two groups at times. The park homeless frequently accused the more violence-prone anarchists of stirring up trouble in the park and thereby making things even more unlivable for their community which was already under siege. The epitome of this tendency was the looting of May 27, which, according to many observers, forced Dinkins' hand in finally moving to decisively clean up Tompkins Square.

The neighborhood conservatives in such groups as Democratic Action Committee merely wanted the homeless out of their sight, portraying them as a menacing threat. The encampment made this park dangerous and unpleasant, goes the line. They claim that the encampment was infested with drugs and prostitution, despite the fact that such activities were at least ostensibly barred by the shantytown's own internal rules.

The liberals on the other hand, frequently felt torn on the issue. Many sought a compromise solution. Said CB3's Sandy Anderson on a June 8 WBAI talk show hosted by sometime *Downtown* contributor Paul DeRienzo: "The homeless can be helped. There are advocate groups in the neighborhood who are willing to work with them . . . People are very scared to go into the shelters. When we have four hospitals stating over the television that there is an incurable form of tuberculosis loose — if that's going on at NYU Hospital, you can imagine what the City shelters are like. I wouldn't go in there. I'd rather take my chances with the fresh air and sunshine if I were homeless . . .

> The neighborhood groups are willing to walk the homeless through the system, help get them on welfare. The system is very scary. They have to go to step one and prove who they are — find birth records and social security numbers and stuff like that. It's going to be a long process, but there's people in the community who are used to that and can help these people . . . If the city doesn't do that, we've lost all semblance of civilization. Civilizations are supposed to take care of the unfortunate, the old, the young, those that can't help themselves. We have to accept responsibility for these people. We just can't push them aside, hope they'll go away. They're not going to go away without our help — and not

just giving them a bowl of soup and saying 'Oh aren't we good?' — serious help to
get them back on their feet and bring back their humanity — and bring back our
neighborhood and neighborhood control.

409

Many find a grisly irony in the fact that the Tompkins Square homeless have been evicted at
precisely the moment that the Dinkins "doomsday" budget is leading the City to massively
cut back on the already overburdened health care and shelter systems. Proposed cuts now on
the table would mean the elimination of all walk-in clinics, including the Bellevue AIDS clinic, and drastic roll-backs of the Community Based Organizations and Community Family
Planning Council programs which provide primary health care and AIDS counseling to thousands of homeless. The cuts would mean the closing of City hospital outpatient pharmacies,
and most of all, the elimination of 10 homeless shelters, which would mean adding hundreds
of beds to the most overcrowded and dangerous HRA shelters. The shelters slated for elimination are the relatively human-scale ones, while it is the massive and impersonal congregate shelters which would be further bloated. HRA healthcare facilities for the homeless
would also be gutted.

Phil Van Aver, a Lower East Side resident for over 20 years and a close observer of neighborhood politics, had this to say on DeRienzo's WBAI special: "As a person who is concerned
with homeless people, I'm of two minds. I've discussed this with many friends in the neighborhood, and many of us feel that we would actually rather have the homeless people in
Tompkins Square Park, because at least we know what's happening to them, rather than having them shipped off to someplace like the camp up near Monroe, New York, or the facility
for Vietnam veterans at St. Albans, Queens, which was described to me by a friend of mine
who was formerly homeless as a *hell hole*. At least we know what is happening to people if
they're in the park. And, as a person of Jewish background, I'm absolutely shocked at the
idea that people are being sent to out-of-the-way places where they have no access to
social services or legal help. I feel that this is criminally monstrous. And it is going on sort
of without any kind of discussion."

Some of the Tompkins Square homeless have accepted placement in HRA or community shelters. Many more have erected new encampments in vacant lots in the east of the park —
which, like the Hoovervilles of the '30s, are simultaneously the most expedient means of
physical survival and a form of political protest, arguably protected by the First Amendment.
It remains to be seen whether these new encampments will be tolerated.

The Face of the New Police State

Since the park was seized, there has been a virtual army of police stationed in the area.
Helmeted riot cops frequently circle the park, plainclothes officers mill around on street corners, brass in white shirts walk the avenues and survey the scene. The park is ringed by
police barricades, and a mobile command post has been established in the 9th Street walkway. Emergency Services Units and sophisticated communications vehicles are frequently in
the area — a City Emergency Management Office bus seems to have taken up residence on
the corner of Avenue A and 10th Street, bristling with video cameras and computers. This is
the same vehicle which reared its ugly head during last winter's squatter evictions in the

A Radical Political and Social History of the Lower East Side

South Bronx. Everything surveyed by its camera is believed to be simulcast to the video screens of the city's "War Room" at 1 Police Plaza. Several times a day, police helicopters survey the park from the air.

How much is this costing the City at this moment of dire budgetary crisis? Bureaucrats are not forthcoming with this information, but after two days of continuous phone calls I was able to arrive at some figures.

Detective Joseph Gallagher of the NYPD Public Information Office declined to give a daily figure, but said that "during one 24 hour period the cost was as high as $100,000." He also declined to say how many police had been assigned to the Tompkins Square area, saying only that it was "an appropriate number."

Michael Jacobson of the Mayor's Office of Management & Budget arrived at a figure through mathematics over the phone. "There are 400 cops each day in the Tompkins Square area, and somewhat less than half are on overtime. The plan is to rapidly as possible discontinue that." If 150 of the cops assigned to the area are on overtime — that is, wouldn't normally be on the job during those hours anyway — and the overtime wage is $28 per hour, then we arrive at a figure of just under $31,000. What about the communications equipment, the choppers, the emergency units? That, according to Jacobson, gets into the "budget ephemeral," where costs are not easily calculated. Presumably, these costs are not configured into the $2.3 million Kharfen assures us was slated for Tompkins Square reconstruction in 1984.

Many see a special irony in the fact that this expensive operation is being undertaken at a time when the Parks Department budget may be slashed from $187 million to $12 million. John Bachman, parks manager for Lower Manhattan, says he expects two thirds of his workforce to be laid off in the coming months — "including guys who have been on the job over 40 years."

There is also an irony in the behavior of the hundreds of police assigned to the area — especially in the street protests which have been held on an almost nightly basis since the closing of the park. The anarchists, many of them horrified by the May 27 looting and its outcome, have thus far refrained from their usual tricks of hurling bottles at the cops and lighting bonfires in the middle of Avenue A. But the police evidently see the siege of Tompkins Square as an open season on their political opponents.

The latest trick seems to be having plainclothes officers follow an activist home from a demonstration, and make the arrest when he or she is alone without witnesses. Chris Flash, editor of the local anarchist newspaper *The Shadow*, was arrested by undercovers as he was walking home alone from a demonstration at Avenue A and 7th street on the night of June 7. He was charged with felony "criminal mischief" for an act the police say he had committed several hours earlier — jumping up and down on a car hood. Flash denies he committed the act at all. Two other local activists were arrested in connection with this act while walking home alone at approximately the same time.

One activist who prefers to remain anonymous says that she and a friend were trailed by undercovers all the way to the doorstep of their building as they left the May 27 riot. At the doorstep, they were assaulted by the plainclothes officers, and her companion was arrested for his alleged role in the riot.

St Brigid's church, which is across Avenue B from Tompkins Square and has supported the struggle to reopen the park, has become a special focus of police harassment. On two occasions since the park closing, police have tried to gain entry to the church against the wishes of Father George Kuhn, the St Brigid's priest who has taken to ringing the church bells to announce demonstrations to reopen the park.

The first time they came, it was during the June 7 demonstration. Several undercovers knocked at St. Brigid's side door on 7th Street and demanded access to the building's roof. According to Maria Tomin, a St. Brigid's parishioner who was preparing food in the church that night and met the officers at the door, they said "We're homeless," an apparent factitious reference to St. Brigid's tradition of providing shelter and food for the neighborhood's homeless. Tomin says that when she refused to let them in and attempted to close the door, one cop forced it back open and shoved her in the face, sending her stumbling backwards. "The children went hysterical, hiding in closets --- it was not a pretty sight."

Shortly thereafter, Father Kuhn and Father Pat Moloney arrived on the scene, and asked the offending officer to identify himself. The cop asked fathers Kuhn and Moloney to step outside onto the street where the demonstration was taking place, and then to step away from the door of the church. The priests followed, and persisted in asking for the cop's ID, says Father Kuhn. The cop refused to respond, and after some angry words were exchanged he shoved Father Moloney in the stomach. An angry crowd gathered and for a few minutes it seemed like the demonstration would explode into a riot. The cop got lost in the crowd, the priests returned to the church and activists defused tensions by leading the demonstration away.

Father Kuhn had this to say about the incident which nearly provoked a riot right outside his church:

> The anger is a result of frustration. We've tried every legal means to get the park opened up to the people and returned to the community. The state Supreme Court [which granted a temporary restraining order barring further demolition in the park] understands the problem, but the appeals court [which overturned the order the next day] is apparently very politicized. This would seem to lend justification to some of the slogans you see around here about Nazism.

Father Kuhn says, "I would just like to see the police out of here," and decries what he sees as the "trampling of rights. Since when do police in our city have the right to demand ID of people entering their homes?"

Kuhn also decries what he calls the "military terminology," noting that the City has dubbed the park seizure and reconstruction "Operation Restore." "This sounds like calling the

A Radical Political and Social History of the Lower East Side

Panama invasion 'Operation Just Cause,' or the war against Iraq 'Operation Desert Storm' — and we see the same tactics of control of the press and the use of power and force without regards to rights."

Indeed, many see the same "national security" mentality behind both Operation Restore and Operation Desert Storm. The City Office of Emergency Management which is apparently directing and closely monitoring the Tompkins Square seizure maintains close links with its federal equivalent, the Federal Emergency Management Agency (FEMA). FEMA has drawn up elaborate strategies for dealing with domestic dissent in the event of a national emergency, and almost certainly had agents present at the high-level meetings which took place in New York on the eve of the Persian Gulf War in January between top Police Department officials, federal antiterrorist experts, and leading metropolitan area business figures. It was precisely at this moment that the Lower East Side's 9th Precinct commander, Inspector Michael Julian, was rotated out and replaced with Captain Michael Esposito.

The charismatic and idealistic Julian had been appointed to head the 9th Precinct in an effort to chill out a shocked and outraged community in the wake of the 1988 police riot. Over the following two years, even anarchists came to appreciate Julian's comparatively easygoing style. When he was rotated out (apparently into a desk job at police HQ) in January 1991, many anarchists suspected that the velvet glove was about to be removed from the iron fist.

Suspicions that Julian had been transferred out just in time to squelch community opposition to the Persian Gulf War are also granted credibility by the timing of the Tompkins Square seizure — exactly one week before the "Operation Welcome Home" tickertape parade. Local anarchists had been planning to meet in the park on the morning of the parade, and then march downtown to confront and disrupt it.

It is also probable that there is a direct federal presence at the Tompkins Square barricades. The NYPD has cooperated with the FBI in the Joint Terrorist Task Force, and federal agents have been involved in drug sweeps in Washington Square Park. Veterans of the Washington Square sweeps have also been involved in policing Tompkins Square.

Suspicions of 9th Precinct complicity with the conservative agenda for the neighborhood were heightened when the precinct's P.O. Joe Quinn brought suit against the city earlier this year, demanding to be excused from patrolling Tompkins Square until the homeless are evicted. Quinn claims that breathing the smoke from trash barrel fires that the homeless light to warm themselves in the park are a threat to his health.

Deborah Wallace, an air quality specialist with the Center for the Biology of Natural Systems, Dr. Barry Commoner's environmental think tank at Queens College, says: "He's got a case. It is an occupational hazard. Treated wood would have chlorinated hydrocarbons or arsenic compounds, and the smoke would be quite toxic. There is a potential for cancer. The problem is complicated by the fact that the people are homeless in the first place due to public policy."

By way of analogy, Wallace points to Bridge & Tunnel Authority officers and toll takers who have disproportionately high rates of cardiovascular disease due to chronic carbon monoxide exposure from car fumes. Pressure and threatened litigation is forcing the City to install air conditioners at toll places.

But the view that Quinn's case has some political motivation seems to have substance. At the April press conference in Tompkins Square announcing the suit, Quinn was flanked by several Democratic Action Club supporters who collared any reporter who would listen to complain about how the homeless had taken over the park. "When I bring my children to the park I don't want to see some black man with his schlong sticking out," one told me.

While Quinn's health concerns may be valid, there appeared to be little concern at his press conference for the fact that the homeless themselves suffer from even greater exposure to the toxic fumes, and that their only alternative in winter may be freezing to death — as one Ed Rutter, a Tompkins Square homeless man, did one night in December of 1988, after the police extinguished his fire.

The Face of the New Resistance

The seizure of the park has sparked a realignment in the Lower East Side's anarchist community. Aware of how deeply disgusted community residents were by the Memorial Day looting, for the first time many of the anarchists are openly disavowing violence. The possibility that the looting was done by paid provocateurs is being strongly considered --- especially since it fit so well into the conservative agenda for the neighborhood, providing the justification for Dinkins' police action. But whether the looting was perpetrated by police agents or kneejerk nihilists, it has been disavowed by the majority of anarchists and squatter scene. For the first time, anarchist and squatter leaflets calling for protests to reclaim the park are using the word "nonviolent."

Of course there is a hardcore nihilist faction which remains intransigent. Unable to move beyond the politics of adrenaline, this faction continues to revel in throwing bottles and M-80 firecrackers around at demonstrations, heedless to the danger that this poses even to their fellow demonstrators, and the degree to which this alienates them from the community at large. This faction also continues to liberal-bait its critics, charging them with naiveté in believing that anything short of violence can change things.

But these nihilists now seem to be alienated from most of their anarchist comrades as well as the more mainstream neighborhood residents. At a strategy meeting in St. Brigid's, called in the aftermath of the park seizure and attended by many neighborhood anarchists, one nihilist was met with boos when he responded to calls for nonviolence with the comment that "the police aren't nonviolent."

For the moment, the nihilists have been effectively reined in. At the almost nightly neighborhood demonstrations since the park closing, there has been a noticeable change in tone. The drum beating and chanting is spirited and exuberant rather than menacing. There have been no flying bottles and few M-80s. On the afternoon of June 8, nearly 1,000 neighbor-

A Radical Political and Social History of the Lower East Side

hood residents turned up to join hands in a circle around the park. Organized almost entirely by word of mouth, the event seemed to be about 100 participants shy of actually encircling the six-block square park — there was a gap, which was never quite filled on the northeast corner.

If the new tone can be maintained, there is the possibility of a broad-based community coalition emerging to demand the return of the park with a unified voice — especially considering that the conservatives now seem to have been effectively iced from the established community organizations. But it remains to be seen how long the nihilists and hotheads will behave. If the bandshell is demolished, or if the park remains closed as balmy June gives way to scorching July, tempers will explode.

Patience is already being tested by the intimidating police presence around the park. Coming on the heels of the killing of Grady Alexis, a neighborhood artist and Haitian émigré, apparently by an off-duty cop, the police cordon around Tompkins Square is escalating anti-police sentiment in the community. The potential for serious violence is very real.

Attorney Stan Cohen is challenging the Tompkins Square demolition in court on behalf of a group of neighborhood residents including George Kuhn, Pat Moloney, Dave Tompkins, Donna Ellaby and Phil Van Avers. Cohen is arguing that under the new City Charter and the Uniform Land Use Review Process (ULURP) there must be public hearings and an environmental impact statement before demolition of a city park can be undertaken. The City argues that what is being undertaken in Tompkins Square is merely "renovation in kind," and is therefore exempt from ULURP and the hearings requirement.

Cohen succeeded in getting a temporary restraining order (TRO) to halt demolition on June 3, arguing that the City's action was "arbitrary, capricious unilaterally undertaken, and illegal." The TRO was extended two days later by State Supreme Court Judge Martin Schoenfeld, who called the action "a shortsighted solution to a difficult problem. I enjoy parks and I like them when they're nice and renovated, but that's no substitute for human beings and human dignity." But the next morning the TRO was overturned by State Appellate Division Justice Joseph Sullivan. Demolition resumed.

Cohen has also been trying to procure a copy of the City contract with the crew now working in Tompkins Square. Back in the Supreme Court on June 10, City Corporation Counsel attorneys admitted that the demolition crew had been contracted for work elsewhere in the city and had been transferred to Tompkins Square when the administration decided to move — the usual bidding process had not taken place. The city attorneys also admitted that there was still no contract for the reconstruction. Yet Judge Schoenfeld said his hands were tied by the Appellate Court's decision, which he decried as "pure power politics."

Says Cohen: "The demolition in the park was begun for one reason — it's more difficult to stop it once it gets started. The City just got finished laying 100 tons of asphalt on the same areas they're now ripping up. They just got finished repairing benches they're now destroying."

Cohen says that Corporation Counsel attorney Leonard Koerner told him that the Tompkins Square action was "semi-surreptitious," which is why the usual hearings and contract bidding were dispensed with.

Cohen also says that a City Attorney who he declined to name told him that "We expect an acceptable level of casualties" from unrest in the neighborhood sparked by the park closing.

Heading off the impending violence is going to take some creative organizing and fast coalition building by the various forces in the neighborhood. The incongruous sight of helmeted riot police barring the way to a demonstration of neighborhood mothers wheeling baby carriages, which we witnessed on the afternoon of June 7 along Avenue B, can be used as political leverage. The incongruous reality of a budget-strapped city spending $100,000 a day to protect a park from its own community can be similarly used.

Differences can be put aside for the immediate goal of halting further destruction and getting the park back open. But once again the World War II analogy presents itself. In the '40s, the left closed ranks with the Allied governments in order to fight the common fascist enemy. But after the victory, the Allies carved up the world and the left was almost completely eclipsed in the subsequent era of red-baiting and blacklists.

Now that the City has seized Tompkins Square, it can use it as a bargaining chip. The basically progressive forces on the Lower East Side may, with enough creativity and commitment, succeed in getting the park back open. But will the price be the imposition of the very curfew, which the community rejected back in 1988? Will the price be a park permanently off limits to the homeless, who many would prefer remain conveniently invisible?

As I write, demolition continues, and these questions may seem rather premature. By the time you are reading this, a week will have passed, and we may have a clearer picture of where we stand. With any luck, those questions will be more relevant.

(*Downtown*, June 19, 1991)

SECTION FOUR - MEDIA

Chapter 1

The Anarchic Politics of Clayton Patterson and the Lower East Side
By Alan Moore with Allan Antliff

What kind of artist is this large man, with his hipster beard and embroidered baseball cap who wanders the streets of the Lower East Side, magnetically drawn to every street situation? Clayton Patterson is known as a photographer, although he draws, collages and assembles, curates and agitates. He relies on his skills of description, following that path wherever it leads, into the streets and down the corridors of power. Clayton's documentary project is ethically driven, and he is fearless before the outcomes of his descriptive actions when they draw him into the legal realm.

Clayton is a documentarian of the Lower East Side. Clayton and his partner of many years, Elsa Rensaa, have built a major Lower East Side archives. One section of the archives deals with the criminal and creative margins. For Clayton, this necessarily includes the structures of power who police those margins — police and courts, lawyers and reporters. This has been then an ongoing work of committed public art: engaged photography. Clayton's extensive involvement in the legal system, and his regular interventions into government are outgrowths of his documentary work. These engagements were not initially chosen by him, although later he seems to have regularly stepped up to the plate to duel with the law. But, in picking him out as an exemplary case after the 1988 police riot in Tompkins Square Park, NYC prosecutors made Clayton a kind of "jailhouse lawyer," and a very effective gadfly. Depositions skilled him in the art of sarcastic counter-interrogation.

What kind of artist is Clayton Patterson? He is a documentary photographer, but he draws upon the greatly expanded brief that conceptual art gave to documentary photography. In the last 30 years, conceptual art has become a well-plowed byway of the political in art. The strategies that evolved lend themselves continuously to the expression of fractious contents, critique and intervention. This now seems self-evident, although it was not American artists whose art was most succinctly and pointedly political, but conceptual artists working in totalitarian states. Despite his engagements, Clayton rejects the label "political" for his work. He writes:

> My art is not purely political. The hardcore politics was mostly spread over a 17-year period. My street video uses consumer products. It's a simple process. The equipment is meant for most people on the street to use. It is being there and documenting the event or situation that is necessary and makes the difference. The technology is accessible. I did other artwork during this time.
>
> I did approach television. I had a meeting with Dan Rather's agent. I had a television producer (who won Emmys, did Morton Downey) take my work to TV station

A Radical Political and Social History of the Lower East Side

heads. I was told nobody would watch a man on the street moving with a camera or following the cops. The viewing audience had to have processed studio material. This was before 'Real TV', 'Cops', and all the reality shows. Someone eventually understood the vision and was able to sell the concept and made millions of dollars.

My video had a style, a point of view, and a lot of practice. It was not the Rodney King tape. The man who shot that tape had never used the camera before. I did hard core music shows for over a year. I had practice in chaotic places and a point of view about what and how I was shooting. I was ready when the riot happened.

During this period, Elsa and I manufactured the Clayton caps. We were the first to put a label and a signature on personalized custom caps with embroidery going around the cap. *GQ magazine* said that we were one of the two best baseball cap makers in America; as small potatoes we changed the whole concept of the baseball cap and made it into a fashion and art item. I was also president of the New York City Tattoo Society then. I helped make a few artists famous and helped some good people get into the business. Wes Wood, City Councilwoman Kathern Freed and I were instrumental in legalizing tattooing in NYC. I became, along with the owners Steve Bonge and Butch Garcia, an organizer of the New York City Tattoo Convention. I put together the American tattoo and sideshow talent for Jochen Auer's Austrian show '"Wildstyle,'" that helped change the public's awareness about tattoos, it increased the level of quality in tattooing by bringing master tattoo artists to the public, and this new energy was instrumental in changing the direction of tattooing and piercing in parts of Europe.

So to say that my art is only political is misses all this. The court cases and such are important because I was consciously using the court as a vehicle to add to my art. Not only the paper work from the cases, but I used more tapes in court against rogue cops than anyone in the history of America. Most people do only one case. I had numerous cases using my material. My riot tape got five cops criminally indicted and also exposed a dysfunctional police force and a lot of misconduct. A chief retired, a captain was moved out of the precinct, numerous cops were up on disciplinary charges. And the most drastic change was that the NYPD decided to enforce a more paramilitary type of approach, a change in police philosophy.

I was arrested a lot. I was the only recognizable figure in the movement who was really beaten up by the cops. I can direct you to testimony from a person that thought I was dead after the cops beat me on the street. I had teeth knocked out, and more. I was not an important figure of the movement. Not at all. I was only a documentarian with a point of view."

Clayton speaks constantly of the totality of his engagements. For him, everything he does is related. His body of work and his engagements have evolved through a particular interlocked set of possibilities on the Lower East Side, a historic seedbed of creative and political radicalism, and a neighborhood constantly undergoing change. Like many artists, Clayton was swept up in his greatest, albeit most scandalous success, his video documentation of the Tompkins Square Park police riot. This experience was by no means celebratory. Instead, he was inducted into a brutal maze of legal entanglements, and led on to many further struggles. His case was an early signal of the artist's right to photograph crime and other activity on the streets, police actions, — in this case, abuse by civil authorities — and retain rights to the document as "artistic property."

Clayton's experience is in the realm of relations between art and the law,[1] and, given subsequent developments in matters of intellectual property, his case is a significant part of the culture wars. It was understood as a part of the muffled subdued class war then raging in NYC, that the battles against the forces of law were being used to soften up the working class neighborhood of the Lower East Side in anticipation of gentrifying. The neighborhood was already degenerated by a post-Vietnam War influx of heroin, and this was a long, tough and ugly struggle, during which the city bent and broke many laws and customs in the single-minded pursuit of improving the tax base. Clayton was there to document one of the bigger outbreaks in the course of this process, a police riot which became a signature event in the gentrification process. The subsequent struggle with the New York City district attorney over possession of his videotapes was an important case in intellectual property law, and the prerogatives of the independent journalist. A prime motive for editing this book — pushing it into being — has been that he wants the context behind his documentary work of the last few decades to be understood.

Clayton loves to talk, and he spends many days sitting in his storefront window with visitors. Since 1986, he had his tiny gallery there; now his partner Elsa Rensaa does tattoos in a back part of that room. He might be a raconteur, but he is usually too impatient to move on to the point of the matter. In fact, Clayton is a polemicist. In conversation, he stakes out a position like jamming a pike into the sand, and then rotates around it.

He understands art as an outsider. His aesthetic is founded in disdain for the art world of the elites. But of course even an anti-art position is an art position, and this may be Dada — he claims kinship, after all, with the No! art movement of the 1950s and '60s (which combined American-produced pornographic imagery with photos of the holocaust to shock and challenge status-quo complacency in the art world and society generally), and that is, arguably, a lineal outgrowth of Dada. But if Clayton is Dada, an idea that he rejects, it is just as another outsider garment. He has no program of revolutionary or sensual derangement, nor does he delight in making confusion. He likes life in its rougher aspects — featuring crime and punishment. The aleatory mechanic is reportorial — "shit happens."

Clayton formed his aesthetic, that is to say, his sense of what he feels he is up against, through his experiences in art education. He disparages what he calls the "A student mentality":

> The art world has too much social tactical thinking. To make art-world art is to be
> compromised by social niceties, rather than social issues. Everything in the art
> world has a subtext attached to it. It is like the `A student' mentality. I taught

A Radical Political and Social History of the Lower East Side

high school. The `A students' were organized, had all the proper social attributes necessary to be appealing to the teacher, and they were focused on their goal. The `A students' were not necessarily the brightest or the best. Even in a small country school, the `A student' personality would be very warm and cuddly when they had you as a teacher. Then, like changing channels, when they got their `A,' when you saw them in the hall, there is no recognition of you. Your use had been accomplished.

When I taught art at college, I found that the radical students were gone. The real seekers of truth, the questioners, were wiped out, if not by the end of the first year, then certainly by the end of the 4th term. The target-hitting champions were there. But these kinds of students just perfect and perpetuate the status quo. The same opinions, same way of thinking, same answers. The creatively wild had been failed out, could not handle the socialization process, or just lost interest.

Clayton believes contemporary art education fails artists by not teaching them basic skills. This is an outcome of the "curse of modernism."

Modernism was a blight on society. They kept stripping it down and making it less and less and less, and that's really just a corporate way of thinking. You eliminate the artist, you eliminate anything decorative in the environment, you make it totally sterile, and you take away from the common man. You keep on eliminating public aesthetics. And you have this whole conformity.

In art school, you think you're learning something, but you're learning conformity. Maybe you're learning how to see blocks of ideas, but whose ideas are they? The Museum of Modern Art is a corporation. And the only thing you can do is copy that aesthetic, get involved in it, and then you're appreciated where you are within the university and the art school, because the outside public doesn't get it at all. So send your kid to art school, they train him to do these drip paintings, he's getting A's, and nobody in the general society knows what he's talking about whatsoever. It's lunacy.

Then they got into conceptual art where you didn't have to do anything, you have to come up with an idea. For a small elitist group of people who have access to the privileged galleries it's fine. For all those kids outside the city and in other places it just robs them of everything. If you take the Rivington School which was our Watts Tower, it had a real aesthetic and creativity attached to it, you couldn't get the Whitney, the Modern or any art people — none of them would have anything to do with any of it. And they just bulldozed it under. You have only the documentation, and that becomes all that remains of the art. There's something between the real thing and the picture. The pictures are great, they have their own unique aesthetic and individual importance, but they're not the 3-D object. Somebody should have saved that sculpture park.

Alan Moore with Allan Antliff

This rebellion against the postwar art elite is pure punk. Clayton seeks the revenge of life experience over corporate art and stands for a do-it-yourself approach that echoes the anarchism at the core of the punk ethos.[2] He wants art that is anti-corporate and impossible to "mainstream," art created by self-sufficient producers who are dangerous to the market-driven corporate art system because they are engaged in free, unfettered expression rooted in life on the edge of everything that system stands for. As an on-site witness to the crash and burn of the 1980s East Village galleries, Clayton acquired a hearty contempt for the corporate-aspiring art scene and its workings. He questions the integrity of the critics of that moment for abandoning the artists they had championed. One may argue that the position of the art critic dwindled fast during that decade, and that outlets for these among the poorest of writers to publish had dried up. But in his insistence that writers, journalists, and promoters of a scene should stick with it no matter what, Clayton evinces his sense of responsibility. He is dogged.

> Much of the commercial East Village scene of the early '80s was a collaboration or a parallel with a real estate movement. You had the news and magazines pumping up these people who brought in the galleries which brought up the real estate, and it was also about selling real estate. Some of those magazines, and the people writing for them, were hypesters. If it isn't rock and roll it's running shoes. Many of those articles in that period had nothing to do with art, because those people would still be writing about this art if it did, there would be something intrinsically important to them. They turned their eyes somewhere else. To make something happen you have to continue pushing it. These things are like shopping carts, and as soon as you stop pushing they don't move anymore. They're not self-propelled. And those writers and people who created that fervor dropped it as soon as the real estate moved. Where is the honesty in that?

Clayton is pretty crusty. He has cultivated a strong, flavorful street persona — he's a guy who knows his way around a hassle. Clayton wears a cap with a skull motif front and center, a vestige of his trade in embroidered baseball caps.

> Most cultures use the skull as an image. If you go to Tibet, much of any their art has skulls in it. In American tattoo iconography, tattoos always had skulls attached to them. In the Renaissance every famous artist put a skull in their work. It stands for a lot of things. And, in another way, you have to have a strong persona if you're going to be doing this kind of work. Having them know you're there is not a bad thing. Having them know that if they attack you, you will respond, that's not a bad thing.

This is machismo, for sure, although it is vested in image and attitude and a long list of conflicts — many of which he came out of on the winners' side.

> "Yes, it is true that I have a strong presence, but I have never pushed my art around. We [Clayton and Elsa] have almost never shown our material, other than what has been on the news."

A Radical Political and Social History of the Lower East Side

His community involvement notwithstanding, Clayton's work as a documentarian has been criticized as disengaged, ruthless, like a war photographer; in fact , he has been accused of documenting a fatal beating.

In that particular incident, I did not document a murder. I heard screaming outside. I ran to the window and saw an elderly man on the ground. I did not even have time to grab my camera. When I got outside, a young Hispanic man was standing with his grandmother, and the youth said the elderly man had pushed and spit on his grandmother. I helped the man get up. He had an asthma inhaler in his hand. He was gasping for breath. As soon as I got him up, he leaned on a car hood. I watched as the tip of his nose turned blue, and the blue moved up his nose, like a thermometer, and he was dead.

The cops arrived, laid the man on the ground and did heart massage. The cops brought the man back to life. The ambulance arrived. The cops asked for oxygen. I yelled to the ambulance to bring oxygen. I put my hand up by my nose and signaled oxygen. They did not have it. They got the man into the ambulance. He died and they tried electric shock treatment. Elsa videotaped the incident out our window across the street. I had no camera. Later I found out in an NY Times article that the man's sister said that I was a callous person for videotaping this fight.

I can only assume that she got this information from the police, since the woman was on the community board, and there were few witnesses, and everyone there knew that I did not have a camera. I think that the man was having a stroke or something, fell into the youth's grandmother, and was spitting. The youth pushed the man to the ground, thinking his grandmother was being attacked. Unfortunately, the kid copped a plea, got a couple of years in jail and was deported back to the Dominican Republic. A detective later told me that he wished the case had gone to court. I said, 'So did I,' as I would have been a witness for the kid. The tragedy, I believe, was all a mistake.

But in his talk, Clayton expresses his moral indignation, his passion, that which led him to look at and imagine so much of what he did. He has a sense of adventure, and the devil-may-care insouciance of a large man. He feels at home in his adopted neighborhood, another immigrant to bohemia, and he feels entitled to see what's going on and take it home with him in his photography.

His reason for making this book is the urgency of recording the history of a resistance movement which that he sees has slipped away. His photographs of that time record a street theater with no script, whose participants mostly played no second acts. Like many longtime Lower East Side residents, Clayton is haunted by the erasure of the scenes of the past in the meat grinder of New York City development.

For Clayton, the long-running battles between police and street people that were a constant feature of the East Village during the late '80s and early '90s amounted to a movement.

This movement was not an art movement. If you look at most of the posters that come from this period they're like cut and paste. The Xerox machine became the printing press of that period. This is pre-user friendly home computers. There were a few artists on the scene. Eric Drooker did posters that were critical to the recognition of the movement. Peter Missing and his graffiti, the upside down champagne glass with the contents pouring out, was immediately recognized by numerous mainstream news people who saw it as a frightening revolutionary symbol against gentrification. And then you had the highly imaginative political art of Seth Tobocman, with his ability to print his volume of work which included his *World War 3* publications (started in 1979 with Peter Kuper), that involved many artists and was very effective at bringing attention to the cause.

Seth was inspired by his association with Dutch artist Anton Van Dalen, who years before created a school because his ideas were copied, and his stencil art opened up a whole new way of doing street art. Anton's metamorphic imagery influenced Seth's distinctive style. Lawrence Van Abbema and Cosmo were important poster artists, and eventually Fran Luck tried her hand at doing drawing on her own posters. Out of the hundreds of posters most are rather mundane, but they all have a feeling of the streets and were extremely necessary to scare people, get the message out, and to help organize. Some are like manifestos and speeches.

David Peel was constantly there with his guitar, and at different moments folksinger Roger Manning also showed up with his guitar. The anarchists would have concerts in the park usually put together by Jerry the Peddler and/or Lori Rizzo. They did an annual Squatters Mayday, and bands and the speech makers would show up for that. But many speeches became political rants. Jorge Brandon [aka, El Coco que Habla] who lived in one of the squats also showed up and gave poetic rants in Spanish.

The Shadow was critically important. They would get stories and ideas out from an anarchist point of view. Another big part of it was Bob Fass, who had the 1 a.m. WBAI radio program and would invite a lot of the activists there. Paul DeRienzo of WBAI was an essential radio news broadcaster. Robert Knight of WBAI was helpful. Sarah Ferguson and Bill Weinberg, journalists, got information out in print. The photographers like Q Sakamaki, John Penley, John McCabe, Peter Levasseur, Paul Kneisel, David Sorcher, Andrew Lichtenstein, Cecil Price, Brian Palmer, and Chris Flash were critically important to getting the message out. In the first year of the struggle, especially with his 20-minute TSP police riot video, Paul Garrin, the video artist, got the pot cooking. From the Revolutionary Communist Party perspective, Paul and Cathy Shay were strong allies. Blackout Books, the Anarchist collective bookstore, was a meeting and thinking place. And unique for me, St. Brigid's church was a meeting place. Interesting that St.

426

Brigid's church has been so eminent in the struggles of the poor and the disadvantaged and now that the drugs, the largest business in the neighborhood, have been taken off the table, and the poor are being suppressed and dislocated as much as ever, the archdiocese, wants to tear down the church and build some new gentrifying for-profit, money-making business.

The Shadow was critically important. They would get stories and ideas out from an anarchist point of view. Another big part of it was Bob Fass, who had the 1:00 a.m. WBAI radio program and would invite a lot of the activists there. Paul DeRienzo of WBAI was an essential radio news broadcaster. Robert Knight of WBAI was helpful. Sarah Ferguson and Bill Weinberg got a lot of journalism out to the world. The photographers like Q Sakamaki, John Penley, John McCabe, Peter Levasseur, Paul Kriesal, David Sorcher, Andrew Lichtenstein, Cecil Price, Chris Flash and, Elsa Rensaa (also video), were critically important to getting the message out. In the first year of the struggle, especially with his 20-minute TSP police riot, Paul Gavin, the video artist, was critically important to getting the pot cooking. From the Revolutionary Communist Party perspective, Paul and Cathy Shay were strong allies and an important part of the struggle. Blackout books, the Anarchist collective bookstore, was a meeting and thinking place. And unique for me, St. Brigid's church was a meeting place. Interesting that St. Brigid's church has been so eminent in the struggles of the poor and the disadvantaged and now that the drugs, the largest business in the neighborhood, have been taken off the table, and the poor are being suppressed and dislocated as much as ever, the archdiocese wants to tear down the church and build some new gentrifying for-profit, money-making business.

Many would have difficulty with the idea of leadership at that period of time, but there is no doubt that a number of people were key players; Jerry the Peddler, Fran Luck (Rage On), Lorrie Rizzo, Little Kirk, Alan Kronstadt, Eric Rossie, Seth Tobocman, Michael Shanker, Ron Casanova, Keith Thompson, Frank Morales, John Penley, Elsa Rensaa, the trio of John the Communist, Karl Rosenberg and Joel Myers (Class War Organizer). Chris Flash, and all *The Shadow* people did a lot of media maneuvers. You would often have all these people milling around, making speeches or giving rants, having political conversations and debates, many times disagreeing with each other, but once the cops show up, there was automatic unity, then the show would start.

It is easy to romanticize this period. This was a kind of marginal radicalism. This off-and-on 10-year period of protest (most intense during 1988-'92) had a very ragtag look to it. Yes, wingnuts and eccentrics were the order of the day. This was no academic paradise or Sunday picnic. Many of the protesters were people living desperate lives. There is not a library shelf full of books written by activists from the period. This group, it seems, did not have the makings of the Situationists amongst themselves. This movement was outside of the mainstream. The *Village Voice* hardly supported what was happening, nor did any faction of the left want to be seen joining hands with this ugly rank collective.

There were numerous problems, dealing with this group of protest people. Seth Tobocman, so far, has issued the only objective history, or partial history, of what went on during this difficult era (the graphic novel *War in the Neighborhood*]. You may say Seth's written words and illustrations are only comic book art, not a real history, but the book gives a very brutal look at the truth from that period in time. This 'movement' was a really strong force for the cops to overcome. These people were great resisters. Many of the squatters won the rights to the property that they were squatting. But try to get them to write a book about their own history which includes them, they can't do it."

It is easy to romanticize this period. This was a kind of marginal radicalism. This off and on 10 year period of protest (most intense from 1988-1992) had a ragtag look to it. Yes, wing nuts and eccentrics were the order of the day. This was no academic paradise or Sunday picnic. Many of the protesters were people living desperate lives. There is not a library shelf full of books written by activists from the period. Members of this group, it seems, did not have the makings of the Situationists. This movement was outside the mainstream. The *Village Voice* hardly supported what was happening, nor did any faction of the left want to be seen joining hands with this ugly rank collective. There were numerous problems dealing with this group of protest people. Seth Tobocman, so far, has issued the only objective history, or partial history, of what went on during this difficult era [the graphic novel *War in the Neighborhood*]. You may say Seth's written words and illustrations are comic book art, not a real history, but the book gives a very brutal look at the truth from that period in time. This 'movement' was a really strong force for the cops to overcome. These people were great resisters. Many of the squatters eventually won the rights to the property that they were squatting. But try to get them to write a book about their own history and they can't do it.

This resistance movement did not get support from New York's Democratic machine in decline or the "community worker" leftists allied with Democrat politicians in the name of "radical reform." It was a movement that mirrored the lives and perspectives of those who had nothing to gain from the compromises the politicians thrived on, compromises for which their community associations were supposed to grease the LES. The rebels of the LES resembled the déclassé urban "rabble" Marx famously dismissed as counter-revolutionary because they were insufficiently "proletarian," the same "rabble" whose rebellious élan 19th-century anarchism celebrated. The divisions in the LES reflected a long-standing battle between the real radicals (the anarchists, the squatters, street-people, the under-employed, the psychologically unbalanced) and the sell-out reformers, between the sometimes incoherent initiatives of the rabble and the politicking that masked increasingly brutal assaults on the social viability of the LES's marginals. For Clayton, the defeat of the LES rebellion carries serious implications.

[Lower East Side City Councilwoman] Miriam Friedlander split off very early on, about 1987, over the squats. But what you had was a Democratic administration. [The Republican administration of] Giuliani broke that mold. He plays a very important part in destroying the Democratic kingdom. This whole neighborhood

A Radical Political and Social History of the Lower East Side

was totally wrapped into the Democratic party. It was little pockets of people each fighting for their own little piece of the pie, and any concepts dealing with idealism, ethics, morality, were all focused on their own group project . . . groups like CHARAS, Cooper Square, Joint Planning Council, all of these collectives were threatened by and opposed the people in the park and the squatters. Some of the people from Met Council, and GOLES (Good Old Lower East Side) were supportive of the struggle, but for a person from one of the usual communist cell democratic factions to show up and be a part of the strug-gle — never. They were too busy trying to eat up the pie. The Democrats to this day still have not gotten a people's agenda formulated.

I believe that the Left was totally wrong not to get involved in this ground floor protest movement. The protesters have been proved right in what they were say-ing. Crazies or not, even if they were only going on intuition and feelings, they were right. The Left is still not conscious of this period in history. The Right is awake and they are now totally in charge. The Left is still in the losing position and they are not awake yet. In all their fake glory and stupidity, the Left pulls out the old '60s political people and modes of protest. Dragging out all the accoutrements that go with that bygone period of time. This is a new decade, century, and millennium. Things have changed. We need new thinkers. I can imagine America using Israeli or even Iraqi means and tactics to suppress dis-sent and protest. These are different times and we are living in a very dangerous period of social change.

Clayton's political analysis is ultimately not broad-brush. It is always very particular. It comes from walking the streets.

I don't understand how people lose their memory about what happened in the city. [Mayor Edward] Koch, whose administration was a complete failure, was a nice guy, going around saying 'Hey, how'm I doing?' But as a leader, he was destructive to the city and had a very corrupt and criminal administration, although the local Democrats loved Uncle Ed. A number of cops were completely corrupt by the third term of Koch. Drugs were rampant everywhere in the city. Heroin and cocaine were being sold right next to schools where police patrolled and even in buildings close to the precinct. On 7th street half a block from Tompkins Square Park a world-famous drug spot the "Laundromat," sold heroin called "Bag in a Bag." The local priest, Father Kuhn, used to take his parish-ioners on a march through the neighborhood and the cops would accompany him, and he'd stop on his block and say this is the Laundromat. They sell heroin here from 6 at night until 6 in the morning, they're here everyday. And the peo-ple would move on to the next spot. Detective Richie Johnson the community affairs officer, who had been in the 9th Precinct his whole career, would go to meetings with community and block associations, to discuss drug locations, and business always went on as usual.

It was that obvious. Drugs had been a ruling street presence since the end of the Vietnam War. When the cops were completely surrounding Tompkins Square Park, I used to rag them when I took their picture. They'd say, "Why are you taking my picture?" I'd say, "I don't know, why are these people going down this block?" I see all these white kids from all over the world, England, Germany, wherever, and they're walking half a block down this dark street, empty of any legitimate business, and coming right back. There's no theater down there, no pizza parlor, no store, there's nothing down there except guys standing around on the street. And this would go on past the cops all night long. "Golly, Mr. Dillon, why are these people going down there?" But there was no answer for it. You'd have these bodegas that would have a whole long shelf of nothing but toilet paper. They'd have no milk. It was obvious that these were all drug locations. Drugs were everywhere. This was the complete collapse of what most Americans think of as law, morality or ethics in the city.

My protesting the drugs was not to get the dealers busted, but to show the relationship between the drugs and the police department. The drugs were the largest and most profitable business in the community. Community people were just victims of a much larger plot. The drug trade was obvious. The local minorities involved in the trade eventually ended up in jail and most cool white people and the corrupt cops had few problems. Local drug dealers are an understandable part of the community, and are nothing compared to the sinister side of corrupt cops ruling the business.

When I captured the three hours and thirty three minutes police riot on tape, it exposed all kinds of things. In a lot of ways, the boring parts were equally as important as the violent parts. If you look at the riot tapes, the significant video isn't only the people being beaten up, but it was the police running around out of control. The captains, the white shirts, the chiefs could not stop the patrolman. One of the most critical shots in the tape is the white shirts, the inspectors and the chiefs chasing down the street, trying to get the patrolmen to come back. This is supposed to be a community police force, structured like a military organization. When the chief comes into the room you're supposed to stand at attention. These guys got their hats on backwards, some of them don't have caps or badges, they have their shirt badge numbers covered, or they switched badges with other cops, and it's all under the watchful eye of the chief and the sightseeing brass. The system was totally out of control.

This political struggle on the street went on for five years, there were hundreds of arrests, thousands of police, they had a tank down there. Out of this long and arduous and difficult period, a good number of the more intelligent cops rose up the ladder. This area was the golden ladder. Lots of media and attention. The LES was used as a forum to practice police tactics, a useful arena for all of America law enforcement. This began to manifest after the Columbine tragedy unfolded on television; all the cops dressed like the NYPD cops and followed the same formations. The LES was a learning pool. Uniforms went through changes.

A Radical Political and Social History of the Lower East Side

Dinkins started the real structural change in the police department. He created the Mollen Commission, which gutted a good cross-section of police corruption. I believe that I had a hand in getting this investigation started. In many depositions and in open court during my cases, I used to ask the city lawyers why we had all these drugs and all these police at the same spot. By the time Giuliani got into power, it took him just three months to clear the streets of drugs. The system does not work for anyone if the police are the criminals. This is far too dangerous a situation for everyone.

Prior to the police riot of August 6th and 7th, Mayor Koch visited Amsterdam to learn about squat evictions and street protests. Our protests became an educational platform for many groups, but the group that was able to learn most from this struggle was the cops. The cops became a razor sharp paramilitary force after five years of fighting the protesters on the LES. This massive, now totally awake giant of a police force, well trained, heavily armed, fully equipped with every modern and old technical equipment and device, had reached maturity. Remember that in 1988 hundreds of police with all kinds of ranking brass, could not close a small 10-acre city park. On the night of the police riot, many of the druggies and homeless people were allowed to stay in the park, the police were selective as to who they drove out into the streets. Since September 11, 2001, the police can now shut down NYC in a couple of hours. This ability to completely shut down NYC, including airports, bridges, tunnels, all cross streets and avenues, was a totally foreign concept to many New Yorkers. Other than some futuristic books and movies who would have believed NYC could be shut down at all? Very few people. The LES protesters witnessed this metamorphosis, the strengthening of the slack muscles. I have a lot of photographic and video documentation of the NYPD going through rebirth, passing through adolescence to become a fully-grown giant. This reorganized force now rules the city. I do not think many people understand how much things have changed. A police state or marshal law could be put into effect in just a few hours.

In the 1980s, Clayton's kind of provocative journalism was a pimple on the Spectacles. Today it seems like a precursor of the kind of independent, radical "fifth estate," which has become a vital part of the strategy of the contemporary anti-multinational capitalist movement (anarchist publications, websites, and so on). TV in the United States first saw big changes, and was then radically reordered in the last few decades. As documentarians shadowed the newsreel opportunities within theatrical film exhibition in the modernist era, so the introduction of cable TV in the 1970s saw the rise of a nationwide creative resistant alternative in community media.[3] The quick growth of camcorder technology through, the 1980s, vastly accelerated the democratization of the documentary image. Public access TV production was a nationwide, even international, movement. In NYC, making TV was approached variously and idiosyncratically in a unique brand of urban artists' television. A practiced community activist videographer, Clayton was a TV journalist since he made television shows for Manhattan Cable's non-commercial public access channel.[4] Unaccredited, to be sure, and relentlessly independent, he talked to print journalists and appeared on broadcast TV talk shows during the height of his involvement in the issues of police brutality. His work on cable TV anticipated the broadcast reality shows that have become staples today. As Clayton defines his work in relation to and in contrast with mainstream journalism:

It shouldn't matter if you're documenting a neighborhood, whether you have a press pass or not. One of the excuses cops always used is that they're doing this for the photographers' safety. Across the street from 537 E. 13th Street, between A and B, there was a raised entrance to a building, it was about eight feet tall, it was completely caged in, but gave an excellent view of the street, there was somebody there from Channel 11, and there was no way they would have impeded the action. But the police kicked in the caged gate and made the journalists get out and sealed that area. There was no reason for that to happen.) During the eviction of the 13th St. squats, Elsa and I were able to document the police assault on the press, because we were barricaded in a squat across the street from this incident. We were able to evade arrest.

What some journalists do is get all their information from the police agency, DCPI (Deputy Commissioner of Public Information) who tells them what "happened," from a police point of view. Another serious impediment to civil rights are "press pens," the barricaded areas on the street into which the "Press" is herded. Why the press ever acceded to this is beyond me — it ridicules the concept of freedom: the caged press. DCPI also issues and controls press passes; so if they don't like you, you may not be renewed.

We have been ruined by television, which is a drug that has formed how we think. It gave us perfect images of police work and we have bought that. We have bought it through [TV cops] Kojak and Columbo and all those crime-solving people. When you get into the real world, as the OJ Simpson trial proved, then you realize that it's just a myth. A lot of white Americans don't get it.

We can't live in a civilization, be civilized and be safe, if we don't examine what really happened, or if those in charge of law and justice are corrupt. The relationship between journalists and government should, by nature, be somewhat adversarial. It should be, `I don't go to your parties, I'm not your friend, and I'm here to investigate.' But in order to get the inside scoop, you have to schmooze but you should not become an elitist insider.

Remember, I do not follow anyone's doctrine or political philosophy. Emma Goldman started in the LES, as did Dorothy Day. Both were individualists and resolved many of their firmly held convictions, although Day was definitely Catholic, but an anarchist Catholic — now that is a paradox. I guess in certain ways growing up in Western Canada, having parents who were pioneers and homesteaders in a new, mostly unsettled land, meant that one had to be independent, think for oneself, be conscious of others, and not rely too much on government or police. You had to be self-sufficient, and make rules that worked with others. Of course there is a difference between squatting on land and homesteading, but in those days the land was basically free anyway.

432

I see myself as an individualist, a small-time capitalist who believes that every-one should own their own home. I came to my own conclusions and observa-tions on what makes a better life, correcting the ills of society. In some ways, I have been lucky growing up in Canada, which had a mixture of socialism and capitalism, where as in the USA, the capitalist philosophy is a much bigger part of the indoctrination. No system is perfect, and I tend to be an outsider to all of them.

In the 1980s and 90s, being an outsider in the midst of the Lower East Side squatting movement was natural. And if there was a politics to it all, it was anarchist. Resistance in the LES was shot through with anarchism: that is, a critical stance towards the state and capitalism and a positive affirmation of the peoples' right to govern their own lives. The tenuous consciousness of what was at stake found expression in the protest posters of the period, which Clayton — in a far-sighted move — has saved for posterity. These posters, suf-fused with circle-A and squatter tags, contain hard-hitting analysis of the city government's incremental gentrifying campaign, the CIA conspiracy to keep the poor down by flooding depressed urban neighborhoods with drugs, and the use of the LES as a training ground for the militarization of the state's domestic police apparatus.

This is the agitational side of the resistance. But, side-by-side, with the critique of the capitalist present, people were building glimpses of the anarchic alternative, forms of lived resistance, always under siege. In the LES, people were reclaiming abandoned buildings for housing, clearing vacant lots and establishing community gardens, sustaining not-for-profit projects like *The Shadow* newspaper, and organizing protests where absolutely everyone had the right to a voice, no matter how off center. Clayton was one of those voices, and his weapon of choice was his video. Through his video documentation, he took the struggle of the LES into the establishment's turf, and won some important victories.

My using the video as a successful activist tool proved how valuable the camera can be in court cases, both criminal and civil, and so on. My example paved the way for others to understand the power of the consumer-available, hand-held video camera, and its use as a neutralizing tool against the state's one-sided advantage. The tapes are valuable in so many ways. They work as history, tools for defense in court, teaching tools, tools for spreading the information, raising money, and so on. They helped to neutralize criminal behavior from the cops — they understand that they are being held accountable for their actions. Holding the cops and system accountable put me in some very difficult situations. I was arrested numerous times, had teeth knocked out, was knocked unconscious and so on. The evidence was important and, when buttressed with an article in a newspaper then things were hopeful. A record was made anyway.

Clayton was part of the resistance, but was his resistance anarchic by proxy or by choice? Where does Clayton Patterson stand, politically? Is he an anarchist?

Alan Moore with Allan Antliff

I do not think of myself as an anarchist, although the cops said that I am one. I considered myself to be an artist. Being an artist to me means seeking original answers. You are an independent, one who thinks for oneself, who has the right to choose to go in whatever direction one wants. I have my own political positions. Art can be anything that one chooses to do, although I do think that there are skills, a point of view, a consistency of theme. But in the end it is up to us to find other like-minded people to appreciate our aesthetic positions. Anarchy to me means a historical position and a given point of view. There are a lot of biases attached to the concept — the stereotypical anarchist bomber, for example. I respect Emma Goldman and what she did, but I am not a follower of anyone or their point of view. I think for myself. I am an independent and the art that I show is about independence.

"Think for yourself," of course, is an anarchist slogan coined by Peter Kropotkin. In fact, Clayton may not think of himself as an anarchist, but his attitude embodies the anarchic spirit of LES and the individualistic independence at the heart of anarchism in practice. This gives what he does its community vitality — and that comes through loud and clear in his videos. In the video of the Tompkins Park Police Riot, for example, one is struck by how people respond to his presence. Strangers aren't threatened by him — they urge him on in documenting what is happening. Plainly, this solidarity was a factor in how his filming became "political," either when presented as evidence to convict unlawful police behaviour or as a record of what was going on from the perspective of the protesters and bystanders. There was a politics to this "point of view" and Clayton is well aware of it.

My point of view was guided by how I thought about the system, and what is right and what is wrong. I was in touch with community people, and that is reflected in all of the videos. The street presence of a video camera worked also as a referee. When we showed up the police usually behaved better keeping the power in check. Cops can easily break the law, if that is their attitude, so having a counter-balance was important. We were one of the first to do "Cop Watch," So not only were we a diversionary presence on the street but our footage often showed up on "*Clayton Presents*" our weekly MNN (Manhattan Neighborhood Network TV series). I was also able to get my footage on many television news programs, as well as be a guest talking about the use of video in the struggle against police misconduct. I was on shows like Oprah, Geraldo, all of the local morning TV shows, numerous specials and so on.

Apart from the videos of demonstrations, Clayton took it upon himself to video life in the squats and on the streets as an act of faith in its value. Some videos trace the evolution of a scene over years, leaving us with a remarkable archival record of LES history in the making.

I have some ABC No Rio video. It is a hard place to get a grip on. The space changes and is very much alive with each youth group that comes through its doors. I have different histories over long periods. I have some tape on Jack Waters' struggles with government bureaucracy, Red Ed's New Years Eve and other moments. Squatter shows and so on. Video of Mickey the Pope, Don Yippie, Jerry the Peddler's involvement in the squatter wars, the homeless struggles, the park curfew battles, and tapes of the police from post riot on. The squats were what they were. Some were very anarchistic, free choice, some were battlegrounds. Some were artistic and productive, other squats were bureaucratic. There is quite a bit of material about the squats. I do have material on just about all of the major squat actions during that period. Evictions, demolitions, standoffs and so on.

What makes Clayton especially distinct as an engaged video journalist of a radically different stripe is his willlingness to take busts through his work, for the principle that he has a right to film actions by public servants, and that the dramatic images he gathers are his. He documented the workings of the state on the street. But in so doing, he undoubtedly provoked many of the cops he taped by the very act of making them his subjects. Clayton also has delighted in submitting artist's briefs to Judges.

Since everyone has the right to hand in court papers, I would do my own and hand them in. I would have a written part, the body of the case. I would put in a photographic part, a visual, recognizable, easy to read, realistic flavor, visual content, of what was being explained. And I would do an art work collage, for a cover -- some times do the back cover and add some art on the inside pages as well. The art was usually made as a color copy from a collage. There would be three or four copies made: one for the Judge, one for the prosecutor, one for the defendant's lawyer, and one for me. The art would have an aesthetic visual representation of what the case was about. Some of these were highly charged art works. Art with content, and social impact. Artwork not meant to be one of the niceties in galleries but as a scream in the courthouse. Art for busting balls so to speak. All legal and within the rights of the person going to court, all free speech, not always socially appreciated by the court, but legal.

I made a collage for a federal case with Judge Leisure, who, because of the imagery, went totally ballistic. A friend of mine, a Hassid from Brooklyn, had an appointment in the Javits Federal Building downtown but was not allowed entry and was wrongfully arrested. He wanted me to help him with his case. So we made a written part and I did a collage and added in photographs. The judge intuitively understood the message, but saw it as a threat against the U.S. government; mentally, he went totally into fear, heart fibrillations and near cardiac arrest. And it turns out, with 9-11, that the content of the collage, in fact, came true — an artistic prophesy. And the premise of our case was correct. Everything was wrong with the security of the building. Just as the police riot tape exposed the collapse of order in the police department, this collage exposed a totally inept security system at a federal building. As in the riot tape, I was blamed — kill the messenger. The Judge and the federal prosecutor said my collage was a threat against the U.S. Government, but — it was not a threat, — it was a warning which was ignored. The Judge went on to say that all of my collages must be destroyed. I should not be allowed to hand in another paper. This was serious censorship. This was no hillbilly art show, this was a federal court case.

The judge had me escorted out of the building. This was about 1998, five years after the 1993 World Trade Center bombing. This was an open, public courthouse, and I was not allowed to be there. I wasn't screaming obscenities;, I was doing something that was on a piece of paper. The judge was destroying court documents. A lot of the things that I've done have created real havoc within the system. In a number of my court cases the Corporation Council said that I was an excellent provocateur and used that as propaganda against me. I look at that federal court collage as an artwork that's important, made noise, and woke people up. And of course, I made and handed in a follow-up collage that included a burnt flag with bullet holes symbolizing the judge's lack of understanding dealing with the security collapse. And then we had 9-11. Elsa and I were documenting at 7 World Trade Center during the air attack and mass murder of our friends and neighbors. Elsa suffered a concussion, a torn rotator cuff, an injured wrist, and serious shock on this dreadful day. I still feel like going back into that courthouse and shoving that court paper into the faces of the federal judge and the prosecutor. — They were wrong, — period. The arrogance and ignorance of elitist power.

The court papers are content/concept. The papers are highly eccentric and unusual because of the format, probably one of the strangest court papers ever handed in. There are three parts to the papers. One is the art, which is on the cover and the art speaks to the subject at hand, the written part which is the main theme, and the photographs that give another kind of interpretation, three totally different ways of dealing with the same concept.

In 1992 cops told a *Newsday* reporter that I had videotaped the Rakowitz murder and that I was a satanist; they then used the newspaper article as their basis to obtain a search warrant. Two detectives came to my house looking for a tape which had never existed. I had nothing to do with this or any other murder.

Lawyers, you really have to kick 'em to make 'em move or you need to have a lot of press. I also found the NYACLU to be a useless organization who made compromises and defended a system and individuals they knew to be corrupt. This, of course is the role of a defense lawyer, but it is not what is expected of an organization allegedly based on a broader social consciousness.

Political lawyers, Kunstler, Maddox, Mason, Sharpton, Lynne Stewart, Ron Kuby, Stanley Cohen, Michael Kennedy, I had them all. The strongest, the most supportive, I felt were Lynn Stewart, and Alton Maddox. Al Sharpton was the best, the brightest and the bravest, and one of the most committed in dealing with police brutality. I'm winding off cases from that period. I've gone to court for over 17 years. I had more videotapes used in court than anybody else in the history of America.

436

As an editor, Clayton had a difficult time assembling the texts for this book. People moved on, can't get it together, and have myriad reasons not to put something in. Maybe it is that those who can stand on the front lines, exhort the rabble, scream at the cops and "take a bust" again and again are special — it's a skill, a talent. And for some, revolutionary provocation is a vocation with few opportunities for expression. These just may not be the kind of people who can years later endure the pangs of recollection and face their own history.

Alan Moore thanks Michael Carter for editorial assistance and Richard Singer for transcription. Thanks to Allan Antliff for his deep understanding of the anarchist project. Clayton Patterson's words are from interviews by Alan Moore, an unidentified interviewer, and from e-mailed interviews with Allan Antliff, Alan Moore and Sarah Ferguson.

Endnotes:

1. Other artists have found their work unexpectedly — or predictably — joined to law, like the Guerrilla Art Action Group (see *Guerrilla Art Action Group, GAAG The Guerrilla Art Action Group* (Printed Matter, NY 1978)).

2. On D-I-Y economics, anarchism and punk see Graig O'Hara, *The Philosophy of Punk: More than Just Noise!* (AK Press: Edinburgh, 1999).

3. Deirdre Boyle, *Subject to Change: Guerrilla Television Revisited* (Oxford University Press, NY, 1997).

4. Many others produced cable TV shows for Manhattan Cable's public access. Prominent among the wild variety of NYC cable producers who followed legendary breast-voyeur Ugly George into the public eye are Lannes Kenfield with Tuli Kupferberg and Coca Crystal, Mitch Corber, Rik Little, Dave Channon, and today Doug Kelley and Penny Arcade. These were joined by collectives like Potato Wolf, Communications Update and the long running Paper Tiger.

Chapter 2

Trial and Error
By Elsa Rensaa

TRIAL and ERROR
INDEX No. 99/114572

In July 1998, Clayton Patterson was arrested for trespassing, disorderly conduct and he was subsequently charged with three counts of second-degree assault on three police officers. We raised bail and paid a hefty legal fee to defend the assault charges, which were dropped after Clayton proceeded with a civil lawsuit against the City of New York. The following is an excerpt from a letter I wrote to Judge Jaffe who presided over Clayton's civil jury trial in 2004. Since March 2006, I've had the opportunity to watch the Moussaoui trial, reflect, and compare what happened to Clayton, who is my partner of 35 years.

One Police Plaza[1]

In 1998, Clayton and I had attended the annual auction of city owned properties at One Police Plaza with two business associates who bought a vacant lot in Brooklyn that day. There had been a good deal of outrage and protest over several community gardens cultivated in abandoned city owned lots that were also to be auctioned. Television and newspaper stories appeared on the days before the pending sales. We knew that sales of the gardens would cause a protest. PS 64, a Lower East Side public school abandoned by the City for years, was also up for grabs. Renamed "Charas," it was an artist space and creative center run by local Puerto Ricans. We were early, one of the first in line, because the middle-aged perspective buyers who accompanied us wanted to secure a seat close to the front of the auditorium. Outside, one large noisy group, some dressed like plants or flowers and holding skyscrapers drawn on foamcore boards had gathered, playing musical instruments, distributing posters, waving banners and chanting "Don't bid on the Gardens" while another group chanted, "Don't bid on Charas."

Not wanting to disrupt the auction, the Charas leadership did not continue protesting inside. Clayton, as he always does, took a few photographs outside. Although we knew some of the protesters, we had no idea what they'd planned; neither Clayton nor I was connected in any way with the Garden's Movement or this protest. We went inside and, after sending our cameras through the conveyor magnetometer, under the watchful eyes of police inspectors, we took seats in the third row front. The auditorium was divided into right, middle and left sections, like a theater, and it quickly filled up with standing room only at the back. An hour or so into the auction, when bidding came up on community gardens, pandemonium ensued after people began screaming and standing on their chairs several rows behind us. Someone had released live crickets under the seats in many locations throughout the auditorium. Those with cameras, including Clayton and me, walked around videotaping and taking photos. Clayton had no idea who'd caused this action until later, after he and some of the "cricket people" were incarcerated in the 5th Precinct. Officers with brooms and plastic bags

437

438

picked up the crickets. After documenting this chaos, we sat down and the auction contin-ued. When bidding for "Charas" came up, a well-known East Village activist and artist-cartoonist began false bidding to jam the process. He later said that he was merely asked to leave the building, despite an earlier announcement that anyone interfering with bidding would be arrested.

As the auction continued, Lt. Richard Herndon, a white shirt, appeared briefly on my video-tape pointing Clayton out to two fellow officers: PO Hayward and PO Elizabeth Castro, who can be seen brusquely leaning over spectators in front of us. Hayward pointed his finger at me while speaking to Clayton and told him: "Stop filming unless you have a valid press pass." However, I happened to be the person who was actually holding the camera and he never said a word to me. I could have continued videotaping, as this clearly was not about me. Yet, Clayton said, "Turn the camera off." And I did. Suddenly, Lieutenant Herndon popped out of nowhere and told Clayton, "I want to talk to you outside."

We left the auditorium walking in front of Herndon with the camera still turned off. Halfway to the exit, when Herndon became aggressive, Clayton said, "Turn on the camera." It had been off for exactly one minute and fourteen seconds. Herndon began shoving Clayton from behind toward the entrance lobby that was divided by a retractable belt barri-cade.

"I thought you wanted to talk to me?" Clayton asked as Herndon lifted the catch, pushed Clayton through into the lobby, reattached it to the pole, turned and walked away. Clayton then said rather loudly to Herndon's back, "You said you wanted to talk to me?"

Without a word, Herndon turned, walked back past the barricade, and shoved Clayton roughly across the lobby into the revolving door. Officer Castro escorted me out the door, so I began to videotape through the windows. Clayton did a three-sixty around the revolv-ing door, but stopped short of entering the building. Herndon grabbed Clayton from behind in an illegal chokehold, dragging him out of the revolving door, and said to Clayton, "You're going down."

PO Herndon motioned to three short female officers who began pulling at Clayton from behind as he held on to papers in one hand, his other hand on the metal bar in the revolv-ing door to keep from falling over, and his camera bouncing around his neck. Clayton was never told that he was under arrest. I was outside but could see in. Herndon then fixated on me and tried to block my (video camera) view by standing in front of me; if I moved so did he. When I tried to come into the building, another officer blocked me; so I continued to videotape through the glass. The video shows the lobby filled with at least ten officers, including two who had just entered through the revolving door. They rushed Clayton in what looked like a football pile up -all on top of Clayton. Remarkably, Clayton was not critically injured, although he hurt his hand, had neck problems for some years after and the camera around his neck was broken. Several officers claimed injury, some claimed to have gone to the hospital.

We had the right to be at this public auction and were not disrupting anything — no other documentarians were restricted from photographing this event. There were no signs or written instructions requiring "valid press credentials." Special events telecast from Police Headquarters always display people freely taking photographs and our cameras were inspected and permitted without comment. This was simply the police response to the cricket incident in which we were not participants. It was 1998, five years after the first World Trade Center attack, so we assumed those in charge of security at Police Headquarters understood their jobs.

Ten years before, on August 6-7th 1988, Officer Herndon was then a supervisor with Brooklyn Highway Unit 2, stationed at Tompkins Square Park. He claimed to have sat on his motorcycle inside the park most of the night (while chaos was raging on the streets). Two officers under Herndon's supervision, PO Giglia and PO Gatto, were indicted for criminal assault on a bystander during the riot, after being identified on Clayton's videotape beating and kicking the man. PO Herndon, as the Highway Unit 2 Supervisor at Tompkins Square was no doubt called during the Giglia and Gatto investigation and trials and must have seen Clayton's 1988 videotape. However, under oath, before the jury in Clayton's civil trial, Lieutenant Herndon denied knowing Clayton at all. It is impossible that Herndon did not see ANY of these newspaper articles about Clayton:

08.21.1988	NY Daily News	Twana Team in Park Case (photo of Clayton, Sharpton and Maddox)
08.14.1988	NY Times	Tompkins Sq.: Provocation and Violence
09.01.1988	NY Times	Man Held for Not Giving Jury Tompkins Sq. Tape (photo of Clayton)
09.02.1988	NY Post	Defiant Tompkins Riot Photog Busted (photo of Clayton)
09.02.1988	NY Newsday	Man Arrested Over Tape of Park Melee
09.02.1988	NY Times	Grand Jury Denied Videotape
09.04.1988	NY Times	Artist With Tape of Melee Faults Prosecutor
09.07.1988	NY Times	Man Jailed for Refusing To Give Up Melee Tape (photo of Clayton)
09.07.1988	NY Post	Park Riot Photog Jailed for Contempt (photo of Clayton)
09.14.1988	NY Magazine	7 Days in New York Person of the Week (photo of Clayton)
09.14.1988	NY Newsday	Accord on Park Tape (photo of Clayton)
09.14.1988	NY Post	Tompkins Riot Fotog Freed Must Hand Over Tape (photo of Clayton)
09.24.1988	NY Daily News	Tale of the Tompkins Tape (photo of Clayton)
09.17.1988	NY Times	Artist Surrenders Videotape of Clash in Tompkins Sq
09.17.1988	NY Post	Riot Photog in Tape Deal
09.23.1988	NY Post	Not in the Bronx
09.19.1988	NY Newsday	He Gave Up His Liberty Over a Videotape (photo of Clayton)
09.21.1988	Downtown	The Clayton Patterson Case (photo of Clayton)
10.03.1988	City Week	The Conscience of Tompkins Square? Page 1-10 (photos of Clayton)
12.00.1988	Spy Magazine	Naked City - The Fine Print
12.15.1988	NY Times	2 Policemen (Giglia and Gatto) Are Indicted in Park Melee
12.15.1988	NY Post	2 Cops (Giglia and Gatto) Indicted in Tompkins Sq. Riot
12.15.1988	NY Daily News	2 Cops Indicted in Riot (Giglia and Gatto)
04.19.1989	NY Times	17 Officers Named in Tompkins Sq. Riot (includes Giglia

A Radical Political and Social History of the Lower East Side

		and Gatto)
05.23.1989	NY Newsday	Part II The Squatter Wars Front Cover (large photo of Clayton)
07.00.1989	NY Post	Man Arrested At City Hall (photo of Clayton)
08.07.1989	NY Post	6 Arrested in Tompkins Anniversary Protest
09.01.1989	NY Newsday	Front Cover New York Newsday (photo of Clayton)
09.02.1989	NY Post	Cops Bust Activist Fotog At Riot (full page photo of Clayton)
09.26.1989	NY Times	Seeking the Truth Amid a Chorus of Video Voices (photo of Clayton)
10.02.1989	NY Newsday	Accidental Newsmen On the Scene (photo of Clayton)
07.25.1990	NY Post	Video Witness of Tompkins Square will Roll the Tapes (photo of Clayton)

Newspapers, often with Clayton's picture, continued to cover events at Tompkins Square for years. Clayton appeared on many local news channels as well as Oprah Winfrey, Sally Jesse Raphael, Gerardo Rivera, and CNN.

Because Clayton's 1988 videotape was the main item of evidence, Clayton was subpoenaed to attend several criminal and civil trials. After the dust had settled, the City was forced to pay Tompkins Square victims in excess of 2.2 million dollars. Bob Arihood, kicked and beaten by the Brooklyn Highway 2 officers on Officer Herndon's watch, received $300,000.00.

Clayton was vocal about police brutality. Whenever he showed up at a police action, cops immediately recognized him, pointed him out to other officers and made comments about him, some positive but most were negative. Cops like to gossip within their own closed society and Clayton was high profile in that circle for some years. It's obvious that Herndon knew exactly who Clayton was when he forcibly evicted him from the auction in July 1998.

Fast-forward to Clayton's false-arrest trial against the City on October 22-29, 2004.

Herndon was in charge of the 1998 auction and he deliberately singled Clayton out: "I want to talk to you outside." No other person taking pictures or video, with or without a press pass, was made to leave. In his depositions and again in court, Herndon came up with the most bizarre reason to explain why he removed Clayton from the auditorium on the pretext of "speaking to him outside." Herndon swore under oath that:

> There came a time when I noticed Mr. Patterson sitting there and between his leg was a brown manila envelope with crickets coming out of the envelope. I walked over to Mr. Patterson and I fairly noticed his feet, both his left foot and right foot shoelaces were tied to the chair. I am saying to myself, people don't tie their shoestrings to the chair. I asked him how his shoes got tied. I begged another officer to come over. We had to cut the shoestrings and have Mr. Patterson leave. I told him on several occasions to leave the building.[2]

A year before, on May 5, 2003, in his CCRB report in response to the complaint made by Clayton, Herndon said "First thing, I guess that he was sitting down letting live crickets out from a manila envelope that were all over him and all over the floor. He was tied to the chair, believe his main function was to disrupt the proceeding, which he did. So we untied him and we escorted him out the door.

Of course, there was no collaborative testimony of this occurrence, no other officer saw this, nor was there any physical evidence of the "manila envelope" or the "cut shoelaces," because NONE OF THIS HAPPENED. In fact, PO Castro and I were both standing inches away from Clayton the entire time; and when asked specifically about it in her 2003 deposition, Castro said: "*I did not see if Clayton had tied his sneaker shoelace to the chair.*"[3] Castro failed to appear at the trial, so her deposition was read in her absence. Neither she nor any other officer saw the shoe incident, as it did not happen to Clayton. In my videotape, both of Clayton's shoes are on, with laces intact, as he's walking out of the auditorium, and they were still on when he was arrested. That's because Herndon actually approached Clayton AFTER the crickets had been removed and order had long been restored. He simply couldn't think of any other plausible reason for losing it on Clayton that day.

For his day at the auction, Clayton was charged with resisting arrest, trespassing, disorderly conduct and three counts of assaulting an officer, a second-degree felony; each count brought a sentence of two to seven years, so times three equals six years minimum or twenty one years maximum. The three counts of assault made us seek expensive legal advice. Had it not been for having to raise bail and expensive lawyers fees, Clayton may have just let this whole event pass.

The trial began ten years after the Mollen Commission gave NYPD another black eye, as had the 1971 Knapp Commission over Frank Serpico. Until the Mollen Commission, Clayton had been outspoken about the relationship between the police and street drug sales that proliferated in plain sight on the Lower East Side. The 9th precinct, where many Lower East Side protests took place, had its own chapter in the final Commission report. But Clayton's trial was three years after 9-11, so NYPD had a newly found supportive public, not inclined to question police authority. Our lawyer, Myron Beldock, had a reputation as a winner among his peers. I thought there might be some hope. During my sojourn on the "bench," outside the courtroom waiting for my turn to testify, I overheard a passing lawyer say, "Although not well known, Mr. Beldock is often cited by other lawyers." In retrospect, I have no idea why Beldock asked me to attend court everyday and sit in the cold damp narrow hallway. He should have had some inkling as to when I would be called. Sitting there idiotically, I was put in a psychologically disadvantaged position with the jury who looked down on me as they frequently left and entered the court. I also ended up with a case of shingles.

The Jury

Unfortunately, Mr. Beldock's selection of Clayton's jury fell short of his reputation. Clayton had asked to participate in the selection process, but somehow that did not happen. One juror had the same family name as the main defendant and, although she swore no relationship, a Google search turned up only seventy-eight people in all of New York State with the same name. We felt that she should not have been selected.

442

Clayton is a recognizable figure, looking a little eccentric with gold teeth, his baseball cap embroidered with skulls, and his long hair and goatee. Because Clayton is a street photographer, dealing with loads of people, he's familiar with those who react negatively to him and those who can identify with him. Beldock chose people with whom Beldock felt personally comfortable. The City attorney liked the same people, so the jury mainly consisted of young professionals: a teacher, an investment banker, an advertising sales rep, a lab technician, and an airport ramp worker. Most jury members appeared to be in the upper socio-economic bracket. Clayton would not have chosen any of them, excepting the airport ramp worker. From the outset, this was not Clayton's jury.

When Mr. Beldock remarked to us after the verdict, "I guess the jury didn't like you," it really meant that Beldock had no empathy for Clayton, and absolutely no understanding of who Clayton was. As we left Court, Clayton told me that he was appalled by Beldock's immediate reaction, thought Beldock weak for passing the buck when it had been Beldock's job to make Clayton look good. Why blame Clayton? I wondered. We had very few meetings, and usually met with Beldock's paralegals in the office. Beldock was not really prepared to present Clayton to this jury. He blamed us for his quick loss. I always fretted why Officer Hayward was never deposed. I considered him the most important witness and the leading instigator acting in concert with Herndon against Clayton. From the beginning, Beldock claimed that Hayward was out of the country, unavailable, or that NYPD was unable to identify him; although he was seen clearly on my video. Beldock did not pursue this.

While attempting to put Clayton in a bad light, corporation counsel DePugh accused him of using lawsuits against NYPD as a form of protest. But when an officer harms you physically, and ruins your property, should you stand outside the precinct screaming insults, or sue for justice? What option does one have in dealing with the government? Suing is the only way to rectify injury, wrongful arrest or harassment. Court actions are not good on cops' records, if they want to advance, especially if the City has to pay money. A corporation counsel once said that if a cop costs the city more then $100,000.00, chances are, he will be "retired."

Clayton was once arrested with a Nikon camera; an officer took off the lens, tore out the internal curtain and mirror with a metal object, and put the lens back on so it looked ok. We sued the City in Small Claims Court and won, no questions asked. There was a visible fingerprint on the inside of the lens, but no officer wanted to find out whose it was. Also, contrary to DePugh's accusation, Clayton does not complain or go to a doctor unless he has sustained a serious injury, and he has never faked one. Clayton did not sue the City after the police riot, even though lawyers made it very easy to submit injury claims.

Still, the problem at Clayton's false arrest trial was not with lawyers or the cops, as much it was with two of the jurors.

Friday, October 29, 2004 PROCEEDINGS[4]

COURT OFFICER:　The juror wants to speak with you.

THE COURT:　　Juror No. 2, Ms. _____. Now, Ms. _____, I've been informed by

	the court officer that you have a problem with Monday, tell me what is going on.
JUROR NO. 2:	My mom has kidney cancer. She is coming back here to visit with the neurologist and oncologist. She is coming Monday for pre-opt screening and blood work. So that is on Monday and then she is having her kidneys removed the following Tuesday.
THE COURT:	I am very sorry to hear that and I hope she is better. Is it at all possible for you to come Monday in the afternoon, maybe after the appointment?
JUROR NO. 2:	The appointment is 9:30. By the time I go there and bring her back home, I guess after lunch.
THE COURT:	Attorneys, Juror No. 2, as you know we are going to very shortly start summations and jury charge, hopefully, we will see what happens. If we have to go in to Monday, we will of course start later in the day.
JUROR NO. 2:	That will be helpful.
THE COURT:	Really, are you sure you could devote your undivided attention?
JUROR NO. 2	Yes.
THE COURT:	I appreciate your willingness and spirit. We all wish your mother the best. (The Juror exits the courtroom.)
THE COURT:	It will be good if you hold off on objecting. Just be judicious on your objections on that score. We will bring the Jury in.
COURT OFFICER:	We have another Juror. (She follows IMMEDIATELY after Juror No. 2 has finished speaking to the Judge).
THE COURT:	Ms. _____. Do you want to tell me something?
JUROR NO. 5:	I have my engagement party. I have a plane to catch. I have people coming in from all over the country.
THE COURT:	I wish I had learned about this earlier.
JUROR NO. 5:	They said it was going to be over yesterday.
THE COURT:	I told the jury by the end of business, Friday. What time do you have to leave?
JUROR NO. 5:	I have to catch a 5:30 shuttle.
THE COURT:	And you have to leave at what time?
JUROR NO. 5:	4:15.
THE COURT:	We will have to do it.
COURT OFFICER:	All rise. Jury entering. (Jury enters the courtroom.)

On Monday, Juror No. 2's mother was traveling here to visit with her neurologist and oncologist in a condition described by Juror No. 2 as complete kidney failure. Was she really having BOTH her kidneys removed on Tuesday? I used to watch Juror No. 2 and Juror No. 5 walking together in the hall, sitting on the benches, talking during recesses, or waiting to enter the courtroom. It was really strange that they both needed to be excused at exactly the same time on the same day. Why hadn't Juror No. 5 said anything to the judge about her engagement party? At the end of the day, on Thursday, Judge Jaffe told the jury, "We will see you tomorrow at 9:45."[5]

Jurors Nos. 2 and 5 could have said something on Thursday, or at 9:45 on Friday morning, but they opted to approach the Judge, just before summations later on Friday, one

444

immediately after the other. Not only did Juror No. 2 not devote her undivided attention to the trial, as she swore before the Judge, but even BEFORE deliberations began, she reportedly stated in the jury room, "I know what I think, I'm getting antsy about being here and I can't be here on Monday. I have to be `somewhere else' on Monday." She didn't mention her mother to the other jurors at all. Juror No. 1 picking up on the pessimistic vibe in the jury room remarked, "Yeah, it's a sham."

Summations: Friday, October 29, 2004

DePugh's summation lasted one hour and Beldock was finished at 1:30 PM. Beldock's part-ner spoke for an additional twenty minutes. After the luncheon recess, the jury was charged and deliberations commenced at 3:40 PM. This left Juror No. 5 barely enough time to make her engagement party, and she was stressed.

The verdict sheet contained 62 questions, structured so that jurors were required to answer only seven questions relating to four issues: excessive force, the legality of plaintiff's arrest, the legality of plaintiff's expulsion, and malicious prosecution:

1. Was plaintiff Clayton Patterson subjected to excessive use of force in violation of his Fourth Amendment rights?

12. Was plaintiff Clayton Patterson subjected to the use of unnecessary or exces-sive use of force during his arrest?

22. Was plaintiff Clayton Patterson unlawfully arrested in violation of his Fourth Amendment rights?

29. Was plaintiff Clayton Patterson falsely arrested?
36. Was plaintiff Clayton Patterson deprived of his constitutional rights to free-dom of assembly and speech?

41. Was plaintiff Clayton Patterson prosecuted maliciously in violation of his Fourth Amendment rights?

52. Was plaintiff Clayton Patterson prosecuted maliciously?[6]

Judge Jaffe suggested substituting Juror Nos. 2 and Juror 5 for two alternates, but Beldock and DePugh objected to discharging either juror, agreeing to suspend deliberations at 4:00 PM until Monday at 2:30 PM, in order to accommodate the two jurors. Judge Jaffe did offer alternates, but it seems that Beldock underestimated "his jury." He failed to understand that they wanted to leave and Justice and Deliberations meant nothing to them.

Deliberations Friday, October 29, 3:40 PM

After Judge Jaffe read the jury instructions, deliberations began and the jurors were in and out of the Courtroom in 13 minutes! Wow!! 13 minutes!!!

This was a jury who had sworn not to discuss the case before deliberation began, but had already said it was a sham.

3 minutes to stand up and walk single file into the jury room.

2 minutes to sit down and pass papers.

2 minutes to deliberate (deliberate means long careful consideration).

Were these people all speed-readers who understood all aspects of the law? Did they comprehend beforehand the significance of each of those 62 questions, or was it easier to check "no" on seven boxes?

6 minutes to gather papers, put on coats, leave the jury room, sit down in their chairs, pass the forms to the clerk who passed them to the Judge who read the verdict, be questioned individually by the Judge and walk out of the court room single file.

The jurors did not have time to read or discuss the questions, but automatically checked the boxes that allowed Juror No. 2 and Juror No. 5 to leave immediately.

If Jurors Nos. 1, 3, 4, and 6 had any input at all it was not reflected by their "deliberations."

Obviously, the jury did not deliberate AT ALL.

"After they learn their ABC's whose going to teach them to think?"

Friday, October 29, 2004 6:30 PM

Following the verdict, in a really unusual move, alternate Juror No. 10 left a message on our answering machine that she disagreed with the verdict. She contacted Beldock and gave an affidavit, saying, "She "was surprised and upset by the short time the jury was out before announcing a verdict. While the jurors were assembled in the jury room, she heard Juror No. 2 say that she was "getting antsy about being there, that she couldn't be there on Monday and that she had to be somewhere else on Monday." The Juror expressed anger about having to return to court on Monday, and said that if she had known it would go on so long, she would have said something about it at voir dire. The juror also complained that the trial was supposed to have been over by Thursday and that now it might be Monday. She wondered aloud about what the timing would be if the jury were to deliberate on Friday, and stated that if deliberations were to commence on Friday, she did not think it would take her long, adding that "I know what I think." Juror No. 1 (who Judge Jaffe had elected to preside in the jury room) then said, "Yeah, it's a sham." Juror No. 5 said that she had to be in Boston on Friday evening. Several jurors, including alternate Juror No. 10, then advised Juror No. 5 about how best to reach Boston on a Friday evening. According to Juror No. 10's affidavit, there was absolutely NO way Juror No. 2 planned to return at all on Monday even though she told Judge Jaffe that she would.[7]

We have great respect for what Juror No. 10 did; it took real conviction on her part. Most people would not have bothered. The jury's decision was the "sham" and a complete disregard of the jury concept and the legal system.

I'd like to compare the manner in which Clayton's jury was handled with the Moussaoui trial that we watched on CCTV at the Federal Court Building on Pearl Street. Moussaoui's trial followed all the rules by optimum standards because it was heavily scrutinized. On 9-11, after

A Radical Political and Social History of the Lower East Side

the first plane hit, Clayton and I went to the World Trade Center feeling it was important to be there. We were beside 7 WTC when Tower 2 started to crumble and roar towards the ground, and in the ensuing panic I was knocked down. I suffered a concussion, a cracked eye-socket, an injured wrist, had a large lump below my eye, and I tore a rotator cuff, requiring an operation that has taken my shoulder years to return to normal. As survivors we were encouraged to attend the Moussaoui trial.

Judge Brinkema's Instructions to Moussaoui's Jury:

A jury theoretically represents all the people of the United States. It is their sworn duty to consider the evidence received without bias or sympathy and to seek the truth from the evidence presented.

Jurors are to:

Listen to each other while deliberating and to consult with each other and decide the case after considering all the evidence not for the mere purpose of making a decision.

Compare notes of testimony either written or from memory. This is one of a juror's greatest assets.

Take into account the credibility of testimony of each witness and the weight it deserves: was all of the testimony, some of the testimony, or none of the testimony credible?

You must consider all the testimony of all the witnesses. Examine each witness as to his/her tendency to falsify, and his or her tendency to favor one side or the other, and to his or her relationship to each side.

Test the accuracy of the memory of each witness based upon the evidence.
When filling out jury forms:

Examine the facts and evidence with reason and fair consideration.

Evaluate the testimony by the quality not the quantity of the evidence.

Do not be swayed by the speech or action of the attorneys.

Do not discuss this case with each other, with the press or with people outside.

Judge Brinkema told the jurors to elect one member to preside in the jury room.

Judge Jaffe chose Juror No. 1 to preside. I think this was a mistake; an appointee has less power and culpability than someone who has been elected from within the group. It merely served to speed up deliberating.

In light of Judge Brinkema's articulate description of how a jury should review a case, I was shocked that Judge Jaffe went along with the jury who complied with NONE of the above guidelines.

Overturning the decision required all kinds of extra work and proving that it was based only on getting Juror No. 2 and Juror No. 5 out of there as soon as possible, without deliberating, for personal reasons having absolutely nothing to do with the issues of the trial. Beldock immediately appealed but so much for the letter and the spirit of the Law!

Judge Brinkema's jury deliberated. Judge Jaffe's jury did not!

Having lived through this experience, I believe that capital punishment should be abolished. How many innocent people have been executed because the jury is already brain dead, could care less, or simply wanted to leave and the Judge went along with them. This trial was more about the personal needs of two jurors than it was about the case. The verdict was reached for all the wrong reasons. When Juror No. 1 was leaving the courtroom, post verdict, he made a gesture at Clayton, as if he was boxing, and said, "Keep up the fight."

THIS WAS ONE OF THE SHORTEST VERDICTS IN HISTORY!!!!!

Should we contact the Guinness Book of World Records?

Endnotes:

1. One Police Plaza is the New York City Police Department headquarters, housing a large main floor auditorium where official police ceremonies, graduations or presentations of medals are held. Certain city auctions are also held there.

2. 10.27.04 Direct-Herndon-DePugh p 555 lines 22-25, p 556 lines 2-12

3. 10.28.04 Castro Deposition Reading p 749 lines 2-4

4. 10.29.04 PROCEEDINGS p. 807 line 17 to p. 810 line 3

5. 10.28.04 p. 794 lines 4-5

6. 10.20.05 Decision and Order on Motion to Set Aside Verdict p 6

7. 10.20.05 Decision and Order on Motion to Set Aside Verdict p 7

Chapter 3

Guerrilla Video and the Battle of Tompkins Square Park
By Richard Porton

Written in 1990

"... The Big City has hot cobblestones
Despite your showers of petrol
And decidedly we have to
Shake you up in the roles you play ... "

Arthur Rimbaud
"Chant de guerre parisien"
(May 1871)

One of our wittiest journalists has recently observed that "these days, all art aspires to the condition of real estate."[1] While it is not difficult to concede that Steven Spielberg's films have become the cinematic equivalent of Trump Tower, the same sort of aesthetic gentrification is apparent in the tendency of even the supposedly "oppositional" realm of the avant-garde to be sucked into the high priced real estate of gallery "spaces" and public television. Clayton Patterson's compelling video document, Tompkins Square Park Police Riot, can be cited as an intriguing counter-example.

Patterson's work is as divorced from the machinations of the art world as it is alien to the infinitely recuperable concerns of commercial cinema. Patterson has been referred to as a "videographer," and his nearly four hour video chronicle of what might be considered an embryonic "urban revolution," cannot be facilely assigned to any one of the by now moldy subdivisions of political documentary. Patterson's tape, however unwittingly, explodes Louis Marcorelles' distinction between American direct cinema's rather naive appeal to authenticity, and the quasi-Brechtian strategies of directors such as Rouch.[2] The tape shares direct cinema's concern with immediacy and the contours of the "life world," but Patterson's low-key, but still apparent, participation in the spirit of communal solidarity as a member of the Lower Fast Side community is far different from the anthropological detachment of filmmakers such as Pennebaker and Leacock.

To invoke an old manifesto, Patterson is "neither a leader nor a bystander but part of the struggle," and his unwillingness to hide behind a veil of objectivity or passionlessness makes his work a synthesis of direct cinema's concern with documentation and the Rouch-Godard tradition of committed reflexivity. Nineteenth century writers such as Henry Mayhew, and recent documentarians such as Frederick Wiseman, have attempted to explicate urban strife from the clinical perspective of the outsider.[3] Patterson's tape is distinctive in that it is the work of a community activist who documents the ongoing struggles over homelessness and corporate greed (the most recent fruits of what has been called the 'recapitalization of the city') without the condescension of the traditional participant-observer.

The unedited version of Tompkins Square Park Police Riot exemplifies the seriousness of Patterson's political commitment, since the use of real time (the camera was turned off only when the necessity to change tapes arose) is not a product of a dogmatic insistence to capture the nuances of lived experience, but of a pragmatic desire to recount the truly marathon nature of the city's assault on its own citizens.

The videographer's compulsion to immerse himself in struggle makes him vulnerable to the police aggression that he is chronicling. and Aa police assault on fellow video artist Paul Garrin is, in fact, depicted in Patterson's tape. Nonetheless, since a three hour and forty five 45 minute tape can prove unwieldy for exhibition at certain gatherings, two abridged versions of ninety 90 and twenty five 25 minutes, respectively, have been edited by Elsa Patterson. Although these briefer versions present highlights of the tumultuous evening in a manner that approaches a lucid narrative, the fact that the Tompkins Square bloodshed was not a brief, somewhat transitory event, but the result of a lengthy operation to transform a neighborhood into a kind of 'strategic hamlet' using counterinsurgency techniques, is minimized in the shorter versions.[4]

Ironically enough, if East Village art gleefully embraces its status as high-priced real estate, Patterson's tape, as ingenuously artful as any *Art in America*[5] sanctioned gallery product, has been reduced by the courts, the FBI, and the police to the status of documentary chattel. Although both the local police and the FBI eventually made copies of the tape, Patterson has been subjected to a barrage of subpoenas from the local U.S. attorney in an attempt (which has so far been successfully resisted) to coerce him to relinquish the tape's master as well as his video camera.

The supposed logic of what Patterson himself believes is a "scam" to destroy evidence (as of this writing [1990] not one of the victims of the now notorious night of police carnage has received any compensation) is extremely muddled. The Court has put forward the outrageous pretext that the transfer of video from master to copy results in a thirty five 35 per cent loss in definition. Although the Court almost certainly views the "riot tape" as an object that can be impounded and tampered with at will, Patterson is mounting a defense which quite legitimately claims that his rights as an artist are being violated by the heavy-handed attempts of the local authorities to seize a document that can be deemed both evidence and aesthetic artifact.

This confusion of realms — the conflict between bad faith legalistic maneuvers and the anti-hierarchical aims of community video — can be viewed as a curious rehash of the Frankfurt School debates concerning the schism between classical bourgeois art, and a more recent "post auratic" reproducible variant. If Judge Alfred Kleiman and the other local authorities who have continued to harass Patterson refuse to acknowledge that Tompkins Square Park

A Radical Political and Social History of the Lower East Side

Police Riot is art, their conception of what can be deemed mechanically reproducible art is undoubtedly confined to photographs and tapes displayed at museums or galleries.
Yet an "original" tape is nonetheless fetishized, although the idea of trying to determine police badge numbers (or any other damning visual evidence that could conceivably be culled from an exceptionally sharp image) is as far from the minds of the local authorities as any desire for disinterested aesthetic contemplation. Jurgen Habermas has observed that "as long as avant-garde art is not completely deprived of its semantic content . . . it strengthens divergence between the values offered by the socio-cultural systems and those demanded by the political and economic systems."[6] While Patterson's determination to chronicle community activism on the Lower East Side is antithetical to the goals of the "culture industry," his interventionist aesthetic is far different from the autonomous "art traditionally promoted by the avant-garde. Community video is neither mass culture nor "bohemianism" (to use Habermas' rather simplistic term for twentieth 20th-century avant-garde tendencies), but it certainly promotes a type of documentary practice that marks a sharp divergence from the ideologies of the "political and economic systems."

Before examining the tape in any detail, it is necessary to contextualize the events of August 6 and 7, 1988, since what ensued that evening, as well as the polemics that followed, have become linked to a constellation of tendencies such as "anarchism," squatting, and punk which have been much maligned by the mainstream press and need to be differentiated from each other.

Local television newsman Mike Taibbi and The *New York Times* have lost little time in claiming that "anarchists" (and by implication anarchism) were responsible despite obvious abuses of police power for the bloody outcome of the Tompkins Square Park fracas. While the conclusions of these mainstream journalists seem to have been inspired more by Alice in Wonderland than by careful research, this. denigration of social victims is part of a long urban tradition. After the Tompkins Square "riot" of 1974,[7] an event which was the culmination of the demands of thousands of unemployed workers for public assistance, the leaders of the unemployed committee were branded "Communists," "loud mouth demagogues," and "enemies of society." The imposition of a park curfew served as the catalyst for the 1988 conflict, while the refusal of the police to grant permits for a demonstration inflamed the working class struggles of 1874. Of course, it is worth noting that the earlier police riot was a response to individuals, who had been made "redundant" (to use the British euphemism) by a crisis of production, while the recent police melee victimized many (the homeless and the. marginal), who were made to feel literally redundant by those who wanted to turn the Lower Fast Side into a bohemian Disneyland for yuppie consumption.

Although the banner, "Gentrification is, Class War," expressed a genuine rage and pithily summarized one political viewpoint, class animosities are merely one component of the rage that fuels activism on the Lower East Side. The continuing struggles in the Tompkins Square Park area are, without question, struggles against domination as well as attempts to puncture, however modestly, the logic of capital. The efforts of squatters to reclaim abandoned buildings exemplify the anarchist emphasis on "self-activity," a notion that seeks to prove that individuals are capable of creating autonomous zones, free from the bureaucratic Intervention intervention that characterizes both "liberal" capitalism and state socialism.

This desire for new forms of communal organization recalls the anarchist writer P.M.'s concept of the word "bolo," a re-invention of the familiar ideal of the "intentional community" that, stripped of all vestiges of hippie pastoralism, strives to dismantle the "planetary work-machine." In his manifesto, Bolo=Bolo,[8] P.M. suggests the possibility of international links between local "bolos." Intimations of this sort of communitarian internationalism are apparent in a recent statement by independent dissident groups in Poland that expressed solidarity with the "alternative culture people"[9] who are being harassed in the Tompkins Square Park area.

The type of urban insurrection and self-activity that "boloism" encourages is not entirely new. It is reminiscent of the desire to re-appropriate social space that inspired the French Revolution and the Paris Commune of 1871. The Commune, for example, urged the "permanent intervention of citizens in the communal affairs, by the free expression of their ideas and the free defense of their Interests."— Manuel Castells[10] conclusion that the Commune was not a movement of the industrial proletariat but of an eclectic agglutination of social groups that directed their rage against the gendarme and landlord rather than the corporate boss has echoes in the quintessentially urban tenor of the Tompkins Square Park events. The recent heralding of "Class War," for example, has ambiguous resonances, since it might well refer to a short-lived British sect of the same name which united militant anarchists and punks,[11] as well as to the classical injunction to marshal forces for a "final conflict." The recent anarcho-punk alliance (also evident in West Germany's Autonomen movement), although undoubtedly difficult to grasp for anarcho-syndicalists and anarcho-communists weaned on Bakunin and Kropotkin, points to the fact that contemporary urban movements are something of a 'transclass' phenomenon, at least when viewed from the perspective of both orthodox Marxism and classical anarchism.

All of these currents —radical urbanism, squatting, communal self-activity and the anarcho-punk synthesis —coalesce in a startling and sometimes even comic fashion in Tompkins Square Park Police Riot. The tape provides a remarkably accurate portrait of the ebb and flow of state violence: the sporadic, seemingly spontaneous outbursts are evident, as well as the eerily quiet lulls. Patterson's, lightweight camera is in almost constant motion, and at times we are presented with a frenetic blur of pavement, blue uniforms, horses, and blood. As the tape progresses, several basic patterns of visual choreography emerge. The camera zooms in to capture the impact of police attacks, remains in close-up for the testimony of witnesses, and pans from stone-faced police on horseback to animated demonstrators to illustrate the chasm between an indigenous population and what amounts to an occupying army. The occasional low angle shots (and perpetual drone) of an overhead helicopter reminds the spectator of the programmatic nature of the violence, engendered more by meticulously planned surveillance[12] than by the impetuous errors of judgment invoked by Mayor Koch and Police Commissioner Ward.

The numerous shots of police vans interspersed throughout Patterson's tape are not gratuitous. *The Shadow*, a Lower East Side anarchist newspaper, reported evidence of police mobilization for "trouble" several days before the police riot, proving that while violence from the "bottom up" is often spontaneous, violence ordained "from above" is rarely the result of mere brute instinct. The tape's soundtrack records many of these antithetical currents, The

A Radical Political and Social History of the Lower East Side

demonstrators" slogans — "Hell no, we won't won't go" (the anti-war chant displaced into another context) and "horse Horse shit out of the park" have the quality of incantatory slogans, while the police retorts of "clear Clear the street" and "Do you think this is some fucking game?" seem both impersonal and prefabricated.

When Patterson's camera lingers on individuals rather than crowds, the tone is in sharp contrast to the smart-alecky omniscience of television news. His queries are not part of a pre-determined agenda, but only try to capture the flux of a neighborhood under siege. A bemused man, half shrugging, announces that he's "from Russia." A homeless man named Spider seems shy and vaguely uncomfortable. An anguished woman leans over a stoop and wails "We are so ashamed." Instead of forcing people to provide facile distillations of events, Patterson engages them in dialogue and teams of recent events with the curiosity of a fellow citizen and neighbor. This is particularly true of his encounter with "Tex," a freelance reporter. Tex reports that "an officer made death threats," and was observed remarking that he "would kill" people if they "didn't move." Although Tex is black, he concludes that Mayor Koch allowed citizens, black and white, to be mercilessly bludgeoned. Patterson agrees that "It's not a race issue," and thanks Tex for his assistance. (Although the complex issues that led to the Tompkins Square. Park riot cannot be reduced to merely the dynamics of class, race, and gender, it is surely not coincidental that the majority of the victims of police violence were either blacks or women.)

The atmosphere of both repression and insurrection rather paradoxically leads to festive moments, as if some brief glimpses of the carnival-esque urge to turn the world upside down are deemed necessary to repel the police artillery. After the French Revolution, "festivals of mockery" flourished, mock pageants in which the church and aristocracy were relentlessly ridiculed. Something of the same buoyant disrespect can be discerned as the crowds sing a mangled, parodic version of the "Star-Spangled Banner" and chant "This Land is Your Land." (The New Deal ballad takes on new meanings in what is considered a post-industrial era.) These "patriotic" ditties are reclaimed by individuals who, more often than not, are vilified as "unpatriotic." In the tradition of Situationist detournement, a banner reading "Real Men Don't Eat Quiche" appropriates the faux macho title of a bestseller in order to condemn the quiche-ification of the Lower Fast Side.

An historian of the French Revolution has observed that the task of the revolutionary festival includes "saving the isolated individual from himself . . . and reconstructing a new sacrality."[13] It might seem curious, or even reactionary, to label black anarchist flags and chants of "It's our fucking park" emblems of a new sacrality, but they can nevertheless be regarded as antidotes to the all too secular implements of social control: the billy club and the armored truck. The. clash between demonstrators and police reminds various participants of different sites of urban struggle. One man likens the bloodshed to "Harlem 1966," another bystander compares the police onslaught to "Chicago 1968," while another sees a recapitulation of the French Revolution. The "subjective factor" that comes to the fore during struggles of this sort is capable of both immersing individuals in the event, and allowing them the perspective of this type of impromptu historicization.

While some local residents saw themselves as latter-day sans culottes or, —however hyperbolic it may sound, participants in a "Loisaida intifada," the tape also recounts the attempts of community leaders to defuse the crisis in the name of a bogus pluralism. This yearning for a bland reasonableness is represented in Patterson's tape by the laughably inept attempts of a local priest, Father Kennington, to reach a consensus that proves both elusive and illusory. Kennington claims that "the people who really want this [the riot] are anarchists," and his preoccupation with "cool heads" seems to make him oblivious to the provocation of a massive police presence. (Toward the end of the tape, a protracted shot of a policeman breaking bottles in order to simulate traces of a riotous melee depicts the chaotic inclinations of those who promote order.)

Kennington's contempt for anarchism recalls the calumny heaped upon the left libertarian movement after the Haymarket riot of 1886, while his agitated search for leaders ("Where are the leaders?" is his mournful refrain) belies an ignorance of anarchism's anti-hierarchical impetus. Yet Matthew Courtney, of the performance space ABC No Rio, puts Kennington's vague humanistic mutterings in perspective by pointing out that the volatile atmosphere was not caused by an anarchist cabal, but by high rents and the sudden high-handed imposition of a park curfew. After Kennington's futilely conciliatory talk of meetings at the 'Boys Club' and resolution of differences, the tape seems tinged with inadvertent narrative irony when the subsequent sequences document one of the evening's most savage incidents, the brutal police attack on a local resident named Ken Fish, who continues to suffer what appears to be irreversible brain damage.

The tape concludes with the storming of the lavish Christodora condominium complex, an exercise in spatial voluntarism which is by now a legendary event. The local insurgents do little actual damage to this yuppie refuge; a close-up of an overturned flower pot reveals the extent of the assault's impact. One of the most comically perverse moments in the Christodora sequence occurs when "Rudolph," the well-heeled rock club entrepreneur, incites the crowd to return "every night, every night!" If Rudolph's new-found militancy (which has subsequently remained dormant despite his exhortation) seems symptomatic of the tendency of some social movements to implode into mere spectacle, the tangible suffering caused by the city's policy of total mobilization cannot be forgotten.

Some of this anguish can be observed in a subsequent Patterson tape, Slaughter of the Innocents, in which officials of the Housing Police Department (HPD), demolish a building on East Eighth Street, in which squatters had been living peacefully. The juxtaposition of a distraught woman, Tya Scott, who weeps at the sight of her demolished building and the impassive face of Deputy Inspector Julian (who had supervised the demolition) eloquently sums up the gap between human needs and bureaucratic insensitivity which that continues to plague the Lower East Side community.

Although more than a year has elapsed since Tompkins Square. Park earned a national reputation as an urban battleground, the struggles against police encroachment and the fight for local autonomy continues. If the mass-media — our society's primary mode of ideological reproduction — remains largely impervious to the kind of local struggles personified by the Tompkins Square. events, Clayton Patterson's ongoing efforts as an indefatigable video guerrilla at least help to crack the veneer of the consciousness industry. Despite the attempts of corporate New York and local officials to displace the residents of one of the city's most

A Radical Political and Social History of the Lower East Side

vibrant neighborhoods (the strategy which has become known as "spatial deconcentration"), Patterson's work on behalf of his community, and his passionate belief in the necessity of documenting the city's assault on Lower Manhattan, should prove cause for restrained optimism. It is possible for individuals to work in concert, and begin the task of reclaiming their neighborhoods. As the nineteenth 19th-century geographer Élisée Reclus observed: "Geography is not an immutable thing. It is made, it is remade every day; at each instant, it is modified by men's actions."[14]

Endnotes:

1. Alexander Cockburn, "Sex, Guys, and High Bohemia," *Interview* (September 1989), p. 150

2. Louis Marcorelles, *Living Cinema,* trans. Isabel Ouigley (London: George Allen and Unwin Ltd., 1973).

3. See Deborah Epstein Nord, *"The Social Explorer as Anthropologist: Victorian Travelers Among the Urban Poor,"* in William Sharpe and Leonard Wallock ed., *Visions of the Modern City* (Now York: Proceedings of the Heyman Center of the Humanities, 1982).

4. The complete version was exhibited at several traditionally avant-garde venues in New York namely the Millennium Film Workshop and the Kitchen Center for Music, Video and Dance, but these screenings became opportunities for spectators to acquaint themselves with the indignities of recent history rather than occasions for the usual post-modernist shop talk.

5. For an example of this magazine's cheerleading for the East Village art scene, see Walter & Robinson and Carlo McCormick, "Slouching Toward Avenue D," *Art in America* (esp. p. 138).

6. Jurgen Habermas, *Legitimation Crisis,* trans. Thomas McCarthy (Boston: Beacon. Press, 1975): pg. 86.

7. For a detailed chronicle of the Tompkins Square event see Herbert G. Gutman, "The Tompkins Square 'Riot' in New York City on January 13,1874: A Re-Examination of its Causes and its Aftermath, *Labor History* (Winter 1965).

8. See P.M., *Bolo=Bolo* (New York; Semiotext(e), 1985).

9. See Bob McGlynn, "From Tompkins Square to Gdansk" *Black Eye*, #6, pp. 14-15.

10. Manuel Castells, *The City and the Grassroots*. (Berkeley and Los Angeles: University of California Press, 1983).

11. See Stewart Home, T*he Assault on Culture: Utopian currents from Lettrisme to Class War* (London: Aporia Press and Unpopular Books, 1988), pp. 95-101.

12. See *The Shadow*, Issue 2 (April 1989).

13. See Mona Ozouf, *Festivals and the French Revolution* (Cambridge and London: Harvard University Press, 1988), pp. 83-105.

14. Reclus is quoted in Kristin Ross, *The Emergence of Social Space* (Minneapolis: University of Minnesota Press, 1988), p. 91.

I would like to express my thanks to Clayton and Elsa Patterson for their hospitality and assistance during the preparation of this article.

Chapter 4

Radical Artifacts
　　　　By Richard Porton

In 1989, the anarchist newspaper *The Shadow*, in a preamble to an attack on its journalistic rival, The NY Press, proclaimed that the "Lower East Side is a big place, and diverse enough to handle many points of view." Even a cursory examination of the political posters (posters can be seen following this chapter) assembled for this anthology makes it clear that often-heated exchanges of diverse points of view reached something of a boiling point during the 1980s and 1990s. And the historical record reveals that the neighborhood's lively and contentious ambience can be traced back to at least the mid-nineteenth 19th century.

To a certain extent, each generation creates its own Lower East Side — and its own form of radicalism. For the author of an entry on the Lower East Side in Encyclopedia of the American Left, the activities of German immigrant socialists — founders of a cultural center called the Socialistische Turnverein — marked a crucial, radical turning point during the 1850s and 1860s. But for many commentators, the "Tompkins Square 'Riot'" of 1874 represents a more obvious harbinger of recent events. Furious workers, incensed at the inability of the local government to address the travails of the burgeoning ranks of the unemployed, fought the police in a protracted battle that the labor historian Herbert Gutman deemed one of the pivotal events in late nineteenth 19th century labor history.

Of course, political ferment has often been combined with artistic endeavors on the Lower East Side. Despite the many clichés surrounding the concept of "Bohemianism," it is undoubtedly true that a synthesis of art and politics has become an almost endemic part of the Lower East Side landscape. Anarchists were often the primary mediators between political and artistic sub-cultures. Less puritanical and more open to artistic expression than the majority of socialists and Marxists, the anarchists often proved receptive to avant-garde tendencies in literature, music, and painting.

By the early twentieth 20th century, the United States's most prominent anarchist, Emma Goldman, (known in the popular press as "Red Emma,") had emerged as a figure who successfully combined a commitment to political action with an interest in the arts. The home she shared with her partner Alexander Berkman at 210 East Thirteenth Street came close to being an anarchist salon and their magazine, Mother Earth, was unique in at least striving to include both the work of anti-authoritarian thinkers and outstanding examples of the most innovative art and literature. (Peter Glassgold, in introducing an excellent recent anthology of pieces from Mother Earth points out that "the pages given to topical pieces and essays on anarchism and related matters far outnumbered those reserved for poetry, fiction, and other literary writings."

A Radical Political and Social History of the Lower East Side

One figure who combined both the idealism of an anarchist and the discernment of an aesthete was Hyppolyte Havel, one of the most colorful contributors to Mother Earth. The model for the aging (and alcoholic rabble-rouser) Hugo Kalmar in Eugene O'Neill's play "The Iceman Cometh," the actual Havel was a considerably more complex figure. The anarcho-syndicalist Sam Dolgoff (a much younger man who was a longtime resident of East Broadway until his death) described him as a "man of broad culture . . . who fit the bourgeois image of an anarchist . . . with long hair, a thick moustache, spade beard."

Dolgoff, despite a certain grudging respect for Havel, was far more interested in pragmatic matters of anarchist organization. By the 1960s, despite the enthusiasm for anarchism and other forms of radicalism evinced by many notable members of the Lower East Side's arts community — Julian Beck and Judith Malina of the Living Theater on Third Street, and, Tuli Kupferberg of the anti-authoritarian rock group, "The Fugs come easily to mind — a certain chasm between "Bohemians" and "leftists" was becoming apparent. This tension was at least partially attributable to the schism between the two main alternative currents of the period— the New Left and the counterculture. To cite only one example, Lower East Side resident Allen Ginsberg's Buddhist-inspired mysticism was unacceptable to the hard-line Leninists of the period, who despite their association with a New Left, often reverted to Old Left platitudes. In fact, one of the ironies of the time was that the New Left, in rejecting the anachronistic moralism of the Communist Party, often ended up re-inventing it in the form of Trotskyism, Maoism, or the Weather Underground's porridge of Third Worldist bromides. Quite typically, anarchism often bridged the gap between the avant-garde and political radicalism. In the late 1980s, a local chapter of the IWW — Industrial Workers of the World — was meeting in the Lower East Side headquarters of the Living Theater.

While many of these divisions remain relevant today, the resurgence of interest in anarchism during the Eighties '80s and Nineties '90s led to something of a rapprochement between the arts community and activists. Just as artists such as Robert Minor and Man Ray illustrated the anarchist broadsides included in Mother Earth , contemporary artists, most notably Seth Tobocman and Eric Drooker, chronicled the struggles on the Lower East Side in World War 3 and other local publications.

The most obvious difference between the Lower East Side of previous eras and the '80s, '90s, and our present post-millennial moment, is the passing of cheap rents that were once taken for granted and made the neighborhood somewhat of a refuge for dissidents and the poor. Consequently, it's not surprising that many of the posters and leaflets in this collection are at times incendiary, at times coolly factual, responses to the housing crises of New York's post-gentrification epoch. A list of warehoused apartments (an apartment defined as "livable," but "purposely kept empty by a landlord for reasons of speculation") on the Lower East Side served as a form of informal pedagogy — and expresses the hope that the public will be outraged after learning that homelessness is not a natural state of being, but a plight created by concrete economic and political interests. On the other hand, a poster that exhorts the residents of the Lower East Side to "fight the power" (invoking the famous "Public Enemy" song) is not meant to encourage mere reflection but to promote concerted direct action.

Inevitably, despite the housing battles that took precedence in the '80s and '90s, more traditional countercultural themes also surface in these documents. An announcement of a Halloween "marijuana march" ("All Hallows Weed") evokes similar "smoke-ins" that date back to the '60s. A leaflet addressing the city's threat to clamp down on what were perceived as "problems" in Washington Square. Park pleads for "co-operation not curfew" and brings to mind attempts of the city to suppress the supposed "noise" of folksingers in the same park during the early 1960s. And a playful comic strip by Eric Drooker and Paul Hewitt (circa 1985) starts out by depicting the grim realities of warehousing and gentrification before moving on to a final panel that hints at the utopian possibility that Lower East Side denizens will rise up and reclaim their community. (This somewhat wistful vision is mirrored in another poster issued by "Lower East Side Class War" that urges residents to "Build an army of the poor.")

Confrontations with the police — the most spectacular being the now legendary "Battle of Tompkins Square Park" in the summer of 1988 — are, inevitably, an important motif in these posters' "hidden history" of the Lower East Side's recent past. Several of the posters also reiterate the fact that local activists viewed equivalent upheavals in other parts of the country and world as extensions of their own bailiwick. As a case in point, a "Tompkins Square Alert" from 1992 coupled support for the LA rebellion that was simmering in anticipation of the verdict in the Rodney King trial with a reference to the "police riot" documented in Clayton Patterson's "4-hour videotape of the August 6, 1988 uprising."

Patterson, both artist and activist, exemplifies the inextricability of politics and art on the contemporary Lower East Side — a continuation, whether conscious or not, of the preoccupations that suffuse the work of earlier Lower East Siders like Goldman, Berkman, and Havel. Occasionally, even well-known cultural institutions on the order of ABC No Rio have been forced to fight for their survival — they too are part of the teeming army of the poor. (A poster in this collection reminds us that, at one crucial juncture in their history, city bureaucrats mercilessly harassed this vibrant cultural center.)

Restaurants on Avenue B now offer menus with Upper East Side prices and many fear that the Lower East Side is slowly becoming a countercultural theme park. Bohemian chic notwithstanding, the spirit of resistance is still alive despite the best efforts of hack politicians and slick developers. In recent years, the Lower East Side has survived Mayors Koch, Dinkins, and Giuliani, and it will probably survive whatever the new millennium has up its sleeve.

Notes:

"NY Press Busters," *The Shadow* (Issue No. 2, April 1989), p.2

Annette P. Bus, "Lower East Side, New York: Turn of the Century," in Mari Jo Buhle, Paul Buhle, and Dan Georgakas eds., *Encyclopedia of the American Left* (Urbana and Chicago: University of Illinois Press, 1990), pp.437-439.

Herbert G. Gutman, "The Tompkins Square 'Riot" in New York City on January 13, 18 74: A Re-examination of its Causes and its Aftermath," *Labor History 6*, NO. 1 (Winter 1965)

Peter Glassgold ed., Anarchy: An Anthology of Emma Goldman's Mother Earth (Washington, D.C.: *Counterpoint*, xix.

The quotation is from an interview with Dolgoff anthologized in Paul Avrich, *Anarchist Voices* (Princeton, NJ: Princeton University Press, 1995), p. 420.

**NO COPS
NO CURFEW
NO RIOT**

Tompkins Square Liberation Front

A Radical Political and Social History of the Lower East Side

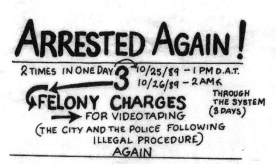

Poster by Elsa Rensaa

460

SUNDAY AUGUST 12: CONDO PICKET/ DRIVE OUT THE RICH RALLY
MEET AT E. 7th ST. & AVE. A, 2:00 pm MARCH TO CONDO SITE

Don't let them burn the neighborhood down--
SAVE THE FIRE STATION

A special hearing to stop City government plans to remove Engine Co. #17 from its Pitt Street station in the heart of the Latin community in New York's Lower East Side will be held in New York State Supreme Court, 60 Centre Street, NYC, Room 412, before Judge Diane Lebedeff, on January 31, 1991.

A success in this case will help save the Lower East Side from a fate similar to South Bronx, Brownesville, and East New York where communities denied fire protection were burned off the map.

The community, however, cannot simply place itself at the mercy of the court. In order to win, the community must demonstrate its determination to fight for its safety as a human right. In order to organize needed support, the Lower East Side Committee for Engine #17, which launched the case (Meyers and Patterson vs. City of New York) will hold

An Evening of Entertainment, Discussion and Organization
at
10pm, Tuesday, January 29, 1991
at
The Limelight, 47 W.20 St. (off 6th Ave.)

We urge the entire community, particularly small business people, along with friends and family

We love this neighborhood, and will not leave it!

We don't want defeat on this issue!

Lower East Side Committee for Engine #17,   161 Essex,   212 / 477-1363

Poster By Clayton Patterson

Artwork by Seth Tobocman

A Radical Political and Social History of the Lower East Side

Vertical text left: DROP THE CHARGES AGAINST THE ABC 43!

Top left panel: THE GOVERNMENT WANTS TO PUSH THE HOMELESS, THE SQUATTERS, AND THE POOR OUT OF N.Y.C.

Bottom panel: TO STOP THEM WE MUST BE UNITED AND ORGANIZED!

Vertical text right: COME TO COURT-DEFEND FREEDOM FIGHTERS!

FIGHT THE POWER RALLY

MONDAY, NOV 27, 9:00 AM - 100 CENTRE ST. COURTROOM AP5 AND AP 9   9:30

In late August of this year a group of neighborhood residents in partnership with a score of homeless persons and organizers from TENT CITY, TOMPKINS SQUARE PARK, entered into the long abandoned premises of PS 105 on East Fourth Street. Within weeks they evicted drug dealers, removed mounds of rubble and debris, sealed the windows, and wired up the building for light.

On October 26 the City's Department of Housing 'Preservation and Development' (HPD) in conjunction with the NYC Police Department descended en masse upon the ABC Community Center. In a twelve hour seige they forcibly evicted all members of ABC. Violence between police and protestors was the inevitable result of an extra-legal administrative eviction.

Without legal recourse and being thrown into the streets by military force, members of the ABC Center physically resisted and at times attacked battalions of police sent to enforce an unjust usurpation of the neighborhood's right to make decisions concerning the disposition of major parcels of its own common property.

TOMPKINS SQUARE EVERYWHERE

Artwork by Seth Tobocman

Chapter 5

Chris Flash
Interviewed by Aaron Jaffe

Q: Tell me about yourself, how you became interested in journalism and how you came to do *The Shadow.*

Chris Flash: I'm a lifelong native New Yorker. I've always been very curious and analytical about things going on around me, and I've been a reader of newspapers and the main-stream media. I developed an interest in how they presented the news to us, and what they were really telling us — not necessarily what, but how. For example, if the media wanted to demonize somebody, they would say, "So-and-so killed 20 people, comma, police said." If they wanted to make the person look better, they would say, "Police claim so-and-so killed 20 people." They have little devices like that to create or, let's say, guide public opinion. I've always had an interest in journalism. I just never knew I was going to apply it by put-ting out an underground newspaper.

Q: As an activist, you make news. As someone who puts out *The Shadow*, **you present news. How are these approaches different?**

CF: I was always kind of a peripheral activist. I always had lots of friends on the Lower East Side. But it was the Tompkins Square Park riot, the night of August 6, 1988, that was the turning point. As a result of that riot *The Shadow* came into being. A week earlier, there was a miniature version of that riot when the cops tried to clear the park by arbitrarily imposing this false midnight curfew. Me: "false curfew?" We protested against that and they started cracking heads. The police were beating all my friends, and everyone just retreated. And over the next seven days, there was this huge military buildup in the park, with police trailers, cops on horseback beginning maneuvers, cops on foot getting into various wedge formations, police vehicles all over the perimeter of the park and around the neighborhood, parking. The buildup implied that, "This Saturday, we're enforcing that curfew," and on our end, we also made it clear to them that we were gonna fight the curfew. As a result of the distorted and twisted media coverage from and in the aftermath of the 1988 riot, we real-ized the need for an underground newspaper in our scene, as had existed in the late 1960s and early '70s — there was the *East Village Other* and the *Rat*. Having just lived through that riot ourselves, we knew what really had happened, and the mainstream press was not reporting the news truthfully.

Q: By "they," do you mean the daily papers here? Or weeklies, like the *Village Voice***?**

CF: At the time the worst transgressors were, of course, the *New York Post*, which I call "the Compost," the *Daily News*, which I call "the Snooze," and the *New York Times*, which I call "the Slimes." Their initial reports were sympathetic to people who had been beaten by the pigs. In the next few days after the riot, their tone shifted dramatically, and suddenly, we were the instigators. We had caused it. We were rich kids from Scarsdale, to use [then] police commissioner Ben Ward's terminology, who had provoked these poor, innocent police into rioting and fighting us. But they neglected to point out that the cops had covered their badges. This all came out later. Cops had come in from every borough in the city. There were no officers supervising the cops or assigning them to a specific task. It was basically a free-for-all, a rumble. The cops versus the people in the neighborhood, is what it came down to.

With *The Shadow*, we are activist-journalists. In our hearts, our real thing is muckraking, investigative, underground journalism that the mainstream press won't touch or bother to do. It's much easier for them to report or regurgitate the official line fed to them at press conferences or through press releases, than to go out and investigate a piece, to find out what really happened. Alert: The next sentence doesn't logically follow the preceding one. I think he means to say, "Whereas, having witnessed it ourselves, we can report truthfully, without having to worry . . . " Or, having witnessed it themselves, report truthfully without having to worry about an editor, without having to worry about advertising base being reduced by reporting the true news, no matter how controversial it might be. We've always maintained an observer's point of view, despite the temptation to get involved in fighting the cops like other activists. We report what we've seen and experienced. We may have chanted "Fuck the pigs," but we never threw a bottle.

Q: How did *The Shadow* come out of the riots? What were the steps that led to issue number one?

CF: It took a while because we had no experience putting out a newspaper. We had no knowledge of how the whole thing worked. I knew someone was putting out a neighborhood newspaper that was kind of a little four-pager, kind of an ad sheet. I picked should be "his" or "her" their brain a little bit. They turned me on to their printer. This elderly Korean man, very nice guy, who has never raised his paper prices with us all these years. Fourteen years. He gave me these huge tabloid-size sheets, 10 inches wide by 15 inches high with blue lines that are non-reproducing, to facilitate pasting up, which we still use. We had Word Perfect. We printed the articles on that. We cut them with scissors. We rubber-cemented them onto the sheet. We just learned the process as we went along. Friends turned us on to paste-up techniques, how to make photographic prints in a darkroom, to make Veloxes, which is turning photographs into dots, so newspaper presses can print it and it won't come out all muddy. At the time that we launched *The Shadow*, we had a rich base of artists, writers, and photographers with a political conscience, who were happy and willing to help us learn. We learned from scratch. The first paper looks very amateurish. All our recent issues are very good. I'm very proud of *The Shadow* for the past five or six years.

Q: How many people were involved at the beginning?

CF: At the beginning, a handful of us. In terms of editorial decisions and production, I'd say three to five people. That doesn't count all the artists who gave us artwork, the writers who covered stories, the photographers who donated shots. People who did cartoons on spec. Here's an interesting story: There was this Yuppie guy who really loved the police, believed

A Radical Political and Social History of the Lower East Side

in them. Ultraconservative Yuppie scumbag. And he's walking down Avenue A in the middle of the riot and he gets his ass beaten by the cops. After that, he became an activist and he hates the police. His politics went 180 degrees, totally opposite to what they had been. So we did a cartoon about him called "One Fine Day on Avenue A." We had a little bull session, and the artist just drew this. So, here's the guy walking down the street, cops are beating him, and he's telling them how much he loves them. He loves the police, and they're still beating him up. Finally, he's been reduced to a pile of rubble. Ugh, he's all twisted. And he says "Fucking pigs!" Which is kind of a great end line.

The Rat was really our main influence. Let's not say influence, but rather something we aspired to become.

Q: Were any of you old enough to remember *The Rat* **first-hand?**

CF: Unfortunately no, but I have copies of it because I collect tons of newspapers and magazines, especially old stuff. *The Rat* was more politically oriented radical than the *East Village Other*. The funny thing about those two papers is they had real mainstream advertising. Big, big money was pouring in from the record and movie companies. They wanted to advertise to the youth market. As radical as those papers were, saying "Fuck the pigs" and "This is how you fight a cop in the street," "This is how you can shoplift and get away with it," jumping turnstiles, and shit like that, and also covering riots and demonstrations, they were the only vehicle to advertise to the youth market. What happened not too long after that was that this asshole Jann Wenner created *Rolling Stone*, Actually, no: *Rolling Stone* began publishing in 1967, *The Rat* in 1968 which started as an underground newspaper Also, no: it was a raggle-taggle paper, to be sure, but Wenner always maintained that he wanted it to become commercially successful, and he tried to distance himself from the underground press from the very beginning. By the late "60s, early "70s, it was failing. Also not true, it grew steadily. They guy can say all this if he wants, but you might want to ask him to reconsider. I know a good amount about this because one of my students wrote a senior thesis on *Rolling Stone* last spring. He had no base in the underground community. He was a spoiled Yuppie college kid. What happened was Warner Brothers came in, the studios, and they had a meeting with them and said if he just avoided controversial politics, they would give him all the ad money. The Nixon administration had some operation — I forget the name of it — that was aimed at basically telling mainstream advertisers to pull their money out of the underground press and put it in safe advertising vehicles, which *Rolling Stone* became. A safe youth-advertising vehicle. As a result, the underground press, which was dependent on that money, was suddenly without that money. It's like when you give artists NEA grants and they depend on that. And the NEA tells them, "Well, we don't want you doing that kind of artwork anymore." And the artist is faced with a choice: continuing to practice their art, or changing what they do to keep getting funds. And if you don't have the funds, since you get so accustomed to it, you become crippled.

Unfortunately, the underground press grounded out shortly after that. Everything was based on this advertising income. And *The Shadow* has had a hard time getting ads because people are afraid of anything that's really political or too heavy.

Chris Flash Interviewed by Aaron Jaffe

Q: There isn't a lot of local news in today's *Shadow*. What was the editorial approach at the get-go, and how has that changed in terms of who you want your audience to be and the kinds of stories you wanted to cover?

CF: Initially, very local because things were happening. In the aftermath of the apostrophe should be facing the other way '88 riot, up until around same here '91, things were heavy in the neighborhood. Every other weekend was a riot. There were fires in the street, pigs chasing you. Everything, you name it. Garbage pails overturned, cops cracking people in the head. Demonstrations to get Washington Square Park freed. Because in the end, we won the battle of Tompkins Square Park. We had the curfew repealed, and the park was wide open. Of course, the city's strategy at the time was to flood the park with homeless people, kick them out of every other park in the city and then create an intolerable situation by closing the bathrooms and refusing to remove the garbage. Let things get really horrible and people would demand that the homeless people be removed. It was a good trick on the city's part, and then people went for the curfew, subsequently, down the road. But initially, *The Shadow* was created for local coverage. It still is.

Our readership is basically the politically aware, the politically curious. *The Shadow*'s selling better now (which is weird), than it ever did back then, when things were really happening. I'd say for the past three or four years, local activism has not been as active as it used to be. We'll still cover stories about rent control and rent laws, and local demonstrations against the war. But there's not as much happening locally. So now we're covering more national stories, and more investigative pieces about the true nature of government. What they're up to, like Operation Garden Plot, which is using the military to repress domestic dissent. Militarizing local police forces with U.S. military budgets, money, equipment and training, the erosion of the Posse Commitatus Act. I think that news appeals because New York City's always been a hotbed of political activity. So far, the New York City police force hasn't really implemented those methods. But during the World Trade Organization demonstrations in Seattle a couple of years ago, they were. Pigs in New York, to their credit, have never shot rubber bullets, thrown smoke bombs or tear gas at us. They'll spray you with pepper spray, but that's as far as they've gone. I think it's only a matter of time before they do. We're telling our audience what's happening already and they come here next.

Q: So when you started the newspaper, you had an editorial vision . . .

CF: Just an alternative to the mainstream press. As outrageous as the mainstream press, with loud, blaring headlines. The same way the *Post* does it or the *News*, but coming from the opposite direction. You know, like "PIGS ATTACK THE HOMELESS" in gigantic letters. The mainstream press will say, "Homeless Evicted From Tompkins Square Park" in teeny-weeny letters on page 58 underneath the brassiere ads from Macy's. That kind of shit.

Q: But it is advocacy . . .

CF: We don't deny it. We advocate a certain position.

A Radical Political and Social History of the Lower East Side

Q: When I went to journalism school, we were taught that to write, certainly for the mainstream press, one must be objective . . .

CF: That's the problem with journalism schools. They tell you that you have to maintain neutrality. Now, if you're living in a neighborhood that's been attacked by the pigs on a regular basis, you see people getting evicted from their homes, homeless people getting beaten up. You see the park being closed. You see the bandshell getting demolished. You see suspicious fires in the middle of the night with squats burning down and the pigs knocking down buildings in violation of court orders, and cordoning off the neighborhood and beating people up. When you live that, how can you be an impartial journalist? How can you report on what you've seen happen and then have to get police department's side of it? It's ridiculous. You don't need their point of view. If you've lived it and you've witnessed it and you have eyewitness reportage and you have documentation The preceding is not a complete sentence. You have photographs and you've seen it and lived through it, you've experienced it. If a cop cracks you on the head with a club, or clubs you in the ribs, or if you get sprayed in the face with tear gas, then you don't need to be impartial. You know what happened. It's the truth.

Q: Have you ever interviewed anyone from the Ninth Precinct?

CF: We have. Of course, you get the official line. But the mainstream press just regurgitates the official line. The government puts out press releases or they have press conferences. The police department does the same thing. So the press duly reports whatever they say as if that's news. Do they bother to investigate what the truth is behind what they say? No, they just duly report what's being said. People don't notice the "comma, police spokesmen said." They just see the sensational lie that the police spokesperson says. We do the opposite. We'll report on what we've seen, we'll go down to city hall, we'll pick up public records. We'll do muckraking journalism that the mainstream press doesn't bother to do. Yeah, we're gonna be called advocacy journalism, but we're living it.

Q: From March '89 (when the first issue came out) through '91, there was a lot of stuff going on in the area. Was it a conscious decision to change the way you covered things and the scope of what you covered?

CF: Truth be told, the political scene here died for a while. One of the factors, which was very disturbing to us, was a lot of in-fighting over strategy, over direction, over who had more say. So we circumvented that by running other news. We tried to avoid getting involved in the fray. Bridges could have been built with more mainstream members of the community. We could've had a larger movement. It didn't happen. The turning point was the closing of the park in 1991 by the city for alleged renovations. Well, they closed the park for a year and a half. They demolished the bandshell, which they considered a focal point for trouble. There was one major riot — the Memorial Day riot in apostrophe goes other way '91, and it involved the pigs rushing the stage to turn the power off and kick people off instead of saying, "Hey, your permit is over. Your sound permit is ended. Please turn the music off." Instead, they bum-rushed the stage, purposely with the idea of provoking a confrontation, which succeeded. A major, insane riot ensued, which we covered in *The*

Shadow. The trick behind closing the park and destroying the bandshell was to change the demographics of the park, which the pigs in the police department succeeded in doing. I hate to give them any credit, but they succeeded. People kind of drifted away. People started finding other things to do. The scene changed. For a while, *The Shadow* stopped publishing. We took a break, like six months, and reassessed. We decided we wanted to cover a wider range of issues. Not just local politics, but more national stuff. We increased our range of coverage beyond the neighborhood.

Q: Do you know what your circulation is?

CF: Our circulation is currently 5,000 an issue. We count it ourselves. We have a small number, maybe 50 left over. It's the copies we keep for archives. And people order them through the mail. We've frozen the price at 50 cents all these years. Thankfully, our printer's never raised his price. He's a really decent guy for that. I think he really digs what we do. Initially, we were going to stick to an issue a month. Then, we started coming out as the need arose. When things started happening, we found ourselves writing like crazy, and when we had 24 pages of news, we'd publish. Sometimes, that meant coming out every two or three weeks. Sometimes, every one or two months. I have a philosophical problem with killing trees just to fill newspapers on a regular cycle, whether you have anything to say or not. We don't have the pressure of advertisers, so we publish as the news warrants. Currently, we get our 5,000 copies and stores sell us, and we have the mail-order business to supplement the cost of putting the paper out. We just about break even with the cover price.

Q: What was the initial reaction to the paper, both from the people you were targeting and the people you were going after?

CF: We were an immediate success. People really dug us, which was gratifying. The right people liked us and the right people hated us. Those that we were investigating, they despised us. They threatened to sue us. We had evidence that former city councilman Antonio Pagan actually has a townhouse in the East 90s, which of course puts him out of the residential requirement. He needs to live in Community Board 3's district, in order to be elected as a City Council member. He flipped out and threatened to sue us. We said, "Come on. We've got the evidence." Wouldn't do it. Wonder why. We exposed members of Community Board 3 that were the ones behind that arbitrary curfew on Tompkins Square Park, they issued secret memos against the squats, against homesteaders and the homeless. It was supposed to be public information, but they'd hide it. We had to really muckrake to go find it.

Q: Did the people you were targeting show enmity or ignore you entirely?

CF: A combination. We had people who ignored us, people who were outraged, and people who really hated us. They were elected officials on the community board and on the city council. But also the cops. We had some cops who hated us. A cop would follow me around with one of those huge Maglites and say "I'm gonna get you in a dark alley and I'm gonna fuck you up." We used to get hate mail. We got a Polaroid photograph of somebody holding up a gun, pointing it at the camera. On the other hand, we'd get cops that said, "I agree with what you say, but I can't say that publicly because I have a job and I have to do what

I'm told. I don't want to be fucking with squatters. I want to be in Midtown where I can get pickpocketers and muggers and thieves." On a real human level, they would explain their guilty feelings about squatters and homeless activists and anarchists in and around Tompkins Square Park. They didn't want their talents wasted doing that. Or sitting outside all night in their car to make sure no one's sneaking into the park. They thought it was ridiculous.

Q: Did any of your readers say you weren't going far enough?

CF: Some people, yeah. We were writing from anger back then. Now we don't say "pig" as much. Fourteen years later, you're older, wiser. Back then we were in our early 20s, and we wanted to express an anger we felt at being chased, being harassed, being beaten up, and all the other abuses by the pigs. And their higher-ups ordering these abuses.

Q: What kind of staff did you have over the years?

CF: Amazingly, the same people. And new people coming in all the time. Some of them want their names in *The Shadow*, some want to remain pseudo-anonymous.

Q: You've got Lamont Cranston . . .

CF: Lamont Cranston was the original *Shadow*, his real identity, on the old-time radio series. Carl Kolchak, the Night Stalker, y'know? He was a muckraking journalist in a TV show.

Q: He never wrote anything!

CF: He did! They refused to publish his articles! He always got the truth behind everything, and the police department would bullshit everybody at press conferences. He'd be the only one to stand up and ask a question. they'd They'd always shut him up or jail him. Or an editor would cut his shit and get rid of him because he's a pest. Look at the stories. Look at the reruns. He would persevere anyway. He would persist. He wouldn't stop. And he'd always get in trouble with the editor. The editor and him would always lose their jobs and get kicked out of the city, and he'd have to go to another city and get another job. He'd go from city to city because he was too controversial, he refused to pull his punches. And there's a little of the spirit of Carl Kolchak when *The Shadow* comes out. Another woman who just joined *The Shadow*, she's going to go by the name Torchy Blaine, which was the name of a 1930s serial newspaper woman, a fictional character, but that's going to be her handle. Some people write for newspapers like the *Village Voice*, but they write for us on the side.

Q: You've got Sarah Ferguson.

CF: Right. We've also got people writing for us from the mainstream media who don't want to use their real names because they don't want to jeopardize their job. These are people whose editors refused to run certain stories, or whose editors watered down the stories beyond recognition. We'll publish the full version, unedited, with all the facts complete.

Chris Flash Interviewed by Aaron Jaffe

Q: What type of organizations were they working for?

CF: Different magazines. News magazines. Different newspapers. I will mention that *High Times* is one of them. But *High Times* has pretty much fired all of its news reporters, and now it's party-oriented coverage. Which is bullshit. They've lost sight of their original mission. The people who used to write for *High Times* still write for us. So we're really blessed. But we get new blood all the time. It's a great thing.

Q: But nobody's making a living off working at *The Shadow*.

CF: It's a labor of love.

Q: Where does the paper actually get done?

CF: Literally in an office under the ground, under street level somewhere. It is literally an underground newspaper.

Q: After 1991, when things began to die down, what was your vision of the way the Lower East Side was going to develop and how did it match what has happened?

CF: The original riot was over the rising gentrification in the neighborhood, not only pushing out squatters from homesteaded buildings, but also low-rent-paying tenants. After the 1988 riot, we had a major recession in the United States, up until around 1991 or '92. We realized why the pigs were doing all these attacks on squats and squatters, political activists, homeless. It was basically to create a safe environment for real-estate developers in the aftermath of a recessive economy. You know, after every recession, there's an upswing, a sudden spike. It happens every 10 years or so. I knew that was coming. Sure enough, by the early '90s, the economy was back on the upswing again, with the election of Clinton and changes to domestic policies. Also, the economy had nowhere to go but up at that point. It was pretty much rock-bottom horrible. Since then, I guess what we saw coming happened. I could say proudly that our scene, our people, our political activist allies basically kept the heat up in the neighborhood successfully, from the '80s to the early '90s, to sort of forestall the rise of gentrification and pretty much stopped the Yuppie invasion for a certain number of years. But you can only keep up the heat for so long. Sooner or later, you settle down. You start a family. You get older. You want to move on. You can't maintain the heat every single day. Every single weekend a riot. And keeping things unstable or let's say, maintaining a Yuppie hostile environment. Sooner or later, the place becomes safer for development, for gentrification, Yuppie invasion, Eurotrash coming in and opening their little cafes, bars, restaurants, their little dives and keeping out people that actually make things and do things that serve the neighborhood. These gentrifying forces are irreversibly altering and harming the delicate economic balance of the neighborhood. And when mom-and-pop shops go out, soon apartments start going up in rent, and when the neighborhood can't be served by certain services and people have to go further to get what they need, it has a multiplicative effect.

A Radical Political and Social History of the Lower East Side

Q: In 1992, I did a piece for *City Limits* on a plan called the cross-subsidy program, and I closed the story with a quote from someone saying "There will never be market-rate housing on Avenue D." And sure enough . . .

CF: Forget about it! You can't recognize Avenue A or B. First Avenue used to be the line of demarcation in the '80s. Nobody went beyond First Avenue. Avenue A was scary. B, C, D, nobody went there. That was no man's land. Now, you can't recognize the place. There's little frat rats running down the street drunk off their asses. You've seen the bars and dives and little Yuppie restaurants. It's insane. Yeah, they made their way there. The economy improved. Interest rates are down. And every jackass is opening a little shop there. You see the prices they're demanding for buildings now, the rent roll doesn't cover the debt service! People are buying for insane prices and they think they're going higher still. It's being underreported that all those housing projects on Avenue D are being slowly privatized little by little. The ones that are still under the city's control are being vacated one by one and not re-rented. They're warehousing those units, with an eye toward possibly selling them to private developers and then making market-rate housing with a view of the East River. It's already happening. They're slowly displacing low-income people, low-rent-paying people and changing the demographics again. We saw this coming. We tried to forestall the Yuppie development as best we could by maintaining a hostile environment. But you can only do it for so long. Now developers have succeeded in invading all the way to Avenue D. There's still a lot of people around. There's still a lot of political activity going on. We're still doing *The Shadow*. We are still political activists, people with a social and political conscience who are acting on their conscience. We haven't completely lost the battle yet. What we need is a good recession, more defaults by all these Yuppie investing assholes and more foreclosures by banks to kind of level the playing field again.

Q: It would seem that a lot of your readership base is no longer even on the Lower East Side, yet you say your readership is as high as it's ever been?

CF: Go figure! I think we're getting more average people who see after that all these years we were right. And maybe we're appealing to some because they see that the mainstream press is full of shit and want an alternative. Maybe because we've frozen our price at 50 cents they'll take a chance on this newspaper. There are some papers that publish for a dollar or two, and just have ranting rhetoric about the masses uprising against their oppressors, blah blah blah, or are calling for revolution, and we're just muckraking journalism, and I think people notice that. Maybe the fact that we've stayed in the game so long is because people remember us. I don't know. But we're selling more issues now than ever before.

Q: You're not giving them free to prisoners anymore. How many were you giving away?

CF: We can't afford to. I'd say a couple hundred of each printing. Without some kind of funding we just can't do it anymore. It breaks my heart.

Q: You walk up Avenue C today. How does the feeling compare with walking in 1988, when it was a war zone?

Chris Flash Interviewed by Aaron Jaffe

CF: I wouldn't call it a war zone. I'd say it was a very different place. You still had plenty of locally owned businesses and shops. The drug dealing was still pretty rampant then. It's a mixed feeling. You could say, "This feels a little dangerous. This feels a little shaky, and I wish it wasn't so scary." I'm talking about your average person on the street, because I don't get afraid. But it's a tradeoff. Do you want an area that's rundown and grungy and a little unsafe, and still be able to afford to live there? Or do you want a neighborhood that's completely safe, totally renovated, Yuppified, gentrified? A million stores, all sparkly clean and sterile, but now, you can't afford to live there any longer. The rent is impossible. You're being pushed out. in favor of a high-rent-paying tenant, a higher income demographic. So, when you see improvements, of course the price is that you're gonna pay higher rent if you want to stay. If you can't afford it, you're gonna have to get the fuck out. It's a real mixed blessing. You can't even call it blessing. Call it a curse. A mixed curse.

Q: I have a certain romantic memory of the Lower East Side in the late '80s and early '90s, when I had a friend who lived on Avenue D and he didn't have a phone. If I wanted to see him, I'd put on all my dark clothing and slink down there and try to look tough and buzz his intercom. He'd be home one out of every six times.

CF: You always look back with rose-tinted glasses, with a romantic view. I do. Everybody does. But I would still take that over the current situation because if you remove the character and culture of a neighborhood, and you replace it with something that's alien, it's not your neighborhood anymore. There's nothing meaningful there any longer. It's like what they've done to Times Square. They used out-of-town developers to design a new Times Square for out-of-towners to visit New York. There's nothing New York about Times Square anymore. They destroyed most of the buildings. The few that are still there have been transformed beyond recognition. It's not Times Square. There's no homegrown New York culture there any longer. For better or worse, Times Square was like Avenue D. All the porn, all the red-light district, it was like all in one cluster. The seamy underbelly of New York. New Yorkers generated it for themselves. Tourists would come and say, "Wow, I want to see this" because they dug New York. As crazy and wild as it was, they dug it. The same with the Lower East Side. Now it's a shell of its former self, just like Times Square. You want to cry. It's alien. Corporate-sponsored theme-park restaurants. It's horrible.

There's nothing New York there any longer. and And what's on Avenue D now? There's this German place [Zum Schneider, on Avenue C and Seventh Street]. That's not New York. None of those people are New Yorkers. They have this gigantic, monolithic police station right across the street to further ensure a safe environment for Yuppie invaders. And all these little alien frat-rats who are just passing through, these transient bastards who rent apartments for a year or two and split because college is over and now the landlord can jack the rent up because they moved out so quickly. They're forever altering the delicate economic balance of our neighborhood, to make it an unaffordable place to live. In their wake, the Yuppies are attracted by the notoriety of the Lower East Side. Everything they've heard and seen, and they want to experience this notorious, crazy, wild, cool scene, with anarchists and everything. But when too many Yuppies populate the area, they displace the very scene they want to try to be a part of. When it becomes nothing, Yuppies get bored with each other. They don't want to be around themselves, so they move on. In their wake, they've dis-

A Radical Political and Social History of the Lower East Side

placed all the mom-and-pop shops, lower-income tenants, artists and writers and musicians and creative people who actually made this type of cultural scene. So they're all gone. It started in Soho and then they came to the East Village. Now they've gone to Williamsburg. Now people are trying to move out to Crown Heights in Brooklyn. Wherever the new wave goes, the Yuppies and Eurotrash follow. In the aftermath of their invasion, you have the neighborhoods devastated. You've got to realize that as that wave approaches, lower-income people, people of color, they're gonna get pushed out. Working-class people, you know people who actually make and build and create things. They're being pushed out. So where do people keep going when rents go astronomically higher and higher? These were the prevailing factors leading to the '88 riots. The park scene was at its peak and gentrification was at its peak at that time. And people were fighting and rebelling. The '88 riot was the sparkplug that jump-started the whole political scene here, which was already happening here on a small and low-key level. After the '88 riot, all these other issues came into play and they were addressed.

Q: How do you feel about the 12 squat buildings gaining title last year [2002]?

CF: Once again, people get older. They start families. How many years can you keep fighting in the street? And that's my feeling with *The Shadow* — if you hang in there long enough, you attain a certain legitimacy because you've just persevered and refused to give up. Before the squatters had their scene, there was a homesteading program which that the city killed where they were giving people buildings for a dollar. By the '80s, they realized they could sell them to developers. So they started taking the buildings back from the homesteaders. You couldn't get the financing to fix up your building, to do it yourself, and you couldn't get insurance for your building, so you failed HPD's requirements, giving them the opportunity to kick you out and take your building back. So squatters just decided to take matters into their own hands. A lot of politically connected housing groups were warehousing buildings. They were getting what is known as "site control," enabling them to hold onto a building and seal it up, hold it for 10 years until they eventually can get financing to do something with it. Meanwhile, homeless families or low-income families were put on vacancy waiting lists to get housing. And squatters said, "Fuck that, we're going to house people right now." They popped the buildings open and took them over. They should be commended, not demonized. Of course, the press did demonize them. I saw no difference between homesteaders and squatters. Both groups were trying to rehab vacant city-owned buildings that were taken in lieu of real-estate taxes. And they were rehabbing the buildings with no expense to the city and taxpayers, unlike the politically connected housing groups.

Q: You were covering this . . .

CF: Our position was that the squatters were heroes, especially those squatters who were beyond political activism. These were squatters that didn't want the controversy. they They wanted quietly, low-key, to occupy their buildings, and not be targets of pigs. Other squatters felt, "Well, squatting's a political statement, and we want to go beyond that and be political on a higher level." But to answer your question, yeah, I think it's a good thing. I think they took the deal because it involved the city getting into the TIL program, which a lot of politically connected people on Community Board 3 did, to get their city-owned buildings rehabbed at taxpayer expense. For $250 out of their own pocket, you get a brand-new apartment renovated. Multimillion-dollar renovation for $250. And 10 years later, sell their units for a profit, which they've done. I can mention several houses: 52 East First Street., and Seven East Third Street, where Pagan has an apartment. Three Community Board 3 members have apartments on East First Street. These are the most anti-squatter people, yet they had a city-owned building designated for low-income tenants, but they're not lower-income people. They're on the community board and they stole housing from the city meant for low-income people, and they got the TIL program to renovate them for free. It's disgusting. So I'm glad the squats gained title.

Chapter 6

The Underground Press vs The Mainstream Media: The Story Of The Shadow or "Freedom Of The Press" Is Guaranteed To Anybody Who Owns One
By Chris Flash, Editor

The Shadow, New York City's only underground newspaper, came about as a result of the Tompkins Square Police Riot on the night of August 6-7, 1988 on the street s of the Lower East Side. Having experienced the riot running from charging cops on foot and horseback and watching friends and strangers being chased and beaten bloody at random by cops all night long, we knew first hand what the riot had been all about.

In the days following the riot, the mainstream media was at first seemingly sympathetic toward those who had been victimized by the police violence, mostly as a result of videos and photos provided by neighborhood residents and freelancers.

However, within a week, things changed dramatically as the mainstream media echoed the mayor and police in blaming the riot on those beaten by the police, labeling them "rich kids from Scarsdale," and backing cop claims that they were provoked into beating people senseless that night.

As a result of the twisted and distorted mainstream media coverage stemming from the riot, we realized that there were no alternative media sources in our neighborhood, where underground newspapers like *The Rat* and *East Village Other* had flourished from the late 1960s through the early '70s. So, we decided to fill the void.

The Shadow has been publishing steadily as a newspaper since March of 1989. Our reporters, artists and photographers are mostly from the Lower East Side, and all are committed political activists who share our mission to expose, inform and entertain our readers with news, graphics and photos they will never see in the mainstream media.

The Shadow will print anything of interest to our readers as long as it is true and can be documented. Surprisingly, several mainstream media reporters have written stories for us that their editors have refused to print due to their controversial nature!! *Shadow* reporters are dedicated to their roles in the alternative press and some of us have been paying the price for exercising First Amendment rights — we have been arrested in the process of covering riots and demonstrations and we occasionally receive death threats from the police and their sympathizers.

The Shadow is now expanding its Internet news operations so that we can provide up-to-the-minute reportage of news events on the Lower East side and anywhere else we have correspondents.

Our ultimate goal is seeing an underground/alternative newspaper/zine in every town and city in the country. We can no longer rely on the mainstream media for the real news, so it is up to the underground press to fill the void!!

477

Chapter 7

Activism By an Activist Kenny Tolia
By Kenny Tolia

It was the early 1980s and I was a young punk-rocker: I was welcomed into my first home on the Lower East Side by the clank of a chain hitting the door as it was closed behind me, leaving me in complete darkness with a homeless man who actually giggled crazily as the padlock clicked behind us. There was only the crack of bright sunlight coming in from East Fifth Street, laughter echoing into the emptiness over our heads, and the overpowering, ancient plaster smell of the long-sealed tenement building opening up before us, like a crypt. As I was coming to terms with wanting to tell the man, Robert, to let me the hell out of there — in spite of my long quest for a residential opportunity in an abandoned building —I heard something come rippling down from the gaping hole where the stairway should have been, a sound, like rain: someone was playing a bamboo flute.

The breeze blowing down from above was mixed with the smoke of sandalwood and patchouli incense, as though I were inside some forgotten temple in the jungles of Asia. I said nothing, and waited as Rob lit a candle and led me through the trash strewn entryway, up a broken carpenter's ladder to the second floor landing. There were no stairs or railings anywhere and looking up, you could see a cloud floating above, where a skylight should have been. It had the feeling of diving in a great shipwreck. I later found out the old building had been gutted, stripped, and abandoned, not by the ever-present junkies as I had naively thought, but instead, by New York City's Department of Housing Preservation and Development.

Rob guided me through a room where a thin passageway led, cave-like, through garbage and paper stacked to the ceiling. As he blew out the candle stub and showed me onto the fire escape, the only way up, I hoped this was not the room he had told me might be available. As we climbed the fire escape, which was mostly missing its steps, we passed a number of open windows from the apartments in the building behind us on Sixth Street, and I waved half-heartedly, I remember, at a woman washing her dishes in the window not five feet away. She ignored us completely.

When we came to the penthouse, in a candlelit room, I met the others, a group of shadowy looking figures who had lived, it seemed, forever, in the forgotten corners of the city. Even among them, I must have looked odd, in my raggedy-andy punk-rock gear, a bike lock for a necklace and a home-made bloody shirt reading: EAT THE RICH. They were certainly an unusual bunch though. There was: Webb, an old, old man with eyebrows like Merlin, who painted ghostly Martian landscapes in oil sheen on black plastic which he sold on St. Marks place. His hair, appropriately, was gathered in one long spidery dreadlock; Hiroki, the flautist, a clean cut Japanese dope fiend; Crazy Eddie, still a neighborhood fixture, who at the time, dressed and decorated entirely in red; Don Houston, one of the greatest street musicians to ever wander the streets of the Lower East Side, straight from the stanzas of Howl; Roy, who was actually scary, a 7-foot-tall white homeless guy who spoke in grunts and later took to leaving presents of unidentifiable pieces of flesh on the doorstep of my apartment, for my girlfriend and myself. And, of course, Jim and Judy, who lived on the top floor in a viking-like hall, where Jim had constructed a giant wood burning stove and a wide table, at which he sat looking for all the world like some Scottish highlander as he listened to my plea for shelter. Judy's son, Sean, also lived in the building: he was a young computer-obsessed oddball, about my age, and he had rigged the electricity in the room from a car battery.

I don't know why they decided to let me in the building: Just looking at me at that time would not have inspired great confidence, I think. Maybe the retiring Judy intervened on my behalf, because it was Jim's decision ultimately, as he had been the first to open the building and let everyone else in, and had chased the junkies out himself with a great ax handle, it was said. Or maybe it was just not a big deal to him, but it was to me. By the end of the meeting, Jim decided the third floor eastern front apartment would be given to Kathleen, my girlfriend, and myself. Jim! If you read this: thank you. Kathleen and I set up our strange household with Coleman lamps and tapestries, sheets of plastic and votive candles. Kathy, at that time, looked like an Irish princess who had been dressed by Vampirella and Dr. Seuss. During the long, cold winter, which Kathy and I survived by pitching a tent in the living room and firing up an old kerosene heater, we took to calling him, Jim of the Mountain.

The path leading me to the building, which later became the well known Fifth Street Squat, was a roundabout, difficult one. It had brought me through the anti-apartheid rallies of the early '80s, which first awakened for me the thrill of protest, past the broken bottle strewn sidewalks in front of CBGB's, and the Yippie House at 9 Bleecker Street. The last stop was particularly important for me, because it was a reading of Abbie Hoffman's autobiographical book Soon to Be a Major Motion Picture, which first gave a name for me to the craft to which I would apprentice myself: activist. What inspired me most was the story of the dollar bills dropped in the stock exchange: to protest the war, Abbie and company had gone to the exchange and dropped dollar bills on the heads of the stockbrokers who immediately stopped buying stocks and started running around grabbing at the floating bills, thus illuminating in one moment the almost comical greed of the men financing the Vietnam War machine. I was hooked.

One day, at Number 9, I discovered, in the musty pages of an old Overthrow, the Yippie newspaper of the '80s, some stories abut the anarchist squatting movement in Europe. And so it was, when, a few weeks later, I came at last to the musty old building on East Fifth Street that would be my home for the next three and a half years, it was with a sense of mission. I wanted to bring the unity and political consciousness of the European squatters (in places like Christiania in Denmark, where squatters had created whole autonomous zones) to the abandoned buildings of the Lower East Side.

I took to preaching the reformed gospel of the European Squatters with the irritating zeal of some television preacher. Many a house meeting in Fifth Street, potluck dinners, something like mad tea parties, ended with the other members telling me, well, to shut up really.

A Radical Political and Social History of the Lower East Side

During this period of relative innocence, I organized to help save Adam Purple's world-famous Garden of Eden, a composted earthwork where birds flew and flowers grew in between alleyways of garbage cans with junkies in them shooting up gutter water. The Garden, an urban oasis as it was called in National Geographic, was of course, exactly the sort of thing the Community Board and the HPD could not tolerate, and after a series of kangaroo community board meetings, it was summarily bulldozed. On Equinoxes thereafter, we had parades to commemorate the garden (in cooperation with the Purple Feet People, who plastered a trail of purple footprints to the Garden's site). There are some very funny pictures out there somewhere of us battling the police in the streets during that playful period, with an enormous purple ball we bounced through the streets and over buses during the Equinox Parades. My new religion, however, I can tell you, was not spreading, at least at first.

I will tell you when it did though, and suddenly it seemed as though everyone had gotten religion. In April of '85, the HPD moved in on our building, in a big way — the first squat eviction of its kind, ever. And, in a fiercely contested battle in the media, in which I first learned what a press release is and how *New York Times* reporters conduct themselves, something amazing happened: we won. During one of that fight's more bizarre moments, Don Houston, having awaken from some three-day coke-and-alcohol binge, only to find the house surrounded by armed riot police, single-handedly faced them down with his guitar, leading the entire block in a rousing chorus of "We Don't Need No Gentrification." Out of a building without a stairwell, we battled the city so fiercely, like some ragtag alternative Alamo, the city actually withdrew and left us alone in our homes for more than a year. Avenue A had become some strange Hadrian's Wall, and beyond it we were left alone for some time.

Fifth Street held out for a year and a half or so, long enough for the other buildings, many of which I helped open in this period, to become established. Kathy and I broke up about the time the squat was finally closed by HPD. (It had another, briefer incarnation at some point later). My path led me through East Eighth Street to East Ninth Street and in the spring following the closure of the building, I organized the first squatter MayDay Concert in Tompkins Square Park. We erected a tepee in the park, to represent the struggle of the homeless to find shelter, and, after the concert weekend was over, I took the tepee I had built and set it up in an abandoned lot on East Ninth Street and lived there for the summer. This tepee eventually became the tepee-village-soup-kitchen, which figured so strongly in the fight for La Plaza Cultural, the community park on East Ninth Street.

There are so many people who gave their sweat and blood in that time to advance our cause in the city. I remember all of you, everyone, I do, (some days better than others) when I run into you in odd places. And, since my own path has led me away, I see now what a wonderful, strange group of people we were, so brave and talented as a bunch, but also how deeply we became divided later, and how bitterly our injuries stung one another in the aftermath. At its most shining moments, at the risk of sounding ridiculous, I think our little uprising resembled some post-modern Paris Commune (in its better aspects, of course), so strong was the bravery and self-sacrifice I saw over and over again during that period on the streets of the Lower East Side.

With so many brave friends giving so deeply of themselves, it is strange to me that, again, I had a key hand in the beginnings of what became real Lower East Side history. With the help of two or three others (who will remain nameless at this time, although you can ask me if you see me), the Tompkins Square Park curfew protest was organized — it was the protest which became forever known as the Police Riot of '88. We referred to it on the Lower East Side as "The Big One." And although this incident — which spawned the FIRST usage of video technology to document out-of-control police violence (drunken police indiscriminately beat up the entire neighborhood) — was recently removed from any *New York Times* chronology of the period, at that point, The *Times* saw fit to call it the largest street protest of its kind since the Vietnam War era. My contribution to the organizing was picking the day and time: A curfew protest should happen at night, when the curfew goes into effect, I reasoned, and not in the afternoon even though we could likely depend on more supporters to come out. And which night should it be? Well, pretty obviously, Friday night.

We held a small, typical Friday night protest. For us, at that point in time, this meant a rather typical assortment of die-hard squatter radical activist types (MARTIAL LAW TODAY BROUGHT TO YOU BY US was, strangely, often the gist of a lot of our flyers), mixed in with your usual East Village Friday night crowd of drunken maniacs, nice old Socialist ladies, industrial rock musicians banging garbage can lids, unusual families with children in strollers, and a mixture of people selling some radical newspapers and reporting for others, all coming together to the sound of people chanting, fireworks exploding, police radios, and bottles smashing somewhere. Somehow, the police managed to over-react to this very standard, loose-knit rally, the sort of thing we had, well, at least weekly. Some scuffles developed during the night. A few people were arrested throwing bottles.

The next day, Saturday, August 6th, the police began filling the park in the afternoon, waiting for the follow-up protest the crowd had called for at the end of the night. During the day, the police brass had gotten their hands on some particularly ominous and lurid flyer circulated by Missing Foundation, a popular local band. They were particularly disturbed by MF's tagline, (Your House is Mine), for reasons known only to the NYC Red Squad. I know it is a cliché, but it really was like thunderclouds filling the sky. I read somewhere that Samuel Gompers, the great union organizer, in one of those weird repetitious waves in history, witnessed a police riot in Tompkins Square in 1874 which was so brutal (he called it an orgy of brutality) it led him to forever abandon radicalism and socialism. This led eventually to the founding of the AFL-CIO. Well, in 1988, I had already abandoned socialism some time earlier, and the police riot, if anything, was not a welcome for me into the fold of mainstream politics, at any rate.

Our little movement became fodder for the headlines after that. It was at this time that the media first coined the abominable redundancy, "self-described anarchist," which is a little like calling someone a "black African-American," if you think about it. This adjective has stuck to the noun like glue ever since, becoming an over-used cliché even of coverage of the protests of the World Trade Organization, and it will doubtlessly live forever in the media because of its incendiary meaninglessness. Typically, after already having been labeled as such in the press, a reporter once asked me if I was an anarchist (see above) and I told him:

A Radical Political and Social History of the Lower East Side

Isn't everyone an anarchist at heart, really? He smiled, conspiratorially. Today, I would answer, Don't let people label you, a very good piece of advice from Malcolm X (and smile).

Three years after the Tompkins Square Riot of '88 found me on trial for inciting a different police riot in the park in '90. Strangely, I had already begun making my way slowly out of the Lower East Side — it had become too much of a progressive Peyton Place for me. The movement, as such, had been taken over by lawyers who proceeded to lead an army of homeless people into the park, a useless struggle that ended inevitably in the parks closing and total renovation. It always struck me as strange that the squatters movement, which had quite reasonably demanded the right of homeless people to take over and renovate abandoned publicly owned property became, overnight, about the right to live in the park! While I beat the felony charges, along with my co-defendants, after a four-and-a-half month trial, I alone was convicted of the misdemeanor crime of inciting to riot, for which I was given the maximum sentence, one year in jail. I became the Lower East Side's only political prisoner, and I spent a year being moved from cage to cage, from Riker's Island up to Riverview in Ogdensburg and back. I remember, for a brief moment, I was oddly comforted when a friend sent me a copy of Emma Goldman's autobiography *Living My Life* and I learned she had also done a year in jail for the same misdemeanor crime.

My life hasn't been exactly easy, but at the same time, I've always had the sort of luck my Irish relatives would say God gives to drunks and fools and widow's sons. Just having lived through all of this is more than I ever expected. So many of my friends eventually succumbed to the Lower East Side's monotonous siren-song of heroin and alcohol and drugs. Their ghosts now haunt the renovated stairways of the new Lower East Side. The last time I went by East Fifth Street — and for the life of me, almost like an old man, I could not tell you what kind of building actually stands there now — there was no trace left at all of the old building where I passed through the doors of adulthood. It was gone without having left any sign at all of having ever been there, as gone as the apple-cart crowded streets of the immigrant's Lower East Side, or the forgotten neighborhood of Five Points. Recently, I searched the internet, that library of the 21st century, and, not only was there nothing at all about the long and lonely year I spent in jail, but there was also nothing, nothing, about the nearly six months I and my co-defendants waited to see if we would be convicted of felonies in the only political trial of its kind in that period. Even Tompkins Square Park itself has only the slimmest of historical references and is mostly listed in terms of its location to various fine eateries and such.

Chapter 8

Villains or Victims: Are East Village Artists Willing Agents for Gentrification and the Displacement of the Poor?
By James Cornwell (aka Jim C.)

"In a world of victims and executioners it is the job of thinking people not to be on the side of the executioners" (Camus, 1986).

In the 1990s an academic critique of urban gentrification was framed using the case of the Lower East Side/East Village in New York City. Studies by Neil Smith, Rosalind Deutsche and Christopher Mele blame the artists of the East Village in the '80s for the population shift from working class poor to young upwardly mobile middle class people (aka "yuppies"). Journalist Steven Hager in *Art After Midnight* (1986) argues otherwise:

> The rapid gentrification of the neighborhood was largely blamed on art galleries, but they probably played only a minor role in a process that had been taking place throughout the city for over four years. A new white-collar labor force had moved into the city, a group dubbed the yuppies, and in order to make room for them, the city was driving the lower class out of the inner city. Before long, the police launched a campaign to displace the East Village drug trade (a major source of youth employment in the area). Titled Operation Pressure Point, the program was widely seen as an important step in making the neighborhood safe for yuppies (Hager, 1986).

As an East Village resident, I clearly remember the changes that Operation Pressure Point brought. Police lined up hundreds of people in the streets, regardless of whether or not they were involved in the drug trade. Scores of police vans shuttled to jail whomever happened to be hanging out in the wrong place at the wrong time. This was in 1984, a very Orwellian year for the East Village. The word on the street was that the East Village as we knew it, as a safe haven for artists and the working poor, would not last. With Pressure Point, illegal after-hours art clubs that were integral to the creative community, like 8 B.C. on East 8th Street and the Limbo Lounge on East 10th Street, were forced to close. The local economy was impacted, as Pressure Point winnowed out those who made money peddling drugs.

Christopher Mele, in *The Selling of the Lower East Side,* asks the question: were the East Village artists "culpable" (Mele, 2000) — involved as accomplices in a crime or wrongdoing — or were the artists unwitting victims of speculation and opportunism? "The debate over artists as willing agents or unwitting pawns in arts-driven urban development overlooked the evolution of underground subcultures that included not only artists but also other creative actors and their relationship to place. Deutsche and Ryan's central argument that artists were culpable was correct for the scene after 1980. The complicity of the key East Village artists with the commercial agenda and class interests of the established art world most

483

A Radical Political and Social History of the Lower East Side

certainly necessitated that the neighborhood's pressing social and economic conditions would not be addressed" (Mele, 2000).

Mele, Smith, Deutsche and Ryan overlook the fact that in the progress of gentrification artists and galleries are eliminated as well as low-income residents. Operation Pressure Point is seldom addressed as a focal point in the gentrification process, but those who lived through the experience of police indiscriminately arresting people on the street know better. Walter Robinson, onetime art editor of the *East Village Eye* monthly, critiques the theoretical tactics of Frankfurt School-influenced social criticism like that of Deutsche and Ryan:

> I'd say that of course artists are as naïve, self-centered and ideologically blinded as anybody else. Personally I feel helpless. Because I'm a college-educated white male I should somehow be able to exercise more control over my destiny than those less privileged — that's the leftists' version of the Protestant ethic. It's worth noting that the basic argument of all those critics — forcing individuals to identify with a social group, and then telling that group to go live somewhere else — is the same one made by Hitler, Stalin and racists of every stripe. Actually, it's symptomatic of what you could call the art world's East Village syndrome — a projection of negative qualities characteristic of the entire body onto a small segment of it, a scapegoat (Siegel, 1988).

To identify artists in the inner city as being of the returning white middle class ignores the many native-born youths active as artists who attempted to transform their environments through their art. In a 1984 interview with the author, graffiti artist Tracy 168 (aka Wild Style) explained, "I look out my window and I see a gate. After the riots in the 1960s they put gates in front of all the stores. Now, the guy who owns the store lives up in Westchester. When he looks out his window he sees a tree. So I paint a tree on the gate. Now, when I look out my window I see a tree." Artists of the inner city transformed a barren, foreboding urban landscape into a riot of color and possibilities. The power to alter the visual terrain is in the hands of artists, those whom Pierre Bourdieu calls the "producers of culture." Yet this activity has been deemed illegal, an act of vandalism, the desecration of public and private property. Enforcement of the laws throughout the United States against graffiti work to criminalize the expression of any local visual imagery and content, leaving urban walls clear for advertising and corporate messages. It is a legal version of visual monopoly capitalism. The position of "cultural producer," as sanctioned by society, is highly specialized. In the East Village art movement artistic production became democratized. It was a populist movement, where the field of cultural production was opened to many, not only to specialists. Tracy and others migrated their work from the streets to the galleries during the early part of the 1980s. The Fun Gallery, the first of the East Village artist-run galleries to open, dedicated much of its space to graffiti art. Artist-run galleries created an alternative mode of distribution for the emerging artists of the East Village scene. This alternative network of distribution competed directly with the established network of distribution of New York City's art world.

If the artists were in league with real estate interests, they must have had something to gain from escalating property values. Artists did not profit from real estate development.

The galleries were forced out more quickly than were tenants, as there was never any rent stabilization or protection for renters of commercial space (Smith, 1996). Steven Hager writes:

> The infusion of so much new capital into the neighborhood pushed storefront rents to unexpected levels. Local Polish and Ukrainian shops were driven out of business with alarming speed as chain stores moved in. New restaurants opened almost daily on St. Marks Place, but established punk boutiques like Manic Panic could no longer afford the rent (Hager, 1986).

The notion of artists' complicity with gentrifiers assumes some kind of long-range vision. Artists live notoriously from day to day. Commercially successful gallerists and dealers were relative neophytes with regard to the business world. They made errors in judgment and marketing, sometimes misreading collectors' real motives for buying artwork. East Village artists turned gallery owners actually thought that collectors' interest in art was "pure," unmotivated by speculation and investment concerns. The prime movers who ran the East Village's first galleries were artists who thought of their businesses more as a kind of conceptual art than a purely commercial enterprise. Two such artist/gallery owners were the collaborative team of Gracie Mansion and Sur Rodney Sur:

> Gracie: Collectors that were into buying this new work always wanted something new. When the East Village first started, I really didn't know anything about running a gallery. It became clear early on that most of these collectors were the same. I had a friend who worked at Sonnabend [gallery]. When somebody would come in and talk to me about buying all this stuff, I'd call my friend and say, "Do you know so and so?" And she'd say, "Oh, yes." It was really all the same people. So, they had been in SoHo, they were now buying in the East Village. I thought that they sincerely loved everything and that's why they were buying. When the stuff turned up at auction I realized that they were speculating. When the International With Monument [gallery] started happening the collectors saw this as something new, something that was going on. They moved toward that. This one collector said, "I used to buy feeling art, but now I only buy thinking art." They couldn't even think for themselves! It's like, "This is the new thing, so this is what we're into" (author's interview, in Cornwell, 2002).

The Gracie Mansion Gallery was one of the first of the East Village galleries; its history mirrors that of the entire scene. Gracie Mansion was pivotal in the creation of an artist-driven movement, which rapidly became subsumed by commercial interests:

> J.C.: So there were these poor artists who were scraping by, in these cheap, tiny storefronts, who create a "scene," then a more moneyed population of art entrepreneurs moves into the scene. These are people who either had money or had financial backing.

> Sur: These were real business people. Maybe they'd never done a gallery before, but they recognize that there's something happening here, that they can create a

A Radical Political and Social History of the Lower East Side

viable business. They were of that kind of mindset. They were thinking of the gallery as a potential business thing, not a kind of an exploration or experiment that could "go out of control."

J.C.: How did the scene get so energetic that it seemed like people were doing "too much, too soon?" And why did the scene peak and then go down?

Gracie: Real estate. There was also a move to get bigger spaces, to move out of your original space and move to another space. By the time people made that second move, the rents were really high. The landlords wanted a lot of money for the spaces. Jamie Wolff figured out this Broadway thing. Then it became clear that you could get a space on Broadway for cheaper than what you were paying in the East Village. Psychologically, the move to SoHo would look very good. Like you've really made it, your artists are in the mainstream, because now they are over with the other mainstream artists. There was a lot of pressure to make that move, whether you wanted to or not. We really resisted for a long time (Cornwell, 2002).

Both artists and landowners were speculators and opportunists on the Lower East Side, but their brands of speculation and opportunism were quite different. Artists saw a chance to take distribution into their own hands with their do-it-yourself galleries. They took a speculative risk that these galleries would be lucrative venues for their art. In taking real space, the East Village artists transformed the imagined or representational landscape of the East Village into an atmosphere, milieu, or environment. Poet and cartoonist Tuli Kupferberg, speaking about the East Village of the 1960s, said that the artists were engaging in the creation of "momentary utopias" (Cornwell, 2002). This utopian vision was manifested by transforming a social landscape inhospitable to creativity into transmuted space, which embraces and reflects, fosters, even promotes creative endeavors and thinking. This was the East Village gestalt.

The radical transformation of urban space by the East Village artists is best reflected in street level art, painting the bricks and mortar. The blank walls of the city were imbued with signs and color. The effect is much as Claes Oldenburg (a Pop artist who transformed a storefront on 2nd Street in the East Village of the '60s into an art installation) said when he described his feelings at seeing subway cars covered with graffiti:

You're standing in a subway station, everything is gray and gloomy, and all of a sudden one of those graffiti trains slides in and brightens the place like a big bouquet from Latin America (Guernsey's, 2000).

The East Village artists' street manifestations more often reflected the dark reality of dissolution, the smell of death that pervaded the abandoned buildings that scarred the streets.

Abandoned Building on East 6th Street between Avenues
C and D, 1984. Video photograph by James Cornwell

Day of the Dead by Michael Roman, 1984, The
Magic Gallery, New York. Video photograph by
James Cornwell.

You Will Never Succeed in Joining Their Club by Seth Tobocman, The Magic Gallery, New York. Video photograph by James Cornwell, 1984.

Starving Dog by Scot Borofsky, 1983 spray paint on exterior gate, Avenue B between 10th and 11th Street. Video photograph by James Cornwell, 1984.

Many of the artists absorbed and then reflected the dystopic reality around them in all of its morbidity and sense of impending doom. This manifestation of the "dark side" shows the serious intentions of artists to change social landscapes by reflecting, intentions like those of the Mexican muralistas (Jeanne Simonelli, personal communication).

For example, *Day of the Dead* by Michael Roman, a Chicano artist working in New York, arises from Latin culture using the rich graphic symbolism attached to indigenous Mexican mythologies. Seth Tobocman, a publisher of the collectively edited *World War III Illustrated*, embodies his radical political message in a work such as *You Will Never Succeed in Joining Their Club*, replete with dollar signs and the yearning "everyman" who will never reach the top (Tobocman, 1999). (Both artists painted and postered on the streets.) Scot Borofsky's mural *Starving Dog* questions how any humane individual could let a dog starve, much less the people of the neighborhood. Richard Hambleton's shadow figures dotted the urban landscape of New York's foreboding streets. These and many other works with political and social content were generated out of the East Village movement.

With the 1984 Operation Pressure Point, police began to arrest artists for defacing public and private property, mostly lampposts and abandoned buildings. Blank brick walls it seemed needed protection as much as the upscale residents who came to reside behind them. Rather than co-conspirators in the impending real estate boom, East Village artists and their art were more pawns to the power brokers who would alter the human geography of the neighborhood. East Village art and its particular transformation of the environment was on its way out. "Momentary utopias" cannot last.

The image of the East Village artist as complicit with gentrification reflects the resentment our society shows towards art and artists. Many artists are socially aware, and try to use their art to do something about their social environments. A prime example of this is the return of Judith Malina's profoundly political Living Theatre to the East Village after years abroad. [See Hanon Reznikov, Section 5].

Rosalyn Deutsche's *Evictions* gives a particularly reductive portrayal of the East Village artist and the '80s art boom as being in league with real estate development in the neighborhood. Deutsche describes the East Village art scene as helping to create "an atmosphere favorable to the interests of big capital" (Deutsche, 1998):

> As part of the unique packaging of this commodity, the new commercial art
> scene, emerging in its full outlines by 1982, helped facilitate gentrification. The
> physical preconditions had been prepared years in advance by the abandonment
> or neglect of the area's existing housing stock and consequent devalorization of
> real estate. When galleries, and artists, assuming the role of the proverbial
> "shock troops" of gentrification, moved into inexpensive storefronts and apart-
> ments, they aided the mechanism by driving up rents and displacing residents
> (Deutsche, 1998).

A Radical Political and Social History of the Lower East Side

490

From my point of view as a participant and documenter of the East Village scene, Deutsche's view appears incomplete and shallow. Rather than glorifying this trend, as Deutsche intimates, many East Village artists were showing their concern with the social and economic conditions of urban decay. Many more were politically motivated, and contested the processes of gentrification happening all around them. The artists were witnessing their world crumbling. The term "East Village" was invented in the early 1960s by the real estate broker and landlord D.D. Stein (Sukenick, 1987). As Christopher Mele points out, the neighborhood had been a haven for artists and creative bohemians since the advent of the beat poets of the '40s and '50s. Even earlier, the Lower East Side was influential in the construction of a New York bohemia at the turn of the century (Stansell, 2000). Irving Sandler (Kardon, 1984) understands the Tenth Street School of artist studios and galleries as spanning a time from the 1850s and the Hudson River School painters through to the East Village scene. The East Village '80s, then, was an extension of previously generated art scenes.

"The Triumph of Death" by James Romberger, 1988 (*Redtape Magazine*, 1992: cover art) Michael Carter, publisher.

"Mounted Police With Attack Dogs" by James Romberger, 1984, The Magic Gallery. Video photograph by James Cornwell, 1984.

Videoportrait of Peter Missing, Nada basement by James Cornwell, 1984.

A Radical Political and Social History of the Lower East Side

Democracy at Work by David Wojnarowicz, from
Your House is Mine, a book and street project,
published by Bullet Space, 1989, 1991.
Reprinted in *Redtap Magazine*, 1992: inside
cover. Michael Carter, publisher.

Deutsche's implication that artists are in league with real estate interests marks much of the academic critique of urban gentrification. This critique of the East Village artists is limited since knowledge of the artist movement is largely coming from the outside. An insider's view would show that the artists were usually radically opposed to the process of gentrification which dissolved the East Village experiment. But where is "inside"? At one point in her text, Deutsche discusses Louise Lawler's "Interesting" exhibition. Here she allies herself with an internal art world critique of the expansive East Village movement, generated in service to the interests of the small, aesthetically unified "Neo-Geo" contingent, identified with photography and neoconceptual strategies like appropriation. Deutsche's critique of the East Village art movement reveals a conflict of interest. In her own words, this critique itself created "an atmosphere favorable to the interests of big capital" — that of investment in the neoconceptual art movement that she serves. Lawler contributed to the ongoing cultural critique of East Village artists that was generated by the Neo-Geo camp. These artists and their allies disparaged the larger scene, displacing it with the tight-knit conceptual group, represented by conceptually oriented galleries such as International With Monument, Nature Morte, Jay Gorney Fine Arts, Cash/Newhouse and others. The Neo-Geo critique of "New Wave" art (Halley, 1987) and of East Village art in general, is contradictory in that the Neo-Geo camp was itself part of that same movement. A great diversity of genres and styles or "schools" existed simultaneously, due to the hyper-democratic and all-inclusive mindset of the East Village scene's prime movers.

Wide-scale resistance to urban gentrification on the part of the East Village artists is best exemplified by the artists' involvement in the so-called Tompkins Square police riot of 1988 (Abu-Lughod, 1996). Artist James Romberger produced a macabre rendition of the razing of the Tent City homeless encampment in Tompkins Square, which followed the riot of '88. Romberger based his pastel on *The Triumph of Death* by Renaissance artist Peter Breugel, transposing the scene to Tompkins Square. David Wojnarowicz, a notable East Village artist who died of AIDS, is pictured in the foreground as a skeleton cuts his throat. Romberger was also prescient in his 1984 pastel depicting mounted police in riot gear close behind their attack dogs.

The author was close to many artists who participated in the 1988 riot. Clayton Patterson made the videotape. I showed at Clayton's storefront gallery in 1984. The sculptor Ken Hiratsuka, who showed at my Nada gallery, lost the tip of a finger that night. Artist and musician Peter Missing created the iconography which came to symbolize the struggle against gentrification.

Peter Missing's slogan "1933-1988" was painted onto large banners during the riot of '88, equating the year of the police riot with the rise of the Nazi Third Reich in Germany. An upside-down martini glass with the words "The Party's Over" alludes to the disintegration of the artist movement as a result of rising rents and widespread real estate development. While putting the blame for gentrification on the artists (Smith, 1996), Neil Smith ironically uses Missing's iconography in a photograph showing a bit of the graffito "MF, Total War for Living Space" with an upturned martini glass. MF stands for "Missing Foundation," the name of Peter Missing's band, a loosely connected underground and a comment on the times. MF

A Radical Political and Social History of the Lower East Side

graffiti is an example of the iconography created by East Village artists to signify cultural resistance to gentrification on the Lower East Side. Smith cites Andrew Castrucci's Bullet Space collective as a rare exception to the rule of artist complicity with real estate development and gentrification. *Your House Is Mine* was the title of a portfolio of art works (and a tabloid newspaper) edited by Castrucci showing artists' resistance to gentrification. *Your House Is Mine* represented the work of many artists, including Peter Missing, Martin Wong and David Wojnarowicz, not only those who worked out of the squatted building Castrucci called Bullet.

Castrucci admits to having problems with Smith's assessment of artist complicity with the process of gentrification:

J.C.: Can you tell me what you think about the demise of the East Village?

A.C.: When the hype was over a lot of people couldn't market it anymore. A lot of people left. On the one hand I kind of liked it when everyone left. It wasn't economical. A lot of people just used it as a stage. They were insincere.

J.C.: Those were the people who left first.

A.C.: Yeah.

J.C.: The ones who are erasing the East Village off their resumes, as Liza Kirwin says [Kirwin, 1999].

A.C.: I think it was a valid movement. There was also a side to it where it was used. The developers and real estate people. It happens all the time. It's been happening since the beginning of time. They would use artists to decorate. That's just life. We were the villains and we were the victims of that whole circle (Cornwell, 2002).

While contemporary critiques of the East Village movement attempt to brand the artists as apolitical, many were politicized. Furthermore, the East Village artists' participation in the 1988 police riot, coupled with the appearance of imagery which created a visual vocabulary for that rebellion, place the East Village artists squarely in the center of a resistance movement. Yet, these artists went beyond a common notion of politics and dissent. For the East Villagers, the creation of art itself was a rebellion in the face of a culture which relegated artistic production to a privileged elite. East Village art, true to its bohemian roots, was a popular movement that gave artistic production back to common people.

Andrew Castrucci, a squatter, political artist and protester, adamantly adheres to a belief in "art for art's sake." People should be free to create art, any art, without the constraint of an exclusively political message. This sentiment recalls the post-World War II debate between Albert Camus and Jean-Paul Sartre (Bree, 1972). Sartre believed that an artist must produce art in service to a proletarian revolution, that art to be valid must contain political meaning. Camus, the editor of *Combat*, the newsletter of the French Resistance, felt that artistic freedom itself would be a freeing force, that an artist's inherent freedom to create would manifest a freeing force for society at large (Camus, 1986). A critique of East Village art which condemns the scene for its supposed ambivalence toward social and political issues is a stand which sides with the Sartrean view. As an artist, a participant and observer of the art scene, I tend to side with Camus' view that the true revolution lies in the freeing of the artist, the individual, to perform the creative act unfettered by "isms" and the schisms of a perceived political correctness. Many East Village artists did, in fact, put social, economic and political concerns at the center of their creative agendas, while many others simply focused on "art for art's sake," the creative act itself. The East Village art movement's meteoric ascendance was quickly extinguished as a result of forces of gentrification, critical barbs from within the established art world, and the devastation and cost in human lives brought on by the AIDS epidemic. Publisher of the *East Village Eye*, Leonard Abrams traces the East Village art movement from its inception through its rapid demise. Abrams observed that the initial scene became inundated with more commercial, entrepreneurial galleries, an opportunistic group attracted to the East Village because of its rapid success. Abrams' East Village Eye was the mouthpiece of the East Village movement, and the monthly rose and fell alongside it.

J.C.: Tell me something about how this art movement peaked, then imploded, or fell apart very rapidly.

L.A.: Yeah. That was amazing. What happened, as far as I could tell, was that there were a handful of people. Like Wojnarowicz, Keith Haring and Kenny Scharf and Jean-Michel Basquiat and a handful of other people who were doing great work . . . . They inspired many people to make art in this environment and to show art in this environment. I swear to you, around 1980, I don't think there were five galleries in the East Village. In 1985, at the peak of the East Village art "thing" there probably was, no exaggeration, 100 galleries. . . . Now we may be back to five here . . . I don't think there are a dozen. So, what happened was that there was this core of people who were doing great work and this group surrounding them, shall we say, who were inspired by them to make art, and there was a larger group around that, who was inspired by whatever they saw, which they might not have even comprehended, to be part of the art scene. This always happens in our society, you get the geeks, the charlatans, the mountebanks, the exploiters. The East Village was the psychedelic haven in the '60s and it became a smack [heroin] killing field. There was a point where there were so many people involved in this scene that had no comprehension of the meaning of art. The weight of that sank the entire scene. It didn't help that people started dying of AIDS. I guess a lot of key people felt they couldn't function here anymore. Another thing happened. There was a winnowing out where some key people were seduced into the SoHo scene. One of the things that happened to the East Village Eye was that we were doing great with those art ads. Eighth pages, quarter pages. People would spend 100, 150 bucks for an ad in the *East Village Eye*. We would write about the art. We didn't write favorable reviews if we didn't want to, I am happy to say. But we wrote about it. These ads were supporting the paper for a good three years. When this winnowing out process happened, the artists, the gallery owners were pulled into the SoHo art sphere. As they abandoned the East Village they also abandoned the *East Village Eye*, in many cases. Our advertising plummeted as a lot of the galleries started to move out. The wannabes, when they saw the key players leave, they didn't want to be there. It was kind of a rush to the exits. . . . and in no time there was a deafening silence in the East Village art scene.

Remarkable. It was over in less than two seasons. I'm talking about, maybe, fall and spring [of 1986-87] (Cornwell, 2002).

An article entitled *"Art Plays on Broadway"* by Judd Tully describes the flight of galleries from the East Village in terms of economics:

Gracie Mansion still has three years left on her Avenue A lease. "Upstairs on Broadway you pay half the price for space. Brokers call me constantly. . . it's very smart for the landlords to attract other galleries. Galleries want raw spaces and make beautiful clean white boxes out of them. You can't do that in the East Village." Mansion quoted Broadway prices at $10 to $12 per square foot versus storefront East Village rents at $20 to $25. "Eventually I'll have to move. They could get three times the money I'm paying and bring in a restaurant. Why, they're asking $4,000 for spaces half this size!" (Her street level gallery is a shade under 2,000 square feet) (Tully, 1987).

An ensuing flight of galleries to Lower Broadway (most notably 560 Broadway), as Doug Milford intimates, took the heart out of the scene:

Then in '86, '87 there were opportunities in East SoHo on Broadway to rent larger spaces for less money than in the East Village. There was an opportunity for those galleries that were successful enough, that had the wherewithal to move there. That cut the commercial heart out of the scene in the sense that the top galleries moved there (Cornwell, 2002).

Peter Missing's upside-down martini glass spray painted on the city streets symbolized "The Party's Over" for the East Village. Economic shifts moved the successful East Village galleries to Lower Broadway, the poorer artist-run galleries were either evicted as rents increased (as had happened to my gallery, Nada and to many others) and disappeared, or moved across the East River to Williamsburg, Brooklyn (as Annie Herron and her Test Site and Eye Wash galleries had done). The art movement in the East Village section of the Lower East Side was essentially finished. The closing of Tompkins Square Park after the 1988 police riots, coupled with recession in the early 1990s effectively sealed the East Village's fate. For a few years the East Village became a literal "no-man's-land." The East Village art scene had been dead for several years in the early 1990s before the final wave of gentrification set in. Today's view from Avenue A through to Avenue B is upscale and well heeled, a far cry from the East Village of the '80s art scene. Where can one find breakfast specials for $2.00 anymore? The gentry, indeed, have landed.

BIBLIOGRAPHY:

497

Abu-Lughod, Janet L. *From Urban Village to East Village*. New York:
    Blackwell Publishers, Inc., 1995.

Bourdieu, Pierre. *Distinction: A Social Critique of the Judgment of Taste*. Cambridge,
    Massachusetts: Harvard University Press, 1984.

_____.*The Field of Cultural Production*. New York: Columbia University Press, 1999.

_____.*The Rules of Art*. Stanford: Stanford University Press, 1992.

Bree, Germaine. *Camus and Sartre: Crisis and Commitment*. New York: Delacorte Press, 1972.

Camus, Albert, et al. *Neither Victims Nor Executioners*. New York: New Society
    Publishers: 1986.

Carter, Michael. *Redtape #7: Tragicomix*. New York: Redtape Publications, 1992.

Cornwell, James. *When Out Was In: The Rise and Fall of the East Village Art
    Movement*. Winston-Salem: Wake Forest University Press, 2002.

Deutsche, Rosalyn and Cara Gendel Ryan. "*The Fine Art of Gentrification.*"
    October, No. 31 (Winter, 1984).

Deutsche, Rosalyn. *Evictions*. Cambridge: The MIT Press, 1998.

Guernsey's. *Graffiti Art: The Auction*. New York: Guernsey's, 2000.

Hager, Steven, *Art After Midnight: The East Village Scene*. New York: St. Martin's Press, 1986.

Halley, Peter. *Collected Essays*, 1981-87. Venice, CA: Lapis Press, 1991.

Kardon, Janet. *The East Village Scene*. Philadelphia: Institute of
    Contemporary Art, 1984.

Kirwin, Elizabeth Seton. *It's All True: Imagining New York's East Village Art Scene
    of the 1980s*. Ann Arbor: UMI Dissertation Services, 1999.

Mele, Christopher. *Selling the Lower East Side*. Minneapolis:
    University of Minnesota Press, 2000.

Scholder, Amy, ed. *The Art of David Wojnarowicz*. New York: Rizzoli
    International Publications, 1999.

Siegel, Jeanne, ed. *Art Talk: The Early 80's*. New York: Da Capo
    Press, Inc., 1988.

Smith, Neil. *The New Urban Frontier*. New York: Routledge, 1996.

Stansell, Christine. *American Moderns: Bohemian New York and the Creation of a New
    Century*. New York: Henry Holt and Company, 2000.

Sukenick, Ronald. *Down and In: Life in the Underground*. New York: William Morrow, l987.

Tobocman, Seth. War in the Neighborhood. *Brooklyn: Autonomedia*, 1999.

Tully, Judd. "Art Plays: On Broadway: Speculations on Real Estate in New York."
    New Art Examiner (November, 1987): 30-31.

Chapter 9
Poems
    By Peter Missing

FROM **IGNORE THE WHITE CULTURE ALBUM** ..

IGNORE THE WHITE CULTURE
THERE IS NO LOVE
 WHEN YOU ONLY FEEL NUMB
EVERYTHING LOOKS WHITE
IT'S TIME TO MOVE FAST
IGNORE THE WHITE CULTURE
LOOT THE STORES
FORGET BIG BUSINESS
FEEEEED START RUNNING
RUNNING THIRTY STRONG
RUNNING
LET'S GO SHOPPING
GOT TO STAY ALIVE
LOOT THE STORES
LOOT THE STORES
FEED YOURSELF
IGNORE THE WHITE CULTURE
FIND A WAY TO STAY ALIVE
THORN IN MY SIDE
LOOT THE STORES
TAKE WHAT'S YOURS
FEEEEEEED START RUNNING
RUNNING
LOOT THE STORES
IGNORE THE WHITE CULTURE
IGNORE THE WHITE THE WHITE THE WHITE

RISE UP

SHIT AND MORE SHIT
WE ALL ADD TO THE HEAP
BOREDOM PILED HIGH
RISE UP
THE WORST HAS MADE ITS MARK
ANYONE CAN TAKE COMMAND
THIS IS A GHOST TOWN
THE MYSTERY IS YOUR MIND

500

IN YOUTHVILLE EVERYTHING IS WRONG
YOU GOT TO FEEL ALIEN
CLUBS BARS RESTAURANTS
WHY ARE WE HERE?
NO ONE HAS TO CARE
CITIES IN ASHES
WE'LL BUILD FROM THERE
BURY IT AGAIN
WE KNOW WHO WON THE BATTLE
WE DISRUPT ANOTHER DAY
FOOLS RUN AMOK
BRING THIS CITY TO THE GROUND
YOUR FEAR IS GONE
WE KILL OURSELVES
IN THE CITY OF THE DEAD.
RISE UP RISE UP   CIRCA UDUB PUBLISHING 1990

I WALK ALONE

A GREY SKY A WORLD THAT'S WORN
WATCH THE TREES DIE AND LOOK ABOVE
GREEN ANGELS FALLING
OUR EARTH TRAMPLED FROM STONE TO STONE
LOVE OF NATURE TOO FAR GONE
MY LAST APPLE AND GRAPES DESTROYED
I WALK ALONE
MANKIND DESTROYS DESTROYS
OUR WATER OUR AIR OUR SOIL
CAN GO NO MORE
PLANES FLYING BY WITH SMOKE EVERYWHERE
MY CONTRIBUTION TO HUMANITY
ONLY A SPECK OF DUST
THERE'S NO TURNING BACK
THE HANDS OF TIME
WE CREATED A HOLE
TO PUT US ALL AWAY
THE FOOD MAKES ME ILL
SO I STARVE AGAIN
WITH LIGHTS GOING OUT
CHILDREN HIDE
DARKNESS CREEPS IN   THE SUN GOING DOWN
PLANTED A TREE BUT IT DOES NOT GROW
SAW A BIRD DYING ON THE ROAD
IT DIED IN MY HAND
I WALK ALONE

SURROUNDED BY INVISIBLE WARS
I CANNOT SEE RADIATION OR BIO CHEMICAL
OR BOMBS DROPPING FROM THE AIR
OUR PLANET NOW AN EMPTY VOID
ITS SPIRIT DESCENDED A TIME AGO
FOR YEARS WILL TELL IF IT STARTS OVER AGAIN
THE DAMAGE WE MADE CAN NEVER BE FIXED
WE ARE THE LAST GENERATION
TO WATCH IT ALL GO DOWN
TO HAVE FUN WE IGNORE IT ALL
AND LIVE IN A GLASS BALL
SOON TO TURN INTO FLAMES OF
YELLOW AND GOLD
MY WORLD IS ONLY A BURNT EMBER
SPRAWLED ACROSS THE LAND
I DIDN'T SURVIVE . . . I WENT OUT QUICK
SO READ THIS ALL
AND FIND THE LIGHT
SEE IT NOW   SPARKLING AFAR
REACH FROM THE DEPTHS TO TRY AND FLY
THE LIGHT GETS BRIGHTER INTERNAL EVOLUTION
THEN DISAPPEARS
YOU ONLY GET ONE CHANCE
THE HUMAN RACE STOPPED IN THEIR CARS
AND THE GUNS GO UP
VANISHING POLITICS TAKING THE PLANET WITH THEM
TURN AWAY
MONEY ALL OVER
MELTING INTO THE GROUND

SECTION FIVE - BIOGRAPHY

Chapter 1

Alfredo Irizarry
Profile:

Born in the United States in the early fifties, I am the first generation Puerto Rican. My mother's mother, Ague, the daughter of a house Indian slave was the first to arrive here in the late '40s. At an early age she became an expert housekeeper like her mother and raised the money to send for her entire family of six daughters and four sons. We lived in the Barrio for a while then moved to the Lower East Side when I was five.

Growing up in the Lower East Side, predominantly a culturally mixed neighborhood, one learns early the lesson of banding together and fighting for just causes. It's impossible not to gain a perspective on social justice while growing up during the Civil Rights era. Being part of a minority places you in a position to either fight for equality or swallow the injustices and prejudices constantly thrown at you by society. At the age of 13, I became a member of L.E.A.P after my first brother Luis. The Lower East Side Action Project. The director Larry Cole, a Black Belt in Judo working on his PhD from California, wanted to teach inner city kids the value of academics through Martial Arts.

Leap taught kids a way out of the gangs and violence consuming our neighborhoods at the time. Leap provided training in Arts, Academics trades, education, music, photography, and Martial Arts. My brother and I both played the Conga Drums after my father who had played and sang in a band with my political uncle called "Los Imperial's," The Imperials.

While at Leap I got involved in organizing and recruiting teenage kids from the neighborhood to dissuade them from becoming gang members. At this time around 1965, I become aware of the Real Great Society during a college forum we both attended on gang related activities and organizing. At the time, we were the only organizations working to stop gangs, violence and the drug epidemic, which wiped out half our generations. Leap taught me how to defend myself with Martial Arts; it also showed me how to become proactive in my community. Paul Goodman, my tutor in the *First Street School* from age 10 to 13, reinforced these life long values. These are the two most significant turning points in my life, which make me the person I am today. Both Paul and Larry were radical thinkers who put their lives on the line to prove a point. Anyone can excel given the right opportunities even under the most harsh conditions.

In Leap I helped establish three clubhouses in LES. We had one on Seventh and B, Second and B, and Broome and Forsyth. By the time 1969 came around we had over a hundred people involved. That's when my Counselors Paul Ramos and Don Turner helped me get into the Navy to avoid being drafted and directly sent to Vietnam. So Leap helped save my life, as many people were getting drafted and killed in the war. When all is said and done Leap helped save many other kids like myself in LES way before there were any crisis intervention programs for inner city youth.

A Radical Political and Social History of the Lower East Side

In 1972 I arrived back to the neighborhood and it resembled Dresden, Germany after the bombings. Many returning Veterans like me felt the same desolation and despair. Our neighborhood was almost in complete ruins. The war on drugs and gangs had taken a toll. Hundreds of my friends were dead or dieing.

I immediately got into College at Old Westbury and started the college newspaper called, *"The Catalyst."* I got involved in the struggle for equal rights and equal opportunity in the school. Fighting for equal representation of the Latino Faculty. We had several school shut downs and huge Campus demonstrations that paralyzed the entire school system, until Superintendent Maguire gave us what we needed and wanted. Old lessons do come in handy.

During the mid '70s I got involved in CHARAS/El Bohio. CHARAS represented the Leap movement on another level. Larry Cole represented the status club with money, helping inner city kids. CHARAS represented Latinos for Latinos. It gave me a great sense of Pride meeting Bittman Rivas, Sal Becker, Armando Perez, Chino Garcia, Luis Lopez, and Jorge Brandon. They were helping the next generation of Latino kids, that didn't have half the opportunities we had had. I wanted to create a neighborhood magazine to help out with the communications part of a housing movement we started to restore our dignity and self-respect in the city. Taking matters into our hands and with the help of Borough President Andrew Stein and councilwoman Miriam Friedlander. We were able to save our entire neighborhood from total destruction and City neglect. Saving the abandoned Ps 64 School building on East Ninth Street and creating a community center to address the issues, became our Alamo. It became our last stand to fight the city and the developers, to prevent them from bull dozing our LES neighborhood.

In 1977, I met Mary McCarthy who helped me organize and raise the necessary funds for a community magazine we agreed to call, *"The Quality Of Life In Loisaida."* After a poem written, and called *"Loisaida"* by the late great Playwright-Poet-Actor-Dancer-Performer Bittman Rivas, my theater mentor for over 15 years.

It was free and published for 18 years with the dedicated love and commitment of Mary, myself, and many others. Mary sold her two-car garage house upstate and moved into a homesteading building on the LES because she believed in what we were doing and wanted to help us. All my life in the Lower East Side there has always been great people like Paul Goodman, Larry Cole, Buckminster Fuller, Margaret Mead, and Mary McCarthy, who made the difference between living on full and living on empty. The sixties were very turbulent but also innovative and unique.

My life in the Lower East Side would not be what it is today, if not for these great people that also saw and understood the true value of social justice and righteousness. Would I consider myself a radical community activist? If you can honestly call Benjamin Franklin a radical social activist then I guess I am. If you can call Buckminster Fuller a radical social activist then so am I. I consider myself an activist for social change to help less fortunate people than me to have the opportunities I had to excel and make something of themselves worthwhile in our great society. I am a true product of my neighborhood called the Lower East Side, LOISAIDA. . .

Chapter 2

A Brief History of The Yippies and An Interview With Dana Beal
By Cheryl Guttman

In late-1967 Abbie Hoffman and Jerry Rubin co-founded the Yippies, a countercultural political group that emphasized theatricality and a sense of humor, in an East Village apartment.
While they eventually had between 30 and 40 chapters all around the country, the Yippies
remained a presence in the Lower East Side. Some of their most famous antics were throwing
dollar bills at the Stock Exchange in an effort to incite a greed-induced frenzy; running a
pig-Pigasus-for president; and, before they were officially formed, members were involved
with the 1967 levitating of the Pentagon. The Yips (which the Yippies preferred to call
themselves) brought Pigasus to the Democratic Convention in 1968 with the slogan, "They
nominate a president and he eats the people. We nominate a president and the people eat
him."[1] However, the Yippies — who came to Chicago to participate in a "Festival of Light" as
opposed to a "Convention of Death" — and other anti-war demonstrators were met by a large
force of intransigent police and the result was violence against the demonstrators and rioting.

In the subsequent "Chicago 7" trial for conspiracy to riot, Abbie Hoffman, one of the defendants (along with six other radical leaders), eloquently and at times humorously used his
chance to speak to explain his movement. For instance, when a prosecutor asked him,
"Where do you live?" Hoffman replied, "The Woodstock Nation . . . which is a state of
mind."[2] He explained that some of the suggested activities that appeared outrageous — like
putting acid in the water supply and having a public "fuck in" were not to be taken seriously but were "just for fun." He then went into theories of why Yippies considered "fun" subversive: the average person was conditioned to postpone pleasure, which had the effect of
making them conform to the system while thinking that only people on television who buy
consumer goods can have fun. The idea was that showing young people having fun while
protesting the system would "turn people on" and radicalize them. Furthermore, the anarchic
sensibility of Yippie antics could serve to break down traditional ways of thinking and therefore open people up to new ways of seeing.

Defendants Hoffman and Rubin wore hippie attire and behaved in turn very casually or in a
theatrical manner; they wore judicial robes, blew kisses to the jury, made faces, and put a
Vietnamese National Liberation Front flag on the defense table (which was usually cluttered
with stuff, including, once, a package of marijuana that spilled out of a package someone
had sent them).

One of the defense's positions was that the defendants had never met or agreed on a plan
before the riots. Norman Mailer, a witness for the defense, explained, "Left wingers are incapable of conspiracy because they're all egomaniacs," while Hoffman made the observation,
"Conspiracy! Hell, we couldn't agree on lunch!"[3] The charges were reversed on appeal based

on the defense's inability to exclude jurors based on their "cultural biases." Some of the jurors were heard to remark after the trial that the defendants "should be convicted for their appearance, their language, and their lifestyle," and that the "demonstrators should have been shot by the police."[4] In a related development, the seven police officers who were charged with violating the civil rights of the demonstrators were all acquitted.

Other Yippie events included sponsoring a rat-shaped float made up to look like Nixon, and a contingent of Yippie "boat people" that attempted to seek asylum in Canada during Nixon's inaugural; attempting to get a "bombing permit" to blow up the General Motors building in Detroit; and making another foray to Wall Street in April 1991 during a market dip where Yippies yelled, "Jump!" to the onlooking Wall Streeters.

"Paul Krassner, the satirist and founder of the magazine *The Realist*, came up with the word 'Yippie.' The word was originally chosen for the spirit it conveyed. However, Abbie's wife Anita suggested the word should have a specific meaning or it would not be taken seriously by the mainstream, so she came up with the formulation, 'Youth International Party.' This appealed to Abbie who realized that it would be understood as a political party structure, whereas he had more of a recreational 'party' in mind.[5]" A. J. Weberman, the inventor of the "garbology" technique of journalism, i.e., searching his subject's (e.g., Nixon's) trash, also had a reputation for taking paranoid conspiracy theories too far — quite a feat considering the credence given the many conspiracy theories among Yips. He eventually denounced the Yippies for not taking seriously his theory that the death of prominent Yip Tom Forcade was not a suicide, but a murder committed by Forcade's wife.

Aron Kay, the Yippie "Pie Man," threw pies at people such as anti-Equal Rights Amendment activist Phyllis Schlafly, right wing commentator William Buckley, two former CIA directors (Richard Helms and William Colby), E. Howard Hunt, G. Gordon Liddy, John Dean and John Ehrlichman of Watergate fame, Governor Jerry Brown, former NY Mayor Abe Beame, former Senator Daniel Patrick Moynihan, countercultural icons Timothy Leary and Andy Warhol, and anti-abortion activist Randall Terry (his last "victim" in 1992) to make a political statement. Although other Yippies have thrown pies to make a point, Aron threw the most, always made sure camera people had great shots of the action, consulted the most Yippies' opinions before he took aim, and had the best rationales. He once said, "You've got to use the right pie for the right person." He used an apple pie on Schlafly and Liddy because of their embrace of American Values, and an apple crumb cake for Beame because "he's such a crumb in the Big Apple."[6]

Another well-known Yippie is Dana Beal. Dana has been described by the *New York Times* as "one of the first movement writers to argue for a merger of political radicalism and the psychedelic lifestyle." Abbie Hoffman once called him "a unique blend of street person and theoretician," and Jerry Rubin has said that Beal's writings "were a strong force in helping us [as Yippies] understand who we are."[7] Beal's writings included "Right On, Culture Freaks" and "Weather Yippie," which were reprinted in most of the underground newspapers in this country and abroad, and he wrote under the pseudonyms George Metesky and Leon Yipsky. Beal argued for militancy without elitism and with more humanity than the violent radical groups seemed to offer. He preferred "alternative cultural actions" rather than getting involved in political violence. "Weather Yippie" referred to the alliance that many Yip collectives around the country made with the Weather Underground — a group that advocated revolutionary violence. In November of '69, Weather people and East Coast Yippies together trashed the Justice Department and the South Vietnamese Embassy after a peace march in D.C. The "Weather Underground released its first bombing communiqués through a NY Yippie office run by Abbie and Jerry [and] *Rolling Stone* even claimed Yip superstars financed Weather people."[8] By the spring of 1970, there were many Yippie/Weather collectives and affinity groups around the country. In Wisconsin on July 17th, 1970, Randy Anderson, a member of one such group, was shot dead by the police after trying to take the "riot to the suburbs."[9]

Beal thought it was a "military error" for Yippies or others in the counter culture to get involved in violence. Although he felt that LSD could radicalize hippies and he consistently championed the legalization of marijuana, he has always disdained "death drugs"—heroin and speed. A. J. Weberman has said that the police were out to get him because he "organized the freak quarter."[10] The Yippies also tried to distinguish themselves from the "old left" — which viewed all issues through the prism of Marxism with its emphases on worker rights and class differences. The Yippies were firmly in the "new left" camp of campaigning against sexism, racism, etc.

Mr. Beal is also associated with a Yippie faction called the Zippies — the Zeitgeist International Party — started by the younger Tom Forcade, who eventually founded the magazine *High Times*. Mainstream liberal groups criticized the Zippies for causing chaos at the Miami Republican and Democratic Conventions — like beating up Republican delegates and stealing Lyndon Johnson's picture from the Democratic Convention while chanting "We are not McGovernable."[11] These groups contended that these actions served to delegitimize Senator McGovern, the peace candidate. Mike Royko of the *Chicago Daily News* even wrote that Tom Forcade might be on the government payroll, but Jack Anderson of the *Washington Post* debunked this theory.[12]

Forcade has said that the "concept of Zippie" was invented to gain media attention at the 1972 presidential conventions and to distinguish this group from Abbie, Jerry, and the "Albion Yips" (who spent the Miami Convention in the Albion Hotel) because of their endorsement of McGovern and a payment dispute about the book *Steal This Book*, put out by Hoffman and edited by Forcade. He said, "After the '72 Conventions, the organization was returned to Yip."[13] The McGovern endorsement was very controversial among the Yips and led to a Yip "National Conclave" in Columbus Ohio, representing Yippies in 23 states in November 23, 1972, to "require the resignation of Abbie Hoffman and Jerry Rubin as party spokespeople."[14] Besides strong disagreement about the endorsement, the Yips felt they wanted a more grassroots decision-making structure and were resentful of Abbie's and Jerry's control of Yip resources.

In May of '72, there was escalation of the Vietnam War and subsequent demonstrations, riots, and police brutality against demonstrators. In Madison, Wisconsin, a Yip named Ollie Steinberg shot at police while in an LSD daze, mistaking them for the local Nazis who had been phoning death threats to his group, the "Wide-Eyed Revolutionary Movement" (WERM). Cops then savagely beat WERM members and arrested Ollie. As one Yip put it, "Vietnam was less of an issue than a metaphor for what . . . young American rebels now wished would happen in their hometowns: wear down the Death Machines and seize control of their lives in a burst of heroism."[15]

However, after the tumult of the late sixties and early seventies, the Yippies settled down to "smoke-ins, rock concerts, underground papers and pieings . . . revolution as entertainment."[16] In 1973, with the exception of Ollie Steinberg and a few others who received significant jail time, many Yips successfully defended themselves against riot charges from 1972. Tom Forcade and Cindy Orensteen were also acquitted of charges that stemmed from the incendiary devices they were found with at the Miami Convention. The prosecution's expert witness admitted the device was not a bomb.

While Jerry Rubin went from Yippie to Yuppie, and Abbie Hoffman took his own life in 1989, Dana Beal continues to carry on the Yippie spirit at 9 Bleecker St., the same East Village location that the Yippies have been working out of since Dana started residing there in 1973. Nowadays he works with his group "Cures Not Wars," an organization with 150 chapters around the county that was started in 1994 to encourage legalization of medical marijuana and to promote Ibogaine, a substance which purportedly helps heroin addicts get over their addiction. It was at 9 Bleecker St. that the Yippies published the *Yipster Times*, which became *Overthrow* in 1979. Topics included conspiracy theories about the JFK and Malcolm X assassinations and an alleged CIA cocaine connection in South East Asia; advice on such subjects as how to make free calls through false credit card numbers — complete with a page of Justice Department numbers — or ride free in boxcars; and urging readers to call members of the Ku Klux Clan and Nazi party to harass them; as well as criticizing every current president and their drug policies.

The Yippies — and now Cures Not Wars — have planned countless demonstrations at Number 9 including their annual May 1st marijuana smoke-ins — which in New York have been held at Washington Square Park and more recently at Battery Bark — and have been a presence at just about every national presidential convention since 1968. Although Beal has admirers, some feel he has been a divisive influence in different progressive movements that he has joined, such as the Greens, Act Up, and the Tompkins Square Park movement after the riots in late '80s. Beal has had some animosity directed against him in the Yippie movement as well. There have been many faction fights and personal animosities, usually resulting in people not talking to each other. However, in 1977 a revolt against Dana by the leaders of a younger D.C. collective turned ugly: he was beaten behind a stage by a "goon squad" at a July 4th Smoke-In. The D.C. collective ultimately expelled the two goon squad leaders.

Mr. Beal has also been embroiled for years in a fight to stop his eviction from 9 Bleecker Street and to enable him to buy the building from his landlord.

I was able to interview Dana, an unforgettable presence with his white hair and long droopy handlebar mustache, reminiscent of a less bushy-haired Mark Twain with hangdog eyes.

We met on the second floor of 9 Bleeker Street, a musty-smelling, ramshackle building that once housed the Yippies, and now is home to Cures Not Wars, whose variously-aged, colorful members were about have a meeting to plan the latest May Day smoke-in.

Cheryl: How did you get involved in the Yippies?

Dana: The Yippies were a successor to a couple of early groups, and when they started it they wanted the biggest coalition possible for the protest in Chicago for the Democratic Convention [in 1968] and they came to me because I was the head of the other faction and they wanted to form one thing.

Abbie was in the Diggers. The real Diggers were in San Francisco so it was really Abbie and Joe . . . using the cache of the Digger name. They did a free store and they used to joke that they kept the good tvs to themselves.

C: Did they have a free store in the Lower East Side?

D: They tried to do something on 43 First St. They didn't have the infrastructure, they were young, they didn't have the work ethic.

C: What was your faction called?

D: We called ourselves Provos. Not like the Provos of Northern Ireland, but like the Provos of Holland. They had pot parades and rode white bicycles. There were free bicycles; you would leave them on the street and then someone else would drive them . . . . They were able to overthrow a conservative administration. They were provocateurs — they were always provoking shit.

You have this repressive liberalism, right? I believe the exact words were "repressive tolerance" — wasn't that Marcuse's formulation of it? Anyway, the idea of it is that it was supposed to provoke them into dropping their mask, their liberal mask, to show them to be the true fascists they were . . .

Where we are coming from is that we believe in something called the psychedelic revolution.

In 1966 this thing blooms in the summer 'cause there was a riot in Tompkins Square Park where they dragged these war resisters from their picnic to those fences and there was a pregnant woman and the Puerto Ricans were incensed at the treatment of this obviously pregnant woman and there was a riot and it went on for three days. And at the end of that time we suggested that we all retire and smoke a joint and we had this big peace . . . around the issue; how can we all be so different if we are all smoking a joint together? . . . Pot was really cheap which brought in a lot of economic activity . . .

C: Tell me about meeting Abbie Hoffman.

D: It was advertised in *Hippie Councils* and I said "We're a little hippie tribe, can we go?"

A Radical Political and Social History of the Lower East Side

Me and [A. J. Weberman], our scam is that we were getting peyote and we were distilling mescaline out of it on a stove. And the people we knew were from Texas — they were Texas hippies and the main difference is that they were down on the civil rights movement, which was shocking to us because we couldn't imagine anyone not being part of the civil rights movement.

But the point is that we met Abbie in the park and he was opposed to the smoke-in in the park but after about three weeks of it being a success he came down with a cigar box full of joints. People held them up and took them and after that it got big and the Grateful Dead came to the park and there were 3,000 people smoking weed and it got into the *New York Times* and of course the inevitable counterrevolution happened and the DEA targeted me and I got set up. And that led to 3,000 people marching because we were putting out a street sheet.

C: The *Yipster Times?*

D: No, a mimeograph. All the stuff was done on a mimeograph.

C: Do you have any anecdotes about Abbie?

D: Well he was in between these different groups. He knew a lot of people.

He was taking people from the Lower East Side to Newark and giving them food during the Newark riots, directly from Tompkins Park.

But there was some tension between these two events because we [the Provos] were into mass events and we were more populist.

The Provos were able to get 3,000 people because we gave the flyer out to everyone regardless of whether it looked like you smoked pot or not, but it turned out a lot of people were smoking pot.

Whereas Abbie was doing more advanced stuff but they never had more than 20 or 30 people in his things . . . but they were so outrageous, like throwing money at the stock exchange — it only took 20-30 people. He didn't want to invite a lot of people because he didn't want to lose control. They needed us [the Provos] to do stuff for the Pentagon. They had us promote it at the smoke in. So the night before, 3,000 people had a smoke before the march to the Pentagon.

C: How was levitating the Pentagon?

D: You could get fucked up there.

C: Was it scary?
D: Oh yeah, it was scary shit. People sat there and got arrested. I did not because I had my federal thing, but I had my 15 minutes of fame and I was only 20. They [Abbie and the

other Yippies] were 27, 28. They were able to deal with it better. I didn't have a good support system — if I knew then what I knew now! I didn't have really good advice then. Anyway . . . I was arrested in December and then I split, but before then, Abbie had me over to St. Marks Place and inducted me into the Yippie Hall of Fame in January 1968. It wasn't more than two weeks before they came up with it — during Christmas while I was in jail.

C: Do you mean the action at the Democratic National Convention?

D: Well, also they came up with a new thing they called "The Death of Hippie." We've all been reborn as Yippies.

They also joked that they were Jewish hippies. The problem was that there was cultural dissonance because they were really expecting all these kids from the Midwest to join them who were not Jewish while radical. There was tension between the New York guys and everyone else.

C: Because they were mostly Jewish?

D: Every single one of them was Jewish except me and my friends.

I was dragooned to go to a Seder [because] they didn't have a 10th guy [needed for the ceremony]. And they put this thing on my head.

C: How did that make you feel?

D: Like an honorary Jew I guess . . . . I'm from a Baptist background so it's easy for Baptists to identify with Jews . . . It's the first story of national liberation.

C: So you weren't involved in the Chicago riot?

D: No, I was on the lam. I didn't surface again till next year just before SDS broke up. I came back from Canada. And I was around but I wasn't really around and what happened was I established contact with these guys just about the time that John Sinclair was setting up this thing that ultimately became the fusion of the Panthers and the Yippies. And I went to that — the "White Panthers."

The White Panthers had a charter from Oakland and John Sinclair was considered to be a separate radical hero and actually because he was into jazz, he was considered to be a soul brother, a fellow traveler.

He was the chairman and I was the field marshal of the Central Committee of the White Panther party because of my legend, because of the Provos. Abbie and Jerry [Rubin] said that — Oh, you should deal with this guy, he's a legend.

C: So the White Panthers were fully in support of the Black Panthers?

A Radical Political and Social History of the Lower East Side

D: Yeah, but what happened is that they merged with the Yippies in 1969 to become the Youth International Party, in December in 1969 on 17th St. — the Tom Forcade block.

C: What did the Black Panthers think of the White Panthers and the Yippies?

D: Well, the Black Panthers at this point were having the Panther 21 trial — they needed all the help they could get . . . .

C: And *so* —

D: And so what happened was that I ended up putting on some stuff in Madison. In 1970 the main stuff that happened was like the bombing in Cambodia, Kent State. I was up here at this big rally for a Bobby Seale demonstration in New Haven. That's when Tom Forcade and I became the Zippies. At that time Tom was still working with Abbie. Then they had a falling out. The falling out I recently found out was provoked by another guy named Michael Forman. Forman was the one who got John Lennon to fly in to do a concert for John Sinclair that got him out of jail for 10 years for pot. [Thirteen thousand people showed up for this concert. The FBI harassed John and Yoko, who cancelled their second scheduled concert for the Yippies. Sinclair was freed with 7 years left on his sentence.] But when he got out he wasn't doing [the political organizing] anymore, so I kind of inherited that whole national organization that had been set up.

[In the spring of 1971, Dana Beal and Tom Forcade organized a theatrical demonstration of 3,000 pot smokers who marched from a D.C. smoke-in to the east side of the capital — where Vietnam Vets had thrown their medals a few months earlier — and smashed huge hypodermic needles used for rhinos in an effort to highlight the allegation that the CIA was bringing in heroin from South East Asia. Ten days later Beal was arrested for organizing Midwest Yippies for a protest at the upcoming Republican convention.]

I set up a Yippie conference . . . in 1971 and that became the seed for the protest in '72. But then I was busted — they caught up to me — and I didn't get out until the protest started. [In September 2001, two thousand people held a smoke-in outside the jail in which Dana was being held.] And I went to Miami and we got into a lot of trouble because of the smoke-in [in Miami]. And people said, "How can you detract from the issue of Vietnam?", and the answer was that Vietnam was over. [In a metaphorical sense; Dana was implying that it was "winding down," because technically it wasn't over at that point].

C: Is this when you were with the Zippies?

D: No, the Zippies were started in my absence and the thing that hamstrung my efforts is that there was this big faction fight and it was impossible to be on one side without being trashed by the other.

They were using the marijuana thing to trash me — they didn't really care about marijuana. But they started a controversy in the movement that dogged the New Left for 30 years about whether marijuana was a legitimate issue or not.

I would basically say in 1979 NORML (The National Organization for the Reform of Marijuana Laws) and the gay movement were about equal in their status. In fact NORML passed up a chance to work with the gay movement in a big demo in '79. Ten years later no one really focused on drug legalization effort. There was a new group, Drug Policy Organization. They lost a tremendous amount of clout and the gays were still going strong. So the gays pulled ahead of the drug legalization effort. In 1968 it was more taboo to be queer than it was to be smoking pot. All kind of people smoked pot-it was considered to be a regular thing.

C: Do you want to talk about the Zippies and why it was started?

D: Well it was started because Tom felt that . . . . There were some legitimate differences, but Tom felt he could replace Abbie Hoffman. And the fact was that Abbie Hoffman was never the same after the trial. [The Chicago 7 trial in 1968]

C: And what do you mean by that?

D: Well, it freaked him out when he was indicted and convicted. And he lost some of his, you know, spirit for life. . . . In Chicago . . . it was a huge thing . . . Abbie always had a problem with manic depression . . . and he eventually committed suicide. He didn't draw enough strength from the people around him. He had a tremendous persona but at the same time you could alienate him.

C: So you think the split was more —

D: The split was because Michael Foreman was an absolute asshole who took some money and then Tom thought he should be paid.

C: You mean for the book *Steal This Book*.

D: He took money for work that Tom did and Tom never got it. Yeah, about the book.

C: So you think it was more of that kind of stuff rather than the political differences?

D: Well, he did put some stuff in the Zippy manifesto that pissed Abbie off. There were a lot of people who accused him of using kids for cannon fodder. He was still upset about it 10 years later — he was even mad at me — because a lot of people got hurt in Chicago. And they weren't really told, according to many people, what they were getting into. There were kids coming from all around the Midwest and there was rioting in the street . . . The violence was not stopping, it was getting bigger.

C: As I understand it, the Zippies considered themselves less into compromise with the system. [Abbie and Jerry Rubin had endorsed McGovern in early May.]

D: The Zippies thought of themselves as younger and more radical. . . . We actually came up with some fairly good positions. Like our position on marijuana. It was different than hard drugs. . . . You know about the charges of heroin being smuggled in from South East Asia through some Defense Department pipeline.

If our own government is going to deal drugs, how are you going to protect the kids who are smoking pot who are in a drug milieu unless it's sold over the counter as a regulated substance? Because otherwise the dealer is going to offer them heroin . . .

C: To get back to the Yippies and the Zippies —

D: The big thing was we started the paper. We went to Miami and after Miami there was this huge fucking alienation between the Yippies and the Zippies. So we started a paper called the *Yipster Times* because we wanted to go back to being the Yippies of 1969 when it wasn't factionalized, it was all one thing. The problem was that neither Tom nor Abbie was interested in that. Abbie was in the underground because he got busted for coke-selling coke to an undercover cop because he needed money. Tom started *High Times*.

C: Anything else about the factionalism?

D: Well it went on for years and basically different wings of the movement wouldn't talk to each other.

C: What was that about?

D: They were really upset about what happened in Miami — talk to Sam Leff. He'll give a whole denunciation word for word.

The point is that we started the paper. The paper really consumed a lot of our efforts. We did a lot of stuff like that the Watergate burglars were also involved in the JFK assassinations. . . . And we did smoke-ins. We did the first smoke in at the White House in 1977. And in 1978 we did a benefit for Abbie at the Felt Forum.

The "Bring Abbie Home" benefit — it was an anniversary of Chicago. And it was fairly successful but we lost a lot of money because it was set up so that we wouldn't make any money. It happened that there was a newspaper strike and he didn't get the kind of coverage he wanted and he was fairly disgruntled. So it didn't really solve the factionalism problem. And then Tom shot himself in the head in the fall. And we were getting a lot of support from Tom Forcade in *High Times* and it wasn't the same after that.

C: Do you have any idea why he committed suicide?

D: They were closing in on him.
C: The government?

D: Yeah.

C: And that was real?

D: That was real. And he figured that way they couldn't take the magazine—put it out of business.

[A few weeks before Forcade shot himself, his wife Gabrielle Shang-Forcade interviewed him. In one quote he said, "Effectively, I've already spent the last ten years in jail—I've been under such surveillance."[16] Then he goes on to say that almost everyone around him is a government agent.]

C: And after that . . . ?

D: After that we just didn't get the same kind of support. Tom was a friend. He would just give you $5,000 dollars.

C: So what about Studio 10?

[Ten Bleecker St. housed the Studio 10 Rock Club and the Tom Forcade Media Center which was "part of the Rock Against Racism strategy" that the Yippies used in 1979, an homage to the European group "Rock Against Racism."]

D: Well that's when we set up Studio 10. That gave us a couple of good years. There was a guy named Hank who Aron could tell you about. He first got kicked out in 1976. They thought he was a plant. He wandered back in a few years later through A.J. We were doing this thing across the street. And it was a great deal. For three dollars if you were a member, you got to see five bands. Beer is a dollar. And there was free pot. Everywhere you looked was pot. This was an era where there was Colombian and it had a lot of seed so you'd end up with a lot of seed with some pot in it. So they weren't taking it home.

C: Did you have any problems with the police?

D: No, because no one was selling it; they were just smoking it.

C: And when did that scene start?

D: It started with the Abbie Hoffman benefit. We wanted to have the after-party here but it was too big. And what happened was that Hank went and fucking called the fire department when there was a little problem with an electric fire because of the refrigerator. That got everybody closed. Alice was mad because he was stealing the beers. And this went on for 20 years until 1995. And a lot of people thought this was just a continuation of the Yippie/Zippie split. But this guy was making obscene calls to little kids and stalking Alice [Torbush, a longtime Yippie who lives on the 3rd floor of 9 Bleecker]. This was really patho-logical behavior. Saying things like he's going to put Aron's family back in the gas chambers. [Aron Kay's mother survived Auschwitz.] Aron was firmly convinced he was a Nazi. So [Hank] finally got to the point at about 1991, during Desert Shield . . . he would put up stuff on telephones in Brooklyn. Stickers that would say bomb Mecca and Medina. Nuke

A Radical Political and Social History of the Lower East Side

the Dome of the Rock. Gas the Arabs. And he was putting this in the Arabic areas and we were getting death threats.

He had Aron's name and this address and phone number and he did that with Alice —[calling her] Anal Alice, [posting flyers for] Alice's Hillbilly Hookers. She was getting hundreds of sexually harassing phone calls. And she would very nicely talk each guy down . . . .

So he was doing all this really nasty stuff and finally he put this thing that said "Drug mules earn big bucks." In Brooklyn. This guy calls up. He was from the *Philadelphia Inquirer* . . . . And I said, "Oh, that, that was put up by this crank. What he was really trying to do was discredit this thing we were working on, which is Ibogaine." And he was so interested – – we were working with the NIH (National Institute of Health) at the time — that he ended up doing a story and we were on the front page of the *Philadelphia Inquirer* on the 4th of July, 1991.

But what happened was that we called Hank. And we said, "Hey, we're on the front page of the *Philadelphia Inquirer*." And he went bonkers. He went nuts. Cranky crank crank. Like the time we handed the stuff about Ibogaine to Nelson Mandela and he saw us . . . . And he just cranked us for days.

But what happened was that he started going after the religion — the Bwidi [the African tribe associated with Ibogaine] religion. He didn't have any problem going after Islam, so why not this obscure African religion?

[Dana then tells a story about how Hank invited bad luck to himself by dissing the Bwidi and was subsequently discovered with bomb-making materials in his home. As a result, Dana is convinced Hank is the one who put a bomb in front of 9 Bleecker, which caused severe injury to two police officers investigating it.]

C: So how did you get into the Ibogaine issue?

D: When Tom Forcade shot himself in the head, that's when the Ibogaine story started, because it forced us out on our own. There was a deal in the movement to only seek the legalization of pot. But other people breached it by also seeking the legalization of coke and when Carter won and Reagan lost, we knew there was no chance. Even before that we had a big falling out with *High Times* with the Heroin Chic. [He showed me a picture from *High Times* with heroin cut in lines like coke] . . . You can do coke and not get seriously fucked up but you cannot do heroin and not get strung out. People were bringing heroin into Studio 10.

C: In hindsight do you think that the critics had some validity to their claim that behavior such as the Zippie actions in the Miami Republican convention served to delegitimize McGovern and caused a counter reaction that helped elect Nixon?

D: No . . . There were two principle complaints about the Zippies: that we were too wild and undisciplined and that we were changing the conversation from Vietnam to the war on drugs. But the war in Vietnam was winding down.

C: Who felt that way?

D: Most of the people making the complaints had a weird, [puritanical] attitude about drugs . . . We were blamed for helping bring down McGovern. But then again, Abbie's brother Jack is still beating his brow about the Chicago protesters causing the Democrats to lose in '68. But I think what brought McGovern down was that he picked the wrong Vice President-and then mishandled the situation by saying he was behind Eagleton "1,000%" and dumping him. Showed he was unsteady.

We did have a higher percentage of our people busted, non-violently, than any of the other groups. We were there to get busted.

C: Did the "mainstream" Yippies blame the Zippies for being too violent in Miami?

D: They blamed us for changing the conversation to the war on drugs. Period. Some people say I personally derailed McGovern because I asked McGovern about the heroin coming in from Vietnam — "In a situation where our own government is dealing hard drugs, how are we going to protect kids who already smoke pot unless it can be sold legally over the counter like alcohol?" — when he came down and spoke to protesters in the lobby of the Doral Hotel during the Miami Convention.

He was being raked over the coals by the Progressive Labor Party — and the conversation was going around in circles — and I broke in and asked him a question that could make him shine. He said, "I'm the guy who first spoke out about the heroin in Vietnam on the floor of the Senate," but then he said, "Even though we disagree about marijuana legalization, we both agree that heroin is bad." It's not my fault he didn't answer my question.

C: How many Yippie chapters were there around the country?

D: Never more than 30 or 40 chapters. We have more affiliates today. There are 150 Million Marijuana March events this May around the world.

C: But Cures Not Wars is not the Yippies is it?

D: CNW is what the Yippies have become. . . "Yippie" was stereotyped by the media, but we have evolved. After Abbie came back we took a detour through the Greens and then Act Up. We were also involved in Rock Against Reagan, Nicaragua, the Great Peace Walk, etc.

C: When did Cures Not Wars start?

D: In 1994, when Act Up broke apart into three factions, the smallest of which was us.

A Radical Political and Social History of the Lower East Side

C: In the Greens, etc., was there a faction known as "the Yippies"?

D: No, although some people identified me as a Yippie. Only the head of NORML, Keith Stroup, still calls us "the Yippies."

C: How's the fight for your building going?

D: We buy the building on Monday.

And Dana is still working on buying his building.

Endotes:

1. *"Pigasus the Immortal and the 1968 Democratic Chicago Convention,"* Porkopolis, April 2004 (Copyright 2004 Glamorous Pig Ranch Productions, Inc.),
http://www.geocities.com/TheTropics/Shores/7484/ftr/pigasus.html

2. "Testimony of Abbie Hoffman," *Famous American Trials, The Chicago 7 Trial 1969-70*, April 2004,
http://www.law.umkc.edu/faculty/projects/ftrials/Chicago7/Hoffman.html

3. Douglas O. Linder, "A Trial Account," *Famous American Trials, The Chicago 7 Trial 1969-70*, April 2004,
http://www.law.umkc.edu/faculty/projects/ftrials/Chicago7/Account.html

4. http://www.law.umkc.edu/faculty/projects/ftrials/Chicago7/Account.html

5. "Testimony of Abbie Hoffman," *Famous American Trials, The Chicago 7 Trial 1969-70*, April 2004,
http://www.law.umkc.edu/faculty/projects/ftrials/Chicago7/Hoffman.html

6. Youth International Press Information Service, *Black Listed News Secret History, From Chicago 1968 to 1984*, (Bleecker Publishing, 1983), Page 288.

7. Associated Press, "A Major Yippie Theorist Seized on Drug Charges," *New York Times*, 7/26/71.

8. Youth International Press Information Service, 407.

9. Youth International Press Information Service, 660.

10. Youth International Press Information Service, 372.

11. Jack Anderson, "Young Radicals," *The Washington Post*, November 5, 1972.

12. Youth International Press Information Service, 548.

13. Youth International Press Information Service, 386.

14. Youth International Press Information Service, 398.

15. Youth International Press Information Service, 407.

16. Youth International Press Information Service, 547.

Chapter 3

The Living Theatre on Third Street
By Hanon Reznikov

From 1989 until 1993, The Living Theatre lived in New York in a storefront on East Third Street, between Avenues C and D. We did plays dealing with the realities of people's lives in that neighborhood, including homelessness, unemployment and police repression. We held poetry readings, music and dance concerts and political meetings. The Living Theatre on Third Street became one of the many venues on the Lower East Side where revolutionaries got together to talk shop and to have a good time.

The Living Theatre on Third Street was born in New York in 1947, but after the group's fourth theater in the city was closed by the authorities in 1963, the company began a life in exile, mostly in Europe. In 1983, an offer came to bring the whole group back to New York for a two-month run of four plays at the Joyce Theater in 1984. The critics were savage and founder Julian Beck was looking forward to returning to Paris when he died of colon cancer in 1985, leaving it to me to pick up where he had left off in seeing to the needs of Judith and the company. Co-founder Judith Malina was always more eager than Julian to be working in New York, and I, a Brooklyn boy, was glad to search with her for a permanent space for the company in its hometown. For several years, we campaigned to in order to rally community boards, block associations and city council members to allow us to purchase one of several interesting city-owned properties. At the time, these included an abandoned synagogue on East 7th Seventh Street, an unused school on Forsyth Street and an empty bathhouse on Allen Street. In each instance, competing interests prevailed, leaving moot the question of whether we would have been able to raise the necessary cash. We kept our sights focused on the East Village/Lower East Side area, which seemed to us to harbor the most volatile mix of artists, poor people and political activists, a mixture which we hoped our theater would ignite. By 1989, we were ready to change our strategy from permanent acquisition to a simple rental. We walked up and down every block, looking at likely and unlikely sites. ·

The recession had taken its toll on the East Village real estate market; almost all of the art galleries that had mushroomed into the neighborhood in the early '80s were out of business or had moved to SoHo. There was hope of finding something affordable. After looking at a few available rentals, including a former fish smokehouse on East 12th Twelfth Street and a loft above a furniture store on Avenue A, Judith and I spotted the empty store at 272 East Third Street. The gate was down, but through the windows we could make out that the space extended significantly into the back. We called the posted realtor's number and arranged to look inside.

This was a storefront whose rear wall boasted a light-studded arch opening onto a back room of minimally satisfactory dimensions for a 74-seat theater. The laws governing spaces

521

rated at occupancy of 75 or greater are much more stringent, requiring sprinkler systems and so on. We also discovered that according to the building code, premises on side streets are not required to have a second means of egress if they happen to be situated within 30 feet of an avenue. 272 East Third fit the bill. Most importantly, we liked the feel of the place. The front room, which occupied the ground floor of a four-story turn-of-the-century apartment building, would make a good-sized lobby/office. The rear room, a single-story extension into the backyard with a square cupola rising from the center promised to make a fine little black box theater. Further, there was a stairway in the rear leading to a large, moldy basement that would serve as dressing room, shop and storage. The real estate agent quoted us a monthly rent of $3,000. We managed to talk the owner, Jerry Atkins, into agreeing to $2,000. He seemed sympathetic enough, for a landlord. "I'm getting out of residential buildings," he told us. "I don't like dealing with people who can"t pay the rent on their home." We handed him a certified check for $6,000 (two months' rent and a month's security deposit) and he handed us the keys to 272 East Third Street. It was curious about the starting sum — $6,000 was the exact amount Julian had inherited from an aunt in the 1940s; that was the sum with which he and Judith had launched The Living Theatre.

We rushed downtown immediately, our hearts pounding as we lifted the security gate protecting the new plate-glass storefront. We moved slowly past the archway into the mysterious gloom of the soon-to-be-a-theater chamber and sat on the floor for a few quiet minutes, our arms tight around each other. Another chapter had begun.

In the weeks that followed, we cleaned and painted, did wiring and plumbing, and began to get to know our neighbors. The starving young artists made themselves known in short order, though the most politically correct among them, many of them recent graduates of expensive schools, kept a certain distance, regarding us as another regrettable instance of gentrification. Just a few doors down there was a municipal family shelter and right across the street, a public health facility. A newsstand occupying the stretch of sidewalk between our front windows and the pawnshop on the corner was rented by a local artist, Jim C (named for the avenue), who used it for installations. The current version consisted of strobe-lit styrofoam wigstands whirling on turntables against an expressionistically painted backdrop. At the eastern end of the mostly Spanish-speaking block, toward the public housing project on Avenue D (very much like the one in which I grew up in East New York in the '50s), there was a performance venue called the Bullet Space. A block to the west was the very hip and successful Nuyorican Poets Café, and a block further, was Delia's, a fashionable late-night spot named after its debutante owner. The area was chock-full of beautifully maintained community gardens sprung up in vacant lots where, during the preceding summer, in 1988, we had done a number of performances of *Turning the Earth*, a street play about the nutritive potential of urban soil. And all around the neighborhood, a number of abandoned tenements had been occupied by squatters. Some of these, like the 13th Street building that had housed the Alchemical Theater, were outfitted rather inventively. Electricity could be procured by tapping into the nearest streetlight, sometimes with the illicit cooperation of disgruntled Con Ed employees. Heating was often supplied by burning scrap wood scavenged from vacant lots in oil-drum furnaces. The toilets, typically, were bucket-flushed. LaMama was one block north, four blocks west, and light-years upscale of us. The drug dealers were everywhere, as were the rats and roaches. We tried to get along with everybody.

Neighbors filled us in about the site's history. It began as the Happy Days Bar and Grill, serving the neighborhood since the end of Prohibition. Sometime in the 1960s, the popular local restaurant shut its doors, after a run-in with local racketeers who had some kind of problem with the crap shoots traditionally held in the back room. One night, someone wandered in and told us of a night more than twenty years before when a gang of thugs with sawed-off shotguns had forced he and his companions to strip naked and lie on the basement floor while they made off with their cash and jewelry. There I was, lying right on top of my buddy John's girlfriend, both of us butt-naked, he laughed hoarsely. The owners took fright and closed. A couple of years later, when hip-dom had bled east deep into Alphabet City, the place reopened as The Sin Club, where off-off-off "events" were spawned. This arrangement gave way to an after-hours joint known as Stupid/Fresh, where, we were told, a patrol car would stop by at least once a night to collect a share of the proceeds. And now it was The Living Theatre.

The East Village in 1989 was a place in ferment. The "gentrification" of large stretches of the neighborhood during the boom years of the eighties had come to a virtual halt after the stock market crash of 1987. Much had already been invested in renovating newly upscale buildings, such as Christodora House on Tompkins Square which had attempted to sell apartments for upwards of a million dollars. A sizeable contingent of people with disposable income remained. The East Village and Lower East Side were unique in the city in offering a dense concentration of artists decidedly anti-establishment in their leanings, as well as certain middle-class working people (teachers, computer wonks, advertising account execs and so on) who liked to live among such artists, as well as the larger stratum of poor people, mostly Puerto Ricans and Dominicans. And beyond the bodega on every block was a vast supply of experimental performance venues, offbeat shops, bars and restaurants, all located halfway between midtown and the financial district.

The neighborhood is famous for its vocal contingent of activists of many stripes: environmentalists, feminists, squatters, old guard anti-imperialists and anti-authoritarians of every kind, many of whom call themselves anarchists (distressingly, when they respond in kind to violent challenges by the police). The Tompkins Square police riot of 1988, memorably documented by Clayton Patterson, during which the homeless were evicted from the park, was still fresh in everyone's mind.

We created theatrical projects designed to reach out to all these groups. When we were performing *Tumult*, or *Clearing the Streets* or *The Body of God*, plays which address the problems of housing and the use of public spaces, we were able to afford to members of the squatters' movement and to those campaigning for aid to the homeless the opportunity to address audiences directly about these concerns. When we mounted our environmental epic, *Waste*, in various outdoor locations in the neighborhood, we were able to create a forum for local environmental groups like the Green Guerrillas. During the run of *Waste*, we opened the doors of the theater to local artists, transforming the space into a Waste Museum of paintings, sculpture and performance events all on the theme of waste. During the initial run of

A Radical Political and Social History of the Lower East Side

Rules of Civility, which coincided with the first American war in the Persian Gulf, we ended the show with a candle-lit peace vigil in the street in coordination with War Resisters League and other protest groups.

Our sojourn on Third Street was virtually coterminous with the first Bush administration. Thus the voices that spoke up at the theater (as they did, for instance, during audience-discussion segments of plays like *The Body of God* and *The Zero Method*) were speaking to the reality of a conservative regime in Washington whose politics our audience blamed for most of the world's problems. It was the recessionary economic cycle, however, which brought down public funding for social programs, for the arts, and finally, brought down the Republican White House itself.

Shortly after we moved in, Ed Koch was succeeded by David Dinkins, and ten months after we moved out, Rudy Giuliani defeated Dinkins. It was instructive to our audiences to see how ineffective well-meaning and, ostensibly progressive political leaders like Dinkins were in making any dent in the city's problems and how such lack of progress ended in abetting the conservative "revolution," as the right-wingers so distressingly call it.

In November, 1989, five months after we moved in, the Berlin Wall fell. John Farris, a neighborhood poet, had done us the great service of taking up residence in the basement dressing room, in exchange for which (plus a small weekly cash sum) he kept watch over the premises, and hosted a regular late-night salon with the wide range of his acquaintances. It was in the basement dressing room where John slept that he had set up a little black-and-white television with a wire-hanger antenna and it was here that we witnessed the astonishing moments when the East Berliners scaled the wall and stood victorious atop it. I remember in particular the amazement of two of our actors, Martin Reckhaus from West Germany, and Elena Jandova from Bulgaria, as we watched the ecstatic crowds surging over the Wall, in disbelief of their own situation.

On Third Street we could for the first time set our own opening dates and , repertory schedule, and rehearse at times that suited our own needs and desires. These were important advantages for us, and we made the fullest use of them, designing every major production as a unique use of the space, placing the audience now on bleachers, now in opposing camps, and then in a circle around us on the floor, or grouped about little cabaret tables, or adrift during *Body of God* like the homeless, required to get up and move again and again through a shifting environment. Further, the space became a real point of reference for the struggling community of East Village/Lower East Side artists and activists. All manner of extra-theatrical events took place under The Living Theatre's banner, or rather, behind the brightly elegant yellow neon sign that sculptor Rudi Stern had made for us. We became a job branch of the I.W.W. and the old anarcho-syndicalist union held regular meetings there. With Michael Shenker's guidance we created the Wobbly Chorus, a political *a cappella* singing group that appeared, among other places, in East River Park during the Fourth of July fireworks and downtown during the Shut Down Wall Street demonstrations, singing, among other things, "I Don't Want Your Millions, Mister!" The artists from World War III filled the lobby with provocative, lurid murals. And a number of street people found that we were a place that could offer them bathrooms and temporary shelter from the cold.

The re-implantation of *The Living Theatre* into the creative soil of downtown New York produced a sizable body of unique theatrical invention. In less than four years, we created a dozen major productions and many more readings and events of all kinds. *The Tablets*, Armand Schwerner's consideration of the earliest roots of civilization, was the opening production and was followed by Else Lasker-Schüler's *I and I*, a retelling of Faust as the modern story of the divided self. Both plays toured successfully through Europe in 1990, the year following their Third Street opening. It was for the first time in twenty years that the company had created plays in New York that then traveled around the world.

Toward the end of 1992, we were presenting *Echoes of Justice*, Exavier Wardlaw Muhammad's docu-drama about Larry Davis, in jail for shooting several policemen when, according to Davis, those same policemen tried to kill him for threatening to pull out of their drug operation. The production featured a number of first-time actors recruited from the projects as well as CHARAS organizer Bimbo Rivas and WBAI broadcaster Bob Fass. As audiences continued to pour in in early 1993, a late-night avant-garde music performance that involved the demolition of a washing machine with sledgehammers drove the upstairs neighbors to distraction. Desperate for sleep, they called the police. Besides putting an end to the performance, the raid revealed that the landlord did not possess a valid certificate of occupancy. The Living Theatre on Third Street soon became the fifth home of the company in New York to be shut down by the authorities. First in 1948, then in 1953, then in 1956, then in 1963 and finally in 1993. Still, much was accomplished. I miss working there, but I'm glad that the premises now house a family aid agency.

More than ten years have passed since then, during which we have worked mostly in other countries (Italy, Brazil and Lebanon, to name a few). But given what's going on out there in the world, we've decided that the time has come to take a stand here, where the trouble starts. We are ready to open another space in New York.

Chapter 4

Jerry the Peddler
The Squatter Movement, Its Anarchist Roots, and Its Conductor
Interview by John Beresford

The peddlers on St. Mark's Place and Cooper Union were a tattered lot in the late 1970s, all but run out by the police. To Jerry Holtzclaw, who peddled comic books, collectible cards, and buttons, this didn't make any sense. He wanted to put an end to the harassment and so organized New York City's peddlers, leafleting and "postering" the city, as well as using letter campaigns and petitions. And, of course, there were the demonstrations and marches with their ambiguous form that Jerry, dubbed the Peddler, would give direction and purpose to, then and over the next two decades, like a man who could have just as easily been dubbed the Conductor.

Jerry, through the way he has chosen to live-as a squatter-represents what some in society might call an element of anarchy. After all, his lifestyle suggests that homeless people have rights, especially to live in buildings that are abandoned and empty. For him, having the right to squat is only logical. At the same time, he eschews the status quo by questioning how society looks at ownership of property.

With empty buildings, squatting makes all the sense in the world, says Jerry, 53. "A lot of people need a pair of boots before they can grab themselves by the bootstraps and pull themselves up, and squatting provides that."

Not loud when engaged in conversation, the Peddler is more a mild-mannered gentleman, with a pointed, salt-and-pepper beard to complement wise, sparkling eyes. But put him on the street, willing host of a crowd, and he won't even need a bullhorn.

Nowadays, Jerry the Peddler rarely leads New York's squatter events. He gets permits for the shows, such as Squatter's May Day, and handles the parks department, the police department, and the bureaucrats, but the crews he assembles do the rest of the work. Over the years, homelessness and other issues such as the environment and racism have been given a voice through the squatters' annual parades, demonstrations, and marches-and through the occasional riot.

"I used to take control of just about any mob around," says Jerry, during an interview on the roof of his building, C-Squat, on Manhattan's Lower East Side. "I don't need to do it now-there are tons of people out doing things. Yes, they're not throwing garbage like we used to, but there's the whole garden movement, the Times Up thing, and in my mind these are much bigger versions of our Purple Parades back in the 1980s."

Although its origins can be traced to an activist group called Everything for Everybody in the mid 1960s, the New York squatting movement crystallized in late 1984, and Jerry was

Jerry the Peddler Interview by John Beresford

there. When two friends, Paul DeRienzo and John Entwhistle, mentioned an English couple looking to open a squat, he told them about a building between Avenue B and C: 327-329 East Eighth Street. He had previously noticed people going in and out of its back entrance, the front of the building being all boarded up.

Taking Jerry's sledgehammer, the three of them went to the back of the building, eventually to be known as the Mother Squat. As Jerry knocked out the bricks from the inside, his friends watched for police coming along Avenues B and C.

This was the moment the movement went public, when homeless people first came together to decide that they would call themselves squatters. The scene took off, with people coming in droves. "This is the heart of it," says Jerry, "where we organized and started becoming active, marching in the street, publicly advocating squatting."

Shortly after the birth of the Mother Squat, empty buildings opened up along Eighth Street. Jerry, who started squatting in February 1984, established himself in a building on Ninth Street, and others important to the movement, such as John the Communist and Don Yippie, were settling into the neighborhood as well, liberating the discarded. While living free meant dances with authority, these people made a point of having fun on the way.

*****

Three years before the dramatic Tompkins Square Park riots of 1988 — over the right of the homeless to sleep in the park — the Purple Parade came about, its cause being to save Adam Purple's garden. Adam Purple was a superintendent in a building who kept expanding his garden when the buildings behind his were torn down. When the City planned to build over the garden, which it succeeded in doing in 1986, the community cried out in protest. During the Purple Parade, people demonstrated by dressing up as fruits, flowers, and vegetables and parading around the Lower East Side.

"We used to have a big, six-foot purple earth ball," says Jerry. "We used to take it across town on St. Mark's Place, and we would turn around Broadway, with a mob against the traffic."

Behind Jerry's Ninth Street squat — where he stayed for 11 years before it burned down — Jerry took care of a garden, the first of four. Now a gravel parking lot, it was, in the mid 1980s a communal meeting place, open 10 hours a day, seven days a week. As long as there were no hard drugs or violence, people could come and go as they pleased," said Jerry. "It was a real autonomous zone."

Gardens took on real significance for the squatters, and the second one Jerry tended, North Star, a couple of doors down from the first, introduced community cooking to the experience. The squatters set up a kitchen, thanks largely to a squatter named Kalif, who had run dozens of Rainbow kitchens. Each morning, Kalif would stand on the corner of Ninth Street and Avenue C, bumming spare change. When he got enough money, the squatters bought a bag of rice and beans. They'd cook and serve the food to anyone who needed a meal.

A Radical Political and Social History of the Lower East Side

One night in 1986, after the second and final Purple Parade, Jerry and others pitched three teepees in the back of the North Star lot. It was an indication of things to come. When the local community board announced its intention to build in the plaza on the other side of Avenue C — something unpopular with neighborhood residents — Jerry decided to make a stand.

Since, as word of it spread, the communal kitchen was outgrowing its lot, the time seemed right to move the operation to the plaza across the street, called La Plaza. In its garden section stood the empty lot that the city wanted to turn into a senior citizen's home. The squatters pitched five teepees there and started putting in the homeless, which was easy to do with hundreds of people sleeping in the park around the clock. The kitchen operation flourished in its new location.

"Nobody's against housing and senior citizen centers, but at that time, you could stand right in the heart of La Plaza and count 10 empty buildings," says Jerry, adding that most of them eventually become housing for low to moderate income earners under a cross-subsidy plan.

At the time, the buildings could house the homeless, but soon enough the city came out with a truck and started drilling holes to begin construction.

"We had just dumpstered like eight dozen eggs the night before, while we were in the original teepee lot," says Jerry. "So we went up on the roof of my building and started throwing eggs at these guys. The workers ducked under their trucks. They left in such a hurry that they abandoned all their samples."

The incident repeated itself a couple of days later when the workers returned with a police officer who, by choosing the wrong place to stand, received most of the egging. The police officer gave Jerry a ticket for disorderly conduct. It was a small price to pay for making the squatters' presence felt. New York City squatters could claim success in their first real encounter with the community board. The senior citizens' home, Casa Victoria, was eventually built — but not in La Plaza.

* * * * *

With opinions and a voice, Jerry and friends appeared on the "Morton Downey, Jr., Show" several times in the mid 1980s. They participated in discussions including the cannabis debate and fascist-bashing; whenever someone was needed, they'd be there.

Although Jerry made over 10 personal appearances, he would often just sit in the audience. He felt most comfortable in a crowd. In an early appearance, old friend Paul DiRienzo took center stage, sitting between two opponents — Curtis and Lisa Sliwa — the former being the founder of the Guardian Angels. At one point, Downey walked up behind DiRienzo and pointed down at him, saying, "This is what's known as a shit sandwich." Jerry yelled from

Jerry the Peddler Interview by John Beresford

the audience, "Yes, but the shit's on the outside." Downey looked up, surprised, and said, "Shut up, weird beard."

"I'm better in the audience than up on stage behind a mic," says Jerry. "I get all tense. I'm absolutely terrible in front of an audience."

Jerry's got a bad tooth these days and, during the interview on his rooftop — in front of a microphone — he occasionally winces in pain. Rather than go to a dentist, he'll eventually yank the tooth out himself. He doesn't have Medicaid, or coverage from the Veteran's Administration. Although he served in the army, Jerry has "bad papers," because he refused to go to Vietnam. In fact, when the army heard he was planning riots to protest the war, he spent time in solitary confinement.

Born and raised in San Angelo, Texas, in the western part of the state, Jerry seems to have always had a contrary streak in him. Or, more accurately, something that made him different from everyone else he met. Kids picked on him mercilessly in elementary school, and pretty soon he had had enough. From the seventh grade on, Jerry found himself getting in and out of trouble.

The day Kennedy was assassinated, he got kicked out of school. A fellow student had made a negative comment about Kennedy, saying something like, "Yea, the nigger lover's dead." Jerry popped him in the mouth for it.

Going from greaser to mod, Jerry ran away from home a lot. In the ninth grade, he led a smoke-in for the right of students to smoke cigarettes on school grounds. And then, at 17, he did something stupid: he joined the army as a condition for marrying a girl he had fallen in love with. The marriage never worked out, and war did Jerry no good. Stationed in Germany from 1967-1970, the day Russia invaded Czechoslovakia, Jerry realized that he was now a soldier close to a war zone. In shock, Jerry sat behind a machine gun in a jeep, looking at the destruction and smoking a bowl of hash.

While still in the army, back on American soil, Jerry joined the Southern Student Organizing Committee and later the Student Mobilization Committee. He learned how to organize the masses. The leafleting strategy he picked up helped him once to blanket his army base with antiwar literature.

In Fort Worth, Jerry joined the White Panther group, but their approaches didn't jive. The White Panthers didn't believe in demonstrating, and that was what Jerry was all about. He soon hooked up with the Yippies. Then, from Fort Worth to Atlanta to Washington, D.C., Jerry established the way of life he leads to this day: community kitchens and gardens. Finally, in the mid 1970s, Jerry headed to New York for good.

"I came here to get away from honky America," he says. "I like hanging out with hippies, punks, beatniks, and freaks, and that's pretty much what I've always been into down here."

*****

A Radical Political and Social History of the Lower East Side

Jerry has never been on probation, done more than five days of community service, or spent more than 12 hours on Riker's Island, but, all told, he has been arrested over 200 times.

So law enforcement knows him well and doesn't need an invitation to charge him. That, however, is exactly what they got in 1997 when a picture of Jerry and pot plants appeared in a local paper, *The Shadow*. Jerry had been growing the plants for three years and had some 200 of them. When the police showed up, they shut down Jerry's block — with officers on the rooftops and behind buildings, a helicopter circling overhead. A truck from the Emergency Services Unit (NYC's version of a SWAT team) sat on the corner.

Jerry had gotten rid of most of the plants, but the police picked up enough of them to charge him with felony possession of over ten pounds, later lowered to misdemeanor possession of less than five pounds. Eighteen months later, however, the court dropped his case for lack of speedy trial.

A proponent of legalizing weed, Jerry considers this kind of bust pointless, a big waste of taxpayers' money. The pot wasn't meant for sale. "It was party pot that everybody knew about," says Jerry, "for events like the smoke-ins on Halloween." They would also make a couple gallons of a marijuana liquor every year, baking brownies, bread, and making spaghetti with it. "We were just doing the hippie thing," says Jerry, who would also fashion bongs out of the dried branches of the larger plants.

Over the years, not everyone wanted to do "the hippie thing" with Jerry. Some people came in to turn the squats into shooting galleries. Four or five buildings opened up on Eighth Street, and a landlord, a bunch of kids, and a junkie mechanic pretty much controlled the crack scene, says Jerry. "They burned a couple of buildings down, ran people out." That started the migration of squatters from Eighth Street to Thirteenth Street in the late 1980s.

At that time, crack was so rampant that a relationship between drugs in the neighborhood and the police began to reveal itself. Open drug dealing was tolerated. According to this book's editor, Clayton Patterson, "it illustrated how dysfunctional, disorganized, and corrupt the police were at that time." He referred to the Mollen Commission, which came out in 1994. The report dedicated a chapter to the Ninth Precinct, which, it turned out, was not held accountable to the extent that other precincts were. Added Jerry: "The Mollen Commission came along and pretty much confirmed everything we'd been saying for seven, eight years."

But the squatters soldiered on, continuing to demonstrate, while constantly tying their message to social issues, primarily the gentrification of society. Indeed, New York City squatters were a primary force for getting the word "gentrification" out into the public mindset, and becoming a household word.

The word, which came into existence sometime between 1975 and 1980, refers to the displacement of the poor by the affluent who buy up and renovate run-down urban neighbor-

Jerry the Peddler Interview by John Beresford

hoods. Jerry and friends did everything they could to defeat gentrification. Jerry's old friend John the Communist, for example, would be out postering three to four times a week, and sometimes everyday, spreading the message that the war on the poor had to stop.

John the Communist's greatest contribution to the squatter movement, perhaps was in adding an image to those voices of protest coming from people like Jerry. He covered the neighborhood not just with posters but graffiti. "He always had cans of spray paint," says Jerry. "After the Tompkins Square Park riots, Henry Stern remarked that if you drove around the neighborhood and looked at the graffiti and the posters, you'd think that the revolution was going to start tomorrow."

When Jerry and John would sit together in the old days, they'd talk about uniting the diverse political types they knew and forming "an army of the poor." Says Jerry: "We never realized we were building just that, an army of the poor."

Chapter 5

Garbage Guerrilla:
The Mystery Man Behind the East Village Art Gang with the Unprintable Name
By John McMillian

"Hey John, it's not too late to call you, is it?"

It's nearly midnight on a Sunday. Normally I'd be asleep (or at least in bed, drifting toward sleep) but tonight I'm awake and, for whatever reason, feeling a little lonesome. So I welcome the call. But who is it? The voice is older, conspicuously friendly, with a languid southwestern drawl. Nobody I know talks like this.

"It's Ben Morea."

* * * * *

Ben Morea is an ex-junkie who, in the late-1960s, was the notorious leader of an entirely unsavory, Lower East Side anarchist collective called Up Against the Wall, Motherfucker. I'm a young historian who studies American radicalism in that period, and I'd been trying to locate him — obviously unsuccessfully — for almost three years. All the leads I followed went nowhere. From my perspective, it was as if Morea had vanished, every bit as thoroughly and irrevocably as a jet contrail.

Not that this was terribly surprising. Even in his heyday, Morea cultivated an air of mystery. In the early-1960s he was an abstract expressionist painter known for dressing completely in black; someone who has seen his work described it as "very unusual. It consisted of *vast panels* of black. Swirling nebulae. Completely black."[1] Later in the decade, Morea used to strut around St. Mark's Place and Second Avenue, longhaired and bearded like any number of hippies, but instead of adorning himself in flowers and beads, he wore a leather jacket, carried a switchblade knife, and peddled manifestos full of cryptic poetry and angry agitprop. The Motherfuckers described themselves as a kind of politicized street gang, but in the media they were known only as "a group with a certain unprintable name."[2] Their general attitude toward the counterculture calls to mind something Patti Smith later said about rock 'n' roll: "We created it; let's take it over!"[3]

This is a group whose members once protested the Vietnam War by unfurling banners of napalmed children during High Mass in St. Patrick's Cathedral; who threw cow's blood on Secretary of State Dean Rusk and his black-tied guests at the New York Hilton; who set up crash pads for teenage runaways, ran "stores" where everything was free, organized community feasts in Tompkins Square Park, taught karate classes, and printed newsletters and broadsheets that trumpeted the most extreme formulations of the counterculture cosmology.

"We are the ultimate Horror Show," read one. "Hideous Hair & Dangerous Drugs . . . Armed Love striking terror into the vacant hearts of the plastic Mother & pig-faced Father."[4]

In 1967, during a New York City garbage strike, they carried piles of stinking, festering trash uptown on the subway and dumped it on the steps and in the fountain of Lincoln Center. ("WE PROPOSE A CULTURAL EXCHANGE," they declared in an accompanying leaflet: "garbage for garbage.")[5] In 1968, they rallied in support of Valerie Solanas, the tormented psychopath who shot Andy Warhol, because they thought that was a *good thing*. In 1969, the Motherfuckers cut the fences at Woodstock, helping to turn it into a free concert for hundreds of thousands.

Then they disappeared — or, some said, escaped. Morea had already been acquitted of attempted murder after allegedly stabbing a Vietnam veteran who was part of a group known for preying on hippies and draft resisters in Boston. After that came a highly publicized turf war between the Motherfuckers and rock impresario Bill Graham, who owned New York City's hippest club, the Fillmore East. At issue was whether or not the East Village's denizens could have free use of the Fillmore one night each week, for revelry and community organizing. Promises were broken, words were exchanged, threats were made, and eventually someone shattered Graham's nose by smashing him in the face with a chain. Another time, a Puerto Rican who oversaw a building where the Motherfuckers were squatting was found stabbed to death. Osha (née Tom) Neumann, the only Motherfucker to ever write about the group in retrospect, said this: "We had shouted 'Off the Pig!' but the first person to die was a Puerto Rican superintendent. The killing never made the papers, no one was ever arrested, and none of us was ever questioned by the police. Within the group, at least in my presence, the matter was not discussed. My tentative inquiries were met with curt impatience: It was necessary; you cannot live on the streets and allow yourselves to be attacked without defending yourself."[6]

Remnants of the group later appeared at a countercultural "gathering of the tribes" in New Mexico. Some of them affiliated with a famous hippie commune called the Hog Farm. Others spent time in Canjilón, among followers of Reies Tijerina (a.k.a. "King Tiger"), an Indio-Hispanic activist who, in an effort to win back land that the United States wrangled from Mexico in 1848, led an armed raid on a county courthouse that ended in a wild shootout. As Neumann recalled, they lived off food stamps, occasionally rustled cattle, and flirted with Native American lifestyles. "But the truth of the matter was we were isolated and self-destructing."[7]

And at some point, Ben Morea drifted off. One rumor suggested he was living a threadbare existence in the Rocky Mountains, traveling by horseback and sleeping in teepees. Another legend had it that he had become a kind of countercultural Col. Kurtz, leading mystical ceremonies in the desert. Not knowing very much about him in the first place, it was easy to imagine the worst: that he'd descended back into heroin, or that he was addlepated or institutionalized. Several years ago a friend of mine, also a historian, tried reaching him as well; he told me he'd heard Morea was dead.

A Radical Political and Social History of the Lower East Side

But of course, he was not dead. In fact, he was coming to New York City soon, and he wanted to meet me.

* * * * *

I was a senior in high school when I first became interested in the Motherfuckers, after reading just a couple of paragraphs about them in Todd Gitlin's elegant popular history, *The Sixties*. Gitlin described a time when "clusters of smart and rough cultural revolutionaries, aiming to carry the avant-garde spirit into the streets," began appearing on the activist scene. "Their common thrust was to overcome the distances between art and everyday life, artists and audience," he wrote. "One Lower East Side cluster, formed in the fall of 1967, became movement legend. Their name alone guaranteed it: Up Against the Wall, Motherfucker, taken from a line in a poem by beat-turned-black nationalist Leroi Jones." Elsewhere he described the group as "postbeat, postbiker, would-be Hells Angels with manifestos . . . deploying direct action against strategy, extravagance against tedium."[8]

I don't know that I was reading carefully enough to grasp that Gitlin didn't mean this as praise, but rather as a vinegary condemnation. Today the Motherfuckers are rarely mentioned in the historiography of the 1960s, and where they do appear, they're almost always portrayed, *pace* Gitlin, as a demented corruption of the gauzy idealism that fueled the Port Huron Generation. If Camelot, the Freedom Riders, and the Beatles in their loveable mop-top phase are commonly summoned to mind to represent the principled and optimistic 1960s, then the Motherfuckers — if they are remembered at all — are lumped in with the Weather Underground, Altamont, and Charles Manson as paradigm examples of the bad, destructive, nihilistic 1960s. But questions about how they ought to be assessed in the scholarly literature were not yet a preoccupation of mine. I was a teenager living in small town Michigan, and I thought they sounded just great.

Flash forward fifteen years: I'm a part-time instructor of history and literature at Harvard, and one of my students — my favorite student, Caitlin Casey — is searching for a senior thesis topic. We discuss a number of ideas, but the Motherfuckers is the one she latches onto. It turns into a brilliant essay that helped her to graduate *magna cum laude* in 2003. (Today she is a history graduate student at Yale.) Hers remains the only scholarly examination of the Motherfuckers that has ever been written; she had no substantive books, no dissertations, not even any journal articles to draw from, and so I encouraged her to scrounge for scraps of information from other sources — various 1960s memoirs, defunct underground newspapers, and above all, oral history interviews. She ended up talking with several New Yorkers who traveled in the Motherfuckers' orbit, but we could locate only three cooperative former members. One was also a former Weatherwoman; the other two, whose identities we never confirmed, went by the names "Travis Motherfucker," and "Creek."

* * * * *

"There's no way you could recognize me now compared to then," Ben tells me when we finally meet for breakfast at a diner in Chelsea. "I was just *heavy*."

He's 63 years old, small and wiry, with a dark tan and jet-black hair that he combs backward, just long enough to fall over the collar. He has a Fu Manchu moustache, wears a western shirt, and so long as we're indoors, he politely keeps his cowboy hat on the bench beside him. For all his past reticence, he strikes me as a classic extrovert; he's an effusive talker and a gifted raconteur, and the more he talks, the more revved up he becomes. If he'd been born just a little earlier, I could imagine him showing up in one of Jack Kerouac's road novels; he'd be one of the "mad ones . . . who never yawn or say a commonplace thing but burn, burn, burn like fabulous yellow roman candles . . . "[9] Sometimes he recounts his past exploits with exactly the type of joyful, stiff-necked pride one might expect to find in an ex-prizefighter. He smiles easily and impishly, his eyes twinkle. I like him immensely.

Right upfront, he tells me what I already know—that but for one recent exception, he hasn't appeared in public as "Ben Morea" in 35 years. So why the change of heart? His answer unfolds gradually, and betrays a genuine ambivalence. On the one hand, he's always been reluctant to be singled out in any manner; even during the late-Sixties, when his revolutionary credentials were such that his East Broadway apartment was a veritable way station for radicals across the world—including European Situationists, Japanese Zengaukoren, and a leader of the Paris uprising of May, 1968—he preferred to remain in the background. He tells me how he made a point of avoiding the cameras when he was backstage at Woodstock, and how he turned down an offer to play a part in Michelangelo Antonioni's film, *Zabriskie Point*.

On the other hand, he regrets that the Motherfuckers remain obscure and poorly understood. Partly this is because the counterculture has proven itself so pliable in the public memory. Whether in films, memoirs, or scholarly monographs, the youth rebellion has been domesticated by those who look favorably upon the 1960s, and vilified by those who do not. But the Motherfuckers pose a special problem; they were so extreme and iconoclastic within the counterculture that even 1960s partisans seem not to know what to do with them. At one point, I nervously gave Morea a copy of Caitlin's thesis, which put forth several crisply formulated criticisms of the group. To my surprise, Ben liked it, and perhaps even felt flattered. It seems strangely paradoxical that those scholars who have skewered the Motherfuckers are more willing to grapple with the counterculture's conundrums than those who have overlooked them.

Over several conversations, Morea sketches a brief outline of his life: He spent his early childhood in a quasi-rural area around Virginia and Maryland, and he moved to New York City at the age of 10. He hung out with mostly black and Puerto Ricans street kids around Hell's Kitchen, where he got mixed up with heroin, off and on, between the ages of 15 and 20. While in treatment for his addiction, he was introduced to two of his longstanding passions (which, I surmise, were also his salvation): painting and reading. He doesn't quite posture himself as an intellectual—he speaks plainly and clearly—yet he sprinkles his conversation with references to thinkers as diverse and obscure as Michael Bakunin, Guy Debord, Franz Fanon, and Herbert Marcuse (the latter of whom was stepfather to the aforementioned Osha Neumann.) When Morea finds out I'm unfamiliar with Wilhelm Reich's work, he describes his theory of orgone energy and recommends his book *The Murder of Christ*.

A Radical Political and Social History of the Lower East Side

In the early-1960s, Morea was befriended by Julian Beck and Judith Malina, the co-founders of the Living Theater — a pioneering, anarchistic experimental theater company that was founded in 1951, whose loose and challenging performances forecast the coming counter-cultural style. In 1966, he helped launch *Black Mask*, a short-lived, crudely mimeographed magazine that he peddled in the East Village for a nickel. The very first issue underscored his faith in the power and agency of the creative spirit. "With this we can change the stultifying classrooms, the inhuman city, the concept of work when it is unnecessary and everything else which is crushing life instead of allowing it to grow fully."[10] Morea was also peripherally involved in Angry Arts Week — a January 1967 festival that brought hundreds of New York City filmmakers, photographers, musicians, painters and sculptors together in condemnation of the Vietnam War. Out of *Black Mask*, Angry Arts Week, and the potent influence of the Black Power Movement emerged Up Against the Wall, Motherfucker.

Privately, the Motherfuckers referred to their group as "the Family." There were perhaps a couple dozen members, although many more dropped in and out or hovered around the margins. Their ranks included Ivy League dropouts, autodidacts, and barely literate street people, and in all the counterculture there was nothing quite like them. They were sympathetic with the hippies, but they mocked their flowery fantasies and chided them for their weakness. They had a tenuous connection to Students for a Democratic Society (SDS), but they recoiled from the new left's sectarian intellectual debates, and regarded even the most militant students as cloistered and unreliable. The media-obsessed Yippies, of course, were far too playful; the White Panthers, too full of hot air. The Black Panther were sufficiently ferocious but deemed too rigidly hierarchical and doctrinaire. Probably the group that they most closely resembled was the San Francisco Diggers, an artistically inclined, utopian-minded collective who, like the Motherfuckers, championed an ethos of maximum personal freedom, staged guerrilla theater performances, and set up various "counter institutions" around Haight-Ashbury. Both groups had a darker side as well; each lost members to narcotics addiction and the apolitical criminal underworld.

But here again, there was a key difference of temperament: The Motherfuckers were tougher and angrier. "They lived like gutter rats," Abbie Hoffman once recalled.[11] Susan Stern, a former Weatherwoman, called the Motherfuckers "the downright dirtiest, skuzziest, and loudest group of people [she'd] ever laid eyes on."[12] Journalist Thai Jones (whose father knew Morea) quipped that although the Motherfuckers "referred to themselves as 'a street gang with an analysis' . . . they seemed to emphasize the street gang part."[13] Yippie Stewart Albert, whom Caitlin interviewed in her thesis, put the difference between the Diggers and the Motherfuckers this way: "In the West Coast, there were flower children. In the East Coast, there were weed children. They just grew out of the sidewalk."[14] In one of their broadsheets, the Motherfuckers romanticized themselves as "outlaws in the eyes of America" — and with good reason. Some of their writings betrayed a violence of feeling that seems almost psychopathic. One leaflet conjured the image of a police officer "sweating over a nite stick, grinding it into the vagina of some hippiess."[15]

After the Motherfuckers disbanded, Morea and his wife lived on horseback for five years in the Sangre de Cristo Mountains, illegally hunting and gathering and constantly evading the

Forest Service. Occasionally they had visitors in their camps, but none who were ever willing to tough it out with them through the brutal winters. Later he became a lumberjack—a job he now admits he wasn't well suited for, given his slight frame. Today he limps because he once sliced his leg with a chainsaw, and he's deaf in one ear because, he says laughingly, he was "too macho to wear earplugs."

When Morea finally begins describing his life in the 1980s and 1990s, I listen with a certain *frisson*. Some of these details . . . they sound vaguely familiar. But how? Later I mention that one of the people I consulted when I was looking for him was the actor Peter Coyote, who is also the author one of my favorite books—an achingly beautiful countercultural memoir called *Sleeping Where I Fall.*

"I'm in that book!" Ben says.

And so he is. Only none of its readers could have known that the "Ben" that is described there is Ben Morea. Coyote never used his last name. He said only this:

> The way life braids experience, strands disappear and then surface unexpectedly. In 1993 I was walking on the Rue Princesse in Paris when two strangers in 1940s retro Western garb approached me from the opposite direction, saying, "Hey Peter" as they passed. Assuming it was someone recognizing me from films, I acknowledged the greeting but did not stop until they both began laughing, and the man said, "You don't know me, do you?" Ben was beardless now, in his mid-forties; [his wife] still petite and attractive. They manufacture earrings . . . employ six hundred people, and sell them all over the world. They no longer live in a wikiup but in a modern, high-tech house they'd built and showed me photographs. Both are still on the peyote road. Both are still grand and fearless. We spent the evening in Paris eating Mexican food and reminiscing about the life we had shared thousands of miles and many years ago.[16]

* * * * *

Ben hadn't even finished his pancakes when I asked him about Valerie Solanas—the disturbed radical feminist who presided over her own one-woman organization: the Society for Cutting Up Men (SCUM). After Solanas shot Andy Warhol in June 1968, the Motherfuckers staged a street performance on her behalf in Washington Square Park. Morea drew up an accompanying leaflet, wherein he described Warhol as a "nonman shot by the reality of his dreams," and lionized Solanas as a "cultural assassin—a tough chick with a bop cap and a thirty eight." "America's white plastic cathedral is ready to burn," Morea concluded. *"Valerie is ours and the Sweet Assassin lives. SCUM in exile."*[17]

I put the question bluntly: How could you rationalize supporting Valerie Solanas?

"Rationalize? I didn't rationalize anything," Ben says. "I loved Valerie and I loathed Andy Warhol, so that's all there was to it." A few seconds later he shrugs and adds, "I mean, I didn't want to *shoot him*." But then he doubles back again. "Andy Warhol ruined art."

A Radical Political and Social History of the Lower East Side

I want to protest: *But she tried to kill him*! She shot him three times at close range and left him for dead. Warhol never fully recovered from his wounds, and the shooting haunted him for the rest of his life. Valerie was sent to a mental hospital and then to prison; she later died penniless and obscure in a San Francisco flophouse. It takes a certain kind of brazenness to spin this as anything other than a tragedy.

"But let me tell you how I met her," Ben says, excitedly. He was selling his nickel copies of *Black Mask* on the corner of 8th St. and 5th Ave.

> I didn't care about the money. But I felt if I handed it out for free, it would end up in the trashcan. In those days, if you handed out something, everyone would take it. So I felt if I charged a nickel [only] those who really wanted it, would take it. Then Valerie came by and said, "Hey, I'd like to get one of those, [but] I don't have a nickel." So I said, "Oh, that's alright, you can have one, you don't need a nickel." She said, "Wait here!" And she ran into the bookstore and she stole a copy of her [SCUM] manifesto — stole it! — and came out and said "Here, I wrote this," in exchange for the nickel paper. And see, she used to stay with me after that.

Ben's smile is infectious.

> And I said to her one time, "You know Valerie, I want to ask you a question." I said, "You know, your belief system and your manifesto is about killing men, cutting up men." I said "What about me, I'm a man?" And she thought about it a minute, pensive, you know, like she'd never thought about it before. And she said, "I'm gonna promise you something." I said "What?" She said, "You'll be the last man we kill." And I said to her, jokingly, "Can you put it in writing?"

We both laugh. "And I wish I had it to this day," he muses softly. "Can you imagine what that would be, the beauty of having something written by her?"

*****

In the 1995 film *I Shot Andy Warhol*, there appears a character identified in the screenplay as "Mark Motherfucker," who, director Mary Harron tells me, was modeled after Morea. In one scene, the two are together in Morea/Mark Motherfucker's "chaotic tenement apartment. It is strewn with laundry, books, posters, empty bottles, overflowing ashtrays, revolutionary posters, combat gear." They vamp around the room, mouthing revolutionary platitudes and striking cartoonish, militant poses with guns to the tune of Jimi Hendrix's "Wild Thing." When they finally collapse into bed, the screenplay calls for "Strobe cuts of more banal sex action." Later, while Morea/Mark Motherfucker is asleep, Valerie steals his gun — the gun she uses to shoot Andy Warhol.[18]

Ben enjoyed the film — but he says none of this happened. "First of all, Valerie was my dearest friend, and we had guns all over the place, but she would never steal a gun from me." And Ben denies they had any sexual relations, although he explains "in a sense I didn't feel [the portrayal] was an error. I took it to mean that we were so close that that was the only way they could be depict that closeness. . . . I really liked her." He smiles warmly and, for a moment, says nothing more.

* * * * *

In Neumann's essay-length memoir about his Motherfucker days, he describes Ben this way:

> He walked with a slight swagger and had a way of cocking his head and hitching himself up for a confrontation that would have seemed ridiculous in anyone else. But Ben took people seriously. Ben projected danger, risk, the commitment to turn rhetoric into real action. The style of the group became, under his influence, one of intense confrontation. . . Ben rewarded us with the promise to protect us with his life. He could be withering about our weaknesses, taunt us with our cowardice, but if we measured up he would reward us with a look of intense affection that became the most valued currency of the group.[19]

I've seen all of these qualities. Even today, Ben relishes having lived, in the late-1960s, at the edge of parapet. "I honestly did not expect to survive it," he says to me. "And you know, a lot of 'em didn't make it. And you know, I wonder about that sometimes . . . "

His voice starts to trail off, and I reflexively change the subject. I wonder if he knows that I know how his brother was killed: In a drug deal.

In this light, the limitations and fallouts of the Motherfucker program seem so obvious they're scarcely worth mentioning. Their arrogance, cantankerousness, nihilism, recklessness, violence, and shabby treatment of women — all of this was egregious even by the counterculture's loosest standards. Their avant-garde protests generally lacked even a pretense of strategic efficacy, and were entirely unsuited toward their goals of fomenting a genuine revolution. They might as well have dedicated themselves to changing the colors of a rainbow.

Nevertheless, Ben inspires a strong bond of trust. And that look of intense affection? I've seen it several times —usually when he describes old friends, and especially when he talks about Valerie. I like to think I've seen it directed toward myself as well; certainly, he's capable of tremendous warmth and sincerity. The second-to-last time I saw him, I brought Caitlin along. We talked for three hours before our conversation wound down to a tender, cusp moment. "I'm just so happy to meet you," Ben said solemnly. "I've been really enjoying it. It really tortured me for 35 years if I could ever talk to anybody [about the Motherfuckers]. And I'm just *thrilled*" — he pauses for a moment, and looks each of us in the eyes —"to meet you."

* * * * *

"I saw recently, in fact yesterday, that *Hippie* book," Ben says. He's referring to a slick, best-selling coffee table book by Barry Miles, which was released this year by Sterling Publishing Company, a subsidiary of Barnes & Noble. "And there was a picture of Jerry Rubin with a [National Liberation Front] flag wrapped around his shoulders, holding a plastic machine gun. And it's like, 'Wow, I have to smile.' . . . Our idea was, if you're gonna pick up a machine gun, it shouldn't be plastic." Later on he makes the same point again, in reference to the Motherfuckers existentially flavored willingness to take such tremendous personal risks. "We weren't like Jerry Rubin walking around with a plastic machine gun and a flag draped on [his] shoulder. If you really feel that way," he says provocatively, "there's a machine gun somewhere. You know?"

Then he brings up Jerry Rubin a *third* time, after describing one of the Mothefuckers' most legendary actions: On October 21, 1967, Morea and several others were beaten by American soldiers after they broke into the Pentagon during an antiwar rally. There were no eyewitnesses to the clash, but the *Washington Post* reported that near the vestibule through which they were evicted, "Blood was spotted on the floor," and Norman Mailer deployed his powers as a novelist to imagine the confrontation in his Pulitzer prize-winning *Armies of the Night*.[20] "It didn't bring the world any closer to [betterment]" Ben shrugs, but "it just showed that if you want to do like Jerry Rubin and walk around with a plastic machine gun and an NLF flag on your shoulder," that was just but one option. Another was "to put your life on the line. I mean, we didn't know if they would start shooting! They could have . . . We really thought they might."

I used to wonder whether the Motherfuckers weren't a bit of a put-on (and in this sense, also a little proto-punk) — more like the Ramones than Jacobins. Ben bristles at the notion. "If you had any instinct of self-preservation you couldn't do what we did," he says. But for all of their pick-up-the-gun militance and acid-fueled rhetoric, today he is proudest of their contributions to the community — giving comfort and shelter to teenaged runaways who flocked to the Lower East Side's mean streets, feeding vagabonds, hippies, and the homeless, counseling people who were experiencing bad acid trips, and having the pluck to stand up to the Ninth Precinct's notoriously gruff Tactical Police Force.

It's no wonder, then, that Rubin should make such a convenient foil. The politicized wing of the counterculture may have postured itself as radically decentralized and virtually lead-erless, but this high ideal was constantly monkeywrenched by self-aggrandizing icons like Rubin. What's more, the Yippies' well publicized and cartoonish antics constantly called into question the movement's authenticity — was it a populist rebellion or a commodfied trend? Who knew? By contrast, the Motherfuckers immunized themselves from any possi-bility of cooptation by virtue of their name alone. The one thing Morea seems determined to convey — through all of his boasts about his street fighting days, his unrepentant loyalty to Valerie Solanas, and his heckling of Jerry Rubin — is the depth of his sincerity. Unlike Rubin — or for that matter, Malcolm X, Che Guevara, Huey Newton, or the Weather Underground — the Motherfuckers have thus far managed to avoid becoming an empty signi-fier. The flipside, however, is that even though they played a unique and important role in the counterculture, very few people know about them. It's a thorny problem; they only way to remedy it is by writing about them, and yet to do so is to grant them a status they never coveted.

Recently I walked into a Barnes & Noble and noticed "that *Hippie* book" Ben was referring to. In fact, there was a whole stack of them, prominently displayed at a table near the front of the store, alongside piles of several other self-congratulatory books on the counterculture, including *The Hippie Dictionary* and *The Hippie Handbook* (which promises to teach its readers how to "tie-dye a t-shirt, flash a peace sign . . . and other essential skills for a carefree life.") I looked in the index of *Hippie* for any mention of Up Against the Wall, Motherfucker, and to my surprise, there seemed to be one, on page 282. So I turned to that page, only to find that the reference is not to Morea's group, but rather to the banal slogan, "Up against the wall, motherfucker!" — just five words ripped from a Leroi Jones' poem. But you'll never guess what is on the opposite page. It's a giant photograph of Jerry Rubin, with an NLF flag draped around his shoulders, holding a toy machine gun.

Endnotes:

1. Murray Bookchin, as quoted in Haden-Guest, Anthony, *True Colors: The Real Life of the Art World* (New York: Atlantic Monthly Press, 1996), p. 30.

2. Hoffman, Abbie, *The Autobiography of Abbie Hoffman* (New York: Four Walls, Eight Windows, 1980), p. 123.
3. Smith, Patti, *"Gloria"/"My Generation,"* (1976), Arista Records AS 0171.

4. In *Black Mask* and *Up Against the Wall, Motherfucker: The Incomplete Works of Ron Hahne, Ben Morea and the Black Mask Group* (London: Unpopular Books and Sabotage Editions, 1993), p. 114.

5. Ibid., p. 75.

6. Neumann, Osha, *"Motherfuckers Then and Now: My Sixties Problem,"* in Darnovsky, Marcy, Barbara Epstein, and Richard Flacks, eds., *Cultural Politics and Social Movements* (Philadelphia: Temple University Press, 1995), p. 64.

7. Ibid., p. 64.

8. Gitlin, p. 241.

9. Kerouac, Jack, *On the Road.* See *Columbia World of Quotations* (New York: Columbia University Press, 1996), no. 32478 (www.bartleby.com/66/78/32478.html).

10. In *Black Mask* and *Up Against the Wall Motherfucker*, p. 9.

11. Hoffman, p. 123.

12. Stern, Susan, *With the Weathermen: The Personal Journey of a Revolutionary Woman* (New York: Doubleday, 1975), p. 22.

13. Jones, Thai, *A Radical Line: From the Labor Movement to the Weather Underground, One Family's Century of Conscience* (New York: Free Press, 2004), p. 182.

14. Stewart Albert, as quoted in Casey, Caitlin, *"Up Against the Wall, Motherfucker: the Life and Times of a 'Street Gang with an Analysis,'"* (Senior Thesis, Harvard University, 2003), p. 16.

15. In *Black Mask* and *Up Against the Wall Motherfucker*, p. 105.

16. Coyote, Peter, *Sleeping Where I Fall: A Chronicle* (Washington, D.C.: Counterpoint, 1998), p. 255.

17. Solanas, Valerie, *S.C.U.M. Manifesto* (New York: Olympia Press, 1968), p. 104.
18. Harron, Mary, and Daniel Minahan, *I Shot Andy Warhol* (New York: Grove Press, 1995), pp. 123-124.

19. Neumann, p. 62.

A Radical Political and Social History of the Lower East Side

20. Chapman, William, "*55,000 Rally Against War; GI's Repel Pentagon Charge,*" *Washington Post* (October 22, 1967), p. A1; Mailer, Norman, *The Armies of the Night: History as a Novel, /the Novel as History* (New York: New American Library, 1968), p. 252.

Chapter 6

Ben Eagle
        By Eve Hinderer

The following is a report of a meeting held recently in a New York City restaurant.

"Up Against the Wall, Motherfucker" member Ben Eagle (aka Ben Morea) described some actions that would classify as playful sabotage. He said that although the Motherfuckers were serious, they could also be "lighthearted."

·   Distributed a flyer along the Bowery falsely advertising that a gallery opening on Manhattan's upscale East 57th Street would have free liquor and food. When the group arrived on the scene to see what had transpired, "there were 1000 people there," with the Tactical Police Force everywhere.

·   Closed off St. Mark's Place between 2nd and 3rd Avenues, which ultimately resulted in a riot. Ben said that when Abbie Hoffman emerged out of his apartment on the same block, he immediately joined in. When Jerry Rubin showed up, however, he took off. Ben used that incident to illustrate the difference between the two. He was close with Hoffman, but disliked Rubin. He recalled Abbie's involvement with the Civil Rights struggle in the South.

·   Cut the cyclone fence at Woodstock in 1969, opening the door for the mass phenomenon that followed. That action was never publicly acknowledged by Wavy Gravy, another friend.

·   During NYC garbage strike in 1968, brought garbage up to Lincoln Center where it was dumped in the fountain. This event was filmed by the Newsreel collective, and they released "*Garbage*" as a short film.

·   Did a mock shooting of poet Kenneth Koch during at reading at St. Mark's Church in the Bowery. A Motherfucker pulled out a fake gun and shouted "Kenneth" and shot a blank. The poet was so shocked. Leaflets were then thrown from the balcony with photos of LeRoi Jones and the slogan "poetry is revolution."

The group specialized in what Ben referred to as "breakaways." During the Pentagon demonstration in the fall of '67, for example, they actually forced an entry into the building.

Ben was always interested in the history of the anti-Leninist left. He looked up old anarchists and went to see them. He was interested in Alexandra Kollantai, who was suppressed by Lenin. He went to see Raya Dunaskaya, Trotsky's secretary, in Detroit. Raya and Ben argued, and she threw him out.

543

A Radical Political and Social History of the Lower East Side

Ben has been a painter since the '60s. He's had a show at the Open Center on Spring Street. In connection with his involvement in the arts, he met with Richard Huelsenbeck of the Berlin Dada movement. Also visited Nicholas Calas, the critic who supported the surrealists. He knew Sam Goodman of "No!" art, and Ralph Ortiz of Destruction art.

Ben left home at 17 and was taken in and mentored by Julian Beck and Judith Malina of the Living Theatre, who always considered themselves anarchists. At one point, Judith Malina, a pacifist, was raped on stage during a performance of *Paradise Now*. Ben said that after that incident, there was always someone from "the family" (the name Ben often used when referring to the group) present during those performances.

The Becks assisted Ben and The Motherfuckers in taking over the Fillmore East, and pressured Bill Graham into letting "the community" have it free one night a week. Ben understood that "revolution and theater went together. A lot of left people didn't believe that."

Many politicized people and groups passed through Ben's East Broadway loft:

· Leader of the Japanese Zengakuren, a group that frequently engaged in pitched battles with the police. This fellow later joined Che in Bolivia;

· King Mob, from the UK, "a wonderful guy."

· The Situationists. Ben corrected a popular misconception that the Situationists had rejected a Motherfucker request for membership: they never asked to join. He said Guy DeBord sent someone to check them out-a Dutch Provo. Later DeBord concluded they were "too mystical." Ben, who later became interested in Native American culture, allows that there is some truth in this allegation.

· Valerie Solanas was a close friend. [She was the author of the *SCUM Manifesto* — the Society for Cutting Up Men. She later made an assassination attempt on Andy Warhol.] His character appears in the movie made of her life (*I Shot Andy Warhol*); however although the relationship was platonic, it was portrayed as being sexual — the only way Hollywood could conceive of it. Ben remembers asking Valerie, "You're about cutting up men, that means killing them, right? What about me?" She said, "I promise you Ben, you'll be the last man to go."

· People from Weatherman.

Ben coined the phrase "affinity group." It was during a meeting between Herbert Marcuse and Murray Bookchin: Marcuse had talked at SVA (School for Visual Arts) and after the talk went down to Bookchin's apartment. Tom Neuman, Marcuse's stepson, was part of MFR (The Motherfuckers) and was also present at the meeting. Ben heard the Spanish term *aficionado* repeatedly as part of the dialogue between Marcuse and Bookchin. He then approximated the term in the word *affinity*. He also gave the term its definition: "a street gang with an analysis," later attributed to and used by King Mob.

Ben and the Motherfuckers supported crash pads, and fed hundreds of people twice a week with mislabeled yogurt from Dannon and stews made with fish market surpluses. They hooked people up with doctors, worked with lawyers and ran a free store. They did this with grants from Judson Church, through ESSO-East Side Services, the moniker they adopted in order to apply for money.

Ben was active in NYC between 1959 and 1969, participating in the '50s Beat scene — he was good friends with Allen Ginsberg and LeRoi Jones (aka Amiri Baraka). In 1969, he left the city for the West and never looked back, living in the wilderness and riding horseback for six years. He became involved with Native Americans and began to raise homeless children, more than 50 over the years. He has dozens of children who call him "grandfather."

Chapter 7

Taking The Plunge
    By Osha Neumann

My arrival on the Lower East Side coincided with that of a new wave of immigrants. They were mostly white, long-haired, dropouts who originally had no collective name for themselves, but whom the media, when it woke up to their existence, called "hippies." They set up crash pads in rundown tenements, dragged their mattresses onto the floor, and formed fragile, everchanging communities. They sent many hours hanging out on St. Marks Place, panhandling in front of Gem's Spa, and getting stoned on the benches of Tompkins Square Park.

They were like confetti blown from a party in some other part of town onto the Puerto Rican streets of the ghetto. By and large they were oblivious to their neighbors. They stayed because the rents were cheap and the Lower East Side didn't seem to belong to anybody. They could do more or less what they wanted and dress as they pleased. No one was going to tell them to get a job. Their migration reversed the route of their predecessors. To prior generations of immigrants the Lower East Side had been the gateway to America. For the dropouts of the Sixties, it was an exit door. They came to the ghetto fleeing America, not trying to gain entrance. They were escaping from the emotional dust bowl of their families, their schools, their jobs. Stoned at night, they would stare in the windows of the corner bodega, watch the mice scurrying over piles of green plantains and sweet potatoes, and breathe a sigh of relief.

Most of them were younger than I, but they had a lot to teach me. They brought the political counterculture of the Sixties to my doorstep. They were an infectious ferment spreading through the bowels of the ghetto. They agitated the intricate privacy of my apartment, which was now full to overflowing with enormous assemblages of Lower East Side garbage.

I began writing an extended essay about the end of avant-garde art. I wrote that painting was lost in a meaningless play with limits that no one cared about any longer. The liberatory promise of art was now to be achieved outside the frame of the canvas by the total imaginative transformation of reality. I typed away in my apartment, setting the typewriter on the lid of the bathtub, but never finished. I was like a nervous swimmer arguing myself into jumping from a high rock into the river. Once I jumped there was no reason to continue the argument.

Somewhere a dam had broken. The miasma of alienation that had enveloped a generation, condensed into a great flood of disaffection. The rising waters swept the hippies out of their homes and into the ghetto. It threatened to tear the rotting clapboard of public and private life from its foundations. It seemed only a matter of time before the tide would reach everywhere. There was no escaping, and on my part, at least, no desire to escape.

I was like a prisoner locked in his cell, who realizes that the jail, which holds him, is directly in the path of a flood. He sees both the danger and the possibility of freedom. He is exhilarated and terrified. The prison is in chaos. The guards desert the watchtowers. He waits for the walls to crack. It's time to choose: Stay or jump. Cling to the remains of the prison, or let yourself be swept downstream, no telling where.

What broke the dam? Too many rotting corpses dragged through the rice fields of Vietnam? Too many black children beaten on the evening news? Who knows? We, who are in the business of undermining dams, don't really know what makes them go. We're always taken by surprise when they do.

In order to stay afloat in the flood it was necessary to discard some baggage. All the accoutrements with which we protected our privacy had to go. It was like a baptism. We immersed ourselves in the water and emerged as members of a new tribe. We left the old behind. We would have new friends, new relations, a new family. The Vietnamese peasant harvesting rice with a rifle on her shoulder, the civil rights worker registering voters in Mississippi — they were our brothers and sisters. We would share with them the danger and the victory. I had missed the first half of the Sixties. SNCC (Student Nonviolent Coordinating Committee) had been founded in 1960, the year of the first sit-ins. In 1961 black and white Freedom Riders sitting together on Greyhound buses drove into Birmingham, Alabama and were beaten with pipes and chains by a Ku Klux Klan led mob. In 1963 Vietnamese Buddhist monks turned themselves into the flaming torches to protest the war. President Johnson began bombing North Vietnam in 1965. It was now waning months of 1966. I was preparing to make up for lost time.

My plunge into the countercultural politics of the Lower East Side began in January 1967 when I noticed fliers posted around the streets calling for artists to participate in an Angry Arts Week to protest the war in Vietnam. I started going to organizing meetings. The artists who attended the meetings on the Lower East Side were an oddly assorted mix of actors in street theater groups, stray poets and painters. Michael Brown was there from the Pageant Players and Peter Schumann from the Bread and Puppet theater. And there was Ben Morea, an anarchist painter.

We met in crowded apartments. Some of us squatted on the bare floor while others of us sat on tables and leaned against radiators. We smoked and talked about the need for art to be a tool of the struggle. As artists, we had an obligation to use our skills in support of the movement. Our angry art had a purpose — to encourage people to oppose the war in Vietnam. The orthodoxy of the avant-garde establishment held that true art doesn't do. It is. Art is for art's sake. Propaganda and pornography, tools to arouse the masses on the one hand and the penis on the other, were excluded from the temple of true art and confined to squat outbuildings on its outskirts. We could care less.

The avant-garde artists sipping cocktails in the living rooms of wealthy patrons, and guzzling wine at Fifty-seventh Street gallery openings, were irrelevant. They played at revolutionary intent while cultivating marketable outrages. We were the real thing. We had little time to waste on subtle theoretical discussions of aesthetics. There were demonstrations to organize, leaflets to produce.

I listened to the organizers express their opinions. I compared myself to them. They all seemed very strong, certain of themselves, formed. There were no famous artists in the room. But

A Radical Political and Social History of the Lower East Side

famous artists had bought their fame at too heavy a price. Here was something potentially better, a group to belong to with a handle on history.

Sometime in my childhood I discovered a book of Goya's etchings in a bookcase in our living room. When I reached puberty, I would sneak the volume down from its shelf and take it up to my room. I would close the door and leaf through the unflinching depictions of murder and sexual violence. Naked headless armless corpses, impaled on sharpened stumps, hung on trees like meat in a butcher shop window; bodies of slaughtered prisoners lay heaped in tangled piles like garbage; a firing squad executed blindfolded prisoners tied to stakes. Women were raped and women begged not to be raped. In one etching two soldiers held a naked prisoner upside down with his legs apart so a third could split him down the middle with a sword. In another a mob exacted revenge on a soldier who was being dragged along the ground by a rope tied to his legs. He had been stripped of his pants and a man shoved a stake into his anus, The captions beneath the pictures were terse: "What Madness," "A Cruel Shame," "Forced to Look." They neither explained nor consoled.

I remember in particular an etching of a child being spanked. The child has broken a pitcher which can be seen in the background. His punishment is being administered by an old woman who pins him across her knees with her left hand. She holds his skirts up in her teeth revealing his buttocks. In her right hand she holds a shoe with which she beats him. I masturbated to this image. Goya was my first pornographer, but his work, since it was on the shelves of my parents' house was part of my cultural heritage, unlike the tattered photograph of chained naked woman that I picked up on the street one evening as I walked home from the subway and secreted away behind a bookshelf in my room.

Sitting in my Lower East Side flat after our meetings, I thought about Goya. He went deaf and mad. The title plate of his *Caprichios* bears the caption: "The dream of reason brings forth monsters." I imagined him hunched over his etching plate, gouging into it by candle light, gouging, gouging deep into the night. He clenches his etching burin until his hand aches. Spreads out on his work table are his acids, his unused copper plates, all the reassuring solid materials of his art. He digs his burin into the plate. As he draws the groove of the buttocks his burin pushes into it. Who is he at that moment? The child who is being beaten or the one who beats him? Is he the penis of the rapist and the vagina of the raped? Is he the sword of the dismemberer and the body of the dismembered? Is he the hangman's noose and the neck of the man who is hung, the gray sky in which the hanged man hangs and his dead eyes that no longer see the sky? Is he all of these or none of them? Whose side was Goya on? Was he angry when he drew, or lost in a more complex mood?

SACRILEGE

On Monday, January 23, 1967, the *New York Times* reported on a demonstration organized by the Lower East Side contingent of Angry Arts Week:

> Twenty-three peace demonstrators unfurled posters portraying a maimed
> Vietnamese child in the central aisle of St. Patrick's Cathedral during the ten
> o'clock high mass yesterday morning, causing the celebrant to interrupt the

liturgy . . . In a statement they left with a friend, the protesters said they were leaving the church in the midst of the ceremony 'out of disrespect for Cardinal Spellman' to protest his recent statement that 'the war in Vietnam is a war for civilization.' The paper posters carried the fifth of the Ten Commandments, "Thou shall not kill" above the child's photograph and below it the legend, 'Vietnam.' They were no sooner unfurled than the demonstrators were surrounded by detectives and plain-clothes patrolmen who had been tipped off that a demonstration would take place.

The *Times*, at least in this instance, was a model of journalistic accuracy. No sooner had I stood up and begun to extract the rolled cardboard from under my tweed overcoat, than I was surrounded by burly men in black trench coats. I was passed from one of them to the other out into the vestibule, where I was I.D.'d and informed I was being charged with disorderly conduct, unlawful assembly in a church, and disruption of a religious ceremony. Then in the firm grip of my arresting officer, I was escorted out of the dark church into bright winter sunlight. As I was being loaded into the paddy wagon I managed to catch a glimpse of photographers, a picket line, and a crowd of onlookers standing on the sidewalk. The door slammed shut and the van drove off, carrying my fellow arrestees and me first to the local precinct and then to a holding cell at the Central Police Station, 100 Center Street, affectionately known as "the Tombs."

We spent the night in jail. A jailer brought us pineapple marmalade sandwiches and cocoa. We talked quietly among ourselves and then someone began chanting "Hare Krishna, Hare Krishna, Hare Rama Hare Rama." We all joined in, and as we chanted I relaxed, the tension flowed out of me, and I began to feel an enormous peace, as if a tense journey that had consumed my entire life was coming to an end. I had arrived at my destination. I gave in to eastern mysticism, to religion, to superstition.

I chanted quietly along with the rest of my cellmates. And as I chanted, all at once, it seemed that the harsh light in the cell — glaring on the naked walls, reflecting off the stainless steel toilet —underwent a transformation, becoming simultaneously brighter, clearer, and softer. There I was, having a "mystical experience." I felt a twinge of disloyalty to the rationality I had learned to admire while listening to the dinner table conversation of my parents. But they were far away and I was on a journey. There was no need to feel ashamed in any case. Such experiences were a sign of the times. The membranes separating various compartments of the counterculture were permeable. Their contents flowed together. Just let yourself go, the times were whispering, and you'll be saved.

We were bailed out the next day. I returned, reluctantly, to the solitude of my railroad flat with its familiar mess, canvases stacked against the wall, and roaches feeding in the garbage. I set my typewriter on the enamel cover of the bathtub next to the sink in my kitchen, pushed away the dishes, and wrote:

> I imagine Cardinal Spellman stripped naked in front of his congregation, beaten, defiled, shit upon, forced to kneel down in a circle of raw bleeding assholes of the sodomized choir boys and be farted upon, forced to eat the flesh of burnt children, forced to shiver in icy puke for all eternity.

A Radical Political and Social History of the Lower East Side

550

His congregation will observe this spectacle while submitting themselves to a number of tortures. Their clothes will be taken away from them and they will be made to beat each other with whips. Their children will be brought to them and before their eyes married to dope-addicted . . . prostitutes. The marriages will be consummated in the aisles.

One must be just in one's fantasies. One must not allow oneself to be lenient. Difficult as it may be one must force oneself to imagine ever new indecencies to inflict on criminals who are the embodiment of real obscenity. Only in one's fantasies can one preserve for future generations the image of justice that perhaps it will be their joy to inflict. It is an obligation which one must fulfill in private.

Nothing inhibits the carrying out of this obligation more drastically than this action. To give way to the temptation to turn one's fantasies into reality is an unmitigated disaster. For immediately one is lost in a world in which they, the obscene ones rule. Their laws apply, their game is played, their dance is danced. Everything one says is used against one: one must become sincere, witness one's ethical convictions, proclaim oneself willing to suffer for those convictions, make sacrifices.

Beware of action! Beware of its temptations! Preserve the truth inside you! Publish it privately among your friends. Live by it secretly. Draw strength from it. Reveal it to broader circles only in veiled allegories. But do not act on it. Do not witness it. Deny it under oath.

And if the desire to act is too strong, do something half-hearted. Picket outside the Cathedral. Run the peace candidate. Proclaim the possibility and necessity of moral outrage (do not admit that you have passed beyond outrage to something harder, glittering, vicious) Do not show your teeth. Be very careful. Shake hands with the right people. Smile. But inside, keep the faith.

Ethics is a bog. They have made it an instrument against us. They have poisoned its waters. It is the most tempting part of their system and the most dangerous. In defense one must become inhuman. One must cling to one's inhumanity, spit full in the face of their poisoned platitudes so that beyond those platitudes, beyond our own inhumanity there is preserved the possibility of a true ethics that will exist not in the minds of the moralist, but in our mutual happiness.

A-men
Fuck off!

The outrages I perpetrated in my imagination far outdistanced the mild disturbance we had created in reality. Our disruption of Cardinal Spellman's mass —a moral act, committed in the name of napalmed babies whose pain and suffering we asked the world to witness — had another dimension. It was an intrusion, a rending of the veil of civility, an invasion of the rabble into the sanctimonious safe house of the hypocrites.

It was not extraordinary that I, in the seclusion of my apartment, wrote "unacceptable" reflections in my journal. It was extraordinary how quickly, and with how little mediation, these private fantasies would enter the arena of public political discourse. In the mimeographed fliers I produced for the Motherfuckers, they emerged almost verbatim. Private fantasy freed itself to roam the streets, titillating the police who picked my ravings out of the gutter and preserved them in their files as evidence of the terrible menace we represented.

BEN MOREA AND THE FOUNDING OF THE MOTHERFUCKERS

When Angry Arts week ended, a group of Lower East side artists decided to continue meeting to carry on where Angry Arts week had left off. We called ourselves "the Motherfuckers," short for "Up Against the Wall Motherfucker." We took the name from a line in Amiri Baraka's prose poem "Black People!" composed as his hometown, Newark, was erupting in a riot sparked by police brutality:

> . . . you can't steal nothin from a white man, he's already stole it he owes you anything you want, even his life. All the stores will open if you will say the magic words. The magic words are: Up against the wall mother fucker this is a stick up!

Our name had the advantage that it could not be spoken in polite company. That which could not be spoken, could not be co-opted.

The unacknowledged leader of our group was Ben Morea. His life story could not have been more different from my own. He had grown up in Hell's Kitchen on the West Side of Manhattan and lived all his life on the streets of New York. He never knew his father. He loved jazz and learned to play a little vibes. He hung out in clubs where heroin was hip and got hooked. That period of his life ended after he was busted for possession. He kicked his heroin habit cold turkey in prison, but in the process became so sick that he almost died. He was transferred from his cell to the prison ward of a hospital. There, in the art therapy room, he did his first paintings.

Ben had tried to kick his habit many times, but always he would go back to the jazz scene and get hooked again. When he left the hospital, he decided he was done. He put away his vibes, stopped going to the clubs, and started painting. While looking to fill the void in his life left when he abandoned the jazz world, he met Judith Malina and Julian Beck, the founders of the Living Theater, an improvisational anarcho-pacifist theater of communal ritual and provocation. Judith and Julian were Ben's introduction to anarchism. After meeting them he joined a study group organized by Murray Bookchin.

It met in Murray's apartment on 9th Street east of 1st Avenue. Murray was a pugnacious working class intellectual, committed to anarchism and interested in technology and ecology. Ben was never entirely comfortable with the intellectual theorizing that went on in the group. According to Murray, he would show up, listen impatiently for a while and then start screaming. He'd call everybody a petty bourgeois white honky and storm out. Everyone thought that was the last they'd see of him, but the next meeting he would be back, and go through the same ritual. Even after the group disbanded, Ben would show up regularly at Murray's home to talk and argue politics.

Ben began searching for a way to turn art into an instrument of revolution, which meant to turn art against itself. He wanted to destroy art in the name of art and life. With Roy Hahne he put out *Black Mask*, a four-page magazine in which he published his manifestos. Ben gathered together a group of like minded artists. They called themselves Black Mask after the magazine and proceeded to stage a series of theatrical provocations. On October 10, 1966, they handed out fliers announcing their intention to shut down the Museum of Modern Art, traveled uptown from the Lower East side and marched towards the entrance to the museum where they were met by a line of cops and barricades. Art, which refused engagement, now required police protection. It was a victory. On another occasion they announced they would change the name of Wall Street to "War Street." On February 10, 1967, Ben and his fellow provocateurs concealed their faces behind black woolen ski masks and paraded down the street carrying skull masks on stakes, while handing out their fliers proclaiming the name change.

A 1967 action targeted the poet Kenneth Koch. Koch was a friend of abstract expressionists. His poems were witty, somewhat obscure, and apolitical. Newark was erupting in riots, and Leroi Jones had just been arrested for carrying firearms and resisting arrest. Black Maskers came to the Koch reading armed with a flier consisting of a picture of Leroi and the words "Poetry is Revolution." They took seats in the balcony. One member of the group, a man over six feet tall with a great head of tousled black hair, wore a trench coat. He looked impressively sinister, the very image of a turn-of-the-century anarchist bomb thrower. Concealed under his coat was a pistol that fired blanks. Koch began to read. The man stood up, shouted out "Koch!" and when the poet looked up aimed the pistol and fired. The audience thought he had been shot. Ben and his cohorts threw their fliers from the balcony and ran out of the church.

Ben was short, wiry, and intense. He spoke in little thrusts and jabs that mirrored his physical mannerisms. His walk had a slight swagger and he had a way of cocking his head to one side and hitching himself up when preparing for a confrontation that might have seemed ridiculous in someone else.

But Ben was not ridiculous. Ben's strength lay in the fact that, in a non-trivial sense, he was true to his word. A lot of words flew around recklessly in the Sixties, but the gap between rhetoric and reality seemed smaller with him than with anybody else I knew at the time. He did what he said he would do. This was his code of honor, the code of the street, to which he adhered with the discipline of a martial artist. He was calm and focused in battle, able to calibrate his actions in moments of tension while all around him, less hardened street fighters such as me, panicked and struggled not to flee from danger.

In those moments of confrontation, with the police charging down on us, I was acutely aware of the limits of my courage. The little bird of my being, silent, private, separate, would become frantic to protect itself. I could no more force myself to take risks than a drowning man could keep from struggling for breath.

At the time I thought of Ben as possessing a street intelligence, the equivalent and polar opposite of Herbert's book intelligence. Ben's code of honor challenged all the training of my childhood in the relation of word to deed. As a child, listening to the grownups talk, I concluded
that thought must be isolated from action. My fathers' minds floated from thought to thought
in a thought-world separate from the world of doing and making. Ben's thought flowed naturally
and directly into action. Before joining the Motherfuckers, I had lived isolated in a whirl of
words and guilty fantasies. My encounter with Ben hurled me from my isolation with awful sud-
denness. I felt I could only imitate, posture, make tentative steps to follow where he led, and
hope that no one would notice my cowardice, my fear, my innocence.

Very quickly under Ben's leadership, so quickly that I no longer remember the transition, the
Motherfuckers was transformed from a group which met to plan activities into something quite
different — an identity. Involvement stopped being a matter of merely attending meetings. It
became a question of "being" a Motherfucker. We lived to throw ourselves into the fray. We gave
up attachments to the past. We abandoned our family names in favor of "Motherfucker." Tom
Neumann died and Tom Motherfucker was born.

Women played a distinctly ancillary role in all matters. Their most acceptable role was to be
someone's girlfriend or "old lady." If the relationship ended, they tended to drift away. They did
the traditional women's work of cooking for the group, helping to prepare the community feasts
we organized, nursing babies, tending to the bruised egos of the men. This was expected,
acceptable and went without comment. They might hawk our fliers, get arrested (rarely) at our
demonstrations, yell at the cops, seethe with their own personal brew of anger at all the institutions of wealth and power, but with few exceptions their role was largely unacknowledged. They
rarely participated in our long tense political arguments, in which the stakes would gradually
rise to the point where the issue was no longer a disagreement about strategy or tactics, but
one's character and commitment. Political argument was men's work.

The vicissitudes of male emotional life dominated the Motherfuckers. Ben was always vigilant for
weakness, insistent in his demands for loyalty. The commitment he demanded, and that we were
quick to demand of each other, knew no boundaries. We concealed our vulnerability. We were
relentless in testing ourselves, and in ferreting out each other's weakness. Ben rewarded us with
the promise to protect us with his life. He would be withering about our weaknesses and taunt
us for our timidity. But when we did well in his eyes he would reward us with a look of intense
affection that became the most valued currency of the group.

What were we? Ben used the term "affinity group," a translation of "groupa affinidad" used by
Spanish anarchists to describe the cellular structures of their underground movement. He was
introduced to the term in discussions with Murray Bookchin. In a manifesto printed in the form
of a flier Ben wrote:

> The affinity group is the seed/term/essence of organization. It is coming togeth-
> er out of mutual Need or Desire: cohesive historical groups unite out of the
> shared necessities of the struggle for survival, while dreaming of the possibility
> of love.

A Radical Political and Social History of the Lower East Side

> In the pre-revolutionary period affinity groups must assemble to project a revolutionary consciousness to develop forms for particular struggles. In the revolutionary period itself they will emerge as armed cadres at the centers of conflict, and in the post-revolutionary period suggest forms for the new everyday life.

Someone in SDS described us as a "street gang with an analysis." In retrospect, I think we had some of the characteristics of a cult. But for Ben — the Italian street kid, who grew up, as he says, "pretty much on his own," who did not know his father; who, even when he was sitting in jail in Boston and facing 25 years for stabbing a man did not want to tell his mother about the Motherfuckers because he did not want to disappoint her — we were first and foremost, and remain to this day, "the family." Family. Not a word that connotes politics, or the organizations which "do" politics. The same word the Manson clan used. The same word the Mafia uses. A word that implies fierce commitment and ties as thick as blood.

At the core of the Motherfuckers were ten to fifteen of us fully committed regulars around which there gathered a group of fellow travelers whose commitment varied, and who preferred to keep some level of safe distance. College students were drawn to us by the possibility of living the total revolution. We were adopted by a group of Puerto Rican street kids. They came to our events, ate at our community feasts, and hung out in our crash pads. The winos with whom we shared the streets, organized themselves into the "Wine Group for Freedom" a.k.a. "The Wine Nation." Ben folded them under our wing. Except for our core group, it was never entirely clear who was and was not a Motherfucker. We didn't have membership cards. If you spent enough time with us, and you wished to be a Motherfucker, and participated in our actions, you became part of the family.

We in the Motherfuckers knew each other through the daily life we shared. We did not engage in long conversations about where we came from and how we got to where we were. We shed our anchors to the past in private. The Marines take in new recruits and systematically strip from them the traces of their former identities. They are given crew cuts, and handed a uniform. So the Motherfuckers took in recruits for a quite different army, a long-haired army of urban guerrillas. The new identities we adopted did not, of course, obliterate the old. Little as we cared to dwell on our differences, the mix of self-doubt and assurance with which we entered into our new life depended in part on whether we were men or women, middle class or working class, college educated or not, in our teens or twenties. It mattered whether we were raised in the country or the city, and whether we were white — almost all of us were, at least in the core group — or a person of color. It's hard to find a common thread in our backgrounds or in the paths that led us to the Motherfuckers. We were like the cast of characters in a Hollywood disaster movie, thrown together by circumstances, forced to depend upon each other, and bringing to our predicament a range of strengths and weaknesses.

The disaster that threw us together was America. We left homes, jobs, high schools and colleges driven by a diversity of dissatisfactions. Vietnam was a big part of the problem. The war was immoral, pointless, and obscene. Each invitation to come to our local draft board for a physical was a stepping-stone into a gaping maw that would chew us up and turn us into bloody chowder. But Vietnam, awful as it might be, was only a symptom of a larger problem.

Osha Neumann

We were repelled by the world our parents had, to one degree or another, accepted. And we were attracted by the promise of a better world awaiting.

For those of us who grew up with parents who espoused some form of radical politics becoming a Motherfucker was our way to strike out on our own path, and re-imagine a revolutionary tradition. For others, whose parents were Goldwater Republicans, the Motherfuckers was a parallel universe. But in all cases the choice to join the Motherfuckers was a rejection of our families of origin. No one joined the Motherfuckers with the blessing of their parents, be they Goldwater Republicans or card-carrying Communists.

Chapter 8

Once Here and Again
    By Michael Rosen

I grew up with stories of the Lower East Side. And with three memories, blurred photographs in the way of earliest childhood.

These photographs are in black and white. The first is of my great grandfather sitting in his living room. We were visiting, and I'm three years old. He's dressed in black pants and jacket, and a white button down shirt. His beard is long and white. His dress is the uniform of a certain type of male Orthodox Jew.

My two other memories are of the elevator in his hallway, one of those old school types with grates instead of doors, and of the pull chain toilet is his bathroom, with the water tank far overhead. It was almost certainly the first time I'd seen such a toilet.

My parents assure me that we did visit my father's grandfather at 57 1/2 Second Avenue, in 1959 or 1960, so my memories hold.

The building is still there. I stop in front of it from time to time, to recollect family. The stories I remember were told by that cabal of progeny from that same great grandfather. He had nine children, and by the time I existed there was a plethora of great aunts and uncles and regular aunts and uncles and gaggles of cousins once and twice and not at all removed.

Great Uncle Al, who died before I was born, was brought out to Tompkins Square Park to sober up during one particularly raucous Passover seder decades before my parents were born.

My grandfather, whom some called Sam and others called George, had the shortest thumbs. Grandpa was a shortish, thick man of few words. "Taciturn" was beyond my vocabulary, but in reconstruction is certainly true. Making fists and extending his thumbs out, pressing them down on a table, he explained that they were so short because he was selling newspapers on the corner one day when he was young, lost a nickel and reached out into the street and had his thumbs squashed by a rolling car.

I knew he was playing with me. Though I did look for damage and scars on his thumbs. The streets he was on became real for me, nevertheless. I imagined a time of ancient cars and crowded streets. And those streets are now my streets.

Great Uncles Harry and Ben were fourteen and twelve, respectively, when their father (after whom I'm named, with the complications of family) got remarried and, at the stepmother's direction, dismissed his two boys from their home. Harry and Ben had no choice but to go off on their own in this neighborhood. Selling newspapers, shining shoes, doing all those things too young children did then to survive if abandoned.

All the early family stories took place here, in the Lower East Side. This is where these relatives grew up and had their first households and first children. East Second and Avenue B, East 4th Fourth between A and B, East 6th Sixth between A and B; all these places and certainly more became part of an inchoate topography I carried from childhood, places my family lived before moving to the Grand Concourse and later beyond that.

I moved to New York in 1983. For the first five years, I was a professor at NYU. I taught in the business school, while my own research was as an anthropologist of contemporary organizations.

My wife and I lived uptown, near her parents, on the east side.

I passed through the Lower East Side each day on the way to work, riding my motorcycle — then a 750 cc Yamaha, an "Interceptor" — down the FDR, getting off at Houston Street and taking various routes west.

I quit NYU in 1988. I'm a little vague on the exact year, but I'm reasonably certain it was five years after starting there. I quit to so that I could develop a piece of property my wife's grandfather had bought on the north side of East Houston Street, between Avenues A and B, in or around 1961. He purchased the property at a City city auction. The City city had condemned buildings on the north side of Houston Street to widen it there. The City city took a strip of property and auctioned the remains.

I built a thirteen-story "luxury" residential rental building on that site, massing the air rights on the west side of the property to gain height and the ability for double-loaded corridors — the latter being the major motivator for the design. Construction started in February, 1989. I filled the ground floor, beside the lobby and related residential areas, with a commercial wing running the full five hundred feet of frontage we owned.

The western part of the site had, for years previous, been rented as a Merit gas station. The eastern part of the site was fenced off and left in a stand of dead trees. Merit wanted to renew its lease, and my father-in-law, managing the site after his father had died, was also entertaining a proposal from McDonald's to put in a drive-through restaurant.

I was then, in addition to my NYU work, developing a largish hotel in a ski area in Vermont. My father-in-law, seeing the hotel, asked me to develop the gas station.

Eighteen months later, in late June, the storefront contractor went bankrupt as we were pressing our July 1st finishing deadline. Without the aluminum storefront, we couldn't complete the building, get our certificate of occupancy ("C of O") and let people move into the building.

A Radical Political and Social History of the Lower East Side

I say "let people move into the building" because we'd started our rental campaign in anticipation of a Temporary C of O, which allows occupancy. I had a bunch of people expecting to move in, and was in a sudden bind. We were putting these people up in hotels.

The storefront fabricator, whom I'd contacted, assured me that the contractor had the storefront in his South Bronx shop. But the contractor wouldn't talk with me. I found where he lived and went out late one evening, rang his doorbell till his wife and then he answered, in his bathrobe, assuring me that he had, yes, taken our money but, no, he didn't have our storefront.

The fabricator again assured me that the contractor had that needed storefront.
The tenants we were putting up in a hotel wanted their apartments.

Johnny Swing, who was then one of the metal artists working in the 2B space, came out to the South Bronx with his gas canisters and blow torche very late one night and burned off the lock to the door of the storefront contractor's warehouse.

Johnny left and a friend and I crow-barred our way through one set of doors then another, only to set off an alarm.

We ran back to sit in our car, watched the cops come and leave, went for some food in an all night Italian restaurant then came back and got further in, so to speak. We broke our way through to the office of the man who'd declared bankruptcy, went through drawers hoping to find a key to the storeroom, which we did eventually come across all to naught, learning that no storefront was ours.

We solved our C of O problem on July 5th, 1991, when the City city agreed to give us a Temporary C of O for the residential tower, separate from the commercial wing. We were failing on one issue, an exhaust vent for a clothes drier in the basement laundry room. There was enough time left in the afternoon for me to race — I do mean "race" — my motor-cycle up to a hardware store on Union Square that carried the particular type of fuse we needed to correct the problem. The City city inspector agreed to stay until I got back from my motorcycle run. We inserted the fuse, the circuit worked, and the inspector wrote out our Temporary C of O. He agreed to stay while I ran down the block to Mrs. Zawin's, on the corner of B, and bought a bottle of champagne for all of us to share a drink.

Mr. Zawin and the Blasof brothers were always kind with me. They were amazed and amused, I think, that I was building "luxury" in the East Village.

What I eventually named "Red Square" was "luxury" in the sense of having elevators, a full time doorman and contemporary, efficiently laid out apartments.

We did not get our C of O for the commercial part of the building until December. I'd decided, until that time, to accommodate the homeless men in the eastern part of the space we'd built out. I say "accommodate" in that we could have built a fence and done other things to keep these men out. But I wanted to keep the space open, as some form of shelter.

We also encouraged an art show in this space during that summer or autumn. But I don't remember any details related to that.

I'm happy that the firm hired to plan Red Square, SLCE Architects, had a young designer, Rick Yestadt, who willingly spent a large amount of time riding on the back of my bike around the City, looking at samples and examples of designs and materials I wanted to consider.

I also had the luck to befriend Johnny Swing, a metal artist working in the extraordinary 2B, the "Gas Station." Johnny and I both grew up in Vermont, and that connection bridged what might otherwise have been a too wide artist/businessman gap.

I asked Johnny to create some of the railing space of Red Square as metal sculpture. Johnny agreed, and we worked out that he'd put in four pieces — one pair of opposing sculptures facing each other along the commercial section and the other pair facing each other at the top of the residential tower.

I anticipated that convincing the contractor and the railing subcontractor would be a problem, but they were intrigued. They worked on the fabrication with Johnny, explaining that the City's city's rule allowed no space to remain open that a ball of a certain size could be passed through it. I no longer remember the size of the ball, but it was somewhere between a golf ball and basketball.

Johnny's railing led to other art of his in the building, and to a great deal of work by others. Ken Hiratsuka spent the summer of 1991 cutting into the five hundred feet of sidewalk and making a serpentine sculpture filled with colored concretes. Johnny, John Carter and another friend of theirs made handles for lobby doors. Julie Dermansky spent months making an ocean of steel sea creatures for the lobby. Judith Robertson, before she left for the art scene in Miami, built a picket fence of ceramic tiles and cut mirrors for the chair rail of the lobby. Claudia Nagy built water-creature filled ponds as total environments in both elevators. She also created twelve astounding mosaics, one on each of the residential floors of the residential tower.

The clocks on Red Square are vestiges of my relationship with Tibor Kalman, the deservedly famous designer. I hired Tibor to "brand" Red Square. He — or more correctly, all the gifted people then at M&Co, and in our case, specifically Marlene McCarty, later from Bureau and Gran Fury, and Emily Oberman, later from Number 17-created our brochure, signage and much in the design work of the rental office. Tibor also insisted we pay him to paint two of his "askew" watches atop the building, on the walls of our water tower. Which have never worked well, but that's another tale.

Tibor was a man of immensely strong convictions. He insisted, I'm certain in full belief, that we needed to tear out our entire lobby just as it was finished. That Rick Yestadt's look was a disaster, and the building would never rent up.

A Radical Political and Social History of the Lower East Side

I didn't tear out the lobby. I did agree to leave one residential apartment "unfinished." Or more correctly, if it was twenty feet from the front door of an apartment to the outside wall and windows, I agreed to complete the first fourteen feet as if the apartment were ready for occupancy and to leave the remaining six feet completely raw-concrete floor and ceiling, masonry block exterior walls and steel stud interior demising walls. Painted sheet rock finished walls and wooden parquet floors ending in total deconstruction.

Tibor had introduced me to Ross Anderson and Fred Schwartz, who were then partners. They had the idea of deconstructing our rental office, which included designing specific furniture to fit the space and painting much of the text of our rental brochure on the windows and raw concrete floor of the unfinished part of that suite of rooms.

I'm asked, from time to time, "Who named Red Square?"

I want to answer, "I did." But the longer truth is that I entered a "naming contract" with Tibor, back in 1990 or so, for $10,000, which I had to pay only if I accepted one of his suggestions. He asked for ideas from me and I sent many, some like Red Circle and Red Box and red this and red that.

Tibor, meaning M&Co, came back with "Red Square."

He sent three suggestions on oversized white cards, not through fax or e-mail — though this was before e-mail existed (at least for me).

The USSR was still in existence. It was clear that the world was changing, and though 1991 doesn't seem so long ago, the geopolitical world was radically different then than it is now. "Red Square" was still a dramatic name, in a neighborhood where it would touch many people in different ways.

I picked "Red Square," as Tibor had hoped.

The Lenin statue on the roof came some years later. I'd been doing some work with three guys in Russia, who said they could buy a heretofore unrealized Kandinsky but didn't have the money.

Being too much impressionable and liking these three, I lent the money.

I also asked if they could locate a monumental Lenin. I thought it would be interesting to have an enormous Lenin waving to Wall Street.

They located a copper Lenin that had been commissioned for the USSR, but left to its sculptor when the USSR disappeared.
It cost us more to ship the Lenin than to purchase it.

These young men also convinced me to purchase a Grandfather Lenin sitting on a park bench, for my desk.
The Kandinsky, of course, was stolen after they purchased it. So they say. In any case, my loan was lost.

The rigging company that lifted a lot of things onto Red Square as we were constructing it agreed to lift the Lenin. They never charged for doing so.

For anyone bothering to notice, there are three or four "flag posts," for lack of a better term, running along the residential portion of the building between the first and second floors. I had the illusion that we could use the building as a living text, from time to time hanging artistically and politically motivated two-sided banners for passersby.

With the input of Marlene McCarty and Bureau, we installed one set of banners in 1992 or 1993. These had a dry feminist overtone, with such messages as "keep them barefoot and pregnant" and "where is RU486?"

I remember one tenant objecting, a woman who clearly wanted her home to be her home separate from a political text.

At least one Catholic priest also objected.

~~

A year earlier, my wife and I purchased an apartment in the Christodora House in 1989. It was one of the penthouses. The apartment was available because the person who'd had it in contract lost his money in the 1989 stock market downturn, or so we were told.

We didn't move in to the apartment until mid-1990, in part because our construction build-out was painfully slow and in part because our older son was born in early 1990. We were thus in no hurry to make more changes to our lives than a child already does.

I was not in the neighborhood for the August, 1988 riots.

I was in the park on December 14, 1989, the day the cops and an army of other city workers destroyed the homeless encampment. I stood here watching this army fill garbage trucks with the possessions of other people's lives and escort the homeless to the boundaries of the park and their nothingnesses. I walked around the neighborhood for much of the rest of that evening, spending time in the vacant lots east of Avenue B where some of the homeless had gone.

I was trying to wrap my understanding more around homelessness. I'd previously volunteered in a homeless shelter, spending nights there. I am concerned with how we treat each other, and watching the police that day was deeply disturbing. I remember some cops taking one man's shopping cart and chucking the whole of it into a garbage truck. I watched the man at the same time as I watched the hydraulic crusher dispose of the material aspects

A Radical Political and Social History of the Lower East Side

of his life, trying to feel at least a bit of how he must feel, remembering that he was once someone's baby, hopefully cuddled and loved.

I wondered about those who made the political decisions these cops and the army of city employees were carrying out.

I knew of the Christodora, in large part, because I had friends living there. Only on occasion did I feel the community animosity beyond the front door of our home. In New York, we often don't know our next-door neighbors, to speak nothing of people in the next building and the next avenue over.

In Vermont, where I grew up, people would bring a cake to a next-door neighbor who moved in. In the Christodora, cobble stones and steel trash cans thrown through the front door glass took the place of chocolate cake with vanilla frosting, and paint balloons tossed across the front façade took the place of an invitation to dinner.

I was, during this time, deeply involved with working to earn a living and raising our family. I did not attend Community Board meetings, nor other community-based gatherings. I do not believe, other than on a very temporary basis, that the Tompkins Square riots and the local homeless issues affected the price of Christodora apartments. The collapse of the national housing markets in the late 1980s and early 1990s, then the sell-offs and restructurings into the mid-1990s through the RTC and FDIC affected real estate prices much more dramatically than any local issues.

I figured, in response to my surroundings then, that human life is best measured in decades, not generally in moments. My wife and I chose to move into this neighborhood and raise our family here. Others' stereotypes need not become mine.

After completing Red Square, I earned a living as one of the principal owners of a construction company that built a large amount of publicly assisted housing, including housing for mentally ill homeless veterans, shelters for battered women, transitional housing for women coming out of the prison system, low income housing, and many other projects. Most of these buildings are in the Lower East Side.

After the contracting experience, I bought buildings, and after that I did other things. Now I'm primarily raising children, our family having grown to include five boys from this neighborhood, whom we met playing baseball in Tompkins Square seven seasons ago.

~

Perhaps having arrived with some grace at middle age, I've come to appreciate that a true sadness of humanity is our propensity to draw boundaries focusing on our "differences" rather on our sameness, our propensity to focus on exclusion over inclusion, on domination over love and compassion. I don't pretend an argument to argue that we don't exist as individuals. We clearly do, just as we clearly exist as communities and as a species. It is inevitable that we differentiate ourselves, as individuals and as group members through affiliation, from other individuals and groups.

But the majesty sought in achieving such differentiation, it seems to me, is to achieve a place of grace focusing on the interior spaces of practical compassion.

Living in the Lower East Side now, well over a decade after completing Red Square, I believe that our political leaders have a profound responsibility to adapt zoning regulations limiting building height and design to neighborhood context. Buildings should be no more than six stories tall, and should be built to the street wall. Tower-in-the-Park style design, built into a zoning code allowing tower construction through such programs as Tower Regulations, set-back and sky exposure plane regulations and more are sad vestiges of Le Corbusier's "Brilliant City" dreams. This architecture is a crime against urban neighborhood vitality.

It is the responsibility of our locally elected leaders to put aside political differences (based, truth be admitted, on class and race) and adopt a zoning code already embraced by the leaders of many other New York City neighborhoods.

As a corollary, I should not have been allowed to build Red Square so tall.

Knowing he was dying too early, Tibor Kalman worked with Princeton Architectural Press to publish *Tibor*, a visually stunning collection of his life work. Four pages are given to Red Square. Never mind that in one place I'm called "Michael Rosen" and in another "Michael Rosenberg." Two pages are given to a photograph of the Red Square brochure, and two pages are given to a photograph of the signage that once hung from the front of the building. Tibor calls our Red Square project "the most masterful deceit of all" (2000:49). I'm not certain of Tibor's meaning, and he's no longer alive to ask, but I'm sure he intended a mixed meaning regarding ethical concerns. Tibor worked from a place of ethics.

Marlene McCarty came to carry no such ambiguity:

> It was difficult for me because I had friends who lived in little buildings behind Red Square, and whose views or light were being blocked. Michael Rosen was saying he was making the economy of the neighborhood healthier, which is probably true on paper — it was an extremely poor neighborhood. But of all my jobs at M&Co, I was always most embarrassed about this one. I live in that neighborhood. Every day when I look out of the window, I see Red Square. It's my punishment (2000:49).

I first felt betrayed by Marlene, when I read her sentences. We'd worked very closely together, both at M&Co and once she'd left to create Bureau with Donald Moffet. She and Donald created the political banners I've described above. She created a good number of post cards for Red Square, and eventually my own stationery, envelopes and business cards when I started a company called Sundered Ground.

But with my own development, I believe Marlene is correct. I should lead my life, and affect others, as I would want to be affected. Practical compassion means amassing the residential square footage differently than I did.

A Radical Political and Social History of the Lower East Side

564

Fred Schwartz, of all the people I met and worked with in developing and then renting Red Square, has continued to be a good friend. Fred was the founder of the Think Group, which won the design contest for the Ground Zero site until the Pataki administration overruled the LMDC (Lower Manhattan Development Council) commission it had created. Fred's work, regardless has gained the recognition it deserves and, Fred, himself, has gained the recognition that should be his.

That's all.

Bibliography:

Hall, Peter and Michael Bierut (Editors), *Tibor: Perverse Optimist*, 2000, Princeton Architectural Press, New York

Chapter 9

Changing the World From His Couch
By Virginie Rocky

"Young people are the only ones who still believe they can change things," Steve Cannon once told me. What are they looking for in this novelist (*Groove, Bang, and Jive Around*, 1969), who is also a playwright, poet, retired professor, and editor? They may find in him the figure who makes them feel like they are able to change the world, as he asks the right questions, listens to everyone with attention and enthusiasm, encourages people to do what they really want to do, and puts them to work. When asked how he wanted the world to be when he was in his twenties, Cannon told me he hoped to make New York "more likable" for him: he wanted people to be able to exchange their ideas and to talk, "instead of being locked in from 9 to 5." He laughed, as he is blindly spreading ashes around him, and noticed: "Instead of changing New York, I had to change myself!" Looking at what he has achieved, in his now-famous brownstone building on East Third Street where he created a non-profit organization called *A Gathering of the Tribes* in 1991, many would disagree. The 70-year-old grandfather and mentor of many young artists has changed what became his world "a century ago" (as he often says) — the Lower East Side of Manhattan.

Cannon arrived here not a century ago, but 43 years ago, a long time considering all that has happened here since. He was involved in many political rallies against the war in Vietnam in the 1960s and was here for the riots in Tompkins Square Park in the late 1980s, when a crowd of protesters exclaiming "No police state!" faced off with an army of police officers. He has observed the changes that have affected the neighborhood, but talks about the past decades without nostalgia. He is one of those people who still believes in the creativity and unique energy of the Lower East Side.

Born and raised in New Orleans, Cannon moved to New York in 1962. "I am a writer, and I wanted to be around other writers — people who are interested in the same thing I am interested in — meaning reading good books and creating good literature. I thought New York would be the right place," he recalls. First, he moved to Harlem but soon settled in the Lower East Side, without knowing he would there meet his "Tribe" and find a lasting home. "I moved with a couple of students from Columbia University to a place on East Houston and Clinton Street. They were very politically active in the civil rights movement and against the war in Vietnam. Through them I met radicals, activists, and artists because they told me the places where all these people used to hang out. I first mingled with them at Stanley's bar on Avenue B and East Twelfth Street."

Since then, Cannon has been very involved in the community, enough to be widely recognized today as an institution of the Lower East Side. Through his participation in the neighborhood cultural and political scene, he has proved to be a strong defender of integration of all ethnicities in society, and multiculturalism — such a rich quality in his opinion. These values led him to writers who shared the same faith in multiculturalism, particularly

A Radical Political and Social History of the Lower East Side

in the arts. Through poet Ishmael Reed, who became a close friend and is a member of Tribes' board of directors, Cannon was introduced to the Umbra movement. This collective of young Black artists of all disciplines and based in the Lower East Side, was the first post-civil rights Black literary group to have a radical impact on the artistic canon of the time, and was one of the first at forging truly multicultural aesthetics. These young artists, including LeRoi Jones (Amiri Baraka), Calvin Hernton, Tom Dent, David Henderson, Al Haynes, Joe Johnson, Lorenzo Thomas, Archie Shepp (a musician/writer), James Johnson, Roland Snellings (a visual artist), and Victor Hernandez Cruz imposed their voice and differed from the establishment. "I first heard them at the St. Mark's Poetry Project making the connection between music and literature, and asking all the right questions about racism and the war in Vietnam," Cannon wrote in an article in 1997. The influential Umbra workshop met on the Lower East Side from 1962 to 1964, and from the workshop came *Umbra* magazine. Cannon was solicited to write book reviews for them. "The core of Umbra was Black males, but the manager was a young Egyptian lady, and we also had a Jewish guy, who was a union activist, and many other different people supported us. It was primarily a literary movement but we did political statements through the arts, with poetry dealing with the segregation in this country, stories about Vietnam . . . "

Divided in its goal, Umbra faced a classic split: One faction was more concerned with political activism and the other one with literature. As part of the latter, Cannon described the former as "Black nationalists who didn't believe in integration," and we can sense some bitterness in his voice when he talks about the exodus from the Lower East Side to Harlem of many members of Umbra, in 1964. Led by Askia Touré and Al Haynes, they launched there the "Uptown Writers Movement," a much more nationalist-oriented organization than Umbra. Accompanied by young "New Music" musicians, they performed poetry all over Harlem. Members of this group joined LeRoi Jones in founding the Black Arts Repertory Theatre/ School (BARTS). Cannon, as a Lower East Sider and a proponent of integration, took a different path and had no link with BARTS. Nonetheless, anxious to recall an often forgotten part of history, he explains that "the irony is that all this came out of Umbra." BARTS was short-lived, but the Black Arts Movement, proclaimed by Larry Neal to be the "aesthetic and spiritual sister of the Black Power concept," was irrepressible and was extremely influential and active until the mid 1970s.[1]

Although he was not involved with the Black Panthers, Cannon, as part of the Black community of the Lower East Side, was familiar with some of them. Members of this African-American militant party, founded in 1966 in Oakland, California, by Huey P. Newton and Bobby Seale, lived in the neighborhood back in the '70s. The Black Panthers called on African-Americans to arm themselves for the liberation struggle. Cannon denounced this violent aspect of their action, as well as their link to Marxist ideology. But he recognized the positive elements of their action:

The positive thing about them is that they were concerned with policing the whole neighborhood, making sure there was a certain peace and prosperity, making sure kids were going to school. The other good thing is that they were concerned with the whole idea of equality, and democracy. They thought that everyone should participate in the democratic process. You are not supposed to pull yourself away from society but you are supposed to integrate society in order to change it from within instead of trying to change it from outside.

Cannon observes the lasting political impact of this radical movement in the hip-hop generation who learn about the Black Panthers in school. "Lots of these kids are very politically aware and realize the importance of being involved with local political issues because of what came out of this experience in the '60s."

Interested in the creativity and energy of young people, Cannon listens carefully to them. As a professor for 20 years, Cannon had the opportunity to observe the evolution of political engagement from generation to generation. He began teaching in 1972 at the City University of New York and recalls: "I enjoyed teaching at that time: Students had a lot of passion and energy, and they were concerned with social issues. That generation was very idealistic; they actually believed they could change things, without being sarcastic." As Cannon smiles, one can feel how close he felt to this spirit and how much he misses it. "When I got to the '80s, that passion was not there. For those students, social issues were something you read about in the newspapers. They didn't have the feeling, whether it's true or not, that if you go to a demonstration it's gonna change things, if you write a poem, make a movie, it's gonna change things." Cannon admits he was hurt by this change in mentality. Even if he mentions young people's engagement after September 11 or post-Hurricane Katrina, one can guess he would like to hear more hope and radicalism among new generations. Being blind now for 15 years (because of glaucoma), Professor Cannon spends most of his time on his couch. He accepts whoever enters his informal "salon" in the same way, no matter who they are and where they come from. Often welcoming you with a direct: "How is your world?" Cannon proves to be supportive of all kinds of initiatives, and admits he can rarely say "No." Thanks to him, young artists find at Tribes Gallery a place to expose their work, and writers can publish poetry and fiction in *A Gathering of the Tribes* magazine. These artists, also an eclectic crowd, join Cannon from time to time around his table. Sitting next to him on the couch, you can look at all these different people trying to catch Cannon's attention. There, you can often expect to hear lively and excited exchanges of viewpoints. Here is the proof if needed that Cannon cannot wait to see radical politics flourish on the Lower East Side.

NEO GEO
Africa in Asia
Asia in America
America in Arabia
Indonesia
Malaysia
Maylasia
Euthainasia
In America, in Asia, in Africa, in Arabia
Neo Geo Geo Neo
YOYOYO
Steve Cannon

1. Larry Neal, *The Black Arts movement*, 1968 http://aalbc.com/authors/blackartsmovement.htm

Virginie de Rocquign

Chapter 10

My Loisaida
An Overview
    By Mary McCarthy

One of the best decisions I made in my life was to move to Loisaida in the late 1970s. I moved there as a stranger and found many friends. You may wonder why a former housewife from Larchmont, New York would want to do such a thing, in the first place.

It wasn't the first time I had made a big change in my life. A couple of years after WWII, while attending graduate school in New York and working as assistant editor of *Good Housekeeping*, I represented the magazine at a writers workshop meeting at St. Albans Veterans Hospital. That was how the recently-discharged Jack McCarthy, wounded veteran of Omaha Beach in Normandy, and I met. It was love at first sight for both of us, and I left behind the unfinished MA, and *Good Housekeeping*, so we could be married. We eventually had three sons and spent most of our married life in Larchmont, N.Y..

Some years later, when the boys were in high school, I went back to work as New York editor and movie reviewer for a magazine for visitors. A few years later, the idea for a low-income magazine came to me. The visitors' magazine was distributed in the best hotels, free. Covering all those early '70s movies raised my consciousness about the injustice in the world. I wondered why nobody was putting out a free magazine for people who couldn't afford magazines while the one I was editing was going to people who could. I tested some of my ideas on a public access TV show I started called *"The Quality of Life."*

At this time, my life changed its quality. My husband of over twenty years left, and, soon after that, I was fired from my job. Even though I had an offer for another good position, I wanted to pursue the free magazine idea. At first, I imagined a midtown office, from which I would edit a nation-wide magazine. I believed it was such a good idea that I would have no trouble raising money from foundations. Reality kicked in when no sources were willing to subsidize this venture. I revised my plan to a city-wide magazine, and, when that wouldn't fly, a magazine for one neighborhood.

I discovered Loisaida for myself through a woman I met at a party in Larchmont. She sent me to a young man who had installed a windmill on a roof there, and I went down and found him and the windmill. There were solar panels on the same roof. The neighborhood was dotted with community gardens. People in the street looked cheerful. And I found out they had a lot of meetings about improving things. It would be a good place to start the magazine.

I incorporated as a not-for-profit organization and began to recruit a board of directors. I realized that it wouldn't make sense to edit a publication for Loisaida while living in

Larchmont. That's how I wound up living on East Fourth Street, with the bathtub in the kitchen. As I settled in, scraping paint and tearing down cracked plaster, I completed the board. A few donations trickled in from well-wishing friends and local banks.

The housing organization, Loisaida, which had helped me find my apartment, put me in touch with Alfredo Irizarry, an enthusiastic young man who rounded up a team of people he knew. Brent Sharman, a young native of England, joined the staff, and brought with him an old press that a local church gave him for the taking. He'd been printing the church's bulletins on it, and now he volunteered to print the magazine on his press. Carmelo Quiñones joined us early as an important contributor of articles. Tony La Sala, art director of a commercial magazine, volunteered to be art director. Adopt-a-Building let us have a free room in the building they were using at Avenue C and East 4th Fourth Street for our press and office. We all volunteered our time. In short, the eight page issue, Vol. I, No. 1 of *The Quality of Life in Loisaida*, came out in March, 1978, with two thousand copies. I must explain about the name: Loisaida is a Spanish-flavored way of saying Lower East Side, and the word was first publicized in Bimbo Rivas' poem "Loisaida." He and Alfredo and others insisted we call the magazine "Loisaida" and I had planned to call it "The Quality of Life," so we put both titles together.

On the cover was a photo of a CitiArts mural at Madison and Pike Street, with a logo by Freddie Hernandez of the word "Loisaida" contained in a silhouette of a row of neighborhood buildings. The mural depicted a pyramid of people, poor immigrants at the bottom, workers with better living conditions on succeeding layers, and, at the top, happy young persons of assorted cultures, cheering. Inside we had a couple of line drawings from Tony, plus text (in English and Spanish) and three photos from the staff.

The first year we were a quarterly, and then switched to bi-monthly. One of our early issues contained a profile of Bimbo Rivas, poet, playwright, actor, known for appearing in *Short Eyes*, a play by Miguel Piñero, another Loisaideño, and his work "with El Teatro Ambulante," Miguel Algarín's Nuyorican Poet's Café, the Nuyorican Village, CHARAS, Seven Loaves, City Arts, Plaza Cultural, and on and on. Bimbo was a great supporter and friend of the magazine until his death in May 1992.

In the early issues, we had a cartoon strip, *"Adventures in Loisaida,"* by Freddie Hernandez and Pete Tirado. One showed a funny little character carrying what seemed to be an unnecessary umbrella on a sunny day, going home and having to put the umbrella up because the ceiling was leaking from a pipe. We went up to fourteen, then to 16 pages, writing about people and events in the neighborhood. Our print run gradually increased, too.

A whole team of us turned out to interview Sarah Berman Beach, who had been a WPA (Works Projects Administration) artist during the Depression. She had lived in the neighborhood in her youth and returned in later years. Another article, on the East 12th St. community garden between Avenues A and B, was by Linda Cohen, who was in charge. It told how an empty plot where two buildings had been demolished was cleaned up and turned into garden space by volunteers. We published a directory of local health care services. We showed how to use a sheet of plastic as an improvised storm window in winter.

A Radical Political and Social History of the Lower East Side

Significantly, we covered the Three Kings celebration, January 6, 1979, which included a march around local streets to present Loisaida Miracle awards to various organizations and people. The march ended at the Nuyorican Poets' Café where three costumed kings gave out small presents to children. The awards were given to such organizations as Cuando, for building the first urban application of passive solar energy in the U.S.; Grupo Cemi for folkloric dance; CHARAS for its recycling center; Tu Casa for providing a place for musicians to meet and rehearse; Nuyorican Poets Café for "bringing us together to reflect upon our vision, and give it song"; and three buildings whose residents had rehabilitated them with sweat equity.

We covered Community Board #3 meetings, which were well attended by neighborhood people, and in 1979 wrote up a new organization, Fight Back for Children, for education. We interviewed our councilwoman, Miriam Friedlander, who asked residents to bring her their problems about housing.

Somewhere along the way, Brent stopped printing. He married and got a full-time job, so he didn't have time. Gradually, others of the first staff people had to drop off for similar reasons. But other people came along and we kept going. We struggled through the 1980s when it was especially hard to get donations and grants.

In February, 1980, about to start our fourth year, we began doing issues devoted to a single theme. These included a "Special Economic Development Issue," "School Board Election," "Summer in Loisaida," and the "Special Issue on Education for Women."

As we began our fifth year, our cover featured one word: "Jobs." The issue told about the various kinds of jobs available and places to go for advice on getting them, about free workshops and assistance in finding jobs and preparing for interviews. It included Bimbo's memorable poem "A Job" (later printed in the anthology *Nuyorican Poetry*) as well as a piece by Chino Garcia, Coordinator coordinator of CHARAS. He wrote, "We have on our hands a very ignorant government, a government that does not feel for the human needs of the people and thinks that if industry does well, automatically that will solve the needs of the people in this country." In an interview, Friedlander said, "I think the major responsibility of federal, state and city governments is to see that people have jobs."

A great part of another issue was given over to "The Plan by the Joint Planning Council." It was from the Joint Planning Council, and was about saving the Lower East Side from gentrification, suggesting the city rehab and build new affordable housing and use zoning to protect and increase such housing. It also called for enforcement of the housing code to keep buildings from deteriorating.

Squeezed in the back pages of this issues was an ad for the Loisaida International Cultural Festival, sponsored by CHARAS at the end of July. That festival turned out to be a major event for the neighborhood, and rated a cover picture on the next issue. It was a great day. The sky was overcast, but every once in a while a ray of sun would peek through. Wherever I looked, I saw remarkable, charming things: a clown entertaining children by twisting balloons into animals, dancers in white, ruffled dresses (their heads bound in colorful scarves), a flute player and people in extraordinary masks, one a horse's head, another like an insect head.

Our holiday issue for 1985 asked the question: "If you came into lots of money, what would you do for the community?" Roberto Caballero, Democratic District Leader, said he would buy up all the empty buildings and turn them into affordable housing. Carmen Pabon, poet and founder of a community garden, had a plan. She'd found a group of parents to deal with the problem of drugs. She'd obtain a building for housing pregnant young women. She would arrange for part- time, and later, full-time jobs for young people. Robert Nadal, in contrast, a man who ran a little store on Avenue C, would have a Nadal Foundation to provide food, clothes and burial expenses where needed. Karen Firpi, housewife, would repair abandoned buildings and provide jobs for the youth. Luis Guzman, actor on *Miami Vice* and *The Equalizer*, as well as volunteer at Henry St. Settlement, would give a million a year to CHARAS (arts and development) and El Bohio (community center). Lastly, Bimbo Rivas would stabilize the community by developing housing for the people.

By 1986, John Lesch was doing our typing on a computer attached to an electric typewriter, which then printed it out like a player piano. We had enough ads to make the magazine look professional. We were up to twenty-eight pages. We put out a Christmas issue saluting holiday customs of different ethnic groups, including those of Puerto Ricans, Ukrainians, Jews, Africans, Italians, Poles, Germans, Koreans, and Irish. In January 1988, our Music music issue featured Jemeel Moondoc, jazz saxophonist, and Pupa Santiago, head of Tucasa studio, and the band Sonido Costeño, and others.

That spring we celebrated our tenth anniversary with a wingding of a party. The incomparable Johnny Colon and his orchestra provided music in the big El Bohio hall. Chino was master of ceremonies. Bimbo passed out many of the awards. We had a great throng, seated at tables and chairs borrowed from several organizations and churches. Food and most of the drinks were donated by individuals and restaurants, providing a nice ethnic variety. Crowds of the magazine's friends were there, and even members of my family. I was supremely glad that night that I'd come to Loisaida to live and spend what would become the last fourteen years of my working life among the valiant, charming people in this enchanting place.

Chapter 11

Carmen's Garden
Loisaida, 1986
        By Mary McCarthy

Come sit with Carmen in her garden
where chickens, rust, speckled, brown,
and a duck cavort, and children and elders laugh,
on Loisaida Avenue in the Lower East Side.

Plaster statues of the Virgin, Michael
the Archangel, and other santos bless the place,
overseen by a mural showing local children.
Tinsel garlands, two small American flags
and two for Puerto Rico mark the gate
where an armless Barbie in pink net
shares space with roses, morning glories,
and a patch of green beans.

Here's a toy-sized one-room house,
no bigger than a closet, that gave
a homeless family shelter just last week —
two parents and two children.
And there's the grill where meals are cooked
for hungry folks. In the corner, plastic bags
of clothes for people, and a store of bottles
to turn in for needed coins.
Come sit with Carmen in her garden,
this magic place she's made,
on Loisaida Avenue.

Chapter 12

William Parker Interview: Land Without Lords
By Steve Dalachinsky and Jim Feast

On June 2, 2004, Clayton Patterson and the authors interviewed bassist William Parker concerning his quest for art, housing, and sanity on the Lower East Side.

Parker is one of the most prolific, accomplished and important composers/ musicians/ bassists on the jazz scene today. He started playing when he was very young, recording his first record as a sideman for Frank Lowe in the early 1970s. However, he did not come to world prominence until the later 1980s when he began a long stint with Cecil Taylor, and then played with the David S. Ware quartet and with Matthew Shipp. He is regarded as one of the most significant jazz bass players since Mingus, and, indeed, his large ensemble, the Little Huey Orchestra, has been favorably compared with the Mingus big band. He is a great arco player, as well as a man who can play inside (traditional) or outside (free) with equal facility. Aside from mastering the bass, Parker plays instruments he has collected from India, Morocco and other countries in Asia and Africa.

In this interview, though, we are not looking at his playing, but at his attempts to find and support alternative venues at which he and other free jazz players could be heard. For, as it turns out, most commercial spaces lack three qualities, which he finds paramount.

First, he believes in bringing music to the community, which means playing a good percentage of his gigs at places that are low priced or at benefits.

Second, he believes in respecting the musician. This in the spirit of the club, The Stone, recently established by John Zorn, which has the policy that all the door goes to the performers on stage. This practice has been carried out in less radical form in other venues that insist the players get fair pay for their effort.

Third, Parker believes in a mix and match policy for the arts. At the Vision Festival, for example, (which he and his wife Patricia Nicholson helped found ten years ago), artistic confluences are omnipresent. On any and every night, an audience member will be treated to musicians playing with poets (including one of the authors of this piece, Steve Dalachinsky); dancers weaving through the audience and among the instrumentalists, an art gallery of sculpture and paintings on the walls surrounding and on the stage, and (usually) Jeff Schlanger doing portraits of the bands in action.

All this together, in our minds, adds up to Parker's implicit belief that the commercial structures set up to process status-quo-oriented music (of jazz or any other genre) are neither adequate nor viable for music that is consistently challenging and freedom-oriented.

A Radical Political and Social History of the Lower East Side

Perhaps, it's not so surprising, then, that a person who fed so much energy into working with and creating alternative venues for performance, where a music, which though technically rigorous, was informal and loosely spontaneous, would pervade a space that was equally unpretentious and open, would also seek a living situation that glances along the margins of the more well-known options for living in New York City, that is: renting, buying or squatting. This will become evident in the following interview in which we coordinate Parker's dual movement as, starting in the mid-1970s he sought on the Lower East Side a place to live and places to play that re-invented the possible.

Parker moved to the Lower East Side in May 1975 partially to further his musical ambitions. "I was a musician and a lot of the work, gigs, playing possibilities were down in Lower Manhattan," he says. Moreover the rent was reasonable. At his first place, 314 East Sixth Street, between First and Second Avenues, he says, "My rent at that time was 90 dollars a month for a studio." Two years later, he moved further west and obtained "a six-room apartment for which I paid $122 a month." On top of that, he had just gotten married, which also called for a change of residence.

Marriage also demanded full-time occupation. "When I talked to my father in law about getting married, I had to have a job. Simple as that." His preference would have been to devote full time to his music, but since his career was still in its early stages, he couldn't pay the bills that way. As it turns out, he made a fortuitous choice in getting a job in the housing authority.

Parker notes, "I worked in the maintenance department, which was actually very good in my homestead because I learned plumbing. I learned electricity. Putting in locks." This had immediate secondary benefits since, as he says, the first Lower East Side apartment he had rented "had nothing in it, so I had to put my bathtub in it. I had to put everything in that apartment, which was actually pre-training ground for" later work fixing up an apartment.

Even with all the work he had to do on his living space, he felt lucky to be downtown. The neighborhood was everything he expected it to be, a-buzz with creative activity. "There were a lot of interesting people doing interesting things. You know, sculptors, poets, walking around, carrying things, going from here to there." This had been a draw in the first place. "I guess the reason I came down here was — well, all the artists I read about lived in the Village — and I felt it was a place where you could be yourself." He adds, "Of course, that's not really true. You can be yourself anywhere, and do what you want anywhere."

Not only a hotbed of the creative arts, the neighborhood was also awash in progressive politics, as evidenced by the founding of free schools, battles against gentrification and attempts to squat and homestead abandoned buildings. Although Parker was not a political militant, his experience as a music educator and performer in alternative sites brought him in constant contact with the activist core of the area, and, that, in turn, led him to hook up with some urban pioneers.

At the time, the city had a homestead program that helped (relatively) lower-income people obtain abandoned buildings. "They had a list of buildings in all the five boroughs and you needed to put a group together," Parker explains. "The criteria for the group was that you had to not make too much money, prove that you could complete the work on the building or get loans to complete work. You had to get an architect, an electrician. Then you would bid for the building." The city would examine proposals made for each of its buildings, and the best one that met its criteria would obtain the site.

Parker continues, "Now, the group I was with I would not consider a grassroots group. I was the only Black person in the group, only minority in the group."

As an aside, he noted that a program such as this, no matter what its seeming thrust, was really only suitable for people with some financial resources. "The whole program is like a Catch 22. You need money to complete a building, but if you're poor, you don't have anything. You don't have any money. You don't have any time; you might not have any skills." Musicians like Marty Ehrlich or John Zorn, who were also involved in such programs, had some wealth and so more easily could participate in these building takeovers. In Ehrlich's group, they "didn't do any sweat equity. They hired a construction company. They didn't do anything."

Parker was asked to participate in the group forming in his rental building both because they knew him as a neighbor and because of his community involvement. "I had done teaching down at the Sixth Street Community Center" as he had at CHARAS and Cuando. So, as he says, "I knew a lot of the people, the so-called activist people who were doing stuff in the neighborhood, just by playing music," for example, at the original Nuyoricans Poets Cafe. The more immediate trigger to his involvement was this: There "just happened to live in my building an architecture student, who said, `Well, we're putting a group together. Do you want to get in on the group?'"

The question had come at a good time because he had made the decision to set aside his day job. "It was just at a certain point, my wife said to me, `You should just concentrate on playing music.' And I said, 'Okay.' Well, actually, at that point my daughter was born, so I would concentrate on playing music. So, that's what I did."

If he was going to make a living as a musician, he had to keep his expenses low, so falling in with a plan to own his own apartment, where the maintenance fee would stay reasonable, was to his liking.

The collection of people applying to homestead a building was top heavy with those qualified to rebuild. Aside from the architect who spoke to Parker, there were two other architects in the building, plus one professional electrician. "So we bid on this building, and we got it. That was 1983."

With Reagan in power, this might not have seemed a time when such projects that deviated from the norms of the real estate market would get much encouragement, but as Parker explains, the programs "were already set up when Jimmy Carter was president and it just took them a while to cancel them after Reagan became president."

A Radical Political and Social History of the Lower East Side

Having obtained the property, they had their hands full.

Well, this building when we started working on it was just the front facade: no ceiling, no roof, no back wall. Two side walls and that was it. So, we did what was called sweat equity, which was you put in a certain number of hours a week and the requirement was to put in sixteen hours per week, preferably Saturday and Sunday, log it, and you'd keep records. You know the architect had a plan how to repair the building, what was needed. You'd get the building up to the point where . . . it was sealed. What we did, and I didn't put any money in because I didn't have any money but the other people in the group put together an amount of money to get a demolition crew to gut the building, because they felt that . . . a lot of homestead groups spent two years just gutting the building. You know, with no machinery and with the building condition what it was, it was very dangerous. So, they hired someone to gut the building so that when we came in the building was all gutted, all the debris was out, so that saved us quite a bit of time dumping stuff in the dumpster.

Now the work of rebuilding could begin. One of the differences between the homesteads and the squatters was that the squatters usually lived in the buildings and with homesteads you weren't allowed to, but it wouldn't have been possible to live here at that time. There was nothing to live. There was no building.

In 1983, they had the building gutted and could start putting the place together. This included replacing all the beams, laying in floors, putting in chimneys, adding a roof, sheet-rocking the walls, doing the electricity, and adding windows. Most of the work they did on their own, though they needed to hire masons for the chimneys and plumbers for the pipes.

Where Parker's background didn't prepare him for certain jobs, he could sometimes use his musical skills to set up a trade. "I had a guy named Joe Barnes, who asked me to write a piece of music for him, so he came in and showed me how to put in a floor. We did it together." They also exchanged work with others in the building. "Two of the people in the building are potters. We had other people doing the demolition, so while they were doing the demolition, the two made tiles, all the hallway tiles."

What the building could have used more of was sharing. Parker says, "I wish it was more communal, but there was no time to give classes in like how do you do this, how do you do that. How do you design your apartment?" The obstacle preventing more sharing was that everyone was under time constraints and living by different schedules. For Parker, "I was going back and forth to Europe. I was doing a lot of different things. Also I didn't have a day job so I could work at night. I remember the guy next door, banging at 3 in the morning, banging, quiet."

After five years of labor, learning and skill bartering, the building was complete. "At the end, when it was all together, you bought each apartment for $250 from the city. The papers were filed, so everyone owned their apartment."

He emphasized that people did not get involved as some kind of political statement. "When you're putting a building together, it's basically what you're doing . . . you're not thinking that when the building is done, you are going to do something political with the building. People were just going to bring their families in to live.

It wasn't even that they took on the project as a way to beat the real estate market. "I don't know whether people were saying, 'Well, the rents are going to go sky high in five years so we better do this.' I think once we got started we were just trying to finish the building and have the joy of actually owning your own apartment."

What he did have was a stable living situation, so that fluctuations in the housing market would not warp his financial picture and force him to give up music. He had also become a property owner. This did not turn him into a real estate speculator, as it did some who homesteaded and then tried to make a killing by selling their places, but it did help him to fashion a philosophy of how society should be restructured.

> I think people should own where they live. I think it's the most important move you can make, because you live in a place 30 years. You're paying $1,000 a month. You're paying $12,000 a year. Over the years, you've paid all this money, and you don't own any thing. The landlord still owns it. So, I think, the same way you own the shoes you wear and you own your clothing, I think people should own the place they live, because, at least, whatever happens, you have a place to live. There shouldn't be such a thing as a landlord. I mean, landlords, that whole thing should be abolished.

Easier said than done, some would say. But Parker has also considered how a landlord-less society would be fashioned.

"What they [the government] should do is that you should have like a mortgage on your apartment."

> It's like when the landlord replaces your refrigerator and like he raises your rent a $100. Now after a year you paid for that refrigerator like 10 times already. You're still paying for that refrigerator. I mean, that's wrong. When you pay a rent, that rent should go toward your buying the apartment. After 20 years, you paid 20 years of rent, you own the apartment. Now, if the landlord after having all these tenants in his building is collecting all this money, if he doesn't have any money after all of that, then that's his problem.

Parker adds a proviso about how homestead programs could be set up that would not be as middle-class-centered as the ones that were in place when he got involved.

A Radical Political and Social History of the Lower East Side

A lot of people, like a mother that's got four kids, three kids, then having to do sweat equity. [She can't do it, so] sweat equity should be varied according to individuals and should be in favor of people who are poor and who can't really afford to complete a program with high standards but they would vary according to the individual.

Obviously, this populist program has been partially inspired by Parker's experience with homesteading, but it is also rooted in his life in the do-it-yourself music club and festival scene that existed on the Lower East Side in the 1980s. Since at the time the area was not on the radar screens of redevelopers, and, indeed, was being abandoned by landlords and the city, empty buildings could be appropriated as artistic venues.

One such was CUANDO, which used to be the Church of All Nations, on Second Avenue and First Street [demolished in 2005]. Parker describes it as "a very, very big building. It's got two swimming pools, tennis courts on the roof, a chapel, I mean, it's just a tremendous space." In 1983, it was being used by theater groups and other community organizations. Parker continues, "We were looking for a place to do a festival in 1983 going into 1984. So I went to Henry Street Settlement where Luis Guzman worked, cut a deal with him to rent CUANDO. Rented it for $1,000. We did this seven-day music festival, the Sound Unity Festival."

They brought in groups from Europe and around the world.

"And we fixed up the place. We had electricity, which was a major thing, although we did have to do a tap with an electrician to get more electricity for lights and stuff." The only thing they were lacking was a working boiler. "There was never any heat in CUANDO, never, never. So, but the festival was in June, so we didn't have to worry about heat."

Simultaneously, a more ongoing musical scene was starting up at a squat being run by Sarah Farley on East Sixth. Although it was a squat, the tenants obtained grudging permission from the city to occupy it. They had an unoccupied basement, "and this guy from Italy, Sandro Genetti, went to talk to Sarah about using the basement as a performance space." The Shuttle opened shortly after that. Parker gigged there as did Rashid Ali and Charles Gayle. "I played down there with everybody, Miguel Algarin, Allen Ginsberg, Don Cherry," he mentions. "You'd go down there and there was the music, boom. Again, the heat was [nonexistent.] It was a summertime thing."

Although, the basement was the site of some amazing artistic collaboration, a combination of irresponsible tenants and the city's taking advantage of this irresponsibility doomed the space. Parker begins his discussion of The Shuttle's downfall with a wry general observation:

Unfortunately, down here in the East Village, you have characters and you have people. And you have people who are characters. Not everyone in a squat building is the most reliable. Not everyone in a squat building is thinking on their feet and on their toes. So, unfortunately, the building was not housed by the elite, as far as being mentally alert with things. So, they had a guy, he was doing some plumbing on the building with an acetylene torch and he set the building on fire. Once something like that happens then the city has an excuse. If you've got an architectural plan, and you've got an architect and money in the bank, you've got some kind of leverage. But if you've just got spaced-out home-less people in the building, saying we're taking over the squat, it lowers your chance of getting the building.

As a result of the fire, "that just kind of killed things and the city came in and took over the building."

But meanwhile, another space had opened up, one of the dimensions of CUANDO. This was CHARAS, a vacant public school on Ninth Street that had been taken over by a community group, which parceled out the classrooms to activists and artists, including musicians. "Between 1983-1984, Jemeel Moondoc had a studio, the drummer Sonny Murray had a stu-dio, the trumpet player Butch Morris had a studio. Gunter Hampel had a space. And there were some theater people that had studios." Parker not only would do music workshops, as he interjects, "We [his wife and himself] worked a daycare center out of CHARAS for a while. A summer camp, not a daycare center. A summer camp where you have kids 13, 14 kids come over, you take them to the swimming pool, music lessons."

Parents would pay to enroll their kids in the summer camp, but the other programs were *gratis*. "These were all unfunded programs. I mean, we'd go and advertise music workshops, and it was free. We tried to get grants later, but they never came in." Not only would they offer programs for youth, but for older people. "We had a program to teach adults how to read music. And we did concerts there periodically," Parker adds. "We did a Lower East Side music festival out of there up in the classroom or the studio that Jemeel had."

Unlike the two aforementioned properties, this one had heat. "One of their accomplishments over there is that they put in these space heaters that are vented from the window. Then Chino Garcia was able to rent the classrooms and you could use it in the wintertime."

The space had exceptional programs and vitality, but the very grandness of the scale made managing it difficult. Parker comments, "It's a really large building. I mean, it's a school building and it just wasn't functioning. It was functioning on a quarter or less than a quar-ter of capacity." To run such a monster, you have to bring in outsiders, who may not do what they promise. "I mean, the roof was leaking, here, over there, broken windows. So someone comes to you and says, `Can you give me this room, I'll fix it up myself?' So, you give it to them, they don't do it."

He broadens his analysis:

If you're going to have a vision for a building, you have to take chances, but at the same time you could lose it. And that's what happens in the end. Because what happens is that you do need money to make a building work. You need to bring people in at the same time, you want to control the building, and when you bring money in that will take the building away from you. I mean there were a lot of factors involved in this thing. And you really have to be a master, master, master and also very, very lucky to pull off something like that, and also have a rich father. [Moreover, government has to be factored in] Because the city has their own master plan about things. And the city doesn't forget. And especially when Giuliani was mayor and they don't forget things, and they have their own plan.

Still, according to Parker, things might have taken another direction. "I think that if they really used it as a hub for all the community organizations, and giving out space and let everybody develop programs. Let Third Street Music School have a space. Let Henry Street have a space." If some of these "ifs" had materialized, the magnificent space might have stayed in the community's hands.

Eventually, the city repossessed the space and sold the place to developers.

Meanwhile, as all this action was taking place at the larger venues, there were also smaller, apartment-sized places appearing in other squats. Parker points out, "Those places were very easy to start. You had low overhead because you weren't paying any rent. You didn't have any neighbors that were going to complain regardless of what was happening." The format was stark and simple.

> You show up on a particular night and there was the living room. You play. People would come. And you could develop a very good feeling in the time when you were playing and people would hang out. Once the event starts, it's just as nice as Carnegie Hall or any place else that you play music. You play music and you communicate with people. And it was serving a need of the people in the building and the people in the neighborhood because there doesn't seem to be . . . I mean, it's now 2004 and I don't see any music centers opening up past Fifth Avenue.

At this point Steve jumps in to further characterize the squat club scene, epitomized by people like Ray Taylor:

> Steve: "But the difference is that those places, Five Spot, Slugs — I like Slugs a lot — they had their own ambiance. They were great places, but they were not run by independent wacky guys like Ray Taylor.

> The key thing here about political independence is that the spaces were either run by a regular guy — like Ray Taylor's living room was where he lived. You know, it was a squat. That was where he lived. It was kind of both joyful and I don't mean this in a negative sense, but joyful and pathetic going in there to see a gig. I heard some of the best music I heard in the '80s in Ray Taylor's living room. The thing is the guy ran the place. If you wanted to buy wine, you gave him a $1 for wine. These things weren't businesses. Sure, the guy wanted to make a little bread, but they weren't businesses."

Steve Dalachinsky and Jim Feast

Taylor was hardly the only squatter fronting a jazz/new music scene. Parker enumerates a number of other spaces. "There was a place on St. Marks called Some Place Nice. Now it's the Yaffa Cafe." It was run by John Dahl, "a political activist." Like Ray Taylor, Dahl was Black and he believed the community should empower itself by seizing business opportunities. He "would always talk to us about owning stuff. About how come we don't own a grocery store. Or how come we don't own a clothing store." He would then bring the point closer to home. "How come we don't own our own music store. I mean, when you need reeds, how come you have to go all the way up town," he'd say.

Some Place Nice was in operation from about 1974 to 1988, and it had a more professional cast than Ray Taylor's space. "It wasn't funky at all, and always you'd leave out of there with some money in your pocket. He'd always pay the musicians."

Like Ray Taylor, "John just popped out of nowhere. Where'd he come from? I don't know. But from time to time people would just pop up.

Steve reminds us that a jazz drummer also had a place: "Cooper did stuff out of his store-front. . . . Jerome Cooper had this storefront where Other Dimensions played, I mean, everybody played there."

Parker adds, "There was another place, Jarman Jones, another interesting guy, had a place on Fifth Street between Second and Third where we used to play all the time." Jones wasn't a squatter. "It was a storefront. He rented it for $200 a month and he'd just open up the doors. He would fit as many people as you could and you'd have a place to play." However, it was no less precarious than a squat. As Parker sagely says, "He didn't own it. See when you don't own your stuff, the rule is you tend to lose it or it tends to fail."

Moreover, good clubs go under because no one has the money to take them over. As Parker illustrates, "When Rick [Van Valkenberg} was giving up Neither/Nor, he offered it to us. We had a meeting and nobody had any money " to take over the lease. "So, there are just so many opportunities you miss without having any money. But that's what happens when you don't have any organization with any unity and people can't think further than today."

To describe the whole scene as he saw it, Parker says, "The whole thing is very nomadic. Places pop up, they exist for a while and then they fold. And then another place will pop up and then another place will pop up."

This is another feature of the Lower East Side that is less seen nowadays. In comparison to the present, in those decades, "there were more clubs because that was coming as an off-shoot of the [1970s] loft jazz scene so there were still a lot of places but they closed. One by one they closed."

Clayton's take on the near disappearance of the scene is that the independent club was cor-related with both squats and individually owned buildings. He states, "What happened to the neighborhood, it got bought up by either lawyer's groups or corporations or Helmsley types. The whole independent, individual landlord, which you were talking about before with the homesteading thing, is really being lost. Because a lot of these people now like own a 100 buildings."

As opposed to the corporations that now control Lower East Side real estate, Clayton continues, the owners of "those spaces, like Ray Taylor's and all that, like that was an individual guy that had a point of view and a vision."

And such people came from and returned to the community. As Steve sees it, "I think the important thing to tie up politically with all this, whether it's CHARAS or . . . the great political point of all this is that these were all started by people, by this grassroots thing. It's all about being politically independent."

"Grassroots" is a portmanteau term in this context in that we can take it to refer both to homesteading and hole-in-the-wall clubs. In either case, homes and institutions were built up and operated by people on the ground. And if the continuation of this organic, self-reliant community has been stalled on the Lower East Side, the ideal that William Parker holds aloft: a city without landlords where nomadic clubs find impermanent shelter in eccentric living rooms and each neighborhood assembles democratic forms of living and supporting culture, still stands foremost on our social agenda. And the history he has outlined shows that such an environment has been temporarily, but glowingly, achieved.

SECTION SIX - AIDS

Chapter 1

Alphabet City Finishing School: The Education of an AIDS Activist
By Jay Blotcher

Politics make for strange bedfellows. Political crises up the ante. If you were squirming under the boot-heels of New York City's ruling class and their political stooges in the 80s and 90s, you realize the tangible weight of this adage.

In the age of Koch, Dinkins and Giuliani, we were all under fire. And we learned the value of coalition-building to stay alive. Hanging together rather than hanging apart.

It was a magical, absurd time: Black and Latino poor were mixing it up with upper middle class gay people with AIDS (Acquired Immune Deficiency Syndrome). Not as opponents. But as allies. All of us had realized we were dispensable during the Reagan-Bush administration- and were equally unwanted here in New York City. In that era, I was a member of the AIDS activist group ACT UP (the AIDS Coalition to Unleash Power). We were literally fighting for our lives. For everyone's lives. We were going mano a mano with a staggering, crushing bureaucracy on the city, state and federal level. And a bigotry that would prefer to see us vaporized.

I remember the urgency of that era, the weekly casualties, and the thrill of coalition-building. I remember all of this because I was a resident of the Lower East Side back then. This was ground zero. Walk a city block and the reality of the situation hit you smack in the face like a rotting mountain of garbage. Shooting galleries vibrating with the twin demons of AIDS and drug addiction. Neighbors mugging one another to stay alive. Cops who selectively pursued offenders, jumping into action when it was quota time.

How did a well-nourished, middle-class, suburban Jewish gayboy enter the world of Lower East Side street activism? Well, first a clarification: You don't wander into activism by chance. Which of us craves pariah status? No, you prefer to live under the radar. Grab your material joys, pay your taxes and hope they don't see you. But then you're under attack. And you ask, Why me? But after the third time you have to kiss ass, you learn to say, What the fuck? And outrage hopefully marries conviction and idealism gives way to activism. Activism grabs you by the scruff of the neck. It shakes you to shit, insisting you wake the fuck up. Give up the sweet dream of apathy, because you have been classified an enemy of the state. You, the poor. You, the homeless. You, the people of color. You, the ones with HIV/AIDS. You, the fags and dykes. So, now what are you going to do? Roll over and play dead? Not likely.

My transformation came in 1987 when ACT UP was formed. I had personally been spared HIV, and wildly grateful, I pledged myself to helping others. Emptying bedpans for the dying was not my scene; I wanted to be more pro-active. So, I caught the fire. I leaped in, swept up in the white-hot anger of a group of heroes who defied the Reagan-Bush juggernaut. So, I learned to unlearn all the suburban white lies my parents had fed me about how

A Radical Political and Social History of the Lower East Side

the government takes care of good people and punishes the bad and how you wait patiently for your turn and you don't upset the status quo. I learned the adrenaline rush of staging a die-in in the middle of the street, raising my voice in fury over a country that had turned its back on a generation with the plague in their veins.

It was no coincidence that many ACT UP members lived in the East Village and Lower East Side. (I lived on Essex Street, in a lonely, dark one-bedroom that I first rented for $485 per month in May, 1989.) We were artists, writers — mostly hungry, certainly pissed off. Some living with the virus in our veins, which first scared us and then fueled us with a desperation that made us willing to do anything. We were perhaps poseurs at first: suburban kids whose idea of roughing it was wearing a torn leather jacket and avoiding the landlord for two months of rent checks. But you can only stay on the perimeter of reality for so long in Loisaida. We dropped the pose and opened our heart and got busy. We were the latest chapter in a cyclical history lesson that scapegoats and divides and conquers and ends up pulverizing those who are suffering the most. What we hadn't learned in our fancy college classes we learned firsthand by standing on Avenue A across from the park in 1988 as the cops bashed heads and then lied about it under oath. ACT UP gave us a crash course in beating down injustice, in connecting with the spiritual hunger that requires fighting back. Sure, we had been middle-class suburban kids — many of us white and living lives of little discomfort. But now we were sharing turf with the forgotten people. Feigning martyrdom was no longer an option. Living on the LES kept us honest.

ACT UP reached out to the people with AIDS who lived in this battle zone. We marched for better housing. For curtailing police from their manic sweeps of Tompkins Square Park. For sex workers trying to negotiate safer sex. And even for those who weren't, hoping to change their ways. We were bold, loud, and frankly, we were a damned charismatic, good-looking bunch of young queers.

We formed uneasy alliances with the community organizers of the LES. And yeah, frankly some of them were pissed off by us, regarding us simply as a bunch of fabulous fags who had come to the brass tacks of social justice a little late. It was true; we might have enjoyed our vie boheme as a lark until the AIDS epidemic marked us as pariahs. Until we suddenly knew the bitter taste of second-class citizenry. Until we started to see our friends die in hospitals because this government had no interest in saving a bunch of fags, blacks and prostitutes with the virus. So we wised up and learned the basics. But fast.

On the flipside, I think our LES comrades had equally hard lessons to learn. Like dumping their homophobia in order to work with the leather-jacketed fags against a common enemy. This dynamic was true especially in Black and Latino circles, where macho bullshit still swaggered, and where Church-fueled holy roller crapola kept gays in the closet and ignored an epidemic that was eating its congregation whole. We all learned we had to set aside our screwed-up notions. Or lose the battle.

ACT UP's Housing Committee was instrumental in helping people with HIV and AIDS to keep their homes in Alphabet City. When the group spun off to become Housing Works, they became doubly effective. They challenged Mayor Giuliani's proposed Alphabet City give-away. They fought against the greedy developers who wanted to evict the poor, mow down many streets of old walk-ups, and throw up million-dollar condos. Eventually, I became publicist for Housing Works, and marched with my neighbors through the streets of the city, raising our voices to protest the potential — some would say inevitable — fatcat buyout of our homes. And to fight for the creation of a daytime clinic for IV drug users so they could find a way out of their personal hell.

I would never romanticize poverty. But therein lies the irony; we were standing inside a daily inferno and we learned to love the heat as a friend. I must stand and bear witness: for me, there were no happier days than these. I lived in my second-floor cave in an 1889 tenement building. My best pal Mike (author and activist Michelangelo Signorile) lived upstairs. Across from him, ACT UP comrade Jeff Fennelly. And on the fifth floor, ACT UP comrade Jon Winkelman. And belated apologies to my landlord Carlos Talavera, for the increasingly uncreative excuses I proffered for failing to pay my rent for months at a time. I wanted to explain that working full-time as an AIDS activist doesn't pay the bills — although in a better world, it would have.

A typical day for me began and ended with ACT UP, since I was the group's media coordinator. I was usually awakened in the morning by a reporter demanding a reaction to the latest political outrage: an inflated AIDS drug price, a discriminatory law proposed by another self-righteous politician. Eight to ten hours were filled with calls like this. Sometimes, I never got out of the apartment until mid-afternoon, stuck on the phone with reporter after reporter. Mike would come down at least five times a day, sometimes more, even after 2 a.m. because he knew I would still be awake.

When the demos and the meetings were over, the bars and clubs of the East Village became our refuge. Our meeting places. Like our predecessors of The Paris Commune, we met and plotted at our watering holes. Like The Bar at 4th Street and 2nd Avenue. Tunnel Bar on First at 7th Street. Wonder Bar on East Sixth. There, we were stars. Objects of desire. Maybe slightly feared. As AIDS activists, we had cachet. It was the Doc Martens, the leather jacket, the practiced swagger. It was the bragging rights for having spent a few hours in a police cell and singing 60s girl group songs to mindfuck the cops.

We ACT UP folk embodied a variation on the Emma Goldman maxim: If I can't camp it up, I don't want to be in your revolution. The beauty of ACT UP was how we unified life-and-death struggles with a generous dose of black comedy. So, we would drink and carouse and proselytize and tell war stories. We'd dive into debates about gentrification, assimilation and anarchy, and usually snag a sweetie from a barstool to spend the night with us, because even activists out to save the world get damned lonely. Especially activists. Thank you to every man from every bar who followed me home and spent the night, and who energized me for the renewed battle the next day.

I lived on the Lower East Side from 1989 to 1999. I had been coming down there since 1983, when I was a towel boy at The St Marks Baths. In that surreal expanse of time, I made friends with seers, madmen, angels and lost souls. It was a world of addled idealism before young executives moved in, their eyes glazed, with nothing on their mind except to

A Radical Political and Social History of the Lower East Side

make a million before 35. The LES vibe had been changing steadily for years. (The last gasp of the class struggle was perhaps the uprising at the Christodora). Then, in a tidal wave of tainted cash, Avenues A through D were engulfed by self-satisfied folk who feel that the key to happiness is an overpriced condo and a Wall Street job. The Summer of 2004, I was able to exact a symbolic bit of revenge: the night before the big march on the Republican Convention, I held an Emma Goldman memorial party at the apartment of some friends in the Christodora. I invited my comrades from ACT UP and Housing Works in whom the flame has not been snuffed; people who were planning to march against the Bush regime the next day. We drank and laughed and steeled ourselves against the next day's confrontation with an enemy we thought we had beaten back in the early 90s.

As my comrade and neighbor Clayton Patterson reminded me, when you're narcotized by money, you have no desire to address social ills. The rebellious vibe of the LES has been quelled by the greed-hungry crowds. But that doesn't begin to explain where the homeless have disappeared.

I was still in shortpants in the 60s. And perhaps I had a strong case of Vietnam Protestor envy. But when the 80s came, I finally had my chance to spit in the face of the Establishment. I miss the LES of my edgy, idealistic years. I miss the streets that were my finishing school for lefty activism. I miss the sense of unity that marked our struggle. I have been dismayed by the Era of Dubya and pre-emptive war, and equally have I been energized to see my old comrades rise up again to the challenge.

Perhaps that 80s unity has returned as we again face a common enemy. Is it simply chauvinism to suggest that there is a fire lacking in the present-day battles? Are the younger marchers willing to risk it all? Do they know what is at stake? Perhaps you need to taste the bile of utter hopelessness before you can fight back with every last fiber. Maybe the old-time energy of the LES, a dying village fighting against extinction, was the key. But how can you convey to an Avenue A newcomer the nostalgia I feel for an era when we lived on the far edge of hopelessness? How do you explain to an arriviste that hopelessness is sometimes the only thing that engenders hope? Ultimately, some feelings just seem to resist explanation.

This article is dedicated to Keith Cylar (1959-2004), a founder of Housing Works.

Chapter 2

AIDS on the Lower East Side
By Jim Feast

*When I was told that I'd contracted this virus it didn't take me long to realize
that I'd contracted a diseased society as well.*
                    -David Wojnarowicz

I

According to an urban legend, the AIDS virus was created by the U.S. government to eliminate gays, IV drug users and others the authorities found undesirable.

Although there doesn't seem to be any conclusive evidence to support this belief, this is not
to say there are no connections between governmental and institutional policy and the
spread (if not the origin) of the immunodeficiency disease. If we look simply at New York
City, we might note: 1) The city's avowed program of planned shrinkage, by which certain
communities, including the Lower East Side (LES), would be starved for services, such as
garbage collection, building inspection, and fire protection, primed them to be contagious
disease amplifiers, and 2) the two-tiered organization of American medicine (with substandard therapy, routed through hospital emergency rooms, for the poor and powerless; and
high-tech, state-of-the-art healthcare, given via private physicians and managed care plans,
for the middle- and upper-middle classes) meant that an emergent epidemic, like AIDS, as
long as it was confined to the bottom tier, would move beneath the radar of the medical
establishment. In this indirect way, then, it could be said that the government and medical
complex did foster the spread of AIDS.

Concentrating on the Lower East Side, let's examine 1) how benign neglect led to punishing
conditions that abetted deteriorating residential health. We should also look at a part of this
story that is discussed less often: how the actions of varied politicized non-governmental
agencies partially deflected the course of the epidemic. To understand this, we need to also
examine, 2) what were a number of important features that distinguished progressive political formations of the 1990s, traits that stood out particularly in AIDS organizations, but
were also visible in other activist circles on the LES, which made their attempts to stop the
spread of AIDS particularly effective. To bring the discussion down to earth, we can also
look at 3) how, in practice, Lower East Side needle exchange services functioned. We will
contrast the inept program run by the government (begun in 1988) to the more effective
and workable one administered by ACT UP New York (begun in 1990). Finally, 4) we will
describe the decline of protest-oriented AIDS groups in the late 1990s, which took place for
reasons parallel to those which led to a lowering of the temperature of activism on the
Lower East Side itself.

589

A Radical Political and Social History of the Lower East Side

In *A Plague on Your Houses: How New York Was Burned Down And National Public Health Crumbled*, Deborah and Rodrick Wallace make a clear case for a link between the city's service-starvation of select neighborhoods and the creation of disease incubation sites, and we can summarize their argument here. The government's planned shrinkage policy designated "the withdrawal of essential services from sick neighborhoods which were seen as unable to survive or undeserving of survival. . . Of course, the neighborhoods diagnosed as 'sick' were all poor and nonwhite" (24).

One of the first functions to be curtailed was fire service. After 1972, four firehouses were closed on the Lower East Side. (The only neighborhoods losing more were Brownsville and the South Bronx.) Predictably, fires in the neighborhood and the loss of housing stock soared after the cutbacks. "The fire epidemic crested in the 1975-77 period . . . What could burn did burn, leaving behind vast stretches of charred hulks and abandoned shells" (55). During the 1970s, the Lower East Side lost more than 500 units to conflagrations.

Anyone interested in literary reflections of the situation may refer to the introduction to *Nuyorican Poetry* (1975). Editor Miguel Algarín notes that the spark that gave birth to the community organization was the death of a woman in a fire on Fifth Street. Prompt action by the authorities would have prevented it. In an angry mood, a crowd assembles in front of the East Second Street Firehouse (17). This is the first stirring, according to Algarín, of Nuyorican consciousness.

But how does this burning down of the neighborhood connect to AIDS and other diseases? To answer this question, let us follow the story a little further. There were two obvious consequences of the loss of shelter in the Lower East Side. For one, tenants had to find other places to live, often, given the paucity of new buildings in New York City, doubling up with friends and relatives, thus increasing the overcrowding in the neighborhood and surrounding communities. Second, this forced relocation destroys the social networks, which the poor had relied on for material resources, information, and norms. On the last two provisions, the Wallaces note, "vital information is shared along these networks: how to get the children immunized, how to get a job at a local supermarket," and so on (58-59).

Moreover, "these networks and the weaker connections within a community enforce societal norms and acceptable behavior," aiding in the socialization of the young and the behavioral controls on adults (59).

These are the connections that might have supplied warnings about emergent diseases and enforced norms, such as using clean needles to inject drugs. Their loss, combined with the overcrowding that increases person-to-person contact, created conditions highly provocative of disease spread. Lack of information and an alienation from city services, for example, led to a rise in measles in New York City into the late '80s as parents stopped obtaining vaccination for their children. Tuberculosis and AIDS also spread through fire-damaged, poorer areas.

We see, then, that the Wallaces document a cause/effect relationship between the government's downsizing of city services to targeted neighborhoods and disease spread. Regarding tuberculosis, "1975 ushered in a period of great instability and signaled the end of the control over TB. This timing coincides with the great demographic instability of poor neighborhoods during the fire epidemic, and TB incidence follows the Index of Extreme Overcrowding closely" (87).

One might expect a similar pattern among AIDS cases, particularly among IV drug users, seeing as "many more drug users were added to the user population because of the wave of housing destruction and its fallout" (126). That is, there was a correlation between the rise in drug use and loss of neighborhood, housing and social network infrastructure. Looking at the New York State records for the '90s, when the state began keeping these statistics, we do see such a pattern at first. For the Lower East Side/Union Square area, the total new cases of AIDS among adults runs up from 3,053 cases in 1993, to 3,443 in 1994, to 3,850 and 4,205 in 1995 and 1996, respectively. However, by 1997, the figures have dropped to 1,419, followed by 2,921 the following year (see AIDS in New York State). It could be the downturn represented the neighborhoods reaching a saturation point, with no new susceptibles to infect. It could also be that various efforts to turn back the infection rate were having an influence. Let's look at these efforts.

II

Remember that planned shrinkage was not a be-all end-all for our city fathers. The idea was that shrinkage, like the de-industrialization that preceded and continued to accompany it, would empty Manhattan of dirty industries and poor people, so the borough could become the exclusive preserve of yuppies working in the FIRE (finance, insurance, and real estate) businesses. While outer borough communities, such as the South Bronx, could be left as picturesque ruins, the Lower East Side was slated to be an adjunct to Wall Street.

So, there had to be a transition from burned-out hulks and empty lots to converted condominiums and other living space earmarked for the urban well-off. Traditionally, the idle young, students and bohemians needing cheap digs, could form this bridge, moving in and gradually upgrading the environs as in their wake the area filled up with hip, hole-in-the-wall stores and outsider art galleries. However, gentrification of this sort is often a jagged process. In the case of the Lower East Side, which was ripe for upscaling by the mid-'80s, a number of internal and external factors held it back. Externally, a business downturn, which Fitch pegs as beginning in 1987, made real estate investment money less available than it might otherwise be (15).

Internally, a number of factors pulled against the area's complete dissolution, which would have resulted in greater dispersion of its poor tenants. As the tide of homelessness increased, an explosion that really began in the early '80s with the deinstitutionalization of mental patients, was swelled by those on the LES who lost their apartments to urban burnout. Rather than finding places to stay in other impoverished neighborhoods, these people might move into a burned-out squat or join those camped out in Tompkins Square Park. Young activists also joined the squats, bringing with them not only anarchist or autonomous political views, but also a commitment to community building.

A Radical Political and Social History of the Lower East Side

In an interview with *Kick It Over*, LES squatter Rick Van Savage points out how political homesteads would gain the respect of the community. "It is really important to establish yourself quickly and get community support," he says (2). This means grassroots work. "During the Community Board governance process . . . you are trying to build up allies, doing door to door canvassing in the neighborhood, explaining what squatting is . . . so people understand . . . this is your home" (3).

The building squats also reached out to the agricultural ones. These linkages have "been building important bridges between a primarily Hispanic community which squats gardens and a lot of Whites and Blacks who squat housing" (6). The squats also established ties with those "doing AIDS work or needle exchange" (2).

Concurrently, militant organizations, such as ACT UP, who set up needle exchange programs, appeared on the scene. While ACT UP was criticized on a number of grounds for its tendency to under-serve poorer communities (a point we will examine in part IV), it's worth pointing to some of the positive, distinguishing traits of this organization and its people of color affiliates, traits which were visible in social movements throughout the Lower East Side. It was these traits that made the AIDS group's needle exchange program such a success and flashpoint.

ACT UP New York, like the squats and the gardens, opted for a town meeting style of democracy. Founded in 1987 after a call to action by Larry Kramer, the group was all volunteers. At the open weekly meeting, anyone could propose an action. "After all the proposals had been heard and voted on, those wishing to work on them left the main room to make a plan. In this way, ACT UP members literally voted with their feet to determine the amount of resources to be given to any particular project" (Stoller, 120). Even actions that were voted down were often carried out by groups that temporarily split off to carry out the protest (they then returned to the fold to report on their success and, perhaps, receive post facto approval). Although in practice, the better speakers and organizers (who were usually the better educated) tended to gain leadership of committees, the group ideally strove for empowerment of the whole membership.

Secondly, in distinction from the direction of most earlier progressive movements, ACT UP New York demonstrations and "zaps" were pinpointed to attack specific individuals and policies, while making very precise demands. The organization asked the Burroughs-Wellcome company to lower its $10,000-a-year price of AZT, for example, and it demanded the FDA introduce a new method for controlling promising medications. In 1989, ACT UP put forth proposals "for a 'parallel track' for access to new AIDS drugs while they continued to be studied in trials" (Harrington, 278). In other words, such drugs would be administered to desperate cases before they had been fully tested. Just as members of ACT UP were well-informed about the policies and practices which their interventions sought to change, so housing activists on the LES, such as those living in ABC No Rio, for instance, became extremely savvy in relation to city housing policy. This was the period of the radical street expert.

The majority of people involved in ACT UP were white, middle-class gays, and while some have castigated the group for the limited views that resulted from this social composition, others have praised it for being true to its constituency. Successful AIDS groups of all types, whether among women, minorities, or other configurations, share this quality of being close-knit with their community. In studying AIDS-related gay organizations, Stockdill notes, "Most of the activists interviewed emphasized the importance of community immersion and alliances." He explains further, "Strong community ties were extremely important for specific actions that may be at odds with values held by some segments of particular communities" (68). Similarly, as we will explore, the peculiar resilience of activism in the LES in the '80s and '90s was its rootedness in the neighborhood.

Lastly, if we turn to AIDS activists in minority organizations, we find that they, while being victims of multiple discriminations, responded by developing "strategies that . . . challenge different forms of . . . oppression [at the same time] . . . Activists structure their efforts around multiple identities, traditions, community institutions, and networks" (Stockdill, 79). As long as such efforts were centered on the multiple impingements on an activist organiza-tion's reality, rather than dissipating energy, their actions, at best, would strike out power-fully on simultaneous fronts. We saw how Von Savage highlights the same multidimensional struggle carried out by the squats, who ally with as many progressive forces and community groups in the neighborhood as possible to protect themselves.

Don't get the wrong impression here. By pointing out how AIDS groups embodied these four distinctive qualities — broad democracy in running the organization; highly particular protests with carefully worked-out, concrete demands; embeddedness in the community; and fighting on a limited number of fronts concurrently — I don't mean to suggest such groups necessarily spearheaded the development of such dispositions. Rather, I'm saying ACT UP New York and a number of other activist groups such as WHAM! (Women's Health Action Mobilization) were outstanding, but not the only exemplars of an emergent style of progres-sive politics that grew up in the East and West Village. Just as the lower part of the Bronx gave us hip-hop, so lower Manhattan incubated a new way of conducting radical political combat. Hopefully, the second innovation will be as popular as the first.

III

We can see how these attributes were displayed in practice by examining needle exchange programs on the Lower East Side.

The first attempts to distribute clean needles to addicts in the neighborhood as a way to stop the spread of HIV infection was initiated by the Koch administration. The program was a farce from beginning to end.

Early in 1988, the Brooklyn-based drug treatment group ADAPT proclaimed it would violate the law and distribute hypodermics to addicts, but this was later scaled back to providing bleach so users could clean needles. Prompted by this action, but at the same time, backpedaling in the face of pressure from community groups, the church and politicians,

A Radical Political and Social History of the Lower East Side

Governor Cuomo said needle exchange would be tried, "the first time in the U.S. that a government would provide drug paraphernalia to addicts" (Anderson, 164).

It was explained that this was to be a small pilot program, restricted to 400 users who would have to prove they were on waiting lists for drug rehabilitation programs before they would be enrolled. That is, this was sold to the community, not as a way to forestall AIDS per se, but as a scientific study of whether the provision of clean needles would indeed reduce the spread of infection among users, notwithstanding conspicuous evidence from Scotland, Amsterdam, and other places in Europe that needle exchange was an effective preventative. The program was "to draw addicts from targeted neighborhoods [including the LES], rather than from the whole city, in order to make the experiment easier to manage" (ibid.). The exchanges would take place at sites located in the users' neighborhood.

Predictably, even this fumbling attempt was met by self-righteous resistance. The State Senate Majority Leader proclaimed, "The notion of state-subsidized drug abuse is abhorrent"; while Cardinal O'Connor thundered, the city was "dragging down the standards of all society." (ibid.) Less bombastic complaints came from community leaders, such as the principal of P.S. 33 in Chelsea, in areas where exchange centers were to be located. These leaders said, basically, "Not in my backyard."

Bowing to the pressure, the city dropped neighborhood distribution points and decided all addicts would have to travel to the Health Department headquarters at 125 Worth Street in Lower Manhattan. Regulations controlling those who wished to exchange syringes were made even more stringent. "Each participant had an identification card with a photograph attached, to prevent others from getting access to clean needles" (Anderson, 168). The program went so far as checking blood types in returned needles to make sure it jibed with that of the legitimate user.

Critics of the needle distribution program, which began in December 1988, were outraged at even allowing 400 addicts to benefit. On this score, they didn't have to worry. Given the bureaucratic hassles one had to go through, the out-of-the-way location, and other inconveniences, in the first week only eight addicts showed up, and after seven months, a mere 160 were enrolled. When Dinkins became mayor in 1990, he canceled the program.

A month later, ACT UP's Needle Exchange Committee was formed. The group's first act was to distribute syringes on a corner in the Lower East Side. The six people involved were promptly arrested. However, when the case came to trial about a year later, in February 1991, the six were acquitted on their plea of a necessity defense. This defense argued from the judicial premise that one is justified in breaking the law if one is doing so to save a life. As ACT UP continued to distribute in the LES and in the face of this decision, Dinkins backed off and said he now found needle swapping a valid method of preventing HIV transmission. A story in the *Philadelphia Inquirer* describes ACT UP activities in November 1991 as they distributed needles in what the reporter characterized as "the fringes of civilization" (1), i.e., the Lower East Side. "On a recent Saturday, in a littered vacant lot . . . volunteers set out plastic buckets filled with bleach bottles, alcohol pads, condoms and other items — a 'salad bar' from which the addicts can choose the things they need" (ibid.).

Although Dinkins had given these **guerrilla** programs a nod of approval, possessing syringes without a prescription was still illegal, and the police treated it as such. "We've been hassled nonstop," one ACT UP member commented. "Two weeks ago, the police confiscated 600 works" (ibid.). However, the police stopped short of actually busting ACT UP members after another acquittal was handed down in June. In 1992, exchange was made legal.

Rod Sorge, one of the founders of the Needle Exchange Committee, wrote a paper, "The Philosophy of Harm Reduction," in which he lucidly explained the theory and practice of syringe handouts. Given that New York City cannot accommodate users who want to get off drugs, with a nine-month waiting list for those trying to get into rehabilitation, and given that "the life conditions [such as racism, classism, poverty, and heterosexism] that often lead to drug related problems are seldom raised in the mainstream discourse about drug addiction," the central problems that lead to drug taking are left unaddressed. Therefore, Sorge argues, it makes sense to espouse needle exchange, due to the fact that leading institutions are not offering any viable, serious way to help those who want to leave the IV world (3). In these circumstances, he affirms, the only compassionate position is to understand "clean injection equipment for drug users is a form of preventive health care" (6).

In discussing exactly how needle exchange on the LES works, Sorge stressed that this was no simple give-and-take exchange, such as would be found if a person were buying a head of lettuce in a supermarket. Sorge notes that "what is often overlooked or ignored by critics of needle distribution is the interaction that takes place during the encounter." He elaborates: "It is this interaction between the giver and receiver of the needle that is the significant component of needle exchange, especially where encounters are repeated, and trust — maybe even friendship — is established" (8). The rough **camaraderie** that can be established between a needle provider and user is depicted in Arthur Nersesian's novel *Chinese Takeout*, although it needs to be noted that the scene described does not involve ACT UP. His hero approaches the syringe exchange people who have set up shop on the mid-street meridian that runs down Allen Street. A woman, he says, "talked at me for roughly twenty minutes about all the dangers of using drugs" (39). Then, after the initial moves, the talk becomes friendlier, even bantering. After giving him bleach and other goods, she hands him a balloon.

> "What's this for?"
> "That's a balloon for being a good boy," she said with a smile.
> "So where's the heroin?"
> "This isn't a start-up kit." (ibid.)

The fresh-faced girl handing out the supplies is an ex-addict, and this puts her on the same wavelength as her clients. Sorge, himself an addict, makes this point as well as pressing the need for a needle exchange program to be firmly embedded in its environs, something which, as we saw, was a characteristic position of AIDS activist groups in general. As he so eloquently puts it,

> It is clear that the most effective prevention methods and system of care have been community-initiated and based. Needle exchange programs . . . must be located in neighborhoods where people buy and use drugs, be staffed by people

A Radical Political and Social History of the Lower East Side

who know the language spoken there (both the ethnic and street language) and offer points of identification and support to users of the exchange. This means having active and former addicts and HIV-positive people involved as well as residents of the neighborhood in which the exchange site is located. (9)

As noted, another key trait of social movements of the '90s is that their protests, as distinguished from their grassroots activities, were fastidiously crafted to target particularly responsible figures or institutions from whom to demand specific changes.

Taking the story forward a few years, let's see how ACT UP New York, while continuing to distribute syringes, coordinated this with militant, site-specific protests.

In 1992, Congress ruled that the Department of Health and Human Services (HHS) could fund needle exchange programs if they proved prophylactic in containing HIV spread. Ignoring the already-published studies that said exchange was useful in just this purpose, the department embarked on its own study. In 1995, after a number of these studies were completed, the Presidential Advisory Council on AIDS recommended to the secretary of HHS, Donna Shalala, that she fund these programs (which were under a ban), on the grounds that they would substantially reduce disease spread. She ignored these findings. "In September, hundreds of protesters marched in front of Shalala's HHS office demanding that she lift the ban, and 11 were arrested for trying to deliver a gigantic spine to her" ("AIDS ACTIVISTS . . . DINNER," 1). She was then moved to urge President Clinton to lift the funding ban. "Clinton accepted the findings, but stated that in spite of them he would continue to block the use of federal funds for needle exchange programs," claiming handing out clean needles would send the wrong message to the nation's children (ibid.).

Protests against this reprehensible attitude followed, culminating, since Clinton wouldn't budge, in June 1998 when a march of over 1,000 was staged when Clinton spoke at the U.N. "The protesters carried 33 coffins, some of them child-sized, to signify the number of HIV infections resulting every day from Clinton's policy." ("At Massive," 1). Also marching in formation was "a giant puppet of President Clinton as the grim reaper, complete with black robe and bloody hands" (ibid.).

This large action had been preceded by smaller zaps, a whole flurry, for instance, occurring in October/November 1997. One ACT UP member jumped up at a rally and interrupted Clinton, who was endorsing a Democratic mayoral candidate; another broke into an awards ceremony of the AIDS Action Foundation that was honoring George Stephanopoulos, a former White House aide and an opponent of needle exchange. Most dramatically, ACT UP member John Riley grabbed the floor when Clinton was speaking at the Sheraton Hotel. The president had been saying that New Yorkers' lives would depend on who they elected mayor. Riley shouted, "what about the lives of thousands of injection drug users endangered by your Administration's refusal to lift the ban on needle exchange funding?" ("AIDS Activist," 1).

The point to be underlined is this: To fight against the spread of HIV on the Lower East Side, ACT UP advanced two agendas at once: on the community plane, its members passed out syringes two days a week, providing service, information, and contact; while, on the political plane, it strove to make the case for the funding of such programs, often drawing attention by throwing cold water on politicians as they basked in unearned applause at con-gratulatory functions. Such a double-pronged approach is not itself unusual, but it is the way a major player on the Lower East Side conducted itself, with, we might note, pluck and aplomb. And ACT UP's panache was not only exhibited in actions like Riley's, when he con-fronted Clinton, but on the Lower East Side, in the actions of Rod Sorge, whose manner of distributing needles was flamboyant, to say the least. As a friend described to the *Village Voice*'s Sharon Lerner, Rod "would fill his shopping cart with needles and just walk through the neighborhood" (Lerner, 1).

IV

By the end of the '90s, ACT UP faded from the scene to a large extent, though unfortunately not because its work was done.

A quick sketch of some of the reasons that have been given for its decline may not be out of place since the abatement of political activism on the Lower East Side can be attributed to some of the same reasons.

ACT UP was always guided by an outside/inside dialectic. The game plan was that the protests on the outside would shame or threaten medical groups or government agencies into changing policies and allowing ACT UP representatives to move to the inside of these organizations where decisions were made. In fact, "some prominent gay commentators have argued that direct action's strategy of public embarrassment through demonstrations . . . won activists access to a mainstream political process, and that once this access was won, grassroots activism was no longer appropriate" (Oppenheimer, 288).

Although such a viewpoint is unrealistic and ignores the necessity for the continued pressure of grassroots work to keep politicians' feet to the fire, it is true that in the later '90s in the gay community, "organizations committed to street activism, open meetings, and an inside/outside strategy, have been replaced largely by professional office-based bureaucracies where decisions are made from the top down" (Oppenheimer, 289). This might be seen as a regrettable but unavoidable tendency of organizations, which become more formalized and structured as they tried to ensure their continuance. After all, Larry Kramer pushed to found ACT UP in the first place because he had become increasingly disillusioned with the Gay Men's Health Crisis, which he repeatedly accused of becoming timid and bureaucratized.

While ACT UP's ultra-democratic arrangements made it less vulnerable to such encroachments than most organizations, certain conclaves were not so restrained. The Treatment + Data (T+D) Committee was accused of moving toward elitism. "After 1990, T+D's tactical successes and its commitment to seeing them through created ideological and tactical stress within ACT UP" (Harrington, 280). The committee felt "demonstrations and zaps against drug com-panies stopped working," and a purely inside strategy was now the most feasible (ibid). When the general membership disagreed with this position, the committee broke with ACT

A Radical Political and Social History of the Lower East Side

UP and formed a new group, TAG (Treatment Action Group). Members of this new formation became recognized experts on AIDS treatment, partnering with the government's Office of AIDS Research, for instance, to evaluate NIH research effort.

And while some groups broke off from ACT UP as they professionalized, others, such as the Black caucus, split because they felt the group wasn't representing their interests. A Black LA AIDS activist commented, "ACT UP was specifically a group of white gay men . . . Because of that, ACT UP has always not been all that inclusive of everybody who's been affected by AIDS" (Stockdill, 76). Although this may have been less true of the New York chapter, critic Nancy Stoller states, "Though these activists would readily feel comfortable with labeling themselves gay and male, few would think of adding 'white' to their self-description. This lack of consciousness about race reflects a common pattern" (Stoller, 125).

On top of these fissures, Oppenheimer locates a broader shaping force. The visibility of gay activism on the New York scene through the late '80s and '90s had garnered a greater tolerance (if not acceptance) for the upper-class, gay urban lifestyle, a tolerance enhanced by the lessening of activism. These changes also endeared the gay consumer to marketers, and this brought some changes. "To accommodate mainstream advertisers, the [gay] lifestyle magazines went glossy and professional, and the community papers, unable to compete, have all but disappeared" (292). Further, as the creation of a gay identity, which had once been formed in bars, neighborhoods and fringe publications, came into the sights of media and advertisers, it was more liable to manipulation by mass propaganda. "The vast majority of opportunities for gay identification profiled by the lifestyle magazines are not political . . . A lonely new identity is consolidated in this process [of more companies trying to sell to homosexuals]: the gay consumer" (Oppenheimer, 295).

It can be said, analogously, that as memories of the Tompkins Square Park riots faded and as the presence of the homeless dwindled, the Lower East Side became more acceptable as a residential area and the mainstream began buying in. This shifted the neighborhood's ballast as well-heeled apartment dwellers entered and formed alliances with upscaling shopkeepers and new businesses.

At the same time, again analogously, when the riot drew attention to the LES as a trouble area, more funds were released and greater contact between activists and city agencies occurred. Local organizations, such as squatter groups, became more involved in the intricacies of housing policy — Van Savage says as much — and, perhaps, had to struggle to maintain their ties to the community as they were accepted to some extent by those on the other side of the fence.

From the opposite end, Hispanics and other minorities often felt shut out of networks developing between white activists and the city. The case of the Nuyorican Poets Cafe is illustrative. Refounded in the late '80s by Miguel Algarín and white members of the St. Marks Poetry Project, this grouping fractured and the white members left in the '90s.

So, as with New York ACT UP, it seemed the Lower East Side's political core was shedding its top and bottom layers, struggling to retain equilibrium while developers were eating away at its popular base.

Coda

"We are born into a world of absolute silence. And the work of the powers that be is to make this silence deeper still." This is the message of David Wojnarowicz. "I wonder how many people understand what it is to grow up in a society where one is invisible," he wrote in the early '90. "I wake up every day and if I turn on the television set or look through a magazine . . . I see no representations of my sexuality" (155).

In the face of this monoculture, it is the artist's and activist's job to speak from the hidden, blocked-out territories. "BOTTOM LINE — IF PEOPLE DON'T SAY WHAT THEY BELIEVE, THOSE IDEAS AND FEELINGS GET LOST, IF THEY ARE LOST OFTEN ENOUGH, THOSE IDEAS AND FEEL-INGS NEVER RETURN" (153). His reason for creation was then: "To place an object or writing that contains what is invisible because of legislation or social taboo into an environment outside myself . . . [which can] act like a 'magnet' to attract others who carried this enforced silence" (156).

Like queer sexuality, and like the political contestation that went on in the parks and streets of the Lower East Side, the AIDS crisis was something the media, the church, the medical establishment, and the politicians attempted to surround with a canister of silence. Activists, such as those engaged in ACT UP's needle exchange program, acted to violate this silence as well as turn a light on shabby policies and continued injustices of the neighbor-hood, making them into, as Monk had it, brilliant corners.

References:

AIDS Activist Disrupts Clinton Speech. Available at: http://www.actupny.org/reports/Clinton97zap.html.

Clinton Speech at Gay Rights Dinner. Available at: http://www.actupny.org/reports/Clinton97zap.html.

AIDS in New York State Through 1993, 1994 . . . 1999, State of New York Department of Health.

Algarín, Miguel. *"Introduction: Nuyorican Language,"* in Nuyorican Poetry: *An Anthology of Puerto Rican Words and Feelings*. Eds. Miguel Algarín and Miguel Piñero. New York: William Morrow, 1975.

A Radical Political and Social History of the Lower East Side

Anderson, Warwick. *"The New York Needle Trial: The Politics of Public Health in the Age of AIDS,"* in AIDS and Contemporary History. Eds. Virginia Berridge and Philip Strong. Cambridge, Cambridge University Press, 1993, 157-181.

"At Massive Demonstration For Clean Needles for Drug Users, AIDS Protesters Blame Clinton for 1,000 of New HIV Infections." Available at: http://www.actupny.org/reports/Clinton97zap.html.

Corr, Anders, *"Squatting the Lower East Side: An Interview with Rick Van Savage,"* Kick It Over, 35.

Fitch, Robert. *The Assassination of New York*. London: Verso, 1993.

Harrington, Mark, *"Some Transitions in the History of AIDS Treatment Activism: from Therapeutic Utopianism to Pragmatic Oraxis,"* in Acting on AIDS: Sex, Drugs and Politics. Eds. Joshua Oppenheimer and Helena Reckitt. London: Serpent's Tail, 1997, 273-286.

Lerner, Sharon, *"Body Politic."* Village Voice, February 3, 1999. Available at: http://www.actupny.org/indexfolder/rodsorge.html.

Maykuth, Andrew, *"Syringe Swaps: Defying AIDS and the Law,"* Philadelphia Inquirer, November 21, 1991. Available at Andrew Maykuth Online.

Nersesian, Arthur, *Chinese Takeout: A Novel*. New York: HarperCollins, 2003.

Oppenheimer, Joshua, *"Movements, Markets, and the Mainstream: Gay Activism and Assimilation in the Age of AIDS, in Acting on AIDS*, 287-304.

Sorge, Rod, *"Drug Policy in the Age of AIDS: The Philosophy of Harm Reduction."* Available online at: http://www.actupny.org/indexfolder/rodsorge.html.

Stockdill, Brett C. *Activism Against AIDS: At the Intersections of Sexuality, Race, Gender, and Class*. Boulder: Lynne Rienner, 2003.

Stoller, Nancy E. *Lessons from the Damned: Queers, Whores, and Junkies Respond to AIDS*. New York, Routledge, 1998.

Wallace, Deborah and Rodrick, *A Plague on Your Houses: How New York Was Burned Down and National Public Health Crumbled*. London: Verso, 1998.

Wojnarowicz, David, *Close to the Knives: A Memoir of Disintegration*. New York: Vintage Books, 1991.

AUTHOR BIOGRAPHIES

Janet Abu-Lughod is a distinguished urbanist. Over the past half century she has authored 13 books and over 100 articles on cities. She taught at Northwestern University for 20 years where she headed the Urban Studies Program, and retired in 1999 from the Graduate Faculty of the New School as professor emeritus of sociology and historical studies.

Allan Antliff is Research Chair in Modern Art at the University of Victoria, Canada. He is the author of *Anarchist Modernism: Art, Politics and the First American Avant-Garde* (2001) and editor of *Only A Beginning: An Anarchist Anthology* (2004).

John Beresford spent time with his subject Jerry the Peddler on the Lower East Side over a period of several weeks. As a writer, Beresford has penned numerous articles for technology trades in New York City and is the former editor of a national music trade magazine. He now lives in Toronto, Canada.

Jay Blotcher, 46, a frantic Gemini now based in the Mid-Hudson Valley, has lived multiple lives as a collage artist, documentary filmmaker, journalist, AIDS activist, and publicist. His nonfiction appears in six anthologies, and on writer Thomas Beller's website www.mrbeller-sneighborhood.com. His latest essay *"The Day My Past Came Calling"* will be in the 2007 anthology *Identity Envy: Wanting to Be Who We're Not* from Haworth Press. Blotcher has collaborated on projects with hoax film artist Mike Z, whose website Crowded Theater was shut down by the FBI. For more see www.jayblotcher.com.

Chris Brandt has lived in the LES since he moved to NY in 1973. He is a writer, translator, teacher, and carpenter. He has worked as a cabbie, truck driver, upholsterer, factory worker, etc., and he has been associated with *Medicine Shop Theatre Ensemble* since 1973. He has served on the boards of the Cooper Square Committee, the Cooper Square Mutual Housing Association, and MFY Legal Services. He currently teaches literature in the Peace and Justice Program at Fordham University.

A lifelong Lower East Sider, homeless activist **Ron Casanova** was a leader in the Tent City camp in Tompkins Square Park. He wrote *Each One Teach One: Up* and *Out of Poverty Memoirs of a Street Activist with Stephen Blackburn*.

Steve Dalachinsky was born in Brooklyn sometime after the last big war, and has survived lots of little wars. He is a writer of poetry, liner notes and criticism. His most recent book is *The Final Nite & Other Poems: Complete Notes from a Charles Gayle Notebook 1987-2006* (Ugly Duckling Presse).

Daniel Edelman has been a lawyer since 1969. He has defended tenants and accused criminals, and brought suits for those victimized by discrimination and violations of civil rights.

Joanne Edelman was a professional modern dancer for over 20 years. She is currently teaching movement techniques for actors at the Stella Adler Studio of Acting where she is also

A Radical Political and Social History of the Lower East Side

the Director of Student Affairs. Her writing includes *Lipstick Diaries*, a series of essays and short stories depicting life as a single parent living and dating in the East Village of New York City and *The Filmmaker's Cut*, a novel based on the wisdom and joy of allowing the love of your to life slip away.

Seth Farber, Ph.D. is a social critic, an anti-war activist, a mystic/utopian and a resident alien on the planet. Middle age has not made him more "compromising." In 1985 he got his doctorate in psychology and for a few years he thought he could change the system from within. His most well known book to date is *Madness, Heresy and the Rumor of Angels: The Revolt Against the Mental Health System*. See www.SethHFarber.com.

Jim Feast is the author (with Gary Null) of the nonfiction work, *AIDS: A Second Opinion*, and of the murder mystery (with Ron Kolm), Neo Phobe. He is a member of the Unbearables writers group. He is the recent winner of *NYC's Fusion Arts Museum's Kafka Literary Award*.

Sarah Ferguson is a freelance writer who has lived in and written about the Lower East Side for the last two decades. She also writes about politics, activism and artists. Her articles have appeared in the *Village Voice, Esquire, Details, Salon, Spin, Mother Jones*, the *Nation, Utne Reader* and numerous other books and publications.

Jeff Ferrell is a writer whose recent books include *Tearing Down the Streets: Adventures in Urban Anarchy* (Palgrave/Macmillan/St. Martin's) and *Empire of Scrounge* (New York University Press). He is the founding editor of the New York University Press book series *Alternative Criminology*, and a founding editor of the journal *Crime, Media, Culture* (Sage, London).

Chris Flash is an independent publisher and political activist news junkie. He publishes *The Shadow*, "New York's only underground newspaper," since 1989, moved by the distorted mainstream media coverage of the August 1988 Police Riot in Tompkins Square Park.

Joe Flood is a freelance reporter living in New York City. He has written for the *New York Sun, Doubletake* magazine and worked for the *Catholic Worker*.

Fly has been hanging out home-(in)steading in the Lower East Side since the late '80s where she paints and draws comics and illustrations and sometimes paints murals. Her work has been published by *New York Press, Juxtapoz, Comics Journal, Village Voice, San Francisco Bay Guardian, World War 3 Illustrated, Punk*, and *Maximum Rocknroll*. Fly has self-published numerous comics and zines, many collected in *CHRON!IC!RIOTS!PA!SM!* (Autonomedia, 1998). *Peops: Portraits and Stories* was published by Soft Skull Press in 2003. See www.bway.net/~fly.

Eve Hinderer was active in the Lower East Side anarchist community in 1967 and '68. She was a founding member of New York Radical Women. Her papers are being archived at the Sophia Smith Collection at Smith College in Northampton, Massachusetts. She currently resides in Newburgh, New York.

A Radical Political and Social History of the Lower East Side

Fred Good is a first generation American of Belgian descent. After graduating from Georgetown University and serving in the United States Army Artillery as a first and second lieutenant, he moved to New York City. There he helped establish the Real Great Society and the University of the Streets in the late 1960s. He worked for the Fund for the City of New York and was coordinator of the Seven Loaves Neighborhood Arts Coalition in the late 1970s. He moved to Chapel Hill, North Carolina in 1981, where he has pursued watercolor painting, founded a publishing and training company with his wife Perry, and founded a charter school, among other endeavors. Fred continues his associations with Lower East Side organizations, among them CHARAS and the Nuyorican Poets Cafe.

Cheryl Guttman is a political activist and freelance writer based in the East Village who has written for *Downtown* magazine. As an activist she served on the UN's North American Coordinating Committee on the Question of Palestine for the International Jewish Peace Union. She worked as the main organizer for DemocracyMarch, formed in reaction to the Republican effort to stop the recount in Florida during the 2000 election. With DemocracyMarch she organized a NYC "Not My President's Day"; one of the first anti-war demonstrations in response to Bush's speech to the UN; and a demonstration against conservative bias in the news at the headquarters of *Fox Cable News*. She is currently working with New Yorkers for Verified Voting (nyvv.org) and wheresthepaper.org to adopt scanned paper ballots rather than electronic voting machines.

Alfredo Irizarry is first generation American of Puerto Rican decent. He's lived most of his life in the Lower East Side. He served in the U.S. Navy during the Vietnam War. After graduating from College at Old Westbury he help found *CUANDO* and the *Quality Of Life In Loisaida* magazine. For over twenty five years he worked in television production, on *"District Nine At A Glance"* on channel 25, and for Manhattan Neighborhood Network where he taught and helped produce thousands of TV shows. Currently he is working on independent films, most recently Looking for Work and Boston Road. He is a life long member of CHARAS and the Nuyorican Poets Cafe.

Aaron Jaffe is an editor on the news desk of the *Wall Street Journal*. A lifelong New Yorker, he has spent more than two decades poking around the nooks and crannies of the Lower East Side.

Michael Julian trained as a lawyer, and was then appointed the youngest captain, then youngest deputy chief inspector, then youngest chief (Chief of Patrol) in New York Police Department history. He taught at the NYPD academy, and served as head of security at Rockefeller Center. He now lives in Australia with his wife and child.

Yuri Kapralov was born in Stavropol, Russia in 1933 and died in New York in 2005. He came to the U.S. in 1949 and fought in Korea with the 101st Airborne Division. He moved to the Lower East Side in 1965. In 1967 he was one of the white "revolutionaries" who, along with the Young Lords and Black Panthers, occupied the Christodora House on Avenue B. Kapralov worked as an artist, illustrator, poet, historian and author. He wrote *Once There Was A Village*, and *Devil's Midnight*. During the 1980s he ran the Sixth Sense Gallery in the East 6th street building he had homesteaded.

A Radical Political and Social History of the Lower East Side

Individual entries on **Richard Kostelanetz** appear in *Contemporary Poets, Contemporary Novelists, Postmodern Fiction, Baker's Biographical Dictionary of Musicians, Reader's Guide to Twentieth-Century Writers,* the *Merriam-Webster Encyclopedia of Literature, Webster's Dictionary of American Authors, HarperCollins Reader's Encyclopedia of American Literature, NNDB.com* and the *Encyclopedia Britannica,* among other distinguished directories. Otherwise, he survives in New York, where he was born, unemployed and thus overworked.

A. Kronstadt is a 30-year resident of the Lower East Side. He has been a participant in local battles against gentrification and police state tactics. He is currently a writer and editor for *The Shadow,* a local newspaper known for investigative articles, including Kronstadt's recent contributions on voting machine fraud, sinister science, and big pharmaceuticals.

Fr. George Kuhn was born in 1939. He was pastor of St. Brigid's Church on Tompkins Square Park during the years of turmoil.

Richard Kusack, born on the LES in NYC during the 1950s has a graduate degree in finance and urban planning. He organized the Committee For Zoning Inaction to challenge the illegal development at 81 East 3rd Street (the Half Dorm). The legal fight led eventually to the issuance of a new rule for the development of community facilities in NYC. He is the father of two sons and has lived in the East Village since the early 1980s.

Roland Legiardi-Laura is a filmmaker and poet. He teaches empowerment through writing to high school kids around the city. He is on the board of directors of the Nuyorican Poets Café, the East Village Parks Conservancy and the East Village Community Coalition. He has lived at 8th Street and Avenue B since 1978.

Mary McCarthy was born in Toledo, Ohio. She worked as a reporter on the *Toledo Times,* then moved to a job in New York as assistant editor on *Good Housekeeping* magazine. She did graduate work in political science at Fordham University, then married and moved to Columbia, Missouri. She returned to New York when her husband took a job in advertising, and lived in Westchester. Mary returned to work when her three sons were in college and high school. In 1977, she founded *The Quality of Life in Loisaida* magazine in the Puerto Rican community of the Lower East Side and published it until 1991. While there she also worked part-time at The Sixth Street Community Center.

Thomas McEvilley is Distinguished Lecturer in Art History at Rice University, where he has been on the faculty since 1969. The author holds a PhD in classical philology. In addition to Greek and Latin, he has studied Sanskrit and has taught numerous courses in Greek and Indian culture, history of religion and philosophy, and art. He has published scholarly monographs and articles in various journals on early Greek poetry, philosophy, and religion as well as on contemporary art and culture. He has been a visiting professor at Yale University and the School of the Art Institute of Chicago, among others. He was the recipient of a *Fulbright Grant* in 1993 and has been awarded an *NEA* critic's grant and the *Frank Jewett Mather Award for Distinction in Art Criticism* by the College Art Association. He lives in New York City.

A Radical Political and Social History of the Lower East Side

Mac McGill's artwork has been published by many publications. He lives and works on the Lower East Side.

John McMillian is a lecturer in history and literature at Harvard University. He has published numerous reviews and essays, and he has co-edited two books: *The Radical Reader* (with Timothy Patrick McCarthy) and *The New Left Revisited* (with Paul Buhle). His book *Tom Paine's Children: The Sixties Underground Press and the Rise of Alternative Media* will be published by Oxford University Press. He is also researching a book on the Lower East Side in the 1960s. Send to mcmill@fas.harvard.edu.

Christopher Mele is Associate Professor of Sociology at the State University of New York at Buffalo. He is author of *Selling the Lower East Side: Culture, Real Estate, and Resistance in New York City* (University of Minnesota Press, 2000).

John Mellon is a New York City police patrolman studying at John Jay College, City University of New York.

Eric Miller works with verbal arts and videoconferencing, as a scholar and artist. A native New Yorker and long-time East Village resident, he has moved to Chennai (formerly called Madras), capital of the state Tamil Nadu on India's southeast coast. Eric's Ph.D. research was with tribal people in the state's mountainous interior. He is currently working with people in fishing communities in Chennai. See www.storytellingandvideoconferencing.com .

Peter Missing was a squatter on the LES and in Germany for many years. He was the leader of the industrial noise band Missing Foundation, founded in Hamburg in 1984. A banner for the MF— "1988-1933"— shows up prominently in the Patterson 1988 TSP police riot video tape. His symbol, the upside down champagne glass, was extensively used as a political graffiti tag. Disheartened by the gentrification on the LES, Peter has moved again to Europe.

Alan Moore was active in the artists' groups Colab and ABC No Rio in the 1980s. He edited *ABC No Rio: Story of a Lower East Side Art Gallery* with Marc Miller in 1985. His doctoral thesis (Graduate Center, City University of New York 2000) concerned New York City artists' organizations. He wrote ``*Local History: The Art of Battle for Bohemia in New York*" (with James Cornwell) for Julie Ault, editor, *Alternative Art New York: 1965-1985*. Recent work includes: *"Political Economy as Subject and Form in Modern Art,"* for the *Review of Radical Political Economics; "Being There: The Tribeca Neighborhood of Franklin Furnace"* (with Debra Wacks), for *The Drama Review*, and a chapter for the forthcoming *Collectivism After Modernism* edited by Greg Sholette and Blake Stimson.

Colin Moynihan is a writer in New York City and has worked for the New Yorker, *New York Times*, *Village Voice* and *New York Magazine*. He has reported on various stories that took place on the Lower East Side, including the eviction of squatters, the bulldozing of a community garden, deaths caused by heroin overdoses and a clash in Tompkins Square Park between police and punk rockers.

A Radical Political and Social History of the Lower East Side

Ellen Moynihan is a writer and former resident of the Lower East Side. She has been involved in tenants' rights, community organizing, and counter military recruitment, and is an ex-Radical Cheerleader. Her first book will be published in 2007. She currently lives in Brooklyn.

Al Orensanz was born in Larués, Spain. He studied at the London School of Economics and took his Ph.D. at the New School for Social Research in New York. Between 1987 and '99 he taught sociology at the New School and New York University. He is director of the Angel Orensanz Foundation for the Arts on the Lower East Side.

Clayton Patterson is an ex-teacher, an artist, photojournalist and a documentarian. He is president of the New York Tattoo Society, and the organizer of the first nine NYC International Tattoo Conventions. He runs the Outlaw Art Museum, and maintains his Clayton Archives, a large collection of photos, videos, and paper material representing aspects of the Lower East Side during the 1980s, '90s and 2000s. He has done much work in collaboration with Elsa Rensaa. He is the editor of *Captured: A Film/Video History of the Lower East Side* (Seven Stories Press, 2005).

Richard Porton is author of Film and the Anarchist Imagination (Verso) and a member of *Cineaste* magazine's editorial board. He has taught at various universities including New York University, Hunter College and Rutgers.

David Pultz has been a resident of the East Village since 1978. Born in Greensburg, PA in 1952, he has worked in the motion picture industry for nearly 30 years. In 1997 he completed the feature length documentary *Eternal Memory: Voices from the Great Terror*, which was selected for inclusion in the *1998 Human Rights Watch International Film Festival*. He is married to the artist and calligrapher Elizabeth White-Pultz.

Carolyn Ratcliffe is a photographer, writer, community activist and gardener. She moved to New York in 1974, and has resided in the Lower East Side off and on since 1976. She was chair of the 9B-C Garden, and secretary of the New 600 B-C E. 9th Neighborhood Association, executive director of La Plaza Cultural Armando Perez Community Park and Garden, and vice president of the NYC Garden Coalition. She formed the La Plaza Performance Project to showcase local artists, and is founder and coordinator of Artistas de Loisaida (www.artistasdeloisaida.org), an artists' collaborative. She is a founding member of the Committee to Save St. Brigid's Church. She is one of five co-authors of The *Thin Green Line, A History of Community Managed Greenspace in New York City*, published by Artistas de Loisaida in 2001.

Elsa H. Rensaa is a painter, print maker; Lower East Side photo and video documentarian and video editor. She is vice president of the N.Y. Tattoo Society and chromiste for the Marina Picasso Estate. She helped to develop the Clayton Archive, and has been Clayton's partner for 34 years.

Hanon Reznikov was born in Brooklyn in 1950. He first met the *Living Theatre* at their performances at Yale in 1968. He soon joined the company and became director after the

A Radical Political and Social History of the Lower East Side

death of Julian Beck in 1985. Reznikov and Judith Malina have been life partners since 1973. He has written many of the company's plays including *The Money Tower*, *The Yellow Methuselah*, *The Body of God*, *Anarchia*, *Utopia*, *Capital Changes* and *Resistenza*.

Virginie de Rocquigny was born in Paris in 1984. She studied literature and politics at the Sorbonne, then came to New York to study journalism. She worked at *A Gathering of the Tribes* where she met Steve Cannon. She currently lives in Paris.

Michael Rosen grew up in Vermont, where he hiked, camped in all seasons, skied and became an Eagle Scout. He attended the University of Pennsylvania in Philadelphia where he took a masters degree in anthropology. He then earned a PhD from the Wharton School, and became a junior professor at NYU. He abandoned the academy to develop Red Square on East Houston Street. He has also run a Wall Street firm, and a software company destroyed in the events of September 11th, 2001. He is currently a community organizer and activist, a father to seven boys, and a struggling author. He writes: "I studied Mandarin Chinese for six years, but stopped a year ago to begin Japanese, because it seems harder and I love frustration. I've found plenty of that in our community, and it's good."

Joshua Rothenberger has published numerous essays and articles on film criticism, film theory, political aesthetics and musicology. He is also a proud member of the New York City film production community, a screenwriter and the guitarist for *Bloody Panda*, a New York City experimental metal band.

Will Sales is a poet of city life — of the streets, of poverty, of racism of childhood, of love, of heroism. He lives on the Lower East Side, in the heart of one of the most vibrant art communities in New York City. Will is a city homesteader, and much of the inspiration for his poetry has come out of that experience.

Tom Savage has published eight books of poetry including *Bamiyan Poems* (Sisyphus Books 2004), *Brain Surgery Poems* (Linear Arts, 1999), and *Political Conditions/Physical States* (United Artists Books, 1993). His poems have appeared in the *New York Times*, *Black Box*, *Unlikely Stories*, *Hanging Loose* and *The World*.

Lynne Stewart was a public school librarian in Harlem (1962) then a teacher at PS 64 (which later became CHARAS El Bohio) when she began her career as a community activist. She and her husband Ralph have lived in the Gompers Housing on the LES for three decades. Stewart went on to become one of the most successful human rights attorneys in New York. She represented ex-Weather Underground revolutionary David Gilbert, and Richard Williams who bombed military and corporate buildings. Recently Stewart was convicted on five federal charges — including "providing material support" to terrorism, conspiracy to abet terrorism, and lying to the government about her actions. She faces up to 30 years in prison.

Aldo Tambellini is a lifelong activist and artist. During the 1960s, he set up the *Gate Theater* on the Lower East Side which introduced many important film, video and performance artists. He was involved in protests against the Museum of Modern Art, and started the activist Group Center. Born in Italy, Aldo joined in the fight to end discrimination against Italian Americans.

Seth Tobocman In 1980 Seth Tobocman was one of the founding editors of the political comic book *World War 3 Illustrated*, a challenge to the politics and morals of the Reagan era. His illustrations have appeared in the *New York Times* and many other magazines. Tobocman has written three graphic books: *You Don't Have to Fuck People Over to Survive*, *War in the Neighborhood*, and *Portraits of Israelis and Palestinians*. He has major exhibitions at at *ABC No Rio and Exit Art in New York*, and been in group shows at the *Museum of Modern Art* and the *New Museum of Contemporary Art*. His images have been used in posters, pamphlets, murals, graffiti and tattoos by peoples' movements around the world from the African National Congress in South Africa to the squatters on the Lower East Side.

Kenneth Toglia (pronounced TOLL yah) was born in the year of the firehorse. Known to everyone as Kenny, he was one of the original organizers of the Lower East Side squatters' movement of the '80s and '90s, as well as the anti-curfew movement. In 1991 he was convicted of misdemeanor incitement to riot after a four month trial, and sentenced to a year in prison, much like his anarchist forebear Emma Goldman at the turn of the century. Toglia has since worked in the field of progressive substance abuse treatment (harm reduction). His organization, the New York Medical Marijuana Patients Cooperative, was raided by police and in a recent historic victory for anti-drug war activists, all charges against him were dismissed.

Bill Weinberg is author of *Homage to Chiapas: The New Indigenous Struggles in Mexico* (Verso Books, 2000), and is currently working on a new book for Verso on indigenous resistance to Plan Colombia in the Andean nations. He also co-hosts the *Moorish Orthodox Radio Crusade* talk show, Tuesdays at midnight on *WBAI, 99.5 FM*, in New York City. A native New Yorker, he has lived in the East Village since 1989.

Peter Lamborn Wilson (b. New York, 1945) is an American political writer, essayist and poet. He developed the idea of the *Temporary Autonomous Zone* (TAZ) writing as Hakim Bey.

JoAnn Wypijewski is a freelance writer and regular columnist for *Mother Jones*. Her work has also appeared in *Harper's, CounterPunch*, the *Los Angeles Times* and the *Nation*. She is president of the board of Good Old Lower East Side (GOLES), with which she has been involved since organizing her building in 1980.

Laura Zelasnic is a slum goddess from the Lower East Side and proud of it. She finds herself between the 19th century and the Milky Way. She is also a poet and an architectural historian. She is a contributor to the *Encyclopedia of New York State*. The signage identifying the monuments in Tompkins Square Park is based on her research for the Smithsonian Institution's Save Outdoor Sculpture Project. As for history, she believes with Heraclites that you cannot step twice into the same river, and with Rumi that the whole of our lives and activities is a frantic fleeing from silence.

A Radical Political and Social History of the Lower East Side

Steve Zehentner is an independent video producer and theater designer. With Penny Arcade, he is co-producer of the Lower East Side Biography Project, a series of video oral histories. His collaboration with Ms. Arcade originated in the theater, where he has designed stage, video and sound for all of Arcade's major productions since 1992. His video The Color Line: *Racism in America* was broadcast by PBS, and screened at the *New York Film Festival*. In 2002 he received a *Bogliasco Fellowship* to develop his piece *The Money Machine*, a video that parodies the talk radio format to present a debate about the culture of "free market" capitalism.

609

INDEX

A Radical Political and Social History of the Lower East Side

A Radical Political and Social History of the Lower East Side

A Radical Political and Social History of the Lower East Side

A Radical Political and Social History of the Lower East Side

A Radical Political and Social History of the Lower East Side

A Radical Political and Social History of the Lower East Side